2nd edition

DATA STRUCTURES USING PASCAL

AARON M. TENENBAUM

MOSHE J. AUGENSTEIN

Department of Computer and Information Science
Brooklyn College
City University of New York

PRENTICE-HALL INTERNATIONAL, INC.

Editorial/production supervision and
  interior design: Marina Harrison
Manufacturing buyer: Ed O'Dougherty

PRENTICE-HALL SOFTWARE SERIES
Brian W. Kernighan, advisor

© 1986, 1981 by Prentice-Hall
A Division of Simon & Schuster, Inc.
Englewood Cliffs, New Jersey 07632

Printed in the United States of America

10 9 8 7 6 5 4 3 2

ISBN 0-13-196684-7

Prentice-Hall International (UK) Limited, *London*
Prentice-Hall of Australia Pty. Limited, *Sydney*
Prentice-Hall Canada Inc., *Toronto*
Prentice-Hall Hispanoamericana, S.A., *Mexico*
Prentice-Hall of India Private Limited, *New Delhi*
Prentice-Hall of Japan, Inc., *Tokyo*
Prentice-Hall of Southeast Asia Pte. Ltd., *Singapore*
Editora Prentice-Hall do Brasil, Ltda., *Rio de Janeiro*
Whitehall Books Limited, *Wellington, New Zealand*
Prentice-Hall, Inc., *Englewood Cliffs, New Jersey*

To my daughter, Sara Tova   A.T.

To my sons, Menachem, Yaakov, and Elchonon   M.A.

CONTENTS

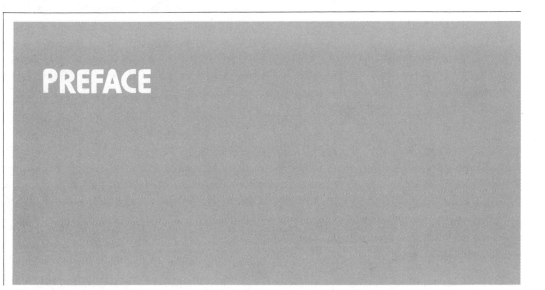

PREFACE

This text is designed for a two-semester course in data structures and programming. For several years, we have taught a course in data structures to students who have had a semester course in high-level language programming and a semester course in assembly language programming. We found that a considerable amount of time was spent in teaching programming techniques because the students had not had sufficient exposure to programming and were unable to implement abstract structures on their own. The brighter students eventually caught on to what was being done. The weaker students never did. Based on this experience, we have reached the firm conviction that a first course in data structures must go hand in hand with a second course in programming. This text is a product of that conviction.

The text introduces abstract concepts, shows how those concepts are useful in problem solving, and then shows how the abstractions can be made concrete by using a programming language. Equal emphasis is placed on both the abstract and the concrete versions of a concept, so that the student learns about the concept itself, its implementation, and its application.

The language used in this text is Pascal. Pascal is well suited to such a course since it contains the control structures necessary to make programs readable and allows basic data structures such as stacks, linked lists and trees to be implemented in a variety of ways. This allows the student to appreciate the choices and tradeoffs which face a programmer in a real situation. The only prerequisite for students using this text is a one-semester course in programming. Students who have had a course in programming using such languages as FORTRAN or PL/I can use this text together with one of the elementary Pascal texts listed in the bibliography. Chapter 1 and the Appendix also provide information necessary for such students to acquaint themselves with Pascal.

Chapter 1 is an introduction to data structures. Section 1.1 introduces the concept of an abstract data structure and the concept of an implementation. Sections 1.2 and 1.3 introduce arrays and structures in Pascal. The implementations of these two data structures as well as their applications are covered. Chapter 2 discusses stacks and their Pascal implementation. Since this is the first new data structure introduced, considerable discussion of the pitfalls of implementing such a structure is included. Section 2.3 introduces postfix, prefix, and infix notations. Chapter 3 covers recursion, its applications, and its implementation. Chapter 4 introduces queues, priority queues and linked lists and their implementations using an array of available nodes. Chapter 5 discusses Pascal dynamic storage and the implementation of stacks, queues, and linked lists using dynamic storage. Chapter 6 discusses trees, chapter 7 introduces Q notation and covers sorting, while chapter 8 covers both internal and external searching. Chapter 9 introduces graphs, and chapter 10 discusses storage management.

The Appendix discusses a number of topics related to the Pascal language and its usage that are relevant to data structures. Some students have encountered some of these topics in an introductory Pascal course but many have not. The instructor can assign sections of the Appendix as independent reading or can integrate them into the body of the course. At the end of the text, we have included a large bibliography with each entry classified by the appropriate chapter or section of the text.

A one-semester course in data structures consists of section 1.1, chapters 2–7, and sections 8.1, 8.2 and part of 8.4. Parts of chapters 3, 6, 7 and 8 can be omitted if time is pressing.

In the second edition, we have added a number of important topics. The formal concept of an abstract data type has been introduced in section 1.1 and is used throughout the book to specify a number of data structures formally. The priority queue has been introduced in Section 4.1 and is also heavily used in the remainder of the text, particularly in chapters 4, 6, 7 and 8. The material in chapter 6 has been substantially reworked for easier pedagogy and a general approach to list representation of binary trees has been introduced in section 6.4. In addition, we have added several algorithms for in order traversal and a discussion of recursion vs. iteration for traversal algorithms.

In chapter 7, the material on Q notation has been expanded substantially. The selection and insertion sorts are introduced as general techniques involving a priority queue, and quicksort and heapsort have been substantially modified. A number of quicksort variations have also been added.

Substantial additions have been made to chapter 8 (Searching). This includes material on interpolation search and the complexity of binary tree search, as well as a great deal of material on external searching. Substantial material has been added on B-trees (section 8.3), and the section on hashing (section 8.4) has been greatly expanded to include material on hashing algorithms, reordering of hash tables, and various forms of dynamic hashing for external storage. The chapter on graphs (now chapter 9) has been placed after the chapters on sorting and searching and now includes complexity analysis and Dijkstra's algorithm. A new section (section 9.4) has been added on graph traversal and spanning trees. Finally, we have added a new chapter (chapter 10) on dynamic storage management.

The text is suitable for course I1 of Curriculum 68 (Communications of the ACM, March 1968), courses UC1 and UC8 of the Undergraduate Programs in Information Systems (Communications of the ACM, Dec. 1973) and course C82 and parts of courses C87 and C813 of Curriculum 78 (Communications of the ACM, March 1979). In particular, the text covers parts or all of topics P1, P2, P3, P4, P5, S2, D1, D2, D3, and D6 of Curriculum 78.

Algorithms are presented as intermediaries between English language descriptions and Pascal programs. They are written in Pascal style interspersed with English. These algorithms allow the reader to focus on the method used to solve a problem without concern about declaration of variables and the peculiarities of a real language. In transforming an algorithm into a program, we introduce these issues and point out the pitfalls which accompany them.

The indentation pattern used for Pascal programs and algorithms is based on a format suggested by Peterson (SIGPLAN Notices, December 1977) and which we have found to be quite useful. We also adopt the convention of indicating in a comment the construct being terminated by each instance of the keyword END. Together with the indentation pattern, this is a valuable tool in improving program comprehensibility. We distinguish between algorithms and programs by presenting the former in italics and the latter in roman.

Most of the concepts in the text are illustrated by several examples. Some of these examples are important topics in their own right (e.g. postfix notation, multi-word arithmetic, etc.) and may be treated as such. Other examples illustrate different implementation techniques (such as sequential storage of trees). The instructor is free to cover as many or as few of these examples as he wishes. Examples may also be assigned to students as independent reading. It is anticipated that an instructor will be unable to cover all the examples in sufficient detail within the confines of a one or two semester course. We feel that, at the stage of a student's development for which the text is designed, it is more important to cover several examples in great detail than to cover a broad range of topics cursorily.

All the programs and algorithms in this text have been tested and debugged. We wish to thank Kai Ming Lee and Professor Allen J. Schreier for their invaluable assistance in this task. Their zeal for the task was above and beyond the call of duty and their suggestions were always valuable. Of course, any errors that remain are the sole responsibility of the authors.

The exercises vary widely in type and difficulty. Some are drill exercises to ensure comprehension of topics in the text. Others involve modifications of programs or algorithms presented in the text. Still others introduce new concepts and are quite challenging. Often, a group of successive exercises includes the complete development of a new topic which can be used as the basis for a term project or an additional lecture. The instructor should use caution in assigning exercises so that an assignment is suitable to the student's level. We consider it imperative for students to be assigned several (from five to twelve, depending on difficulty) programming projects per semester. The exercises contain several projects of this type. The instructor may find a great many additional exercises and projects in the Exercise Manual of our earlier text, Data Structures and PL/I Programming. Although the exercises in that manual are presented using PL/I, they can readily be recast in a Pascal setting. The Exercise Manual for Data Structures and PL/I Programming is available from the publisher.

We have attempted to use "standard" Pascal, as specified in the Pascal Manual and Report and in the ISO standard. We have tried to use no feature about which these two sources differ and have attempted to use the strictest possible assumptions about implementation-dependent features, or have noted the use of such features. (The primary exception to this is the occasional use of a packed array of a subrange of characters as an argument to the *write* procedure.) You should, of course, warn your students about any idiosyncracies of the particular compiler which they are using. We have included material on conformant array parameters in Section 5 of the Appendix but have not used this controversial feature in the text. We have also added some references to several personal computer Pascal compilers.

Itchy Goldbrenner, Simon Krischer, and Carl Markowitz spent many hours typing and correcting the original manuscript. Andrew Berkowitz and Yevgeny Logvinsky worked on the changes for the second edition. Their cooperation and patience as we continually made up and changed our minds about additions and deletions are most sincerely appreciated.

We would also like to thank J. Barone, A. Ciappina, J. Davis, R. Gerard, T. Goldfinger, W. Lee, G. Markowitz, M. Maurer, D. Rybstein, G. Schechter, R. Teich, D. Zaslowsky, and B. Zusin for their invaluable assistance.

The staff of the City University Computer Center deserves special mention. They were extremely helpful in assisting us in using the excellent facilities of the Center. The same can be said of the staff of the Brooklyn College Computer Center.

We would like to thank the editors and staff at Prentice-Hall and especially the reviewers for their helpful comments and suggestions.

Finally, we thank our wives, Miriam Tenenbaum and Gail Augenstein, for their advice and encouragement during the long and arduous task of producing such a book.

AARON TENENBAUM

MOSHE AUGENSTEIN

1

INTRODUCTION TO DATA STRUCTURES

A computer is a machine that manipulates information. The study of computer science includes the study of how information is organized in a computer, how it can be manipulated, and how it can be utilized. Thus it is exceedingly important for a student of computer science to understand the concepts of information organization and manipulation in order to continue study of the field.

1. INFORMATION AND MEANING

If computer science is fundamentally the study of information, the first question that arises is: What is information? Unfortunately, although the concept of information is the bedrock of the entire field, this question cannot be answered precisely. In this sense, the concept of information in computer science is similar to the concepts of point, line, and plane in geometry—they are all undefined terms about which statements can be made but which cannot be explained in terms of more elementary concepts.

In geometry, it is possible to talk about the length of a line despite the fact that the concept of a line itself is undefined. The length of a line is a measure of quantity. Similarly, in computer science, we can measure quantities of information. The basic unit of information is the *bit*, whose value asserts one of two mutually exclusive possibilities. For example, if a light switch can be in one of two positions but not in both simultaneously, the fact that it is either in the "on" position or the "off" position is one bit of information. If a device can be in more than two possible states, the fact that it is in a particular state is more than one bit of information. For example, if a dial has eight possible positions, the fact that it is in position 4 rules out seven other possibilities, whereas the fact that a light switch is on rules out only one other possibility.

Another way of thinking of this phenomenon is as follows. Suppose that we had only two-way switches but could use as many of them as we needed. How many such switches would be necessary to represent a dial with eight positions? Clearly, one switch can represent only two positions (see Figure 1.1.1a). Two switches can represent four different positions (Figure 1.1.1b), and three switches are required to represent eight different positions (Figure 1.1.1c). In general, n switches can represent 2^n different possibilities.

The binary digits 0 and 1 are used to represent the two possible states of a particular bit (in fact, the word "bit" is a contraction of the words "binary digit"). Given n bits, a string of n 1s and 0s is used to represent their settings. For example, the string 101011 represents six switches, the first of which is "on" (1), the second of which is "off" (0), the third on, the fourth off, and the fifth and sixth on.

We have seen that three bits are sufficient to represent eight possibilities. The eight possible configurations of these three bits (000, 001, 010, 011, 100, 101, 110, and 111) can be used to represent the integers 0 through 7. However, there is nothing intrinsic about these bit settings that implies that a particular setting represents a particular integer. Any assignment of integer values to bit settings is equally valid as long as no two integers are assigned to the same bit setting. Once such an assignment has been made, a particular bit setting can be unambiguously interpreted as a specific integer. Let us examine several widely used methods for interpreting bit settings as integers.

Binary and Decimal Integers

The most widely used method for interpreting bit settings as non-negative integers is the *binary number system*. In this system each bit position represents a power of 2. The rightmost bit position represents 2^0, which equals 1; the next position to the left represents 2^1, which is 2; the next bit position represents 2^2, which is 4; and so on. An integer is represented as a sum of powers of 2. A string of all 0s represents the number 0. If a 1 appears in a particular bit position, the power of 2 represented by that bit position is included in the sum, but if a 0 appears, that power of 2 is not included in the sum. For example, the group of bits 00100110 has 1s in positions 1, 2, and 5 (counting from right to left with the rightmost position counted as position 0). Thus 00100110 represents the integer $2^1 + 2^2 + 2^5 = 2 + 4 + 32 = 38$. Under this interpretation, any string of bits of length n rep-

Switch 1

OFF

ON

(a) One switch (two possibilities).

Switch 1	Switch 2
OFF	OFF
OFF	ON
ON	OFF
ON	ON

(b) Two switches (four possibilities).

Switch 1	Switch 2	Switch 3
OFF	OFF	OFF
OFF	OFF	ON
OFF	ON	OFF
OFF	ON	ON
ON	OFF	OFF
ON	OFF	ON
ON	ON	OFF
ON	ON	ON

(c) Three switches (eight possibilities).

Figure 1.1.1

resents a unique nonnegative integer between 0 and $2^n - 1$, and any non-negative integer between 0 and $2^n - 1$ can be represented by a unique string of bits of length n.

There are two widely used methods for representing negative binary numbers. In the first method, called **ones-complement notation**, a negative number is represented by changing each bit in its absolute value to the opposite bit setting. For example, since 00100110 represents 38, 11011001 is used to represent -38. This means that the first bit of a number is no longer used to represent a power of 2, but is reserved for the sign of the number. A bit string starting with a 0 represents a positive number, while a bit string starting with a 1 represents a negative number. Given n bits, the range of numbers that can be represented is $-2^{n-1} + 1$ (a 1 followed by $n - 1$ 0s) to $2^{n-1} - 1$ (a 0 followed by $n - 1$ 1s). Note that under this representation, there are two representations for the number 0: a "positive 0" consisting of all 0s and a "negative 0" consisting of all 1s.

The second method of representing negative binary numbers is called **twos-complement notation**. In this notation, 1 is added to the ones-complement representation of a negative number. For example, since 11011001 represents -38 in ones-complement notation, 11011010 is used to represent -38 in twos-complement notation. Given n bits, the range of numbers that can be represented is -2^{n-1} (a 1 followed by $n - 1$ 0s) to $2^{n-1} - 1$ (a 0 followed by $n - 1$ 1s). Note that -2^{n-1} can be represented in twos-complement notation but not in ones-complement notation. However, its absolute value 2^{n-1} cannot be represented in either notation using n bits. Note also that there is only one representation for the number 0 using n bits in twos-complement notation. To see this, consider 0 using 8 bits: 00000000. The ones complement is 11111111, which is "negative 0" in that notation. Adding one to produce the twos-complement form yields 100000000, which is 9 bits long. Since only 8 bits are allowed, the leftmost bit (or "overflow") is discarded, leaving 00000000 as minus 0.

The binary number system is by no means the only method by which bits can be used to represent integers. For example, a string of bits may be used to represent integers in the decimal number system, as follows. Four bits can be used to represent a decimal digit between 0 and 9 in the binary notation just described. A string of bits of arbitrary length may be divided into consecutive sets of four bits, where each set represents a decimal digit. The string then represents the number that is formed by those decimal digits in conventional decimal notation. For example, in this system, the bit string 00100110 is separated into two strings of four bits each: 0010 and 0110. The first of these represents the decimal digit 2 and the second represents the decimal digit 6, so that the entire string represents the integer 26. This representation is called **binary-coded decimal**.

One important feature of the binary-coded decimal representation of nonnegative integers is that not all bit strings are valid representations of a decimal integer. Four bits can be used to represent one of 16 different possibilities since there are 16 possible states for a set of four bits. However, in the binary-coded decimal integer representation, only 10 of those 16 possibilities are used. That is, codes such as 1010 and 1100 whose binary values are 10 or larger are invalid in a binary-coded decimal number.

Real Numbers

The usual method used by computers to represent real numbers is floating-point notation. There are many varieties of floating-point notation, and each has individual characteristics. The key concept is that a real number is represented by a number, called a *mantissa*, times a *base* raised to an integer power, called an *exponent*. The base is usually fixed, and the mantissa and exponent vary to represent different real numbers. For example, if the base is fixed at 10, the number 387.53 could be represented as 38,753 times 10 to the -2 power. (Recall that 10^{-2} is .01.) The mantissa is 38753 and the exponent is -2. Other possible representations are $.38753 \times 10^3$ and 387.53×10^0. We choose the representation in which the mantissa is an integer with no trailing zeros.

In the floating-point notation that we describe (which is not necessarily implemented on any particular machine exactly as described), a real number is represented by a 32-bit string consisting of a 24-bit mantissa followed by an 8-bit exponent. The base is fixed at 10. Both the mantissa and the exponent are twos-complement binary integers. For example, the 24-bit binary representation of 38753 is 000000001001011101100001, and the 8-bit twos-complement binary representation of -2 is 11111110, so the representation of 387.53 is 00000000100101110110000111111110.

Other real numbers and their floating-point representations are

0	00000000000000000000000000000000
100	00000000000000000000000100000010
.5	00000000000000000000010101111111
.000005	00000000000000000000010101111010
12000	00000000000000000000110000000011
-387.53	11111111011010001001111111111110
-12000	11111111111111111111010000000011

The advantage of floating-point notation is that it can be used to represent numbers with extremely large or extremely small absolute values. For example, in the notation presented here, the largest number that can be represented is $(2^{23} - 1) \times 10^{127}$, which is a very large number indeed. The smallest positive number that can be represented is 10^{-128}, which is quite small. The limiting factor on the precision to which numbers can be represented on a particular machine is the number of significant binary digits in the mantissa. Not every number between the largest and the smallest can be represented. Our representation allows only 23 significant bits. Thus a number such as 10 million and 1, which requires 24 significant binary digits in the mantissa, would have to be approximated by 10 million (1×10^7), which requires only one significant digit.

Character Strings

As we all know, information is not always interpreted numerically. Items such as names, job titles, and addresses must also be represented in some fashion within a computer. To enable the representation of such nonnumeric objects, still another method of interpreting bit strings is necessary. Such information is usually represented in character string form. For example, in some computers, the eight bits 00100110 are used to represent the character '&'. A different eight-bit pattern is used to represent the character 'A', another to represent 'B', another to represent 'C', and still another for each character that has a representation in a particular machine. A Russian machine uses bit patterns to represent Russian characters; an Israeli machine uses bit patterns to represent Hebrew characters. (In fact, the characters being used are transparent to the machine; the character set can be changed by using a different set of printer characters.) If 8 bits are used to represent a character, up to 256 different characters can be represented, since there are 256 different 8-bit patterns. If the string 11000000 is used to represent the character 'A' and 11000001 is used to represent the character 'B', the character string 'AB' would be represented by the bit string 1100000011000001. In general, a character string *str* is represented by the concatenation of the bit strings that represent the individual characters of *str*.

As in the case of integers, there is nothing intrinsic about a particular bit string which makes it suitable for representing a specific character. The assignment of bit strings to characters may be entirely arbitrary, but it must be adhered to consistently. It may be that some convenient rule is used in assigning bit strings to characters. For example, two bit strings may be assigned to two letters so that the one with a smaller binary value is assigned to the letter that comes earlier in the alphabet. However, such a rule is merely a convenience; it is not mandated by any intrinsic relation between characters and bit strings. In fact, computers even differ over the number of bits used to represent a character. Some computers use 7 bits (and therefore allow only up to 128 possible characters), some use 8 (up to 256 characters), and some use 10 (up to 1024 possible characters). The number of bits necessary to represent a character in a particular computer is called the *byte size*, and a group of bits of that number is called a *byte*.

Note that using 8 bits to represent a character means that 256 possible characters can be represented. It is not very often that one finds a computer which uses so many different characters (although it is conceivable for a computer to include upper- and lowercase letters, special characters, italics, boldface, and other type characters), so that many of the 8-bit codes are not used to represent characters.

Thus we see that information itself has no meaning. Any meaning can be assigned to a particular bit pattern as long as it is done consistently. It is the interpretation of a bit pattern that gives it meaning. For example, the bit string 00100110 can be interpreted as the number 38 (binary), the number 26 (binary-coded decimal), or the character '&'. A method of interpreting a bit pattern is often called a *data type*. We have presented several data types: binary integers, binary-coded decimal nonnegative integers, real numbers, and character strings. The key questions are how to determine what data types are available to interpret bit patterns and which data type to use in interpreting a particular bit pattern.

Hardware and Software

The *memory* (also called *storage* or *core*) of a computer is simply a group of bits (switches). At any instant of the computer's operation any particular bit in memory is either 0 or 1 (off or on). The setting of a bit is called its *value* or its *contents.*

The bits in a computer memory are grouped together into larger units such as bytes. In some computers, several bytes are grouped together into units called *words*. Each such unit (byte or word, depending on the machine) is assigned an *address*, which is a name identifying a particular unit among all the units in memory. This address is usually numeric, so that we may speak of byte 746 or word 937. An address is often called a *location*, and the contents of a location are the values of the bits that make up the unit at that location.

Every computer has a set of "native" data types. This means that it is constructed with a mechanism for manipulating bit patterns in a way that is consistent with the objects they represent. For example, suppose that a computer contains an instruction to add two binary integers and place that sum at a given location in memory for subsequent use. Then there is a mechanism built into the computer to

1. Extract operand bit patterns from two given locations.
2. Produce a third bit pattern, representing the binary integer that is the sum of the two binary integers represented by the two operands.
3. Store the resultant bit pattern at a given location.

The computer "knows" to interpret the bit patterns at the given locations as binary integers because the hardware which executes that particular instruction is designed to do so. This is akin to a light "knowing" to be on when the switch is in a particular position.

If the same machine also has an instruction to add two real numbers, there is a separate built-in mechanism to interpret operands as real numbers.

Two distinct instructions are necessary for the two operations, and each instruction carries within itself an implicit identification of the types of its operands as well as their explicit locations.

Therefore, it is the programmer's responsibility to know which data type is contained in each location that is used. It is the programmer's responsibility to choose between using an integer or real addition instruction to obtain the sum of two numbers.

A high-level programming language aids in this task considerably. For example, if a Pascal programmer declares

var x, y: integer;
a, b: real;

space is reserved at four locations for four different numbers. These four locations may be referenced by the *identifiers* x, y, a, and b. An identifier is used instead of a numerical address to refer to a particular memory location because of its convenience for the programmer. The contents of the locations reserved for x and y will be interpreted as integers, and the contents of a and b will be interpreted as real numbers. The compiler responsible for translating Pascal programs into machine language will translate the "+" in the statement

x := x + y

into integer addition and will translate the "+" in the statement

a := a + b

into real addition. An operator such as "+" is really a *generic* operator because it has several different meanings, depending on its context. The compiler relieves the programmer of specifying the type of addition that must be performed by examining the context and using the appropriate version.

It is important to recognize the key role played by declarations in a high-level language. It is by means of declarations that the programmer specifies how the contents of the computer memory are to be interpreted by the program. In doing this, a declaration specifies how much memory is needed for a particular entity, how the contents of that memory are to be interpreted, and other vital details. Declarations also specify to the compiler exactly what is meant by the operation symbols which are subsequently used.

The Concept of Implementation

Thus far, we have been viewing data types as a method of interpreting the memory contents of a computer. The set of native data types which a particular computer can support is determined by the functions that have been wired into its hardware. However, we can view the concept of "data type" from a completely different perspective—not in terms of what a computer can do, but in terms of what the user wants done. For example, if a human being wishes to obtain the sum of two integers, he or she does not care very much about the detailed mechanism by which the sum will be obtained. The person is interested in manipulating the mathematical concept of an "integer," not in manipulating hardware bits. The hardware of the computer may be used to represent an integer and is useful only insofar as the representation is successful.

Once the concept of "data type" is divorced from the hardware capabilities of the computer, there are a limitless number of data types that can be considered. A data type is an abstract concept defined by a set of logical properties. Once such an abstract data type is defined and the legal operations involving that type are specified, we may **implement** that data type (or a close approximation to it). An implementation may be a **hardware implementation**, in which the circuitry necessary to perform the required operations is designed and constructed as part of a computer. Or it may be a **software implementation**, in which a program consisting of already existing hardware instructions is written to interpret bit strings in the desired fashion and to perform the required operations. Thus a software implementation includes a specification of how an object of the new data type is represented by objects of previously existing data types, as well as a specification of how such an object is manipulated in conformance with the operations that have been defined for it. Throughout the remainder of this text, the term "implementation" is used to mean "software implementation."

An Example   Let us illustrate these concepts with an example. Suppose that the hardware of a computer contains an instruction

MOVE (SOURCE, DEST, *length*)

which copies a character string of *length* bytes from an address specified by SOURCE to an address specified by DEST. We present hardware instructions and locations using uppercase letters. The length must be specified by an integer, and for that reason we indicate it with lowercase letters. SOURCE and DEST can be specified by identifiers that represent storage locations. An example of this instruction is MOVE (A, B, 3), which copies the three bytes starting at location A to the three bytes starting at location B.

Note the different roles played by the identifiers A and B in this operation. The first operand of the MOVE instruction is the contents of the location specified by the identifier A. The second operand, however, is not the contents of location B, since these contents are irrelevant to the execution of the instruction. Rather, the location itself is the operand, since the location specifies the destination of the character string. Although an identifier always stands for a location, it is common for an identifier to be used to reference the contents of that location. It is always apparent from the context whether an identifier is referencing a location or its contents. The identifier appearing as the first operand of a MOVE instruction refers to the contents of memory, whereas the identifier appearing as the second operand refers to a location.

We also assume that the computer hardware contains the usual arithmetic and branching instructions, which we indicate by using Pascal-like notation. For example, the instruction

$$Z := X + Y$$

interprets the contents of the bytes at locations X and Y as binary integers, adds them, and inserts the binary representation of their sum into the byte at location Z. (We do not operate on integers greater than one byte in length, and we ignore the possibility of overflow.) Here again, X and Y are used to reference memory contents and Z is used to reference a memory location, but the proper interpretation is clear from the context.

Sometimes, it is desirable to add a quantity to an address to obtain another address. For example, if A is a location in memory, we might want to reference the location four bytes beyond A. We cannot refer to this location as A + 4 because that notation is reserved for the integer contents of location A plus four. We therefore introduce the notation A[4] to refer to this location. We also introduce the notation A[X] to refer to the address given by adding the binary integer contents of the byte at X to the address A.

The MOVE instruction requires the programmer to specify the length of the string to be copied. Thus it deals with an operand that is a fixed-length character string (i.e., the length of the string must be known). A fixed-length string and a byte-sized binary integer may be considered native data types of that particular machine.

Suppose that we wished to implement varying-length character strings on this machine. That is, we want to enable programmers to use an instruction

$$MOVEVAR(SOURCE, DEST)$$

to move a character string from location SOURCE to location DEST without being required to specify any length.

To implement this new data type, we must first decide on how it is to be represented in the memory of the machine and then indicate how that representation is to be manipulated. Clearly, we must to know how many bytes must be moved to execute this instruction. Since the MOVEVAR operation does not specify this number, the number must be contained within the representation of the character string itself. A varying-length character string of length l may be represented by a contiguous set of $l + 1$ ·

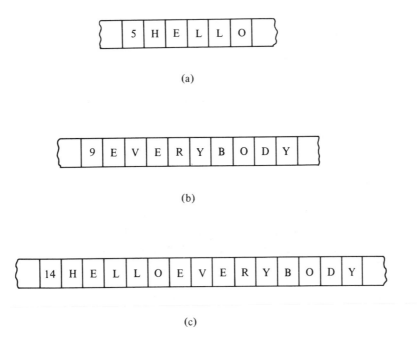

(a)

(b)

(c)

Figure 1.1.2 Varying-length character strings.

bytes ($l < 256$). The first byte contains the binary representation of the length l, and the remaining bytes contain the representations of the characters in the string. Representations of three such strings are illustrated in Figure 1.1.2. (Note that the digits 5 and 9 in these figures do not stand for the bit patterns representing the characters '5' and '9' but rather for the patterns 00000101 and 00001001—assuming eight bits to a byte—which represent the integers five and nine. Similarly, 14 in Figure 1.1.2c stands for the bit pattern 00001110.)

The program to implement the MOVEVAR operation can be written as follows (I is an auxiliary memory location):

```
MOVE(SOURCE, DEST, 1);
for I:= 1 to DEST
    do MOVE(SOURCE[I], DEST[I], 1)
```

Similarly, we can implement an operation CONCATVAR (C1, C2, C3) to concatenate two varying-length character strings at locations C1 and C2 and place the result at C3. Figure 1.1.2c illustrates the concatenation of the two strings in Figure 1.1.2a and b:

```
    {     move the length     }
Z:= C1+C2;
MOVE(Z, C3, 1);
    {   move the first string   }
for I:= 1 to C1
    do MOVE(C1[I], C3[I], 1);
    { move the second string }
for I:= 1 to C2
    do begin
            X:= C1+I;
            MOVE(C2[I], C3[X], 1)
        end {for . . . do begin}
```

However, once the operation MOVEVAR has been defined, CONCAT-VAR can be implemented using MOVEVAR as follows:

```
MOVEVAR(C2, C3[C1]);  {     move the second string     }
MOVEVAR(C1, C3);       {     move the first string      }
Z:= C1+C2;             { update the length of the result }
MOVE(Z, C3, 1)
```

Figure 1.1.3 illustrates phases of this operation on the strings of Figure 1.1.2. Although this latter version is shorter, it is not really more efficient, since all the instructions used in implementing MOVEVAR are performed each time that MOVEVAR is used.

The statement $Z:= C1+C2$ in both of the foregoing algorithms is of particular interest. The addition instruction operates independently of the use of its operands (in this case, parts of varying-length character strings). The instruction is designed to treat its operands as single-byte integers regardless of any other use that the programmer has for them. Similarly, the reference to C3[C1] is to the location whose address is given by adding the contents of the byte at location C1 to the address C3. Thus the byte at C1 is treated as holding a binary integer, although it is also the start of a varying-length character string. This illustrates the fact that a data type is a method of treating the contents of memory and that those contents have no intrinsic meaning.

Note that this representation of varying-length character strings allows only strings whose length is less than or equal to the largest binary integer that fits into a single byte. If a byte is eight bits, this means that the largest such string is 255 (which is $2^8 - 1$) characters long. To allow for longer strings, a different representation must be chosen and a new set of programs must be written. If we use this representation of varying-length character strings, the concatenation operation is invalid if the resulting string is more than 255 characters long. Since the result of such an operation is

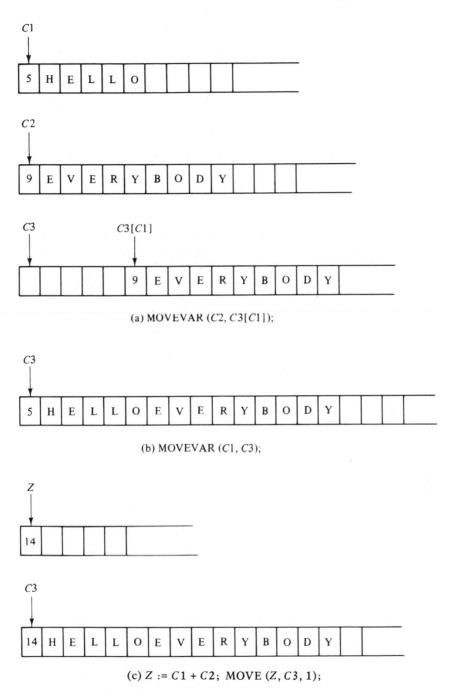

(a) MOVEVAR ($C2, C3[C1]$);

(b) MOVEVAR ($C1, C3$);

(c) $Z := C1 + C2$; MOVE ($Z, C3, 1$);

Figure 1.1.3 The CONCATVAR operation.

undefined, there are a wide variety of actions that an implementor can take if that operation is attempted. One possibility is to use only the first 255 characters of the result. Another possibility is to ignore the operation entirely and not move anything to the result field. There is also a choice of printing a warning message or of assuming that the user wants to achieve whatever result the implementor decides on.

Yet another technique for representing varying-length character strings is to use a special character (such as the **null character**, all of whose bits are zero) as a terminating character for the string. For example, 'hello' is represented by its five characters followed by a null character. We invite the reader to implement MOVEVAR and CONCATVAR for this representation and to compare the efficiency of this representation with the representation that uses a preceding length field.

Once a representation has been chosen for objects of a particular data type and routines have been written to operate on those representations, the programmer is free to use that data type to solve problems. The original hardware of the machine plus the programs for implementing more complex data types than those provided by the hardware can be thought of as a "better" machine than the one consisting of the hardware alone. The programmer of the original machine need not worry about how the computer is designed and what circuitry is being used to execute each instruction. He or she need only know what instructions are available and how those instructions can be used. Similarly, the programmer who uses the "extended" machine (which consists of hardware and software) need not be concerned with the details of how various data types are implemented. All the programmer needs to know is how they can be manipulated.

Abstract Data Types

A useful tool for specifying the logical properties of a data type is the **abstract data type** or **ADT**. Fundamentally, a data type is a collection of values and a set of operations on those values. That collection and those operations form a mathematical construct that may be implemented using a particular hardware or software **data structure**. The term "abstract data type" (ADT) refers to the basic mathematical concept that defines the data type.

In defining an abstract data type as a mathematical concept, we are not concerned with space or time efficiency. Those are implementation issues. In fact, the definition of an ADT is not concerned with implementation details at all. It may not even be possible to implement a particular ADT on a particular piece of hardware or using a particular software system. For example, we have already seen that the ADT *integer* is not implementable in full generality. Nevertheless, by specifying the mathematical and logical properties of a data type or structure, the ADT is a useful guideline to implementors and a useful tool to programmers who wish to use the data type correctly.

There are a number of methods for specifying an ADT. The method we use is semiformal and borrows heavily from Pascal notation but extends that notation where necessary. To illustrate the concept of an ADT and our specification method, consider the ADT *rational*, which corresponds to the mathematical concept of a rational number. The operations we define on rational numbers are creation of a rational number from two integers, addition, multiplication, and testing for equality. The following is a specification of this ADT:

{value definition}
abstract type *rational* = (*integer, integer*);
condition *rational*(2) $<> 0$;

[operator definition]
abstract function *makerational*(a, b: integer): rational;
precondition $b <> 0$;
postcondition *makerational*(1) = a;
           makerational(2) = b;

abstract function *add* (a, b: rational): rational;   { **written** a+b }
postcondition $add(2) = a(2)*b(2)$;
           $add(1) = a(1)*b(2) + b(1)*a(2)$;

abstract function *mult*(a, b: rational): rational;   { **written** a*b }
postcondition $mult(1) = a(1)*b(1)$;
           $mult(2) = a(2)*b(2)$;

abstract function *equal*(a, b: rational): boolean;   { **written** a=b }
postcondition $equal = (a(1)*b(2)=b(1)*a(2))$;

An ADT consists of two parts: a **value definition** and an **operator definition**. The value definition defines the collection of values for the ADT and consists of two parts: an **abstract type** clause and a **condition** clause. For example, the value definition for the ADT *rational* states that a *rational* value consists of two integers, where the second does not equal zero. Of course, the two integers that comprise a rational number are the numerator and the denominator.

The keywords **abstract type** introduce a value definition, and the keyword **condition** is used to specify any conditions on the newly defined type. In this definition, the condition specifies that the denominator may not be zero. The abstract type clause is required, but the condition clause may not be necessary for every ADT.

Immediately following the value definition comes the operator definition. Each operator is defined as an abstract procedure or function with three parts: a **header**, the optional **preconditions**, and the **postconditions**.

For example, the operator definition of the ADT *rational* includes the operations of creation (*makerational*), addition (*add*), and multiplication (*mult*), as well as a test for equality (*equal*). Let us consider the specification for multiplication first, since it is the simplest. It contains a header and postconditions, but no preconditions.

> **abstract function** $mult(a, b: rational): rational;$ { **written** $a * b$ }
> **postcondition** $mult(1) = a(1) * b(1);$
> $mult(2) = a(2) * b(2);$

The header of this definition is the first line, which is just like a Pascal function or procedure header. The keyword **abstract** indicates that this is not a Pascal function, but an ADT operator definition. The comment beginning with the new keyword **written** indicates an alternative way of writing the function.

The postcondition specifies what the operation does. That is, it specifies what conditions become true after the operation is executed. In this example, it specifies that the numerator of the result of a rational multiplication equals the integer product of the numerators of the two inputs and that the denominator equals the integer products of the two denominators.

The specification for addition (*add*) is straightforward and simply states that

$$\frac{a1}{a2} + \frac{b1}{b2} = \frac{a1 * b2 + a2 * b1}{a2 * b2}$$

The creation operation (*makerational*) creates a rational number from two integers and contains the first example of a precondition. In general, preconditions specify any restrictions that must be satisfied before the operation can be applied. In this example, the precondition states that *makerational* cannot be applied if its second parameter is zero.

The specification for equality (*equal*) is more significant and more complex in concept. In general, any two values in an ADT are "equal" if and only if the values of their components are equal. Indeed, it is usually assumed that an equality (and inequality) operation exists and is defined that way, so that no explicit *equal* operator definition is required. The assignment operation (setting the value of one object to the value of another) is another example of an operation that is often assumed for an ADT and is not specified explicitly.

However, for some data types, two values with unequal components may be considered equal. Indeed, such is the case with rational numbers, where, for example, the rational numbers 1/2, 2/4, 3/6, and 18/36 are all equal despite the inequality of their components. Two rational numbers are considered equal if they are equal when reduced to lowest terms (that is, when their numerators and denominators are both divided by their greatest common divisor). One way of testing for rational equality is to reduce the two numbers to lowest terms and then test for equality of numerators and denominators. Another way of testing for rational equality is to check if the cross products (that is, the numerator of one times the denominator of the other) are equal. This is the method that we used in specifying the abstract *equal* operation.

The abstract specification illustrates the role of an ADT as a purely logical definition of a new data type. As collections of two integers, two ordered pairs are unequal if their components are not equal; yet as rational numbers, they may be equal. It is unlikely that any implementation of rational numbers would implement a test for equality by actually forming the cross products; they might be too large to represent as machine integers. Most likely, an implementation would first reduce the inputs to lowest terms and then test for component equality. Indeed, a reasonable implementation would insist that *makerational*, *add*, and *mult* only produce rational numbers in lowest terms. However, mathematical definitions such as abstract data type specifications need not be concerned with implementation details.

Sequences as Value Definitions

In developing the specifications for various data types, we often use set-theoretic notation to specify the values of an ADT. In particular, it will be helpful to use the notation of mathematical *sequences*, which we now introduce.

A sequence is simply a numbered set of elements. A sequence S is sometimes written as the enumeration of its *elements* such as

$$S = \langle s_1, s_2, \ldots, s_n \rangle$$

If S contains n elements, then S is said to be of *length n*. We assume the existence of a length function *len* such that $len(S)$ is the length of the sequence S. We also assume functions *first*(S) which returns the value of the first element of S (s_1 in the example) and *last*(S) which returns the value of the last element of S (s_n in the example). There is a special sequence of length zero, called *nilseq*, that contains no elements. The values *first*$(nilseq)$ and *last*$(nilseq)$ are undefined.

We wish to define an ADT *stp*1 whose values are sequences of elements. If the sequences can be of arbitrary length and consist of elements all of which are of the same type, *tp*, then *stp*1 can be defined by

abstract type $stp\,1$ = *sequence of* tp ;

Alternatively, we may wish to define an ADT, *stp2*, whose values are sequences of fixed length whose elements are of specific types. In such a case, we would specify the definition

abstract type $stp\,2$ = *sequence* (n) *of* $(tp1, tp\,2, \ldots, tpn)$;

Of course, we may want to specify a sequence of fixed length all of whose elements are of the same type. We could then write

$$abstract\ type\ stp3 = sequence\,(n)\ of\ tp;$$

In this case *stp3* represents a sequence of length *n*, all of whose elements are of type *tp*.

For example, using the preceding notation, we could define the following types:

$abstract\ type\ intseq = \textbf{\textit{sequence of}}\ integer;$

{ *sequence of integers of* }
{ *any length* }

$absract\ type\ seq3 = sequence\,(3)\ \textbf{\textit{of}}\ (integer,\ char,\ boolean);$

{ *sequence of length 3* }
{ *consisting of an integer,* }
{ *a character and a boolean* }

$abstract\ type\ intseq10 = \textbf{\textit{sequence}}\,(10)\ \textbf{\textit{of}}\ integer;$

{ *sequence of 10 integers* }

$abstract\ type\ pair = \textbf{\textit{sequence}}\,(2);$

{ *arbitrary sequence of* }
{ *length 2* }

We say that two sequences are **equal** if each element of the first is equal to the corresponding element of the second. A **subsequence** is a contiguous portion of a sequence. If S is a sequence, then the function $sub(S, i, j)$ refers to the subsequence of S starting at position i in S and consisting of j consecutive elements. Thus if $T = sub(S, i, k)$ and $T = <t_1, t_2, \ldots, t_k>$, then $t_1 = s_1$, $t_k = s_{i+k-1}$. If i is not between 1 and $len(S)-k+1$, then $sub(S, i, k)$ is defined as *nilseq*.

The concatenation of two sequences, written $S+T$, is the sequence consisting of all the elements of S followed by all the elements of T. It is sometimes desirable to specify insertion of an element in the middle of a sequence. $place(S, i, x)$ is defined as the sequence S with the element x inserted immediately following position i (or into the first element of the sequence if i is 0). All subsequent elements are shifted by one position; that is, $place(S, i, x)$ equals $sub(S, 1, i) + <x> + sub(S, i+1, len(S)-i)$.

Deletion of an element from a sequence can be specified in one of two ways. If x is an element of sequence S, then $S - <x>$ represents the sequence S without all occurrences of element x. The sequence $delete(S, i)$ is equal to S with the element at position i deleted; $delete\,(s, i)$ can also be written in terms of other operations as $sub(S, 1, i-1) + sub(S, i+1, len(S)-i)$.

An ADT for Varying-Length Character Strings

As an illustration of the use of sequence notation in defining an ADT, we develop an ADT specification for the varying-length character string. There are four basic operations (aside from equality and assignment) normally included in languages that support such strings:

length   a function that returns the current length of the string

concat a function that returns the concatenation of its two input strings

substr a function that returns a substring of a given string

pos   a function that returns the first position of one string as a substring of another.

abstract type string = *sequence of* char;

abstract function length (s: string): integer;
postcondition length = len (s);

abstract function concat (s1, s2; string); string;
postcondition concat = s1+s2;

abstract function substr (s1; string; i, j: integer): string;
precondition $0 < i <= len(s1)$;
$$0 <= j <= len(s1) - i + 1;$$
postcondition substr = sub (s1, i, j);

abstract function pos (s1, s2: string); integer;
postcondition $\{lastpos := len(s1) - len(s2) + 1\}$
    $((pos = 0)$ *and* $($*for* $i := 1$ *to* lastpos
                $(s2 <> sub(s1, i, len(s2)))))$

   or
   $((pos >= 1)$ *and* $(pos <= lastpos)$
      and $(s2 = sub(str1, pos, len(s2)))$
      and for $(i := 1$ *to* $pos - 1$
            $(s2 <> sub(s1, i, len(s2)))));$

The postcondition for *pos* is complex and introduces some new notation, so we review it here. First, note the initial comment whose content has the form of a Pascal assignment statement. This merely indicates that we wish to define the symbol *lastpos* as representing the value of $lens(s1) - len(s2) + 1$ for use within the postcondition to simplify the appearance of the condition. Here, *lastpos* represents the maximum possible value of *pos* (that is, the last position of *s1* where a substring whose length equals that of *s2* can start); *lastpos* is used twice within the postcondition itself. The longer expression $len(s1) - len(s2) + 1$ could have been used in both cases, but we choose to use a more compact symbol (*lastpos*) for clarity.

The postcondition itself states that one of two conditions must hold. The two conditions, which are separated by the *or* operator, are

1. The function's value (*pos*) is zero, and *str2* does not appear as a substring of *str1*.
2. The function's value is between 1 and *lastpos*, *str2* does appear as a substring of *str1* beginning at the function value's position, and *str2* does not appear as a substring of *str1* in any earlier position.

Note the use of a pseudo *for* loop in a condition. The condition

$$for\ i := x\ to\ y$$
$$(condition\,(i))$$

is *true* if *condition*(i) is *true* for all i from x to y inclusive. It is also *true* if $x > y$. Otherwise, the entire *for* condition is *false*.

Data Types in Pascal

A type definition in Pascal specifies two things. First, it specifies the amount of storage that must be set aside for objects declared with that type. For example, a variable of type *integer* must have enough space to hold the largest possible integer value, whereas a variable of type *boolean* needs only a single bit. Second, it specifies how data represented by strings of bits are to be interpreted. The same bits at a specific storage location can be interpreted as an integer or a real number, yielding two completely different numeric values. For a discussion of the scalar data types available in Pascal, see Section 1 of the Appendix.

A variable declaration specifies that storage be set aside for an object of the specified type and that the object at that storage location can be referenced with the specified variable identifier.

A Pascal programmer can think of the Pascal language as defining a new machine with its own capabilities, data types, and operations. The user can state a problem solution in terms of the more useful Pascal constructs rather than in terms of lower-level machine language constructs. Thus problems can be solved more easily because a larger set of tools is available.

The study of data structures therefore involves two complementary goals. The first goal is to identify and develop useful mathematical entities and operations and to determine what classes of problems can be solved by using those entities and operations. The second goal is to determine representations for those abstract entities and to implement the abstract operations on those concrete representations. The first of these goals views a high-level data type as a tool that can be used to solve other problems, whereas the second views the implementation of such a data type as a problem to be solved using already existing data types. In determining representations for abstract entities, we must be careful to specify what facilities are available for constructing such representations. For example, it must be stated whether the full Pascal language is available or if we are restricted to the hardware facilities of a particular machine.

In the next two sections we examine several data structures that already exist in Pascal—the array, the set, and the record. We describe the facilities that are available in Pascal for utilizing these structures. We also focus on the abstract definitions of these data structures and how they can be useful in problem solving. Finally, we examine how they could be implemented if Pascal were not available (although a Pascal programmer can simply use the data structures as defined in the language without being concerned with most of these implementation details).

In the remainder of the book, we develop more complex data types and show their usefulness in problem solving. We also show how to implement these data types using the data types that are already available in Pascal. Since the problems that arise in the course of attempting to implement high-level data structures are quite complex, this will also allow us to investigate the Pascal language more thoroughly and to gain valuable experience in the use of that language.

Often, no implementation, hardware or software, can model a mathematical concept completely. For example, it is impossible to represent arbitrarily large integers on a computer, because the size of such a machine's memory is finite. Thus it is not the data type "integer," which is represented by the hardware but rather the data type "integer between x and y," where x and y are the smallest and largest integers representable by that machine.

It is important to recognize the limitations of a particular implementation. Often, it will be possible to present several implementations of the same data type, each with its own strengths and weaknesses. One particular implementation may be better than another for a specific application, and the programmer must be aware of the possible trade-offs that might be involved.

One important consideration in any implementation is its efficiency. In fact, the reason that the high-level data types which we discuss are not built into Pascal is the significant overhead that they would entail. There are languages of significantly higher level than Pascal which have many of these data types already built into them, but many of them are highly inefficient and are therefore not in widespread use.

Efficiency is usually measured by two factors: time and space. If a particular application is heavily dependent on manipulating high-level data structures, the speed at which those manipulations can be performed will be the major determinant of the speed of the entire application. Similarly, if a program uses a large number of such structures, an implementation that uses an inordinate amount of space to represent the data structure will be impractical. Unfortunately, there is usually a trade-off between these two efficiencies, so that an implementation that is fast uses more storage than does one which is slow. The choice of implementation in such a case involves a careful evaluation of the trade-offs among the various possibilities.

EXERCISES

1. In the text, an analogy is made between the length of a line and the number of bits of information in a bit string. In what ways is this analogy inadequate?

2. Determine what hardware data types are available on the computer at your particular installation and what operations can be performed on them.

3. Prove that there are 2^n different settings for n two-way switches. Suppose that we wanted to have m settings. How many switches would be necessary?

4. Interpret the following bit settings as binary positive integers, binary integers in twos-complement notation, and binary-coded decimal integers. If a setting cannot be interpreted as a binary-coded decimal integer, explain why.

    (a) 10011001   (b) 1001   (c) 000100010001
    (d) 01110111   (e) 01010101   (f) 100000010101

5. Write Pascal routines *add*, *subtract*, and *multiply* that read two strings of 0s and 1s representing binary nonnegative integers and print the string representing their sum, difference, and product, respectively.

6. Assume a ternary computer in which the basic unit of memory is a "trit" (ternary digit) rather than a bit. Such a trit can have three possible settings (0, 1, and 2) rather than just two (0 and 1). Show how nonnegative integers can be represented in ternary notation using such trits by a method analogous to binary notation using bits. Is there any nonnegative interger which can be represented using ternary notation and trits that cannot be represented using binary notation and bits? Are there any which can be represented using bits that cannot be represented using trits? Why are binary computers more common than ternary computers?

7. Write a Pascal program to read a string of 0s and 1s representing a positive integer in binary and to print a string of 0s, 1s, and 2s representing the same number in ternary notation (see Exercise 6). Write another Pascal program to read a ternary number and print the equivalent in binary.

2. ARRAYS AND SETS IN PASCAL

In this section and the next we examine several data structures which are an invaluable part of the Pascal language. We see how to use these structures and how they can be implemented. These structures are *composite* or *structured* types; that is, they are made up of simpler data types which exist in the language. The study of these structures involves an analysis of how the simple structures combine to form the composite and how to extract a specific component from the composite. We expect that you have already seen these data structures in an introductory Pascal programming course and that you are aware of how they are defined and used in Pascal. In these sections, therefore, we will not dwell on the many details associated with these structures but instead will highlight those features that are interesting from a data structure point of view.

The first of these data types is the *array*. The simplest form of an array is a *one-dimensional array*, which may be defined abstractly as a finite, ordered set of homogeneous elements. By "finite" we mean that there is a specific number of elements in the array. This number may be large or small, but it must exist. By "ordered" we mean that the elements of the array are arranged so that there is a first, second, third, and so on. By "homogeneous" we mean that all the elements in the array must be of the same type. For example, an array may contain all integers or all characters but may not contain both.

However, specifying the form of a data structure does not yet completely describe the structure. We must also specify how the structure is accessed. An array has two data types associated with it. The first type, called the **base type** (or **component type**) of the array, is the type of the elements, or components, of the array. For example, we can have an array of integers, or reals, or even of arrays. The second type, called the **index type** of the array, is the type of values used to access individual elements of the array. For example, the Pascal declaration

var a: array[1..100] of integer;

specifies that *a* is an array whose base type is *integer* and whose index type is the subrange type 1..00. The declarations

type fruittype = (apple, orange, pear, banana);
     season = (winter, spring, summer, fall);
var   ripe: **array**[fruittype] **of** season;

specify that *ripe* is an array whose base type is *season* and whose index type is *fruittype*.

The two basic operations that access an array are **extraction** and **storing**. The extraction operation is a function that accepts an array *a* and an element of its index type *i* and returns an element of the array's base type. In Pascal, the result of this operation is denoted by the expression $a[i]$. The storing operation accepts an array *a*, an element of its index type *i*, and an element of its base type *x*. In Pascal, this operation is denoted by the assignment statement $a[i] := x$. This operation is defined by the rule that after this assignment statement has been executed, the value of $a[i]$ is *x*. Before a value has been assigned to an element of the array, its value is undefined and a reference to it in an expression is illegal.

The index type of an array may be any ordinal type, and the base type may be any valid Pascal type. (For a definition of ordinal types and the *ord* function, see Section 1 of the Appendix.) Although *integer* is prohibited as a base type by many Pascal implementations, a subrange of the *integer* type is permitted and is most useful. The smallest element of an array's index type is called its **lower bound**, and the highest element is called its **upper bound**. If *l* is the lower bound of an array and *u* is the upper bound, the number of elements in the array, called its **range**, is given by $ord(u) - ord(l) + 1$.

For example, in the array *a*, the lower bound is 1, the upper bound is 100, and the range is $ord(100) - ord(1) + 1$, which equals $100 - 1 + 1$, which is 100. In the array *ripe*, the lower bound is *apple*, the upper bound is *banana*, and the range is $ord(banana) - ord(apple) + 1$, which equals

$3 - 0 + 1$, or 4. The four elements of *ripe* are *ripe[apple]*, *ripe[orange]*, *ripe[pear]*, and *ripe[banana]*.

An important feature of a Pascal array is that its upper bound, lower bound, and range are fixed at the time a program is written. They cannot be changed without modifying the program. The size of a Pascal array cannot change during a program's execution. One very useful technique is to declare a bound as a constant identifier, so that the work required to modify the size of an array is minimized. For example, consider the following program segment to declare and initialize an array:

```
var i: 1..100;
    a: array[1..100] of integer;
begin
    for i:= 1 to 100
       do a[i]:= 0;
```

To change the array to a larger (or smaller) size, the constant 100 must be changed in three places: twice in the declarations and once in the *for* statement. Consider the following equivalent alternative:

```
const numelts = 100;
var i: 1..numelts;
    a: array[1..numelts] of integer;
begin
    for i:= 1 to numelts
       do a[i]:= 0;
```

Now, only a single change in the constant definition is needed to change the upper bound. Still another suggestion for improving the modifiability of the program would be to introduce a new type identifier, *indextype*, as follows:

```
const numelts = 100;
type indextype = 1..numelts;
var i: indextype;
    a: array[indextype] of integer;
begin
    for i:= 1 to numelts
       do a[i]:= 0;
```

By explicitly defining the index type and declaring all variables used as indexes to be of that type, you will detect the error of using an illegal index value earlier (at the time that the variable is assigned an illegal value rather than at the time that it is used as an index). It is also common for several arrays in a program to have the same index type. By defining that type explicitly, it is possible to modify the size of all the arrays with a single change in the index type definition. See Section 2 of the Appendix for a discussion of the use of one-dimensional arrays.

There is a special kind of array in Pascal called a *packed* array which may be used to save space. The details of how such an array is used and implemented are presented in Section 3 of the Appendix, which the reader is encouraged to review. For now, however, we merely indicate that an array *a* can be declared as packed by a declaration such as

$$\text{var } a: \textbf{packed array } [1..10] \text{ of integer};$$

Such an array may be used exactly as any other array (with slight exceptions, as noted in Section 3 of the Appendix). As we shall see later, the Pascal language requires some arrays to be declared as packed in certain contexts.

The Array as an ADT

We can represent an array as an abstract data type with a slight extension of the conventions and notation discussed earlier. We assume the function *type(arg)*, which returns the type of its argument *arg*. Of course, such a function cannot exist in Pascal since Pascal cannot dynamically determine the type of a variable, and the type of every variable must be known when a program is written. However, since we are not concerned here with implementation, but rather with specification, the use of such a function is permissible.)

Let *arrtype(lb, ub, eltype)* denote the ADT corresponding to the Pascal array type

$$\textit{array} \, [lb..ub] \; of \, eltype$$

This is our first example of a *parameterized ADT*, in which the precise ADT is determined by the values of one or more parameters (in this case, *lb*, *ub*, and *eltype*; note that *eltype* is a type indicator, not a value). We may now view any one-dimensional array as an entity of the type *arrtype*. The specification follows:

> *abstract type* arrtype (lb, ub, eltype) =
>   *sequence* (ord(ub) − ord(lb)+1) *of* eltype;
> *condition* type (lb) = type (ub);
>
> *abstract function* extract (arrtype (lb, ub, eltype); i : type (lb)): eltype;
>   { *written* arr [i] }
> *precondition* lb <= i <= ub;
> *postcondition* extract = $arr_{ord(i) - ord(lb)+1}$;
>
> *abstract procedure* store (arr: arrtype (lb, ub, eltype); i : type (lb); elt : eltype);
>   { *written* arr [i] := elt }
> *precondition* lb <= i <= ub;
> *postcondition* $arr_{ord(i) - ord(lb)+1}$ = elt

The *store* operation is our first example of an operation defined as procedure rather than as a function. An operation defined as a procedure usually modifies one of its parameters, in this case, the array *arr*. This is indicated in the postcondition by specifying the value of the array element to which *elt* is being assigned. Unless a modified value is specified in a postcondition, we assume that all parameters retain the same value after the operation is applied in a postcondition as before. It is not necessary to specify that such values remain unchanged. Thus, in this example, all array elements other than the one to which *elt* is assigned retain the same values.

Implementing One-Dimensional Arrays

A one-dimensional array can be easily implemented. Let us first consider arrays whose index types are subranges of integers. The Pascal declaration

var b: **array** [1..100] **of** integer;

reserves 100 successive memory locations, each large enough to contain a single integer. The address of the first of these locations is called the **base address** of the array *b* and is denoted by *base(b)*. Suppose that the size of each individual element of the array is *esize*. Then a reference to the element $b[1]$ is to the element at location *base(b)*, a reference to $b[2]$ is to the element at *base(b)* + *esize*, and a reference to $b[3]$ is to the element *base(b)* + 2*esize. In general, a reference to $b[i]$ is to the element at location *base(b)* + $(i - 1)$*esize. Thus it is possible to reference any element in the array, given its index.

To implement an array declared with a lower bound other than 1, there is one minor change in the formula for computing the address of an element. For example, if the array *c* is declared by

var c: **array** [10..100] **of** integer;

then *base(c)* refers to the location of $c[10]$ which is the first element of the array *c*, $c[11]$ is at location *base(c)* + *esize*, $c[12]$ at *base(c)* + 2*esize, and $c[i]$ is at location *base(c)* + $(i - 10)$*esize. In general, if *l* is the integer lower bound of an array *d*, then $d[i]$ is located at *base(d)* + $(i - l)$*esize.

The foregoing formulas can be modified easily for an array whose index type is not a subrange of the integers. If *l* is the lower bound of the array *e*, the position of $e[i]$ in the array is $ord(i) - ord(l) + 1$. Thus $e[l]$ is in position $ord(l) - ord(l) + 1$, which is the first position; $e[succ(l)]$ is in position $ord(succ(l)) - ord(l) + 1$, which is the second position; and so on. Therefore, the location of $e[i]$ is given by *base(e)* + $(ord(i) - ord(l))$*esize. When *i* is an integer, $ord(i) = i$, so that this formula holds generally for arrays with any index type including integer subranges. Note, however, that the Pascal programmer can use arrays without being concerned with these implementation details. The Pascal system automatically computes the appropriate location for each array reference.

In Pascal, all elements of an array have the same fixed, predetermined size. Some programming languages, however, allow arrays of objects of differing sizes. For example, a language might allow arrays of varying character strings. In such cases, the method just described cannot be used to implement the array. This is because this method of calculating the address of a specific element of the array depends upon knowing the fixed size *esize* of each preceding element. If not all the elements have the same size, a different implementation must be used.

One method of implementing an array of varying-sized elements is to reserve a contiguous set of memory locations, each of which holds an address. The contents of each such memory location is the address of the varying-length array element in some other portion of memory. For example, Figure 1.2.1a illustrates an array of five varying-length character strings under this implementation. The arrows in that diagram indicate addresses of other portions of memory. The character ' ƀ ' indicates a blank.

Since the length of each address is fixed, the location of the address of a particular element can be computed in the same way that the location of a fixed-length element was computed in the previous examples. Once this location is known, its contents can be used to determine the location of the actual array element. This, of course, adds an extra level of indirection to referencing an array element by involving an extra memory reference, which in turn decreases efficiency. However, this is a small price to pay for the convenience of being able to maintain such an array.

A similar method for implementing an array of varying-sized elements is to keep all fixed-length portions of the elements in the contiguous array area, in addition to keeping the address of the varying-length portion in the contiguous area. For example, in the implementation of varying-length character strings presented in the previous section, each such string contains a fixed-length portion (a one-byte length field) and a variable-length portion (the character string itself). One implementation of an array of varying-length character strings keeps the length of the string together with the address, as shown in Figure 1.2.1b. The advantage of this method is that those parts of an element that are of fixed length can be examined without an extra memory reference. For example, a function to determine the current length of a varying-length character string can be implemented with a single memory lookup. The fixed-length information for an array element of varying length which is stored in the contiguous memory area of the array is often called a *header*.

Character Strings

A *string* is defined in Pascal as a packed array of characters whose lower bound is 1. A string constant is denoted by any set of characters included in single quote marks. A single quote within a string constant is denoted by two consecutive single quotes. Each such string constant repre-

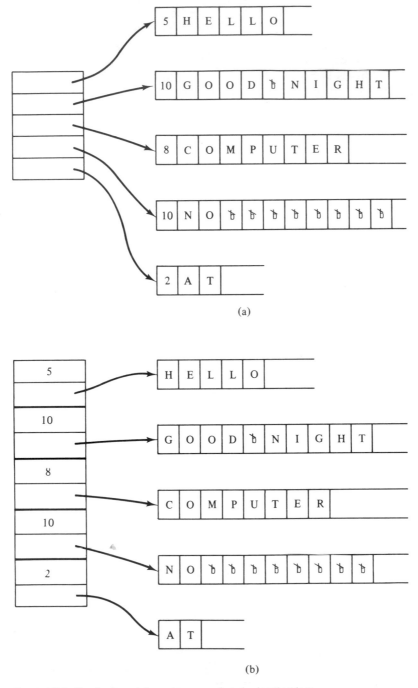

(a)

(b)

Figure 1.2.1 Two implementations of an array of varying-length strings.

sents an array whose lower bound is 1 and whose upper bound, or *length*, is the number of characters in the string. For example, the string *'hello there'* is a packed array of 11 characters (the blank counts as a character), and *'i don''t know'* is a packed array of 12 characters (the two quotes represent the single quote character).

We may define a string type explicitly, as in

> **type** string = **packed array** [1..80] **of** char;

Note that any variable of type *string* has a fixed length of 80. The length of a string cannot vary during a program execution. This is sometimes extremely annoying. For example, if we declared

> **var** s: string;

and wished to assign the string *'hello'* to *s*, the statement

> s:= 'hello'

would be invalid. The reason for this is that the type of *s* is *packed array* [1..80] *of char*, whereas the type of *'hello'* is *packed array* [1..5] *of char*. Thus the two objects have different types, and one cannot be assigned to the other. Seventy-five blanks would have to follow the letters *hello* in order to make the assignment valid. One solution to this problem is to define a new type by

> **type** shortstr = **packed array**[1..10] **of** char;

and write a procedure *assign* as follows:

```
procedure assign(ss: shortstr; var s: string);
var i: 1..80;
begin
    for i:= 1 to 10
        do s[i]:= ss[i];
    for i:= 11 to 80
        do s[i]:= ' '
end {procedure assign};
```

Then we could assign the string *'hello'* to *s* as follows:

```
var ss: shortstr;
    s: string;
begin
    ss:= ' hello   ';
    assign(ss, s)
```

Note the five blanks used to pad *'hello'* to a length of 10.

(Some versions of Pascal, such as UCSD Pascal and Turbo Pascal, allow the predefined type *string[n]*, where *n* is an integer, to represent a varying-length string of up to *n* characters. The assignment of a short string to a long string is then allowed. The current length of the target string becomes equal to the current length of the source string. Microsoft Pascal contains a similar predefined type, *lstring(n)*. However, these features and capabilities are nonstandard.)

The comparison operators may be used to compare two packed character arrays. For example, if $s1 = $ 'hello' and $s2 = $ 'helio', the expression $s1 > s2$ has the value *true* because *hello* comes later in alphabetic order than *helio*. The comparison proceeds character by character until a character in one string is not equal to the corresponding character of the second. If that character in the first string follows the character in the second string in the ordering of characters on the particular machine being used, the first string is greater than the second; otherwise, the first string is less than the second. If all the characters are equal, the two strings are equal. Pascal requires that two strings being compared have equal length, but some nonstandard compilers permit comparison of strings of different lengths.

Another special provision made for strings is that they can be passed as arguments to the *write* and *writeln* procedures for text files. This allows printing an entire message in a single call to one of these procedures. However, an unpacked array of characters may not be passed to these procedures.

Under compilers that implement all arrays of characters as packed arrays, any array of characters may be used as a string even if it is not explicitly declared packed. That is, it can be the target of an assignment statement from a string constant, it can appear as an operand of a comparison, and it can be passed as an argument to *write* and *writeln*. Similarly, under many such compilers, an element of a character array (whether or not declared packed) can be passed as a variable parameter to a function or procedure. However, these features are nonstandard. A Pascal programmer should know how character arrays are handled by the compilers available and which Pascal rules and exceptions apply.

According to the definition of a Pascal string, a variable such as *number*, declared by

var number: **packed array** [1..10] **of** '0'..'9';

is not a string, because its base type is '0'..'9' rather than *char*. Therefore, it cannot be assigned a string value and cannot appear as an argument to the procedures *write* and *writeln*. However, many Pascal compilers do treat such a variable as a string. We will occasionally use such a variable as an argument to *write* and *writeln*, but the reader should be aware that this is a minor extension to standard Pascal.

Character String Operations

In the previous section, we saw how we could define an ADT for a varying-length string type *string* with operations *length*, *substr*, and *pos*. Let us examine how this ADT can be implemented in Pascal.

A string in Pascal has a fixed length. However, we can treat a string as having a varying length if we choose to ignore all trailing blanks. Under such a system, the string '*hello   *' may be considered to have a length of five, since all the remaining characters are blanks. Of course, embedded blanks do count, so that a string such as '*a b*' with two blanks between the *a* and *b* has a length of four. The declaration of a string variable would then define only the maximum length of a string; its actual length would be the declared length minus the number of trailing blanks. It is important to note that this method of implementing varying-length character strings does not represent an addition or a change in the Pascal language, but only a new method of using the language in a specific way.

Note also that the Pascal implementation is only an approximation of the ADT for varying-length character strings. This is because the ADT did not specify a maximum length, but the Pascal implementation permits only strings up to a certain length. This is not at all unusual; most implementations impose practical limitations on theoretically unbounded abstract types.

To illustrate the use of such strings, let us present Pascal routines to implement the primitive operations on varying-length character strings. For all these routines, we assume the global declarations

```
const strsize = 80;
type string = packed array [1..strsize] of char;
```

The first routine is a function to find the current length of a string interpreted as a varying-length character string:

```
function length(s: string): integer;
var i: integer;
    found: boolean;
begin
    i:= strsize;
    found:= false;
    while (i > 0) and (not found)
        do begin
            if s[i] <> ' '
                then found:= true
                else i:= i-1
        end {while...do begin};
    length:= i
end { function length};
```

The second routine is a function that accepts two strings as parameters. The function returns an integer which indicates the starting location of the first occurrence of the second parameter string within the first parameter string. If the second string does not exist within the first, 0 is returned.

```
function pos(s1, s2: string): integer;
var i, j, len1, len2: integer;
    found, finis: boolean;
begin
    len1:= length(s1);
    len2:= length(s2);
    i:= 0;
    found:= false;
    while (i+len2 <= len1) and (not found)
        do begin
            finis:= false;
            j:= 1;
            while (j <= len2) and (not finis)
                do if s1[i+j] = s2[j]
                    then j:= j+1
                    else finis:= true;
            if j > len2
                then found:= true
                else i:= i+1
        end {while...do begin};
    if found
        then pos:= i+1
        else pos:= 0
end { function pos};
```

(UCSD Pascal, Turbo Pascal, and Microsoft Pascal provide versions of both *length* and *pos* as predefined functions. The Microsoft version of *pos* is called *positn* and requires a third parameter that is the integer position of the target string at which the search begins. Both the Turbo *pos* and Microsoft *positn* functions also reverse the order of the string parameters so that the first parameter is the pattern being searched for and the second is the string being searched.

Another common operation on strings is concatenation. The result of concatenating two strings is a third string, consisting of the characters of the first followed by the characters of the second. The following procedure sets *s3* to the concatenation of *s1* and *s2*.

```
procedure concat(s1, s2: string; var s3: string);
var len1, len2, len3, i: integer;
```

```
begin
    len1:= length(s1);
    len2:= length(s2);
    len3:= len1 + len2;
    if len3 > strsize
       then writeln('error - strings are too long')
       else begin
               s3:= s1;
               for i:= len1+1 to strsize
                   do s3[i]:= s2[i-len1]
            end {else begin}
end {procedure concat};
```

Note that the operator definition for *concat* in the ADT *string* returned the concatenated result as a function value, whereas the Pascal implementation is a procedure that sets a parameter to the result. The reason for this is that standard Pascal may not return an array. UCSD Pascal and Turbo Pascal implement *concat* as a predefined function accepting any number of strings as input and returning their concatenation. UCSD Pascal exempts certain built-in functions, including *concat*, from the restriction that a Pascal function may not return an array. Microsoft Pascal includes a version of *concat* whose first parameter is a varying-length string that is modified to contain the concatenated result.

The last operation we present on strings is the substring operation. *substr*($s1, i\ j, s2$) sets the string $s2$ to the j characters beginning at $s1[i]$. If fewer than j characters remain in $s1$, $s2$ is padded with blanks.

```
procedure substr(s1: string; i,j: integer; var s2: string);
var k,limit: integer;
begin
    if i+j-1 <= strsize
       then limit:= i+j-1
       else limit:= strsize;
    for k:= i to limit
        do s2[k-i+1]:= s1[k];
    for k:= limit-i+2 to strsize
        do s2[k]:= ' '
end {procedure substr};
```

(UCSD Pascal contains a built-in function similar to *substr*, called *copy*, which returns a substring of a given string. UCSD Pascal also contains two other built-in string routines: *insert*, to insert one string into the middle of another, and *delete*, to remove a portion of a string.)

While the routines we have presented give us the capability of implementing varying-length character strings, there is one basic flaw with the representation that we have chosen. Under our representation, trailing blanks are not significant. Very often, it is desirable to include trailing blanks as part of a character string. For example, given a long character string, we might wish to break the string into words separated by blanks. The *pos* function, however, cannot be used to locate a blank in a string. As another example, consider extracting the first six characters from the string '*today is a nice day*' using *substr*. The resultant string will have a length of only five characters. In the next section we see how varying-length character strings can be represented to include trailing blanks.

Varying-Sized Arrays and Pascal

The amount of work necessary to provide for varying-length character strings in Pascal is clearly excessive. This is symptomatic of a generally recognized problem with the Pascal language. The size of an array in a Pascal program must be known at compile time. There is no way to change the size of an array during the program's execution. If the number of elements needed in a particular situation depends on the input, the Pascal programmer must estimate the maximum number that will ever be required and declare an array of that size. If the program is used repetitively in a production environment, it will eventually be presented with input for which the estimate is not large enough and will fail. On the other hand, in most cases the estimate is a gross exaggeration, and all the extra space in the array is wasted. Unfortunately, there is no remedy for this situation in Pascal, because the language does not allow the size of an array to be determined dynamically during execution. (However, some personal computer Pascal compilers do allow arrays to be created dynamically with a size specified during program execution. This is a nonstandard feature.) There is a data structure that can be used instead of an array in situations where the number of elements varies dramatically from run to run. This data structure is a linked list and will be examined in Chapters 4 and 5.

Two-Dimensional Arrays

The component type of an array can be another array. For example, we may define

type matrix = **array** [1..3] **of array** [1..5] **of** integer;

This defines a new array type containing three elements. Each of these elements is itself an array containing five integers. This definition may be abbreviated to

type matrix = **array** [1..3, 1..5] **of** integer;

Figure 1.2.2a illustrates an array declared by

var a: matrix;

An element of this array is accessed by specifying two indices—a row number and a column number. For example, the darkened element in Figure 1.2.2a is in row 2 and column 4 and may be referenced as $a[2]$ $[4]$ or as $a[2, 4]$. Note that $a[2]$ refers to the entire row 2, but there is no equivalent way to reference an entire column. Figure 1.2.2b illustrates an array declared by

var b: array [-3..3, 2..5] of integer;

and names each element of the array. Such an array is called a ***two-dimensional*** array. The number of rows or columns is equal to the upper bound minus the lower bound plus 1. This number is called the ***range*** of the dimension. In the array a, the range of the first dimension is $3 - 1 + 1$,

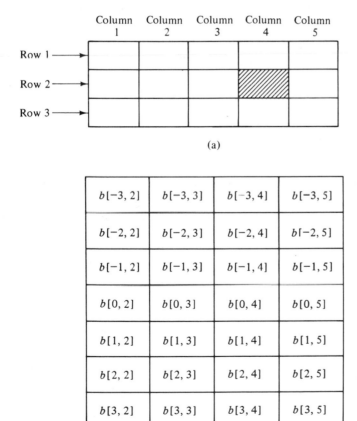

(a)

(b)

Figure 1.2.2 Two-dimensional arrays.

which is 3, and the range of the second dimension is $5 - 1 + 1$, which is 5. Thus the array a has three rows and five columns. In the array b, the number of rows is $3 - (-3) + 1 = 7$, and the number of columns is $5 - 2 + 1 = 4$. The number of elements in a two-dimensional array is equal to the product of the number of rows and the number of columns. Thus the array a contains $3 \times 5 = 15$ elements, and the array b contains $7 \times 4 = 28$ elements. If the index type of either dimension is not an integer subrange, the range of that dimension equals the number of elements in that index type. This can be computed as *ord* of the upper bound, minus *ord* of the lower bound, plus 1.

A two-dimensional array clearly illustrates the differences between a *logical* and a *physical* view of data. A two-dimensional array is a logical data structure which is useful in programming and problem solving. For example, such an array is useful in describing an object that is physically two-dimensional, such as a map or a checkerboard. It is also useful in organizing a set of values that are dependent upon two inputs. For example, a program for a department store that has 20 branches, each of which sells 30 items, might include a two-dimensional array declared by

var sales: array[1..20, 1..30] of real;

Each element *sales*[i, j] represents the amount of item j sold in branch i.

However, although it is convenient for the programmer to think of the elements of such an array as being organized in a two-dimensional table (and programming languages do indeed include facilities for treating them as a two-dimensional array), the hardware of most computers has no such facilities. An array must be stored in the memory of a computer and that memory is usually linear. By this we mean that the memory of a computer is essentially a one-dimensional array. A single address (which may be viewed as a subscript of a one-dimensional array) is used to retrieve a particular item from memory. To implement a two-dimensional array, it is necessary to develop a method of ordering its elements in a linear fashion and of transforming a two-dimensional reference to the linear representation.

One method of representing a two-dimensional array in memory is the *row-major* representation. Under this representation, the first row of the array occupies the first set of memory locations reserved for the array, the second row occupies the next set, and so on. There may also be several locations at the start of the physical array which serve as a header and which contain the upper and lower bounds of the two dimensions. (This header should not be confused with the headers discussed earlier. This header is for the entire array, wheras the headers mentioned earlier are headers for the individual array elements.) Figure 1.2.3 illustrates the row major representation of the two-dimensional array b just declared and illustrated in Figure 1.2.2b. Alternatively, the header need not be contiguous to the array elements, but could instead contain the address of the first element of the array.

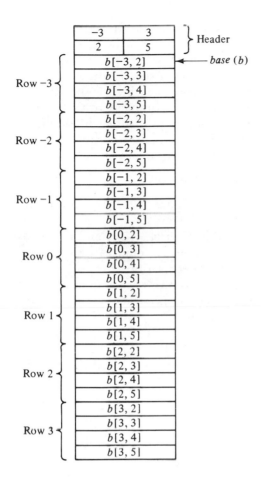

−3	3
2	5

⎱ Header

base (b)

b[−3, 2]
b[−3, 3]
b[−3, 4]
b[−3, 5]
b[−2, 2]
b[−2, 3]
b[−2, 4]
b[−2, 5]
b[−1, 2]
b[−1, 3]
b[−1, 4]
b[−1, 5]
b[0, 2]
b[0, 3]
b[0, 4]
b[0, 5]
b[1, 2]
b[1, 3]
b[1, 4]
b[1, 5]
b[2, 2]
b[2, 3]
b[2, 4]
b[2, 5]
b[3, 2]
b[3, 3]
b[3, 4]
b[3, 5]

Row −3
Row −2
Row −1
Row 0
Row 1
Row 2
Row 3

Figure 1.2.3 Representing a two-dimensional array.

Additionally, if the elements of the two-dimensional array are variable-length objects, the elements of the contiguous area could themselves contain the addresses of those objects in a form similar to those of Figure 1.2.1 for linear arrays.

Let us suppose that a two-dimensional array with integer index types is stored in row-major sequence, as in Figure 1.2.3, and let us suppose that, for an array ar, $base(ar)$ is the address of the first element of the array. That is, if ar is declared by

var ar: **array** $[l1..u1, l2..u2]$ **of** integer;

where $l1$, $u1$, $l2$, and $u2$ are the integer lower and upper bounds, then $base(ar)$ is the address of $ar[l1, l2]$. For example, for the array a of Figure 1.2.2a, $base(a)$ is the address of $a[1, 1]$, and for the array b of Figure 1.2.2b, $base(b)$ is the address of $b[-3, 2]$. Let us define $r2$ (the range of the second dimension) as $u2 - l2 + 1$. We also assume that $esize$ is the size of each element in the array. Let us calculate the address of an aribtrary element, $ar[i1, i2]$. Since the element is in row $i1$, its address can be calculated by computing the address of the first element of row $i1$ and adding the quantity $(i2 - l2)*esize$ (this quantity represents how far into row $i1$ the element at column $i2$ is). But to reach the first element of row $i1$ (which is the element $ar[i1, l2]$), it is necessary to pass through $i1 - l1$ complete rows, each of which contains $r2$ elements (since there is one element from each column in each row), so that the address of the first element of row $i1$ is at $base(ar) + (i1 - l1)*r2*esize$. Therefore, the address of $ar[i1, i2]$ is at

$$base(ar) + [(i1 - l1)*r2 + (i2 - l2)]*esize$$

As an example, consider the array b of Figure 1.2.2b, whose representation is illustrated in Figure 1.2.3. In this array, $l1 = -3$, $u1 = 3$, $l2 = 2$, and $u2 = 5$, so that $base(b)$ is the address of $b[-3, 2]$ and $r2$ equals 4. Let us also suppose that each element of the array requires a single unit of storage, so that $esize$ equals 1. (This is not necessarily true, since b was declared as an array of integers and an integer may need more than one unit of memory on a particular machine. For simplicity, however, we accept this assumption.) Then the location of $b[0, 4]$ may be computed as follows. To reach row 0, we must skip over rows -3, -2, and -1. Each of those rows contains four elements, consisting of one memory location each. Thus the first element of row zero (which is $b[0, 2]$) is 12 elements past the address of $b[-3, 2]$, which is $base(b)$. The element $b[0, 4]$ is two elements past $b[0, 2]$. Use of this formula yields the address of $b[0, 4]$ as

$$base(b) + [(0 - (-3))*4 + (4 - 2)]*1$$

which is

$$base(b) + 12 + 2 = base(b) + 14$$

You may confirm the fact that $b[0, 4]$ is 14 units past $base(b)$ in Figure 1.2.3. The formula for the location of an element of a two-dimensional array is easily modified to accommodate noninteger ranges as index types. $i1$, $i2$, $l1$, $u1$, $l2$, and $u2$ are all members of the index types. $r2$, the range of the second dimension, is now defined as the integer $ord(u2) - ord(l2) + 1$. $i1$, $i2$, $l1$, and $l2$ are replaced in the formula by $ord(i1), ord(i2), ord(l1)$, and $ord(l2)$. This yields

$$base(ar) + [(ord(i1) - ord(l1))*r2 + (ord(i2) - ord(l2))]*esize$$

as the location of $ar(i1, i2)$.

Multidimensional Arrays

Pascal also allows arrays with more than two dimensions. For example, a three-dimensional array may be declared by

var c: **array**[3..5, 1..2, 1..4] **of** integer;

which is equivalent to

var c: **array**[3..5] **of array**[1..2] **of array**[1..4] **of** integer;

and is illustrated in Figure 1.2.4a. An element of this array is specified by three subscripts such as c[4] [1] [3] or c[4, 1, 3]. The first subscript specifies a plane number, the second subscript a row number, and the third a column number. Such an array is useful when a value is determined by three inputs. For example, an array of temperatures might be indexed by latitude, longitude, and altitude.

   For obvious reasons, the geometric analogy breaks down when we go beyond three dimensions. However, Pascal does allow an arbitrary number of dimensions. For example, a six-dimensional array may be declared by

var d: **array**[1..7, 1..15, 1..3, -2..2, 1..8, 5..6] **of** integer;

Referencing an element of this array would require six subscripts, such as d[3, 14, 1, -1, 7, 6]. The number of different subscripts which are allowed in a particular position (the range of a particular dimension) equals the upper bound of that dimension, minus its lower bound, plus 1. The number of elements in an array is the product of the ranges of all its dimensions. For example, the array c contains $(5 - 3 + 1) \times (2 - 1 + 1) \times (4 - 1 + 1) = 3 \times 2 \times 4 = 24$ elements; the array d contains $7 \times 15 \times 3 \times 5 \times 8 \times 2 = 25,200$ elements.

   The row-major representation of arrays can be extended to arrays of more than two dimensions. Figure 1.2.4b illustrates the representation of the array c of Figure 1.2.4a. The elements of the six-dimensional array d just described are ordered as follows:

$$d[1, 1, 1, -2, 1, 5]$$
$$d[1, 1, 1, -2, 1, 6]$$
$$d[1, 1, 1, -2, 2, 5]$$
$$d[1, 1, 1, -2, 2, 6]$$
$$d[1, 1, 1, -2, 3, 5]$$
$$\cdots$$
$$\cdots$$
$$d[7, 15, 3, 2, 6, 5]$$
$$d[7, 15, 3, 2, 6, 6]$$
$$d[7, 15, 3, 2, 7, 5]$$
$$d[7, 15, 3, 2, 7, 6]$$
$$d[7, 15, 3, 2, 8, 5]$$
$$d[7, 15, 3, 2, 8, 6]$$

That is, the last subscript varies most rapidly and a subscript is not increased until all possible combinations of the subscripts to its right have been ex-

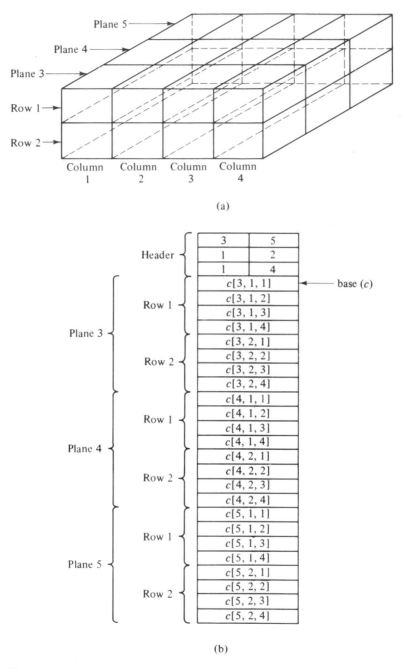

(a)

(b)

Figure 1.2.4 A three-dimensional array.

hausted. This is similar to an odometer (mileage indicator) of a car, where the rightmost digit changes most rapidly.

What mechanism is needed to access an element of an arbitrary multidimensional array? Suppose that ar is an n-dimensional array declared by

$$\text{var } ar: \textbf{array}\,[l_1..u_1, l_2..u_2, ..., l_n..u_n]\ \textbf{of integer};$$

which is stored in row-major order. Each element of ar is assumed to occupy $esize$ storage locations and $base(ar)$ is defined as the address of the first element of the array (which is $ar[l_1, l_2, ... , l_n]$). r_i is defined as $u_i - l_i + 1$ for all i between 1 and n. Then to access the element

$$ar[i_1, i_2, ..., i_n]$$

it is first necessary to pass through $(i_1 - l_1)$ complete "hyperplanes," each consisting of $r_2*r_3*...*r_n$ elements, to reach the first element of ar whose first subscript is i_1. Then it is necessary to pass through an additional $(i_2 - l_2)$ groups of $r_3*r_4*...*r_n$ elements to reach the first element of ar whose first two subscripts are i_1 and i_2, respectively. A similar process must be carried out through the other dimensions until the first element whose first $n - 1$ subscripts match those of the desired element is reached. Finally, it is necessary to pass through $(i_n - l_n)$ additional elements to reach the element desired.

Thus the address of $ar[i_1, i_2, ... , i_n]$ may be written as $base(ar) + esize*[(i_1-l_1)*r_2*...*r_n + (i_2 - l_2)*r_3*...*r_n + ... + (i_{n-1}-l_{n-1})*r_n + (i_n - l_n)]$, which can be evaluated more efficiently by using the equivalent formula

$$base\,(ar) + esize * [i_n - l_n + r_n*(i_{n-1} - l_{n-1} + r_{n-1}*(...$$
$$... + r_3*(i_2 - l_2 + r_2*(i_1 - l_1)))...))]$$

This formula may be evaluated by the following algorithm, which computes the address of the array element and places it into $addr$ (assuming that arrays i, l, and r of size n hold the indices, lower bounds, and the ranges, respectively):

$$offset := 0;$$
$$for\ j := 1\ to\ n$$
$$\quad do\ offset := r[j] * offset + (i[j] - l[j]);$$
$$addr := base\,(ar) + esize * offset$$

Sets in Pascal

A *set* is a collection of objects. In Pascal, all the objects in a set must be of the same **base type**. This base type can be any scalar or subrange type. However, the number of values that the type includes can be severely restricted by an implementation. For example, every Pascal implementation would permit a declaration such as

var x: set of 1..10;

The base type of the set *x* is the subrange type 1..10, which includes only 10 values. However, a declaration such as

var y: set of 1..100;

may be invalid in a Pascal implementation that allows fewer than 100 values in the base type of a set. We will shortly examine the reasons for this restriction. Note that the base type of a Pascal set may not be a composite type such as an array or another set.

A set can be specified by enumerating its elements in brackets. An example of this is the following program segment:

```
type days = (sun, mon, tues, wed, thur, fri, sat);
     dayset = set of days;
var    weekdays, weekend: dayset;
begin
     weekdays := [mon, tues, wed, thur, fri];
     weekend := [sun, sat]
```

It is also permissible to use a subrange to specify a group of set elements. For example, the variable *weekdays* could have been initialized as follows:

weekdays := [mon..fri]

All values of type *days* between the values *mon* and *fri* are elements of *weekdays*. The two ways of specifying set elements can be mixed, as in [1..4, 6, 9..11, 14..20], which contains 15 elements. The set with no elements is called the *empty set* and is denoted by [].

[The restriction on the number of elements in the base type of a set often causes a problem in enumerating elements of a set. For example, one popular Pascal compiler permits up to 60 elements in the base type of a set. Under this compiler, the set [1,100] is illegal, although it contains only two elements. The reason for this is that the type of such a set must be *set of* 1..100 and the base type 1..100 contains too many values. In fact, it might be the case that even the set [99,100] is illegal. Despite the fact that a base type of 99..100 or even 51..110 would make such a set valid, the compiler may assume that any enumerated set containing integers has a base type 1..60, so that any set containing an integer larger than 60 is invalid.

This problem is also prevalent in sets containing characters. The type *set of char* may be prohibited because the number of characters of type *char* is greater than the maximum allowable in the base type of a set. This may imply that such useful sets as ['0'..'9'] or ['a'..'z'] are invalid. (In any case, the subrange 'a'..'z' may include characters which are not letters, although the subrange '0'..'9' includes only digits.)

A Pascal programmer should determine the maximum number of values allowed in the base type of a set by the compiler being used and the implications of that number on enumerated sets.]

Operations on Sets

If a and b are sets, their **union** is a new set which contains every element that is in a or b. In Pascal, the union of two sets a and b is written as $a+b$. The **intersection** of two sets a and b is a new set containing every element that is in both a and b. In Pascal, the intersection of a and b is written $a*b$. The **difference** of two sets, a and b, is a new set containing every element of a that is not in b. In Pascal, the difference of a and b is written as $a-b$. Note that $a-b$ is not equal to $b-a$. The base types of the two operands of the union, intersection, and difference operators must be either identical or subranges of the same type, in which case the types are said to be **compatible**. However, some Pascal compilers prohibit operands whose base types are not identical.

As an illustration of these three operations, consider the integer sets $a = [1..5]$, $b = [1, 3, 5, 7, 9]$, and $c = [2, 4, 6, 8]$. Make sure you understand why each of the following expressions has the value indicated:

$$a+b = [1..5, 7, 9] \qquad b+c = [1..9]$$

$$a*b = [1, 3, 5] \qquad b*c = [\ ]$$

$$a-b = [2, 4] \qquad b-a = [7, 9]$$

$$b-c = b \qquad c-b = c$$

There are also four comparison operators defined on sets. $a = b$ is *true* if every element of a is an element of b and every element of b is an element of a; otherwise, it is *false*. $a <= b$ is *true* if every element of a is an element of b; otherwise, it is *false*. $a >= b$ is *true* if every element of b is an element of a; otherwise, it is *false*. If $a >= b$ is *true* (which is the same as saying that $b <= a$ is *true*), then set a **contains** set b (or, equivalently, set b **is contained in** set a). $a <> b$ is *true* if there is an element in one of the two sets that is not in the other; otherwise, $a <> b$ is *false*. As is the case with union, intersection, and difference, these operations may be applied in Pascal only to two sets of compatible base type.

Referring to the sets a, b, and c, make sure you understand why each of the following boolean expressions has the value indicated:

$$(a >= b) = \textit{false} \qquad (b+c >= a) = \textit{true}$$

$$(a-c <= b) = \textit{true} \qquad ((b+c)*a = a) = \textit{true}$$

$$(b*c <> [\ ]) = \textit{false} \qquad (a-b = c) = \textit{false}$$

Note that the set operators $+$, $*$, and $-$ have precedence over the set comparison operators $=$, $<=$, $>=$, and $<>$. Note also that the set operator $*$ takes precedence over the set operators $+$ and $-$, so that $(b+c)*a$ is not the same as $b+c*a$. All other mixtures of set operators are evaluated by performing the leftmost operation first.

The final set operation determines whether an object is an element of a set. *x in s*, where *x* is an object of the base type of the set *s*, is *true* if *x* is an element of *s*, and *false* otherwise. The *in* operator is at the same precedence level as the other comparison operators.

Implementation of a Set

Many peculiarities of sets in Pascal become clearer by looking at their implementation. Given the base type *B* of a set type *T*, any set of type *T* may be specified by its **characteristic function**. This function is defined for all values of type *B*. Given a set *s* of type *T*, the characteristic function of *s*, called *c*, is defined as follows. If *b* is of type *B*, then *c(b)* is 0 if *b* is not in *s* and is 1 if *b* is in *s*. For example, suppose that *B* is the type $1..10$, so that *T* is the type *set of* $1..10$. Suppose also that *s* is a variable of type *T* and that the value of *s* is $[1..3, 5, 9, 10]$. Then the characteristic function of *s* is as follows:

$$c(1) = 1 \quad c(4) = 0 \quad c(7) = 0 \quad c(10) = 1$$

$$c(2) = 1 \quad c(5) = 1 \quad c(8) = 0$$

$$c(3) = 1 \quad c(6) = 0 \quad c(9) = 1$$

The characteristic function of every element in the set is 1 and of every element not in the set is 0.

The most convenient way to represent a single characteristic function value is by a single bit. The most convenient way to represent the entire characteristic function is by a string of bits, one for each element in the base type of the set type. In the example, where the base type is $1..10$, a string of 10 bits is needed. For the set $[1..3, 5, 9, 10]$, the characteristic bit string is 1110100011. A 1 appears in every position, corresponding to an element of the set. The characteristic bit string of the set $[2, 4, 6, 8]$ is 0101010100, the string of the set $[1, 2, 5, 9]$ is 1100100010, the string of $[1..10]$ is 1111111111, and the string of $[\ ]$ is 0000000000. Every set on a given base type corresponds to one and only one characteristic bit string.

One of the reasons that a characteristic bit string is a useful method for representing a set is the ease with which the set operations can be performed using that method. Given two bit strings, $b1$ and $b2$, of the same length, their **disjunction** is the bit string of that length which contains a 1 in every position in which either $b1$ or $b2$ (or both) contains a 1. For example, if $b1 = 0101010100$ and $b2 = 1100100010$, their disjunction is

1101110110. (Note that disjunction is a natural extension of the boolean *or* operation, where if 1 represents *true* and 0 represents *false*, the disjunction of two bits is the *or*ing of the two boolean values they represent.) The disjunction of two characteristic bit strings representing two sets is the characteristic bit string of the union of those two sets. For example, $b1 = 0101010100$ represents the set [2, 4, 6, 8], $b2 = 1100100010$ represents [1, 2, 5, 9], and their disjunction, 1101110110, represents [1, 2, 4, 5, 6, 8, 9], which is the union of [2, 4, 6, 8] and [1, 2, 5, 9]. This fact is not at all surprising when we realize that an element is in a union if it is in either of two sets, and a bit is 1 in a disjunction if it is 1 in either of two bit strings.

Similarly, the ***conjunction*** of two bit strings, $b1$ and $b2$, is defined as a bit string containing a 1 in every position in which both $b1$ and $b2$ have a 1. For example, if $b1 = 0101010100$ and $b2 = 1100100010$, their conjunction is 0100000000. (Note that conjunction is a natural extension of the boolean ***and*** operation, where if 1 represents *true* and 0 represents *false*, the conjunction of two bits is the ***and***ing of the two boolean values they represent.) The conjunction of two strings represents the intersection of the two sets they represent, in the same way that their disjunction represents the union. For example, using $b1$ and $b2$ as above, their conjunction is 0100000000, which represents [2], the intersection of [2, 4, 6, 8] and [1, 2, 5, 9]. Again, this relationship is clear when we realize that an element is in an intersection if it is in both of two sets and a bit is 1 in a conjunction if it is 1 in both of two bit strings.

The ***difference*** of two bit strings, $b1$ and $b2$, is defined as the bit string containing a 1 in every position in which $b1$ contains a 1 and $b2$ contains a 0. The difference of two bit strings corresponds to the set difference of the two sets they represent. Again using $b1$ and $b2$, their difference is 0001010100, which represents [4, 6, 8], which equals [2, 4, 6, 8] − [1, 2, 5, 9]. (If 1 represents *true* and 0 represents *false*, the difference of two bits representing two boolean values, $x1$ and $x2$, represents the value of $x1$ ***and not*** $x2$.)

Most computers have hardware instructions (called ***logical operations***) to form the conjunction, disjunction, and difference of bit strings. For this reason, representation of sets by bit strings leads to efficient operation on sets. Similarly, comparison operations are easily implemented, because most computers have hardware operations to compare two bit strings for equality. For the set-containment operations ($<=$ and $>=$), the fact that $a <= b$ is *true* if and only if $a*b=a$, and $a >= b$ is *true* if and only if $a*b=b$ leads to the efficient implementation of these operations. The condition x *in* a is equivalent to $[x] <= a$, so this operation can also be implemented efficiently.

The reason for many restrictions on the use of sets in Pascal now becomes apparent. The limitation on the number of elements in the base type of a set stems from the maximum length of bit strings on which the logical operations may be performed efficiently. In general, this length varies from machine to machine and is usually related to the number of bits in a machine word. Some implementations allow larger base types by extending the hardware logical operations using software routines. Also, composite types such as arrays, sets, or records are not permitted as the base type of a set, because the possible values of such a composite type are too numerous for efficient implementation of a set by a characteristic bit string.

Similarly, the base types of two sets that participate in a set operation must be compatible to allow the same bit position in two bit strings representing the sets to represent the same element of the base types of the two sets.

Choosing Elements from a Set

Because of the Pascal implementation of a set, there are no built-in mechanisms for choosing an arbitrary element from a set or for performing some process for every element of a set. These are extremely useful operations in manipulating sets. Let us see how they can be implemented by Pascal routines.

Assume a set *s* declared as follows:

```
const lowval = ...;
      hival = ...;
type t = lowval..hival;
     stype = set of t;
var s: stype;
```

The function *arb* returns an arbitrary element of *s*. (Actually, *arb* returns the smallest element of *s*, but if we desire any element of the set, it is irrelevant which is returned.)

```
function arb(s: stype): t;
var i: t;
    found: boolean;
begin
    if s = [ ]
        then writeln('the set is empty')
        else begin
                found:= false;
                i:= lowval;
                while (i <= hival) and (not found)
                    do if i in s
                        then begin
                                arb:= i;
                                found:= true
                            end {then begin}
                        else i:= succ(i)
            end {else begin}
end {function arb};
```

Suppose that we wish to apply a routine *process* to every element of
s. We can do this using the following procedure:

```
procedure procset(s: stype)
var i: t;
begin
      for i:= lowval to hival
            do if i in s
                  then process(i)
end {procedure procset};
```

Note that there is no method of processing all the elements of a Pascal set
without checking every value in the base type of the set. This is an inefficiency in Pascal set processing.

Another common operation on a set is to find an element *i* in *s* such
that some condition on *i* is *true*. Let *cond* be a function defined for all values
of type *t* which returns a boolean value. Then a function to return an element
i of *s* for which *cond*(*i*) is *true* may be written as follows:

```
function find(s: stype): t;
var i: t;
      found, completed: boolean;
begin
      found:= false;
      completed:= false;
      i:= lowval;
      while (not completed) and (not found)
            do if (i in s) and cond(i)
                  then begin
                              find:= i;
                              found:= true
                        end {then begin}
                  else if i < hival
                        then i:= succ(i)
                        else completed:= true;
      if not found
            then writeln('no such element exists')
end {function find};
```

EXERCISES

1. (a) The *median* of an array of numbers is the element *m* of the array such that
half the remaining numbers in the array are greater than or equal to *m* and

half are less than or equal to m, if the number of elements in the array is odd. If the number of elements is even, the median is the average of the two elements $m1$ and $m2$ such that half the remaining elements are greater than or equal to $m1$ and $m2$ and half the elements are less than or equal to $m1$ and $m2$. Write a Pascal function that accepts an array of numbers and returns the median of the numbers in the array.

(b) The *mode* of an array of numbers is the number m in the array which is repeated most frequently. If several numbers are repeated with equal maximal frequency, there is no mode. Write a Pascal subroutine which accepts an array of numbers and returns the mode or an indication that the mode does not exist.

2. Write a Pascal program to read a group of temperature readings. A reading consists of two numbers, an integer between -90 and 90 representing the latitude at which the reading was taken and the observed temperature at that latitude. Print a table consisting of each latitude and the average temperature at that latitude. If there are no readings at a particular latitude, print *no data* instead of an average. Then print the average temperature in the northern and southern hemispheres (the northern consists of latitudes 1 through 90 and the southern consists of latitudes -1 through -90). (This average temperature should be computed as the average of the averages, not the average of the original readings.) Also determine which hemisphere is warmer. In making the determination, take the average temperatures in all latitudes of each hemisphere for which there are data for both that latitude and the corresponding latitude in the other hemisphere. (For example, if there are data for latitude 57 but not for latitude -57, the average temperature for latitude 57 should be ignored in determining which hemisphere is warmer.)

3. Write a program for a chain of 20 department stores, each of which sells 10 different items. Every month, each store manager submits a data card for each item, consisting of a branch number (from 1 to 20), an item number (from 1 to 10), and a sales figure (less than $\$100,000$) representing the amount of sales for that item in that branch. However, some managers may not submit cards for some items (e.g., not all items are sold in all branches). You are to write a Pascal program to read these data cards and print a table with 12 columns. The first column should contain the branch numbers from 1 to 20 and the word *total* in the last line. The next 10 columns should contain the sales figures for each of the 10 items for each of the branches, with the total sales of each item in the last line. The last column should contain the total sales of each of the 20 branches for all items, with the grand total sales figure for the chain in the lower right-hand corner. Each column should have an appropriate heading. If no sales were reported for a particular branch and item, assume zero sales. Do not assume that your input is in any particular order.

4. Show how a checkerboard can be represented by a Pascal array. Show how to represent the state of a game of checkers at a particular instant. Write a Pascal routine which inputs an array representing such a checkerboard and prints all possible moves which black can make from that position.

5. Write a routine *printar(a)* that accepts an m by n array a of integers and prints the values of the array on several pages as follows. Each page is to contain 50 rows and 20 columns of the array. Along the top of each page, headings COL 1, COL 2, and so on, should be printed, and along the left margin of each page, headings ROW 1, ROW 2, and so on, should be printed. The array should be printed by subarrays. For example, if a were a 100 by 100 array, the first page contains $a[1..50, 1..20]$, the second page contains $a[1..50, 21..40]$, the third page contains $a[1..50, 41..60]$, and so on, until the fifth page contains $a[1..50,$

81..100], the sixth page contains $a[51..100, 1..20]$, and so on. The entire printout occupies 10 pages. If the number of rows is not a multiple of 50, or the number of columns is not a multiple of 20, some pages of the printout should contain fewer than 100 numbers.

6. Assume that each element of an array a stored in row-major order occupies four units of storage. If a is declared by each of the following, and the address of the first element of a is 100, find the address of the indicated array element:

    (a) **var** a: **array**[1..100] ... ;   address of a[10]

    (b) **var** a: **array**[10..200] ... ;   address of a[100]

    (c) **var** a: **array**[-100..1, 1..100] ... ;   address of a[1, 12]

    (d) **var** a: **array**[1..10, 1..20] ... ;   address of a[1, 1]

    (e) **var** a: **array**[1..10, 1..20] ... ;   address of a[2, 1]

    (f) **var** a: **array**[1..10, 1..20] ... ;   address of a[5, 1]

    (g) **var** a: **array**[1..10, 1..20] ... ;   address of a[1, 10]

    (h) **var** a: **array**[1..10, 1..20] ... ;   address of a[2, 10]

    (i) **var** a: **array**[1..10, 1..20] ... ;   address of a[5, 3]

    (j) **var** a: **array**[1..10, 1..20] ... ;   address of a[10, 20]

    (k) **var** a: **array**[5..10, 1..20] ... ;   address of a[5, 13]

    (l) **var** a: **array**[5..10, 1..2] ... ;   address of a[7, 1]

    (m) **var** a: **array**[5..10, -10..20] ... ; address of a[5, -5]

    (n) **var** a: **array**[5..10, -10..20] ... ; address of a[7, 7]

7. Write a Pascal procedure *listoff* which accepts three one-dimensional array parameters of the same size: *lb*, *ub*, and *sub*. *lb* and *ub* represent the lower and upper bounds of an integer array. For example, if the elements of *lb* are

1 3 1 1 1

and the elements of *ub* are

3 5 10 6 3

then *lb* and *ub* represent an array a declared by

var a: **array**[1..3, 3..5, 1..10, 1..6, 1..3] of integer;

The elements of *sub* represent subscripts to this array. If *sub*[i] does not lie between *lb*[i] and *ub*[i], all subscripts from the *i*th onward are missing. In the preceding example, if the elements of *sub* are

1 3 1 2 0

then *sub* represents the expression $a[1, 3, 1, 2]$. The procedure *listoff* should print the offsets from the base of the array a represented by *lb* and *ub* of all the elements of a that are included in the array (or the offset of the single element if all subscripts are within bounds) represented by *sub*. Assume that the size (*esize*) of each element of a is one. In the example, *listoff* would print the values 4, 5, and 6.

8. (a) A *lower triangular* array a is an n by n array in which $a[i, j] = 0$ if $i < j$. What is the maximum number of nonzero elements in such an array? How can these elements be stored sequentially in memory? Develop an algorithm for accessing $a[i, j]$ where $i \geq j$. Define an *upper triangular* array in an analogous manner and do the same as described above for such an array.

(b) A *strictly lower triangular array* a is an n by n array in which $a[i, j] = 0$ if $i \le j$. Answer the questions of part (a) for such an array.

(c) Let a and b be two n by n lower triangular arrays. Show how an n by $n + 1$ array c can be used to contain the nonzero elements of the two arrays. Which elements of c represent the elements $a[i, j]$ and $b[i, j]$, respectively?

(d) A *tridiagonal* array a is an n by n array in which $a[i, j] = 0$ if the absolute value of $i - j$ is greater than 1. What is the maximum number of nonzero elements in such an array? How can these elements be stored sequentially in memory? Develop an algorithm for accessing $a[i, j]$ if the absolute value of $i - j$ is 1 or less. Do the same for an array a in which $a[i, j] = 0$ if the absolute value of $i - j$ is greater than k.

9. (a) Show how to represent a set of integers between 1 and n by a boolean array in Pascal.

(b) Write Pascal routines to implement the union, intersection, and difference operations and tests for equality, containment, and membership for sets represented by boolean arrays.

(c) Rewrite the routines of part (b) if the sets are represented by packed boolean arrays.

10. Assume the following type definitions and declarations:

```
type basetype = 1..25;
     settype = set of basetype;
var s1, s2, s3: settype;
```

Write Pascal routines to

(a) Form the set of all elements that are in $s1$ or $s2$, but not both.

(b) Form the set of all elements that are in a single one of $s1$, $s2$, and $s3$.

(c) Form the set of all elements that are in exactly two of $s1$, $s2$, and $s3$.

(d) Form the set of all elements of type *basetype* that are not in $s1$.

(e) Form the set of all elements of type *basetype* that are not in any of $s1$, $s2$, or $s3$.

(f) Form the set of all elements of type *basetype* that are not in all three sets $s1$, $s2$, and $s3$.

11. Write a Pascal program to create and print the following set s. s contains the integers 1 and 2. s also contains all integers (less than the upper bound u allowed by your compiler for the type $1..u$ as the base type of a set) of the form $3*x + y$, where x and y are distinct elements of s. (That is, s contains 1, 2, 5, 7, 8, 10, 11, 13, 14, 16, 17, ...)

3. RECORDS IN PASCAL

In this section we examine the Pascal data structure called a *record*. A record is a group of items in which each item is identified by its own *field identifier*. For example, a record for a name can be defined by the type definition:

```
type nametype = record
                first: packed array [1..10] of char;
                midinit: char;
                last: packed array [1..20] of char
                end;
```

This definition may now be used to declare a variable such as

> **var** myname: nametype;

Alternatively, *myname* could have been declared directly as

> **var** myname: **record**
>> first: **packed array** [1..10] **of** char;
>> midinit: char;
>> last: **packed array** [1..20] **of** char
>
> **end**;

As in the case of arrays, the two basic operations on records are *extraction* and *storing*. *Fields* of a record are referenced by specifying the variable name followed by the field identifier separated by a period. For example, the middle initial of *myname* could be extracted by

> mid:= myname.midinit

and could be assigned the letter '*j*' by

> myname.midinit:= 'j'

We assume that you are familiar with the record from an introductory course. Sections 6 through 12 of the Appendix describe the facilities available in Pascal for defining and using records. In the remainder of this section, we examine how records can be specified as an abstract data type. We then illustrate the use of records in implementing varying-length character strings and contrast the record implementation with the array implementation of the previous section. We also discuss the implementation records.

Record ADTs

A single abstract data type cannot be used to specify the general record type. The reason for this is that each record definition is a different data type rather than an instance of a single general record data type. We present a specification for a sample record data type, one that contains two simple fields:

> **type** rf1f2type = **record**
>> f1: field1type;
>> f2: field2type
>
> **end**;

The ADT specification for the record type *rf1f2type* is as follows. A similar ADT could be defined for other record types.

> ***abstract type*** *rf*1*f*2*type* = ***sequence*** (2) ***of*** (*field*1*type*, *field*2*type*);

> ***abstract function*** *extract*1 (*r*: *rf*1*f*2*type*): *field*1*type*;   { *written r.f*1 }
> ***postcondition*** *extract*1 = r_1 ;

abstract function extract2 (r: rf1f2type): field2type;   { **written** r.f2 }
postcondition extract2 = r_2 ;

abstract procedure store1 (r: rf1f2type; val1: field1type);
{ **written** r.f1 := val1 }

postcondition r_1 = val1;

abstract procedure store2 (r: rf1f2type; val2: field2type);
{ **written** r.f2 := val2 }

postcondition r_2 = val2;

Note that there is a separate *store* and *extract* operation for each field.

Character Strings Using Records

In the preceding section, we presented an implementation of varying-length character strings using arrays. To refresh your memory, a string was represented by a fixed-length array of characters with trailing blanks. All trailing blanks were considered insignificant and not part of the string. There are two drawbacks to that method. First, it is sometimes desirable to include trailing blanks in a string. Second, to determine the length of the string, the trailing blanks must be traversed until the last nonblank position is found. Since finding the length of a string is such a common operation, this method may be too inefficient.

The record type is extremely convenient for defining new data structures, such as varying-length strings. We illustrate its usefulness in this section by defining varying-length character strings using a record type. The technique that we present here will be repeated throughout the book to define new and complex data structures.

A record representing a varying-length character string consists of two fields. One of these fields is an array containing the actual characters of the string, and the other is an integer representing the current length of the string:

```
const strsize = 80;
type string = record
                  ch: packed array [1..strsize] of char;
                  length: 0..strsize
              end;
```

For example, to represent the string '*john smith*' of length 10 in a string variable s, the 10 elements s.ch[1] through s.ch[10] are set to the 10 characters '*j*' through '*h*', and s.*length* is set to 10. The values of s.ch[11] through s.ch[*strsize*] are irrelevant to the value of the string. The string '*john smith* ' with 3 trailing blanks is represented in a string variable s by setting s.ch[1] through s.ch[10] to the 10 characters '*j*' through '*h*', s.ch[11], s.ch[12], and *s.ch*[13] to blanks, and *s. length* to 13. Under such a scheme, trailing blanks are significant because they are included in the length of the string.

Let us now write routines similar to those of the preceding section for this representation. It is no longer necessary to write a function *length* to determine the length of a string *s*, since the variable *s length* can be used directly. The function *pos(s1, s2)* accepts two varying-length character strings *s*1 and *s*2 and returns the position of the first occurrence of *s*2 in *s*1 if *s*2 appears as a substring of *s*1. If *s*2 is not a substring of *s*1, then *pos* returns 0.

```
function pos(s1, s2: string): integer;
var i, j, len1, len2: integer;
    found, finis: boolean;
begin
     len1:= s1.length;
     len2:= s2.length;
     i:= 0;
     found:= false;
     while (i+len2 <= len1) and (not found)
          do begin
                 finis:= false;
                 j:= 1;
                 while ( j <= len2) and (not finis)
                      do if s1.ch[i+j] = s2.ch[j]
                            then j:= j + 1
                            else finis:= true;
                 if j > len2
                      then found:= true
                      else i:= i + 1
          end {while...do begin};
     if found
        then pos:= i + 1
        else pos:= 0
end {function pos};
```

The procedure *concat(s1, s2, s3)* sets *s3* to the concatenation of *s*1 and *s*2:

```
procedure concat(s1, s2: string; var s3: string);
var len1, len2, len3, i: integer;
begin
     len1:= s1.length;
     len2:= s2.length;
     len3:= len1+len2;
     if len3 > strsize
        then writeln('error - strings are too long')
```

```
                    else begin
                         s3.ch:= s1.ch;
                         for i:= len1+1 to len3
                              do s3.ch[i] := s2.ch[i-len1] ;
                         s3.length:= len3
                    end {else begin}
          end {procedure concat};
```

The procedure *substr(s1, i, j, s2)* sets the string *s2* to the substring of *s1* of length *j* beginning with the *i*th character. If fewer than *j* characters remain in *s1*, *s2* is padded with blanks.

```
          procedure substr(s1: string; i, j: integer; var s2: string);
          var k, limit: integer;
          begin
               if i+j-1 <= s1.length
                    then limit:= i+j-1
                    else limit:= s1.length;
               for k:= i to limit
                    do s2.ch[k-i+1]:= s1.ch[k];
               for k:= limit-i+2 to j
                    do s2.ch[k]:= ' ';
               s2.length:= j
          end {procedure substr};
```

Another routine becomes necessary under the record representation of character strings. This is a function to determine if two strings are equal. Under the array representation, the two packed arrays could be tested for equality using the Pascal = operator. However, under the record representation, if *s1* and *s2* are two records representing strings, the arrays *s1.ch* and *s2.ch* might be identical, yet *s1* and *s2* represent different strings. For example, suppose that both *s1.ch*[1] through *s1.ch*[26] and *s2.ch*[1] through *s2.ch*[26] contain the letters of the alphabet (and *s1.ch*[27] through *s1.ch*[*strsize*] and *s2.ch*[27] through *s2.ch*[*strsize*] are blank). If *s1.length* is 4 and *s2.length* is 5, then *s1* represents the string '*abcd*' while *s2* represents '*abcde*', so the strings are unequal. Similarly, if *s1.ch*[1] and *s2.ch*[1] both equal '*a*' and all the remaining characters of both arrays are blanks but *s1.length* is 3 and *s2.length* is 2, then *s1* and *s2* are unequal since *s1* represents '*a*' with two trailing blanks, while *s2* represents '*a*' with only one trailing blank. Note that under the array representation of the previous section, the two strings are equal, because trailing blanks are insignificant and both arrays (*s1.ch* and *s2.ch*) represent the string '*a*' of length 1.

It is also possible for the two arrays *s1.ch* and *s2.ch* to be unequal, yet for the two strings to be equal. For example, if *s1.ch* starts with '*abcde . . .*' and *s2.ch* starts with '*abcdf . . .*' but *s1.length* and *s2.length* are both 4, both *s1* and *s2* represent the string '*abcd*'.

Thus a function to determine whether two strings are equal is clearly necessary.

```
function equalstr(s1, s2: string): boolean;
var i, len1: integer;
    equal: boolean;
begin
    len1 := s1.length;
    if s2.length <> len1
      then equalstr := false
      else begin
              i := 1;
              equal := true;
              while (i <= len1) and (equal)
                  do if s1.ch[i] = s2.ch[i]
                       then i := i + 1
                       else equal := false;
              equalstr := equal
           end {else begin}
end {function equalstr};
```

Implementing Records

Let us now turn our attention from the definition and application of record types to their implementation. Any type in Pascal may be thought of as a pattern or a template. By this we mean that a type is a method for interpreting a portion of memory. When a variable identifier is declared as being of a certain type, we are saying that the identifier refers to a certain portion of memory and that the contents of that memory are to be interpreted according to the pattern defined by the type. The type specifies both the amount of memory set aside for the variable and the method by which that memory is interpreted.

For example, suppose that under a certain Pascal implementation an integer is represented by 4 bytes, a real number by 8, and a packed array of 10 characters by 10 bytes. Then the variable declarations

```
var x: integer;
    y: real;
    z: packed array[1..10] of char;
```

specify that 4 bytes of memory be set aside for x, 8 bytes be set aside for y, and 10 bytes for z. Once those bytes are set aside for those variables (which occurs just prior to the program's execution), the names x, y, and z will always refer to those locations. When x is referenced, its 4 bytes will be interpreted as an integer; when y is referenced, its 8 bytes will be interpreted as a real number; and when z is referenced, its 10 bytes will be interpreted as a collection of 10 characters in packed format. Note that the amount of storage set aside for each type and the method by which the contents of memory are interpreted as specific types vary from one machine and Pascal implementation to another. But within a given Pascal implementation, any type always indicates a specific amount of storage and a specific method of interpreting that storage.

Now suppose that we defined a record type by

```
type rectype = record
                    field1: integer;
                    field2: real;
                    field3: packed array [1..10] of char
               end;
```

and declared a variable

```
var r: rectype;
```

Then the amount of memory specified by the record type is the sum of the storage specified by each of its field types. Thus the space required for the variable r of type *rectype* is the sum of the space required for an integer (4 bytes), a real number (8 bytes), and a packed array of 10 characters (10 bytes). Therefore, 22 bytes are set aside for r. The first 4 of these bytes are interpreted as an integer, the next 8 as a real number, and the last 10 as a packed array of characters. (This is not always true. On some computers, objects of certain types may not begin anywhere in memory but are constrained to start at certain "boundaries." For example, an integer of length 4 bytes may have to start at an address divisible by 4, and a real number of length 8 bytes may have to start at an address divisible by 8. Thus, in our example, if the starting address of r is 200, the integer occupies bytes 200 through 203, but the real number cannot start at byte 204 because that location is not divisible by 8. Thus the real number must start at location 208 and the entire record requires 26, rather than 22, bytes. Bytes 204 through 207 are wasted space.)

For every reference to a field of a record, an address must be calculated. Associated with each field identifier of a record type is an *offset*, which specifies how far beyond the start of the record is the location of that field. In the example just presented, the offset of *field*1 is 0, the offset of *field*2 (assuming no boundary restrictions) is 4, and the offset of *field*3 is 12. Associated with each record variable is a base address, which is the location of the start of the memory allocated to that variable. These associations are established by the compiler and are of no concern to the user. To calculate the location of a field in a record, the offset of the field identifier is added to the base address of the record variable.

For example, assume that the base address of r is 200. Then what really happens in executing a statement such as

$$r.field2 := r.field1 + 3.7$$

is the following. First, the location of $r.field1$ is determined as the base address of r (200) plus the field offset of $field1$ (0), which yields 200. The 4 bytes at locations 200 through 203 are interpreted as an integer. This integer is then converted to a real number, which is then added to the real number 3.7. The result is a real number that takes up 8 bytes. The location of $r.field2$ is then computed as the base address of r (200) plus the field offset of $field2$ (4), which is 204. The 8 bytes 204 through 211 are set to the real number computed in evaluating the expression.

Note that the process of calculating the address of a record component is very similar to that of calculating the address of an array component. In both cases, an offset that depends on the component selector (the field identifier or the subscript value) is added to the base address of the compound structure (the record or the array). In the case of a record, the offset is associated with the field identifier by the type definition, whereas in the case of an array, the offset is calculated based on the value of the subscript.

These two types of addressing (record and array) may be combined. For example, to calculate the address of $r.field3[4]$, we first use record addressing to determine the base address of the array $r.field3$ and then use array addressing to determine the location of the fourth element of that array. The base address of $r.field3$ is given by the base address of r (200) plus the offset of $field3$ (12), which is 212. The address of $r.field3[4]$ is then determined as the base address of $r.field3$ (212) plus 3 (the subscript 4 minus the lower array bound 1) times the size of each element of the array (1), which yields $212 + 3 * 1$, or 215.

As a further example, consider another variable rr, declared by

var rr: **array** [1..20] **of** rectype;

rr is an example of an array of records. If the base address of rr is 400, the address of $rr[14].field3[6]$ may be computed as follows. The size of each component of rr is 22, so the location of $rr[14]$ is $400 + 13 * 22$, which is 686. The base address of $rr[14].field3$ is then $686 + 12$, which is 698. The address of $rr[14].field3[6]$ is therefore $698 + 5 * 1$, which is 703. (Again, this ignores the possibility of boundary restrictions. For example, although the type *rectype* may require only 22 bytes, each *rectype* may have to start at an address divisible by 4, so that 2 bytes are wasted between each element of rr and its neighbor. If such is the case, the size of each element of rr is really 24, so that the address of $rr[14].field3[6]$ is acutally 729 rather than 703.)

Variant Records

Thus far, each record type we have looked at has had fixed fields and a single format. Pascal also allows another type of record, the *variant record*, which permits a record variable to be interpreted in several different ways.

For example, consider an insurance company that offers three kinds of policies: life, auto, and home. A policy number identifies each insurance policy, of whatever kind. For all three types of insurance, it is necessary to have the policyholder's name and address, the amount of the insurance, and the monthly premium payment. For auto and home insurance policies, a deductible amount is needed. For a life insurance policy, the insured's birth date and beneficiary are needed. For an auto insurance policy, a license number, state, model, and year are requried. For a homeowner's policy, an indication of the age of the house and the presence of any security precautions are required. A policy record type for such a company may be defined as a variant record. We first define four auxiliary types.

```
type addrtype = record
                    streetaddr: packed array [1..50] of char;
                    city: packed array [1..10] of char;
                    state: packed array [1..2] of char;
                    zip: packed array [1..5] of '0'..'9'
                end;
     date = record
                    month: 1..12;
                    day: 1..31;
                    year: 0..2000
                end;
     policytype = (life, auto, home);
     policy = record
                    polnumber: integer;
                    name: packed array [1..30] of char;
                    address: addrtype;
                    amount: integer;
                    premium: real;
                    case kind: policytype of
                        life: (beneficiary: packed array [1..30] of char;
                            birthday: date);
                        auto: (autodeduct: integer;
                            license: packed array [1..10] of char;
                            state: packed array [1..2] of char;
                            model: packed array [1..15] of char;
                            year: 1900..2000);
                        home: (homededuct: integer;
                            yearbuilt: 1700..2000;
                            security: (bolts, alarm, dog, watchman, other))
                end;
```

Let us examine the variant type definition more closely. The definition, between the keywords *record* and *end*, consists of two parts: a fixed part and a variant part. The fixed part consists of all field declarations up to the keyword *case*, while the variant part consists of the remainder of the type definition. The fixed part may be omitted, but, if present, must precede the variant part. The variant part may be omitted, but then the record is no longer a variant record.

The variant part begins with the keyword *case*, followed by a field declaration, followed by the keyword *of*. The field of the record declared after the keyword *case* is called a ***tag field*** and its type is called a ***tag type***. The tag type may not be *real* or a compound type. In the record type *policy*, the tag field is *kind* and its tag type is the enumerated type (*life, auto, home*). Following the keyword *of* is a list of variant declarations. Each variant declaration consists of a constant whose type is the tag type (e.g., *auto*), followed by a colon, followed by a parenthesized list of field declarations. The fields declared in a variant declaration are called ***variant fields***, while those declared in the fixed part of a record definition are called ***fixed fields***. The tag field is also a fixed field. Note that the single keyword *end* ends both the variant part and the entire record definition.

Now that we have examined the syntax of a variant record definition, let us examine its semantics. A variable declared as being of a variant record type *t* (e.g., *var p:policy*) always contains all the fixed fields of *t*, including the tag field. Thus it is always valid to reference *p.name* or *p.premium* or *p.kind*. However, the variant fields contained in the value of such a variable depend on the value of its tag field. In the example, if the value of *p.kind* is *life*, then *p* currently contains variant fields *p.beneficiary* and *p.birthday*, since those are the only fields declared in the variant declaration preceded by the value *life* in the record definition. It is invalid to reference *p.model* or *p.yearbuilt* while the value of *p.kind* is *life*. Similarly, if the value of *p.kind* is *auto*, we may reference *p.autodeduct*, *p.license*, *p.state*, *p.model*, and *p.year*, but may not reference any other variant field. When the value of a tag field is changed, the variant fields associated with the old value cease to exist and the variant fields associated with the new value come into being with undefined values.

Thus a variant record allows a variable to take on several different "types" at different points in execution. It also allows an array to contain objects of different types. For example, the array *a* declared by

var a: **array**[1..100] **of** policy;

may contain life, auto, and home insurance policies.

Suppose that such an array *a* is declared and it is desired to raise the premiums of all auto insurance policies and all home insurance policies for homes built before 1950 by 5%. This can be done as follows: (Note the use of the *with* statement which is discussed in Sections 9 and 10 of the Appendix.)

```
for i:= 1 to 100
    do with a[i]
        do begin
            case kind of
                life:;
                auto: premium:= 1.05 * premium;
                home: if yearbuilt < 1950
                        then premium:= 1.05 * premium
            end {case}
        end {with...do begin}
```

A variant of a record may contain no variant fields, in which case the list of variant fields in the variant declaration consists of an open parenthesis followed immediately by a closed parenthesis. For example, a mailing list may contain both home and business addresses. Business addresses may contain a company name and a department, while home addresses do not. We may define

```
type custype = (home, business);
    customer = record
                name: packed array[1..30] of char;
                address: addrtype;
                case kind: custype of
                    home: ( );
                    business: (company, dept: packed array[1..25] of char)
            end;
```

The tag field is used to determine the variant that the record variable is currently assuming. However, it is possible for a tag field to be omitted from the declaration of a record, although the tag type must be included. For example, the following is a definition of such a record:

```
type tag123 = 1..3;
    vrectype = record
                field1: integer;
                case tag 123 of
                    1: (field11, field12: integer);
                    2: ( );
                    3: (field31: char)
            end;
```

No tag field is included, but the variants are specified by the values of the tag type *tag*123. Any field of any variant may be referenced at any time.

However, that field must be initialized before it can be used meaningfully. Once any field of one variant is referenced, there is no guarantee that the fields of any other variant retain their values.

For example, assume the declaration

var v: vrectype;

and the statements

v.field11:= 7;
v.field12:= 10;
writeln (v.field11, v.field12);

These statements utilize the first variant of the record. Now, if we execute

v.field31:= 'a';

we are utilizing the third variant. If we now again execute

writeln (v.field11, v.field12);

an error may result, because a different variant (variant 3) was referenced between the initialization and current utilization of the current variant (variant 1).

Implementation of Variant Records

To understand fully the concept of a variant record, it is necessary to examine its implementation. A record type may be regarded as a road map to an area of memory. It defines how the memory is to be interpreted. A variant record type provides several different road maps for the same area of memory, and a tag field value determines which road map is in current use. For example, consider the simple variant record type and variable

type tagtype = (first, second);
vtype = **record**
       f1: integer;
       f2: real;
       case c: (tagtype) **of**
       first: (f3, f4: integer);
       second: (f5, f6: real)
    end;
var v: vtype;

Let us again assume an implementation in which an integer requires 4 bytes and a real number 8 bytes. Let us also assume that an enumerated type such as *tagtype* uses 4 bytes (although only a single bit is needed). Then the three fixed fields $f1$, $f2$, and c occupy 16 bytes. The fields of the first variant, $f3$ and $f4$, require 8 bytes, while the fields of the second require 16. The memory actually allocated for the variant part of such a record variable is the maximum of the space needed by any single variant. In this case, therefore, 16 bytes are allocated for the variant part of *v*. Added to the 16 bytes needed for the fixed part, 32 bytes are allocated to *v*.

The different variants of a variant record overlay each other. In the example, if space for *v* is allocated starting at location 100, so that *v* occupies bytes 100 through 131, the fixed fields *v.f*1, *v.f*2, and *v.c* occupy bytes 100 through 103, 104 through 111, and 112 through 115, respectively. If the value of the tag field *v.c* is *first*, bytes 116 through 119 and 120 through 123 are occupied by *v.f*3 and *v.f*4, respectively, while bytes 124 through 131 are unused. If the value of *v.c* is *second*, bytes 116 through 123 are occupied by *v.f*5 and bytes 124 through 131 are occupied by *v.f*6. That is why only one variant of the record can exist at a single instant. All the variants of a record use the same space and that space can be used by only one of them at a time. The value of the tag field determines how that space is organized.

If no tag field exists, any interpretation of the space for a variant record can be used at any time. For example, assume the definition and declaration

```
type tagtype = (first, second);
     vtype2 = record
                  f1: integer;
                  f2: real;
                  case tagtype of
                       first: (f3, f4: integer);
                       second: (f5, f6: real)
              end;
   var v2: vtype2;
```

Then the total of 28 bytes are allocated for *v2* (12 for the fixed part and 16 for the longest variant part). If *v2* begins at location 100, a reference to *v2.f*1 is to bytes 100 through 103, a reference to *v2.f*2 is to bytes 104 through 111, a reference to *v2.f*3 is to bytes 112 through 115, a reference to *v2.f*4 is to bytes 116 through 119, a reference to *v2.f*5 is to bytes 112 through 119, and a reference to *v2.f*6 is to bytes 120 through 127. Because there is no tag type, any field may be referenced at any time. However, an assignment to either *v2.f*3 or *v2.f*4 destroys the value of *v2.f*5, since they occupy the same space. Although this does not destroy the value of *v2.f*6 under the particular implementation we have presented, another implementation (e.g., if an integer requires 6 bytes while a real takes up 8, or if an integer and a real both occupy 4) may not be so kind. A Pascal programmer should be writing programs that are implementation-independent, unless he is writing a systems program for a specific implementation. The Pascal language itself (being, by definition, implementation-independent) leaves the values of the fields of all other variants undefined once a field in a particular variant is referenced.

If a variant record does not contain a tag field, there is no way to determine which variant of a record variable is currently in use. The programmer must keep track of the current variant and make sure not to reference a field of a different variant until the values of the current variant are no longer needed. It is therefore always a good idea to include a tag field in a variant record and to keep that field set to its appropriate value.

EXERCISES

1. A *complex number* is one that contains real and imaginary parts, both of which are real numbers. If $c1$ has real and imaginary parts $r1$ and $i1$, respectively, and $c2$ has real and imaginary parts $r2$ and $i2$, respectively, then
   (a) The sum of $c1$ and $c2$ has real part $r1 + r2$ and imaginary part $i1 + i2$.
   (b) The difference of $c1$ and $c2$ has real part $r1 - r2$ and imaginary part $i1 - i2$.
   (c) The product of $c1$ and $c2$ has real part $r1*r2 - i1*i2$ and imaginary part $r1*i2 + r2*i1$.

   Implement complex numbers by declaring a record with real and complex parts and write routines to add, subtract, and multiply such complex numbers.

2. Suppose that a real number is represented by a Pascal record such as

   ```
   type realtype = record
                     left: integer;
                     right: 0..maxint
                   end;
   ```

   where *left* and *right* represents the digits to the left and right of the decimal point, respectively. If *left* is a negative integer, the represented real number is negative.
   (a) Write a routine to input a real number and create a record representing that number.
   (b) Write a function that accepts such a record and returns the real number represented by it.
   (c) Write routines *add*, *subtract*, and *multiply* that accept two such records and set the value of a third record to represent the number that is the sum, difference, and product, respectively, of the two input records.

3. Assume that an integer needs four bytes, a real number needs eight bytes, an unpacked array of characters takes four times as many bytes as characters in the array, and a packed array takes as many bytes as characters in the array. Assume the following definitions and declarations:

   ```
   type nametype = record
                     first: packed array[1..12] of char;
                     midinit: char;
                     last: packed array[1..20] of char
                   end;
   ```

```
            person = record
                      name: nametype;
                      birthday: array[1..3] of integer;
                      parents: array[1..2] of nametype;
                      income: real;
                      numchildren: integer;
                      address: array[1..20] of char;
                      city: array[1..10] of char;
                      state: array[1..2] of char
                    end;
        var p: array[1..100] of person;
```

If the starting address of p is 100, what are the starting addresses (in bytes) of each of the following?

(a) p[10]

(b) p[20].*name.midinit*

(c) p[20].*income*

(d) p[20].*address*[5]

(e) p[5].*parents*[2].*last*[10]

4. Assuming the space requirements of Exercise 3, what is the starting location of each field of a record variable x declared as in each of the following, if the starting location for x is 100? Assume that an element of an enumerated type requires four bytes.

```
    (a) type abcde = (a, b, c, d, e);
            var x: record
                    f1: real;
                    case f2: abcde of
                        a: (f3, f4: array[1..10] of char);
                        b: (f5, f6: record
                                        f7: real;
                                        f8: integer
                                    end);
                        c: (f9, f10: packed array[1..20] of char);
                        d: (f11, f12: real);
                        e: (f13, f14: integer)
                  end;

    (b) type tagtype = 17..19;
            var x: record
                    case f1: tagtype of
                        17: (f2, f3, f4: char);
                        18: (f5, f6: integer);
                        19: (f7, f8: real)
                  end;
```

(c) **type** abc = (a, b, c);
         var x: **record**
                    f1: integer;
                    case abc **of**
                        a: (f2, f3: real);
                        b: (f4, f5: integer);
                        c: (f6, f7: **packed array** [1..20] **of** char)
                 end;

5. Write a Pascal procedure to print the value of all current fields in the current value of the record variable *x* declared in Exercise 4(a).

Exercises 6 through 8 refer to material presented in Sections 6 through 12 of the Appendix.

6. Which of the following sets of definitions and declarations are invalid, and why?

(a) **type** x = 1..10;
         var z: **record**
                    x: x;
                    y: integer
                 end;

(b) **procedure** sample(x, y: integer);
         type xtype = 1..10;
         var i, j, x: xtype;

(c) **type** oneten = 1..10;
         function sample(x, y: oneten): oneten;
         type oneten = (one, five, ten);
                 rectype = **record**
                              one: oneten;
                              ten: oneten
                          end;

(d) **type** st = **record**
                    x: integer;
                    y: real
                 end;
         var x, y: st;
             st1, st2, st: integer;

(e) **type** xt = 1..10;
         var xt: xt;
         type tag12 = 1..2;

(f) rec = **record**
     f1: integer
     case f2: tag12 **of**
       1: (x, y, z: integer);
       2: (v, w, x: integer)
    end;
(g) **type** rec = **record**
       f1: integer;
       f2: **record**
         f1: integer;
         f2: real;
         rec: char
        end
      end;
   var f1, f2: rec;

7. Assume two arrays, one of student records, the other of employee records. Each student record contains fields for a last name, first name and a grade-point index. Each employee record contains fields for the last name, first name, and salary. Both arrays are ordered in alphabetical order by last name and first name. Two records with the same last name/first name do not appear in the same array. Write a Pascal procedure to give a 10% raise to every employee who has a student record and whose grade-point index is greater than 3.0.

8. Write a procedure as in Exercise 7, but assume that the employee and student records are kept in two ordered external files rather than in two ordered arrays.

2

THE STACK

One of the most useful concepts in computer science is that of the stack. In this chapter we examine this deceptively simple data structure and see why it plays such a prominent role in the areas of programming and programming languages. We shall define the abstract concept of a stack and show how that concept can be made into a concrete and valuable tool in problem solving.

1. DEFINITION AND EXAMPLES

A *stack* is an ordered collection of items into which new items may be inserted and from which items may be deleted at one end, called the *top* of the stack. Figure 2.1.1 illustrates a stack containing items *A*, *B*, *C*, *D*, *E*, and *F*. However, the definition of a stack provides for insertion and deletion of items, so that a stack is really a dynamic, constantly changing object. Figure 2.1.1 is only a snapshot of a stack at a particular point in its continuing evolution. To have a true view of a stack, a motion picture is necessary.

The question therefore arises, how does a stack change? From the definition, note that a single end of the stack must be designated as the stack *top*. New items may be put on top of the stack (in which case the top of the stack moves upward to correspond to the new highest element) or items that are at the top of the stack may be removed (in which case the top of the stack moves downward to correspond to the new highest element). To answer the question "which way is up?" we must decide which end of the

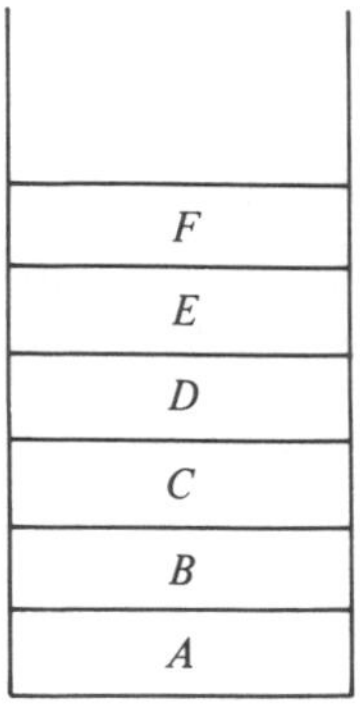

Figure 2.1.1   A stack containing six items.

stack is designated as its top—that is, at which end will items be added or deleted? By drawing Figure 2.1.1 so that *F* is physically higher on the page than all the other items in the stack, we mean to imply that *F* is the current top element of the stack. If any new items are to be added to the stack, they will be placed on top of *F* and if any items are to be deleted, *F* will be the first to be deleted. This is also indicated by the vertical lines which extend past the items of the stack in the direction of the stack top.

Let us now view a motion picture of a stack to see how it expands and shrinks with the passage of time. Such a picture is given by Figure 2.1.2. In Figure 2.1.2a we see the stack as it existed at the time that the snapshot of Figure 2.1.1 was taken. In Figure 2.1.2b, item *G* is added to the stack. According to the definition, there is only one place on the stack where it can be placed—on the top. The top element on the stack is now *G*. As our motion picture progresses through frames (c), (d), and (e), we see items *H*, *I*, and *J* successively added onto the stack. Notice that the last item inserted (in this case *J*) is at the top of the stack. Beginning with frame (f), however, the stack begins to shrink as first *J*, then *I*, *H*, *G*, and *F* are successively removed. At each point, the top element is removed since a deletion can be made only from the top. Item *G* could not be removed from the stack before items *J*, *I*, and *H* were gone. This illustrates the most important attribute of a stack, that the last element inserted into a stack is the first element deleted. Thus *J* is deleted before *I* because *J* was inserted after *I*. For this reason a stack is sometimes called a last-in, first-out (or *lifo*) list.

Between frames (j) and (k), the stack has stopped shrinking and begins to expand again as item *K* is added. However, this expansion is short-lived, as the stack then shrinks to only three items in frame (n).

Note that there is no way to distinguish between frame (a) and frame (i) by looking at the stack's state at the two instances. In both cases, the stack contains the identical items in the same order and has the same stack top. No record is kept on the stack of the fact that four items had been inserted and deleted in the meantime. Similarly, there is no way to distinguish between frames (d) and (f) or (j) and (l). If a record is needed of the intermediate items having been on the stack, that record must be kept elsewhere; it does not exist within the stack itself.

In fact, we have actually taken an extended view of what is really observed in a stack. The true picture of a stack is given by a view from the top looking down, rather than from a side looking in. Thus there is no perceptible difference between frames (h) and (o) in Figure 2.1.2. In each case the element at the top is *G*. While we know that the stack at (h) and the stack at (o) are not equal, the only way to determine this is to remove all the elements on both stacks and compare them individually. Although we have been looking at cross sections of stacks to make our understanding clearer, you should remember that this is an added liberty and there is no real provision for taking such a picture.

Primitive Operations

The two changes that can be made to a stack are given special names. When an item is added to a stack, it is **pushed** onto the stack, and when an item is removed, it is **popped** from the stack. Given a stack *s*, and an item *i*, performing the operation *push(s, i)* is defined as adding the item *i* to the top of stack *s*. Similarly, the operation *pop(s)* removes the top element and returns it as a function value. Thus the assignment operation

$$i := pop(s)$$

removes the element at the top of *s* and assigns its value to *i*.

For example, if *s* is the stack of Figure 2.1.2, we performed the operation *push(s, g)* in going from frame (a) to frame (b). We then performed, in turn, the operations

push (*s, II*);	(frame (c))
push (*s, I*);	(frame (d))
push (*s, J*);	(frame (e))
pop (*s*);	(frame (f))
pop (*s*);	(frame (g))
pop (*s*);	(frame (h))
pop (*s*);	(frame (i))
pop (*s*);.	(frame (j))
push (*s, K*);	(frame (k))
pop (*s*);	(frame (l))
pop (*s*);	(frame (m))
pop (*s*);	(frame (n))
push (*s, G*)	(frame (o)).

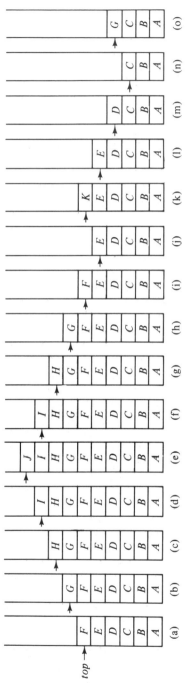

Figure 2.1.2 A motion picture of a stack.

70

Because of the push operation, which adds elements to a stack, a stack is sometimes called a ***pushdown list***.

There is no upper limit on the number of items that may be kept in a stack, because no mention was made in the definition as to how many items are allowed in the collection. Pushing another item onto a stack merely produces a larger collection of items. However, if a stack contains a single item and the stack is popped, the resulting stack contains no items and is called the ***empty stack***. Although the *push* operation is applicable to any stack, the *pop* operation cannot be applied to the empty stack because such a stack has no elements to delete. Therefore, before applying the *pop* operator to a stack, we must ensure that the stack is not empty. The operation *empty(s)* determines whether or not a stack *s* is empty. If the stack is empty, *empty(s)* returns the value *true*; otherwise, it returns the value *false*.

Another operation that can be performed on a stack is to determine what the top item on a stack is without removing it. This operation is written *stacktop(s)* and returns as its value the top element of stack *s*. The operation *stacktop(s)* is not really a new operation, because it can be decomposed into a pop and a push.

$$i := stacktop(s)$$

is equivalent to

$$i := pop(s);$$
$$push(s, i)$$

Like the operation *pop*, *stacktop* is not defined for an empty stack. The result of an illegal attempt to pop or access an item from an empty stack is called ***underflow***. Underflow can be avoided by ensuring that *empty(s)* is *false* before attempting the operation *pop(s)* or *stacktop(s)*.

The Stack as an Abstract Data Type

Now that we have described the stack and its behavior, let us give an ADT specification for the stack using the notation that we introduced earlier. However, there is one new additional notational convention that we must first introduce. The *push* and *pop* operations are procedures that modify the contents (i.e., the value) of a stack. The new stack value is defined as the old stack value with an element added (*push*) or the old stack value with an element deleted (*pop*). The postcondition of an operation must refer to the value of the data object (e.g., the stack) both before and after the operation. The name of an object in a postcondition refers to its value after the operation. To denote in a postcondition the value before the operation, an apostrophe (or a "prime" symbol) is placed after the object's name. Thus, if *s* represents a stack, a reference to *s* in a postcondition is a reference to the stack's value after the operation, and a reference to *s'* is a reference to the stack's value before the operation. In a precondition, of course, the object's name always represents a reference to its value before the operation and no apostrophe is necessary.

With this new notation, here is the ADT specification for a stack:

type *stackitem* = . . .;   { type of item on stack }
abstract type *stack* = **sequence of** *stackitem*;

abstract function *empty* (*s*: *stack*): *boolean*;
postcondition *empty* = (*len* (*s*) = 0);

abstract function *pop* (*s*: *stack*): *stackitem*;
precondition not *empty* (*s*);
postcondition *pop* = *last* (*s*');
                    s = *sub* (*s*', 1, *len* (*s*')-1);

abstract procedure *push* (*s*: *stack*; *elt*: *stackitem*);
postcondition *s* = *s*' + ⟨*elt*⟩

An Example   Now that we have defined a stack and have indicated the operations that can be performed on it, let us see how we may use the stack in problem solving. Consider a mathematical expression with several sets of nested parentheses, for example,

$$7-((X *((X+Y) / (J-3)) + Y) /(4-2.5))$$

and we want to ensure that the parentheses are nested correctly. That is, we want to check that

1. There are an equal number of right and left parentheses.
2. Every right parenthesis is preceded by a matching left parenthesis.

Expressions such as

$$((A+B)   \text{or}   A+B($$

would violate condition 1, and

$$)A+B(-C   \text{or}   (A+B))-(C+D$$

would violate condition 2.

To solve this problem, think of each left parenthesis as opening a scope and each right parenthesis as closing a scope. The ***nesting depth*** at a particular point in an expression is the number of scopes which have been opened but not yet closed at that point. This is the same as the number of left parentheses encountered whose matching right parentheses have not yet been encountered. Let us define the ***parenthesis count*** at a particular point in an expression as the number of left parentheses minus the number of right parentheses which have been encountered in scanning the expression from its left end up to that particular point. If the parenthesis count is nonnegative, it is the same as the nesting depth. The two conditions that must hold if the parentheses in an expression are to form an admissible pattern are

1. The parenthesis count at the end of the expression is 0. This implies that no scopes have been left open or that exactly as many right parentheses as left parentheses have been found.
2. The parenthesis count at each point in the expression is nonnegative. This implies that no right parenthesis has been encountered for which a matching left parenthesis had not previously been encountered.

In Figure 2.1.3, the count at each point in each of the previous five strings is given directly below that point. Since only the first string meets the foregoing two conditions, it is the only one among the five with a correct parentheses pattern.

Let us now change the problem slightly and assume that three different types of scopes exist. These types are indicated by parentheses ((and)), brackets ([and]), and braces ({and}). A scope ender must be of the same type as its scope opener. Thus strings such as

$$(A+B], \quad [(A+B]), \quad \{A-(B]\}$$

are illegal.

It is necessary to keep track not only of how many scopes have been opened, but also of their types. This information is needed because when a scope ender is encountered, we must know the symbol with which the scope was opened to ensure that is is being closed properly.

Figure 2.1.3 Parenthesis count at various points of strings.

```
7 – ( ( X * ( ( X + Y ) / ( J – 3 ) ) + Y ) / ( 4 – 2.5 ) )
0 0 1 2 2 2 3 4 4 4 4 3 3 4 4 4 4 3 2 2 2 1 1  2 2 2   2 1 0


                    ( ( A + B )
                    1 2 2 2 2 1


                    A + B  (
                    0 0 0  1


                ) A  +  B ( – C
               –1 –1 –1 –1 0 0 0


            ( A + B )  )   – ( C + D
            1 1 1 1 0  –1  –1 0 0 0 0
```

A stack may be used to keep track of the types of scopes encountered. Whenever a scope opener is encountered, it is pushed onto the stack. Whenever a scope ender is encountered, the stack is examined. If the stack is empty, the scope ender does not have a matching opener, so the string is invalid. If, however, the stack is nonempty, we pop the stack and check whether the popped item corresponds to the scope ender. If a match occurs, we continue. If it does not, the string is invalid. When the end of the string is reached, we make sure that the stack is empty; otherwise, one or more scopes have been opened which have not been closed, making the string invalid. The algorithm for this procedure is outlined next. Figure 2.1.4 shows the state of the stack after reading in parts of the string $\{x+(y-[a+b])*c-[(d+e)]\}/(b-(j-(k-[l-n])))$.

```
valid := true;
Let s := the empty stack;
while (we have not read the entire string) and (valid)
    do begin
            read the next symbol (symb) of the string;
            if symb in ['(', '[', '{'] then push (s, symb);
            if symb in [')', ']', '}']
                then if empty (s)
                        then valid := false
                        else begin
                            i := pop (s);
                            if i is not the matching opener for symb
                                then valid := false
                        end {else begin}
        end {while...do begin};
    if not empty (s) then valid := false;
    if valid
        then writeln ('the string is valid')
        else writeln ('the string is invalid')
```

Let us see why the solution to this problem calls for the use of a stack. The last scope to be opened must be the first to be closed. This is precisely simulated by a stack where the last element arriving is the first to leave. Each item on the stack represents a scope that has been opened but has not yet been closed. Pushing an item onto the stack corresponds to the closing of a scope, leaving one less scope open.

Notice the correspondence between the number of elements on the stack in this example and the parenthesis count in the previous example. When the stack is empty (parenthesis count equals 0) and a scope ender is encountered, an attempt is being made to close a scope which has never been opened, so that the parenthesis pattern is invalid. In the first example, this is indicated by a negative parenthesis count and in the second example

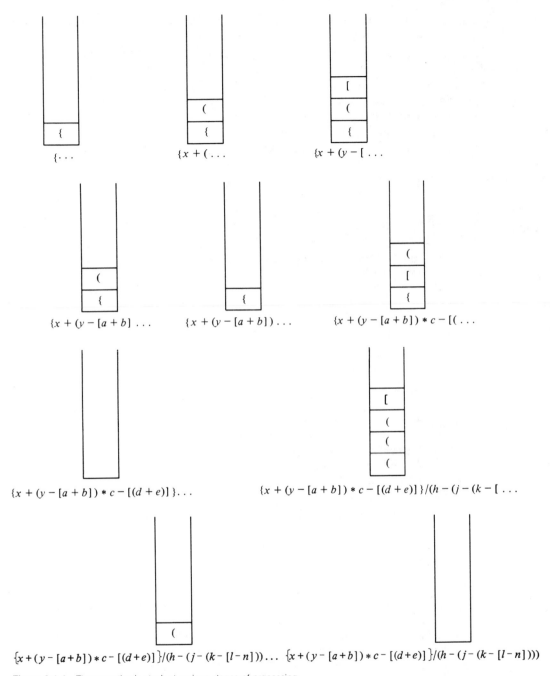

Figure 2.1.4 The parenthesis stack at various stages of processing.

by an inability to pop the stack. The reason that a simple parenthesis count is inadequate for the second example is that we must keep track of the actual scope openers themselves. This can be done by the use of a stack. Notice also that at any point we examine only the element at the top. The particular configuration of parentheses below the top element is irrelevant while examining this top element. Only after the top element has been popped do we concern ourselves with subsequent elements in a stack.

In general, a stack can be used in any situation that calls for a last-in first-out discipline or displays a nesting pattern. We shall see more examples of the use of stacks in the remaining sections of this chapter and, indeed, throughout the text.

EXERCISES

1. Use the operations *push*, *pop*, *stacktop*, and *empty* to construct operations which do each of the following:
   (a) Set i to the second element from the top of the stack, leaving the stack without its top two elements.
   (b) Set i to the second element from the top of the stack, leaving the stack unchanged.
   (c) Given an integer n, set i to the nth element from the top of the stack, leaving the stack without its top n elements.
   (d) Given an integer n, set i to the nth element from the top of the stack, leaving the stack unchanged.
   (e) Set i to the bottom element of the stack, leaving the stack empty.
   (f) Set i to the bottom element of the stack, leaving the stack unchanged. (*Hint*: Use another, auxiliary stack.)
   (g) Set i to the third element from the bottom of the stack.

2. Simulate the action of the algorithm in this section for each of the following strings by showing the contents of the stack at each point.
   (a) $(a + b\})$
   (b) $\{[a + b] - [(c - d)]$
   (c) $(a + b) - \{c + d\} - [f + g]$
   (d) $((b) * \{([j + k])\})$
   (e) $(((a))))$

3. Write an algorithm to determine if an input character string is of the form

$$x \, C \, y$$

   where x is a string consisting of the letters 'A' and 'B' and where y is the reverse of x (i.e., if $x = $ 'ABABBA', then y must equal 'ABBABA'). At each point you may read only the next character of the string.

4. Write an algorithm to determine if an input character string is of the form

$$a \, D \, b \, D \, c \, D \ldots D \, z$$

   where each string $a, b, \ldots, z$ is of the form of the string $x \, C \, y$ defined in Exercise 3. (Thus a string is in the proper form if it consists of any number of such strings separated by the character 'D'.) At each point you may read only the next character of the string.

5. Design an algorithm that does not use a stack which reads a sequence of *push* and

pop operations and determines whether or not underflow occurs on some *pop* operation. Implement the algorithm as a Pascal program.

6. What set of conditions are necessary and sufficient for a sequence of *push* and *pop* operations on a single stack (initially empty) to leave the stack empty and not to cause underflow? What set of conditions are necessary for such a sequence to leave a nonempty stack unchanged?

2. REPRESENTING STACKS IN PASCAL

Before programming a problem solution that calls for the use of a stack, we must decide how to represent a stack using the data structures that exist in our programming language. As we shall see, there are several ways to represent a stack in Pascal. We now consider the simplest of these. As the entire book progresses, you will be introduced to other possible representations. Each of them, however, is merely an implementation of the concept introduced in Section 1 of this chapter. Each has its advantages and disadvantages in terms of how close it comes to mirroring the abstract concept of a stack and how much effort must be made by the programmer and the computer in using it.

A stack is an ordered collection of items, and Pascal already contains a data type that is an ordered collection of items—the array. Whenever a problem solution calls for use of a stack, therefore, it is tempting to begin a program by defining a type identifier *stack* to be an array. Unfortunately, however, a stack and an array are two entirely different things. The number of elements in an array is fixed and is determined by the definition of the array. In general, the user cannot change this number. A stack, on the other hand, is fundamentally a dynamic object whose size is constantly changing as items are popped and pushed.

However, although an array cannot be a stack, it can be the home of a stack. That is, an array can be declared with a range that is large enough for the maximum size of the stack. During the course of program execution, the stack will grow and shrink within the space reserved for it. One end of the array will be the fixed bottom of the stack, while the top of the stack will constantly shift as items are popped and pushed. Thus another field is needed to keep track of the current position of the top of the stack.

A stack in Pascal may therefore be declared as a record containing two objects: an array to hold the elements of the stack and an integer to indicate the position of the current stack top within the array. This may be done by the declarations

```
const maxstack = 100;
type  stack = record
                item: array [1..maxstack] of integer;
                top: 0..maxstack
              end;
var   s: stack;
```

Here we assume that the elements of the stack *s* contained in the array *s.item* are integers and that the stack will at no time contain more than *maxstack* integers. In this example *maxstack* is set to 100. There is, of course, no reason to restrict a stack to contain only integers; *item* could just as easily have been given the type **array** [1..*maxstack*] **of** *real* or **array** [1..*maxstack*] **of** *char*, or whatever other type we might wish to give to the elements of the stack. The field identifier *top*, however, must be declared as an integer between 0 and *maxstack*, because its value represents the position within the array *item* of the topmost stack element. Thus, if the value of *s.top* is 5, there are 5 elements on the stack. These are *s.item*[1], *s.item*[2], *s.item*[3], *s.item*[4], and *s.item*[5]. When the stack is popped, the value of *s.top* must be changed to 4 to indicate that there are now only four elements on the stack and that *s.item*[4] is the top element. On the other hand, if a new object is pushed onto the stack, the value of *s.top* must be increased by 1 to 6 and the new object inserted into *s.item*[6].

The empty stack contains no elements and can therefore be indicated by *top* equaling 0. In order to initialize a stack *s* to the empty state, we may initially execute *s.top*:=0.

To determine, during the course of execution, whether or not a stack is empty, the condition *s.top*=0 may be tested by means of an **if** statement as follows:

```
if s.top=0
    then {    stack is empty    }
    else { stack is not empty }
```

This test corresponds to the operation *empty*(s) which was introduced in Section 1. Alternatively, we may write a function that returns *true* if the stack is empty and *false* if it is not empty. Such a function may be written as follows:

```
function empty (s: stack): boolean;
begin
    if s.top=0
        then empty:= true
        else empty:= false
end {function empty};
```

Once this function exists, a test for the empty stack is implemented by the statement

```
if empty(s)
    then {    the stack is empty    }
    else { the stack is not empty }
```

You may wonder why we bother to define the function *empty* when we could just as easily write *if s.top*=0 each time that we want to test for the empty condition. The answer is that we wish to make our programs more comprehensible and to make the use of a stack independent of its implementation. Once we understand the stack concept, the phrase "*empty(s)*" is more meaningful than is the phrase "*s.top*=0." If we should later introduce a better implementation of a stack so that "*s.top*=0" becomes meaningless, we would have to change every reference to the field identifier *s.top* throughout our entire program. On the other hand, the phrase "*empty(s)*" would still retain its meaning, since it is an inherent attribute of the stack concept rather than of an implementation of that concept. All that would be required to revise our program to accommodate a new implementation of the stack would be a revision of the definition of the type *stack* in the main program and the rewriting of the function *empty*. Aggregating the set of implementation-dependent trouble spots into small, easily identifiable units is an important method of making a program more understandable and modifiable. This concept is know as **modularization**, in which individual functions are isolated into low-level **modules** whose properties are easily provable. These low-level modules can then be used by more complex routines, which do not have to concern themselves with the details of the low-level modules, only with their function. The complex routines may themselves be viewed as modules by still higher-level routines, which use them independently of their internal details.

A programmer should always be concerned with the readability of the code he or she produces. Often, a small amount of attention to clarity will save a large amount of time in debugging. Large and medium-sized programs will almost never be correct the first time they are run. If precautions are taken at the time that a program is written to ensure that it is easily modifiable and comprehensible, the total time needed to get the program to run correctly will be sharply reduced. For example, the *if* statement in the *empty* function could be replaced by the shorter, more efficient statement

$$empty := s.top=0$$

The effect of this statement is precisely equivalent to the longer statement

```
if s.top=0
    then empty := true
    else empty := false
```

This is because the value of the expression *s.top*=0 is *true* if and only if the condition *s.top*=0 is true. However, someone else who reads a program will probably be much more comfortable reading the *if* statement. Often, you will find that if you use "tricks" of the language in writing programs, you will be unable to decipher your own programs after putting them aside for a day or two.

To implement the *pop* operation, the possibility of underflow must be taken into account, because the user may inadvertently attempt to pop an element from an empty stack. Of course, such an attempt is illegal and should be avoided. However, if such an attempt should be made, the user should be informed of the underflow condition. We therefore introduce a function *pop*, which consists of the following three actions:

1. If the stack is empty, it prints a warning message and halts execution.
2. It removes the top element from the stack.
3. It returns this element to the calling program.

Note that in Pascal there is no way to halt execution prematurely from within a function such as *pop*. Therefore, we assume the existence of a library procedure *error(str)*, where *str* is a character string. This routine prints the string *str* as an error message and then halts execution. (You may wish to replace the call to *error* by a compound statement consisting of a call to *writeln* and a **goto** the end of your program. [A call to *exit (program)* in UCSD Pascal or *halt* in Turbo Pascal might be used instead of a **goto**.] Note that despite the fact that *error* ends program execution, we place the remainder of the function in an *else* clause in keeping with the "spirit" of standard Pascal.)

```
function pop (var s: stack): integer;
begin
     if empty(s)
          then error('stack underflow')
          else begin
                    pop:= s.item[s.top];
                    s.top:= s.top - 1
               end {else begin}
end { function pop};
```

Testing for Exceptional Conditions

Let us look at the *pop* function more closely. If the stack is not empty, the top element of the stack is saved as the returned value. This element is then removed from the stack by the statement $s.top := s.top - 1$. Let us assume that when *pop* is called, $s.top$ equals 87; that is, there are 87 items on the stack. The value of $s.item[87]$ is returned and the value of $s.top$ is changed to 86. Note that $s.item[87]$ still retains its old value; the array $s.item$ remains unchanged by the call to *pop*. However, the stack is changed, because it now contains only 86 elements rather than 87. Recall that an array and a stack are two different objects. The array only provides a home for the stack. The stack itself contains only those elements between the first item of the array and the *top*th element. Thus, reducing the value of $s.top$ by 1 effectively. removes an element from the stack. This is true despite the fact that $s.item[87]$ retains its old value.

To use the *pop* function, the programmer can declare *x:integer* and write

x:= pop(s)

x will then contain the value popped from the stack. If the intent of the *pop* operation was not to retrieve the element on the top of the stack but only to remove it from the stack, *x* will not be used again in the program except perhaps to serve once more as the target of a *pop* operation. Of course, the programmer should ensure that the stack is not empty when he or she calls the *pop* operation. If unsure of the state of the stack, the programmer may write

```
if not empty(s)
   then x:= pop(s)
   else { take remedial action }
```

If the programmer unwittingly does call *pop* with an empty stack, the function will print the error message *stack underflow* and execution will halt. Although this is an unfortunate state of affairs, it is far better than what would occur had the *if* statement in the *pop* routine been omitted entirely. In that case, the value of *s.top* would be 0, and an attempt would be made to access the nonexistent element *s.item*[0].

A programmer should always provide for the almost certain possibility of error by including meaningful diagnostics. By doing so, if and when an error does occur, the programmer will be able to pinpoint its source and take corrective action immediately.

However, within the context of a given problem, it may not be necessary to halt execution immediately upon the detection of underflow. Instead, it might be more desirable for the *pop* routine to signal the calling program that an underflow has occurred. Upon detecting this signal, the calling routine can take corrective action. Let us call the procedure that pops the stack and returns an indication as to whether underflow has occurred, *popandtest*.

```
procedure popandtest (var s: stack; var x: integer; var und: boolean);
begin
   if empty(s) then und:= true
         else begin
                 und:= false;
                 x:= s.item[s.top];
                 s.top:= s.top − 1
              end {else begin}
end {procedure popandtest};
```

In the calling program the programmer would write

```
popandtest (s, x, underflow);
if underflow
    then {          take corrective action          }
    else { x is the element popped off the stack }
```

Implementing the *push* Operation

Let us now examine the *push* operation. It seems that this operation should be quite easy to implement using the array representation of a stack. A first attempt at a *push* procedure might be the following:

```
procedure push (var s: stack; x: integer);
begin
    s.top:= s.top + 1;
    s.item[s.top]:= x
end {procedure push};
```

This routine makes room for the item *x* to be pushed onto the stack by incrementing *s.top* by 1, and then it inserts *x* into the array *s.item*.

The procedure directly implements the *push* operation, which was introduced in the preceding section. Yet, as it stands, it is quite incorrect. It allows a subtle error to creep in, caused by using the array representation of the stack. See if you can spot this error before reading further.

Recall that a stack is a dynamic structure that is constantly allowed to grow and shrink and thus change its size. An array, on the other hand, is a fixed object of predetermined size. Thus it is quite conceivable that a stack will outgrow the array that was set aside to contain it. This will occur when the array is full, that is, when the stack contains as many elements as the array—and an attempt is made to push yet another element onto the stack. The result of such an attempt is called an *overflow*.

Assume that the array is full and that the Pascal *push* routine is called. The full array is indicated by the condition *s.top* = 100, so that the 100th (and last) element of the array is the current top of the stack. When *push* is called, an attempt is made to increase the value of *s.top* to 101. Since 101 is outside the subrange 0..100 which is the type of *s.top*, this attempt will result in an error and produce an appropriate error message. This message is totally meaningless within the context of the original algorithm, because it does not indicate an error in the algorithm but rather in the computer implementation of that algorithm. It would be far more desirable for the programmer to provide for the possibility of overflow and to print a more meaningful message.

The *push* procedure may therefore be revised so that it reads as follows:

```
procedure push (var s: stack; x: integer);
begin
    if s.top=maxstack
       then error ('stack overflow')
       else begin
              s.top:= s.top + 1;
              s.item[s.top] := x
            end {else begin}
end {procedure push};
```

Here, a check is made to determine whether the array is full before attempting to push another element onto the stack. The array will be full if $s.top = maxstack$.

You should again note that if and when the overflow condition is detected in *push*, execution will halt immediately after the printing of an error message. This action, as in the case of *pop*, may not be the most desirable. It might, in some cases, make more sense for the calling routine to be able to invoke the push operation with the instructions

```
pushandtest (s, x, overflow);
if overflow
   then {Overflow has been detected. x was not }
        {pushed on stack. Take remedial action.}
   else {x was successfully pushed on the stack }
        {        continue processing.        }
```

This allows the calling program to proceed after the call to *pushandtest* whether or not overflow was detected. The procedure *pushandtest* is left as an exercise for the reader.

Although the underflow and overflow conditions are handled similarly in *pop* and *push*, there is a fundamental difference between the two conditions. Underflow indicates that the *pop* operation cannot be performed on the stack and may indicate an error in the algorithm or the data. No other implementation or representation of the stack will cure the underflow condition. Rather, the entire problem must be rethought. (Of course, underflow might be a signal for ending one task and beginning another, but in that case, *popandtest* rather than *pop* should be used.)

Overflow, however, is not a condition that is applicable to a stack as an abstract data structure. Abstractly, it is always possible to push an element onto a stack because a stack is just an ordered collection and there is no limit to the number of elements such a collection can contain. The possibility of an overflow is introduced when a stack is implemented by an array with only a finite number of elements, thereby prohibiting the growth of the stack beyond that number. It may very well be that the algorithm is correct; the implementation simply did not anticipate that the stack would become so large. Thus, in some cases, a possible way to correct an overflow condition is to change the value of the constant *maxstack* in the program so that the array field *item* contains more elements. There is no need to change the routines *pop* or *push*, because they refer to whatever data structure was declared for the type *stack* in the program declarations. *push* also refers to the constant *maxstack* rather than the actual value 100.

However, more often than not, an overflow does indicate an error in the program which cannot be attributed to a simple lack of space. The program may be in an infinite loop where things are constantly being pushed onto the stack and nothing is ever popped. Thus the stack will outgrow the array bound no matter how high that bound is set. The programmer should always check that this is not the case before indiscriminately raising the array bound.

Let us now look at our last operation on stacks, *stacktop(s)*, which returns the top element of a stack without removing it from the stack. As we noted in the preceding section, *stacktop* is not really a primitive operation, because it can be decomposed into the two operations:

$$x := \text{pop}(s);$$
$$\text{push}(s, x)$$

However, this is a rather awkward way to retrieve the top element of a stack. Why not ignore the decomposition just noted and directly retrieve the proper value? Of course, a check for the empty stack and underflow must then be explicitly stated, because the test is no longer handled by a call to *pop*.

We present a Pascal function *stacktop* as follows:

```
function stacktop (s: stack): integer;
begin
      if empty (s)
            then error('stack underflow')
            else stacktop:= s.item[s.top]
end {function stacktop};
```

You may wonder why we bother writing a separate routine *stacktop* when a reference to *s.item[s.top]* would serve just as well. There are several reasons for this. First, the routine *stacktop* incorporates a test for underflow, so that no mysterious errors will occur if the stack is empty. Second, it allows the programmer to use a stack without worrying about its internal makeup. Third, if a different implementation of a stack is introduced, the programmer need not comb through all the places where he or she referred to *s.item[s.top]* to make those references compatible with the new implementation. The programmer need only change the *stacktop* routine.

Stacks of Differing Types

As we have implemented a stack, a stack can contain only integers. We have noted that a stack of elements of another type may be obtained by altering the type of the *item* field. For example, a stack of real numbers is declared by

```
const maxstack = 100;
type  stack = record
                 item: array[1..maxstack] of real;
                 top: 0..maxstack
              end;
     var   s: stack;
```

However, this would require a change to all the routines that manipulate a stack. For example, the function header of *pop* would now become

```
function pop (var s: stack): real;
```

while the procedure header of *push* must be changed to

```
procedure push (var s: stack; x: real);
```

We would like to specify routines such as *pop* and *push* so that they work regardless of the type of the items on the stack. This can be done very simply in Pascal by introducing a new type *stackitem* and defining a stack in terms of this new type, as follows:

```
type stackitem = integer;
     stack = record
                 item: array[1..maxstack] of stackitem;
                 top: 0..maxstack
             end;
```

The headers of the *pop* and *push* routines would be

```
function pop (var s: stack): stackitem;
```

and

```
procedure push (var s: stack; x: stackitem);
```

The same routines can be used to manipulate a stack of reals by simply changing the type definition of *stackitem* to

```
type stackitem = real;
```

No other change is necessary, neither in the type definition of *stack* nor in the stack manipulation routines. Once these routines have been written in this way, they can be used in any program that manipulates stacks. However, some Pascal compilers may require that any variables popped or pushed off the stack must be declared to be of type *stackitem*.

It is also possible to allow the same stack to contain different types of elements by using variant records. For example, to define a stack that can contain integers and characters, we write

```
type stackitem = record
             case itemtype: (int,ch) of
                 int: (iitem: integer);
                 ch: (citem: char)
      end;
```

No changes need be made to the definition of *stack* or the *push*, *empty*, or *stacktop* routines. However, since a Pascal function may only return a scalar type, we must write a procedure *popsub* to replace the function *pop*. The header for this procedure is

```
procedure popsub(var s: stack; var x: stackitem);
```

We leave the body of the procedure as an exercise for the reader.

Given the foregoing definition for *stackitem*, a program segment to print an item popped off a stack would be

```
var x: stackitem;
    s: stack;
    . . .
popsub(s, x);
case x.itemtype of
    int: write (x.iitem);
    ch: write (x.citem)
end {case}
```

EXERCISES

1. Write Pascal routines that use the routines presented in this chapter to implement the operations of Exercise 2.1.1.

2. Given a sequence of *push* and *pop* operations and an integer representing the size of an array in which a stack is to be implemented, design an algorithm to determine whether or not overflow occurs. The algorithm should not use a stack. Implement the algorithm as a Pascal program.

3. Implement the algorithms of Exercises 2.1.3 and 2.1.4 as Pascal programs.

4. Show how to implement a stack of integers in Pascal by using an array *s:array*[0..100] *of stackitem*, where *s*[0] is used to contain the index of the top element of the stack and where *s*[1] through *s*[100] contain the elements on the stack. Write a declaration and routines *pop*, *push*, *empty*, *popandtest*, *stacktop*, and *pushandtest* for this implementation.

5. Implement a stack in Pascal in which each item on the stack is a varying number of integers. Choose a Pascal data structure for such a stack and design *push* and *pop* routines for it.

6. Consider a language that does not have arrays but does have stacks as a data type. That is, one can declare

var s: stack;

and the *push*, *pop*, *popandtest*, and *stacktop* operations are defined. Show how a one-dimensional array can be implemented by using these operations on two stacks.

7. Design a method for keeping two stacks within a single linear array *s:array*[1 .. *spacesize*] in such a way that neither stack overflows until all of memory is used and an entire stack is never shifted to a different location within the array. Write Pascal routines *push*1, *push*2, *pop*1, and *pop*2 to manipulate the two stacks. (*Hint*: The two stacks grow toward each other.)

8. The Bashemin Parking Garage contains a single lane which can hold up to 10 cars. There is only a single entrance/exit to the garage at one end of the lane. If a customer arrives to pick up a car that is not nearest the exit, all cars blocking its path are moved out, the customer's car is driven out, and the other cars are restored in the order they were in originally.

   Write a program that processes a group of input lines. Each input line contains an 'a' for arrival or 'd' for departure, and a license plate number. Cars are assumed to arrive and depart in the order specified by the input. The program should print a message whenever a car arrives or departs. When a car arrives, the message should specify whether or not there is room for the car in the garage. If there is no room, the car leaves without entering the garage. When a car departs, the message should include the number of times that the car was moved out of the garage to allow other cars to depart.

3. AN EXAMPLE: INFIX, POSTFIX, AND PREFIX

Basic Definitions and Examples

In this section we examine a major application of stacks. Although it is one of the most prominent applications, it is by no means the only one. The reason that we consider this application is that it illustrates so well the different types of stacks and the various operations and functions we have defined upon them. The example is also an important topic of computer science in its own right.

Before proceeding with the algorithms and programs of this section it will be necessary to provide some groundwork. Consider the sum of A and B. We think of applying the *operator* '+' to the *operands* A and B and write the sum as $A + B$. This particular representation is called *infix*. There are two alternative notations for expressing the sum of A and B using the symbols A, B, and $+$. These are

$+ A B$ prefix
$A B +$ postfix

The prefixes "pre," "post," and "in" refer to the relative position of the operator with respect to the two operands. In prefix notation the operator precedes the two operands, in postfix notation the operator follows the two operands, and in infix notation the operator is between the two operands. Prefix is often called **Polish notation** after its inventor, the Polish mathematician Jan Lukasiewicz (1878–1956). Postfix is often called **reverse Polish notation**.

The prefix and postfix notations are not really as awkward to use as they might first appear. For example, if we were using a Pascal function to return the sum of the two arguments a and b, we might invoke it by $add(a, b)$. The operator add precedes the operands a and b. The FORTH programming language uses postfix notation exclusively.

Let us now consider some additional examples. The evaluation of the expression $A + B*C$, as written in standard infix notation, requires knowledge of which of the two operations, $+$ or $*$, is to be performed first. In the case of $+$ and $*$ we "know" that multiplication is to be done before addition (in the absence of parentheses to the contrary). Thus $A + B*C$ is to be interpreted as $A + (B*C)$ unless otherwise specified. We say that multiplication takes **precedence** over addition. Suppose that we would now like to rewrite $A + B*C$ in postfix. Applying the rules of precedence, we first convert the portion of the expression that is evaluated first, namely the multiplication. By doing this conversion in stages, we obtain

$A+(B*C)$	parentheses for emphasis
$A+(BC*)$	convert the multiplication
$A(BC*)+$	convert the addition
$ABC*+$	postfix form

The only rules to remember during the conversion process are that the operations with highest precedence are converted first and that after a portion of the expression has been converted to postfix it is to be treated as a single operand. Let us now consider the same example with the precedence of operators reversed by the deliberate insertion of parentheses.

$(A+B)*C$	infix form
$(AB+)*C$	convert the addition
$(AB+)C*$	convert the multiplication
$AB+C*$	postfix form

In the foregoing example, the addition was converted before the multiplication because of the parentheses. In going from $(A+B)*C$ to $(AB+)*C$, A and B are the operands and $+$ is the operator. In going from $(AB+)*C$ to $(AB+)C*$, $(AB+)$ and C are the operands and $*$ is the operator. The rules for converting from infix to postfix are simple, provided that you know the order of precedence.

We consider five binary operations: addition, subtraction, multiplication, division, and exponentiation. The first four are available in Pascal. The fifth, exponentiation, will be represented by the operator $. The value of the expression $A\$B$ is A raised to the B power, so that $3\$2$ is 9. The other four operations are denoted by the usual operators $+$, $-$, $*$, and $/$. For these binary operators the following is the order of precedence (highest to lowest):

exponentiation

multiplication/division

addition/subtraction

By using parentheses we can override the default precedence.

We give the following additional examples of converting from infix to postfix. Be sure that you understand each of these examples (and can do them on your own) before proceeding to the remainder of this section. We follow the convention that when unparenthesized operators of the same precedence are scanned, the order is assumed to be left to right except in the case of exponentiation, where the order is assumed to be from right to left. Thus $A+B+C$ means $(A+B)+C$ and $A\$B\$C$ means $A\$(B\$C)$.

Infix	Postfix
$A+B$	$AB+$
$A+B-C$	$AB+C-$
$(A+B)*(C-D)$	$AB+CD-*$
$A\$B*C-D+E/F/(G+H)$	$AB\$C*D-EF/GH+/+$
$((A+B)*C-(D-E))\$(F+G)$	$AB+C*DE--FG+\$$
$A-B/(C*D\$E)$	$ABCDE\$*/-$

The precedence rules for converting an expression from infix to prefix are identical. The only change from postfix conversion is that the operator is placed before the operands rather than after them. We present the prefix forms of the foregoing expressions. Again, you should attempt to make the transformations on your own.

Infix	Prefix
$A+B$	$+AB$
$A+B-C$	$-+ABC$
$(A+B)*(C-D)$	$*+AB-CD$
$A\$B*C-D+E/F/(G+H)$	$+-*\$ABCD//EF+GH$
$((A+B)*C-(D-E))\$(F+G)$	$\$-*+ABC-DE+FG$
$A-B/(C*D\$E)$	$-A/B*C\$DE$

Note that the prefix form of a complex expression is not the mirror image of the postfix form, as can be seen from the second of the foregoing examples, $A+B-C$. Henceforth, we shall be concerned with the postfix transformations and will leave to the reader as exercises most of the work involving prefix.

One point immediately obvious about the postfix form of an expression is that it requires no parentheses. Let us consider the two expressions $A+(B*C)$ and $(A+B)*C$. Whereas the parentheses in one of the two expressions are superfluous [by convention $A+B*C = A+(B*C)$], the parentheses in the second expression are necessary to avoid confusion with the first. The postfix forms of these expressions are

Infix	Postfix
$A+(B*C)$	$ABC*+$
$(A+B)*C$	$AB+C*$

There are no parentheses in either of the two transformed expressions. A close look tells us that the order of the operators in the postfix expressions determines the actual order of operations in evaluating the expression, making the use of parentheses unnecessary. In going from infix to postfix we are sacrificing the ability to note at a glance the operands associated with a particular operator. We are gaining, however, an unambiguous form of the original expression without the use of cumbersome parentheses. In fact, you may argue that the postfix form of the original expression might look simpler were it not for the fact that it appears difficult to evaluate. For example, how do we know that if $A = 3$, $B = 4$, and $C = 5$ in the foregoing examples, we have 3 4 5 * + =23 and 3 4 + 5 * = 35?

Evaluating a Postfix Expression

The answer to this question lies in the development of an algorithm for evaluating expressions in postfix. Each operator in a postfix string refers to the previous two operands in the string. (Of course, either of these two operands may itself be the result of applying a previous operator.) Suppose that each time we read an operand we push it onto a stack. When we reach an operator, its operands will then be the top two elements on the stack. We can then pop these two elements, perform the indicated operation on them, and push the result on the stack so that it will be available for use as an operand of the next operator. The following algorithm evaluates an expression in postfix using this method.

```
Initialize a stack, opndstk, to be empty;
    {scan the input string reading one element at a}
    {              time into symb                  }
while there are more characters in the input string
    do begin
            symb := next input character;
            if symb is an operand
                then push(opndstk, symb)
```

else {*symb* is an operator}
  begin
    $opnd2 := pop(opndstk)$;
    $opnd1 := pop(opndstk)$;
    value := result of applying *symb*
          to *opnd*1 and *opnd*2;
    push (*opndstk*, *value*)
  end {else begin}
 end {while...do begin};
$result := pop(opndstk)$

Let us now consider an example. Suppose that we are asked to evaluate the following expression in postfix:

$$6\ 2\ 3\ +\ -\ 3\ 8\ 2\ /\ +\ *\ 2\ \$\ 3\ +$$

We show the contents of the stack *opndstk* and the variables *symb*, *opnd*1, *opnd*2, and *value* after each successive iteration of the loop. The top of *opndstk* is to the right.

symb	opnd1	opnd2	value	opndstk
6				6
2				6,2
3				6,2,3
+	2	3	5	6,5
−	6	5	1	1
3	6	5	1	1,3
8	6	5	1	1,3,8
2	6	5	1	1,3,8,2
/	8	2	4	1,3,4
+	3	4	7	1,7
*	1	7	7	7
2	1	7	7	7,2
$	7	2	49	49
3	7	2	49	49,3
+	49	3	52	52

Let us make some observations about the foregoing example which will aid us in translating the algorithm into a program. As its name implies, *opndstk* is a stack of operands. Each operand is pushed onto the stack when encountered. Therefore, the maximum size of the stack is the number of operands that appear in the input expression. However, in dealing with most postfix expressions, the actual size of the stack needed is less than this maximum, because an operator removes operands from the stack. In the previous example the stack never contained more than four elements, despite the fact that eight operands appeared in the postfix expression.

Program to Evaluate
a Postfix Expression

We are now prepared to plan a program to evaluate an expression in postfix notation. There are a number of questions we must consider before we can actually write the program. A primary consideration, as in all programs, is to define precisely the form and restrictions, if any, on the input. Usually, the programmer is presented with the form of the input and is required to design a program to accommodate the given data. On the other hand, we are in the fortunate position of being able to choose the form of our input. This enables us to construct a program that is not overburdened with transformation problems that overshadow the actual intent of the routine. Had we been confronted with data in a form that is awkward and cumbersome to work with, we could relegate the transformations to various procedures and use the output of these procedures as input to our primary routine. In the "real world," recognition and transformation of input is a major concern.

Let us assume in this case that each input line is in the form of a string of digits and operator symbols. We assume that operands are single nonnegative digits (e.g., 0, 1, 2, ... , 8, 9). For example, an input line might contain $345*+$ in the first five columns with the remaining columns left blank. We would like to write a program that reads input lines of this format, as long as there are any remaining, and prints out for each line the original input string and the result of the evaluated expression.

Since the symbols are read as characters, we must find a method to convert the operand characters to numbers and the operator characters to operations. For example, we must have a method for converting the character '5' to the number 5 and the character '+' to the addition operation. The conversion of a character to an integer can be handled easily in Pascal. If $x:char$ is a digit in Pascal, the expression $ord(x) - ord(`0`)$ yields the numerical value of that digit. To convert an operator symbol into the corresponding action, we use a function *oper* which accepts an operator and two operands as input parameters. The header for this function is

    function oper(operator: char; op1, op2: real): real;

The function returns the value of the expression obtained by applying the operator to the two operands. The body of the function will be given below.

The body of the main program might be the following. The constant *maxcols* is the number of columns in an input line.

```
program evaluate(input, output);
const maxcols = 80;
type exprtype = array[1..maxcols] of char;
var   expr: exprtype;
      position: 1..maxcols;
```

```
      function eval(expr: exprtype): real;
              {body of eval goes here}
begin
   while not eof
      do begin
              {process next expression}
              for position:= 1 to maxcols
                 do read(expr[position]);
              readln;
              writeln('original postfix expression is     ');
              for position:= 1 to maxcols
                 do write(expr[position]);
              writeln('value of expression is     ', eval(expr));
              writeln
         end {while...do begin}
   end {program evaluate}.
```

(Note that we cannot print the value of *expr* in a single statement because its type is an unpacked, rather than a packed, array. If *exprtype* were defined as a packed array, we could print the value of *expr* with the single statement *write(expr)*. However, under some Pascal compilers, we would then be unable to execute *read(expr[position])* but would have to execute *read(c)*; *expr[position]:=c* instead. Some compilers, however, will allow *write(expr)* even if *expr* is not packed.)

The main part of the program is, of course, the function *eval*, which is presented next. The routine is merely the Pascal implementation of the evaluation algorithm, taking into account the specific environment and format of the input data and calculated outputs. *eval* calls on a function *opnd*, which determines whether or not its argument is an operand.

```
      function eval (expr: exprtype): real;
              {eval accepts a postfix expression as input}
              {and returns the value of the expression as}
              {              a real number              }
const maxstack = maxcols;
type  stack = record
                 item: array[1..maxstack] of real;
                 top: 0..maxstack
              end;
var   opndstk: stack;
      opnd1, opnd2, value: real;
      symb: char;
      position: 1..maxcols;
   function pop (var s: stack): real;
      { body of pop }
```

```
procedure push (var s: stack; x: real);
    {body of push}
function opnd (symb: char): boolean;
    {body of opnd}
function oper (symb: char; op1, op2: real): real;
    {body of oper}
begin {function eval}
    opndstk.top:= 0;
    position:= 1;
    symb:= expr[position];
    {position indicates the current position in the}
    { expression and symb is the current symbol. }
    {Start scanning symbols until a blank is found}
    while symb <> ' '
        do begin
                if opnd(symb)
                    then begin {operand is found}
                            value:= ord(symb) - ord('0');
                            push(opndstk, value)
                        end {then begin}
                    else begin {operator is found}
                            opnd2:= pop(opndstk);
                            opnd1:= pop(opndstk);
                            value:= oper(symb, opnd1, opnd2);
                            push(opndstk, value)
                        end {else begin};
                if position < maxcols
                    then begin
                            position:= position + 1;
                            symb:= expr[position]
                        end {then begin}
                    else symb:= ' '
            end {while...do begin};
    eval:= pop(opndstk)
end  {function eval};
```

For completeness, we present the functions *opnd* and *oper*. The function *opnd* simply checks if its argument is a digit:

```
function opnd(symb: char): boolean;
begin
    if (ord(symb) >= ord('0')) and (ord(symb) <= ord('9'))
        then opnd:= true
        else  opnd:= false
end {function opnd};
```

The function *oper* checks to ensure that its first argument is a valid operator and, if it is, determines the results of its operation on the next two arguments. For exponentiation, we assume the existence of a function *expon(op1, op2: real): real*. The function *oper* uses a set of characters which is not implemented in some Pascal compilers, but it can easily be modified to eliminate this feature.

```
function oper(symb: char; op1, op2: real): real;
function expon(op1, op2: real): real;
    {body of expon}
begin
    if symb in ['+', '*', '-', '/', '$']
        then case symb of
                '+': oper := op1 + op2;
                '*': oper := op1 * op2;
                '-': oper := op1 - op2;
                '/': oper := op1 / op2;
                '$': oper := expon(op1, op2)
            end {then case}
        else error ('illegal operator')
end {function oper};
```

Limitations of the Program

Before we leave the program, we should note some of its deficiencies. Understanding what a program cannot do is as important as knowing what it can do. It should be obvious that attempting to use a program to solve a problem for which it was not intended will lead to chaos. Worse still is the case where an attempt is made to solve a problem with an incorrect program only to have the program produce incorrect results, without the slightest trace of an error message. In these cases the programmer has no indication that the results are wrong and may therefore make faulty judgments based on those results. For this reason, it is important for the programmer to understand the limitations of a program.

A major criticism of this program is that it does nothing in terms of error detection and recovery. If the data on each input line form a correct postfix expression, the program will work. Suppose, however, that one input line has too many operators or operands or that they are not in a proper sequence. These problems could come about as a result of someone innocently using the program on a postfix expression that contains two-digit numbers, yielding an excessive number of operands. Or possibly the user of the program was under the impression that negative numbers could be handled by the program and that they are to be entered with the minus sign, the same sign that is used to represent subtraction. These minus signs will be treated as subtraction operators, resulting in an excess number of operators. Depending on the specific type of error, the computer may take one of several actions (e.g., halt execution or print erroneous results). Suppose that at the final statement of the program, the stack *opndstk* is not empty. We will get no error messages (because we asked for none), and *eval* will return a numerical value for an expression that was probably incorrectly stated in the first place. Suppose that one of the calls to the *pop* routine raises the underflow condition. Since we did not use the *popandtest* routine to pop elements from the stack, our program will stop. This seems unreasonable since faulty data on one line should not prevent the processing of additional lines. By no means are these the only problems that could arise. As exercises, you may wish to write programs that accommodate less restrictive inputs and some others that will test for and detect some of the errors just listed.

Converting an Expression from Infix to Postfix

We have thus far presented routines to evaluate a postfix expression. Although we have discussed a method for transforming infix to postfix, we have not as yet presented an algorithm for doing so. It is to this task that we now direct our attention. Once such an algorithm has been constructed, we will have the capability of reading an infix expression and evaluating it by first converting it to postfix and then evaluating the postfix expression.

In our previous discussion, we mentioned that subexpressions within innermost parentheses must first be converted to postfix, so that they can then be treated as single operands. In this fashion, parentheses can be successively eliminated until the entire expression is converted. The last pair of parentheses to be opened within a group of parentheses encloses the first subexpression within that group to be transformed. This last-in, first-out behavior should immediately suggest the use of a stack.

Consider the two infix expression $A+B*C$ and $(A+B)*C$ and their respective postfix versions $ABC*+$ and $AB+C*$. In each case the order of the operands is the same as the order of the operands in the original infix expressions. In scanning the first expression, $A+B*C$, the first operand A can be immediately inserted into the postfix expression. Clearly, the $+$ symbol cannot be inserted until after its second operand, which has not yet been scanned, is inserted. Therefore, it must be stored away to be retrieved and inserted in its proper position. When the operand B is scanned, it is inserted immediately after A. Now, however, two operands have been scanned. What prevents the symbol $+$ from being retrieved and inserted? The answer is, of course, the $*$ symbol, which follows and has precedence over $+$. In the case of the second expression, the closing parenthesis indicates that the $+$ operation should be performed first. Remember that in postfix, unlike infix, the operator that appears earlier in the string is the one that is applied first.

Let us assume the existence of a function *prcd*(op1, op2: *char*): *boolean*, where op1 and op2 are characters representing operators. This function returns *true* if *op1* has precedence over *op2* when *op1* appears to the left of *op2* in an infix expression without parentheses. *prcd(op1, op2)* returns *false* otherwise. For example, *prcd*('*', '+') and *prcd*('+', '+') are *true* while *prcd*('+', '*') is *false*. Let us now present an outline of an algorithm to convert an infix string without parantheses into a postfix string. Since we are assuming no parentheses in our input string, the only governor of the order in which operators appear in the postfix string is precedence.

```
1    initialize the stack opstk to empty;
2    initialize the postfix string to '';
3    while there are more input symbols
4        do begin
5                read(symb);
6                if symb is an operand
7                    then add symb to the postfix string
8                    else { the symbol is an operator }
9                        begin
10                            while (not empty(opstk)) and
                                  (prcd(stacktop(opstk), symb))
11                                do begin
12                                    topsymb := pop(opstk);
                                      { topsymb has precedence over }
                                      { symb so it can be added to  }
                                      {       the postfix string      }
13                                    add topsymb to the postfix string
14                                end {while...do begin};
                              {   At this point, either opstk is empty or   }
                              { symb has precedence over stacktop(opstk). }
                              {   We cannot output symb into the postfix   }
                              {      string until we have read the next      }
                              { operator, which may have precedence. We }
                              {          must therefore store symb          }
15                            push (opstk, symb)
16                        end {else begin}
17            end {while...do begin};
         {   At this point, we have reached the end of the   }
         { string. We must output the operators remaining }
         {        on the stack into the postfix string.        }
18    while not empty(opstk)
19        do begin
20                topsymb := pop(opstk);
21                add topsymb to the postfix string
22            end {while...do begin}
```

Simulate the algorithm with such infix strings as '*a*b+c*d*' and '*a+b*c\$d\$e*' [where '\$' represents exponentiation and *prcd*('\$', '\$')=*false*] to convince yourself that it is correct. Note that at each point of the simulation, an operator on the stack has a lower precedence than all the operators above it. This is because the initial empty stack trivially satisfies this condition, and an operator is pushed onto the stack (line 15) only if the operator currently on top of the stack has a lower precedence than the incoming operator.

You should also note the liberty that we have taken in line 10 in forming the condition

$$(not \; empty(opstk)) \; and \; (prcd(stacktop(opstk), symb))$$

Later in this section, we will explain why such a condition should not be used in an actual program.

What modification must be made to this algorithm to accommodate parentheses? The answer is surprisingly little. When an opening parenthesis is read, it must be pushed onto the stack. This can be done by establishing the convention that $prcd(op, '(') = false$, for any operator symbol op other than a right parenthesis. In addition, we define $prcd('(', op)$ to be $false$ for any operator symbol op. [The case of $op = ')'$ will be discussed shortly.] This ensures that an operator symbol appearing after a left parenthesis will be pushed onto the stack.

When a closing parenthesis is read, all operators up to the first opening parenthesis must be popped from the stack into the postfix string. This can be done by setting $prcd(op, ')') = true$ for all operators op other than a left parenthesis. When these operators have been popped off the stack and the opening parenthesis is uncovered, special action must be taken. The opening parenthesis must be popped off the stack, and it and the closing parenthesis must be discarded rather than placed in the postfix string or on the stack. Let us set $prcd('(', ')')$ to $false$. This will ensure that upon reaching an opening parenthesis, the loop beginning at line 10 will be skipped, so that the opening parenthesis will not be inserted into the postfix string. Execution will therefore proceed to line 15. However, since the closing parenthesis should not be pushed onto the stack, line 15 will be replaced with the statement

15   *if* (empty(opstk)) *or* (symb <> ')')
                 then push (opstk, symb)
                 else topsymb := pop(opstk)

With the foregoing conventions for the *prcd* function and the revision to line 15, the algorithm can be used to convert any infix string to postfix. We summarize the precedence rules for parentheses:

$prcd('(', op) = false$	for any operator op
$prcd(op, '(') = false$	for any operator op other than ')'
$prcd(op, ')') = true$	for any operator op other than '('
$prcd(')', '(') = undefined$	(an attempt to compare the two indicates an error).

We illustrate this algorithm on some examples:

Ex. 1: $A+B*C$

The contents of *symb*, the postfix string, and *opstk* are shown after scanning each symbol. *opstk* is shown with its top to the right.

	symb	postfix string	opstk
1	A	A	
2	+	A	+
3	B	AB	+
4	*	AB	+*
5	C	ABC	+*
6		ABC*	+
7		ABC*⏐	

Lines 1, 3, and 5 correspond to the scanning of an operand, so the symbol (*symb*) is immediately placed on the postfix string. In line 2 an operator was scanned and the stack was found to be empty, so the operator is placed on the stack. In line 4 the precedence of the new symbol (*) was greater than the precedence of the symbol on the top of the stack (+), so the new symbol is pushed onto the stack. In steps 6 and 7 the input string was empty, so the stack is popped and its contents placed on the postfix string.

Ex. 2: $(A+B)*C$

symb	postfix string	opstk
(		(
A	A	(
+	A	(+
B	AB	(+
)	AB+	
*	AB+	*
C	AB+C	*
	AB+C*	

In this example, when the right parenthesis is encountered, the stack is popped until a left parenthesis is encountered, at which point both parentheses are discarded. By using parentheses to force an order of precedence different from the default, the order of appearance of the operators in the postfix string is different than in Example 1. We present an additional example on the next page.

Why does the conversion algorithm seem so involved, whereas the evaluation algorithm seems so simple? The answer is that the former converts from one order of precedence (governed by the *prcd* function and the appearance of parentheses) to the natural order (i.e., the operation to be executed first appears first). Because of the many combinations of elements at the top of the stack (if not empty) and possible incoming symbol, a large number of statements are necessary to cover each possibility. In the latter algorithm, on the other hand, the operators appear in precisely the order they are to be executed. For this reason the operands can be stacked until an operator is found, at which point the operation is performed immediately.

Ex. 3: $((A-(B+C))*D)\$(E+F)$

symb	postfix string	opstk
(		(
(		((
A	A	((
–	A	((-
(	A	((-(
B	AB	((-(
+	AB	((-(+
C	ABC	((-(+
)	ABC+	((-
)	ABC+-	(
*	ABC+-	(*
D	ABC+-D	(*
)	ABC+-D*	
$	ABC+-D*	$
(	ABC+-D*	$(
E	ABC+-D*E	$(
+	ABC+-D*E	$(+
F	ABC+-D*EF	$(+
)	ABC+-D*EF+	$
	ABC+-D*EF+$	

The motivation behind the conversion algorithm is the desire to output the operators in the order in which they are to be executed. In solving this problem by hand, we could follow vague instructions that require us to convert from the inside out. This works very well for human beings doing a problem with pencil and paper (if they do not become confused or make a mistake). However, when writing a program or an algorithm, we must be more precise in our instructions. We cannot be sure that we have reached the innermost parentheses or the operator with the highest precedence until we have actually scanned all the symbols. At this time, we must backtrack to some previous point.

Rather than backtrack continuously, we make use of the stack to "remember" the operators encountered previously. If an incoming operator is of greater precedence than the one on top of the stack, this new operator is pushed onto the stack. This means that when all the elements in the stack are finally popped, this new operator will precede the former top in the postfix string (which is correct, because it has higher precedence). If, on the other hand, the precedence of the new operator is less than that of the top of the stack, the operator at the top of the stack should be executed first. Therefore, the top of the stack is popped and the incoming symbol is compared with the new top, and so on. By including parentheses in our input string, we may override the order of operations. Thus when a left parenthesis is scanned, it is pushed on the stack. When its associated right parenthesis is found, all the operators between the two parentheses are placed on the output string, because they are to be executed before any operators appearing after the parentheses.

Program to Convert an Expression from Infix to Postfix

There are two things that we must do before we actually start writing a program. The first is to define precisely the format of the input and output. The second is to construct, or at least define, those routines upon which the main routine depends. We assume that our input will be strings of characters, one string per input line. The end of the string will be signaled by the occurrence of a blank. For the sake of simplicity, we assume that all operands are single-character letters or digits. All operators and parentheses are represented by themselves and $ represents exponentiation. The output will be an array of characters. These conventions will make the output of the conversion process suitable for the evaluation process, provided that all the single-character operands in the initial infix string are digits.

In transforming the conversion algorithm into a program, we make use of several routines. Among these are *empty*, *pop*, *push*, and *popandtest*, all suitably modified so that the elements on the stack are characters. We also make use of the function *opnd*, which returns *true* if its argument is an operand and *false* otherwise. This function must also be slightly modified from the version introduced in the program for the evaluation algorithm so that it recognizes a letter as well as a digit as an operand. These simple modifications are left to the reader.

Similarly, the *prcd* function is left to the reader as an exercise. It accepts two single-character operator symbols as arguments and returns *true* if the first has precedence over the second when it appears to the left of the second in an infix string and *false* otherwise. The function should, of course, incorporate the parentheses conventions which we previously introduced.

Once these auxiliary subroutines and functions have been written, we can write the program that calls a conversion procedure *postfix* and the function *postfix* itself. We assume that the program reads a line containing an expression in infix, calls the routine *postfix*, and prints the original string and the postfix string. The body of the main routine follows:

```
program conv (input, output);
const maxcols = 80;
type exprtype = array [1..maxcols] of char;
var  instring, poststring: exprtype;
     position: 1..maxcols;
procedure postfix (infix: exprtype; var out: exprtype);
     {body of postfix}
begin {program conv}
     while not eof
          do begin {process next expression}
                    for position:= 1 to maxcols
                         do read (instring[position]);
                    readln;
                    write ('infix expression is    ');
                    for position:= 1 to maxcols
                         do write (instring[position]);
                    writeln;
                    postfix (instring, poststring);
                    write ('postfix equivalent is    ');
                    for position:= 1 to maxcols
                         do write (poststring[position]);
                    writeln;
                    writeln
          end {while...do begin}
end {program conv}.
```

The postfix routine that implements the conversion follows.

```
procedure postfix (infix: exprtype; var out: exprtype);
const maxstack = maxcols;
type  stack = record
                   item: array [1..maxstack] of char;
                   top: 0..maxstack
              end;
var   opstk: stack;
      position, outlen: 0..maxcols;
      und: boolean;
      symb, topsymb: char;

function empty (s: stack): boolean;
          { body of empty }

function opnd (symb: char): boolean;
          { body of opnd }

function pop (var s: stack): char;
          { body of pop }
```

```
function prcd (op1, op2: char): boolean;
        { body of prcd }

procedure push (var s: stack; x: char);
        { body of push }

procedure popandtest (var s: stack; var x: char; var und: boolean);
        { body of popandtest }
begin {procedure postfix}
    topsymb:= '+';
    opstk.top:= 0; { stack is initially empty }
    { initialize postfix string to blanks }
    for position:= 1 to maxcols
        do out[position]:- ' ';
    position:= 1;
    outlen:= 0;
    { begin scanning symbols until a blank is found }
    symb:= infix[position];
    while symb <> ' '
            do begin
                if opnd(symb)
                    then begin {operand is found}
                            outlen:= outlen + 1;
                            out[outlen]:= symb
                        end {then begin}
                    else  begin {operator}
                            popandtest(opstk, topsymb, und);
                            while (not und) and (prcd(topsymb, symb))
                                do begin
                                        outlen:= outlen + 1;
                                        out[outlen]:= topsymb;
                                        popandtest(opstk, topsymb, und)
                                    end {while...do begin};
                            if not und
                                then push(opstk, topsymb);
                            if und or (symb <> ')')
                                then push(opstk, symb)
                                else topsymb:= pop(opstk)
                        end {else begin};
                if position < maxcols
                    then begin
                            position:= position + 1;
                            symb:= infix[position]
                        end {then begin}
                    else symb:= ' '
            end {while...do begin};
```

```
              while not empty(opstk)
                    do begin
                         outlen:= outlen +1;
                         out[outlen]:= pop(opstk)
                   end {while...do begin}
          end {procedure postfix};
```

The program has one major flaw, in that it does not check that the input string is a valid infix expression. In fact, it would be instructive for you to examine the operation of this program when it is presented with a valid postfix string as input. As an exercise you are asked to write a program that checks whether or not an input string is a valid infix expression.

It is useful for you to examine how lines 10 through 14 of the conversion algorithm were implemented. We could not simply code

while (**not** empty(opstk)) **and** (prcd(stacktop(opstk), symb))

because if *opstk* were empty, *stacktop(opstk)* would result in an underflow and halt program execution under those Pascal compilers that evaluate all conditions in any logical expression. Instead, we used *popandtest* to both pop the top element and test for underflow simultaneously. However, if it turns out that the popped element (*topsymb*) has lower precedence than the incoming symbol (*symb*), it must be restored to the stack. That is why we must add the statement

if not und **then** push(opstk, topsymb)

after the inner loop. Such a statement was unnecessary in the algorithm outline, because there the top element of the stack is not popped until it is known that it has higher precedence than the incoming symbol.

One other point to make note of is that *topsymb* is initialized to '+'. The reason that *topsymb* must be initialized is that the statement *popandtest(opstk, topsymb, und)* will be executed upon encountering the first operator. Since *opstk* is initially empty, *topsymb* will not be changed by *popandtest*. If *topsymb* had no initial value, the call to *prcd(topsymb, symb)* in the **while** statement would result in an error. This will occur in spite of the fact that it is the value of *und* which will govern the algorithm's action in this case rather than the value of *prcd*. By initializing *topsymb* to some value, we are sure that *prcd* will return a value on this call, although that value is irrelevant to further processing. Details such as these can often cause errors in program execution.

We can now write a program ro read an infix string and find its numerical value. If the original string consists of single-digit operands with no letter operands, the following program will read the original string and print its value.

```
program convandeval (input, output);
const maxcols = 80;
type exprtype = array [1..80] of char;
var   instring, poststring: exprtype;
      position: 1..maxcols;
      value: real;
procedure postfix (infix: exprtype; var out: exprtype);
            { body of postfix goes here }
function eval (expr: exprtype): real;
            { body of eval goes here }
begin {program convandeval}
    while not eof
        do begin {process next expression}
            for position:= 1 to maxcols
                do read(instring[position]);
            readln;
            write ('infix expression is     ');
            for position:= 1 to maxcols
                do write (instring[position]);
            writeln;
            postfix (instring, poststring);
            value:= eval(poststring);
            writeln ('value is     ', value)
        end {while...do begin}
end {program convandeval}.
```

The stack manipulation procedures (*pop*, *push*, etc.) for the stack of character operators (i.e., *opstk*) are internal to *postfix*, whereas the procedures for manipulating the stack of *real* operands (i.e., *opndstk*) are internal to *eval*. This is necessary to avoid any conflict between the two versions of each procedure. Of cource, it would be possible to use a stack that can contain both reals or characters by defining a type *stackitem* as a variant record, as described at the end of Section 2. This would allow a single set of the stack manipulation routines to be defined in the main program which could be used by both the conversion and evaluation routines.

Most of our attention in this section has been devoted to transformations involving postfix expressions. The algorithm to convert an infix expression into postfix scans characters from left to right, stacking and unstacking as necessary. If it were necessary to convert from infix to prefix, the infix string could be scanned from right to left and the appropriate symbols entered in the prefix string from right to left. Since most algebraic expressions are read from left to right, postfix is a more natural choice.

The programs discussed above are merely indicative of the type of routines one could write to manipulate and evaluate postfix expressions. They are by no means comprehensive or unique. There are many variations of these routines that are equally acceptable. Some of the older high-level language compilers actually used routines such as *eval* and *postfix* to handle algebraic expressions. Since that time, more sophisticated schemes have been developed to handle these problems.

EXERCISES

1. Transform each of the following expressions to prefix and postfix.
   (a) $A+B-C$
   (b) $(A+B)*(C-D)\$E*F$
   (c) $(A+B)*(C\$(D-E)+F)-G$
   (d) $A+(((B-C)*(D-E)+F)/G)\$(H-J)$

2. Transform each of the following prefix expressions to infix.
   (a) $+-ABC$
   (b) $+A-BC$
   (c) $++A-*\$BCD/+EF*GHI$
   (d) $+-\$ABC*D**EFG$

3. Transform each of the following postfix expressions to infix.
   (a) $AB+C-$
   (b) $ABC+-$
   (c) $AB-C+DEF-+\$$
   (d) $ABCDE-+\$*EF*-$

4. Apply the evaluation algorithm in the text to evaluate the following postfix expressions. Assume that $A = 1$, $B = 2$, and $C = 3$.
   (a) $AB+C-BA+C\$-$
   (b) $ABC+*CBA-+*$

5. Modify the routine *eval* to accept as input a character string of operators and operands representing a postfix expression and to create the fully parenthesized infix form of the original postfix. For example, $AB+$ would be transformed into $(A+B)$ and $AB+C-$ would be transformed into $((A+B)-C)$.

6. Write a single program combining the features of *eval* and *postfix* to evaluate a string given in infix. You are to use two stacks, one for operands and the other for operators. You should not first convert the infix string to postfix and then evaluate the postfix string, but rather evaluate as you go along.

7. Write a routine *prefix* to accept an input string in infix and create the prefix form of that string, assuming that the string is read from right to left and that the prefix string is created from right to left.

8. Write a Pascal program to convert
   (a) a prefix string to postfix.
   (b) a postfix string to prefix.
   (c) a prefix string to infix.
   (d) a postfix string to infix.

9. Write a Pascal routine *reduce* that accepts an infix string and forms an equivalent infix string with all superfluous parentheses removed. Can this be done without using a stack?

10. Assume a machine that has a single register and six instructions.
LD	*A*	which places the operand A into the register
ST	*A*	which places the contents of the register into the variable A

AD	*A*	which adds the contents of the variable *A* to the register
SB	*A*	which subtracts the contents of the variable *A* from the register
ML	*A*	which multiplies the contents of the register by the variable *A*
DV	*A*	which divides the contents of the register by the variable *A*

Write a program that accepts a postfix expression containing single-letter operands and the operators +, −, *, and / and which prints a sequence of instructions to evaluate the expression and leave the result in the register. Use variables of the form *TEMPn* as temporary variables. For example, the postfix expression *ABC*∗+*DE*−/ should yield the printout

LD	*B*
ML	*C*
ST	*TEMP1*
LD	*A*
AD	*TEMP1*
ST	*TEMP2*
LD	*D*
SB	*E*
ST	*TEMP3*
LD	*TEMP2*
DV	*TEMP3*
ST	*TEMP4*

3

RECURSION

This chapter introduces recursion, a programming tool that is one of the most powerful and one of the least understood by beginning students of programming. We define recursion, introduce its use in Pascal, and present several examples. We also examine an implementation of recursion using stacks. The programmer should be aware of how recursion is defined in his or her particular programming language because the lack of such knowledge will cause errors that may or may not be readily apparent. Finally, we discuss the advantages and disadvantages of using recursion in problem solving.

1. RECURSIVE DEFINITION AND PROCESSES

Many objects in mathematics are defined by presenting a process to produce that object. For example, π is defined as the ratio of the circumference of a circle to its diameter. This is equivalent to the set of instructions: obtain the circumference of a circle and its diameter, divide the former by the latter, and call the result π. Clearly, the process specified must terminate with a definite result.

The Factorial Function

Another example of a definition specified by a process is that of the factorial function, a function that plays an important role in mathematics and statistics. Given a positive integer n, *n factorial* is defined as the product of all integers between n and 1. For example, 5 factorial is equal to $5 * 4 * 3 * 2 * 1 = 120$ and 3 factorial equals $3 * 2 * 1 = 6$. 0 factorial is defined as 1. In mathematics, the exclamation mark (!) is often used to denote the factorial function. We may therefore write the definition of this function as follows:

$$n! = 1 \text{ if } n = 0$$
$$n! = n * (n - 1) * (n - 2) * \ldots * 1 \text{ if } n > 0$$

Note that the three dots are really a shorthand for the product of all the numbers between $n - 3$ and 2. To avoid this shorthand in the definition of $n!$ we would have to list a formula for $n!$ for each value of n separately, as follows:

$$0! = 1$$
$$1! = 1$$
$$2! = 2 * 1$$
$$3! = 3 * 2 * 1$$
$$4! = 4 * 3 * 2 * 1$$

Of course, we cannot hope to list a formula for the factorial of each integer. To avoid any shorthand and to avoid an infinite set of definitions, yet to define the function precisely, we may present an algorithm that accepts a nonnegative integer n and returns the value of $n!$ in a variable *fact*:

```
x := n;
prod := 1;
while x <> 0
    do begin
            prod := x * prod;
            x := x - 1
    end {while...do begin};
fact := prod
```

Such an algorithm is called *iterative* because it calls for the explicit repetition of some process until a certain condition is met. This algorithm can be readily translated into a Pascal function that will return $n!$ when n is input as a parameter. An algorithm may be thought of as a program for an "ideal" machine without any of the practical limitations of a real computer and may therefore be used to define a mathematical function. A Pascal function, however, cannot serve as the definition of the factorial function because of such limitations as precision and the finite size of a real machine.

Let us look more closely at the definition of $n!$, which lists a separate formula for each value of n. We may note, for example, that 4! equals $4 * 3 * 2 * 1$, which equals $4 * 3!$. In fact, for any $n > 0$, we see that $n!$ equals $n * (n - 1)!$. Multiplying n by the product of all integers from $n - 1$ to 1 yields the product of all integers from n to 1. We may therefore define

$$0! = 1$$
$$1! = 1 * 0!$$
$$2! = 2 * 1!$$
$$3! = 3 * 2!$$
$$4! = 4 * 3!$$

or, using the mathematical notation used earlier,

$$n! = 1 \text{ if } n = 0$$
$$n! = n * (n - 1)! \text{ if } n > 0$$

This definition may appear quite strange, since it defines the factorial function in terms of itself. This seems to be a circular definition and totally unacceptable until we realize that the mathematical notation is only a concise way of writing out the infinite number of equations necessary to define $n!$ for each n. $0!$ is defined directly as 1. Once $0!$ has been defined, defining $1!$ as $1*0!$ is not circular at all. Similarly, once $1!$ has been defined, defining $2!$ as $2*1!$ is equally straightforward. It may be argued that the latter notation is more precise than the definition of $n!$ as $n*(n-1)*\ldots*1$ for $n > 0$, because it does not resort to three dots to be filled in by, it is hoped, the logical intuition of the reader. Such a definition, which defines an object in terms of a simpler case of itself, is called a *recursive definition*.

Let us see how the recursive definition of the factorial function may be used to evaluate $5!$. The definition states that $5!$ equals $5*4!$. Thus before we can evaluate $5!$, we must first evaluate $4!$. Using the definition once more, we find that $4!=4*3!$. Therefore, we must evaluate $3!$. Repeating this process, we have that

(1) $5! = 5*4!$
(2) $4! = 4*3!$
(3) $3! = 3*2!$
(4) $2! = 2*1!$
(5) $1! = 1*0!$
(6) $0! = 1$

Each case is reduced to a simpler case until we reach the case of $0!$, which is, of course, 1. At line (6) we have a value that is defined directly and not as the factorial of another number. We may therefore backtrack from line (6) to line (1), returning the value computed in one line to evaluate the result of the previous line. This produces

(6′) $0! = 1$
(5′) $1! = 1*0! = 1*1 = 1$
(4′) $2! = 2*1! = 2*1 = 2$
(3′) $3! = 3*2! = 3*2 = 6$
(2′) $4! = 4*3! = 4*6 = 24$
(1′) $5! = 5*4! = 5*24 = 120$

Let us attempt to incorporate this process into an algorithm. Again, we want the algorithm to accept a nonnegative integer n and to return in a variable *fact* the nonnegative integer that is n factorial.

1. **if** $n = 0$
2.   **then** $fact := 1$
3.   **else begin**
4. $x := n - 1;$
5.   Find the value of $x!$. Call it y;
6. $fact := n * y$
7.   **end** {else begin}

This algorithm exhibits the process used to compute $n!$ by the recursive definition. The key to the algorithm is, of course, line 5, where we are told to "find the value of $x!$". This requires reexecuting the algorithm with input x since the method for computing the factorial function is the algorithm itself. To see that the algorithm will eventually halt, note that at the start of line 5, x equals $n - 1$. Each time that the algorithm is executed, its input is one less than the preceding time, so that (since the original input n was a nonnegative integer) 0 will eventually be input to the algorithm. At that point, the algorithm will simply return 1. This value is returned to line 5, which asked for the evaluation of $0!$. The multiplication of $y(= 1)$ by $n(= 1)$ is then executed and the result is returned. This sequence of multiplications and returns continues until the original $n!$ has been evaluated. In the next section, we see how to convert this algorithm into a Pascal program.

Of course, it is much simpler and more straightforward to use the iterative method for evaluation of the factorial function. We present the recursive method as a simple example to introduce recursion, not as a more effective method of solving this particular problem. Indeed, all the problems in this section can be solved more efficiently by iteration. However, later in this chapter and in subsequent chapters, we will come across examples that are more easily solved by recursive methods.

Multiplication of Natural Numbers

Another example of a recursive definition is the definition of multiplication of natural numbers. The product $a*b$, where a and b are positive integers, may be defined as a added to itself b times. This is an iterative definition. An equivalent recursive definition is

$$a*b = a \text{ if } b = 1$$
$$a*b = a*(b-1)+a \text{ if } b > 1$$

To evaluate $6*3$ by this definition, we must first evaluate $6*2$ and then add 6. To evaluate $6*2$, we must first evaluate $6*1$ and add 6. But $6*1$ equals 6 by the first part of the definition. Thus

$$6*3 = 6*2+6 = 6*1+6+6 = 6+6+6 = 18$$

The reader is urged to convert the foregoing definition to a recursive algorithm as a simple exercise.

Note the pattern that exists in recursive definitions. A simple case of the term to be defined is defined explicitly (in the case of the factorial, 0! was defined as 1; in the case of multiplication, $a*1 = a$). The other cases are defined by applying some operation to the result of evaluating a simpler case. Thus $n!$ is defined in terms of $(n-1)!$ and $a*b$ in terms of $a*(b-1)$. Successive simplifications of any particular case must eventually lead to the explicitly defined trivial case. In the case of the factorial function, successively subtractng 1 from n will eventually yield 0. In the case of multiplication, successively subtracting 1 from b will eventually yield 1. If this were not the case, the definition would be invalid. For example, if we defined

$$n! = (n+1)!/(n+1)$$

or

$$a*b = a*(b+1)-a$$

we would be unable to determine the values of 5! or 6*3. (You are invited to attempt to determine these values using the definitions just given.) This is true despite the fact that the two equations are valid. Continually adding one to n or b does not eventually produce an explicitly defined case. Even if 100! were defined explicitly, how could the value of 101! be determined?

The Fibonacci Sequence

Let us examine a less familiar example. The ***Fibonacci sequence*** is the sequence of integers

$$0, 1, 1, 2, 3, 5, 8, 13, 21, 34, \ldots$$

Each element in this sequence is the sum of the two preceding elements (e.g., $0 + 1 = 1, 1 + 1 = 2, 1 + 2 = 3, 2 + 3 = 5, \ldots$). If we let $fib(0) = 0$, $fib(1) = 1$, and so on, we may define the Fibonacci sequence by the following recursive definition:

$$fib(n) = n \text{ if } n = 0 \text{ or } 1$$
$$fib(n) = fib(n - 2) + fib(n - 1) \text{ if } n \geq = 2$$

To compute $fib(6)$, for example, we may apply the definition recursively to obtain

$fib(6) = fib(4)+fib(5) = fib(2)+fib(3)+fib(5) =$
$fib(0)+fib(1)+fib(3)+fib(5) = 0+1+fib(3)+fib(5) = 1+fib(1)+fib(2)+fib(5) =$
$1+1+fib(0)+fib(1)+fib(5) = 2+0+1+fib(5) = 3+fib(3)+fib(4) =$
$3+fib(1)+fib(2)+fib(4) = 3+1+fib(0)+fib(1)+fib(4) = 4+0+1+fib(2)+fib(3) =$
$5+fib(0)+fib(1)+fib(3) = 5+0+1+fib(1)+fib(2) = 6+1+fib(0)+fib(1) = 7+0+1 = 8$

Notice that the recursive definition of the Fibonacci numbers differs from the recursive definitions of the factorial function and multiplication. The recursive definition of *fib* refers to itself twice. For example, $fib(6) = fib(4) + fib(5)$, so that in computing $fib(6)$, *fib* must be applied recursively twice. However, part of the computation of $fib(5)$ involves determining $fib(4)$, so that a great deal of computational redundancy occurs in applying the definition. In the example, $fib(3)$ was computed three separate times. It would have been much more efficient to "remember" the value of $fib(3)$ the first time that it was evaluated and reuse it each time that it was needed. An iterative method of computing $fib(n)$, such as the following, is much more efficient (the result is placed in the variable *fib*):

```
if n <= 1
    then fib := n
    else begin
             lofib := 0;
             hifib := 1;
             for i := 2 to n
                 do begin
                        x := lofib;
                        lofib := hifib;
                        hifib := x + lofib
                    end {for...do begin};
             fib := hifib
         end {else begin}
```

Essentially, this algorithm enumerates all the Fibonacci numbers in the successive values of the variable *hifib*.

Compare the number of additions (not including increments of the index variable i) which are performed in computing $fib(6)$ by this algorithm and by using the recursive definition. In the case of the factorial function, the same number of multiplications must be performed in computing $n!$ by the recursive and iterative methods. The same is true of the number of additions in the two methods of computing multiplication. However, in the case of the Fibonacci numbers, the recursive method is far more expensive than is the iterative. We shall have more to say about the relative merits of the two methods in a later section.

The Binary Search

You may have received the erroneous impression that recursion is a very handy tool for defining mathematical functions but has no influence in more practical computing activities. The next example will illustrate an application of recursion to one of the most common activities in computing—that of searching.

Consider an array of elements in which objects have been placed in some order. For example, a dictionary or telephone book may be thought of as an array whose entries are in alphabetical order. A company payroll file may be in the order of employees' social security numbers. Suppose that such an array exists and we wish to find a particular element in it. For example, we wish to look up a name in a telephone book, a word in a dictionary, or a particular employee in a personnel file. The process used to find such an entry is called a *search*. Since searching is such a common activity in computing, it is desirable to find an efficient method for performing it. Perhaps the crudest search method is the *sequential* or *linear* search, in which each item of the array is examined in turn and compared to the item being searched for until a match occurs. If the list is unordered and haphazardly constructed, the linear search may be the only way to find anything in it (unless, of course, the list is first rearranged). However, such a method would never be used in looking up a name in a telephone book. Rather, the book is opened to a random page and the names on that page are examined. Since the names are ordered alphabetically, such an examination would determine whether the search should proceed in the first or the second half of the book.

Let us apply this idea to searching an array. If the array contains only one element, the problem is trivial. Otherwise, compare the item being searched for with the item at the middle of the array. If they are equal, the search has been completed successfully. If the middle element is greater than the item being searched for, the search process is repeated in the first half of the array (since if the item appears anywhere, it must appear in the first half); otherwise, the process is repeated in the second half. Note that each time a comparison is made, the number of elements yet to be searched is cut in half. For large arrays, this method is superior to the sequential search, in which each comparison reduces the number of elements yet to be searched by only one. Because of the division of the array to be searched into two equal parts, this search method is called the *binary search.*

Notice that we have quite naturally defined a binary search recursively. If the item being searched for is not equal to the middle element of the array, the instructions are to search a subarray using the same method. Thus the search method is defined in terms of itself with a smaller array as input. We are sure that the process will terminate because the input arrays become smaller and smaller, and the search of a one-element array is defined nonrecursively since the middle element of such an array is its only element.

We now present a recursive algorithm to search a sorted array *a* for an element *x* between *a*[*low*] and *a*[*high*]. The algorithm places in a variable *binsrch* an *index* of *a* such that *a*[*index*] = *x* if such an *index* exists between *low* and *high*. If *x* is not found in that portion of the array, *binsrch* is set to 0. We assume that *low* and *high* are either both greater or both less than 0, so that there is no element *a*[0].

```
 1    if low > high
 2        then binsrch := 0
 3        else begin
 4                   mid := (low+high) div 2 ;
 5                   if x = a[mid]
 6                      then binsrch := mid
 7                      else if x < a[mid]
 8                              then search for x in a[low] to a[mid-1]
 9                              else search for x in a[mid+1] to a[high]
10            end {else begin}
```

Since the possibility of an unsuccessful search is included (i.e., the element may not exist in the array), the trivial case has been altered somewhat. A search on a one-element array is not defined directly as the appropriate index. Instead, that element is compared to the item being searched for. If the two items are not equal, the search continues in the "first" or "second" half—each of which contains no elements. This case is indicated by the condition *low* > *high*, and its result is defined directly as 0.

Let us apply this algorithm to an example. Suppose that the array *a* contains the elements 1, 3, 4, 5, 17, 18, 31, and 33 in that order and we wish to search for 17 (i.e., $x = 17$) between item 1 and item 8 (i.e., *low* = 1, *high* = 8). Applying the algorithm, we have

line 1: Is *low* > *high*? It is not, so execute the ***else*** clause.
line 4: $mid := (1+8)$ ***div*** $2 = 4$.
line 5: Is $x = a[4]$? 17 is not equal to 5, so execute the ***else*** clause.
line 7: Is $x < a[4]$? 17 is not less than 5, so perform the ***else*** clause at line 9.
line 9: Repeat the algorithm with *low* = *mid*+1 = 5 and *high* = *high* = 8 (i.e., search the upper half of the array).
line 1: Is 5 > 8? No, so execute the ***else*** clause.
line 4: $mid := (5+8)$ ***div*** $2 = 6$.
line 5: Is $x = a[6]$? 17 does not equal 18, so execute the ***else*** clause.
line 7: Is $x < a[6]$? Yes, since 17 < 18, so execute the ***then*** clause.
line 8: Repeat the algorithm with *low* = *low* = 5 and *high* = *mid*-1 = 5. We have isolated *x* between the fifth and the fifth elements of *a*.
line 1: Is 5 > 5? No, so execute the ***else*** clause.
line 4: $mid := (5+5)$ ***div*** $2 = 5$.
line 5: Since $a[5] = 17$, return 5 as the answer. 17 is indeed the fifth element of the array.

Note the pattern of calls to and returns from the algorithm. A diagram tracing this pattern appears in Figure 3.1.1. The solid arrows indicate the flow of control through the algorithm and the recursive calls. The dashed lines indicate returns. Since there are no steps to be executed in the algorithm after line 8 or 9, the returned result is returned intact to the previous exe-

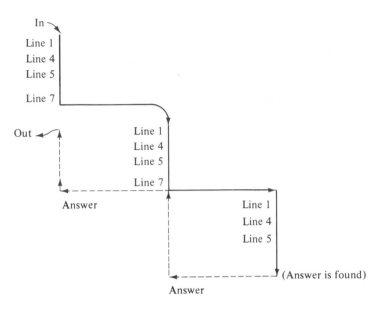

Figure 3.1.1 A diagrammatic representation of the binary search algorithm.

cution. Finally, when control returns to the original execution, the answer is returned to the caller.

Let us examine how the algorithm works in searching for an item that does not appear in the array. Assume the array a as in the previous example and assume that we are searching for $x = 2$.

line 1: Is $low > high$? 1 is not greater than 8, so execute the *else* clause.

line 4: $mid := (1+8)\ div\ 2 = 4$.

line 5: Is $x = a[4]$? 2 does not equal 5, so execute the *else* clause.

line 7: Is $x < a[4]$? Yes, $2 < 5$, so perform the *then* clause.

line 8: Repeat the algorithm with $low = low = 1$ and $high = mid - 1 = 3$. If 2 appears in the array, it must appear between $a[1]$ and $a[3]$ inclusive.

line 1: Is $1 > 3$? No, so execute the *else* clause.

line 4: $mid := (1+3)\ div\ 2 = 2$.

line 5: Is $2 = a[2]$? No, so execute the *else* clause.

line 7: Is $2 < a[2]$? Yes, since $2 < 3$. Perform the *then* clause.

line 8: Repeat the algorithm with $low = low = 1$ and $high = mid - 1 = 1$. If x exists in a, it must be the first element.

line 1: Is $1 > 1$? No, so execute the *else* clause.

line 4: $mid := (1+1)\ div\ 2 = 1$.

line 5: Is $2 = a[1]$? No, so execute the *else* clause.

line 7: Is $2 < a[1]$? 2 is not less than 1, so perform the *else* clause.

line 9: Repeat the algorithm with $low = mid + 1 = 2$ and $high = high = 1$.

line 1: Is $low > high$? 2 is greater than 1, so *binsrch* is 0. The item 2 does not exist in the array.

Properties of Recursive Definitions or Algorithms

Let us summarize what is involved in a recursive definition or algorithm. One important requirement for a recursive algorithm to be correct is that it not generate an infinite sequence of calls on itself. Clearly, any algorithm that does generate such a sequence will never terminate. For at least one argument or group of arguments, a recursive function f must be defined in terms that do not involve f. There must be a "way out" of the sequence of recursive calls. In the examples of this section the nonrecursive portions of the definitions were

factorial: $0! = 1$
multiplication: $a*1 = a$
Fibonacci seq.: $fib(0) = 0;$ $fib(1) = 1$
binary search: **if** $low > high$ **then** $binsrch := 0$
                 if $x = a[mid]$ **then** $binsrch := mid$

Without such a nonrecursive exit, no recursive function can ever be computed. Any instance of a recursive definition or invocation of a recursive algorithm must eventually reduce to some manipulation of one or more simple, nonrecursive cases.

EXERCISES

1. Write an iterative algorithm to evaluate $a * b$ by using addition, where a and b are nonnegative integers.
2. Write a recursive definition of $a + b$, where a and b are nonnegative integers, in terms of the Pascal *succ* function.
3. Let a be an array of integers. Present recursive algorithms to compute
   (a) the maximum element of the array.
   (b) the minimum element of the array.
   (c) the sum of the elements of the array.
   (d) the product of the elements of the array.
   (e) the average of the elements of the array.
4. Evaluate each of the following, using both the iterative and recursive definitions:
   (a) 6!   (b) 9!
   (c) 100 * 3   (d) 6 * 4
   (e) $fib(10)$ (f) $fib(11)$
5. Assume that an array of 10 integers contains the elements

$$1, 3, 7, 15, 21, 22, 36, 78, 95, 106$$

   Use the recursive binary search to find each of the following items in the array
   (a) 1   (b) 20   (c) 36
6. Write an iterative version of the binary search algorithm. (*Hint:* Modify the values of *low* and *high* directly.)

7. Ackerman's function is defined recursively on the nonnegative integers as follows:

$$a(m, n) = n + 1 \qquad\qquad \text{if } m = 0$$
$$a(m, n) = a(m - 1, 1) \qquad \text{if } m \neq 0, n = 0$$
$$a(m, n) = a(m - 1, a(m, n - 1)) \quad \text{if } m \neq 0, n \neq 0$$

  (a) Using the definition just given, show that $a(2, 2) = 7$.
  (b) Prove that $a(m, n)$ is defined for all nonnegative integers m and n.
  (c) Can you find an iterative method of computing $a(m, n)$?

8. Count the number of additions necessary to compute $fib(n)$ for $0 \leq n \leq 10$ by the iterative and recursive methods. Does any pattern emerge?

9. If an array contains n elements, what are the maximum number of recursive calls made by the binary search algorithm?

2. RECURSION IN PASCAL

Factorial in Pascal

The Pascal language allows a programmer to write procedures and functions that call themselves. Such routines are called **recursive.** To present Pascal routines for the algorithms of the preceding section, we first define two global types for the positive and nonnegative integers, respectively:

```
type posint = 1..maxint;
     nonegint = 0..maxint;
```

The recursive algorithm to compute $n!$ may be directly translated into a Pascal function as follows:

```
function fact(n: nonegint): posint;
var x: nonegint;
    y: posint;
begin
    if n = 0
        then fact:= 1
        else begin
                x:= n - 1;
                y:= fact(x);
                fact:= n * y
             end {else begin}
end {function fact};
```

In the statement $y := fact(x)$, the function *fact* calls itself. This is the essential ingredient of a recursive routine. The programmer assumes that the function he or she is computing has already been written and uses it in its own definition. However, the programmer must ensure that this does not lead to an endless series of calls on itself.

Let us examine the execution of the function just shown when it is called by another program. For example, suppose that the calling program contains the statement

write (fact (4))

When the calling routine calls *fact*, the parameter *n* is set equal to 4. Since *n* is not 0, *x* is set equal to 3. At that point, *fact* is called a second time with an argument of 3. Therefore, the block *fact* is reentered and the local variables (*x* and *y*) and parameter (*n*) of the block are reallocated. Since execution has not yet left the first call of *fact*, the first allocation of these variables remains. Thus there are two generations of each of these variables in existence simultaneously. From any point within the second execution of *fact*, only the most recent copy of these variables can be referenced.

In general, each time the function *fact* is entered recursively, a new set of local variables and value parameters is allocated and only this new set may be referenced within that call of *fact*. When a return from *fact* to a point in a previous call takes place, the most recent allocation of these variables is freed and the previous copy is reactivated. This previous copy is the one that was allocated upon the original entry to the previous call and is local to that call.

This description suggests the use of a stack to keep the successive generations of local variables and value parameters. This stack is maintained by the Pascal system and is invisible to the user. Each time that a recursive procedure is entered, a new allocation of its variables is pushed on top of the stack. Any reference to a local variable or parameter is through the current top of the stack. When the procedure returns, the stack is popped, the top allocation is freed, and the previous allocation becomes the current stack top to be used for referencing local variables. This mechanism will be examined more closely in Section 4, but for now, let us see how it is applied in computing the factorial function.

Figure 3.2.1 contains a series of snapshots of the stacks for the variables *n*, *x*, and *y* as execution of the *fact* function proceeds. Initially, the stacks are empty, as illustrated by Figure 3.2.1a. After the first call on *fact* by the calling procedure, the situation is as shown in Figure 3.2.1b, with *n* = 4. The variables *x* and *y* are allocated but not initialized. Since *n* does not equal 0, *x* is set to 3 and *fact*(3) is called (Figure 3.2.1c). The new value of *n* does not equal 0, so *x* is set to 2 and *fact*(2) is called (Figure 3.2.1d). This continues until *n* equals 0 (Figure 3.2.1f). At that point, the value 1 is returned from the call to *fact*(0). Execution resumes from the point at which *fact*(0) was called, which is the assignment of the returned value to the copy of *y* declared in *fact*(1). This is illustrated by the status of the stack shown in Figure 3.2.1g, where the variables allocated for *fact*(0) have been freed and *y* is set to 1.

The statement *fact*:= *n*∗*y* is then executed, multiplying the top values of *n* and *y* to obtain 1, and returning this value to *fact*(2) (Figure 3.2.1h).

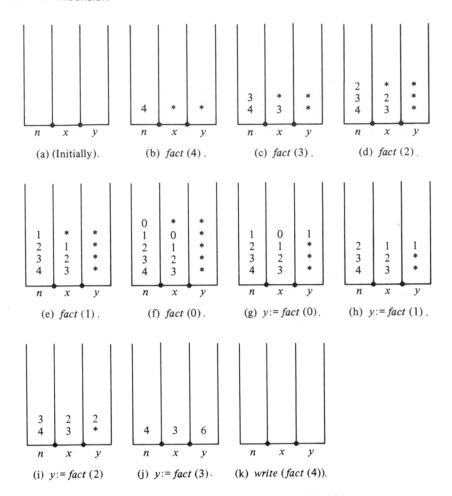

Figure 3.2.1 The stack at various times during execution. (An asterisk indicates an uninitialized value.)

This process is repeated twice more, until finally the value of *y* in *fact*(4) cquals 6 (Figure 3.2.1j). The statement *fact*:= *n**y is executed one more time. The product 24 is returned to the calling procedure, where it is printed by the statement

write(fact(4))

Note that each time that a recursive routine returns, it returns to the point immediately following the point from which it was called. Thus the recursive call to *fact*(3) returns to the assignment of the result to *y* within *fact*(4), but the call to *fact*(4) returns to the *write* statement in the calling routine.

Let us transform some of the other recursive definitions and processes of the previous section into recursive Pascal programs. It is difficult to conceive of a Pascal programmer writing a function to compute the product of two positive integers in terms of addition, since an asterisk can be used to perform the multiplication. Nevertheless, such a function can serve as another illustration of recursion in Pascal. Following closely the definition of multiplication in the previous section, we may write

```
function mult (a, b: posint): posint;
begin
    if b = 1
        then mult := a
        else mult := mult (a, b - 1) + a
end {function mult};
```

Notice how similar this program is to the recursive definition of the preceding section. We leave it as an exercise for you to trace through the execution of this function when it is called with two positive integers. The use of stacks will be a great aid in this tracing process.

This example illustrates that a recursive function may invoke itself even within a statement assigning a value to the function. Similarly, we could have written the recursive *fact* function more compactly as

```
function fact (n: nonegint): posint;
begin
    if n = 0
        then fact := 1
        else fact := n * fact (n - 1)
end {function fact};
```

Note the difference between the uses of *fact* on the left and the right side of the assignment in the foregoing *else* clause; the reference to *fact* on the left is to a local variable; the reference to *fact* on the right is a recursive call. This compact version avoids the explicit use of local variables x (to hold the value of $n - 1$) and y (to hold the value of *fact*(x)). However, temporary locations are set aside anyway for these two values upon each invocation of the function. These temporaries are treated just as any explicit local variable. Thus in tracing the action of a recursive routine, it may be helpful to declare all temporary variables explicitly. See if it is any easier to trace the following more explicit version of *mult*:

```
function mult (a, b: posint): posint;
var c, d: posint;
begin
    if b = 1
      then mult := a
      else begin
              c := b - 1;
              d := mult (a, c);
              mult := d + a
          end {else begin}
end {function mult};
```

Another point which should be made is that it is particularly important to check for the validity of input parameters in a recursive routine. In Pascal, this is easily done by using subrange types such as *posint* and *nonegint* to ensure that parameters are within the proper range. If such subranges are not used, recursive routines can be the source of much grief. For example, consider the *fact* routine if the type *integer*, rather than *posint* and *nonegint*, were used in its declaration. Let us examine the execution of *fact* when it is invoked by a statement such as

write (fact (-1))

Of course, the *fact* function was not designed to produce a meaningful result for negative inputs. However, one of the most important things for a programmer to learn is that a procedure or function will invariably be presented at some time with invalid input and, unless provision is made for such input, the resultant error may be very difficult to trace. For example, when -1 is passed as a parameter to *fact*, so that $n = -1$, x is set to -2 and -2 is passed to a recursive call on *fact*. Another set of n, x, and y is allocated, n is set to -2, and x becomes -3. This process continues until the program either runs out of time or space or the value of x becomes too small. No message indicating the true cause of the error is produced. If *fact* were originally called with a complicated expression as its argument and the expression erroneously evaluated to a negative number, a programmer might spend hours searching for the cause of his error. The problem can be remedied either by using subranges, as we have done, or by revising the *fact* routine to check its input explicitly, as follows:

```
function fact (n: integer): integer;
var x, y: integer;
begin
    if n < 0
      then error ('negative argument passed to the factorial function')
```

```
        else if n = 0
            then fact:= 1
            else begin
                    x:= n - 1;
                    y:= fact(x);
                    fact:= n * y
                end {else begin}
    end {function fact};
```

Similarly, the function *mult* must guard against a nonpositive value in the second parameter.

The Fibonacci Numbers in Pascal

We now turn our attention to the Fibonacci sequence. A Pascal program to compute the nth Fibonacci number can be modeled closely after the recursive definition:

```
function fib(n: nonegint): nonegint;
var x, y: nonegint;
begin
    if n <= 1
        then fib:= n
        else begin
                x:= fib(n-1);
                y:= fib(n-2);
                fib:= x + y
            end {else begin}
end {function fib};
```

Let us trace through the action of the foregoing function in computing the sixth Fibonacci number. You may compare the action of the routine with the manual computation we performed in the last section to compute *fib*(6). The stacking process is illustrated in Figure 3.2.2. When the program is first called, the variables n, x, and y are allocated and n is set to 6 (Figure 3.2.2a). Since $n > 1$, $n - 1$ is evaluated and *fib* is called recursively. A new set of n, x, and y is allocated and n is set to 5 (Figure 3.2.2b). This process continues (Figures 3.2.2c–f) with each successive value of n equaling one less than its predecessor, until *fib* is called with $n = 1$. The sixth call to *fib* returns 1 to its caller, so the fifth allocation of x is set to 1 (Figure 3.2.2g).

The next sequential statement $y:=fib(n-2)$ is then executed. The value of n that is used is the most recently allocated one, which is 2. Thus we again call on *fib* with an argument of 0 (Figure 3.2.2h). The value of 0 is immediately returned so that y in *fib*(2) is set to 0 (Figure 3.2.2i). Note that each recursive call results in a return to the point of call, so that the call of *fib*(1) returns to the assignment to x, while the call of *fib*(0) returns

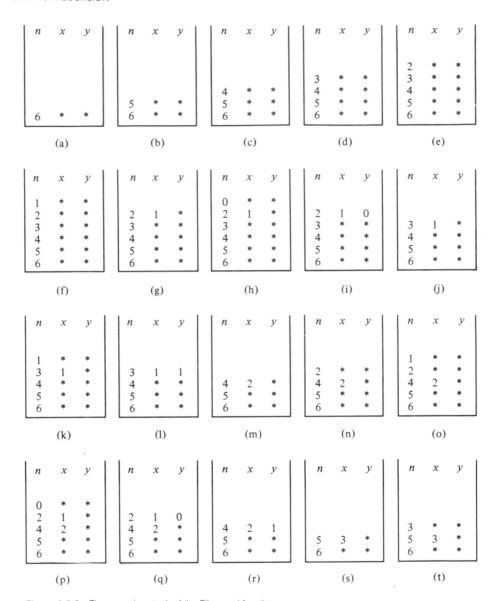

Figure 3.2.2 The recursion stack of the Fibonacci function.

to the assignment to y. The next statement to be executed in $fib(2)$ is the statement that assigns $x + y = 1 + 0 = 1$ to fib and then returns to its invoking statement in the generation of the function calculating $fib(3)$. This is the assignment to x, so that x in $fib(3)$ is given the value $fib(2) = 1$ (Figure 3.2.2j). The process of calling and pushing and returning and popping continues until finally the routine returns for the last time to the main program with the value 8. Figure 3.2.2 shows the stack up to the point where *fib*(5) calls on *fib*(3), so that its value can be assigned to *y*. The reader is urged to complete the picture by drawing the stack states for the remainder of the program execution.

This program illustrates that a recursive routine may call itself a number of times with different arguments. In fact, as long as a recursive routine uses only local variables, the programmer can use the routine just as he or she uses any other and assume that it performs its function and produces the desired value. There is no need to worry about the underlying stacking mechanism.

The Binary Search in Pascal

Let us now present a Pascal program for the binary search. A function to do this would accept an array *a* and an element *x* as input and would return the index *i* in *a* such that $a[i] = x$, or 0 if no such *i* existed. Thus the function *binsrch* might be invoked in a statement such as

$$i := binsrch(a, x)$$

However, in looking at the binary search algorithm of Section 1 as a model for a recursive Pascal routine, we note that two other parameters are passed in the recursive calls. Lines 8 and 9 of that algorithm call for a binary search on only part of the array. Thus, for the function to be recursive, the bounds between which the array is to be searched must also be specified. We assume in the subsequent discussion that the following global definitions appear:

```
const maxarraysize = 500;
      maxplus1 = 501; {array size plus one}
type  arraytype = array[1..maxarraysize] of integer;
      index = 0..maxplus1;
```

The routine is written as follows:

```
function binsrch(a: arraytype; x: integer; low, high: index): index;
var mid: index;
begin
    if low > high
      then binsrch:= 0
      else begin
              mid:= (low+high) div 2;
              if x = a[mid]
                then binsrch:= mid
                else if x < a[mid]
                        then binsrch:= binsrch(a, x, low, mid-1)
                        else  binsrch:= binsrch(a, x, mid+1, high)
      end {else begin}
end {function binsrch};
```

When *binsrch* is first called from another routine to search for *x* in an array declared by

a: arraytype

of which the first *n* elements are occupied, it is called by the statement

i:= binsrch(a, x, 1, n)

You are urged to trace the execution of this routine and follow the stacking and unstacking using the example of the preceding section, where *a* is an array of 8 elements (*n* = 8) containing 1, 3, 4, 5, 17, 18, 31, 33 in that order. The value being searched for is 17 (*x* = 17). Note that the array *a* is stacked for each recursive call. The values of *low* and *high* are declared as being in the range 0 to one more than the maximum array size, because if *x* is less than *a*[1], *high* is set to zero on the last recursive call and if *x* is larger than *a*[*n*], *low* is set to *n* + 1 on the last recursive call.

In the course of tracing through the *binsrch* routine, you may have noticed that the values of the two parameters *a* and *x* do not change throughout its execution. Each time that *binsrch* is called, the same array is searched for the same element: it is only the upper and lower bounds of the search that change. It therefore seems wasteful to stack and unstack these two parameters each time that the routine is called recursively. (In addition, since *a* is a value parameter, it is copied on each call. Of course, *a* could be made a variable parameter.)

One solution is to allow *a* and *x* to be global variables, declared in the calling routine, which includes the function *binsrch* as a subblock. In this case these variables are declared in the surrounding block by

var a: arraytype;
x: integer;

and the header of *binsrch* is replaced by

function binsrch(low,high: index): index;

The routine would be called by a statement such as

i:= binsrch(1, n)

In this case, all references to *a* and *x* are to the single copy which is declared in the outer block but also known in the inner block. This saves the allocation and freeing of multiple copies of these two variables.

However, this solution has some serious drawbacks. The variable *x* must always be set in the calling routine to the variable whose value is being searched for. Another serious objection is one based on logical and aesthetic design factors. Logically, the two parameters to a search function should be the array that is being searched and the object being searched for, in our case *a* and *x*. However, in the current version of *binsrch*, neither of these appears as a parameter. Instead, the two parameters that do appear—the upper and lower bounds—relate to the internal workings of the algorithm and not to the problem specification.

   To remedy all these problems, we may rewrite the *binsrch* function as a nonrecursive routine with parameters *a* and *x*, which calls on an internal auxiliary recursive routine *auxsrch* with parameters *low* and *high*, as follows:

```
function binsrch (a: arraytype; n: index; x: integer): index;
   function auxsrch (low, high: index): index;
   var mid: index;
   begin {function auxsrch}
      if low > high
         then auxsrch:= 0
         else begin
                 mid:= (low+high) div 2;
                 if x = a[mid]
                    then auxsrch:= mid
                    else if x < a[mid]
                            then auxsrch:= auxsrch (low, mid-1)
                            else auxsrch:= auxsrch (mid+1, high)
         end {else begin}
   end {function auxsrch};
   begin {function binsrch}
      binsrch:= auxsrch (1, n)
   end {function binsrch};
```

Using this scheme, the variables *a* and *x* are passed to the binary search routine, as they should be. *a* and *x* do not change their values and are not stacked. The work of stacking, unstacking, and altering the values of *low* and *high* is left to the internal recursive routine *auxsrch*. The programmer wishing to make use of *binsrch* in his program need not even be aware of the existence of *low* and *high*. He merely invokes the routine with a statement such as

$$i:= binsrch (a, n, x)$$

Note that the function *binsrch* is not recursive.

Recursive Chains

   A recursive procedure need not call itself directly. Rather, it may call itself indirectly, as in the following example:

```
procedure a (formal parameters);        procedure b (formal parameters);
   begin                                    begin
      .                                         .
      .                                         .
      .                                         .
      b (arguments);                            a (arguments);
      .                                         .
   end {procedure a};                       end {procedure b};
```

In this example procedure *a* calls *b*, which may in turn call *a*, which may again call *b*. Thus both *a* and *b* are recursive, since they indirectly call on themselves. However, the fact that they are recursive is not evident from examining the body of either of the routines individually. The routine *a* seems to be calling a separate routine *b*, and it is impossible to determine, by examining *a* alone, that it will indirectly call itself.

More than two routines may participate in a *recursive chain*. Thus a routine *a* may call *b*, which calls *c*, ... , which calls *z*, which calls *a*. Each routine in the chain may potentially call itself and is therefore recursive. Of course, the programmer must ensure that his or her program does not generate an infinite sequence of recursive calls.

There is one special rule for recursive chains in Pascal. Ordinarily, a function or procedure must be defined before it can be referenced. But if *a* calls *b* and *b* calls *a*, *a* cannot be defined first because it references *b*, but *b* cannot be defined first either because it references *a*. The solution is to define the procedures as follows:

> **procedure** b(*formal parameters*); forward;
> **procedure** a(*formal parameters*);
> {*body of* a}
> **procedure** b;
> {*body of* b}

The keyword *forward* indicates that the body of procedure *b* will be defined subsequently. Since the parameters of *b* have been declared before *a* is defined, the call on *b* within *a* can be compiled correctly. Then after *a* has been defined, the body of *b* is defined. Note that the parameters of *b* are not redeclared in the header when the body of the procedure is defined.

Recursive Definition of Algebraic Expressions

As an example of such a recursive chain, consider the following recursive group of definitions:

1. An *expression* is a *term* followed by a *plus sign* followed by a *term*, or a *term* alone.
2. A *term* is a *factor* followed by an *asterisk* followed by a *factor*, or a *factor* alone.
3. A *factor* is either a *letter* or an *expression* enclosed in *parentheses*.

Before looking at some examples, note that none of the foregoing three items is defined directly in terms of itself. However, each is defined in terms of itself indirectly. An expression is defined in terms of a term, a term in terms of a factor, and a factor in terms of an expression. Similarly, a factor is defined in terms of an expression, which is defined in terms of a term, which is defined in terms of a factor. Thus the entire set of definitions forms a recursive chain.

Let us now give some examples. The simplest form of a factor is a letter. Thus *A, B, C, Q, Z, M* are all factors. They are also terms, because a term may be a factor alone. They are also expressions, because an expression may be a term alone. Since *A* is an expression, (*A*) is a factor and therefore a term as well as an expression. $A+B$ is an example of an expression which is neither a term nor a factor. $(A+B)$, however, is all three. $A*B$ is a term and therefore an expression, but it is not a factor. $A*B+C$ is an expression that is neither a term nor a factor. $A*(B+C)$ is a term and an expression but not a factor.

Each of the examples is a valid expression. This can be shown by applying the definition of an expression to each of them. Consider, however, the string $A+*B$. It is not an expression, a term, or a factor. It would be instructive for you to attempt to apply the definitions of expression, term, and factor to see that none of them describe the string $A+*B$. Similarly, $(A+B*)C$ and $A+B+C$ are not valid expressions according to the definitions just given.

Let us write a program that reads a character string, prints it out, and then prints *valid* if it is a valid expression and *invalid* if it is not. We will use three functions to recognize expressions, terms, and factors, respectively. However, we first present an auxiliary function *getsymb*, which operates on three global variables: *str*, *length*, and *pos*. The first of these variables, *str*, contains the input character string as an array of characters. *length* represents the number of elements of *str* containing characters. The third of these variables, *pos*, is the position in *str* from which we last obtained a character. Upon entry to *getsymb*, *pos* is incremented by 1. If *pos* ≤ *length*, then *getsymb* returns the character at position *pos* of *str*. If *pos* > *length*, then *getsymb* returns a blank.

```
function getsymb: char;
begin
    pos:= pos + 1;
    if pos > length
        then getsymb:= ' '
        else getsymb:= str[pos]
end {function getsymb};
```

The function that recognizes an expression is called *expr*. It, too, has no arguments and uses *str* and *pos* as global variables. It returns *true* if a valid expression begins at position *pos* of *str* and *false* otherwise. It also resets *pos* to the last position of the longest expression it can find. The program also calls a procedure *readstr* that reads a string of characters, placing the string in *str* and its length in *length*. Having described the function *expr* and the procedure *readstr*, we can write the main routine as follows:

```
program findexp(input,output);
const maxstringsize = 100;
      maxplusone = 101;
```

```
type  arraychar = array[1..maxstringsize] of char;
      index = 1..maxstringsize;
var str: arraychar;
    length: index;
    pos: 0..maxplusone;
    ok: boolean;
function getsymb: char;
          {body of getsymb goes here}
function factor: boolean; forward;
function term: boolean; forward;
function expr: boolean;
          {  body of expr goes here  }
function factor;
          {  body of factor goes here  }
function term;
          {  body of term goes here  }
procedure readstr(var str: arraychar; var length: index);
          {  body of readstr goes here  }
begin  {program findexp}
    readstr(str, length);
    for pos:= 1 to length
        do write(str[pos]);
    writeln;
    pos:= 0;
    ok:= expr;
    if ok and (pos = length)
        then write('valid')
        else  write('invalid')
    {The condition can fail for one (or both) of two}
    {   reasons.  If not ok then there is no valid    }
    {  expression beginning at pos.  If pos < length  }
    {there may be a valid expression starting at pos }
    {   but it does not occupy the entire string.    }
end  {program findexp}.
```

The functions *factor* and *term* are much like *expr* except that they are responsible for recognizing factors and terms, respectively. They also reposition *pos* to the last position of the longest factor or term within the string *str* that they can find.

The code for these routines adheres closely to the definitions given earlier. Each of the routines attempts to satisfy one of the criteria for the entity being recognized. If one of these criteria is satisfied, then *true* is returned. If none of these criteria is satisfied, then *false* is returned.

```
function expr: boolean;
var ok: boolean;
    c: char;
begin {function expr}
    {Look for a term.}
    ok:= term;
    if not ok {no expression exists}
      then expr:= false
      else begin
              {Look at the next symbol.}
              c:= getsymb;
              if c <> '+'
                then begin
                      {We have found the longest expression}
                      {   (a single term).  Reposition pos so   }
                      {        it refers to the last position    }
                      {               of the expression.          }
                      pos:= pos - 1;
                      expr:= true
                    end {then begin}
                else  begin
                      { At this point, we have found a term }
                      { and a plus sign.  We must look for  }
                      {               another term.          }
                      ok:= term;
                      if ok
                        then expr:= true
                        else  expr:= false
                    end {else begin}
          end {else begin}
end {function expr};
```

The routine *term* that recognizes a term is similar, and we present it without comments. Note that the return type of *term* has already been specified as *boolean* and cannot be repeated.

```
function term;
var ok: boolean;
    c: char;
begin {function term}
    ok:= factor;
    if not ok
      then term:= false
```

```
              else begin
                      c:= getsymb;
                      if c <> '*'
                          then begin
                                     pos:= pos - 1;
                                     term:= true
                              end {then begin}
                          else begin
                                     ok:= factor;
                                     if ok
                                          then term:= true
                                          else  term:= false
                              end {else begin}
                  end {else begin}
          end {function term};
```

The function *factor* recognizes a factor and should now be fairly straightforward. It uses a function *letter* which returns *true* if its character parameter is a letter and *false* otherwise.

```
          function factor;
          var ok: boolean;
              c: char;
          function letter(c: char): boolean;
                  {body of letter goes here}
          begin {function factor}
              c:= getsymb;
              if c <> '('
                  then {check for a letter}
                      if letter(c)
                          then factor:= true
                          else  factor:= false
                  else begin {the factor is a parenthesized expression}
                          ok:= expr;
                          if not ok
                              then factor:= false
                              else begin
                                      c:= getsymb;
                                      if c <> ')'
                                          then factor:= false
                                          else  factor:= true
                                  end {else begin}
                      end {else begin}
          end {function factor};
```

All three routines are recursive since each may call itself indirectly. For example, if you trace through the actions of the program *findexp* for the input string '$(A*B+C*D)+(E*(F)+G)$', you will find that each of the routines *expr*, *term*, and *factor* calls on itself.

EXERCISES

1. Determine what the following recursive Pascal function computes. Write an iterative function to accomplish the same purpose.

    ```
    function func(n: nonegint): nonegint;
    begin
        if n = 0
            then func:= 0
            else func:= n + func(n-1)
    end {function func};
    ```

2. The Pascal expression *m* **mod** *n* yields the remainder of *m* upon division by *n*. Define the **greatest common divisor** (**gcd**) of two integers *x* and *y* by

    $$gcd(x, y) = y \qquad\qquad \text{if } y \leqslant x \text{ and } x \bmod y = 0$$
    $$gcd(x, y) = gcd(y, x) \qquad \text{if } x < y$$
    $$gcd(x, y) = gcd(y, x \bmod y) \quad \text{otherwise}$$

    Write a recursive Pascal function to compute $gcd(x, y)$. Find an iterative method for computing this function.

3. Let *comm*(*n*, *k*) represent the number of different committees of *k* people that can be formed, given *n* people to choose from. For example, *comm*(4, 3) = 4, since given four people *A*, *B*, *C*, and *D* there are four possible committees: *ABC*, *ABD*, *ACD*, and *BCD*. Prove the identity

    $$comm(n, k) = comm(n-1, k) + comm(n-1, k-1)$$

    Write and test a recursive Pascal program to compute *comm*(*n*, *k*) for *n*, *k* >= 1.

4. Define a **generalized Fibonacci sequence of** $f0$ **and** $f1$ as the sequence $gfib(f0, f1, 0), gfib(f0, f1, 1), gfib(f0, f1, 2), \ldots$, where

    $$gfib(f0, f1, 0) = f0$$
    $$gfib(f0, f1, 1) = f1$$
    $$gfib(f0, f1, n) = gfib(f0, f1, n-1) + gfib(f0, f1, n-2) \quad \text{if } n > 1$$

    Write a recursive Pascal function to compute $gfib(f0, f1, n)$. Find an iterative method for computing this function.

5. Write a recursive Pascal function to compute the number of sequences of *n* binary digits that do not contain two 1s in a row. (*Hint:* Compute how many such sequences exist that start with a 0, and how many exist that start with a 1.)

6. An **order n matrix** is an $n \times n$ array of numbers. For example,

    $$(3)$$

    is a 1×1 matrix,

$$\begin{pmatrix} 1 & 3 \\ -2 & 8 \end{pmatrix}$$

is a 2 × 2 matrix, and

$$\begin{pmatrix} 1 & 3 & 4 & 6 \\ 2 & -5 & 0 & 8 \\ 3 & 7 & 6 & 4 \\ 2 & 0 & 9 & -1 \end{pmatrix}$$

is a 4 × 4 matrix. Define the **minor** of an element x in a matrix as the submatrix formed by deleting the row and column containing x. In the foregoing example of a 4 × 4 matrix, the minor of the element 7 is the 3 × 3 matrix

$$\begin{pmatrix} 1 & 4 & 6 \\ 2 & 0 & 8 \\ 2 & 9 & -1 \end{pmatrix}$$

Clearly, the order of a minor of any element is 1 less than the order of the original matrix. Denote the minor of an element $a[i, j]$ by *minor* $(a[i, j])$.

Define the **determinant** of a matrix a (written $det(a)$) recursively as follows:

(a) If a is a 1 × 1 matrix (x), then $det(a) = x$.
(b) If a is of order greater than 1, compute the determinant of a as follows:

(i) Choose any row or column. For each element $a[i, j]$ in this row or column, form the product.

$$(-1)^{i+j} * a[i, j] * det(minor(a[i, j]))$$

where i and j are the row and column positions of the element chosen, $a[i, j]$ is the element chosen, $det(minor(a[i, j]))$ is the determinant of the minor of $a[i, j]$.

(ii) $det(a)$ = sum of all these products over the chosen row or column. (More concisely, if n is the order of a, then

$$det(a) = \sum_{i=1}^{n} (-1)^{i+j} * a[i, j] * det(minor(a[i, j])), \quad \text{for any } j$$

or

$$det(a) = \sum_{j=1}^{n} (-1)^{i+j} * a[i, j] * det(minor(a[i, j])), \quad \text{for any } i$$

Write a Pascal program that will read in a, print out a in matrix form, and print out $det(a)$, where det is a function that computes the determinant of a matrix.

7. Write a recursive Pascal program to sort an array a as follows:

(a) Let k be the index of the middle element of the array.
(b) Sort the elements up to and including $a[k]$.
(c) Sort the elements past $a[k]$.
(d) Merge the two subarrays into a single sorted array.

This method is called a **merge sort.**

8. Show how to transform the following iterative procedure into a recursive procedure. $f(i)$ is a function returning a boolean value based on the value of i, and $g(i)$ is a function that returns a value of the same type as i without changing the value of i.

```
procedure iter(n: ntype);
var i: ntype
function f(k: ntype): boolean;
        {body of f goes here}
function g(k: ntype): ntype;
        {body of g goes here}
begin {procedure iter}
    i:= n;
    while f(i)
        do begin
                {    any group of Pascal statements    }
                {which does not change the value of i}
                i:- g(i)
            end {while...do begin}
end {procedure iter};
```

3. WRITING RECURSIVE PROGRAMS

In the preceding section we saw how to take a recursive definition or algorithm and transform it into a Pascal program. It is a much more difficult task to develop a recursive Pascal solution to a problem specification whose algorithm is not supplied. It is not only the program but also the original definitions and algorithms that must be developed. In general, when faced with the task of writing a program to solve a problem, there is no reason to look for a recursive solution. Most problems can be solved in a straightforward manner using nonrecursive methods. We shall have more to say about these "efficiency" considerations in later sections. However, some problems can be solved logically and most elegantly by recursion. In this section we shall try to identify those problems that can be solved recursively, develop a technique for finding recursive solutions, and present some examples.

Let us reexamine the factorial function. Factorial is probably a prime example of a problem that should not be solved recursively since the iterative solution is so direct and simple. However, let us examine the elements that make the recursive solution work. First, we can recognize a large number of distinct cases to solve. That is, we want to write a program to compute 0!, 1!, 2!, and so on. We can also identify a "trivial" case for which a nonrecursive solution is directly obtainable. This is the case of 0!, which is defined as 1. The next step is to find a method of solving a "complex" case in terms of a "simpler" case. This will allow reduction of a complex problem to a simpler problem. The transformation of the complex case to the simpler case should eventually result in the trivial case. This would mean that the complex case is ultimately defined in terms of the trivial case.

Let us examine what this means when applied to the factorial function. 4! is a more "complex" case than is 3!. The transformation that is applied to the number 4 to obtain the number 3 is simply the subtraction of 1. Repeatedly subtracting 1 from 4 eventually results in 0, which is a "trivial" case. Thus, if we are able to define 4! in terms of 3!, and in general $n!$ in terms of $(n - 1)!$, we will be able to compute 4! by first working our way down to 0! and then working our way back up to 4! using the definition of $n!$ in terms of $(n - 1)!$. In the case of the factorial function we have such a definition, since

$$n! = n*(n - 1)!$$

Thus $4! = 4*3! = 4*3*2! = 4*3*2*1! = 4*3*2*1*0! = 4*3*2*1*1 = 24$.

These are the essential ingredients of a recursive routine—being able to define a "complex" case in terms of a "simpler" case and having a directly solvable (nonrecursive) "trivial" case. Once this has been done, one can develop a solution using the assumption that the simpler case has already been solved. The Pascal version of the factorial function assumes that $(n - 1)!$ is defined and uses that quantity in computing $n!$.

Let us see how these ideas apply to other examples of the previous sections. In defining $a*b$, the case of $b = 1$ is trivial, since in that case, $a*b$ is defined as a. In general, $a*b$ may be defined in terms of $a*(b - 1)$ by the definition $a*b = a*(b - 1) + a$. Again the complex case is transformed into a simpler case by subtracting one, eventually leading to the trivial case of $b = 1$. Here the recursion is based on the second parameter b alone.

In the case of the Fibonacci function, two trivial cases were defined: $fib(0) = 0$ and $fib(1) = 1$. A complex case, $fib(n)$, is then reduced to two simpler cases, $fib(n - 1)$ and $fib(n - 2)$. It is because of the definition of $fib(n)$ as $fib(n - 1) + fib(n - 2)$ that two trivial cases directly defined are necessary. $fib(1)$ cannot be defined as $fib(0) + fib(-1)$, because the Fibonacci function is not defined for negative numbers.

The binary search function is an interesting case of recursion. The recursion is based on the number of elements in the array that must be searched. Each time the routine is called recursively, the number of elements to be searched is halved (approximately). The trivial case is the one in which there are either no elements to be searched or the element being searched for is at the middle of the array. If $low > high$, then the first of these two conditions holds and 0 is returned. If $x = a[mid]$, the second condition holds and mid is returned as the answer. In the more complex case of $high - low + 1$ elements to be searched, the search is reduced to taking place in one of two subregions.

1. The lower half of the array from low to $mid - 1$.
2. The upper half of the array from $mid + 1$ to $high$.

Thus a complex case (a large area to be searched) is reduced to a simpler case (an area to be searched of approximately half the size of the original area). This eventually reduces to a comparison with a single element ($a[mid]$) or a search within an array of no elements.

The Towers of Hanoi Problem

Thus far we have been looking at recursive definitions and examining how they fit the pattern we have established. Let us now look at a problem that is not specified in terms of recursion and see how we can use recursive techniques to produce a logical and elegant solution. The problem is the "Towers of Hanoi" problem, whose initial setup is shown in Figure 3.3.1. Three pegs, A, B, and C, exist. Five disks of differing diameters are placed on peg A so that a larger disk is always below a smaller disk. The object is to move the five disks to peg C using peg B as auxiliary. Only the top disk on any peg may be moved to any other peg, and a larger disk may never rest on a smaller one. See if you can produce a solution. Indeed, it is not even apparent that a solution exists.

Let us see if we can develop a solution. Instead of focusing our attention on a solution for five disks, let us consider the general case of n disks. Suppose that we had a solution for $n - 1$ disks and we could state a solution for n disks in terms of the solution for $n - 1$ disks. Then the problem would be solved. This is true because in the trivial case of one disk (continually subtracting 1 from n will eventually produce 1), the solution is simple: merely move the single disk from peg A to peg C. Therefore, we will have developed a recursive solution if we can state a solution for n disks in terms of $n - 1$. See if you can find such a relationship. In particular, for the case of five disks, suppose that we knew how to move the top four disks from peg A to another peg according to the rules. How could we then complete the job of moving all five? Recall that there are three pegs available.

Suppose that we could move four disks from peg A to peg C. Then

Figure 3.3.1   The initial setup of the Towers of Hanoi.

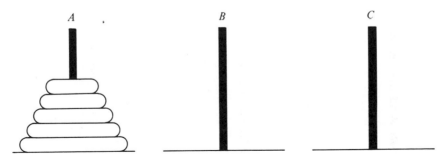

we could just as easily move them to *B*, using *C* as auxiliary. This would result in the situation depicted in Figure 3.3.2a. We could then move the largest disk from *A* to *C* (Figure 3.3.2b) and finally again apply the solution for four disks to move the four disks from *B* to *C*, using the now empty peg *A* as an auxiliary (Figure 3.3.2c). Thus we may state a recursive solution to the Towers of Hanoi problem as follows:

Figure 3.3.2   Recursive solution to the Towers of Hanoi.

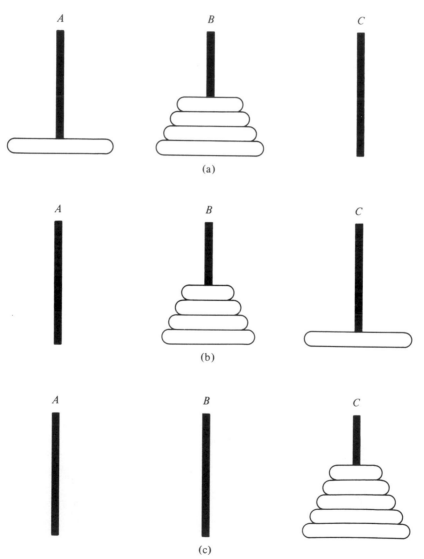

To move n disks from A to C, using B as auxiliary

1. If $n = 1$, then move the single disk from A to C and stop.
2. Move the top $n - 1$ disks from A to B, using C as auxiliary.
3. Move the remaining disk from A to C.
4. Move the $n - 1$ disks from B to C, using A as auxiliary.

We are sure that this algorithm will produce a correct solution for any value of n. If $n = 1$, step 1 will result in the correct solution. If $n = 2$, we know that we already have a solution for $n - 1 = 1$, so that steps 2 and 4 will perform correctly. Similarly, when $n = 3$, we already have produced a solution for $n - 1 = 2$, so that steps 2 and 4 can be performed. In this fashion, we can show that the solution works for $n = 1, 2, 3, 4, 5, \ldots$ up to any value for which we desire a solution. Notice that we developed the solution by identifying a trivial case ($n = 1$) and a solution for a general complex case (n) in terms of a simpler case ($n - 1$).

How can this solution be converted into a Pascal program? We are no longer dealing with a mathematical function such as factorial, but rather with concrete actions such as "move a disk." How are we to represent such actions in the computer? The problem is not completely specified. What are the inputs to the program? What are its outputs to be? Whenever you are told to write a program, you must receive specific instructions as to exactly what the program is expected to do. A problem statement such as "Solve the Towers of Hanoi problem" is quite insufficient. What is usually meant when such a problem is specified is that not only the program but also the inputs and outputs must be designed, so that they reasonably correspond to the problem description. The design of inputs and outputs is an important phase of a solution and should be given as much attention as the rest of a program. There are two reasons for this. The first is that the user (who must ultimately evaluate and pass judgement on your work) will not see the elegant method you incorporated in your program but will struggle mightily to decipher the output or to adapt his or her input data to your particular input conventions. The failure to agree early on input and output details has been the cause of much grief to programmers and users alike. The second reason is that a slight change in the input or output format may make the program much simpler to design. Thus the programmer can make the job much easier if he or she is able to design an input or output format compatible with the algorithm. Of course, these two considerations, convenience to the user and convenience to the programmer, often conflict sharply, and some happy medium must be found. However, the user as well as the programmer must be a full participant in the decisions on input and output formats.

Let us, then, proceed to design the inputs and outputs for this program. The only input needed is the value of n, the number of disks. At least, that may be the programmer's view. The user may want the names of the disks (such as "red," "blue," "green," etc.) and perhaps the names of the pegs (such as "left," "right," and "middle") as well. The programmer can probably convince the user that naming the disks 1, 2, 3, ... , *n* and the pegs *A*, *B*, and *C* is just as convenient. If necessary, the programmer can write a small function to convert the user's names to his own, and vice versa.

A reasonable form for the output would be a list of statements such as

move disk *nnn* from peg *yyy* to peg zzz

where *nnn* is the number of the disk to be moved and *yyy* and zzz are the names of the pegs involved. The action to be taken for a solution would be to perform each of the output statements in the order that they appear in the output.

The programmer then decides to write a procedure *towers* (he is purposely vague about the parameters at this point) to print the output just shown. The main program would be

```
program result(input, output);
var n: 1..maxint;
begin
    read(n); { read the number of disks }
    towers( parameters)
end {program result}.
```

Let us assume that the user will be satisfied to name the disks 1, 2, 3, ... , *n* and the pegs *A*, *B*, and *C*. What should the parameters to *towers* be? Clearly, they should include *n*, the number of disks to be moved. This includes not only information about how many disks there are but also what their names are. The programmer then notices that in the recursive algorithm, he will have to move *n* − 1 disks using a recursive call to *towers*. Thus, on the recursive call, the first parameter to *towers* will be *n* − 1. But this implies that the top *n* − 1 disks are numbered 1, 2, 3, ... , *n* − 1 and that the smallest disk is numbered 1. This is a good example of programming convenience determining problem representation. There is no a priori reason for labeling the smallest disk 1; logically, the largest disk could have been labeled 1 and the smallest disk *n*. However, since it leads to a simpler and more direct program, we will choose to label our disks so that the smallest disk has the smallest number.

What are the other parameters to *towers*? At first glance, it might appear that no additional parameters are necessary, since the pegs are named *A*, *B*, and *C* by default. However, a closer look at the recursive solution leads us to the realization that on the recursive calls, disks will not be moved from *A* to *C* using *B* as auxiliary but rather from *A* to *B* using *C* (step 2) or from *B* to *C* using *A* (step 4). We therefore include three more parameters in *towers*. The first, *frompeg*, represents the peg from which we are removing disks; the second, *topeg*, represents the peg to which we will take the disks; and the third, *auxpeg*, represents the auxiliary peg. This situation is one that is quite typical of recursive routines; additional parameters are necessary to handle the recursive call situation. We already saw one example of this in the binary search program where the parameters *low* and *high* were necessary.

The complete program to solve the Towers of Hanoi problem, closely following the recursive solution, may be written as follows:

```
program result(input, output);
type posint = 1..maxint;
var n: posint;

procedure towers(n: posint; frompeg, topeg, auxpeg: char);
begin
    { if only one disk, make the move and return }
    if n = 1
        then writeln('move disk 1 from peg', frompeg, ' to peg ', topeg)
        else begin
                { move top n-1 disks from A to B, using C as }
                {                auxiliary                   }
                towers(n-1, frompeg, auxpeg, topeg);
                {    move remaining disk from A to C         }
                writeln('move disk ', n, 'from peg ', frompeg, ' to peg ', topeg);
                {   move n-1 disks from B to C, using A as   }
                {                auxiliary                   }
                towers(n-1, auxpeg, topeg, frompeg)
            end {else begin}
end {procedure towers};

begin {program result}
    read(n);
    towers(n, 'a', 'c', 'b')
end {program result}.
```

towers is our first example of a recursive procedure as opposed to a function. It is called by using the name of the procedure, exactly as any other procedure would be called. Trace the actions of the foregoing program when it reads the value 4 for *n*. Be careful to keep track of the changing values of the parameters *frompeg*, *auxpeg*, and *topeg*. Verify that it produces the following output:

```
move disk 1  from peg a to peg c
move disk 2  from peg a to peg b
move disk 1  from peg c to peg b
move disk 3  from peg a to peg c
move disk 1  from peg b to peg a
move disk 2  from peg b to peg c
move disk 1  from peg a to peg c
```

> move disk 4 from peg a to peg b
> move disk 1 from peg c to peg b
> move disk 2 from peg c to peg a
> move disk 1 from peg b to peg a
> move disk 3 from peg c to peg b
> move disk 1 from peg a to peg c
> move disk 2 from peg a to peg b
> move disk 1 from peg c to peg b

Verify that this solution actually works and does not violate any of the rules.

Translation from Prefix to Postfix Using Recursion

Let us examine another problem for which the recursive solution is the most direct and elegant one. This is the problem of converting a prefix expression to postfix. Prefix and postfix notation were discussed in Chapter 2. Briefly, prefix and postfix notations are methods of writing mathematical expressions without parentheses. In prefix notation each operator immediately precedes its operands. In postfix notation each operator immediately follows its operands. To refresh your memory, here are a few conventional (infix) mathematical expressions with their prefix and postfix equivalents:

infix	prefix	postfix
$A+B$	$+AB$	$AB+$
$A+B*C$	$+A*BC$	$ABC*+$
$A*(B+C)$	$*A+BC$	$ABC+*$
$A*B+C$	$+*ABC$	$AB*C+$
$A+B*C+D-E*F$	$-++A*BCD*EF$	$ABC*+D+EF*-$
$(A+B)*(C+D-E)*F$	$**+AB +CDEF$	$AB+CD+E-*F*$

The most convenient way to define postfix and prefix is by using recursion. Assuming no constants and using only single letters as variables, a prefix expression is a single letter or an operator followed by two prefix expressions. A postfix expression may be similarly defined as a single letter, or as an operator preceded by two postfix expressions. The foregoing definitions assume that all operations are binary (i.e., each requires two operands). Examples of such operations are addition, subtraction, multiplication, division and exponentiation. It is easy to extend these definitions of prefix and postfix to include unary operations such as negation or factorial, but in the interest of simplicity, we will not do so here. Verify that each of the foregoing prefix and postfix expressions are valid by showing that they satisfy the definitions and make sure that you can identify the two operands of each operator.

We will put these recursive definitions to use in a moment, but first let us return to our problem. Given a prefix expression, how can we convert it into a postfix expression? We can immediately identify a trivial case: if a prefix expression consists of only a single variable, that expression is its own postfix equivalent. That is, an expression such as *A* is valid as both a prefix and a postfix expression.

Now consider a longer prefix string. If we knew how to convert any shorter prefix string to postfix, could we convert this longer prefix string? The answer is yes, with one proviso. Every prefix string longer than a single variable contains an operator, a first operand, and a second operand (remember that we are assuming binary operators only). Assume that we are able to identify the first and second operands, which are necessarily shorter than the original string. We can then convert the long prefix string to postfix by first converting the first operand to postfix, then converting the second operand to postfix and appending it to the end of the first converted operand, and finally appending the initial operator to the end of the resultant string. Thus we have developed a recursive algorithm for converting a prefix string to postfix with the single provision that we must specify a method for identifying the operands in a prefix expression. We can summarize our algorithm as follows:

1. If the prefix string is a single variable, it is its own postfix equivalent.
2. Let *op* be the first operator of the prefix string.
3. Find the first operand *opnd*1 of the string. Convert it to postfix and call it *post*1.
4. Find the second operand *opnd*2 of the string. Convert it to postfix and call it *post*2.
5. Concatenate *post*1, *post*2, and *op*.

To manipulate the expressions in this program, it will be necessary to store the initial prefix expression and the final postfix expression as strings of characters. The most direct way to do this is by defining a type *string* (as in Section 1.3) by the following:

```
const strsize = 80;
type string = record
                ch: packed array [1..strsize] of char;
                length: 0..strsize
              end;
```

The *length* portion of this record represents the current length of the string, whose characters are stored in the array *ch*. We also define two subrange types:

```
type postype = 1..strsize;
     lentype = 0..strsize;
```

One operation that will be required in this program is that of concatenation. For example, if two strings represented by *a* and *b* of type *string* represent the strings '*abcde*' and '*xyz*', respectively, then the procedure call

concat(a,b,c)

places into *c* (also of type *string*) the string '*abcdexyz*' (i.e., the string consisting of all the elements of *a* followed by all the elements of *b*). We also require a routine *substr* (*s1*, *i*, *j*, *s2*) which sets the string *s2* to the substring of *s1* starting at position *i* containing *j* characters. The routines *concat* and *substr* for this implementation of character strings may be found in Section 1.3.

Before transforming the conversion algorithm into a Pascal program, let us examine its inputs and outputs. We wish to write a procedure *convert* which accepts a character string. This string represents a prefix expression in which all variables are single letters and the allowable operators are ' + ', ' − ', ' * ', and ' / '. The procedure produces a string which is the postfix equivalent of the prefix parameter.

Assume the existence of a function *find* which accepts a string and a position and returns an integer which is the length of the longest prefix expression contained within the input string which starts at that position. For example, *find*('*a*+*cd*', 1) returns 1, since '*a*' is the longest prefix string starting at the beginning of '*a*+*cd*'. *find*(' + *abcd*+*gb*', 1) returns 5, since ' + *abc*' is the longest prefix string starting at the beginning of ' + *abcd*+*gb*'. *find*('*a*+*cd*', 2) returns 3, since ' +*cd*' is the longest prefix string starting at position 2 of '*a*+*cd*'. If no such prefix string exists within the input string starting at the specified position, *find* returns 0. [For example, *find*(' * + *ab*', 1) and *find*(' + *a*−*c**d', 6) both return 0]. This function is used to identify the first and second operands of a prefix operator. Assuming the existence of the function *find*, a conversion routine may be written as follows. *convert* also calls the function *letter*, which determines if its parameter is a letter.

```
procedure convert(prefix: string; var postfix: string);
var post1, post2, opstr, opnd1, opnd2, temp: string;
    op: char;
    m,n: lentype;
begin
    if prefix.length = 1
        then { check for variable }
            if letter(prefix.ch[1])
                then postfix:= prefix
                else error(' illegal prefix string ')
        else begin
                { The prefix string is longer than a single }
                { character. Extract the operator and the }
                {          two operand lengths.          }
                op:= prefix.ch[1];
```

```
        m := find(prefix, 2);
        n := find (prefix, m + 2);
        if not(op in ['+', '-', '*', '/'] ) or
              (m = 0) or (n = 0) or (m+n+1 <> prefix.length)
          then error(' illegal prefix string ')
          else begin
                    substr(prefix, 2, m, opnd1);
                    substr(prefix, m+2, n, opnd2);
                    convert(opnd1,post1);
                    convert(opnd2,post2);
                    concat(post1,post2,temp);
                    opstr.ch[1] := op;
                    opstr.length := 1;
                    concat(temp, opstr, postfix)
                end {else begin}
        end {else begin}
    end { function convert};
```

Note that several checks have been incorporated into *convert* to ensure that the parameter is a valid prefix string. One of the most difficult classes of errors to detect are those resulting from invalid inputs and the programmer's neglect to check for validity.

We now turn our attention to the function *find*, which accepts a character string and a starting position and returns the length of the longest prefix string which is contained in that input string starting at that position. The word "longest" in this definition is superfluous since there is at most one substring starting at a given position of a given string which is a valid prefix expression. We first show that there is at most one valid prefix expression starting at the beginning of a string. To see this, note that it is trivially true in a string of length 1. Assume that it is true for a short string. Then a long string that contains a prefix expression as an initial substring must begin with either a variable, in which case that variable is the desired substring, or with an operator. Deleting the initial operator, the remaining string is shorter than the original string and can therefore have at most a single initial prefix expression. This expression is the first operand of the initial operator. Similarly, the remaining substring (after deleting the first operand) can have only a single initial substring which is a prefix expression. This expression must be the second operand. Therefore, we have uniquely identified the operator and operands of the prefix expression starting at the first character of an arbitrary string, if such an expression exists. Since there is at most one valid prefix string starting at the beginning of any string, there is at most one such string starting at any position of an arbitrary string. This is obvious when we consider the substring of the given string starting at the given position.

Notice that this proof has given us a recursive method for finding a prefix expression in a string. We now incorporate this method into the function *find*:

```
function find(str: string; position: postype): lentype;
var m, n: lentype;
    first: char;
  begin {function find}
      if position > str.length
        then find:= 0
        else begin
              first:= str.ch[position];
              if letter(first)
                then { First character is a letter.  That }
                     {  letter is the desired substring  }
                  find:= 1
                else { otherwise find the }
                     {   two operands    }
                  begin
                      m:= find(str, position + 1);
                      n:= find(str, position + m + 1);
                      if (m = 0) or (n = 0)
                        then find:= 0
                        else find:= m + n + 1
                  end {else begin}
          end {else begin}
  end {function find};
```

Make sure that you understand how these routines work by tracing their actions on both valid and invalid prefix expressions. More important, make sure that you understand how they were developed and how logical analysis led to a natural recursive solution that was directly translatable into a Pascal program.

EXERCISES

1. Suppose that another provision were added to the Towers of Hanoi problem: that one disk may not rest on another disk which is more than one size larger (e.g., disk 1 may rest only on disk 2 or on the ground, disk 2 may rest only on disk 3 or on the ground, etc.). Why does the solution in the text fail to work? What is faulty about the logic that led to it under the new rules?

2. Prove that the number of moves performed by *towers* in moving n disks equals $2^n - 1$. Can you find a method of solving the Towers of Hanoi problem in fewer moves? Either find such a method for some n or prove that none exists.

3. Define a postfix and prefix expression to include the possibility of unary operators. Write a program to convert a prefix expression possibly containing the unary negation operator (represented by the symbol '@') to postfix.

4. Rewrite the function *find* in the text so that it is nonrecursive and computes the length of a prefix string by counting the number of operators and single-letter operands.

5. Write a recursive function that accepts a prefix expression consisting of binary operators and single-digit integer operands and returns the value of the expression.

6. Consider the following procedure for converting a prefix expression to postfix. The routine would be called by *convert(prefix, n, postfix)*, where *n* has been initialized to 1.

```
procedure convert(prefix: string; var n: posint; var postfix: string);
var p1,p2: string;
    c: char;
    len: lentype;
begin
    if n > prefix.length
        then postfix.length:= 0
        else begin
            c:= prefix.ch[n];
            n:= n + 1;
            if letter(c)
                then begin
                    postfix.ch[1]:= c;
                    postfix.length:= 1
                end {then begin}
                else begin
                    convert(prefix, n, p1);
                    convert(prefix, n, p2);
                    concat(p1, p2, postfix);
                    len:= postfix.length + 1;
                    postfix.ch[len]:= c;
                    postfix.length:= len
                end {else begin}
        end {else begin}
end {procedure convert};
```

Explain how the procedure works. Is it better or worse than the method of the text? What happens if the routine is called with an invalid prefix string as input? Can you incorporate a check for such an invalid string within *convert*? Can you design such a check for the calling program after *convert* has returned? What is the value of *n* after *convert* returns?

7. Develop a recursive method (and program it) to compute the number of different ways in which an integer k can be written as a sum, each of whose operands is less than n.

8. Consider an array a containing positive and negative integers. Define *contigsum* (i, j) as the sum of the contiguous elements $a[i]$ through $a[j]$ for all array indexes

$i \leq j$. Develop a recursive procedure that determines i and j such that *contigsum* (i, j) is maximized. The recursion should consider the two halves of the array a.

9. Write a recursive Pascal program to find the kth smallest element of an array a of numbers by choosing any element $a[i]$ of a and partitioning a into those elements smaller than, equal to, and greater than $a[i]$.

10. The Eight Queens problem is to place eight queens on a chessboard so that no queen is attacking any other queen. The following is a recursive program to solve the problem. *board* is an 8×8 array that represents a chessboard. *board*$[i, j]$ equals *true* if there is a queen at position $[i, j]$, and *false* otherwise. *good*(*board*) is a function that returns *true* if no two queens on the chessboard are attacking each other, and *false* otherwise. At the end of the program, the status of *board* represents a solution to the problem.

```
program queens(input, output);
var board: array[1..8, 1..8] of boolean;
    b: boolean;
    i, j: integer;

function try(n: integer): boolean;
var i: integer;
    ans: boolean;
begin { function try}
    if n > 8
      then try:= true
      else begin
                ans:= false;
                i:= 1;
                while (i <= 8) and (not ans)
                    do begin
                            board[n, i] := true;
                            if good(board) and try(n+1)
                              then ans:= true
                              else begin
                                        board[n, i] := false;
                                        i:= i + 1
                                   end {else begin}
                       end {while...do begin};
                try:= ans
             end {else begin}
end { function try};

begin {program queens}
    for i:= 1 to 8
        do for j:= 1 to 8
                do board[i, j] := false;
    b:= try(1)
end {program queens}.
```

The recursive function *try* returns *true* if it is possible, given the *board* at the time that it is called, to add queens in rows n through 8 to achieve a solution. *try* returns *false* if there is no solution which has queens at the positions in *board* that already contain *true*. If *true* is returned, the function also adds queens in rows *n* through 8 to produce a solution. Write the function *good* just used, and verify that the program produces a solution.

[The idea behind the solution is as follows: *board* represents the global situation during an attempt to find a solution. The next step toward finding a solution is chosen arbitrarily. Place a queen in the next untried position in row *n* and recursively test whether it is possible to produce a solution which includes that step. If it is, then return. If it is not, then backtrack from the attempted next step (*board*[*n*, *i*]:=*false*) and try another possibility. This method is called *backtracking*.]

4. SIMULATING RECURSION

In this section we examine more closely some of the mechanisms used to implement recursion so that we can simulate these mechanisms using non-recursive techniques. This activity is important for several reasons. First, many commonly used programming languages (such as FORTRAN, COBOL, and many machine languages) do not allow recursive programs. Problems such as the Towers of Hanoi and prefix-to-postfix conversion, whose solutions can be derived and stated quite simply using recursive techniques, can be programmed in these languages by simulating the recursive solution using more elementary operations. If we know that the recursive solution is correct (and it is often fairly easy to prove such a solution correct) and we have established techniques for converting a recursive solution to a nonrecursive one, then we can create a correct solution in a nonrecursive language. It is not an uncommon occurrence for a programmer to be able to state a solution to a problem in the form of a recursive algorithm. The ability to generate a nonrecursive solution from this algorithm is indispensable if he or she is using a compiler that does not support recursion.

Another reason for examining the implementation of recursion is that it will allow us to understand the implications of recursion and some of its hidden pitfalls. While these pitfalls do not exist in mathematical definitions that employ recursion, they seem to be an inevitable accompaniment of an implementation in a real language on a real machine.

Finally, even in a language such as Pascal which does support recursion, a recursive solution to a problem is usually more expensive than is a nonrecursive solution, both in terms of time and space. Frequently, this expense is a small price to pay for the logical simplicity and self-documentation of the recursive solution. However, in a production program (such as a compiler, for example) which may be run thousands of times, the recurrent expense is a heavy burden on the system's limited resources. Thus a program may be designed to incorporate a recursive solution to reduce the expense of design and certification, and then carefully converted to a nonrecursive version to be put into actual day-to-day use. As we shall see, in performing such a conversion it is often possible to identify parts of the implementation of recursion that are superfluous in a particular application and thereby significantly reduce the amount of work that the program must perform.

Before examining the actions of a recursive routine, let us take a step back and examine the action of a nonrecursive routine. We will then be able to see what mechanisms must be added to support recursion. Before proceeding, we adopt the following convention. Suppose that we have the statement

rout(x)

where *rout* is defined as a procedure by the statement

procedure rout(a: ...);

x will be referred to as an ***argument*** (of the calling routine), and *a* will be referred to as a ***parameter*** (of the called routine).

What happens when a subroutine is called? The action of calling a subroutine (either a procedure or function) may be divided into three parts:

1. Passing arguments.
2. Allocating and initializing local variables.
3. Transferring control to the subroutine.

Let us examine each of these three steps in turn.

1. Passing arguments.

For a value parameter in Pascal, a copy of the argument is made locally within the procedure and any changes to the parameter are made to that local copy. The effect of this scheme is that the original input argument cannot be altered. In this method, storage for the argument is allocated within the data area of the subroutine.

For ***var*** parameters in Pascal, the rule for transmission is different, and we do not consider its effects on recursion here. For a discussion of value and variable parameters, see Section 5 of the Appendix.

2. Allocating and initializing local variables.

After arguments have been passed, the local variables of the subroutine are allocated. These local variables include all those declared directly in the procedure and any temporaries that must be created during the course of execution. For example, in evaluating the expression

$$x + y + z$$

a storage location must be set aside to hold the value of $x + y$ so that z can be added to it. Another storage location must be set aside to hold the value of the entire expression after it has been evaluated. Such locations are called *temporaries*, since they are needed ony temporarily during the course of execution. Similarly, in a statement such as

$$x := fact(n)$$

a temporary must be set aside to hold the value of *fact(n)* before that value can be assigned to *x*.

3. Transferring control to the subroutine.

At this point control may still not be passed to the subroutine because provision has not yet been made for saving the *return address*. If a subroutine is given control, it must eventually restore control to the calling routine by means of a branch. However, it cannot execute that branch unless it knows the location to which it must return. Since this location is within the calling routine and not within the subroutine, the only way that the sub-routine can know this address is to have it passed as an argument. This is exactly what happens. Aside from the explicit arguments specified by the programmer, there are also a set of implicit arguments that contain infor-mation necessary for the subroutine to execute and return correctly. Chief among these implicit arguments is the return address. The subroutine stores this address within its own data area. When it is ready to return control to the calling program, the subroutine retrieves the return address and branches to that location.

Once the arguments and the return address have been passed, control may be transferred to the subroutine, since everything required has been done to ensure that the subroutine will operate on the appropriate data and then return safely to the calling routine.

Return from a Subroutine

When a subroutine returns, three actions are performed. First, the return address is retrieved and stored in a safe location. Second, the subrou-tine's data area is freed. This data area contains all local variables (including local copies of arguments), temporaries, and the return address. Finally, a branch is taken to the return address, which had been previously saved. This restores control to the calling program at the point immediately after the instruction that initiated the call. In addition, if the subprogram is a function, the value returned is placed in a secure location from which the calling program may retrieve it. Usually, this location is a hardware register that is set aside for this purpose.

Suppose that a main procedure has called a subroutine *b*, which has called *c*, which has in turn called *d*. This is illustrated in Figure 3.4.1a, where we indicate that control currently resides somewhere within *d*. Within each

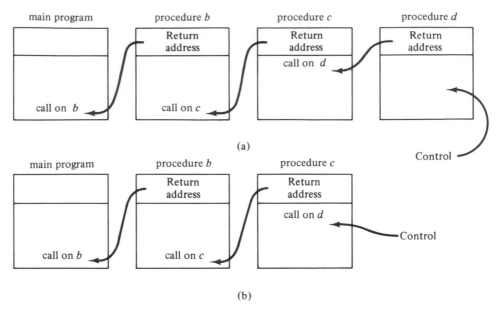

Figure 3.4.1   A series of procedures calling one another.

subroutine, there is a location set aside for the return address. Thus the return address area of d contains the address of the instruction in c immediately following the call to d. Figure 3.4.1b shows the situation immediately following d's return to c. The return address within d has been retrieved and control transferred to that address.

You may have noticed that the string of return addresses forms a stack (i.e., the most recent return address to be added to the chain is the first to be removed). At any point, we can only access the return address from within the subroutine that is currently executing which repesents the top of the stack. When the stack is popped (i.e., when the subroutine returns), a new top is revealed within the calling routine. Calling a subroutine has the effect of pushing an element onto the stack and returning pops the stack.

Implementing Recursive Routines

What must be added to this description in the case of a recursive routine? The answer is, surprisingly little. Each time a recursive routine calls itself, an entirely new data area for that particular call must be allocated. As before, this data area contains all parameters, local variables, temporaries, and a return address. The point to remember is that in recursion a data area is associated not with a subroutine alone, but with a particular call to that subroutine. Each call causes a new data area to be allocated, and each reference to an item in the subroutine's data area is to the data area of the most recent call. Similarly, each return causes the current data area to be freed, and the data area allocated immediately prior to the current area becomes current. This behavior, of course, suggests the use of a stack.

Simulation of Factorial

In Section 2, where we described the action of the recursive factorial function, we used a set of stacks to represent the successive allocations of each of the local variables and parameters. These stacks may be thought of as separate stacks, one for each local variable. Alternatively, and closer to reality, we may think of all of these stacks as a single large stack. Each element of this large stack is an entire data area containing subparts representing the individual local variables or parameters. Each time that the recursive routine is called, a new data area is allocated. The parameters within this data area are initialized to refer to the values of their corresponding arguments. The return address within the data area is initialized to the address following the call instruction. Any reference to local variables or parameters are via the current data area. When the recursive routine returns, the returned value (in the case of a function) and the return address are saved, the data area is freed, and a branch to the return address is executed. The calling routine retrieves the returned value (if any), resumes execution, and refers to its own data area, which is now on top of the stack.

Let us now examine how we can simulate the actions of a recursive procedure. We will need a stack of data areas defined by

```
const maxstack = 50;
type stack = record
                top: 0..maxstack;
                item: array[1..maxstack] of dataarea
             end;
```

dataarea is itself a record containing the various items that exist in a data area and must be defined to contain the fields required for the particular routine being simulated.

Since we do not yet know how to manipulate addresses in Pascal, we cannot simulate the mechanism of a call with *var* parameters. Since all of the recursive routines we have looked at in this chapter used value parameters, we do not address the question of *var* parameters for recursive routines at this time.

Let us look at a specific example—the factorial function. We repeat the code for that function:

```
function fact(n: nonegint): posint;
var x: nonegint;
    y: posint;
begin
    if n = 0
        then fact:= 1
        else begin
                    x:= n - 1;
                    y:= fact(x);
                    fact:= n * y
              end {else begin}
end {function fact};
```

How are we to define the data area for this routine? It must contain the parameter *n* and the local variables *x* and *y*. As we shall see, no temporaries are needed. The data area must also contain a return address. In this case, there are two possible points to which we might want to return: the assignment of *fact*(*x*) to *y* and the main program which called *fact*. Suppose that we had two labels declared by

label 1,2;

and we let the label 2 be the label of a section of code

2: y:= result

within the simulating program. Let the label 1 be the label of a statement

1: fact:= result

This reflects a convention that the variable *result* contains the value to be returned by an invocation of the *fact* function. The return address will be stored as an integer *i* (equal to either 1 or 2). To effect a return from a recursive call, the statement

case i of
1: goto 1;
2: goto 2
end

is executed. Thus, if $i = 1$ a return is executed to the main program which called *fact*, and if $i = 2$, a return is simulated to the assignment of the returned value to *y* in the previous execution of *fact*. Note that since the labels are not integers (even though they look like integers), we cannot write *goto i*.

Thus the data area stack for this example can be defined as follows:

```
const maxstack = 50;
type  dataarea =
          record
              param: nonegint;
              x: nonegint;
              y: posint;
              retaddr: 1..2
          end;
      stack =
          record
              top: 0..maxstack;
              item: array[1..maxstack] of dataarea
          end;
var s: stack;
```

The field in the data area that contains the simulated parameter is called *param* rather than *n*, to avoid confusion with the parameter *n* passed to the simulating routine. We also declare a current data area to hold the values of the variables in the simulated "current" call on the recursive routine. The declaration is

```
var currarea: dataarea;
```

In addition, we declare a single variable *result* by

```
var result: posint;
```

This variable is used to communicate the returned value of *fact* from one recursive call of *fact* to its caller, and from *fact* to the outside calling routine. Since the elements on the stack of data areas are records and a Pascal function cannot return a record, we cannot use a function *pop* to pop a data area from *stack*. Instead, we must write a procedure *popsub* defined by

```
procedure popsub(var s: stack; var area: dataarea);
```

popsub pops the stack and sets *area* to the popped element. We leave the details as an exercise.

A return from *fact* is simulated by the code

```
result:= value to be returned;
i:= currarea.retaddr;
popsub(stack, currarea);
case i of
   1: goto 1;
   2: goto 2
end;
```

A recursive call on *fact* is simulated by pushing the current data area on the stack, reinitializing the variables *currarea.param* and *currarea.retaddr* to the parameter and return address of this call, respectively, and then transferring control to the start of the simulated routine. Recall that *currarea.x* holds the value of $n - 1$ which is to be the new parameter. Recall also that on a recursive call we wish to eventually return to label 2. The code to accomplish this is

```
push(stack,currarea);
currarea.param:= s.item[s.top].x;
currarea.retaddr:= 2;
goto 10 { 10 is the label of the start of the simulated routine }
```

Of course, the *popsub* and *push* routines must be written so that they pop and push entire records of type *dataarea* rather than simple variables. (Another imposition of the array implementation of stacks is that the variable *currarea.y* must be initialized to some value or an error will result in the *push* routine upon assignment of *currarea.y* to *item[top].y*.) Notice that in assigning a value to *currarea.param* we reference the top of the stack. To keep the array implementation of a stack transparent to the program, we should use a version of the *stacktop* function of Chapter 2 to access the top element of the stack. However, in the interest of simplicity, we do not do this here.

When the simulation first begins, the current area must be initialized so that *currarea.param* equals n and *currarea.retaddr* equals 1 (indicating a return to the calling routine). A dummy data area must be pushed onto the stack so that when *popsub* is executed in returning to the main routine, an underflow does not occur. This dummy data area must also be initialized so as not to cause an error in the *push* routine (see the parenthesized comment in the last paragraph). Thus the simulated version of the recursive *fact* routine is as follows:

```
function simfact(n: nonegint): posint;
label 1, 2, 10;
const maxstack = 50;
type dataarea =
        record
            param: nonegint;
            x: nonegint;
            y: posint;
            retaddr: 1..2
        end;
    stack =
        record
            top: 0..maxstack;
            item: array[1..maxstack] of dataarea
        end;
var i: 1..2;
    result: posint;
    currarea: dataarea;
    s: stack;
```

```
begin {initialization}
      s.top := 0;
      currarea.param := 0;
      currarea.x := 0;
      currarea.y := 1;
      currarea.retaddr := 1;
      {  push the dummy data area onto the stack   }
      push (s, currarea);
      {   set the parameter and the return address   }
      { of the current data area to their proper values }
      currarea.param := n;
      currarea.retaddr := 1;
 10:  {     this is the beginning of the simulated     }
      {                  factorial routine             }
      if currarea.param = 0
         then { simulation of fact:= 1 }
              begin
                    result := 1;
                    i := currarea.retaddr;
                    popsub (s, currarea);
                    case i of
                       1: goto 1;
                       2: goto 2
                    end {case}
              end {then begin};
      currarea.x := currarea.param - 1;
      { simulation of recursive call to fact }
      push (s, currarea);
      currarea.param := s.item [s.top].x;
      currarea.retaddr := 2;
      goto 10;
  2:  {      This is the point to which we return      }
      {      from the recursive call.  Set currarea.y  }
      {                 to the returned value.         }
      currarea.y := result;
      {           simulation of fact:= n * y           }
      result := currarea.param * currarea.y;
      i := currarea.retaddr;
      popsub (s, currarea);
      case i of
         1: goto 1;
         2: goto 2
      end {case};
  1:  { at this point we return to the main routine   }
      simfact := result
end { function simfact};
```

Trace through the execution of this program for $n = 5$ and be sure that you understand what the program does and how it does it.

Notice that no space was reserved in the data area for temporaries, since they need not be saved for later use. The temporary location that holds the value of $n*y$ in the original recursive routine is simulated by the temporary for *currarea.param * currarea.y* in the simulating routine. This is not the case in general. For example, if a recursive function *funct* contained a statement such as

```
x:= a*funct(b) + c*funct(d)
```

the temporary for *a*funct(b)* must be saved during the recursive call on *funct(d)*. However, in the example of the factorial function it is not required to stack the temporary.

Improving the Simulated Routine

This leads, naturally, to the question of whether all of the local variables really need to be stacked at all. A variable must be saved on the stack only if its value at the point of initiation of a recursive call must be reused after return from that call. Let us examine whether the variables n, x, and y meet this requirement. Clearly, n does have to be stacked. In the statement

```
y:= n * fact(x)
```

the old value of n must be used in the multiplication after return from the recursive call on *fact*. However, this is not the case for x and y. In fact, the value of y is not even defined at the point of the recursive call, so clearly it need not be stacked. Similarly, although x is defined at the point of call, it is never used again after returning, so why bother saving it?

This point can be illustrated even more sharply by the following realization. If x and y were not declared within the recursive function *fact*, but rather were declared as global variables, the routine would work just as well. Thus the automatic stacking and unstacking action performed by recursion for the local variables x and y is unnecessary.

Another interesting question to consider is whether the return address is really needed on the stack. Since there is only one textual recursive call to *fact*, there is only one return address within *fact*. The other return address is to the main routine which originally called *fact*. But suppose that a dummy data area had not been stacked upon initialization of the simulation. Then a data area is placed on the stack only in simulating a recursive call. When the stack is popped in returning from a recursive call, that area is removed from the stack. However, when an attempt is made to pop the stack in simulating a return to the main procedure, an underflow will occur. We can test for this underflow by using *popandtest* rather than *popsub*, and when it does occur we can return directly to the outside calling routine rather than through a local label. This means that one of the return addresses can be eliminated. Since this leaves only a single possible return address, it need not be placed on the stack.

Thus the data area has been reduced to contain the parameter alone and the stack may be declared by

```
const maxstack = 50;
type stack =
        record
          top: 0..maxstack;
          param: array[1..maxstack] of nonegint
        end;
var s: stack;
```

The current data area is reduced to a single variable declared by

```
var currparam: nonegint;
```

The program is now quite compact and comprehensible.

```
function simfact(n: nonegint): posint;
label 1, 2, 10;
const maxstack = 50;
type  stack =
        record
          top: 0..maxstack;
          param: array[1..maxstack] of nonegint
        end;
var s: stack;
    currparam, x: nonegint;
    y, result: posint;
    und: boolean;
begin {initialization}
    s.top:= 0;
    currparam:= n;
10:    {beginning of the simulated routine}
    if currparam = 0
      then {simulation of fact:= 1}
        begin
            result:= 1;
            popandtest(s, currparam, und);
            if und
              then { return to main routine }
                goto 1
              else {return from recursive call}
                goto 2
        end {then begin};
```

```
          {currparam <> 0}
          x:= currparam - 1;
          {        simulation of recursive call        }
          push(s, currparam);
          currparam:= x;
          goto 10;
    2:    {we return to this point from the simulated}
          {                recursive call              }
          y:= result;
          {        simulation of fact:= n * y;        }
          result:= currparam * y;
          popandtest(s, currparam, und);
          if und
              then {return to main routine}
                  goto 1
              else {return to recursive call}
                  goto 2;
    1:   simfact:= result
   end {function simfact};
```

Eliminating *gotos*

Although the foregoing program is certainly simpler than the previous one, it is still far from an "ideal" program. If you were to look at the program without having seen its derivation, it is probably doubtful that you could identify it as computing the factorial function. The statements

goto 10 and **goto 2**

are particularly irritating, since they interrupt the flow of thought at a time that one might otherwise come to an understanding of what is happening. Let us see if we can transform this program into a still more readable version.

Several transformations are immediately apparent. First, the statements

```
          popandtest(s, currparam, und);
          if und
              then goto 1
              else  goto 2
```

appear twice for the two cases *currparam* $= 0$ and *currparam* $<> 0$. The two sections can easily be combined into one. A further observation is that the two variables x and *currparam* are assigned values from each other and are never in use simultaneously, so they may be combined and referred to as one variable x. A similar statement may be made about the variables *result* and y, which may be combined and referred to as the single variable y.

Performing these transformations leads to the following version of *simfact*:

```
function simfact(n: nonegint): posint;
label 2,10;
const maxstack = 50;
type  stack =
          record
              top: 0..maxstack;
              param: array[1..maxstack] of nonegint
          end;
var s: stack;
    x: nonegint;
    y: posint;
    und: boolean;
begin {function simfact}
      s.top:= 0;
      x:= n;
10:   if x = 0
          then y:= 1
          else begin
                    push(s, x);
                    x:= x - 1;
                    goto 10
               end {else begin};
 2:   popandtest(s, x, und);
      if und
          then simfact:= y
          else begin
                    y:= x * y;
                    goto 2
               end {else begin}
end {function simfact};
```

We are now beginning to approach a readable program. Note that the program consists of two loops:

1. The loop that consists of the entire *if* statement labeled 10. This loop is exited when $x = 0$, at which point y is set to 1 and execution proceeds to the label 2.
2. The loop that begins at label 2 and ends with the statement ***goto 2***. This loop is exited when the stack has been emptied and underflow occurs, at which point a return is executed.

These loops can easily be transformed into explicit ***while*** loops as follows:

```
            { subtraction loop }
        while x <> 0
                do begin
                            push (s, x);
                            x := x - 1
                    end {do begin};
            y := 1;
            popandtest (s, x, und);
            {multiplication loop}
        while not und
                do begin
                            y := x * y;
                            popandtest (s, x, und)
                    end {do begin};
            simfact := y
```

Let us examine these two loops more closely. *x* starts off at the value of the input parameter *n* and is reduced by one each time that the subtraction loop is repeated. Each time *x* is set to a new value, the old value of *x* is saved on the stack. This continues until *x* is 0. Thus after the first loop has been executed, the stack contains, from top to bottom, the integers 1 to *n*.

The multiplication loop merely removes each of these values from the stack and sets *y* to the product of the popped value and the old value of *y*. Since we know what the stack contains at the start of the multiplication loop, why bother popping the stack? We can use those values directly. We can eliminate the stack and the first loop entirely and replace the multiplication loop with a loop that multiplies *y* by each of the integers from 1 to *n* in turn. The resulting program is

```
        function simfact (n: nonegint): posint;
        var x: nonegint;
            y: posint;
        begin {function simfact}
            y := 1;
            for x := 1 to n
                do y := y * x;
            simfact := y
        end {function simfact};
```

But this program is a direct Pascal implementation of the iterative version of the factorial function as presented in Section 1. The only change is that *x* varies from 1 to *n* rather than from *n* to 1.

Simulating the Towers of Hanoi

We have shown that successive transformations of a nonrecursive simulation of a recursive routine may lead to a simpler program for solving a problem. Let us now look at a more complex example of recursion, the Towers of Hanoi problem presented in Section 3. We will simulate its recursion and attempt to simplify the simulation to produce a nonrecursive solution. We present again the recursive procedure of Section 3.

```
procedure towers(n: posint; frompeg, topeg, auxpeg: char);
begin
    if n = 1
        then writeln('move disk 1 from peg', frompeg, ' to peg ', topeg)
        else begin
                towers(n-1, frompeg, auxpeg, topeg);
                writeln('move disk ', n, ' from peg ', frompeg, ' to peg ', topeg);
                towers(n-1, auxpeg, topeg, frompeg)
            end {else begin}
end {procedure towers};
```

Make sure that you understand the problem and the recursive solution before proceeding.

There are four parameters in this subroutine, each of which is subject to change in a recursive call. Therefore, the data area must contain elements representing all four. There are no local variables. There is a single temporary that is needed to hold the value of $n - 1$, but this can be represented by a similar temporary in the simulating program and does not have to be stacked. There are three possible points to which the subroutine returns on various calls: the calling program and the two points following the recursive calls. Therefore, three labels are necessary:

label 1, 2, 3;

The return address will be encoded as an integer (1, 2, or 3) within each data area.

Consider the following nonrecursive simulation of *towers*:

```
procedure simtowers(n: posint; frompeg, topeg, auxpeg: char);
label 1, 2, 3, 10;
const maxstack = 50;
type  dataarea =
        record
            nparam: posint;
            fromparam: char;
```

```
                    toparam: char;
                    auxparam: char;
                    retaddr: 1..3
                  end;
               stack =
                 record
                    top: 0..maxstack;
                    item: array[1..maxstack] of dataarea
                 end;
         var s: stack;
             currarea: dataarea;
             i: 1..3;
         begin {initialization}
             s.top:= 0;
             currarea.nparam:= 1;
             currarea.fromparam:= ' ';
             currarea.toparam:= ' ';
             currarea.auxparam:= ' ';
             currarea.retaddr:= 1;
             {    push dummy data area onto stack     }
             push(s, currarea);
             {set the parameters and the return address}
             { of the current data area to their proper }
             {                values                    }
             currarea.nparam:= n;
             currarea.fromparam:= frompeg;
             currarea.toparam:= topeg;
             currarea.auxparam:= auxpeg;
             currarea.retaddr:= 1;
      10:    {this is the start of the simulated routine}
             if currarea.nparam = 1
                 then with currarea
                     do begin
                         writeln('move disk 1 from peg ', fromparam,
                                              ' to peg ', toparam);
                         i:= retaddr;
                         popsub(s, currarea);
                         case i of
                             1: goto 1;
                             2: goto 2;
                             3: goto 3
                         end {case}
                     end {then with...do begin};
```

```
      {      this is the first recursive call       }
      push(s, currarea);
      currarea.nparam:= s.item[s.top].nparam - 1;
      currarea.fromparam:= s.item[s.top].fromparam;
      currarea.toparam:= s.item[s.top].auxparam;
      currarea.auxparam:= s.item[s.top].toparam;
      currarea.retaddr:= 2;
      goto 10;
  2:  {      we return to this point from the       }
      {            first recursive call             }
      writeln('move disk ', currarea.nparam, ' from peg ',
                   currarea.fromparam, ' to peg ', currarea.toparam);
      {   this is the second recursive call   }
      push(s, currarea);
      currarea.nparam:= s.item[s.top].nparam - 1;
      currarea.fromparam:= s.item[s.top].auxparam;
      currarea.toparam:= s.item[s.top].toparam;
      currarea.auxparam:= s.item[s.top].fromparam;
      currarea.retaddr:= 3;
      goto 10;
  3:  { return to this point from the second  }
      {            recursive call             }
      i:= currarea.retaddr;
      popsub(s, currarea);
      case i of
         1: goto 1;
         2: goto 2;
         3: goto 3
      end {case};
  1:  {      return to the calling program       }
  end {procedure simtowers};
```

Let us attempt to simplify the foregoing program. First, notice that three labels were used for return addresses: one for each of the two recursive calls and one for the return to the main program. However, the return to the main program can be signaled by an underflow in the stack, exactly as in the second version of *simfact*. This leaves two return labels. If we could eliminate one more such label it would no longer be necessary to stack the return address, since there would be only one point remaining to which control may be passed if the stack is popped successfully. We focus our attention on the second recursive call and the following segment:

```
      towers(n - 1, auxpeg, topeg, frompeg)
  end
```

The actions that occur in simulating this call are

1. Push the current data area, $a1$, onto the stack.
2. Set the parameters in the new current data area, $a2$, to their respective values: $n - 1$, *auxpeg*, *topeg*, and *frompeg*.
3. Set the return label in the current data area, $a2$, to the address of the statement immediately following the call.
4. Branch to the beginning of the simulated routine.

After the simulated routine has completed, it is ready to return. The following actions occur:

5. Save the return label, l, from the current data area $a2$.
6. Pop the stack and set the current data area to the popped data area, $a1$.
7. Branch to l.

But l is a label at the keyword **end**. Thus the next step is to pop the stack again and return once more. We never again make use of the information in the current data area $a1$, since it is immediately destroyed by popping the stack as soon as it has been restored. Since there is no reason to use this data area again, there is no reason to save it on the stack in simulating the call. Data need be saved on the stack only if it is to be reused. Therefore, in this case, the call may be simulated simply by

1. Changing the parameters in the current data area to their respective values.
2. Branching to the beginning of the simulated routine.

When the simulated routine returns, it can return directly to the routine that called the current version. There is no reason to execute a return to the current version, only to return immediately to the previous version. Since there is only one possible return address left, it is unnecessary to keep it in the data area, to be pushed and popped with the rest of the data. Whenever the stack is popped successfully, there is only one address to which a branch can be executed: the statement following the first call. If an underflow is encountered, the routine returns to the calling routine. Since the new values of the variables in the current data area will be obtained from the old values in the current data area, it will be necessary to declare an additional variable *temp* so that values can be interchanged.

Our revised nonrecursive simulation of *towers* follows:

```
procedure simtowers(n: posint; frompeg, topeg, auxpeg: char);
label 1, 2, 10;
const maxstack = 50;
```

```
type  dataarea =
        record
          nparam: posint;
          fromparam: char;
          toparam: char;
          auxparam: char
        end;
      stack =
        record
          top: 0..maxstack;
          item: array[1..maxstack] of dataarea
        end;
var s: stack;
    currarea: dataarea;
    und: boolean;
    temp: char;
begin {initialization}
      s.top:= 0;
      currarea.nparam:= n;
      currarea.fromparam:= frompeg;
      currarea.toparam:= topeg;
      currarea.auxparam:= auxpeg;
10:   {the simulated routine begins here}
      if currarea.nparam = 1
          then with currarea
              do begin
                    writeln('move disk 1 from peg ',
                                fromparam, ' to peg', toparam);
                    {simulate the return}
                    popandtest(s, currarea, und);
                    if und
                        then goto 1 { return to main routine  }
                        else  goto 2 {go to point after recursive}
                                     {            call           }
              end {with...do begin};
      {simulation of first recursive call}
      push(s, currarea);
      currarea.nparam:= s.item[s.top].nparam - 1;
      currarea.fromparam:= s.item[s.top].fromparam;
      currarea.toparam:= s.item[s.top].auxparam;
      currarea.auxparam:= s.item[s.top].toparam;
      goto 10;
```

```
  2:   {this is the point of return from the}
       {          first recursive call          }
       writeln('move disk ', currarea.nparam, ' from peg ',
                    currarea.fromparam, ' to peg ', currarea.toparam);
       {simulation of second recursive call}
       currarea.nparam:= currarea.nparam - 1;
       temp:= currarea.fromparam;
       currarea.fromparam:= currarea.auxparam;
       currarea.auxparam:= temp;
       goto 10;
  1:   {   return to the calling program   }
  end {procedure simtowers};
```

Examining the structure of the program, we see that it can easily be reorganized into a simpler format. We begin from the code appearing at the label 10.

```
    und:= false;
repeat
    while currarea.nparam <> 1
        do with currarea
            do begin
                    push(s, currarea);
                    nparam:= s.item[s.top].nparam - 1;
                    fromparam:= s.item[s.top].fromparam;
                    toparam:= s.item[s.top].auxparam;
                    auxparam:= s.item[s.top].toparam
                end {do begin};
        writeln('move disk 1 from peg ', currarea.fromparam, ' to peg ',
                                            currarea.toparam);
        popandtest(s, currarea, und);
        if not und
          then with currarea
                do begin
                    writeln('move disk ', nparam, ' from peg ',
                                        fromparam, 'to peg ', toparam);
                    nparam:= nparam - 1;
                    temp:= fromparam;
                    fromparam:= auxparam;
                    auxparam:= temp
                end {with...do begin}
until und
```

Trace through the actions of this program and see how it reflects the actions of the original recursive version.

EXERCISES

1. Write a nonrecursive simulation of the functions *convert* and *find* presented in Section 3.

2. Write a nonrecursive simulation of the recursive binary search precedure, and transform it into an iterative procedure.

3. Write a nonrecursive simulation of *fib*. Can you transform it into an iterative method?

4. Write nonrecursive simulations of the recursive routines of Sections 2 and 3 and the exercises of those sections.

5. Show that any solution to the Towers of Hanoi problem that uses a minimum number of moves must satisfy the conditions that follow. Use these facts to develop a direct iterative algorithm for Towers of Hanoi. Implement the algorithm as a Pascal program.
   (a) The first move involves moving the smallest disk.
   (b) A minimum-move solution consists of alternately moving the smallest disk and a disk that is not the smallest.
   (c) At any point, there is only one possible move involving a disk that is not the smallest.
   (d) Define the cyclic direction from *frompeg* to *topeg* to *auxpeg* to *frompeg* as ***clockwise*** and the opposite direction (from *frompeg* to *auxpeg* to *topeg* to *frompeg*) as ***counterclockwise***. Assume that a minimum-move solution to move a *k*-disk tower from *frompeg* to *topeg* always moves the smallest disk in one direction. Show that a minimum-move solution to move a (*k* + 1)-disk tower from *frompeg* to *topeg* would then always move the smallest disk in the other direction. Since the solution for one disk moves the smallest disk clockwise (the single move from *frompeg* to *topeg*), this means that for an odd number of disks, the smallest disk always moves clockwise and for an even number of disks, the smallest disk always moves counterclockwise.
   (e) The solution is completed as soon as all the disks are on a single peg.

6. Convert the following recursive program scheme into an iterative version that does not use a stack. *f(n)* is a function that returns a boolean value based on the value of *n*, and *g(n)* is a function that returns a value of the same type as *n* without modifying *n*.

```
procedure rec(n: ntype);
begin
    if not f(n)
        then begin
                { any group of Pascal statements }
                {which does not change the value of n}
                rec(g(n))
            end {then begin}
end {procedure rec};
```

Generalize your result to the case in which *rec* is a function.

7. Let *f(n)* be a boolean-valued function and *g(n)* and *h(n)* be functions that return a value of the same type as *n* without modifying *n*. Let *(stmts)* represent any group of Pascal statements that do not modify the value of *n*. Show that the recursive program scheme *rec* is equivalent to the iterative scheme *iter*:

```
procedure rec(n: type1);
begin
      if not f(n)
        then begin
                   (stmts);
                   rec(g(n));
                   rec(h(n))
              end {then begin}
end {procedure rec};

procedure iter(n: type1);
type stack =
        record
          top: 0..100;
          nvalues: array[1..100] of type1
        end;
var s: stack;
begin
      s.top:= 0;
      push(s, n);
      while not empty(s)
          do begin
                   n:= pop(s);
                   if not f(n)
                     then begin
                                (stmts);
                                push(s, h(n));
                                push(s, g(n))
                           end {then begin}
              end {while...do begin}
end {procedure iter};
```

Show that the *if* statements in *iter* can be replaced by the loop:

```
while not f(n)
    do begin
             (stmts)
             push(s, h(n));
             n:= g(n)
        end {while...do begin}
```

Modify the two iterative versions for the case of a recursive function.

5. EFFICIENCY OF RECURSION

In general, a nonrecursive version of a program will execute more efficiently in terms of time and space than will a recursive version. This is because the overhead involved in entering and exiting a block is avoided in the nonrecursive version. As we have seen, it is often possible to identify a good number of local variables and temporaries that do not have to be saved and restored through the use of a stack. In a nonrecursive program this needless stacking activity can be eliminated. However, in a recursive procedure, the compiler is usually unable to identify such variables, and they are therefore stacked and unstacked to ensure that no problems arise.

However, we have also seen that sometimes a recursive solution is the most natural and logical way of solving a problem. It is doubtful whether a programmer could have developed the nonrecursive solution to the Towers of Hanoi problem directly from the problem statement. A similar comment may be made about the problem of converting prefix to postfix, where the recursive solution flows directly from the definitions. A nonrecursive solution involving stacks is much more difficult to develop and more prone to error.

Thus we have a conflict between machine efficiency and programmer efficiency. With the cost of programming increasing steadily and the cost of computation decreasing, we have reached the point where in most cases it is not worth a programmer's time to laboriously construct a nonrecursive solution to a problem which is most naturally solved recursively. Of course, an incompetent, overly clever programmer may come up with a complicated recursive solution to a simple problem which can be solved directly by nonrecursive methods. (An example of this is the factorial function, or even the binary search.) However, if a competent programmer identifies a recursive solution as being the simplest and most straightforward method for solving a particular problem, it is often not worth the time and effort to discover a more efficient method.

However, this is not always the case. If a program is to be run very frequently (often, entire computers are dedicated to running the same program continually), so that increased efficiency in execution speed significantly increases throughput, the extra investment in programming time is worthwhile. Even in such cases, it is probably better to create a nonrecursive version by simulating and transforming the recursive solution than by attempting to create a nonrecursive solution from the problem statement.

To do this most efficiently, what is required is to first write the recursive routine and then its simulated version, including all stacks and temporaries. After this has been done, eliminate all stacks and variables that are superfluous. The final version is a refinement of the original program, and is certainly more efficient. Clearly, the elimination of each superfluous and redundant operation will improve the efficiency of the resulting program. However, every transformation applied to a program is another opening through which an unanticipated error may creep in.

When a stack cannot be eliminated from the nonrecursive version of a program and when the recursive version does not contain any extra parameters or local variables, the recursive version can be as fast or faster than the nonrecursive version under a good compiler. The Towers of Hanoi is an example of such a recursive program. Factorial, whose nonrecursive version does not need a stack, and calculation of Fibonacci numbers, which contains an unnecessary second recursive call (and does not need a stack either), are examples where recursion should be avoided in a practical implementation. We examine another example of efficient recursion (inorder tree traversal) in Section 6.2.

Another point to remember is that explicit calls to *pop, push,* and *empty,* as well as tests for underflow and overflow, are quite expensive. In fact, they can often outweigh the expense of the overhead of recursion. Thus to maximize actual runtime efficiency of a nonrecursive translation, these calls should be replaced by inline code and the overflow/underflow tests eliminated when it is known that we are operating within the array bounds.

The ideas and transformations that we have put forward in presenting the factorial function and the Towers of Hanoi can be applied to more complex problems whose nonrecursive solution is not readily apparent. The extent to which a recursive solution (actual or simulated) can be transformed into a direct solution will depend in large measure on the particular problem and the ingenuity of the programmer.

EXERCISES

1. Run the recursive and nonrecursive versions of the factorial function of Sections 2 and 4, and examine how much space and time each requires as *n* becomes larger.
2. Do the same as in Exercise 1 for the Towers of Hanoi problem.

4

QUEUES AND LISTS

This chapter introduces the queue and the priority queue, two important data structures often used to simulate real-world situations. The concepts of the stack and queue are then extended to a new structure, the list. Various forms of lists and their associated operations are examined and several applications are presented.

1. THE QUEUE AND ITS SEQUENTIAL REPRESENTATION

A *queue* is an ordered collection of items from which items may be deleted at one end (called the *front* of the queue) and into which items may be inserted at the other end (called the *rear* of the queue).

Figure 4.1.1a illustrates a queue containing three elements, A, B, and C. A is at the front of the queue and C is at the rear. In Figure 4.1.1b, an element has been deleted from the queue. Since elements may be deleted only from the front of the queue, A is removed and B is now at the front. In Figure 4.1.1c, when items D and E are inserted, they must be inserted at the rear of the queue.

Since D has been inserted into the queue before E, it will be removed earlier. The first element inserted into a queue is the first element to be removed. For this reason a queue is sometimes called a *fifo* (first-in, first-out) list, as opposed to a stack which is a *lifo* (last-in, first-out) list. Examples of queues abound in the real world. A line at a bank or at a bus stop, and a batch of jobs waiting to be read by a card reader, are familiar examples of queues.

173

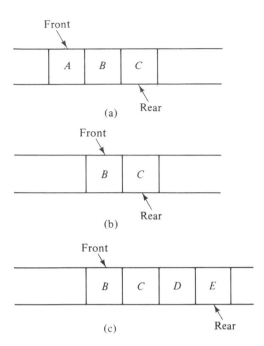

Front

Figure 4.1.1   A queue.

There are three primitive operations that can be applied to a queue. The operation *insert(q, x)* inserts item *x* at the rear of the queue *q*. The operation *x* := *remove(q)* deletes the front element from the queue *q* and sets *x* to its contents. The third operation, *empty(q)*, returns *false* or *true* depending on whether or not the queue contains any elements. The queue in Figure 4.1.1 can be obtained by the following sequence of operations. We assume that the queue is initially empty.

> *insert* (*q, A*);
> *insert* (*q, B*);
> *insert* (*q, C*);   (Figure 4.1.1a)
> *x* := *remove* (*q*);   (Figure 4.1.1b; *x* is set to *A*)
> *insert* (*q, D*);
> *insert* (*q, E*)   (Figure 4.1.1c)

The *insert* operation can always be performed since there is no limit to the number of elements a queue may contain. The *remove* operation, however, can be applied only if the queue is nonempty—there is no way to remove an element from a queue that contains no elements. The result of an illegal attempt to remove an element from an empty queue is called **underflow**. The *empty* operation is, of course, always applicable.

The Queue as an Abstract Data Type

The representation of a queue as an abstract data type is straightforward:

type *queueitem* = ... ;   { type of item on the queue }
abstract type *queue* = **sequence of** *queueitem*;

abstract function *empty*(*q*: *queue*): *boolean*;
postcondition *empty* = (*len*(*q*) = 0);

abstract function *remove*(*q*: *queue*): *queueitem*;
precondition not *empty*(*q*);
postcondition *remove* = *first*(*q'*);
$$q = sub(q', 2, len(q') - 1);$$

abstract procedure *insert*(*q*: *queue*; *elt*: *queueitem*);
postcondition *q* = *q'* + ⟨*elt*⟩;

Pascal Implementation of Queues

How shall a queue be represented in Pascal? An idea that comes immediately to mind is to use an array to hold the elements of the queue, and to use two variables, *front* and *rear*, to hold the positions within the array of the first and last elements of the queue. Thus a queue of integers might be declared by

```
const maxqueue = 100;
type  queue = record
                 items: array[1..maxqucuc] of integer;
                 front, rear: 0..maxqucue
              end;
   var    q: queue;
```

Of course, using an array to hold a queue introduces the possibility of *overflow* if the queue contains more elements than were allocated for the array. Ignoring the possibility of underflow and overflow for the moment, the operation *insert*(*q*, *x*) could be implemented by the statements

```
q.rear:= q.rear + 1;
q.items[q.rear]:= x
```

and the operation *x*: = *remove*(*q*) could be implemented by

```
x:= q.items[q.front];
q.front:= q.front + 1
```

Initially, *q.rear* is set to 0 and *q.front* is set to 1, and the queue is empty whenever $q.rear < q.front$. The number of elements in the queue at any time is equal to the value of $q.rear - q.front + 1$.

Let us examine what might happen under this representation. Figure 4.1.2 illustrates an array of five elements used to represent a queue (i.e., $maxqueue = 5$). Initially (Figure 4.1.2a), the queue is empty. In Figure 4.1.2b, items A, B, and C have been inserted. In Figure 4.1.2c, two items have been deleted, and in Figure 4.1.2d, two new items D and E have been inserted. The value of $q.front$ is 3 and the value of $q.rear$ is 5, so that there are only $5 - 3 + 1 = 3$ elements in the queue. Since the array contains five elements, there should be room for the queue to expand without the worry of overflow. However, to insert F into the queue, $q.rear$ must be increased by 1 to 6 and $q.items[6]$ must be set to the value F. But $q.items$ is an array of only five elements, so that the insertion cannot be made. It is possible to reach the absurd situation where the queue is empty, yet no new element can be inserted (see if you can come up with a sequence of insertions and deletions to reach that situation). Clearly, the array representation as just outlined is unacceptable.

One solution is to modify the *remove* operation so that when an item is deleted, the entire queue is shifted to the beginning of the array. The

Figure 4.1.2

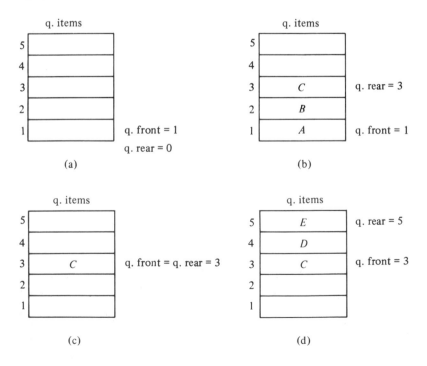

operation $x := remove(q)$ would then be modified (again, ignoring the possibility of underflow) to

```
x:= q.items[1];
for i:= 1 to q.rear - 1
    do q.items[i] := q.items[i+1];
q.rear:= q.rear - 1
```

The field *front* need no longer be specified as part of a queue, because the front of the queue is always at the first element of the array. The empty queue is represented by the queue in which *rear* equals zero. Figure 4.1.3 shows the queue of Figure 4.1.2 under this new representation.

This method, however, is too inefficient to be satisfactory. Each deletion involves moving every remaining element of the queue. If a queue contains 500 or 1000 elements, this is clearly too high a price to pay. Further, the operation of removing an element from a queue logically involves manipulation of only one element—the one currently at the front of the queue. The implementation of that operation should reflect this and should not involve a host of extraneous operations.

Another solution is to treat the array that holds the queue as a circle

Figure 4.1.3

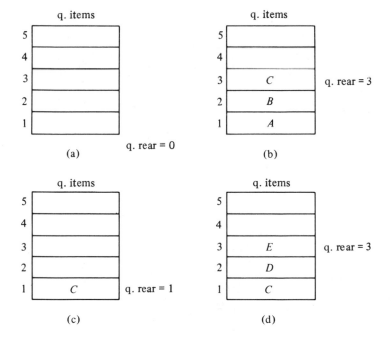

rather than as a straight line. That is, we imagine the first element of the array as immediately following its last element. This implies that even if the last element is occupied, a new value can be inserted behind it in the first element of the array as long as that first element is empty.

Let us look at an example. Assume that a queue contains three items in positions 3, 4, and 5 of a five-element array. This is the situation of Figure 4.1.2d, reproduced as Figure 4.1.4a. Although the array is not full, the last element of the array is occupied. If an attempt is now made to insert item *F* into the queue, it can be placed in position 1 of the array, as shown in Figure 4.1.4b. The first item of the queue is in *q.items*[3], which is followed in the queue by *q.items*[4], *q.items*[5], and *q.items*[1]. Figures 4.1.4c–e show

Figure 4.1.4

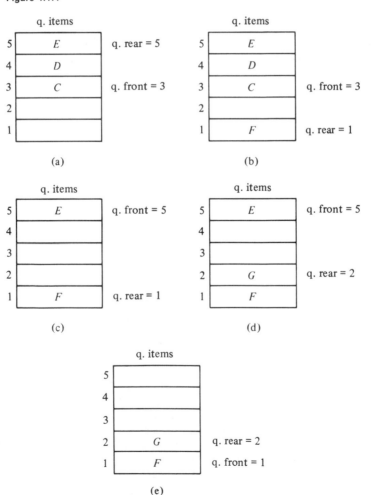

the status of the queue as first two items C and D are deleted, then G is inserted, and finally E is deleted.

Unfortunately, it is difficult under this representation to determine when the queue is empty. The condition $q.rear < q.front$ is no longer valid as a test for the empty queue, since Figures 4.1.4b–d all illustrate situations in which the condition is true, yet the queue is not empty.

One way of solving this problem is to establish the convention that the value of $q.front$ is the index of the array element immediately preceding the first element of the queue rather than the index of the first element itself. Thus since $q.rear$ contains the index of the last element of the queue, the condition $q.front = q.rear$ implies that the queue is empty.

A queue of integers may therefore be declared and initialized by

```
const maxqueue = 100;
type  queue = record
                items: array[1..maxqueue] of integer;
                front, rear: 1..maxqueue
              end;
var   q: queue;
begin
      q.front:= maxqueue;
      q.rear:= maxqueue
```

Note that $q.front$ and $q.rear$ are initialized to the last index of the array, rather than 0 or 1, because the last element of the array immediately precedes the first one within the queue under this representation. Since $q.rear = q.front$, the queue is initially empty.

The *empty* function may be coded as

```
function empty(q: queue): boolean;
begin
      with q
        do if front = rear
             then empty:= true
             else empty:= false
end {function empty};
```

The operation *remove(q)* may be coded as

```
function remove(var q: queue): integer;
begin
      if empty(q)
        then error('queue underflow')
        else with q
          do begin
               if front = maxqueue
                 then front:= 1
                 else front:= front + 1;
```

$$remove := items[front]$$
$$end \ \{else \ with \ q \ do \ begin\}$$
$$end \ \{function \ remove\};$$

Note that *q.front* must be updated before an element is extracted.

Of course, often an underflow condition is meaningful and serves as a signal for a new phase of processing. We may wish to use a procedure *remvandtest* that would be declared by

procedure remvandtest(**var** q: queue; **var** x: integer; **var** und: boolean);

This routine sets *und* to *false* and *x* to the element removed from the queue if the queue is nonempty and sets *und* to *true* if underflow occurs. The coding of the routine is left to the reader.

The *insert* Operation

The *insert* operation involves taking care of overflow. Overflow occurs when the entire array is occupied by items of the queue and an attempt is made to insert yet another element into the queue. For example, consider the queue of Fig. 4.1.5a. There are three elements in the queue: *C, D,* and *E* in *q.items*[3], *q.items*[4], and *q.items*[5], respectively. Since the last item of the queue occupies *q.items*[5], *q.rear* equals 5. Since the first element of the

Figure 4.1.5

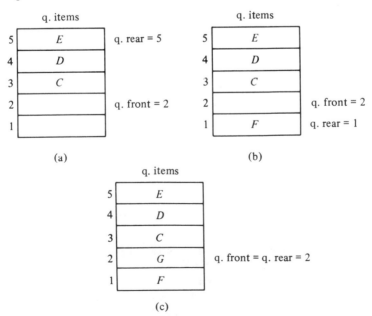

(a)

(b)

(c)

queue is in *q.items*[3], *q.front* equals 2. In Figure 4.1.5b and c, items *F* and *G* are inserted into the queue and the value of *q.rear* is changed accordingly. At that point, the array is full and an attempt to perform any more insertions will cause an overflow. But this is indicated by the fact that *q.front* = *q.rear*, which is precisely the indication for underflow. It seems that there is no way to distinguish between the empty queue and the full queue under this implementation. Such a situation is clearly unsatisfactory.

One solution is to sacrifice one element of the array and to allow a queue to grow only as large as one less than the size of the array. Thus, if an array of 100 elements is declared as a queue, the queue may have up to 99 members. An attempt to insert a hundredth element into the queue will cause an overflow. The *insert* routine may then be written as follows:

```
procedure insert(var q: queue; x: integer);
begin
    with q
        do begin
                if rear = maxqueue
                    then rear:= 1
                    else  rear:= rear + 1;
                if rear = front
                    then error('queue overflow')
                    else  items[rear] := x
        end {with q do begin}
    end {procedure insert};
```

The test for overflow in *insert* occurs after *q.rear* has been adjusted, whereas the test for underflow in *remove* occurs immediately upon entering the routine, before *q.front* is updated.

The Priority Queue

Both the stack and the queue are data structures whose elements are ordered based on the sequence in which they have been inserted. The *pop* operation retrieves the last element inserted, and the *remove* operation retrieves the first element inserted. If there is an intrinsic order among the elements themselves (e.g., numeric order or alphabetic order), it is ignored in the stack or queue operations.

The ***priority queue*** is a data structure in which the intrinsic ordering of the elements does determine the results of its basic operations. There are two types of priority queues: an ascending priority queue and a descending priority queue. An ***ascending priority queue*** is a collection of items into which items can be inserted arbitrarily and from which only the smallest item can be removed. If *apq* is an ascending priority queue, *pqinsert(apq, x)* inserts element *x* into *apq*, and *pqmindelete(apq)* removes the minimum element from *apq* and returns its value. A ***descending priority queue*** is similar but allows deletion of only the *largest* item. The operations applicable to a descending priority queue, *dpq*, are *pqinsert(dpq, x)* and *pqmaxdelete(dpq)*. *pqinsert(dpq, x)* inserts element *x* into *dpq* and is logically identical to *pqinsert* for an ascending priority queue. *pqmaxdelete(dpq)* removes the maximum element from *dpq* and returns its value. The operation *empty(pq)* applies to both types of priority queue and determines whether a priority queue is empty. *pqmindelete* or *pqmaxdelete* can only be applied to a nonempty priority queue [that is, if *empty(pq)* is *false*].

Once *pqmindelete* has been applied to retrieve the smallest element of an ascending priority queue, it can be applied again to retrieve the next smallest, and so on. Thus the operation successively retrieves the elements of the priority queue in ascending order. (However, if a small element is inserted after several deletions, the next retrieval will return that small element, which may be smaller than a previously retrieved element.) Similarly, *pqmaxdelete* retrieves the elements of a descending priority queue in descending order. This explains the designation of a priority queue as either ascending or descending.

The elements of a priority queue need not be numbers or character strings that can be compared directly. They may be complex records which are ordered on one or several fields. Sometimes, the field on which the elements of a priority queue is ordered is not even part of the elements themselves; it may be a special, external value used specifically for the purpose of ordering the priority queue.

For example, a stack may be viewed as a descending priority queue whose elements are ordered by time of insertion. The element with the greatest insertion time value (the "maximum" element) is the only item that can be retrieved. A queue may similarly be viewed as an ascending priority queue whose elements are ordered by time of insertion. In both cases, time of insertion is a field that is not part of the elements themselves but is used to order the priority queue.

We leave as an exercise for the reader the development of an ADT specification for a priority queue. We now look at implementation methods.

Array Implementation of a Priority Queue

As we have seen, a stack and a queue can be implemented in an array so that each insertion or deletion involves accessing only a single element of the array. Unfortunately, this is not the case for a priority queue.

Suppose the *n* elements of a priority queue *pq* are maintained in positions 1 to *n* of an array *pq.items* of size *maxpq*, and suppose *pq.rear* equals the first empty array position, $n + 1$. Then *insert(pq, x)* would seem to be a fairly straightforward operation:

```
if pq.rear > maxpq
   then error('priority queue overflow')
   else begin
           pq.items[pq.rear]:= x;
           pq.rear:= pq.rear + 1
      end
```

Note that, under this insertion method, the elements of the priority queue are not kept ordered in the array.

As long as only insertions take place, this implementation works well. Suppose, however, that we attempt the operation *pqmindelete(pq)* on an ascending priority queue. This raises two issues. First, to locate the smallest element, every element of the array from *pq.items*[1] through *pq.items*[*pq.rear* − 1] must be examined. Therefore, a deletion requires accessing every element of the priority queue.

Second, how can an element in the middle of the set be deleted? Stack and queue deletion involves removal of an item from one of the two ends and does not require any searching. Priority queue deletion, under this implementation, requires both searching for the element to be deleted and removal of an element in the middle of an array.

There are several solutions to this problem, none of them entirely satisfactory:

- A special "empty" indicator can be placed into the deleted position. Insertion proceeds as before, but, when *pq.rear* reaches *maxpq* + 1, the array elements are compacted into the front of the array, and *pq.rear* is reset to one more than the number of elements. The "empty" indicator can be a value that is invalid as an element (e.g., −1 in a priority queue of nonnegative numbers), or a separate boolean field can be associated with each array position to indicate whether it is empty. There are several disadvantages to this approach. First, the search process to locate the maximum or minimum element must examine all the deleted array positions in addition to the actual priority queue elements. Thus if many items have been deleted but no compaction has yet taken place, the deletion operation accesses many more array elements than exist in the priority queue. Second, once in a while insertion suddenly requires accessing every single position of the array, as it runs out of room and begins compaction.
- The deletion operation can label a position empty as in the previous solution, but insertion is modified to insert the new item in the first "empty" position. Insertion would then involve beginning at the start of the array and accessing every element up to the first one that has been deleted. This decreased efficiency of every insertion is a major drawback to this solution.
- Each deletion can compact the array by shifting all elements past the deleted element backward by one position, and *pq.rear* is reduced by one. Insertion remains unchanged. On the average, half of all priority queue elements are shifted for each deletion so that deletion becomes quite inefficient. A slightly better alternative is to shift either all preceding elements forward or all succeeding elements backward, depending on which group is smaller. This would require maintaining both *front*

and *rear* indicators and treating the array as a circular structure, as we did for the queue.

- Instead of maintaining the priority queue as an unordered array, maintain it as an *ordered*, circular array as follows:

```
const  maxpq = ... ;
type   pqueue = record
                    items: array[1..maxpq] of integer;
                    minpos, maxpos: integer
               end;
var    pq: pqueue;
```

pq.minpos is the position of the smallest element; *pq.maxpos* is one greater than the position of the largest. Deletion involves merely increasing *pq.minpos* (for an ascending queue) or decreasing *pq.maxpos* (for a descending queue). However, insertion requires locating the proper position of the new element and shifting the preceding or succeeding elements (again, the technique of shifting whichever group is smaller is helpful). This method moves the work of searching and shifting from the deletion operation to the insertion operation. However, since the array is ordered, the search for the position of the new element in an ordered array is only half as expensive on the average as finding the maximum or minimum of the unordered array. Other techniques that involve leaving gaps in the array between elements of the priority queue to allow for subsequent insertions are also possible.

We leave the Pascal implementations of *pqinsert*, *pqmindelete*, and *pqmaxdelete* for the array representation of a priority queue as exercises for the reader. Searching ordered and unordered arrays is discussed further in Section 8.1.

EXERCISES

1. Write the procedure *remvandtest(q, x, und)*, which sets *und* to *false* and *x* to the item removed from a nonempty queue *q* and sets *und* to *true* if the queue is empty.

2. What set of conditions are necessary and sufficient for a sequence of *insert* and *remove* operations on a single empty queue to leave the queue empty without causing an underflow? What set of conditions are necessary and sufficient for such a sequence to leave a nonempty queue unchanged?

3. If an array is not considered circular, the text suggests that each *remove* operation must shift down every remaining element of a queue. An alternative method is to postpone shifting until *rear* equals the last index of the array. When that situation occurs and an attempt is made to insert an element into the queue, the entire queue is shifted down so that the first element of the queue is in the first position of the array. What are the advantages of this method over performing a shift at each *remove* operation? What are the disadvantages? Rewrite the routines *remove*, *insert*, and *empty* using this method.

4. Show how a sequence of insertions and removals from a queue represented by a linear array can cause an overflow to occur upon an attempt to insert an element into an empty queue.

5. We can avoid sacrificing one element of a queue if a field *empty:boolean* is added to the queue representation. Show how this can be done and rewrite the queue manipulation routines under that representation.

6. How would you implement a queue of stacks? A stack of queues? A queue of queues? Write routines to implement the appropriate operations for each of these data structures.

7. Show how to implement a queue of integers in Pascal by using an array *queue*[−1..100], where *queue*[−1] is used to indicate the front of the queue, *queue*[0] is used to indicate its rear, and *queue*[1] through *queue*[100] are used to contain the queue elements. Show how to initialize such an array to represent the empty queue and write routines *remove*, *insert*, and *empty* for such an implementation.

8. Show how to implement a queue in Pascal in which each item consists of a variable number of integers.

9. A *deque* is an ordered set of items from which items may be deleted at either and into which items may be inserted at either end. Call the two ends of a deque *left* and *right*. How can a deque be represented as a Pascal array? Write four Pascal routines,

remvleft, remvright, insrtleft, insrtright

to remove and insert elements at the left and right ends of a deque. Make sure that the routines work properly for the empty deque and that they detect overflow and underflow.

10. Define an ***input-restricted deque*** as a deque (see Exercise 9) for which only the operations *remvleft*, *remvright*, and *instrleft* are valid, and an ***output-restricted deque*** as a deque for which only the operations *remvleft*, *insrtleft*, and *insrtright* are valid. Show how each of these can be used to represent both a stack and a queue.

11. The Scratchemup Parking Garage contains a single lane that holds up to 10 cars. Cars arrive at the south end of the garage and leave from the north end. If a customer arrives to pick up a car that is not the northernmost, all cars to the north of his car are moved out, his car is driven out, and the other cars are restored in the same order that they were in originally. Whenever a car leaves, all cars to the south are moved forward so that at all times all the empty spaces are in the south part of the garage.

    Write a program that reads a group of input lines. Each line contains an 'a' for arrival or a 'd' for departure and a license plate number. Cars are assumed to arrive and depart in the order specified by the input. The program should print a message each time that a car arrives or departs. When a car arrives, the message should specify whether or not there is room for the car in the garage. If there is no room for a car, the car waits until there is room or until a departure line is read for the car. When room becomes available, another message should be printed. When a car departs, the message should include the number of times the car was moved within the garage (including the departure itself but not the arrival). This number is 0 if the car departs from the waiting line.

12. Implement an ascending priority queue and its operations, *pqinsert*, *pqmindelete*, and *empty* using each of the four methods presented in the text.

13. Show how to sort a set of numbers in a file assuming, that you can use a priority queue and the operations *pqinsert*, *pqmindelete*, and *empty*.

2. LINKED LISTS

What are the drawbacks of using sequential storage to represent stacks and queues? One major drawback is that a fixed amount of storage remains allocated to the stack or queue even when the structure is actually using a smaller amount or possibly no storage at all. Further, no more than that fixed amount of storage may be allocated, thus introducing the possibility of overflow.

Assume that a program uses two stacks implemented in two separate arrays, *s1.items* and *s2.items*. Further, assume that each of these arrays has 100 elements. Then despite the fact that 200 elements are available for the two stacks, neither can grow beyond 100 items. Even if the first stack contains only 25 items, the second cannot contain more than 100. One solution to this problem is to allocate a single array *items* of 200 elements. The first stack will occupy *items*[1], *items*[2], ... , *items*[*top*1], while the second stack will be allocated from the other end of the array, occupying *items*[200], *items*[199], ... , *items*[*top*2]. Thus when one of the stacks is not occupying storage, the other stack may make use of that storage. Of course, two distinct sets of *pop*, *push*, and *empty* routines are necessary for the two stacks, since one grows by increasing *top*1 while the other grows by decreasing *top*2.

Unfortunately, although such a scheme allows two stacks to share a common area, no such simple solution exists for three or more stacks or even for two queues. Instead, one must keep track of the tops and bottoms (or fronts and rears) of all the structures sharing a single large array. Each time that the growth of one structure is about to impinge on the storage currently being used by another, all the structures must be shifted within the single array to allow for the growth.

In a sequential representation, the items of a stack or queue are implicitly ordered by the sequential order of storage. Thus, if $q.items[x]$ represents an element of a queue, the next element will be $q.items[x + 1]$ (or if $x = maxqueue$, $q.items[1]$). Suppose that the items of a stack or a queue were explicitly ordered; that is, each item contained within itself the address of the next item. Such an explicit ordering gives rise to a data structure pictured in Figure 4.2.1, which is known as a *linear linked list*. Each item in the list is called a **node** and contains two fields, an **information** field and a **next address** field. The information field holds the actual element on the list. The next address field contains the address of the next node in the list. Such an address, which is used to access a particular node, is known as a *pointer*. The entire linked list is accessed from an external pointer *list*, which points to (contains the address of) the first node in the list. (By an "external" pointer, we mean one that is not included within a node. Rather its value can be accessed directly by referencing a variable.) The next address field of the last node in the list contains a special value, known as **nil**, which is not a valid address. This **nil pointer** is used to signal the end of a list.

The list with no nodes on it is called the **empty list** or the **nil list**. The value of the external pointer *list* to such a list is the nil pointer. Thus a list can be initialized to the empty list by the operation *list* := *nil*.

We now introduce some notation for use in algorithms (but not in Pascal programs). If p is a pointer to a node, *node*(p) refers to the node

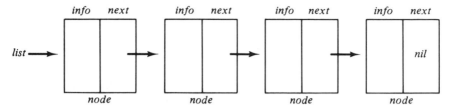

Figure 4.2.1 A linear linked list.

pointed to by *p*, *info*(*p*) refers to the information portion of that node, and *next*(*p*) refers to the next address portion and is therefore a pointer. Thus, if *next*(*p*) is not *nil*, *info*(*next*(*p*)) refers to the information portion of the node that follows *node*(*p*) in the list.

Before proceeding with further discussion of linked lists, we should mention that we are presenting them primarily as a data structure (that is, an implementation method) rather than as a data type (that is, a logical structure with precisely defined primitive operations). We therefore do not present an ADT specification for linked lists here. In Section 10.1, we discuss lists as abstract structures and some primitive operations for them.

Inserting and Removing Nodes from a List

A list is a dynamic data structure. The number of nodes on a list may vary dramatically as elements are inserted and removed. The dynamic nature of a list may be contrasted with the static nature of an array whose size remains constant. For example, suppose that we are given a list of integers, as illustrated in Figure 4.2.2a and we desire to add the integer 6 to the front of that list. That is, we wish to change the list so that it appears as in Figure 4.2.2f.

The first step is to obtain a node in which to house the additional integer. If a list is to grow and shrink, there must be some mechanism for obtaining empty nodes to be added onto the list. Note that, unlike an array, a list does not come with a presupplied set of storage locations into which elements can be placed.

Let us assume the existence of a mechanism for obtaining empty nodes. The operation

$$p := getnode$$

obtains an empty node and sets the contents of a variable named *p* to the address of that node. This means that *p* is a pointer to this newly allocated node. Figure 4.2.2b illustrates the list and the new node after performing the *getnode* operation. The details of how this operation works will be explained shortly.

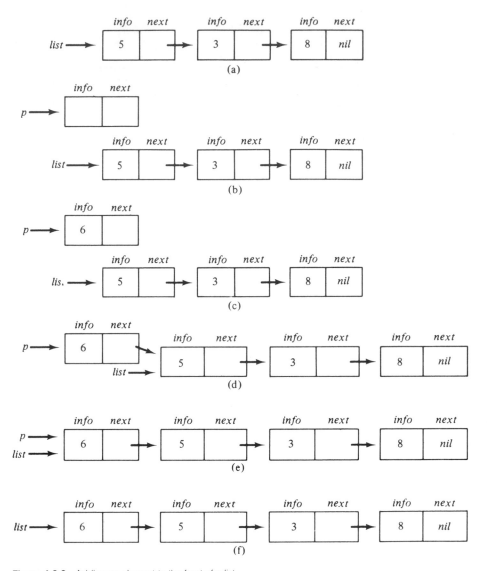

Figure 4.2.2   Adding an element to the front of a list.

The next step is to insert the integer 6 into the *info* portion of the newly allocated node. This is done by the operation

$$info(p):= 6$$

The result of this operation is illustrated in Figure 4.2.2c.

After setting the *info* portion of *node*(p), it is necessary to set the *next* portion of that node. Since *node*(p) is to be inserted at the front of the list, the node that follows should be the current first node on the list. Since the variable *list* contains the address of that first node, *node(p)* can be added to the list by performing the operation

$$next(p):= list$$

This operation places the value of *list* (which is the address of the first node on the list) into the *next* field of *node(p)*. Figure 4.2.2d illustrates the result of this operation.

At this point, *p* points to the list with the additional item included. However, since *list* is the external pointer to the desired list, its value must be modified to the address of the new first node of the list. This can be done by performing the operation

$$list:= p$$

which changes the value of *list* to the value of *p*. Figure 4.2.2e illustrates the result of this operation. Note that Figures 4.2.2e and f are identical except that the value of *p* is not shown in Figure 4.2.2f. This is because *p* is used as an auxiliary variable during the process of modifying the list, but its value is irrelevant to the status of the list before and after the process. Once the foregoing operations have been performed, the value of *p* may be changed without affecting the list.

Putting all the steps together, we have an algorithm for adding the integer 6 to the front of the list *list*:

```
p:= getnode;
info(p):= 6;
next(p):= list;
list:= p
```

The algorithm can obviously be generalized so that it adds any object *x* to the front of a list *list* by replacing the operation *info(p)* := 6 with *info(p)*: = *x*. Convince yourself that the algorithm works correctly, even if the list is initially empty (*list* = *nil*).

Figure 4.2.3 illustrates the process of removing the first node of a nonempty list and storing the value of its *info* field into a variable *x*. The initial configuration is shown in Figure 4.2.3a and the final configuration is shown in Figure 4.2.3f. The process itself is almost the exact opposite of the process to add a node to the front of a list. To obtain Figure 4.2.3d from Figure 4.2.3a, the following operations (whose actions should be clear) are performed:

```
p:= list;        (Figure 4.2.3b)
list:= next(p);  (Figure 4.2.3c)
x:= info(p)      (Figure 4.2.3d)
```

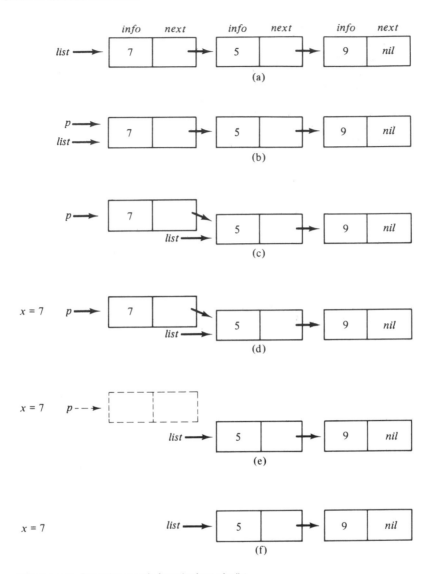

Figure 4.2.3 Removing a node from the front of a list.

At this point, the algorithm has accomplished what it was supposed to do: the first node has been removed from *list* and *x* has been set to the desired value. However, the algorithm is not yet complete. In Figure 4.2.3d, *p* still points to the node that was formerly first on the list. However, that node is currently useless because it is no longer on the list and its information has been stored in *x*. [The node is not considered to be on the list despite the fact that *next(p)* points to a node on the list, since there is no way to reach *node(p)* from the external pointer *list*.] The variable *p* was used as an auxiliary variable during the process of removing the first node from the list. The starting and ending configurations of the list make no reference to p. It is therefore reasonable to expect that p will be used for some other purpose in a short while after this operation has been performed. But once the value of p is changed, there is no way to access the node at all, since neither an external pointer nor a *next* field contains its address. Therefore, the node is currently useless and cannot be reused, yet it is taking up valuable storage.

It would be desirable to have some mechanism for making *node(p)* available for reuse even if the value of the pointer p is changed. The operation that does this is

$$freenode(p) \quad \text{(Figure 4.2.3e)}$$

Once this operation has been performed, it becomes illegal to reference *node(p)*, since the node is no longer allocated. Since the value of p is a pointer to a node that has been freed, any reference to that value is also illegal.

However, the node might be reallocated and a pointer to it reassigned to p by the operation $p := getnode$. Note that we say that the node "might be" reallocated, since the *getnode* operation returns a pointer to some newly allocated node. There is no guarantee that this new node is the same as the one that has just been freed.

Another way of thinking of *getnode* and *freenode* is that *getnode* creates a new node, whereas *freenode* destroys a node. Under this view, nodes are not used and reused but are rather created and destroyed. We shall say more about the two operations *getnode* and *freenode* and about the concepts they represent in a moment, but first we make the following interesing observation.

Linked Implementation of Stacks

The operation of adding an element to the front of a linked list is quite similar to that of pushing an element onto a stack. In both cases, a new item is added as the only immediately accessible item in a collection. A stack can be accessed only through its top element, and a list can be accessed only from the pointer to its first element. Similarly, the operation of removing the first element from a linked list is analogous to popping a stack. In both cases, the only immediately accessible item of a collection is removed from that collection, and the next item becomes immediately accessible.

Thus we have discovered another way of implementing a stack. A stack may be represented by a linear linked list. The first node of the list is the top of the stack. If an external pointer s points to such a linked list, the operation $push(s, x)$ may be implemented by

$$p := getnode;$$
$$info(p) := x;$$
$$next(p) := s;$$
$$s := p$$

The operation *empty(s)* is merely a test as to whether *s* equals *nil*. The operation *x* := *pop(s)* is the operation of removing the first node from a nonempty list and signaling underflow if the list is empty:

> **if** *empty* (*s*)
> > **then** *error* ('stack underflow')
> > **else begin**
> > > *p* := *s*;
> > > *s* := *next* (*p*);
> > > *x* := *info* (*p*);
> > > *freenode* (*p*)
> > **end** {else begin}

Figure 4.2.4a illustrates a stack implemented as a linked list, and Figure 4.2.4b illustrates the same stack after another element has been pushed onto it.

getnode and freenode Operations

We now return to a discussion of the *getnode* and *freenode* operations. In an abstract, idealized world it is possible to postulate an infinite number

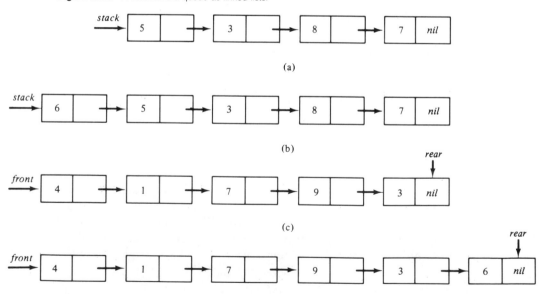

Figure 4.2.4 A stack and a queue as linked lists.

of unused nodes available for use by abstract algorithms. The *getnode* operation finds one such node and makes it available to the algorithm. Alternatively, the *getnode* operation may be regarded as a machine that manufactures nodes and never breaks down. Thus each time that *getnode* is invoked, it presents its caller with a brand new node, different from all the nodes previously in use.

In such an ideal world, the *freenode* operation would be unnecessary to make a node available for reuse. Why use an old secondhand node when a simple call to *getnode* can produce a new, never-before-used node? The only harm that an unused node can do is to reduce the number of nodes that can possibly be used, but if an infinite supply of nodes is available, such a reduction is meaningless. Therefore, there is never any reason to reuse a node.

Unfortunately, we live in a real world. Computers do not have an infinite amount of storage and cannot manufacture more storage for immediate utilization (at least, not yet). Therefore, there are a finite number of nodes available, and it is impossible to use more than that number at any given instant. If it is desired to use more than that number over a given period of time, some nodes must be reused. The function of *freenode* is to make a node that is no longer being used in its current context available for reuse in a different context.

We might think of a finite pool of empty nodes existing initially. This pool cannot be accessed by the programmer, except through the *getnode* and *freenode* operations. *getnode* removes a node from the pool, while *freenode* returns a node to the pool. Since any unused node is as good as any other, it makes no difference which node is retrieved by *getnode* or where within the pool a node is placed by *freenode*.

The most natural form for this pool to take is that of a linked list acting as a stack. The list is linked together by the *next* field in each node. The *getnode* operation removes the first node from this list and makes it available for use. The *freenode* operation adds a node to the front of the list, making it available for reallocation by the next *getnode*. The list of available nodes is called the ***available list***.

What happens when the available list is empty? This means that all nodes are currently in use, and it is impossible to allocate any more. If a program calls on *getnode* when the available list is empty, then the amount of storage assigned for that program's data structures is too small. Therefore, overflow occurs. This is similar to the situation of a stack implemented in an array overflowing the array bounds.

As long as data structures are abstract, theoretical concepts in a world of infinite space, there is no possibility of overflow. It is only when they are implemented as real objects in a finite area that the possibility of overflow arises.

Let us assume that the external pointer *avail* points to the list of available nodes. Then the operation

$$p := getnode$$

is implemented as follows:

> **if** *avail* = *nil*
>   **then** *error*('overflow')
>   **else begin**
>   *p* := *avail*;
>   *avail* := *next* (*avail*)
>   **end** {else begin}

Since the possibility of overflow is accounted for in the *getnode* operation, it need not be mentioned in the list implementation of *push*. If a stack is about to overflow all available nodes, the statement $p := getnode$ within the *push* operation will result in an overflow.

The implementation of *freenode*(*p*) is straightforward:

> *next* (*p*) := *avail*;
> *avail* := *p*

The advantage of the list implementation of stacks is that all the stacks being used by a program can share the same available list. When a stack needs a node, it can obtain it from the single available list. When a stack no longer needs a node, it returns the node to that same available list. As long as the total amount of space needed by all the stacks at any one time is less than the amount of space initially available to them all, each stack is able to grow and shrink to any size. No space has been preallocated to any single stack and no stack is using space that it does not need. Furthermore, other data structures, such a queues, may also share the same set of nodes.

Linked Implementation of Queues

Let us now examine how to represent a queue as a linked list. Recall that items are deleted from the front of a queue and inserted at the rear. Let the list pointer that points to the first element of a list represent the front of the queue. Another pointer to the last element of the list represents the rear of the queue, as shown in Figure 4.2.4c. Figure 4.2.4d illustrates the same queue after a new item has been inserted.

If we let a queue *q* consist of a list and two pointers, *q.front* and *q.rear*, then the operations *empty*(*q*) and $x := remove(q)$ are completely analogous to *empty*(*s*) and $x := pop(s)$, with the pointer *q.front* replacing *s*. However, special attention must be paid to the case in which the last element is removed from a queue. In this case, *q.rear* must also be set to *nil*, since in an empty queue both *q.front* and *q.rear* are *nil*. The algorithm for $x := remove$ (*q*) is therefore as follows:

$$
\begin{aligned}
&\textbf{\textit{if}}\ empty(q)\\
&\quad \textbf{\textit{then}}\ error(\text{`queue underflow'})\\
&\quad \textbf{\textit{else with}}\ q\\
&\qquad\quad \textbf{\textit{do begin}}\\
&\qquad\qquad\quad p := front;\\
&\qquad\qquad\quad x := info(p);\\
&\qquad\qquad\quad front := next(p);\\
&\qquad\qquad\quad \textbf{\textit{if}}\ front = nil\\
&\qquad\qquad\qquad \textbf{\textit{then}}\ rear := nil;\\
&\qquad\qquad\quad freenode(p);\\
&\qquad\qquad\quad remove := x\\
&\qquad\quad \textbf{\textit{end}}\ \{\text{else with } q \text{ do begin}\}
\end{aligned}
$$

The operation *insert(q, x)* can be implemented by

$$
\begin{aligned}
&\textbf{\textit{with}}\ q\\
&\quad \textbf{\textit{do begin}}\\
&\qquad\quad p := getnode;\\
&\qquad\quad info(p) := x;\\
&\qquad\quad next(p) := nil;\\
&\qquad\quad \textbf{\textit{if}}\ rear = nil\\
&\qquad\qquad \textbf{\textit{then}}\ front := p\\
&\qquad\qquad \textbf{\textit{else}}\ next(rear) := p;\\
&\qquad\quad rear := p\\
&\quad \textbf{\textit{end}}\ \{\text{with } q \text{ do begin}\}
\end{aligned}
$$

What are the disadvantages of representing a stack or queue by a linked list? Clearly, a node in a linked list occupies more storage than a corresponding element in an array, since two pieces of information are necessary in a list node for each item (*info* and *next*), whereas only one piece of information is needed in the array implementation. However, the space used for a list node is usually not twice the space used by an array element, since the elements in such a list usually consist of records with many subfields. For example, if each element on a stack were a record occupying 10 words, the addition of an eleventh word to contain a pointer increases the space requirement by only 10%. Further, in many machine languages it is possible to compress information and a pointer into a single word so that there is no space degradation.

Another disadvantage is the additional time that must be spent in managing the available list. Each addition and deletion of an element from a stack or a queue involves a corresponding deletion or addition to the available list.

The advantage of using linked lists is that all the stacks and queues of a program have access to the same free list of nodes. Nodes that are unused by one stack may be used by another, as long as the total number of nodes in use at any one time is not greater than the total number of nodes available.

The Linked List as a Data Structure

Linked lists are important not only as a means of implementing stacks and queues, but as data structures in their own right. An item is accessed in a linked list by traversing the list from its beginning. An array implementation allows access to the nth item in a group using a single operation, while a list implementation requires n operations. It is necessary to pass through each of the first $n - 1$ elements before reaching the nth element, because there is no relation between the memory location occupied by an element of a list and its position within that list.

The advantage of a list over an array occurs when it is necessary to insert or delete an element in the middle of a group of other elements. For example, suppose that we wished to insert an element x between the third and fourth elements in an array of size 10 which currently contains seven items. Items 7 through 4 must first be moved one slot and the new element inserted in the newly available position 4. This process is illustrated by Figure 4.2.5a. In this case, insertion of one item involves moving four items in addition to the insertion itself. If the array contained 500 or 1000 elements, a correspondingly larger number of elements would have to be moved. Similarly, to delete an element from an array, all the elements past the element deleted must be moved one position.

On the other hand, if the items are stored as a list, then if p is a pointer to a given element of the list, inserting a new element after $node(p)$ involves allocating a node, inserting the information, and adjusting two pointers. The amount of work required is independent of the size of the list. This is illustrated in Figure 4.2.5b.

Let *insafter*(p, x) denote the operation of inserting an item x into a list after a node pointed to by p. This operation may be implemented as follows:

$$q := getnode;$$
$$info(q) := x;$$
$$next(q) := next(p);$$
$$next(p) := q$$

An item can only be inserted after a given node, not before the node. This is because there is no way to proceed from a given node to its predecessor in a linear list without traversing the list from its beginning. To insert an item before $node(p)$, the *next* field of its predecessor must be changed to point to a newly allocated node. But, given p, there is no way to find that predecessor. However, it is possible to achieve the effect of inserting an element before a given node in a linked list by inserting the element after the node and then switching the contents of the given node and its newly created successor. We leave the details for the reader.

Similarly, to delete a node from a linear list it is insufficient to be

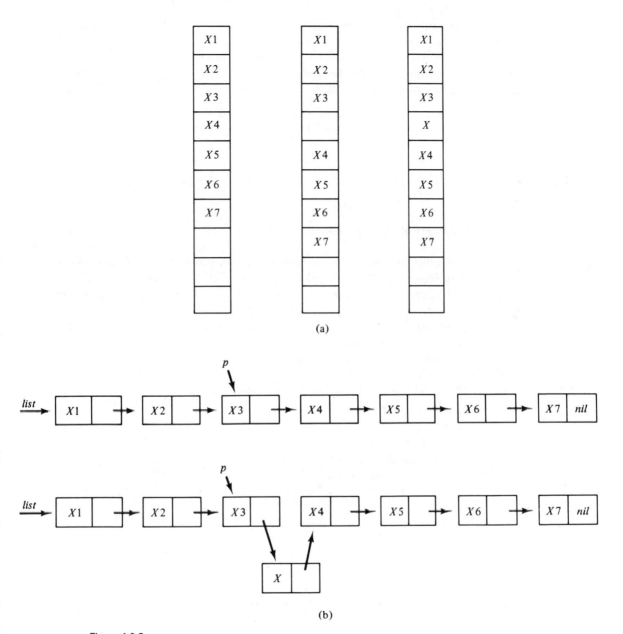

Figure 4.2.5

given a pointer to that node. This is because the *next* field of the node's predecessor must be changed to point to the node's successor, and there is no direct way of reaching the predecessor of a given node. The best that can be done is to delete a node following a given node. (However, it is possible to save the contents of the following node, delete the following node, and then replace the contents of the given node with the saved information. This achieves the effect of deleting a given node.) Let *delafter(p, x)* denote the operation of deleting the node following *node(p)* and assigning its contents to the variable *x*. This operation may be implemented as follows:

$$q := next(p);$$
$$x := info(q);$$
$$next(p) := next(q);$$
$$freenode(q)$$

The freed node is placed back onto the available list so that it may be reused in the future.

Examples of List Operations

We illustrate these two operations as well as the *push* and *pop* operations for lists with some simple examples. The first example is to delete all occurrences of the number 4 from a list *list*. The list is traversed in a search for nodes that contain 4 in their *info* fields. Each such node must be deleted from the list. But to delete a node from a list, its predecessor must be known. For this reason, two pointers, *p* and *q* are used. *p* is used to traverse the list, and *q* always points to the predecessor of *p*. The algorithm makes use of the *pop* operation to remove nodes from the beginning of the list and the *delafter* operation to remove nodes from the middle of the list.

```
q := nil;
p := list;
while p <> nil
    do if info(p) = 4
        then begin
                    p := next(p);    {advance p}
                    if q = nil
                        then {remove the first node of the list}
                            x := pop(list)
                        else {remove the node following q}
                            delafter(q,x)
            end {then begin}
        else {continue traversing the list}
            begin {advance p and q}
                q := p;
                p := next(p)
            end {else begin}
```

The practice of using two pointers, one following the other, is a common one in working with lists. This technique is used in the next example as well. Assume that a list *list* is ordered so that smaller items precede larger ones. Such a list is called an **ordered list**. It is desired to insert an item *x* into this list in its proper place. The algorithm to do so makes use of the *push* operation to add a node to the front of the list and the *insafter* operation to add a node in the middle of the list:

```
q := nil;
p := list;
while (p <> nil) and (x > info(p))
        do begin
                q := p;
                p := next(p)
        end {while...do begin};
{at this point, a node containing x must be inserted}
if q = nil
    then {insert x at the head of the list}
            push(list,x)
    else  insafter(q,x)
```

This is a very common operation and will be denoted by *place(list, x)*.

Note that *x* can be placed in one of $n + 1$ positions; that is, it can be found to be less than the first element of the list, between the first and the second, . . . , between the $(n - 1)$st and the *n*th, and greater than the *n*th. If *x* is less than the first, then *place* accesses only the first node of the list (aside from the new node containing *x*); that is, it immediately determines that $x < info(list)$ and inserts a node containing *x* using *push*. If *x* is between the *k*th and $(k + 1)$st element, then *place* accesses the first $k + 1$ nodes; only after finding *x* to be less than the content of the $(k + 1)$st node is *x* inserted using *insafter*. If *x* is greater than the *n*th element, then all *n* nodes are accessed.

Now suppose that it is equally likely that *x* is inserted into any one of the $n + 1$ possible positions. (If this is true, then we say that the insertion is **random**.) Then the average number of nodes accessed, *a*, equals the sum over all possible positions of the products of the probability of inserting at a particular position and the number of accesses required to insert an element at that position. Because the insertion is random, the probability of inserting at any particular position is $1/(n + 1)$ (there are $n + 1$ positions). If the element is inserted between the *k*th and the $(k + 1)$st position, then the number of accesses is $k + 1$. If the element is inserted after the *n*th element, the number of accesses is *n*. Thus

$$a = (1/(n + 1)) * 1 + (1/(n + 1)) * 2 + \ldots + (1/(n + 1)) * (n - 1)$$

$$+ (1/(n + 1)) * n + (1/(n + 1)) * n$$

or

$$a = (1/(n + 1)) * (1 + 2 + \ldots + n) + n/(n + 1).$$

Now $1 + 2 + \ldots + n$ equals $n*(n + 1)/2$. (This can be proved easily by mathematical induction.) Therefore,

$$a = (1/(n + 1)) * (n * (n + 1)/2) + n/(n + 1) = n/2 + n/(n + 1)$$

When n is large, $n/(n + 1)$ is very close to 1, so a equals approximately $n/2 + 1$ or $(n + 2)/2$. For large n, a is close enough to $n/2$ so that we often say that the operation of randomly inserting an element into an ordered list requires approximately $n/2$ node accesses on the average.

List Implementation of Priority Queues

An ordered list can be used to represent a priority queue. For an ascending priority queue, insertion (*pqinsert*) is implemented by the *place* operation, which keeps the list ordered, and deletion of the minimum element (*pqmindelete*) is implemented by the *pop* operation, which removes the first element from the list. A descending priority queue can be implemented by keeping the list in descending, rather than ascending, order or by using *remove* to implement *pqmaxdelete*. A priority queue implemented as an ordered linked list requires examining an average of approximately $n/2$ nodes for insertion, but only one node for deletion.

An unordered list may also be used as a priority queue. Such a list requires examining only one node for insertion (by implementing *pqinsert* using *push* or *insert*) but always requires examining n elements for deletion (traverse the list to find the minimum or maximum and then delete that node). Thus an ordered list is somewhat more efficient than an unordered list in implementing a priority queue.

The advantage of a list over an array for implementing a priority queue is that no shifting of elements or gaps are necessary in a list. An item can be inserted into a list without moving any other items, while this is impossible for an array unless extra space is left empty. We examine other, more efficient implementations of the priority queue in Sections 7.3 and 8.3.

Lists in Pascal

How can linear lists be represented in Pascal? Since a list is simply a collection of nodes, an array of nodes immediately suggests itself. However, the nodes cannot be ordered by the array ordering; each must contain within itself a pointer to its successor. Thus a group of nodes might be declared as follows:

```
const numnodes = 500;
type  nodeptr = 0..numnodes;
      nodetype = record
                      info: integer;
                      next: nodeptr
                 end;
var   node: array[1..numnodes] of nodetype;
```

In this scheme, a pointer to a node is an integer between 1 and *numnodes* which references a particular element of the array *node*. The nil pointer is represented by the integer 0.

Under this implementation, the Pascal expression *node[p]* is used to reference *node(p)*, *info(p)* is referenced by *node[p].info*, and *next(p)* is referenced by *node[p].next*. *nil* is represented by 0. Let the variable *list* represent a pointer to a list. Suppose that *list* has the value 7. Then *node[7]* is the first node on the list, so that *node[7].info* is the first data item on the list. The second node of the list is given by *node[7].next*. Suppose that *node[7].next* equals 385. Then *node[385].info* is the second data item on the list and *node[385].next* points to the third node. The nodes of a list may be scattered throughout the array *node* in any arbitrary order. Each node carries within itself the address of its successor until the last node in the list, whose *next* field contains 0, which is the nil pointer. There is no relation between the contents of a node and the pointer to it. The pointer *p* to a node merely specifies which element of the array *node* is being referenced; it is *node[p].info* that represents the information contained within that node.

Figure 4.2.6 illustrates a portion of an array *node* that contains four

	info	next
1	26	0
2	11	10
3	5	16
list4 = 4	1	25
list2 = 5	17	1
6	13	2
7		
8	19	19
9	14	13
10	4	22
11		
list3 = 12	31	8
13	6	3
14		
15		
16	37	24
list1 = 17	3	21
18		
19	32	0
20		
21	7	9
22	15	0
23		
24	12	0
25	18	6
26		
27		

Figure 4.2.6   An array of nodes containing four linked lists.

linked lists. The list *list*1 starts at *node*[17] and contains the integers 3, 7, 14, 6, 5, 37, and 12. The nodes that contain these integers in their *info* fields are scattered throughout the array. The *next* field of each node contains the index within the array of the node containing the next element of the list. The last node on the list is *node*[24], which contains the integer 12 in its *info* field and the nil pointer (0) in its *next* field to indicate that it is last on the list. Similarly, *list*2 begins at *node*[5] and contains the integers 17 and 26, *list*3 begins at *node*[12] and contains the integers 31, 19, and 32, and *list*4 begins at *node*[4] and contains the integers 1, 18, 13, 11, 4, and 15. The variables *list*1, *list*2, *list*3, and *list*4 are integers (or *nodeptrs*) representing external pointers to the four lists. Thus the fact that the variable *list*2 has the value 5 represents the fact that the list to which it points begins at *node*[5].

Initially, all nodes are unused, since no lists have yet been formed. Therefore, they must all be placed on the available list. If the global variable *avail: nodeptr* is used to point to the available list, we may initially organize that list as follows:

```
avail:= 1;
for i:= 1 to numnodes-1
    do node[i].next:= i + 1;
node[numnodes].next:= 0
```

The 500 nodes are initially linked in their natural order, so that *node*[i] points to *node*[i + 1]. Thus *node*[1] is the first node on the available list, *node*[2] is the second, and so on. *node*[500] is the last node on the list, since *node*[500].*next* equals 0. There is no reason other than convenience for initially ordering the nodes in this fashion. We could just as well have set *node*[1].*next* to 500, *node*[500].*next* to 2, *node*[2].*next* to 499, and so on, until *node*[250].*next* is set to 251 and *node*[251].*next* to 0. The important point is that the ordering is explicit within the nodes themselves and is not implied by some other underlying structure.

For the remaining subroutines in this section, we assume that the variables *node* and *avail* are global and can therefore be used by any routine.

When a node is needed for use in a particular list, it is obtained from the available list. Similarly, when a node is no longer necessary, it is returned to the available list. These two operations are implemented by the Pascal routines *getnode* and *freenode*. *getnode* is a function that removes a node from the available list and returns a pointer to it.

```
function getnode: nodeptr;
begin
    if avail = 0
        then error('list overflow')
        else begin
                getnode:= avail;
                avail:= node[avail].next
            end {else begin}
end {function getnode};
```

If *avail* equals 0 when this function is called, there are no nodes available. This means that the list structures of a particular program have overflowed the available space.

The procedure *freenode* accepts a pointer to a node and returns that node to the available list:

```
procedure freenode(p: nodeptr);
begin
        node[p].next:= avail;
        avail:= p
end {procedure freenode};
```

The primitive operations for lists are straightforward Pascal versions of the corresponding algorithms. The routine *insafter* accepts a pointer *p* to a node and an item *x* as parameters. It first ensures that *p* is not nil and then inserts *x* into a node following the node pointed to by *p*.

```
procedure insafter(p: nodeptr; x: integer);
var q: nodeptr;
begin
    if p = 0
        then error('void insertion')
        else begin
                q:= getnode;
                node[q].info:= x;
                node[q].next:= node[p].next;
                node[p].next:= q
            end {else begin}
end {procedure insafter};
```

The routine *delafter*(*p*, *x*) deletes the node following *node*(*p*) and stores its contents in *x*.

```
procedure delafter(p: nodeptr; var x: integer);
var q: nodeptr;
begin
    if p = 0
        then error('void deletion')
        else if node[p].next = 0
                then error('void deletion')
                else begin
                        q:= node[p].next;
                        x:= node[q].info;
                        node[p].next:= node[q].next;
                        freenode (q)
                    end {else begin}
end {procedure delafter};
```

Before calling *insafter*, we must be sure that *p* is not nil. Before calling *delafter*, we must be sure that neither *p* nor *node[p].next* is nil.

Queues as Lists in Pascal

We now present Pascal routines for manipulating a queue represented as a linear list, leaving routines for manipulating a stack and a priority queue as exercises for the reader. A queue is represented by a record:

```
type queue = record
                 front: nodeptr;
                 rear: nodeptr
             end;
```

front and *rear* are pointers to the first and last nodes of a queue represented as a list. The empty queue will be represented by *front* and *rear* both equaling 0, the nil pointer. The function *empty* need check only one of these pointers, since in a nonempty queue, neither *front* nor *rear* will be 0.

```
function empty(q: queue): boolean;
begin
    if q.front = 0
        then empty:= true
        else empty:= false
end {function empty};
```

The routine to insert an element into a queue may be written as follows:

```
procedure insert(var q: queue; x: integer);
var p: nodeptr;
begin
    p:= getnode;
    with node[p]
        do begin
            info:= x;
            next:= 0
        end {with...do begin};
    with q
        do begin
            if rear = 0
                then front:= p
                else node[rear].next:= p;
            rear:= p
        end {with...do begin}
end {procedure insert};
```

The function *remove*, which deletes the first element from a queue and returns its value, may be written as follows:

```
function remove (var q: queue): integer;
var p: nodeptr;
    x: integer;
begin
     if empty (q)
       then error ('queue underflow')
       else begin
              p:= q.front;
              with node [p]
                 do begin
                      x:= info;
                      q.front:= next;
                      if q.front = 0
                        then q.rear:= 0
                 end {with...do begin};
              freenode (p);
              remove:= x
       end {else begin}
end {function remove};
```

An Example of a List Operation in Pascal

Let us look at a somewhat more complex list operation implemented in Pascal. We have defined the operation *place(list, x)*, where *list* points to a sorted linear list and *x* is an element to be inserted into its proper position within the list. Recall that this operation is used to implement the operation *pqinsert* to insert into a priority queue.

Ordinarily, the algorithm for performing that operation could be translated directly into Pascal. However, that algorithm contains the line

$$\textit{while } (p <> \textit{nil}) \textit{ and } (x > \textit{info } (p))$$

If p is equal to 0 (which is the nil pointer under this Pascal implementation of lists), then *info(p)* (i.e., *node[p].info*) is undefined and a reference to it will cause an error. Thus we want to avoid the evaluation of *node[p]* in the case that p equals 0. We assume that we have already implemented the stack operation *push*. The code to implement the *place* operation follows:

```
procedure place (var list: nodeptr; x: integer);
var found: boolean;
    p, q: nodeptr;
begin
     found:= false;
     p:= list;
     q:= 0;
```

```
                    while (p <> 0) and (not found)
                        do if x <= node[p].info
                              then found:= true
                              else begin
                                        q:= p;
                                        p:= node[p].next
                                    end {else begin};
                    if q = 0
                        then {insert x at the head of the list}
                              push(list, x)
                        else insafter(q, x)
            end {procedure place};
```

Note that *list* must be declared as a variable parameter since its value is changed if *x* is inserted at the front of the list using the *push* procedure.

Noninteger Lists

Of course, a node on a list need not represent an integer. For example, to represent a stack of character strings by a linked list, nodes containing character strings in their *info* fields are needed. Such nodes could be defined by

```
type nodetype = record
                    info: packed array[1..100] of char;
                    next: nodeptr
                end;
```

A particular application may call for nodes containing more than one item of information. For example, each student node in a list of students may contain the following information: the student's name, college identification number, address, grade-point index, major, and so on. Nodes for such an application may be defined as follows:

```
type nodetype = record
                    info: record
                        name:    packed array[1..50] of char;
                        id:      packed array[1..9] of char;
                        address: packed array[1..100] of char;
                        gpindex: real;
                        major:   packed array[1..20] of char
                    end;
                    next: nodeptr
                end;
```

A separate set of Pascal routines must be written to manipulate lists containing each type of node.

It is possible to use a variant record to define a node that can hold more than one type of item. For example, a node that can hold either an integer or a character might be defined as follows:

```
type nodetype = record
            next: nodeptr;
            case infotype: (ch,int) of
               ch: (cinfo: char);
               int: (iinfo: integer)
         end;
```

Note that the *next* field precedes the variant part of the record in the definition because the fixed part of a variant record must always precede the variant part. We examine nonhomogeneous lists, including lists that can contain other lists and recursive lists, in Section 10.1.

Header Nodes

Sometimes it is desirable to keep an extra node at the front of a list. Such a node does not represent an item in the list and is called a *header node* or a *list header*. The *info* portion of such a header node might be unused, as illustrated in Figure 4.2.7a. More often, the *info* portion of such a node could be used to keep global information about the entire list. For example, Figure 4.2.7b illustrates a list in which the *info* portion of the header node contains the number of nodes (not including the header) in the list. In such a data structure more work is needed to add or delete an item from the list, since the count in the header node must be adjusted properly. However, the number of items in the list may be obtained directly from the header node, so that the entire list need not be traversed.

Another example of the use of header nodes is the following. Suppose that a factory assembles machinery out of smaller units. A particular machine (inventory number $A746$) might be composed of a number of different parts (numbers $B841$, $K321$, $A087$, $J492$, $G593$). This assembly could be represented by a list such as the one illustrated in Figure 4.2.7c, where each item on the list represents a component and where the header node represents the entire assembly. The empty list would no longer be represented by the nil pointer, but rather by a list with a single header node, as in Figure 4.2.7d.

Of course, routines such as *empty*, *push*, *pop*, *insert*, and *remove* must be rewritten to account for the presence of a header node. Most of the routines become a bit more complex, but some, like *insert*, become simpler, because an external list pointer is never nil. We leave the rewriting of the routines as an exercise for the reader. The routines *insafter* and *delafter* need not be changed at all. In fact, *insafter* and *delafter* can be used instead of *push* and *pop*, since the first item in such a list appears in the node that follows the header node, rather than in the first node on the list.

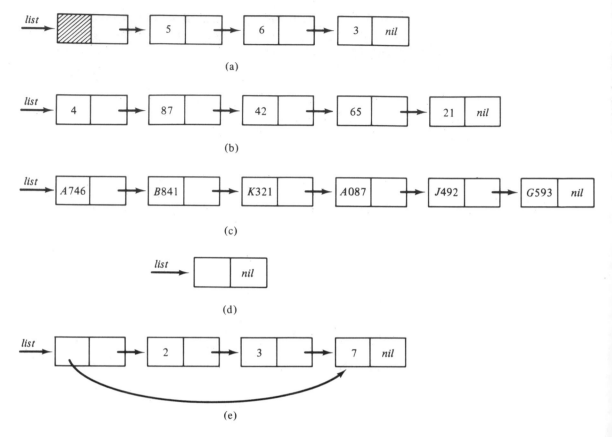

Figure 4.2.7 Lists with header nodes.

If the *info* portion of a node can contain a pointer (as is true in our Pascal implementation of a list of integers where a pointer is represented by an integer), then additional possibilities for the use of a header node present themselves. For example, the *info* portion of a list header might contain a pointer to the last node in the list, as in Figure 4.2.7e. Such an implementation would simplify the representation of a queue. Until now, two external pointers, *front* and *rear*, were necessary for a list to represent a queue. However, now only a single external pointer *q* to the header node of the list is necessary. *next(q)* would point to the front of the queue and *info(q)* to its rear.

Another possibility for the use of the *info* portion of a list header is as a pointer to a "current" node in the list during a traversal process. This would eliminate the need for an external pointer during traversal.

It is also possible for header nodes to be declared as variables separate from the array of list nodes. For example, consider the following set of declarations:

```
const numnodes = 500;
type  nodeptr    = 0..numnodes;
      nodetype  = record
                    info: char;
                    next: nodeptr
                  end;
      charstr   = record
                    length: integer;
                    firstchar: nodeptr
                  end;
var   node: array[1..numnodes] of nodetype;
      s1, s2: charstr;
```

The variables $s1$ and $s2$ of type *charstr* are header nodes for a list of characters. The header contains the number of characters in the list (*length*) and a pointer to the list (*firstchar*). Thus $s1$ and $s2$ represent varying-length character strings. As exercises, you may wish to write routines to concatenate two such character strings or to extract a substring from such a string.

EXERCISES

1. Write a set of routines for implementing several stacks and queues within a single array.
2. What are the advantages and disadvantages of representing a group of items as an array versus a linear linked list?
3. Present four methods of implementing a queue of queues using the list and array implementations of a queue. Write each of the following routines for each implementation:

   remvq(*qq*, *q*)   which removes a queue from the queue of queues *qq* and assigns it to *q*;

   insrtq(*qq*, *q*)   which adds queue *q* to *qq*;

   remvonq(*qq*, *x*)   which removes an element from the first queue of *qq* and assigns it to *x*;

   insrtonq(*qq*, *x*)   which adds an element *x* to the first queue on *qq*.

   Define analogous implementations and operations for a stack of stacks, a stack of queues, and a queue of stacks.
4. Write an algorithm and a Pascal routine to perform each of the following operations:
   (a) Append an element to the end of a list.
   (b) Concatenate two lists.
   (c) Free all the nodes in a list.
   (d) Reverse a list, so that the last element becomes the first, and so on.
   (e) Delete the last element from a list.
   (f) Delete the *n*th element from a list.
   (g) Combine two ordered lists into a single ordered list.

    (h)   Form a list containing the union of the elements of two lists.
    (i)   Form a list containing the intersection of the elements of two lists.
    (j)   Insert an element after the nth element of a list.
    (k)   Delete every second element from a list.
    (l)   Place the elements of a list in increasing order.
    (m) Return the sum of the integers in a list.
    (n)   Return the number of elements in a list.
    (o)   Move $node(p)$ forward n positions in a list.
    (p)   Make a copy of a list.

5. Write an algorithm and a Pascal routine to perform each of the operations of Exercise 4 on a group of elements in contiguous positions of an array.

6. Write a Pascal routine to interchange the mth and nth elements of a list.

7. Write a routine *inssub*($l1$, $i1$, $l2$, $i2$, *len*) to insert the elements of list $l2$ beginning at the $i2$th element and continuing for *len* elements into the list $l1$ beginning at position $i1$. No elements of the list $l1$ are to be removed or replaced. If $i1 > length(l1) + 1$ [where $length(l1)$ denotes the number of nodes in the list $l1$], or if $i2 + len - 1 > length(l2)$, or if $i1 < 1$, or if $i2 < 1$, print an error message. The list $l2$ should remain unchanged.

8. Write a Pascal function *search*(l, x), which accepts a pointer l to a list of integers and an integer x and returns a pointer to a node containing x, if it exists, and the nil pointer otherwise. Write another function *srchinsrt*(l, x), which adds x to l if it is not found and always returns a pointer to a node containing x.

9. Write a Pascal program to read a group of input lines, each containing one word. Print each word that appears in the input and the number of times that it appears.

10. Suppose that a character string is represented by a list of single characters, as described at the end of this section. Write a set of routines to manipulate such lists as follows (where $l1$, $l2$, and *list* are pointers to a header node of a list representing a character string, *str* is a packed array of characters, and $i1$ and $i2$ are integers):

    (a) *convcl(str)*   to convert the character string *str* to a list. This function returns a pointer to a header node.

    (b) *convlc(list, str)*   to convert a list into a character string.

    (c) *posl(l1, l2)*   to perform the *pos* function of Section 1.2 on two character strings represented by lists. This function returns an integer.

    (d) *verifyl(l1, l2)*   to determine the first position of the string represented by $l1$ which is not contained in the string represented by $l2$. This function returns an integer.

    (e) *substrl(l1, i1, i2)*   to perform the *substr* function of Section 1.2 on a character string represented by list $l1$ and integers $i1$ and $i2$. This function returns a pointer to the header node of a list representing a character string that is the desired substring. The list $l1$ remains unchanged.

    (f) *psubstrl(l1, i1, i2, l2)* to perform a pseudo *substr* assignment to list $l1$. The elements of list $l2$ should replace the $i2$ elements of $l1$ beginning at position $i1$. The list $l2$ should remain unchanged.

    (g) *comparel(l1, l2)*   to compare two character strings represented by lists. This function returns -1 if the character string rep-

resented by $l1$ is less than the string represented by
$l2$, 0 if they are equal, and 1 if the string represented
by $l1$ is greater.

3. AN EXAMPLE: SIMULATION USING LINKED LISTS

One of the most useful applications of queues, priority queues, and linked
lists is in *simulation*. A simulation program is one that attempts to model a
real-world situation to learn something about it. Each object and action in
the real situation has its counterpart in the program. If the simulation is
accurate, that is, if the program successfully mirrors the real world, then the
result of the program should mirror the result of the actions being simulated.
Thus it is possible to understand what occurs in the real-world situation
without actually observing its occurrence.

Let us look at an example. Consider a bank with four tellers. A
customer enters the bank at a specific time $t1$, desiring to conduct a transaction with any teller. The transaction may be expected to take a certain
period of time $t2$ before it is completed. If a teller is free, the teller can
process the customer's transaction immediately, and the customer leaves the
bank as soon as the transaction has been completed, at time $t1 + t2$. The
total time spent in the bank by the customer is exactly equal to the duration
of the transaction, $t2$.

However, it is possible that none of the tellers is free; they are all
servicing customers who arrived previously. In that case, there is a line
waiting at each teller's window. The line for a particular teller may consist
of a single person—the one currently transacting business with the teller—
or it may be a very long line. The customer proceeds to the back of the
shortest line and waits until all the preceding customers on the line have
completed their transactions and have left the bank. At that time, the customer may transact his or her business. The customer leaves the bank at $t2$
time units after having reached the front of his or her teller's line. In this
case, the time spent in the bank is $t2$ plus the time spent waiting on line.

Given such a system, we would like to compute the average time
spent by a customer in the bank. One way of doing so is to stand in the
bank doorway, ask departing customers the time of their arrival and record
the time of their departure, subtract the first from the second, and take the
average over all customers. However, this would not be very practical. It
would be difficult to ensure that no customer is overlooked leaving the bank.
Furthermore, it is doubtful that most customers would remember the exact
time of arrival.

Instead, we write a program to simulate the customer actions. Each
part of the real-world situation has its analog in the program. Each line input
to the program represents a customer. The real-world action of a customer
arriving is modeled by an input line being read. As each customer arrives,

two facts are known: the time of his or her arrival and the duration of his or her transaction (since, at the time of arrival, the customer presumably knows what he or she wishes to do at the bank). Thus each input line contains two numbers: the time (in minutes since the bank opened) of the customer's arrival and the amount of time (again, in minutes) necessary for his or her transaction. These input lines are ordered by increasing arrival time. We assume at least one input line.

The four lines in the bank are represented by four queues. Each node of the queues represents a customer waiting on a line, and the node at the front of a queue represents the customer currently being serviced by a teller.

Suppose that at a given instant of time the four lines each contain a specific number of customers. What can happen to alter the status of the lines? Either a new customer enters the bank, in which case one of the lines will have an additional customer, or the first customer on one of the four lines completes his or her transaction, in which case that line will have one less customer. Thus a total of five actions (a customer entering plus four cases of a customer leaving) can change the status of the lines. Each of these five actions is called an *event*.

The simulation proceeds by finding the next event to occur and effecting the change in the queues that mirrors the change in the lines at the bank due to that event. To keep track of events, the program uses an ascending priority queue, called the ***event list***. This list contains at most five nodes, each representing the next occurrence of one of the five types of events. Thus the event list contains one node representing the next customer arriving and four nodes representing each of the four customers at the head of a line completing his or her transaction and leaving the bank. Of course, it is possible that one or more of the lines in the bank are empty or that the doors of the bank have been closed for the day so that no more customers are arriving. In such cases, the event list contains fewer than five nodes.

An event node representing a customer's arrival is called an ***arrival node***, and a node representing a departure is called a ***departure node***. At each point in the simulation, it is necessary to know the next event to occur. For this reason, the event list is ordered by increasing time of event occurrence so that the first event node on the list represents the next event to occur.

The first event to occur is the arrival of the first customer. The event list is therefore initialized by reading the first input line and placing an arrival node representing the first customer's arrival on the event list. Initially, of course, all four queues are empty. The simulation then proceeds as follows. The first node is removed from the event list, and the changes which that event causes are made to the queues. As we shall soon see, these changes may also cause additional events to be placed on the event list. The process of removing the first node from the event list and effecting the changes that it causes is repeated until the event list is empty.

When an arrival node is removed from the event list, a node representing the arriving customer is placed on the shortest of the queues representing the four lines. If that customer is the only one on his or her queue, a node representing his or her departure is also placed on the event list, since he or she is at the front of his or her queue. At the same time, the next input line is read and an arrival node representing the next customer to arrive is placed on the event list. Thus there will always be an arrival node on the event list (as long as the input is not exhausted, at which point no more customers arrive), because as soon as one arrival node is removed from the event list, another is added to it.

When a departure node is removed from the event list, the node representing the departing customer is removed from the front of one of the four queues. At that point, the amount of time that the departing customer has spent in the bank is computed and added to a total. At the end of the simulation, this total will be divided by the number of customers to yield the average time spent by a customer. After a customer node has been deleted from the front of its queue, the next customer on the queue (if any) becomes the one being serviced by that teller and a departure node for that next customer is added to the event list.

This process continues until the event list is empty, at which point the average time is computed and printed. Note that the event list itself does not mirror any part of the real-world situation. It is used as part of the program to control the entire process. A simulation such as this one, which proceeds by changing the simulated situation in response to the occurrence of one of several events, is called an ***event-driven simulation***.

We now examine the data structures that are necessary for this program. The nodes on the queues represent customers and therefore must contain fields representing the arrival time and the transaction duration, in addition to a *next* field to link the nodes in a list. The nodes on the event list represent events and therefore must contain the time that the event occurs, the type of the event, and any other information associated with that event, as well as a *next* field. Thus it would seem that either a variant record or two separate node pools are needed for the two different types of node. Using a variant record would entail setting and checking the tag field before inserting or using a node. Two different types of node would entail two *getnode* and *freenode* routines and two sets of list manipulation routines. To avoid this cumbersome set of duplicate routines, let us try to use a single type of node for both events and customers.

We can declare such a pool of nodes as follows:

```
const numnodes = 500;
type  nodeptr = 0..numnodes;
      nodeinfo = record
                     time: integer;
                     duration: integer;
                     ntype: 0..4
                 end;
```

```
        nodetype = record
                    info: nodeinfo;
                    next: nodeptr
                end;
var   node: array[1..numnodes] of nodetype;
```

For a customer, *time* is the customer's arrival time and *duration* is the transaction's duration. *ntype* is unused in a customer node. *next* is used as a pointer to link the queue together. For an event node, *time* is used to hold the time of the event's occurrence; *duration* is used for the transaction duration of the arriving customer in an arrival node and is unused in a departure node. *ntype* is an integer between zero and four, depending on whether the event is an arrival (*ntype* = 0) or a departure from line 1, 2, 3, or 4 (*ntype* = 1, 2, 3, or 4). *next* holds a pointer linking the event list together.

The four queues are declared as an array by the declaration

```
type queue = record
                front: nodeptr;
                rear:  nodeptr;
                num:   integer
             end;
var  q: array[1..4] of queue;
```

The *num* field of a queue contains the number of customers on that queue. The variable *evlist: nodeptr* points to the front of the event list. The variable *tottime: integer* is used to keep track of the total time spent by all customers, and *count: integer* keeps count of the number of customers that have passed through the bank. An auxiliary variable *auxinfo: nodeinfo* is used to store temporarily the information portion of a node.

The main routine declares all the global variables mentioned, initial-izes all lists and queues, and repeatedly removes the next node from the event list to drive the simulation until the event list is empty. It calls on the procedure *place(evlist, auxinfo)* to insert a node whose information is given by *auxinfo* in its proper place in the event list. The event list is ordered by increasing value of the *time* field. The main routine also calls on procedure *popsub(evlist, auxinfo)* to remove the first node from the event list and place its information in *auxinfo*. This procedure is equivalent to the function *pop*. However, a standard Pascal function may not return an array or a record variable such as *auxinfo*. For this reason, we use a procedure *popsub*. These routines must, of course, be suitably modified from the examples given in the preceding section to handle this particular type of node. Note that *evlist*, *place*, and *popsub* are merely a particular implementation of an ascending priority queue and the operations *pqinsert* and *pqmindelete*. A more efficient representation of a priority queue (such as we present in Sections 7.3 and 8.3) would allow the program to operate somewhat more efficiently.

The main program also calls on procedures *arrive* and *depart*, which effect the changes in the event list and the queues caused by an arrival and a departure. Specifically, procedure *arrive(atime, dur)* reflects the arrival of a customer at time *atime* with a transaction of duration *dur*, and procedure *depart(qindx, dtime)* reflects the departure of the first customer from queue *q[qindx]* at time *dtime*. The coding of these routines will be given shortly.

```
program bank(input, output);
const numnodes = 500;
type nodeptr    = 0..numnodes;
     nodeinfo   = record
                      time, duration: integer;
                      ntype: 0..4
                  end;
     nodetype  = record
                      info: nodeinfo;
                      next: nodeptr
                  end;
     queue = record
                 front, rear: nodeptr;
                 num: integer
             end;
var   node: array[1..numnodes] of nodetype;
      qindx: 1..4;
      q: array[1..4] of queue;
      evlist, avail, i: nodeptr;
      tottime, count, atime, dtime, dur: integer;
      auxinfo: nodeinfo;
procedure place(var evlist: nodeptr; auxinfo: nodeinfo);
          { body of place goes here }
procedure popsub(var evlist: nodeptr; var auxinfo: nodeinfo);
          {body of popsub goes here}
procedure arrive(atime, dur: integer);
          { body of arrive goes here }
procedure depart(qindx, dtime: integer);
          { body of depart goes here }
begin {program bank}
   {initialization}
   evlist:= 0;
   count:= 0;
   tottime:= 0;
   avail:= 1;
   for i:= 1 to numnodes - 1
       do node[i].next:= i + 1;
   node[numnodes].next:= 0;
```

```
        for qindx:= 1 to 4
            do with q[qindx]
                do begin
                            num:= 0;
                            front:= 0;
                            rear:= 0
                end {with...do begin};
    {read the first input line and initialize the event list}
    with auxinfo
        do begin
                    readln(time, duration);
                    ntype:= 0; {an arrival}
                    place(evlist, auxinfo)
            end {with...do begin};
    {run the simulation as long as the event list is not empty}
    while evlist <> 0
        do begin
                    popsub(evlist, auxinfo);
                    {check if the next event is an arrival or departure}
                    if auxinfo.ntype = 0
                        then begin {an arrival}
                                    atime:= auxinfo.time;
                                    dur:= auxinfo.duration;
                                    arrive(atime, dur)
                            end {then begin}
                        else begin {a departure}
                                    qindx:= auxinfo.ntype;
                                    dtime:= auxinfo.time;
                                    depart(qindx, dtime)
                            end {else begin}
            end {while...do begin};
        writeln('average time is ', tottime/count)
end {program bank}.
```

The procedure *arrive(atime, dur)* modifies the queues and the event list to reflect a new arrival at time *atime* with a transaction of duration *dur*. It inserts a new customer node at the rear of the shortest queue by calling the procedure *insert(qq, auxinfo)*, which must be suitably modified to handle the type of node in this example and which also must increase the *num* field of the queue *qq* by 1. If the customer is the only one on his or her queue, a node representing his or her departure is added to the event list by calling on the procedure *place(evlist, auxinfo)*. Then, the next input line (if any) is read and an arrival node is placed on the event list to replace the arrival that has just been processed. If there is no more input, the procedure returns without adding a new arrival node and the program processes the remaining (departure) nodes on the event list.

```
procedure arrive (atime, dur: integer);
var small: integer;
    i, j: 1..4; {global variables: q, auxinfo, evlist}
procedure insert (var qq: queue; auxinfo: nodeinfo);
    {body of insert goes here}
begin {procedure arrive}
    j:= 1;
    small:= q[1].num;
    for i:= 2 to 4
        do if q[i].num < small
            then begin
                    small:= q[i].num;
                    j:= i
                end {then begin};
    { Queue j is the shortest.  Insert a new arrival node. }
    with auxinfo
        do begin
                time:= atime;
                duration:= dur;
                ntype:= j
            end {with...do begin};
    insert (q[j], auxinfo);
    { Check if this is the only node on the queue.  If it }
    {is, the customer's departure node must be placed on}
    {                   the event list.                   }
    if q[j].num = 1
        then begin
                auxinfo.time:= atime + dur;
                place (evlist, auxinfo)
            end {then begin};
    { If any input remains, read the next input line and  }
    {       place an arrival on the event list.           }
    if not eof (input)
        then with auxinfo
                do begin
                        readln (time, duration);
                        ntype:= 0;
                        place (evlist, auxinfo)
                    end {then with...do begin}
end {procedure arrive};
```

The routine *depart(qindx, dtime)* modifies the queue *q[qindx]* and the event list to reflect the departure of the first customer on the queue at time *dtime*. The customer is removed from his or her queue by a call to *remove(qq, auxinfo)*, which must be suitably modified to handle the type of node in this example and must also decrement the queue's *num* field by 1. Note that *remove* must be coded as a procedure rather than as a function, since a Pascal function may not return a record. The departure node of the next customer on the queue (if any) replaces the departure node that has just been removed from the event list.

```
procedure depart(qindx, dtime: integer);
var p: nodeptr; {global variables: q, auxinfo, tottime, count,}
              {                    evlist                     }
procedure remove(var qq: queue; var auxinfo: nodeinfo);
       {body of remove goes here}
begin {procedure depart}
      remove(q[qindx],auxinfo);
      tottime:= tottime + (dtime - auxinfo.time);
      count:= count + 1;
      { if there are any more customers on the queue, }
      { place the departure of the next customer onto  }
      {the event list after computing its departure time}
      if q[qindx].num > 0
         then begin
                   p:= q[qindx].front;
                   with auxinfo
                       do begin
                              time:= dtime + node[p].info.duration;
                              ntype:= qindx
                          end {with...do begin};
                   place(evlist, auxinfo)
              end {then begin}
      end {procedure depart};
```

Simulation programs are rich in their use of list structures. The reader is urged to explore the use of Pascal for simulation and the use of special-purpose simulation languages.

EXERCISES

1. In the bank simulation program of the text, a departure node on the event list represents the same customer as the first node on a customer queue. Is it possible to use a single node for a customer currently being serviced? Rewrite the program of the text so that only a single node is used. Is there any advantage to using two nodes?

2. The program in the text uses the same type of node for both customer and event

nodes. Rewrite the program using two different types of nodes for these two purposes. Does this save space?

3. Revise the bank simulation program of the text to determine the average length of the four lines.

4. Modify the bank simulation program to compute the standard deviation of the time spent by a customer in the bank. Write another program which simulates a single line for all four tellers, with the customer at the head of the single line going to the next available teller. Compare the means and standard deviations of the two methods.

5. Modify the bank simulation program so that whenever the length of one line exceeds the length of another by more than two, the last customer on the longest line moves to the rear of the shortest.

6. Write a Pascal program to simulate a simple computer system as follows. Each user has a unique ID and wishes to perform a number of transactions on the computer. However, only one transaction may be processed by the computer at any given moment. Each input line represents a single user and contains the user's ID, followed by a starting time, followed by a series of integers representing the duration of each of his or her transactions. The input is sorted by increasing starting time, and all times and durations are in seconds. Assume that a user does not request time for a transaction until that user's previous transaction is complete and that the computer accepts transactions on a first-come, first-served basis. The program should simulate the system and print a message containing the user ID and the time whenever a transaction begins and ends. At the end of the simulation it should print the average waiting time for a transaction. (The waiting time is the amount of time between the time that the transaction was requested and the time it was started.)

7. What parts of the bank simulation program would have to be modified if the priority queue of events were implemented as an array or as an unordered list? How would they be modified?

8. Many simulations do not simulate events given by input data, but rather generate events according to some probability distribution. The following exercises illustrate how. Most computer installations have a random number generating function $rand(x)$. (The name and parameters of the function vary from installation to installation. $rand$ is used as an example only.) x is initialized to a value called a *seed*. The statement $x := rand(x)$ resets the value of the variable x to a random uniform real number between 0 and 1. By this we mean that if the statement is executed a sufficient number of times and any two equal-length intervals between 0 and 1 are chosen, approximately as many of the successive values of x fall into one interval as into the other. Thus the probability of a value of x falling in an interval of length $l <= 1$ equals l. Find out the name of the random number generating function at your installation and verify that the above is true.

Given a random number generator $rand$, consider the following statements:

$$x := rand(x);$$
$$y := (b - a) * x + a$$

Show that, given any two equal-sized intervals within the interval from a to b, if the statements are repeated sufficiently often, an approximately equal number of successive values of y fall into each of the two intervals. Show that if a and b are integers, the successive values of y truncated to an integer equal each integer between a and $b - 1$ an approximately equal number of times. The variable y is said to be a *uniformly distributed random variable*. What is the average of the values of y in terms of a and b?

Rewrite the bank simulation of the text assuming that the transaction duration is uniformly distributed between 1 and 15. Each input line represents an arriving customer and contains only the time of his or her arrival. Upon reading an input line, generate a transaction duration for that customer by computing the next value according to the method just outlined.

9. The successive values of y that are generated by the following statements are said to be *normally distributed*. (Actually, they are approximately normally distributed, but the approximation is close enough.)

```
var x: array[1..15] of real;
    sum, y, s, m: real;
    i: integer;
begin
    {statements initializing the values of s, m and}
    {            the array x go here            }
    repeat
      sum:= 0;
      for i:= 1 to 15
          do begin
                  x[i]:= rand(x[i]);
                  sum:= sum + x[i]
          end {for...do begin};
      y:= s*(sum-7.5)/sqrt(1.25) + m;
              {statements that use the value of y go here}
      until {a terminating condition goes here}
end;
```

Verify that the average of the values of y (the mean of the distribution) equals m and that the standard deviation equals s.

A certain factory produces items according to the following process: an item must be assembled and polished. Assembly time is uniformly distributed between 100 and 300 seconds and polishing time is normally distributed with a mean of 20 seconds and a standard deviation of 7 seconds (but values below five are discarded). After an item is assembled, a polishing machine must be used and a worker cannot begin assembling the next item until the item just assembled has been polished. There are 10 workers but only one polishing machine. If the machine is not available, workers who have finished assembling their items must wait for it. Compute the average waiting time per item by means of a simulation. Do the same under the assumption of two and three polishing machines.

4. OTHER LIST STRUCTURES

Although a linked linear list is a rather useful data structure, it has several shortcomings. In this section we shall present other methods of organizing a list and show how they can be used to overcome these shortcomings.

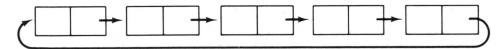

Figure 4.4.1 A circular list.

Circular Lists

One of the shortcomings of linear lists is that given a pointer *p* to a node in such a list, we cannot reach any of the nodes that precede *node*(*p*). If a list is traversed, the original pointer to the beginning of the list must be preserved in order to be able to reference the list again.

Suppose a small change is made to the structure of a linear list so that the *next* field in the last node contains a pointer back to the first node rather than the nil pointer. Such a list is called a *circular list* and is illustrated in Figure 4.4.1. From any point in such a list it is possible to reach any other point in the list. If we begin at a given node and traverse the entire list, we ultimately end up at the starting point. Note that a circular list does not have a natural "first" or "last" node. We must, therefore, establish a first and last node by convention. One useful convention is to let the external pointer to the circular list point to the last node, and to allow the following node to be the first node, as illustrated in Figure 4.4.2. We also establish the convention that a nil pointer represents an empty circular list.

The Stack as a Circular List

A circular list can be used to represent a stack or a queue. Let *stack* be a pointer to the last node of a circular list, and let us adopt the convention that the first node is the top of the stack. The following is a Pascal procedure to push an integer *x* onto the stack, assuming a set of *node*s and an auxiliary routine *getnode* as presented in previous sections. The *push* procedure calls on the function *empty*, which tests whether its parameter is 0.

Figure 4.4.2 The first and last nodes of a circular list.

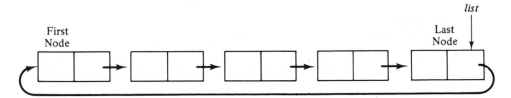

```
procedure push(var stack: nodeptr; x: integer);
var p: nodeptr;
begin
    p:= getnode;
    node[p].info:= x;
    if empty(stack)
       then stack:= p
       else node[p].next:= node[stack].next;
    node[stack].next:= p
end {procedure push};
```

Note that the *push* procedure is slightly more complex for circular lists than
it is for linear lists.

The Pascal *pop* function for a stack implemented as a circular list is
as follows. It calls the procedure *freenode* introduced earlier.

```
function pop(var stack: nodeptr): integer;
var p: nodeptr;
begin
    if empty(stack)
       then error('stack underflow')
       else begin
               p:= node[stack].next;
               pop:= node[p].info;
               if p = stack
                  then { only one node on the stack }
                      stack:= 0
                  else node[stack].next:= node[p].next;
               freenode(p)
            end {else begin}
end {function pop};
```

The Queue as a Circular List

It is easier to represent a queue as a circular list than as a linear list.
As a linear list, a queue is specified by two pointers, one to the front of the
list and the other to its rear. However, by using a circular list, a queue may
be specified by a single pointer q to that list. *node[q]* is the rear of the queue
and the following node is its front. The routine *remove(q)* is identical to
pop(stack) except that all references to *stack* are replaced by q. The Pascal
routine *insert* may be coded as follows:

```
procedure insert(var q: nodeptr; x: integer);
var p: nodeptr;
```

```
begin
    p:= getnode;
    node[p].info:= x;
    if empty(q)
        then q:= p
        else node[p].next:= node[q].next;
    node[q].next:= p;
    q:= p
end { procedure insert };
```

Note that this is equivalent to the code

```
push (q, x);
q:= node[q].next
```

That is, to insert an element into the rear of a circular queue, the element is inserted into the front of the queue and the queue pointer is then advanced one element, so that the new element becomes the rear.

Primitive Operations on Circular Lists

The routine *insafter(p: nodeptr; x: integer)* for a circular list, which inserts a node containing x after *node[p]*, is identical to the routine for linear lists as presented in Section 2. Let us now consider the routine *delafter (p: nodeptr; x: integer)*, which deletes the node following *node[p]* and stores its contents in x. Looking at the corresponding routine for linear lists as presented in Section 2, we note one additional consideration in the case of a circular list. Suppose that p points to the only node in the list. In a linear list, *next(p)* is nil in that case, making the deletion invalid. In the case of a circular list, however, *next(p)* points to *node(p)*, so that *node(p)* follows itself. The question is whether or not it is desirable to delete *node(p)* from the list in this case. It is unlikely that we would want to do so, since the operation *delafter* is usually invoked when pointers to each of two nodes are given, one immediately following another and it is desired to delete the second. *delafter* for circular lists is implemented as follows:

```
procedure delafter(p: nodeptr; var x: integer);
var q: nodeptr;
begin
    if p = 0
        then { an empty list }
            error('void deletion')
        else if p = node[p].next
                then { the list contains only a single node }
                    error('void deletion')
```

```
            else begin
                  q:= node[p].next;
                  x:= node[q].info;
                  node[p].next:= node[q].next;
                  freenode (q)
            end {else begin}
      end {procedure delafter};
```

Note, however, that these routines cannot be used to insert a node following the last node in a circular list or to delete the last node of a circular list. In both cases, the external pointer to the list must be modified to point to the new last node. The routines can be modified to accept *list* as an additional parameter and to change its value when necessary. An alternative is to write separate routines *insend* and *deletelast* for these cases. (*insend* is identical to the *insert* operation for a queue implemented as a circular list.) The calling routine would be responsible for determining which routine to call. We leave the exploration of these possibilities to the reader.

It is also easier to free an entire circular list than to free a linear list. In the case of a linear list, the entire list must be traversed, as one node at a time is returned to the available list. For a circular list, we can write a routine *freelist*, which effectively frees an entire list:

```
      procedure freelist(var list: nodeptr);
      var p: nodeptr;
      begin
            p:= node[list].next;
            node[list].next:= avail;
            avail:= p;
            list:= 0
      end {procedure freelist};
```

Similarly, we may write a routine *concat(list1, list2)*, which concatenates two lists—that is, it appends the circular list pointed to by *list2* to the end of the circular list pointed to by *list1*:

```
      procedure concat(var list1: nodeptr; list2: nodeptr);
      var p: nodeptr;
      begin
         if list1 = 0
            then list1:= list2
            else if list2 <> 0
               then begin
                     p:= node[list1].next;
                     node[list1].next:= node[list2].next;
                     node[list2].next:= p;
                     list1:= list2
               end {then begin}
      end {procedure concat};
```

The Josephus Problem

Let us consider a problem that can be solved in a straightforward manner by using a circular list. The problem is known as the Josephus problem and postulates a group of soldiers surrounded by an overwhelming enemy force. There is no hope for victory without reinforcements, but there is only a single horse available for escape. The soldiers agree to a pact to determine which of them is to escape and summon help. They form a circle and a number n is picked from a hat. One of their names is also picked from a hat. Beginning with the soldier whose name is picked, they begin to count clockwise around the circle. When the count reaches n, that soldier is removed from the circle, and the count begins again with the next man. The process continues so that each time the count reaches n, a man is removed from the circle. Once a soldier is removed from the circle, of course, he is no longer counted. The last soldier remaining is to take the horse and escape. The problem is: Given a number n, the ordering of the men in the circle, and the man from whom the count begins, determine the order in which men are eliminated from the circle and which man escapes.

The input to the program is the number n and a list of names that is the clockwise ordering of the men in the circle, beginning with the man from whom the count is to start. The last input line contains the string '*end*', indicating the end of the input. The program should print the names of the men in the order that they are eliminated and the name of the man who escapes.

For example, suppose that n equals 3 and there are five men named A, B, C, D, and E. We count three men, starting at A, so that C is eliminated first. We then begin at D and count D, E, and back to A, so that A is eliminated next. Then we count B, D, and E (C has already been eliminated) and finally B, D, and B, so that D is the man who escapes.

Clearly, a circular list in which each node represents one man is a natural data structure to use in solving this problem. It is possible to reach any node from any other by counting around the circle. To represent the removal of a man from a circle, his node is deleted from the circular list. Finally, when only one node remains on the list, the result is determined.

An outline of the program might be the following:

```
read(n);
read(name);
while name is not 'end'
      do begin
                  insert name on the circular list;
                  read(name)
          end {while...do begin};
while there is more than one node on the list
      do begin
                  count through n - 1 nodes on the list;
```

```
                    print the name in the nth node;
                    delete the nth node
                end {while...do begin};
            print the name of the only node on the list
```

We will assume that a set of nodes has been declared in a main program by

```
const numnodes = 500;
type  nametype = packed array[1..30] of char;
      nodeptr  = 0..numnodes;
      nodetype = record
                     info: nametype;
                     next: nodeptr
                 end;
var   node: array[1..numnodes] of nodetype;
```

and that an available list has been initialized. We also assume at least one name in the input. The program uses the routine *insert*, *delafter*, and *freenode*. We also assume the existence of a procedure *readname(var name: nametype)*, which reads a name from the input.

```
procedure josephus;
const endname = 'end';
var   name: nametype;
      n, i: integer;
      list: nodeptr;
begin
    read(n);
    list:= 0;
    { read the names, placing each }
    {    at the rear of the list       }
    readname(name);
    while name <> endname
        do begin
                insert(list, name);
                readname(name)
           end {while...do begin};
    { continue counting as long as more }
    { than one node remains on the list }
    while list <> node[list].next
        do begin
                for i:= 1 to n-1
                    do list:= node[list].next;
                { node[list].next points }
                {      to the nth node      }
                delafter(list,name);
                writeln(name)
```

        end   {*while...do begin*};
      {*print the only name on the* }
      {   *list and free its node*   }
      writeln('the man who escapes is: ', node[list].info);
      freenode(list)
    end {*procedure josephus*};

Header Nodes

Suppose that we wish to traverse a circular list. This can be done by repeatedly executing $p := node[p].next$, where p is initially a pointer to the beginning of the list. However, since the list is circular, we will not know when the entire list has been traversed unless another pointer *list* points to the first node and a test is made for the condition $p - list$.

An alternative method is to place a header node as the first node of a circular list. This list header may be recognized by a special value in its *info* field, which cannot be the valid contents of a list node in the context of the problem, or it may contain a flag marking it as a header. The list can then be traversed using a single pointer, with the traversal halting when the header node is reached. The external pointer to the list is to its header node, as illustrated in Figure 4.4.3. This means that a node cannot easily be added onto the rear of such a circular list, as could be done when the external pointer was to the last node of the list. Of course, it is possible to keep a pointer to the last node of a circular list even when a header node is being used.

If a stationary external pointer to a circular list is present in addition to the pointer used for traversal, the header node need not contain a special code but can be used in much the same way as a header node of a linear list, to contain global information about the list. The end of a traversal would be signaled by the equality of the traversing pointer and the external stationary pointer.

Figure 4.4.3 A circular list with a header node.

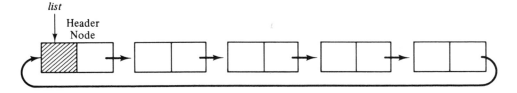

Addition of Long Positive Integers Using
Circular Lists

We now present an example of an application that uses circular lists with header nodes. The hardware of most computers allows integers of only a specific maximum length. Suppose that we wish to represent positive integers of arbitrary length and to write a function that returns the sum of two such integers. To add two integers, their digits are traversed from right to left, and corresponding digits and a possible carry from the previous digits' sum are added. This suggests representing long integers by storing their digits from right to left in a list so that the first node on the list contains the least significant digit (rightmost) and the last node contains the most significant (leftmost). However, to save space, we will keep five digits in each node. (Some implementations of Pascal may not allow integers to be as large as 99999. In such implementations, fewer digits must be kept in each node.) We may declare the set of nodes by

```
const numnodes = 500;
type  nodeptr = 0..numnodes;
        nodetype=record
                    info: -1..99999;
                    next: nodeptr
                end;
var node: array[1..numnodes] of nodetype;
```

Since we wish to traverse the lists during the addition but wish to eventually restore the list pointers to their original values, we use circular lists with headers. The header node is distinguished by an *info* value of -1. For example, the integer 459763497210698463 is represented by the list illustrated in Figure 4.4.4.

Now let us write a function *addint* which accepts pointers to two such lists representing integers, creates a list representing the sum of the integers, and returns a pointer to the sum list. Both lists are traversed in parallel and five digits are added at a time. If the sum of two five-digit numbers is x, the low-order five digits of x can be extracted by the expression $x \bmod 100000$, which yields the remainder of x on division by 100000. The carry can be computed by the expression $x \dv 100000$. When the end of

Figure 4.4.4 A large integer as a circular list.

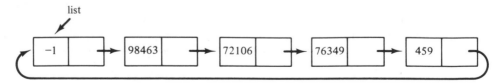

one list is reached, the carry is propagated to the remaining digits of the other list. The function follows and uses the routines *getnode* and *insafter*.

```
function addint(p, q: nodeptr): nodeptr;
const hunthou = 100000;
var    s, pp, qq, r: nodeptr;
       carry: 0..1;
       number: 0..99999;
       total: integer;
begin
       { set pp and qq to the nodes following the headers }
       pp:= node[p].next;
       qq:= node[q].next;
       { set up a header node for the sum }
       s:= getnode;
       node[s].info:= -1;
       node[s].next:= s;
       { initially there is no carry }
       carry:= 0;
       while (node[pp].info <> -1) and (node[qq].info <> -1)
            do begin {traverse the two lists in parallel}
                   { add the info of the two nodes and previous carry }
                   total:= node[pp].info + node[qq].info + carry;
                   { Determine the low-order five digits of }
                   {      the sum. Insert into the list.     }
                   number:= total mod hunthou;
                   insafter(s, number);
                   { determine whether there is a carry }
                   carry:= total div hunthou;
                   s:= node[s].next;    { advance the pointers }
                   pp:= node[pp].next;
                   qq:= node[qq].next
                end {while...do begin};
       { at this point, there may be nodes left in one of the }
       {                   two input lists                    }
       if node[pp].info <> -1
         then r:= pp
         else r:= qq;
       while node[r].info <> -1
            do begin {traverse the remainder of the list}
                   total:= node[r].info + carry;
                   number:= total mod hunthou;
                   insafter(s, number);
                   carry:= total div hunthou;
```

```
                       s:= node[s].next;
                       r:= node[r].next
                  end {while...do begin};
         { check if there is an extra carry from the first five }
         {                      digits                           }
         if carry = 1
            then begin
                       insafter (s, carry);
                       s:= node[s].next
                  end {then begin};
         { s points to the last node in the sum.  next[s] points }
         {            to the header of the sum list.             }
         addint:= node[s].next
     end {function addint};
```

Doubly Linked Lists

Although a circularly linked list has advantages over a linear list, it still has several drawbacks. One cannot traverse such a list backward, nor can a node be deleted from a circularly linked list given only a pointer to that node. In cases where these facilities are required, the appropriate data structure is a ***doubly linked list***. Each node in such a list contains two pointers, one to its predecessor and another to its successor. In fact, in the context of doubly linked lists, the terms "predecessor" and "successor" are meaningless, since the list is entirely symmetric. Doubly linked lists may be either linear or circular and may or may not contain a header node, as illustrated in Figure 4.4.5.

We may consider the nodes on a doubly linked list to consist of three fields: an *info* field, which contains the information stored in the node, and *left* and *right* fields, which contain pointers to the nodes on either side. We may declare a set of such nodes by

```
const numnodes = 500;
type  nodeptr= 0..numnodes;
      nodetype= record
                     info: integer;
                     left, right: nodeptr
                end;
var   node: array[1..numnodes] of nodetype;
```

Note that the available list for such a set of nodes need not be doubly linked, since it is not traversed bidirectionally. The available list may be linked together by using either the *left* or *right* pointer. Of course, appropriate *getnode* and *freenode* routines must be written.

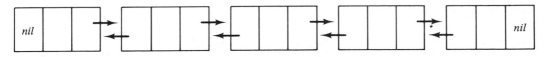

(a) A linear doubly linked list.

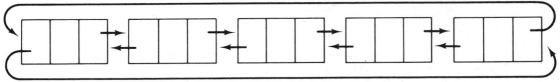

(b) A circular doubly linked list without a header.

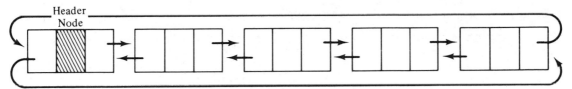

(c) A circular doubly linked list with a header.

Figure 4.4.5   Doubly linked lists.

We now present routines to operate on doubly linked circular lists. A convenient property of such lists is that if p is a pointer to any node in a doubly linked list, then letting $left(p)$ be an abbreviation for $node[p].left$ and $right(p)$ an abbreviation for $node[p].right$, we have

$$left(right(p)) = p = right(left(p))$$

One operation that can be performed on doubly linked lists but not on ordinary linked lists is to delete a given node. The following Pascal routine deletes the node pointed to by p from a doubly linked list and stores its contents in x.

```
procedure delete(p: nodeptr; var x: integer);
var r, q: nodeptr;
begin
    if p = 0
        then error('void deletion')
        else begin
                x:= node[p].info;
                q:= node[p].left;
                r:= node[p].right;
                node[q].right:= r;
```

```
            node[r].left:= q;
            freenode(p)
        end {else begin}
    end { procedure delete};
```

The routine *insertright* inserts a node with information field x to the right of *node[p]* in a doubly linked list.

```
procedure insertright(p: nodeptr; x: integer);
var r, q: nodeptr;
begin
    if p = 0
        then error('void insertion')
        else begin
            q:= getnode;
            node[q].info:= x;
            r:= node[p].right;
            node[r].left:= q;
            node[q].right:= r;
            node[q].left:= p;
            node[p].right:= q
        end {else begin}
    end { procedure insertright};
```

A routine *insertleft* to insert a node with information field x to the left of *node[p]* in a doubly linked list is similar and is left as an exercise for the reader.

When space efficiency is a consideration, a program may not be able to afford the overhead of two pointers for each element of a list. There are several techniques for compressing the left and right pointers of a node into a single field. For example, a single pointer field *ptr* in each node can contain the sum of pointers to its left and right neighbors. (Here, we are assuming that pointers are represented in such a way that arithmetic can be performed on them readily. For example, pointers represented by array indexes in Pascal can be added and subtracted.) Given two external pointers, p and q, to two adjacent nodes such that $p = left(q)$, $right(q)$ can be computed as $ptr(q) - p$ and $left(p)$ can be computed as $ptr(p) - q$. Given p and q, it is possible to delete either node and reset its pointer to the preceding or succeeding node. It is also possible to insert a node to the left of *node(p)* or to the right of *node(q)* or to insert a node between *node(p)* and *node(q)* and reset either p or q to the newly inserted node. In using such a scheme, it is crucial always to maintain two external pointers to two adjacent nodes in the list.

Addition of Long Integers Using Doubly Linked Lists

As an illustration of the use of doubly linked lists, let us consider extending the implementation of long integers to include negative as well as positive integers. The header node of a circular list representing a long integer will contain an indication of whether the integer is positive or negative. When we wanted to add two positive integers, we traversed the integers from the least significant digit to the most significant. However, to add a positive and a negative integer, the smaller absolute value must be subtracted from the larger absolute value, and the result must be given the sign of the integer with the larger absolute value. Thus some method is needed for testing which of two integers represented as circular lists has the larger absolute value.

The first criterion that may be used to identify the integer with the larger absolute value is the length of the integers (assuming that they do not contain leading zeros). Thus we can count the number of nodes in each list, and the list that has more nodes represents the integer with the larger absolute value. However, this count involves an extra traversal of the list. Instead of counting the number of nodes, the count could be kept as part of the header node and referred to as needed.

However, if both lists have the same number of nodes, it is necessary to traverse the lists from the most significant digit to the least significant to determine which number is larger. Note that this traversal is in the opposite direction of the traversal that must be used in actually adding two integers. For this reason, doubly linked lists are used to represent such integers.

Consider the format of the header node. In addition to a right and left pointer, the header must contain the length of the list and an indication of whether the number is positive or negative. These two pieces of information can be combined into a single integer whose absolute value is the length of the list and whose sign is the sign of the number being represented. However, in doing so, the ability to identify the header node by examining the sign of its *info* field is destroyed. When a positive integer was represented as a singly linked circular list, an *info* field of -1 indicated a header node. Under the new representation, however, a header node may contain an *info* field such as 5, which is a valid *info* field for any other node in the list.

There are several ways to remedy this problem. One way is to add another field to each node to indicate whether or not it is a header node. Such a field could be a boolean with the value *true* if the node is a header and *false* if it is not. This means, of course, that each node would require more space. Alternatively, the count could be eliminated from the header node, and an *info* field of -1 would indicate a positive number and -2 a negative number. A header node could then be identified by its negative *info* field. However, this would increase the time needed to compare two numbers, since it would be necessary to count the number of nodes in each list.

(a) A sample node.

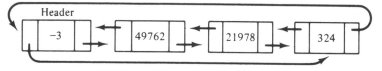

(b) The integer −3242197849762.

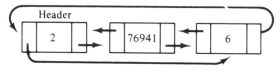

(c) The integer 676941.

(d) The integer 0.

Figure 4.4.6 Integers as doubly linked lists.

Such space/time trade-offs are very common in computing, and a decision must be made as to which efficiency should be sacrificed and which retained. In our case, we choose yet a third option, which is to retain an external pointer to the list header. A pointer p can be identified as pointing to a header if it is equal to the original external pointer; otherwise, the node to which p points is not a header.

Figure 4.4.6 indicates a sample node and the representation of three integers as doubly linked lists. Note that the least significant digits are to the right of the header and that the counts in the header nodes do not include the header node itself.

Using the representation just described, we now present a function *compabs*, which compares the absolute value of two integers represented as doubly linked lists. Its two parameters are pointers to the list headers, and it returns a value indicating whether the first has an absolute value less than, greater than, or equal to the second. The type of this value may be defined in the main program as

```
                  type comptype= (lessthan, equalto, greaterthan);

          function compabs(p, q: nodeptr): comptype;
          var r, s: nodeptr;
              equal: boolean;
          begin { function compabs }
              { compare the counts }
              if abs(node[p].info) > abs(node[q].info)
                then compabs:= greaterthan
                else if abs(node[p].info) < abs(node[q].info)
                      then compabs:= lessthan
                      else { they are of equal length }
                          begin
                              r:= node[p].left;
                              s:= node[q].left;
                              equal:= true;
              { traverse the list from the most significant digits }
                              while (r <> p) and (equal)
                                  do begin
                                      if node[r].info > node[s].info
                                        then begin
                                              equal:= false;
                                              compabs:= greaterthan
                                            end {then begin};
                                      if node[r].info < node[s].info
                                        then begin
                                              equal:= false;
                                              compabs:= lessthan
                                            end {then begin};
                                      if node[r].info = node[s].info
                                        then begin
                                              r:= node[r].left;
                                              s:= node[s].left
                                            end {then begin}
                                  end {while...do begin};
                              if equal
                                then compabs:= equalto
                          end {else begin}
          end {function compabs};
```

We are now ready to write a function *addiff*, which accepts two pointers to lists representing long integers of opposite sign, where the absolute value of the first is not less than that of the second, and which returns a pointer to a list representing the sum of the integers. We must, of course, be careful to eliminate leading zeros from the sum. To do this, we keep a pointer *zeroptr* to the first node of a consecutive set of leading zero nodes and a boolean flag *zeroflag*, which is *true* if and only if the last node of the sum generated so far is zero.

In this function, *p* points to the number with the larger absolute value and *q* points to the number with the smaller absolute value. The values of these variables do not change. Auxiliary variables *pptr* and *qptr* are used to traverse the lists. The sum is formed in a list pointed to by the variable *r*.

```
function addiff(p, q: nodeptr): nodeptr;
const hunthou = 100000;
var   r, s, zeroptr, pptr, qptr: nodeptr;
      zeroflag: boolean;
      borrow: 0..1;
      diff, count: integer;
begin
      { initialize variables }
      count:= 0;
      borrow:= 0;
      zeroflag:= false;
      { generate a header node for the sum }
      r:= getnode;
      node[r].left:= r;
      node[r].right:= r;
      { traverse the two lists }
      pptr:= node[p].right;
      qptr:= node[q].right;
      while qptr <> q
            do begin
                  diff:= node[pptr].info - borrow - node[qptr].info;
                  if diff >= 0
                    then borrow:= 0
                    else begin
                            diff:= diff + hunthou;
                            borrow:= 1
                         end {else begin};
                  { generate a new node and insert it }
                  {    to the left of header in sum      }
                  insertleft(r, diff);
                  count:= count + 1;
                  { test for zero node }
                  if diff = 0
                    then begin
```

```
                                if not zeroflag
                                    then zeroptr:= node[r].left;
                                zeroflag:= true
                            end {then begin}
                        else zeroflag:= false;
                    pptr:= node[pptr].right;
                    qptr:= node[qptr].right
                end {while...do begin};
        { traverse the remainder of the p list }
        while p <> pptr
            do begin
                    diff:= node[pptr].info - borrow;
                if diff >= 0
                    then borrow:= 0
                    else begin
                            diff:= diff + hunthou;
                            borrow:= 1
                        end {else begin};
                insertleft(r, diff);
                count:= count + 1;
                if diff = 0
                    then begin
                            if not zeroflag
                                then zeroptr:= node[r].left;
                            zeroflag:= true
                        end {then begin}
                    else zeroflag:= false;
                pptr:= node[pptr].right
            end {while...do begin};
        if zeroflag { then delete leading zeros }
            then while zeroptr <> r
                do begin
                        s:= zeroptr;
                        zeroptr:= node[zeroptr].right;
                        delete(s, diff);
                        count:= count - 1
                    end {while...do begin};
        { insert count and sign into the header }
        if node[p].info > 0
            then node[r].info:= count
            else node[r].info:= -count;
        addiff:= r
end {function addiff};
```

We can also write a function *addsame*, which adds two numbers with like signs. This is very similar to the function *addint* of the previous implementation except that it deals with a doubly linked list and must keep track of the number of nodes in the sum.

Using these routines, we can write a new version of *addint*, which adds two integers represented by doubly linked lists.

```
function addint(p, q: nodeptr): nodeptr;
type comptype = (lessthan, equalto, greaterthan);
{ definitions for compabs, addiff, and addsame go here }
begin
    { check if integers are of like sign }
    if node[p].info * node[q].info > 0
        then addint:= addsame(p, q)
        else { check which has a larger absolute value }
            if compabs(p, q) = greaterthan
                then addint:= addiff(p, q)
                else addint:= addiff(q, p)
end {function addint};
```

EXERCISES

1. Write an algorithm and a Pascal routine to perform each of the operations of Exercise 4.2.4 for circular lists. Which are more efficient on circular lists than on linear lists? Which are less efficient?

2. Rewrite the routine *place* of Section 2 to insert a new item in an ordered circular list.

3. Write a program to solve the Josephus problem by using an array rather than a circular list. Why is a circular list more efficient?

4. Consider the following variation of the Josephus problem. A group of people stand in a circle and each chooses a positive integer. One of their names and a positive integer n are chosen. Starting with the person whose name is chosen, they count around the circle clockwise and eliminate the nth person. The positive integer which that person chose is then used to continue the count. Each time that a person is eliminated, the number the person chose is used to determine the next person eliminated. For example, suppose that the five people are A, B, C, D, and E; they choose integers 3, 4, 6, 2, and 7, respectively; and the integer 2 is initially chosen. Then if we start from A, the order in which people are eliminated from the circle is B, A, E, C, leaving D as the last one in the circle.

   Write a program that reads a group of input lines. Each input line except the first and last contains a name and a positive integer chosen by that person. The order of the names in the data is the clockwise ordering of the people in the circle and the count is to start with the first name in the input. The first input line contains the number of people in the circle. The last input line contains only a single positive integer representing the initial count. The program prints the order in which the people are eliminated from the circle.

5. Write a Pascal function *multpos*(*p*, *q*) to multiply two long positive integers represented by singly linked circular lists.

6. Write a program to print the 100th Fibonacci number.

7. Write algorithms and Pascal routines to perform the operations of Exercise 4.2.4 for doubly linked circular lists. Which are more efficient on doubly linked than on singly linked lists? Which are less efficient?

8. Assume that a single pointer field in each node of a doubly linked list contains the sum of pointers to the node's predecessor and successor, as described in the text. Given pointers *p* and *q* to two adjacent nodes in such a list, write Pascal routines to insert a node to the right of *node*[*q*], to the left of *node*[*p*], and between *node*[*p*] and *node*[*q*], modifying *p* to point to the newly inserted node. Write an additional routine to delete *node*[*q*], resetting *q* to the node's successor.

9. Assume that *first* and *last* are external pointers to the first and last nodes of a doubly linked list represented as in Exercise 8. Write Pascal routines to implement the operations of Exercise 4.2.4 for such a list.

10. Write a routine *addsame* to add two long integers of the same sign represented by doubly linked lists.

11. Write a Pascal function *multint*(*p*, *q*) to multiply two long integers represented by doubly linked circular lists.

12. How can a polynomial in three variables (*x*, *y*, and *z*) be represented by a circular list? Each node should represent a term and should contain the powers of *x*, *y*, and *z* as well as the coefficient of that term. Write Pascal functions to do the following:

   (a) Add two such polynomials.
   (b) Multiply two such polynomials.
   (c) Take the partial derivative of such a polynomial with respect to any of its variables.
   (d) Evaluate such a polynomial for given values of *x*, *y*, and *z*.
   (e) Divide one such polynomial by another creating a quotient polynomial and a remainder polynomial.
   (f) Integrate such a polynomial with respect to any of its variables.
   (g) Print the representation of such a polynomial.
   (h) Given four such polynomials, $f(x, y, z)$, $g(x, y, z)$, $h(x, y, z)$, and $i(x, y, z)$, compute the polynomial $f(g(x, y, z), h(x, y, z), i(x, y, z))$.

5

PASCAL LIST PROCESSING

This chapter discusses the list processing facilities available in Pascal. Under these techniques, a pointer is the actual address of a portion of storage that can be dynamically allocated and freed. A list can grow and shrink dynamically without tying up valuable storage.

1. IMPLEMENTING LISTS USING DYNAMIC STORAGE

The Need for Dynamic Storage

As we have seen in Chapter 4, the notion of a pointer allows us to build and manipulate linked lists of various types. The concept of a pointer introduces the possibility of assembling a collection of building blocks, called nodes, into flexible structures. By altering the values of pointers, nodes can be attached, detached, and reassembled in patterns that grow and shrink as execution of a program progresses.

In Chapter 4, however, a fixed set of nodes represented by an array and its elements is established for use at the start of execution. A pointer to a node was represented by the relative position of the node within the array. The disadvantage of that approach is twofold. First, the number of nodes that are needed cannot be predicted at the time that a program is written. Usually, the data with which the program is executed determines the number of nodes necessary. Thus no matter how many elements the array of nodes contains, it is always possible that the program will be executed with input that requires a larger number.

The second disadvantage of the array approach is that whatever number of nodes are declared must remain allocated to the program throughout its execution. For example, if 500 nodes of a given type are declared, the amount of storage required for those 500 nodes is reserved for that purpose. If the program actually uses only 100, or even 10, nodes in its execution, the additional nodes are still reserved and their storage cannot be used for any other purpose.

The solution to this problem is to allow nodes that are *dynamic* rather than static. That is, when a node is needed, storage is reserved for it, and when it is no longer needed, the storage is released. Thus the storage for nodes that are no longer in use is available for another purpose. Also, no predefined limit on the number of nodes is established. As long as sufficient storage is available to the job as a whole, part of that storage can be reserved for use as a node.

Pointers in Pascal

The method of access to a node is through a pointer. In the array implementation of Chapter 4, a pointer is simply an index to the array that specifies which of a predefined set of nodes is being accessed. However, if dynamic storage allocation is being used, there is no predefined set of nodes, nor is there a predefined organization among the set of nodes. Therefore, when a portion of storage is reserved for use as a node (i.e., when a node is *allocated*), a method of accessing the node must simultaneously be created. That method of access is a pointer, which may be thought of as the address of the portion of storage allocated to the node.

In Pascal, the type of the node being accessed is part of the type of the pointer. Specifically, we may declare a pointer to an integer by

$$\textbf{var} \; \text{pi: } \uparrow\text{integer;}$$

and a pointer to a real number by

$$\textbf{var} \; \text{pr: } \uparrow\text{real;}$$

The values of *pi* and *pr* will both be addresses, but the value of *pi* must be the address of a portion of storage containing an integer, while the value of *pr* must be the address of a portion of storage containing a real number.

A new kind of variable can be referenced by using a pointer. Given the foregoing declarations of *pi* and *pr*, the constructs *pi*$\uparrow$ and *pr*$\uparrow$ are variables of type *integer* and *real*, respectively. The statement

$$\text{pi}\uparrow\text{:= 6}$$

is executed in two phases. First, the value of *pi* is used to locate the integer variable *pi*↑, and second, the value of that variable is set to 6. Similarly, the statement

$$\text{write (pi↑)}$$

first uses the value of *pi* to locate the integer variable *pi*↑, and then prints the value of that variable.

Note that the statements

$$\text{pi:= 6}$$

and

$$\text{write (pi)}$$

are illegal. *pi* is not an integer, but a pointer to an integer, so that it cannot be given an integer value nor can its value be printed. Its sole purpose is to provide access to the integer *pi*↑. *pi*↑ may be thought of as "the variable to which *pi* points."

Allocating and Freeing Dynamic Variables

Once a variable *p* has been declared as a pointer to a specific type of object, it must be possible to create dynamically an object of the specific type and assign its address to *p*. This may be done in Pascal by calling the standard procedure *new*. If *p* is a pointer to an object of type *t*, *new(p)* creates an object of type *t* and assigns its address to *p*. Thus given the declarations

```
var pi: ↑integer;
    pr: ↑real;
```

executing the statements

```
new(pi);
new(pr)
```

dynamically creates the integer variable *pi*↑ and the real variable *pr*↑.

As an example of the use of pointers and the procedure *new*, consider the following statements:

```
1    var p, q: ↑integer;
2        x: integer;
3    begin
4        new(p);
5        p↑: = 3;
6        q: = p;
7        writeln(p↑, q↑);
8        x: = 7;
9        q↑: = x;
```

```
10          writeln(p↑, q↑);
11          new(p);
12          p↑: = 5;
13          writeln(p↑, q↑)
14     end;
```

In line 4, an integer variable is created and its address is placed in p. Line 5 sets the value of that variable to 3. Line 6 sets q to the address of that variable. The assignment statement in line 6 is perfectly valid, since one pointer variable (q) is being assigned the value of another (p). Figure 5.1.1a illustrates the situation after line 6. Note that at this point, $p↑$ and $q↑$ refer to the same variable. Line 7 therefore prints the contents of this variable (which is 3) twice.

Line 8 sets the value of an *integer* variable, x, to 7. Line 9 changes the value of $q↑$ to the value of x. However, since p and q both point to the same variable, $p↑$ and $q↑$ both have values of 7. This is illustrated in Figure 5.1.1b. Line 10 therefore prints the number 7 twice.

Line 11 creates a new integer variable and places its address in p. The results are illustrated in Figure 5.1.1c. $p↑$ now refers to the newly

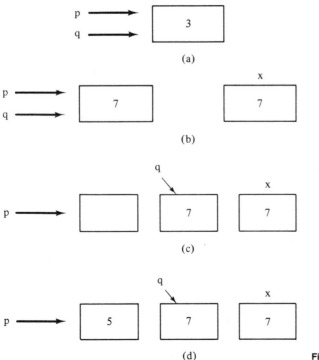

(a)

(b)

(c)

(d)

Figure 5.1.1

created integer variable, which has not yet been given a value. q has not been changed, so the value of $q\uparrow$ remains 7. Note that $p\uparrow$ does not refer to a single, specific variable. Its value changes as the value of p changes. Line 12 sets the value of this newly created variable to 5, as illustrated in Figure 5.1.1d, and line 13 prints the values 5 and 7.

The procedure *dispose* is used in Pascal to free storage of a dynamically allocated variable. The statement

dispose(p)

makes any future references to the variable $p\uparrow$ illegal (unless, of course, a new value is assigned to p by an assignment statement or by a call to *new*). In most Pascal implementations, calling *dispose*(p) makes the storage occupied by $p\uparrow$ available for reuse, if necessary.

To illustrate the use of the *dispose* procedure, consider the following statements:

```
1     new(p);
2     p↑:= 5;
3     new(q);
4     q↑:= 8;
5     dispose(p);
6     p:= q;
7     new(q);
8     q↑:= 6;
9     writeln(p↑, q↑)
```

The values 8 and 6 are printed. Figure 5.1.2a illustrates the situation after line 4, where $p\uparrow$ and $q\uparrow$ have both been allocated and given values. Figure 5.1.2b illustrates the effects of line 5, where the variable to which p points has been freed. Figure 5.1.2c illustrates line 6, where the value of p is changed to point to the variable $q\uparrow$. In line 7, the value of q is changed to point to a newly created variable which is given the value 6 in line 8 (Figure 5.1.2d).

Note that if procedure *new* is called twice in succession with the same parameter, as in

```
new(p);     p↑:= 3;
new(p);     p↑:= 7;
```

the first copy of $p\uparrow$ is lost since its address was not saved. Since the space allocated for these variables can be accessed only through a pointer, unless the pointer to the first variable is saved in another pointer, it will be lost. In fact, the storage cannot even be freed, because there is no way to reference it in a call to *dispose*. This is an example of a memory location that is allocated but cannot be referenced.

There is a special value that any pointer variable may have, denoted

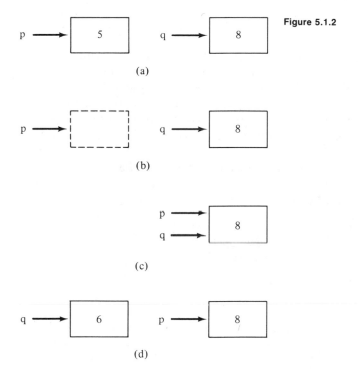

Figure 5.1.2

by *nil*. This pointer value does not reference a storage location but denotes the nil pointer, which does not point to anything. The value *nil* may be assigned to any pointer variable p, after which a reference to $p\uparrow$ is illegal. Note that *nil* is a reserved word in Pascal rather than a predefined identifier such as *true* or *maxint*.

We have noted that a call to *dispose(p)* makes a subsequent reference to $p\uparrow$ illegal. However, the actual effects of a call to *dispose* are not defined by the Pascal language—each implementation of Pascal is free to develop its own version of this procedure. In some Pascal implementations, *dispose* has no effect at all; in others, the storage for $p\uparrow$ is freed, but the value of p is left unchanged. This means that although a reference to $p\uparrow$ becomes illegal, there may be no way of detecting the illegality. The value of p is a valid address and the object at that address of the proper type may be used as the value of $p\uparrow$. p is called a *dangling pointer*. It is the programmer's responsibility never to use such a pointer in a program.

Still other Pascal implementations cause *dispose(p)* to set p to *nil*. In that case a subsequent reference to $p\uparrow$ would be detected as an error, since p no longer points to a valid object. The programmer should determine the effects of the *dispose* procedure in the Pascal implementation that he or she is using. (Some implementations of Pascal contain a different, nonstandard mechanism for freeing storage, the *mark* and *release* procedures, which are not discussed here.)

One other dangerous feature associated with pointers should be mentioned. If p and q are pointers with the same value, then the variables $p\uparrow$ and $q\uparrow$ are identical. Both $p\uparrow$ and $q\uparrow$ refer to the same object. Thus an assignment to $p\uparrow$ changes the value of $q\uparrow$, despite the fact that neither q nor $q\uparrow$ are explicitly mentioned. It is the programmer's responsibility to keep track of "which pointers are pointing where" and to recognize the occurrence of such implicit results.

Note that when a pointer variable is declared in Pascal, the type of the object to which it points must be specified. A single pointer variable may contain a pointer to only one type of object during a program's execution. For example, if we had declared

> **var** pi: ↑integer;
> pc: ↑char;

the statement

> pi:= pc

would be illegal, despite the fact that both *pi* and *pc* are pointers. The reason is that the types of *pi* and *pc* are not simply "pointer" but "pointer to an integer" and "pointer to a character," respectively. Since the two variables have different types, it is illegal to assign a value from one to the other.

Linked Lists Using Dynamic Variables

Now that we have the capability of dynamically allocating and freeing a variable, let us see how dynamic variables can be used to implement linked lists. Recall that a linked list consists of a set of nodes, each of which has two fields: an information field and a pointer to the next node in the list. In addition, there is an external pointer to the first node in the list. We will use pointer variables to implement list pointers. Thus we could define the type of a pointer and a node by

> **type** nodeptr = ↑nodetype;
> nodetype = **record**
>   info: integer;
>   next: nodeptr
>   **end**;

A node of such type is identical to the nodes of Section 4.2, except that the *next* field is a pointer (containing the address of the next node in the list) rather than an integer (containing the index within an array where the next node in the list is kept). Note that in the definition of a pointer type such as *nodeptr*, Pascal permits a reference to the type to which the pointer points (*nodetype*) before the type pointed to has been defined. This is because it is unnecessary to know the details of that type in order to implement a pointer to it. A pointer is, after all, an address. The storage requirements for an address are the same regardless of the object located at that address.

Let us employ the dynamic allocation features to implement linked lists. Instead of declaring an array to represent an aggregate collection of nodes, a node will be referenced through its pointer. Nodes will be allocated and freed as necessary, and the need for a declared collection of nodes is eliminated.

If we declare

var p: nodeptr;

an execution of the statement

p:= gctnodc

should place the address of an available node into *p*. We present the function *getnode*:

```
function getnode: nodeptr;
var p: nodeptr;
begin
    new(p);
    getnode:= p
end { function getnode };
```

Similarly, an execution of the statement

freenode(p)

should return the node whose address is at *p* to available storage. We present the routine *freenode*. *p* is declared as a variable parameter in order to have it reset to **nil** under those implementations in which *dispose* sets its argument to **nil**.

```
procedure freenode (var p: nodeptr);
begin
    dispose(p)
end { procedure freenode };
```

The programmer need not be concerned with managing available storage. There is no longer a need for the pointer *avail* (pointing to the first available node) because the system governs the allocating and freeing of nodes and the system keeps track of the first available node. Note also that there is no test in *getnode* for determining whether overflow has occurred. This is because such a condition will be detected during the execution of the *new* function and is system-dependent.

Since the routines *getnode* and *freenode* are so simple under this implementation, they are often replaced by the inline statements *new(p)* and *dispose(p)*.

The procedures *insafter(p, x)* and *delafter(p, x)* are presented next using the dynamic implementation of a linked list. Assume that *list* is a pointer variable which points to the first node of a list (if any) and is equal to **nil** in the case of an empty list.

```
procedure insafter(p: nodeptr; x: integer);
var q: nodeptr;
begin
    if p = nil
        then error('void insertion')
        else begin
                q:= getnode;
                q↑.info:= x;
                q↑.next:= p↑.next;
                p↑.next:= q
            end {else begin}
end { procedure insafter};

procedure delafter(p: nodeptr; var x: integer);
var q: nodeptr;
begin
    if p = nil
        then error('void deletion')
        else if p↑.next = nil
                then error('void deletion')
                else begin
                        q:= p↑.next;
                        x:= q↑.info;
                        p↑.next:= q↑.next;
                        freenode(q)
                    end {else begin}
end { procedure delafter};
```

Notice the striking similarity between the foregoing routines and those of the second half of Section 4.2. Both are implementations of the algorithms of the first half of that section. In fact, the only difference between the two versions is in the manner in which the list pointers are specified.

Stacks and queues can also be implemented using this new implementation of linked lists. We leave these as exercises for the reader.

List Operations Using the Dynamic Implementation

We now present several small examples to illustrate some features of list manipulation in Pascal. First, let us write a procedure *insend(list, x)* to insert the element x at the end of a list *list*.

```
procedure insend(var list: nodeptr; x: integer);
var p, q: nodeptr;
begin
        p:= getnode;
        p↑.info:= x;
        p↑.next:= nil;
        if list = nil
          then list:= p
          else begin
                      { search for the last node }
                      q:= list;
                      while q↑.next <> nil
                             do q:= q↑.next;
                      q↑.next:= p
                end {else begin}
end { procedure insend};
```

We now present a function *search(list, x)*, which returns a pointer to the first occurrence of x within the list *list* and the **nil** pointer if x does not occur in the list.

```
function search(list: nodeptr; x: integer): nodeptr;
var p: nodeptr;
    found: boolean;
begin
        p:= list;
        found:= false;
        while (p <> nil) and (not found)
               do if p↑.info = x
                      then found:= true
                      else p:= p↑.next;
        search:= p
end { function search};
```

The next routine deletes all nodes whose *info* field contains the value x.

```
procedure remvx(var list: nodeptr; x: integer);
var p, q: nodeptr;
    y: integer;
begin
    q:= nil;
    p:= list;
    while p <> nil
        do if p↑.info = x
            then begin
                    p:= p↑.next;
                    if q = nil
                        then { remove first node }
                             {      of the list    }
                            begin
                                freenode(list);
                                list:= p
                            end {then begin}
                        else delafter(q, y)
                end {then begin}
            else { advance to next node of list }
                begin
                    q:= p;
                    p:= p↑.next
                end {else begin}
end { procedure remvx};
```

Allocating and Freeing Variant Records

A node need not contain a simple item such as an integer or character. As we saw in Chapter 4, the *info* field can be an array or a record. In particular, when we wish nodes of several different forms, a variant record can be used. For example, suppose that the elements of a list can be single numbers or pairs of integers. Then we might declare

```
type nodeptr = ↑nodetype;
     sptype = (single, pair);
     nodetype = record
                    next: nodeptr;
                case sp: sptype of
                    single: (info: integer);
                    pair: (info1, info2: integer)
                end;
var p: nodeptr;
```

A node of this type may be allocated by *new(p)* and freed by *dispose(p)*. When such a node is allocated, enough storage is reserved to hold the largest possible variant of the record—in this case, a pair of integers.

However, suppose we know that the node will only contain a single integer. Then it is wasteful to reserve storage for two integers, since only one is necessary. To assist in conserving storage, Pascal allows another form of the *new* and *dispose* procedures. *new*(*p, single*) allocates a variable of type *nodetype* with only enough storage in the variant part of the record to contain a single integer, while *new*(*p, pair*) allocates a *nodetype* variable with enough storage in the variant part to contain two integers. The tag field *sp* is not assigned a value by the call to *new*. Subsequently, the tag field may only be assigned the value specified in the call to *new* and may not be changed. For its entire lifetime, such a record adopts a single one of its variants.

A node created by the *new* function with two arguments must be freed with the *dispose* function using two arguments. *dispose*(*p, single*) is used to free a record created by *new*(*p, single*), while *dispose*(*p, pair*) is used to free a record created by *new*(*p, pair*). Similarly, if a variant record has more than one tag field (in the case of a variant record which contains a field that is itself declared as a variant record), *new* and *dispose* can be called with more than two arguments.

Another restriction on a variant record variable created by the *new* function with more than one argument is that it cannot appear in an assignment statement. The reason for this is that an assignment statement is usually implemented by copying the contents of memory from one area to another. The amount of memory to be copied is determined from the types of the variables in the assignment. When a variant record is allocated with a specified tag value, it is not always possible to determine in advance (i.e., at compilation time) the size of the record and, therefore, the amount of memory to be copied. Although the source and the target of the assignment might be of the same type, they may be of different sizes since one might be allocated with a specific tag value (two parameters in the *new* function) and the other might be allocated with a different tag value or without any specific tag value (only one parameter in the *new* function). For this reason, standard Pascal prohibits such record assignments. Individual Pascal compilers might implement such assignments consistently "correctly," inconsistently "correctly," consistently "incorrectly," or not at all. Such assignments are therefore not recommended even if, on occasion, your compiler does allow the assignment.

Of course, individual fields of such variant records, including those fields present only in the allocated variant, may be assigned freely, subject only to the general Pascal type-agreement rules for assignment.

Comparing the Dynamic and Array Implementations of Lists

It is instructive to examine the advantages and disadvantages of the dynamic and array implementations of linked lists. The major disadvantage of the dynamic implementation is that it may be more time consuming to call upon the system to allocate and free storage than to manipulate a programmer-managed available list. Its major advantage is that a set of nodes is not reserved in advance for use by a particular group of lists. For example, suppose that a program uses two types of lists: lists of integers and lists of characters. Under the array representation, two arrays of fixed size would immediately be allocated. If one group of lists overflows its array, the program cannot continue. Under the dynamic representation, two node types are defined at the outset, but no storage is allocated for variables until needed. As nodes are needed, the system is called upon to provide them. Any storage not used for one type of node may be used for another. Thus as long as sufficient storage is available for the nodes actually present in the lists, no overflow will occur.

Another advantage of the dynamic implementation is that a reference to $p\uparrow$ does not involve the address computation that is necessary in computing the address of $node[p]$. To compute the address of $node[p]$, the contents of p must be added to the base address of the array $node$, whereas the address of $p\uparrow$ is given by the contents of p directly.

Still another advantage of dynamic variables exists in the case of variant records. If an array of nodes is declared, each node must contain enough storage to hold the largest possible variant. By using the *new* and *dispose* procedures with two arguments, each node need contain only as much storage as the particular variant required for that node.

EXERCISES

1. Write a function *binsrch*, which accepts two parameters, an array of pointers to a group of sorted numbers, and a single number. The function should use a binary search (see Section 3.1) to return a pointer to the single number if it is in the group. If the number is not present in the group, return to the value **nil**.

2. Consider the following implementation of a stack of integers. Declare and initialize an array of pointers, a dynamic array type, and two variables as follows:

```
type nodeptr = ↑nodetype;
     nodetype = array [1..100] of integer;
var p: array [1..10] of nodeptr;
    i, topptr, topitem: integer;
begin
    topptr:= 0;
    topitem:= 100;
    for i:= 1 to 10
       do p [i]:= nil;
```

To push an element onto the stack, *topitem* is incremented and the element is inserted into *p[topptr]* ↑ *[topitem]*. If, however, *topitem* equals 100, *topptr* is increased by 1, *new*(*p*[*topptr*]) is called, *topitem* is reset to 1, and the element is inserted into *p*[*topptr*] ↑ [*topitem*]. The pop operation is implemented analogously.

Write routines *push*, *pop*, and *empty* for this implementation. What is the maximum number of elements that the stack can hold? How are underflow and overflow signaled? What are the advantages and disadvantages of this implementation of stacks compared to the array implementation of Section 2.2, the list implementation of Section 4.2, and the list implementation of this section?

3. Implement the routines *empty*, *push*, *pop*, and *popandtest* using a dynamic storage implementation of a linked stack.

4. Implement the routines *empty*, *insert*, and *remove* using a dynamic storage implementation of a linked queue.

5. Implement the routines *empty*, *pquinsert*, and *pqmindelete* using a dynamic storage implementation of a linked priority queue.

6. Rewrite the list processing exercises of Sections 4.2 and 4.4 using the dynamic implementation of linked lists. Note any differences in space and time usage between the array and dynamic implementations.

7. Rewrite the bank simulation program of Section 4.3 using the dynamic implementation of linked lists. Note any differences in space and time usage between the two implementations.

8. Write Pascal programs to implement the list operations on circular and doubly linked lists using dynamic storage.

9. Rewrite the solution to the Josephus problem presented in Section 4.4 using the dynamic implementation of circular lists. Note any differences in space and time usage between the two implementations.

10. Rewrite the routines to add long integers presented in Section 4.4 using the dynamic implementation of circular and doubly linked lists. Note any differences in space and time usage between the two implementations.

11. Assume that we wish to form *n* lists, where *n* is a constant. Declare an array *list* of pointers by

```
const n = ... ;
type nodeptr = ↑nodetype;
     nodetype = record
                     info: integer;
                     inext: nodeptr
                 end;
var list: array [1..n] of nodeptr;
```

Read two numbers from each input line, the first number being the list into which the second number is to be placed in ascending order. When there are no more input lines, print out all the lists.

2. AN EXAMPLE:
AN AIRLINE RESERVATION SYSTEM

In this section and the next, we consider some examples involving linked allocation that use the dynamic storage implementation of linked lists. The programs could be written equally well using the array representation of

Chapter 4. As exercises, you may wish to implement these programs using the methods of Chapter 4.

Consider the problem of programming an airline reservation system. The input consists of two groups of data: a flight control group containing flight data used to initialize the system followed by a passenger request group containing data on passenger reservations. The flight control group consists of one input line containing a single number (representing the number of flights available that day) followed by a set of input lines (one for each flight) each of which contains a flight number in columns 1 through 3 and the seating capacity for that flight in columns 5 through 7. A sample flight control group is illustrated in Figure 5.2.1a.

Once this flight control group has been read, a separate input line is read for each passenger request for service. The requests may be of three types: reservation, cancellation, or inquiry. The type of each request is indicated by the word *reserve*, *cancel*, or *inquire* beginning in column 1. A request for a reservation or a cancellation is accompanied by a passenger name beginning in column 15 and a flight number beginning in column 50.

Figure 5.2.1

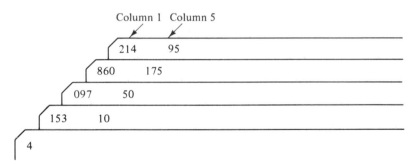

(a) Flight control group for Airline problem.

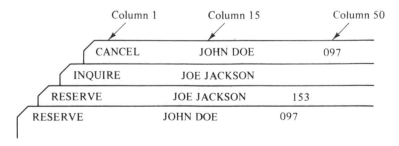

(b) Passenger request group for Airline problem.

An inquiry is accompanied by a passenger name only. (We assume that a passenger inquires about all of the flights on a particular journey, but may cancel one particular leg of the journey.) A sample set of data for a passenger request group is shown in Figure 5.2.1b.

We are to write a program that processes these two groups of input. For each passenger service request, a message describing the action taken is to be printed.

Before designing a program, the requirements of the problem must be defined more precisely. In particular, it must be determined what action is to be taken for each of the possible passenger requests. In the case of a reservation, the passenger is to be placed on a flight list for the flight, if the flight is not full. If the flight is full, the passenger is to be placed on a waiting list and will be placed on the flight if there are any cancellations. In the case of a cancellation, the passenger is to be deleted from the flight list if the passenger is currently booked on the flight, and the first passenger from the waiting list (if any) is to be placed on the flight list. If the canceled passenger is on the waiting list, he must be removed from it. Finally, in the case of an inquiry, a list of all flights on which the passenger is booked is to be printed.

Now that we have defined the actions to be taken for the various requests, we may consider the data structures that will be necessary. Clearly, two lists are required for each flight: a list of passengers currently booked on the flight and a waiting list for the flight. The passenger list has no restrictions as to where a passenger may be inserted or deleted. The waiting list, however, should be a queue, so that if a cancellation occurs, the first person on the waiting list will be the first to be given a seat on the flight. However, we must also have the capability of deleting a passenger from the middle of the waiting list (in case of a cancellation). It will also be necessary to keep a record of the capacity of each flight and of the number of people currently on the flight. We can thus declare the data structures for this program as follows:

```
const numflights = 100; {maximum of 100 flights}
type  nametype = packed array[1..20] of char;
      flightnum = packed array[1..3] of '0'..'9';
      nodeptr = ↑nodetype;
      nodetype = record
                     name: nametype; {    passenger name      }
                     next:  nodeptr    {next passenger on the list}
                 end;
      queue = record
                  front: nodeptr;
                  rear: nodeptr
              end;
```

```
flighttype = record
              fltno: flightnum;   {        flight number        }
              cpcty: integer;     {     capacity of flight       }
              count: integer;     {number of people on flight}
              flthd: nodeptr;     { pointer to first passenger }
                                  {     on the flight list      }
              waitlist: queue     {   queue for waiting list    }
          end;
var    flight: array[1..numflights] of flighttype;
```

Before proceeding to the program, let us consider what routines will be required for manipulating the lists. First, it is necessary to be able to locate the index of the record representing the flight within the array *flight* given its flight number. We call the function that does this *find* and leave its coding as an exercise for the reader. The function accepts a flight number as a parameter and returns the index in the array *flight* of the record representing that flight. We will also need the routines *insert* and *remove* to insert and remove an element from a queue. However, we will see shortly that these routines must be somewhat modified. Because elements will be eliminated from positions other than the front of the waiting queues and also from the flight lists, the *delafter* routine will also be required.

The final decision that must be made relates to the structure of the passenger list. Since deletions can be made from either end or from within the list, our choice of a data structure should depend upon the ease with which other operations can be performed. Aside from deleting an element, the only operations needed are insertion and searching for a name within the list. Keeping the list in order by name will make searching more efficient in the case where a name is not present on the list. (Why?) However, keeping a sorted list will reduce the efficiency of every insertion.

We choose to make all insertions at the head of the list. The following additional routines are therefore needed: a procedure *search* (*listhd*, *nam*, *pred*, *found*), which accepts a pointer, *listhd*, to the head of a list, and the name, *nam*, of a passenger. Upon returning, *pred* contains a pointer to the predecessor of the node containing the name *nam* if the name is present in the list, and *found* will be *true*. If *nam* is not present, then *found* will be *false*. A dummy header node is stored at the beginning of each passenger list so that the output parameter *pred* of *search* can be used as an input argument to *delafter* even if the desired node is first on the list. Such a technique is frequently used to make subroutines applicable to special cases. Similarly, a dummy node is stored at the head of each waiting list so that *delafter* may be used to delete the first passenger on the waiting list. This means that the *remove* routine for the queue must be altered, since *front* points to a header node before the actual front of the queue. It is necessary to rewrite *remove* as a procedure rather than as a function, since a Pascal function cannot return a packed array (of type *nametype*). The *empty* function for queues must also be modified to allow for a dummy node. The routine *insafter* is also used. We now present the main program and the procedure for the *cancel* request. The procedures that handle reservations and inquiries are left as exercises for the reader.

```
program airline (input, output);
const numflights = 100;
      nilname = '                    ';
type  nametype = packed array [1..20] of char;
      flightnum = packed array [1..3] of '0'..'9';
      nodeptr = ↑nodetype;
      nodetype = record
                      name: nametype;
                      next: nodeptr
                 end;
      queue = record
                   front: nodeptr;
                   rear: nodeptr
              end;
      flighttype = record
                       fltno: flightnum;
                       cpcty: integer;
                       count: integer;
                       flthd: nodeptr;
                       waitlist: queue
                   end;
var   flight: array [1..numflights] of flighttype;
      i, nflts: 1..numflights; {nflts is the number of flights}
      prcd: nodeptr;
      d: '0'..'9';
      j: 1..3;
      c: char;
      command: packed array [1..10] of char;
{The following functions and procedures are defined here:}
{   cancel, delafter, empty, find, inquire, insafter, insert,   }
{              remove, reserve, and search                      }
begin {program airline}
      {initialize variables and lists}
      readln (nflts);
      for i:= 1 to nflts
          do with flight [i]
             do begin
                    for j:= 1 to 3
                        do begin
                               read (d);
                               fltno [j] := d
                           end {for...do begin};
```

```
                                      readln(cpcty);
                                      {          flight is initially empty          }
                                      count:= 0;
                                      { insert dummy node at head of list   }
                                      new(pred);
                                      flthd:= pred;
                                      pred↑.name:= nilname;
                                      pred↑.next:= nil;
                                      {insert dummy node at front of queue}
                                      new(pred);
                                      waitlist.front:= pred;
                                      waitlist.rear:= pred;
                                      pred↑.name:= nilname;
                                      pred↑.next:= nil
                          end {with...do begin};
                   {process customer requests}
                   while not eof
                          do begin
                              for i:= 1 to 10
                                  do begin
                                          read (c);
                                          command[i]:= c
                                  end {for...do begin};
                              writeln(command);
                              if command = 'inquire   ' then inquire
                                else if command = 'reserve   ' then reserve
                                    else if command = 'cancel   ' then cancel
                                        else writeln('invalid command');
                              readln
                          end {while...do begin}
                   end {program airline}.
```

We now present the procedure *cancel*. This procedure utilizes the minor Pascal extension which permits a packed array of a character subrange to appear as an argument to the *writeln* procedure.

```
procedure cancel;
{all variables of airline are global to cancel}
var nam: nametype;
    i: integer;
    flt: flightnum;
    c: char;
    d: '0'..'9';
    pred: nodeptr;
    found: boolean;
```

```
begin
    {read the name starting in column 15}
    for i:= 1 to 4
        do read(c);
    for i:= 1 to 20
        do begin
                read(c);
                nam[i] := c
            end {for...do begin};
    {read the flight number starting in column 50}
    for i:= 1 to 15
        do read(c);
    for i:= 1 to 3
        do begin
                read(d);
                flt[i] := d
            end {for...do begin};
    write(nam, ' ', flt);
    i: = find(flt);
    if i = 0
        then writeln('invalid flight')
        else with flight[i]
            do begin
                    search(flthd, nam, pred, found);
                if found
                    then begin {remove from flight list}
                            delafter(pred, nam);
                            writeln(nam, ' deleted from flight ', fltno);
                            if not empty(waitlist)
                                then begin
                                        {remove passenger from}
                                        {  queue and place on  }
                                        {         flight        }
                                        remove(waitlist, nam);
                                        insafter(flthd, nam);
                                        writeln(nam, ' now booked on flight ', fltno)
                                    end {then begin}
                                else count:= count - 1
                        end {then begin}
                    else begin {cancel passenger from}
                            {      waiting list      }
                            search(waitlist.front, nam, pred, found);
                        if found
                            then begin
                                delafter(pred, nam);
                                writeln(nam, 'deleted from waiting ',
                                                    'list of flight ', fltno)
```

end {*then begin*}

end {*else begin*}

end {*with...do begin*}

end {*procedure cancel*};

We leave the coding of the two other major routines, *inquire* and *reserve*, as exercises for the reader. There are more efficient ways of programming the foregoing example so that not so much time is spent in searching for names on lists. Some of these techniques will be examined in Chapter 8.

EXERCISES

1. Write routines *search*, *find*, *insafter*, *remove*, *delafter*, *insert*, *empty*, *inquire*, and *reserve* as called for in the program *airline*.

2. The lists in the airline problem (both passenger lists and queues) all contain a dummy header node. What changes are necessary in the program if no such dummy nodes exist?

3. Modify the airline program to list all the passengers booked or waiting for a given flight upon reading an input line with the command

fltlist   *flight number*

4. Modify the airline program to accept and process a command *chngcpcty* with a flight number and a quantity. The quantity represents an increase or decrease in the number of seats available on that flight.

5. Write a Pascal routine that accepts a passenger name and cancels all reservations (including those on a waiting list) for that passenger.

6. Assume that each fight has a given ticket price. Modify the data structures and write a routine that will print out a separate bill for each passenger.

7. Redesign the data structures, inputs, and programs of the airline system so that it will include for each passenger an indication of whether he is in the first-class or economy section. Each of these two sections has its own capacity. However, if first class is not full but economy class is, an economy passenger will be placed into first class (at economy prices) until a passenger requests a first-class reservation. Make sure that your system is equitable in handling such questions as the relation among passengers on the waiting list, economy passengers in first class, and requests for cancellations and first-class reservations (i.e., who gets bumped from where to where).

8. Rewrite the example of this section using the array implementation of lists.

3. AN EXAMPLE: SPARSE MATRICES

We now consider a second application of linked lists using dynamic variables. As in the preceding section, the main emphasis is on linked lists. Its implementation using dynamic variables is of secondary importance. As exercises, you may wish to implement the routines presented here using the array method of Chapter 4.

A *matrix* is a two-dimensional array. Figure 5.3.1 illustrates some matrices. Each matrix in that figure is a two-dimensional array with m rows and n columns. The values of m and n for each matrix are shown. Matrices are used in many fields, including mathematics, economics, and computer science. There are a number of recognized operations defined on matrices, some of which will be illustrated in this section and others left as exercises.

Suppose that we are programming a problem whose solution calls for the use of matrices. How can a matrix be represented in memory? The simplest and most obvious answer is, of course, to use a two-dimensional array. For example, we might code

```
const m = ...;
      n - ...;
type  rownum = 1..m;
      colnum = 1..n;
      matrix = array [rownum, colnum] of integer;
var   a: matrix;
```

$$A = \begin{bmatrix} 5 \end{bmatrix}$$

$m = 1$
$n = 1$

(a)

$$B = \begin{bmatrix} 1 & 0 & 2 \\ -1 & 4 & 6 \end{bmatrix}$$

$m = 2$
$n = 3$

(b)

$$C = \begin{bmatrix} 1 & 3 & 7 & 5 \end{bmatrix}$$

$m = 1$
$n = 4$

(c)

$$D = \begin{bmatrix} 8 & 7 \\ 2 & 5 \\ 1 & 4 \end{bmatrix}$$

$m = 3$
$n = 2$

(d)

$$E = \begin{bmatrix} 1 & 0 & 0 & 3 & 0 & 0 & 0 & 0 & 0 \\ 0 & 2 & 0 & 0 & 0 & 0 & 0 & 2 & 0 \\ 0 & 0 & 0 & 0 & 0 & 0 & 0 & 0 & 0 \\ 0 & 0 & 0 & 0 & 0 & 0 & 0 & 0 & 0 \\ 0 & 0 & 0 & -1 & 4 & 0 & 0 & 0 & 0 \\ 0 & 0 & 0 & 8 & 0 & 0 & 2 & 0 & 0 \\ 0 & 0 & 0 & 0 & 1 & 0 & 0 & 0 & 0 \end{bmatrix}$$

$m = 7$
$n = 9$

(e)

Figure 5.3.1 Examples of matrices.

Storage for a two-dimensional array of m rows and n columns is allocated. Any element in the matrix can be referenced by $a[i, j]$, where i represents the row number and j the column number of the element. Notice that nothing is assumed about the actual contents of the array except that they are integers. $m*n$ is the number of units of storage allocated. We say the matrix is of *size m* by n (sometimes written as $m \times n$).

The representation of a matrix by an array is certainly satisfactory for small matrices. Very often, however, we deal with a matrix such as the one in Figure 5.3.1e, which contains mostly zeros. A matrix that is filled with mostly zeros is called a *sparse* matrix. The actual amount of nonzero data is small compared with the amount of storage set aside for the matrix. Suppose that the matrix of Figure 5.3.1e were 700 by 900 rather than 7 by 9 and the additional entries were all 0. Such a matrix, if represented as a two-dimensional array, would exceed the storage capacity of most computers existing today. Yet since there are only nine nonzero data items in this matrix, surely there must be some method of representing a matrix in fewer than 630,000 units of storage.

Let us see how a sparse matrix can be represented using linked allocation. We will keep in memory a structure containing only those elements which are nonzero, linked to each other in a way that describes their position in the large matrix. If a position of the matrix is represented in the structure, its value is given within a list node. If a position is not represented in the structure, its value is zero. How should this list be organized? One way is as a single linear linked list consisting of all the nonzero elements of the first row, followed by all the nonzero elements of the second row, and so on. Of course, since not every column is represented in a particular row, each node will also include an indication of the column in which the element appears. It will also be necessary to keep an indication of where a particular row ends. (This indication can consist of a special flag in the last node of each row, or an extra node at the end of each row with a zero value field.) This method has the drawback that the entire list would have to be searched each time a particular element is to be accessed. Also, whereas an entire row can be accessed once its first element has been located, accessing a column is an entirely different matter. To access a column, the entire list must be traversed until that column position is encountered in the last row. This is clearly inefficient. In addition, it does not mirror the two-dimensional nature of a matrix, which implies that either a row or a column can be traversed once its first element has been accessed.

One possible solution is to keep a separate list for each row. This would certainly reduce the time necessary to access a particular element, since only a single smaller list (that of the row in question) would have to be searched rather than a list of all the matrix elements. However, the problem of accessing a column remains. Keeping the matrix in column order rather than row order would merely transfer the problem from that of accessing a column to that of accessing a row.

To allow easy access to any row or column of the matrix, we let each nonzero matrix element appear on two lists, one for its row and one for its column. Thus each node contains two pointers, one to the next element in its row and one to the next element in its column. In addition, each node contains fields for the row number, column number, and the value of its element. Thus the type of a node is defined by

```
const m = ...;
       n = ...;
type rownum = 1..m;
       colnum = 1..n;
       nodeptr = ↑nodetype;
       nodetype = record
                        row: rownum;
                        col: colnum;
                        val: integer;
                        nextrow: nodeptr; {to next element in same column}
                        nextcol: nodeptr { to next element in same row }
                  end;
```

Figure 5.3.2a depicts the fields of a sample node. Figure 5.3.2c illustrates the representation of the matrix of Figure 5.3.2b.

row	col	value
nextrow		nextcol

(a) Fields of a sample node.

$$\begin{pmatrix} 3 & 0 & 2 \\ -1 & 0 & 0 \\ 0 & 0 & 5 \end{pmatrix}$$

(b) Matrix in array format.

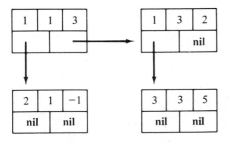

(c) Matrix using linked allocation.   **Figure 5.3.2**

As with any linked list, some method of accessing the first element of each list in the matrix representation is required. This can be done in either of two ways. One method would be to keep two arrays of pointers, *rowfirst* and *colfirst*, where *rowfirst*[*i*] points to the first node in row *i* and *colfirst*[*i*] points to the first node in column *i*.

An alternative method is to keep a dummy column (column 0) containing as many elements as there are rows. Each element in this dummy column points to the first element of its respective row. Similarly, a dummy row (row 0) exists containing as many elements as there are columns. Each element in this dummy row points to the first element of its respective column. Each node in these dummy lists serves as a header node for a row list or a column list. These header nodes may be recognized by a zero value in the column or row field, respectively. Of cource, now the types *rownum* and *colnum* must be defined as

$$\textbf{type } \text{rownum} = 0..m;$$
$$\text{colnum } = 0..n;$$

Since each row and column has a header, they are kept as circular lists. An external pointer points to a dummy element at row 0, column 0. Figure 5.3.3 illustrates this scheme. Figure 5.3.3a illustrates a 4 × 4 matrix, and Figure 5.3.3b illustrates its linked representation. Notice the dummy column on the left and the dummy row on the top, each element of which points to the first nonzero element of a row or column. Since row 1 consists of only zeros, it contains only the dummy node whose *nextcol* field points to itself. Note also that the element pointed to by *a* serves as the "header" node of the matrix. Given *a*, it is possible to reach any node in the matrix. A structure in which nodes appear on more than one list and contain more than one pointer is called a **multilinked list** or a **multilist**.

Before proceeding with some applications of this method, some comments on its use are appropriate. If the matrix of Figure 5.3.3a were to be stored as a two-dimensional array, it would require 16 nodes of storage, each consisting of one field. Using the linked method depicted in Figure 5.3.3b, 15 nodes of storage each consisting of five fields are required. By no stretch of the imagination could this latter method be considered more efficient than the former. Moreover, using the array method, a particular element can be accessed merely be referencing it; to access that same element in the linked method requires a rather elaborate traversal procedure, as we shall see shortly. Thus only where the matrices are very large and sparse (relatively few nonzero entries) is it more efficient to use the linked allocation than the array implementation. All the following routines are simpler to code when the matrix is stored as an array. Thus, although the methods and examples of this section apply to matrices of any size and any number of nonzero elements, applying them to the wrong types of matrices will seriously affect the speed and storage efficiency of the programs involved.

$$\begin{pmatrix} 0 & 0 & 0 & 0 \\ 0 & 2 & 0 & 3 \\ -2 & 4 & 0 & 0 \\ 0 & 0 & -1 & 8 \end{pmatrix}$$

(a) Matrix using array format.

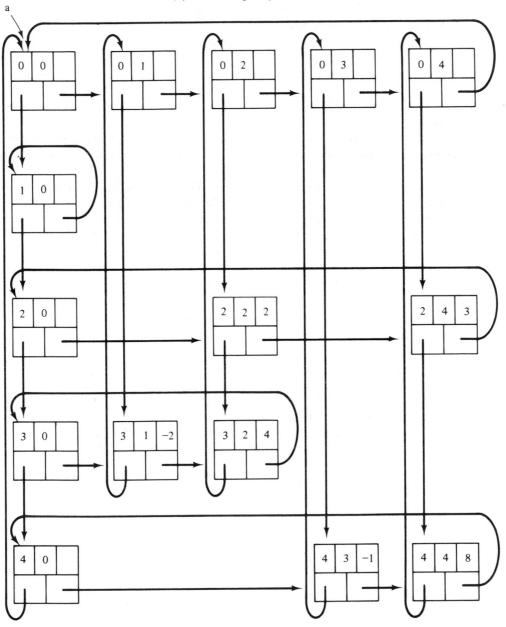

(b) Matrix using linked allocation.

Figure 5.3.3

Let us now consider some transformations on matrices. An ***elementary row operation*** is defined as one of the following:

1. Multiplying any row by a nonzero constant.
2. Interchanging any two rows.
3. Adding a multiple of one row to another.

We consider each of these three operations in turn, and assume the following routines:

findabove(*a*: *nodeptr*; *r*: *rownum*; *c*: *colnum*): *nodeptr*. This function accepts a pointer *a* to a matrix, a row number *r*, and a column number *c*. The function returns a pointer to the node in column *c* that immediately precedes the position where a node at row *r* and *c* would be if it were present in the matrix.

insertafter(*p*, *q*: *nodeptr*; *x*: *integer*). This routine inserts a new node with value *x* into the same row as *p*↑ and the same column as *q*↑, immediately following *p*↑ in its row and *q*↑ in its column.

deleteafter(*p*, *q*: *nodeptr*; **var** *x*: integer). This routine deletes the node pointed to by both *p*↑.*nextcol* and *q*↑.*nextrow*, and places its value into *x*.

We present the routine *findabove* and leave the coding of the other two as exercises:

```
function findabove (a: nodeptr; r: rownum; c: colnum): nodeptr;
var p, q: nodeptr;
begin
      {   find a pointer to the dummy node of column c   }
      p:= a;
      while p↑.col < c
            do p:= p↑.nextcol;
      {p now points to dummy node of column c.  Advance}
      { p through column c until row r is reached or passed }
      q := p;
      p := p↑.nextrow;
      while (p↑.row < r) and (p↑.row <> 0)
            do begin
                  q := p;
                  p := p↑.nextrow
            end {while...do begin};
      findabove := q
end {function findabove};
```

1. Multiplying a row by a nonzero constant.

If the array representation is used, the routine is trivial.

```
procedure mult (var a: matrix; row: rownum; c: integer);
    {multiply row number row by the constant c <> 0}
var j: colnum;
begin
      for j := 1 to n
          do a[row, j] := a[row, j] * c
    end {procedure mult};
```

If the linked representation is used, there are some minor changes necessary in the looping mechanism.

```
procedure mult2 (a: nodeptr; r: rownum; c: integer);
var above, q: nodeptr;
begin
      {set above to the element above row r in the dummy column}
      above := findabove (a, r, 0);
      {          set q to the first nonzero entry in row r          }
      q := above↑.nextrow;
      q := q↑.nextcol;
      {                multiply the entire row by c                 }
      while q↑.col > 0
            do begin
                  q↑.val := q↑.val * c;
                  q := q↑.nextcol
              end {while...do begin}
  end {procedure mult2};
```

Notice that there are no insertions or deletions in *mult2*, since multiplying by a nonzero constant cannot change a nonzero entry to zero, or vice versa. Suppose that we wish to multiply a row by 0. No changes are necessary in *mult* (except that the operation is no longer an elementary row operation). *mult2*, however, must be modified considerably, since an entire row now becomes zero and each of its elements must therefore be removed from the list. We could code *mult0* as follows:

```
procedure mult0 (a: nodeptr; r: rownum);
    {c need not be a parameter; we are multiplying by zero}
var above, p, q: nodeptr;
    x: integer;
begin
      above := findabove (a, r, 0);
      q := above↑.nextrow;
      p := q↑.nextcol;
```

```
        while p↑.col > 0
            do begin
                    above := findabove(a, r, p↑.col);
                    deleteafter(q, above, x);
                    p := q↑.nextcol
            end {while...do begin}
    end {procedure mult0};
```

Of course, *mult*2 and *mult*0 could be combined into a single routine.

2. Interchanging two rows.

If a matrix is stored as a two-dimensional array, the routine *int* interchanging two rows is again straightforward:

```
    procedure int(var a: matrix; row1, row2: rownum);
    var j: column;
        hold: integer;
    begin
        for j := 1 to n
            do begin
                    hold := a[row1, j];
                    a[row1, j] := a[row2, j];
                    a[row2, j] := hold
            end {for...do begin}
    end {procedure int};
```

Storing the matrix as a multilinked list requires a choice between two options. Nodes in *row*1 and *row*2 could actually be allocated and freed as necessary so that the interchange is made. A second option is to keep the two rows intact, adjusting the column pointers to reflect the interchange. We select this second option. Since interchanging two rows is a symmetric operation, we will assume, without loss of generality, that *row*1 < *row*2.

The rows *row*1 and *row*2 are traversed in parallel. As the algorithm proceeds from one column to the next in each of *row*1 and *row*2, one of three conditions may occur:

a. There is an element in a particular column of *row*2, but the corresponding element in *row*1 is 0. The element must be moved from *row*2 to *row*1.
b. There is an element in a particular column of *row*1, but the corresponding element in *row*2 is 0. The element must be moved from *row*1 to *row*2.
c. There are elements in a particular column of both *row*1 and *row*2. The element of *row*1 must be interchanged with that of *row*2.

Figures 5.3.4a–c depict (for an arbitrary column *j*) the situations after the appropriate action is taken. In Figure 5.3.4a the notation (*row*1 =>) means

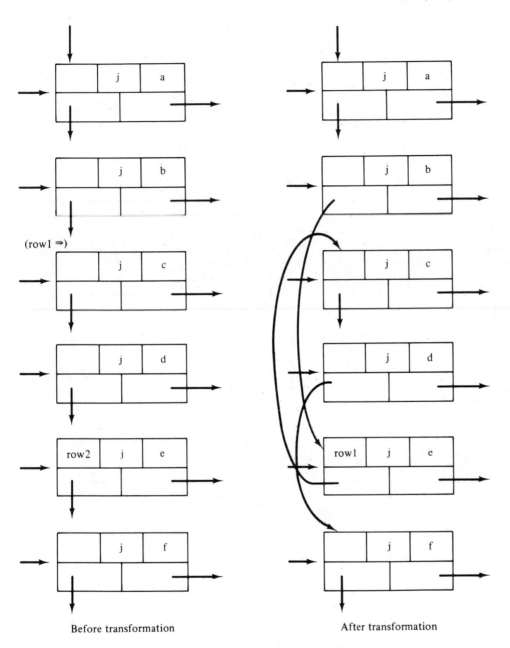

(row1 ⇒)

Before transformation

After transformation

(a) row1 = 0 and row2 ≠ 0.

Figure 5.3.4

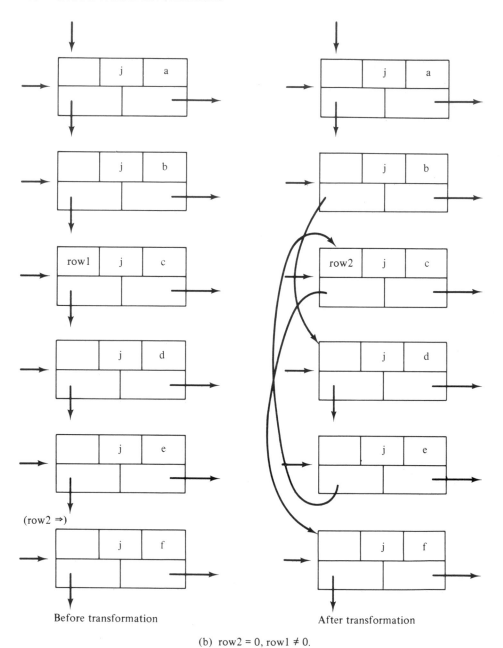

Before transformation   After transformation

(b) row2 = 0, row1 ≠ 0.

Figure 5.3.4   *(cont.)*

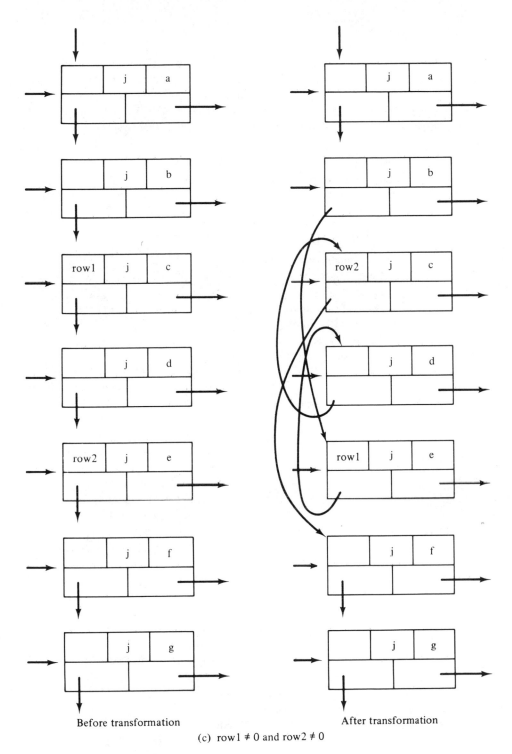

Before transformation

After transformation

(c) row1 ≠ 0 and row2 ≠ 0

Figure 5.3.4 (cont.)

that a nonzero element of *row*1 and column *j* would belong between two elements of column *j* at the point indicated, and similarly for the notation (*row2* = >) in Figure 5.3.4b. (Note that because complete rows are being moved, there is no need to adjust the *nextcol* fields. We begin our loop at the first nonzero column and halt when we reach the dummy column.)

```
procedure int2 (a: nodeptr; row1, row2: rownum);
var above1, above2, r1, r2, temp: nodeptr;
    j: colnum;
begin
  r1 := findabove (a, row1, 0);
  r1 := r1↑.nextrow;
  r2 := findabove (a, row2, 0);
  r2:= r2↑.nextrow;
  repeat
    r1:= r1↑.nextcol;
    r2:= r2↑.nextcol;
    while r1↑.col <> r2↑.col
            do {there is at least one zero}
                if ((r1↑.col < r2↑.col) and (r1↑.col <> 0))
                                            {row1 nonzero, row2 zero}
                or (r2↑.col = 0) {end of row2}
                then begin
                        temp:= r1↑.nextrow;
                        if (temp↑.row < row2) and (temp↑.row <> 0)
                        then begin
                                {r1 and r2 are not adjacent}
                                {move element at r1 to r2.}
                                {    see Figure 5.3.4b      }
                                j:= r1↑.col;
                                above1 := findabove (a, row1, j);
                                above2 := findabove (a, row2, j);
                                above1↑.nextrow:= r1↑.nextrow;
                                r1↑.nextrow:= above2↑.nextrow;
                                above2↑.nextrow:= r1
                            end {then begin};
                        r1↑.row:= row2;
                        {advance r1 to the next column}
                        r1:= r1↑.nextcol
                    end {then begin}
                else begin
                        j:= r2↑.col;
                        above 1 := findabove (a, row1, j);
                        temp:= above1↑.nextrow;
```

```
            if temp↑.row < row2
                then begin
                        {r1 and r2 are not adjacent.}
                        {move the element at r2 to }
                        {   r1. see Figure 5.3.4a   }
                        above2 := findabove (a, row2, j);
                        above2↑.nextrow := r2↑.nextrow;
                        r2↑.nextrow:= above1↑.nextrow;
                        above1↑.nextrow:= r2
                    end {then begin};
                r2↑.row:= row1;
                {advance r2 to the next column}
                r2:= r2↑.nextcol
            end {else begin};
        {at this point, r1 and r2 point to the same column}
        {        swap r1 with r2. see Figure 5.3.4c        }
        j:= r1↑.col;
        above1 := findabove (a, row1, j);
        above2 := findabove (a, row2, j);
        temp:= r2↑.nextrow;
        above1↑.nextrow:= r2;
        if r1↑.nextrow↑.row < row2 {then rows are not adjacent}
            then r2↑.nextrow:= r1↑.nextrow
            else r2↑.nextrow:= r1;
        above2↑.nextrow:= r1;
        r1↑.nextrow:= temp;
        r1↑.row:= row2;
        r2↑.row:= row1
    until r1↑.col = 0
end {procedure int2};
```

3. Adding a multiple of one row to another.

The routine that handles the case where the matrix is stored as an array is straightforward.

```
procedure multiple(var a: matrix; row1, row2: rownum; c: integer);
    {replace row1 by row1 + c*row2}
var j: column;
begin
    for j:= 1 to n
        do a[row1, j] := a[row1, j] + c*a[row2, j]
end {procedure multiple};
```

In the case of the matrix stored as a multilinked list, both rows are again traversed in parallel. As each element of *row2* is reached, *r*1 is advanced to the corresponding column in *row*1. If such an element exists, its value is adjusted, and if it now becomes zero, it is deleted from the list. If such a column element does not exist, a new node with the appropriate value is created.

```
procedure multiple2 (a: nodeptr; row1, row2: rownum; c: integer);
var r1, r2, q, above: nodeptr;
x: integer;
begin
      q:= findabove(a,row1,0);
      r1:= q↑.nextrow;
      r1:= r1↑.nextcol;
      r2:= findabove (a, row2, 0);
      r2:= r2↑.nextrow;
      r2:= r2↑.nextcol;
      {traverse row2}
      while r2↑.col > 0
            do begin
                  while (r1↑.col < r2↑.col) and (r1↑.col > 0)
                        do begin {corresponding element of row2}
                              {         is zero; advance r1         }
                              q:= r1;
                              r1:= r1↑.nextcol
                        end {while...do begin};
                  if r1↑.col = r2↑.col
                        then begin
                              r1↑.val:= r1↑.val + c*r2↑.val;
                              if r1↑.val = 0
                                    then begin
                                          {delete the node}
                                          above:= findabove(a, row1, r1↑.col);
                                          deleteafter (q, above, x)
                                    end {then begin};
                              {update r1 and r2}
                              r1:= q↑.nextcol;
                              r2:= r2↑.nextcol
                        end {then begin};
                  else begin {insert new element}
                              above:= findabove (a, row1, r2↑.col);
                              insertafter (q, above, r2↑.val*c);
                              q:= q↑.nextcol;
```

$$r1 := q\uparrow.nextcol;$$
$$r2 := r2\uparrow.nextcol$$
end {*else begin*}
end {*while...do begin*}
end {*procedure multiple2*};

EXERCISES

1. Rewrite the routines of this section using the array implementation of linked allocation presented in Chapter 4.

2. Write a routine *linktoarr*(*link*, *arr*) to convert a matrix in linked format pointed to by *link* into its array format *arr*. (*arr* is already of the proper dimension.)
   Write a routine *arrtolink*(*arr*, *link*) to convert a matrix stored as an array *arr* into its linked format. *link* should point to the resultant structure.

3. Write a routine *store*(*a*, *i*, *j*, *x*) to set the element of a matrix at row *i* and column *j* to *x*, where the matrix is represented as a multilinked list pointed to by *a*. Write a function *retrieve*(*a*, *i*, *j*) to return the element at row *i* and column *j* in such a matrix.

4. Multiplication of matrices for the array representation is performed by the following routine (*c* is the product of *a* and *b*, where *a* has the same number of columns as *b* has rows):

```
const m = ...;
      n = ...;
      r = ...;
type amatrix = array[1..m,1..n] of integer;
     bmatrix = array[1..n,1..r] of integer;
     cmatrix = array[1..m,1..r] of integer;
procedure prod(a: amatrix; b: bmatrix; var c: cmatrix);
var i, j, k: integer;
begin
    for i:= 1 to m
        do for j:= 1 to r
            do begin
                   c[i, j] := 0;
                   for k:= 1 to n
                       do c[i, j] := c[i, j] + a[i, k] * b[k, j]
            end {for...do begin}
end {procedure prod};
```

   Rewrite this routine using the linked matrix representation.

5. Write a function *det*(*matptr*), which accepts a pointer to a linked list matrix and returns its determinant. (For a definition of the determinant, see Exercise 3.2.6.)

6. Would any harm be done if no dummy node existed in the linked representation of a sparse matrix for a row or column with no elements? Rewrite the elementary row operations and the exercises of this section for this altered representation.

7. Assume that dummy rows and columns did not exist. Instead, assume that there are two arrays *colfirst* and *rowfirst*, as described in the text, and assume that the

row and column lists are linear rather than circular. Rewrite the programs in this section under these conditions.

8. Implement the elementary row operations for a matrix that is stored as a single linked list consisting of all the nonzero elements of the first row followed by all the nonzero elements of the second row, and so on, as described in the text. Implement the exercises in this section for this representation.

9. The following questionnaire containing five questions has been completed by a large number of people:

   (i)   Your sex is (1) male (2) female.
   (ii)   Your income is (1) below $10,000 (2) $10,000 to $20,000 (3) $20,000 to $30,000 (4) $30,000 to $40,000 (5) above $40,000.
   (iii) Your political affiliation is (1) Democratic (2) Republican (3) Independent.
   (iv)   You smoke (1) cigars only (2) pipe only (3) less than one pack of cigarettes a day (4) one to two packs of cigarettes a day (5) more than two packs of cigarettes a day (6) not at all.
   (v)   Your age is (1) below 20 (2) 20 to 29 (3) 30 to 39 (4) 40 to 49 (5) 50 to 59 (6) 60 or above.

   The results have been entered on input lines so that the respondent's name appears in columns 1 to 30, and columns 31 to 35 contain five digits representing the respondent's answers to the five questions. Write a program to read such input and create a data structure in which each node containing a name is on five lists, each list representing those people who answered a particular question the same way.

10. Write a routine that accepts a pointer to the data structure created in Exercise 9 and a five-digit code. The code represents a set of answers to the five questions, but a 0 means that we do not care about a particular answer. For example, the code 14020 represents all male pipe smokers who make between $30,000 and $40,000 a year. The routine should print the names of all respondents who have answered the questionnaire according to the code.

6

TREES

In this chapter, we focus attention on a data structure that is extremely useful in many applications—the tree. We define several different forms of this data structure and show how they can be represented in Pascal and how they can be applied to solving a wide variety of problems. As with lists, we treat trees primarily as data structures rather than as data types. That is, we are primarily concerned with implementation rather than mathematical definition.

1. BINARY TREES

A *binary tree* is a finite set of elements that is either empty or is partitioned into three disjoint subsets. The first subset contains a single element called the *root* of the tree. The other two subsets are themselves binary trees, called the *left* and *right subtrees* of the original tree. Note that a left or right subtree can be empty. Each element of a binary tree is called a *node* of the tree.

A conventional method of picturing a binary tree is shown in Figure 6.1.1. This tree consists of nine nodes with A as its root. Its left subtree is rooted at B, and its right subtree is rooted at C. This is indicated by the two branches emanating from A—to B on the left and to C on the right. The absence of a branch indicates an empty subtree. For example, the left subtree of the binary tree rooted at C and the right subtree of the binary tree rooted at E are both empty. The binary trees rooted at D, G, H, and I have empty right and left subtrees.

Figure 6.1.2 illustrates some structures that are not binary trees. Be

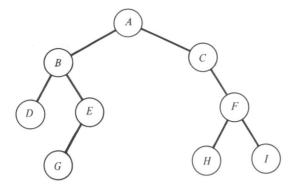

Figure 6.1.1   A binary tree.

sure that you understand why each of them is not a binary tree as was just defined.

If *A* is the root of a binary tree and *B* is the root of its left or right subtree, then *A* is said to be the *father* of *B* and *B* is said to be the *left* or *right son* of *A*. A node that has no sons (such as *D*, *G*, *H*, or *I* of Figure 6.1.1) is called a *leaf*. Node $n1$ is an *ancestor* of node $n2$ (and $n2$ is a *descendant* of $n1$) if $n1$ is either the father of $n2$ or the father of some ancestor of $n2$. For example, in the tree of Figure 6.1.1, *A* is an ancestor of *G* and *H* is a descendant of *C*, but *E* is neither an ancestor nor a descendant of *C*. Node $n2$ is a *left descendant* of node $n1$ if $n2$ is either the left son of $n1$ or a descendant of the left son of $n1$. A *right descendant* may be similarly defined. Two nodes are *brothers* if they are left and right sons of the same father.

Although natural trees grow with their roots in the ground and their leafs in the air, computer scientists almost universally portray tree data structures with the root at the top and leafs at the bottom. The direction from the root to the leafs is "down," and the opposite direction is "up." Going from the leafs to the root is called "climbing" the tree, while going from the root to the leafs is called "descending" the tree.

If every nonleaf node in a binary tree has nonempty left and right subtrees, the tree is termed a *strictly binary tree*. Thus the tree of Figure 6.1.3 is strictly binary while that of Figure 6.1.1 is not (because nodes *C* and *E* have one son each). A strictly binary tree with *n* leafs always contains $2n - 1$ nodes. The proof of this fact is left as an exercise for the reader.

The *level* of a node in a binary tree is defined as follows: The root of the tree has level 0, and the level of any other node in the tree is one more than the level of its father. For example, in the binary tree of Figure 6.1.1, node *E* is at level 2 and node *H* is at level 3. The *depth* of a binary tree is the maximum level of any leaf in the tree. This equals the length of the longest path from the root to any leaf. Thus, the depth of the tree of Figure 6.1.1 is 3. A *complete binary tree of depth d* is the strictly binary tree, all of whose leafs are at level *d*. Figure 6.1.4 illustrates the complete binary tree of depth 3.

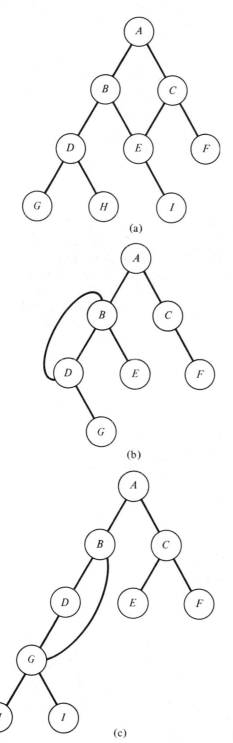

(a)

(b)

(c)

Figure 6.1.2 Structures which are not binary trees.

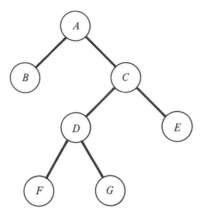

Figure 6.1.3 A strictly binary tree.

If a binary tree contains m nodes at level l, then it contains at most $2m$ nodes at level $l + 1$. Since a binary tree can contain at most one node at level 0 (the root), it can contain at most 2^l nodes at level l. A complete binary tree of depth d is the binary tree of depth d that contains exactly 2^l nodes at each level l between 0 and d. (This is equivalent to saying that it is the binary tree of depth d that contains exactly 2^d nodes at level d.) The total number of nodes in a complete binary tree of depth d, tn, equals the sum of the number of nodes at each level between 0 and d. Thus

$$tn = 2^0 + 2^1 + 2^2 + \ldots + 2^d = \sum_{j=0}^{d} 2^j$$

By induction, it can be shown that this sum equals $2^{d+1} - 1$. Since all leafs in such a tree are at level d, there are 2^d leafs and, therefore, $2^d - 1$ nonleaf nodes.

Figure 6.1.4 A complete binary tree of level 3.

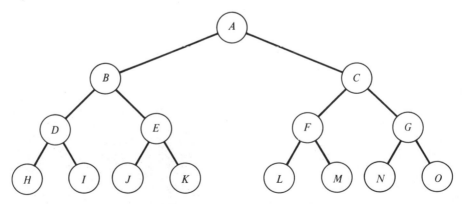

Similarly, if the number of nodes, tn, in a complete binary tree is known, we can compute its depth d from the equation $tn = 2^{d+1} - 1$. d equals one less than the number of times 2 must be multiplied by itself to reach $tn + 1$. In mathematics, $\log_b x$ is defined as the number of times b must be multiplied by itself to reach x. Thus we may say that, in a complete binary tree, d equals $\log_2 (tn + 1) - 1$. For example, the complete binary tree of Figure 6.1.4 contains 15 nodes and is of depth 3. Note that 15 equals $2^{3+1} - 1$ and 3 equals $\log_2 (15 + 1) - 1$.

$\log_2 x$ is much smaller than x; for example, $\log_2 1024$ equals 10 and $\log_2 1,000,000$ is less than 20. The significance of a complete binary tree is that it is the binary tree with the maximum number of nodes for a given depth. Put another way, although a complete binary tree contains many nodes, the distance from the root to any leaf (the tree's depth) is relatively small.

A binary tree of depth d is an ***almost complete binary tree*** if

1. Each leaf in the tree is either at level d or at level $d - 1$.
2. For any node nd in the tree with a right descendant at level d, all the left descendants of nd that are leafs are also at level d.

The strictly binary tree of Figure 6.1.5(a) is not almost complete since it contains leafs at levels 1, 2, and 3, thereby violating condition 1. The strictly binary tree of Figure 6.1.5(b) satisfies condition 1 since every leaf is either at level 2 or at level 3. However, condition 2 is violated since A has a right descendant at level 3 (J) but also has a left descendant that is a leaf at level 2 (E). The strictly binary tree of Figure 6.1.5(c) satisfies both conditions 1 and 2 and is therefore an almost complete binary tree. The binary tree of Figure 6.1.5(d) is also an almost complete binary tree but is not strictly binary since node E has a left son but not a right son. (We should note that many texts refer to such a tree as a "complete binary tree" rather than as an "almost complete binary tree." Still other texts use the term "complete" or "fully binary" to refer to the concept that we call "strictly binary." We use the terms "strictly binary," "complete," and "almost complete" as we have defined them here.)

The nodes of an almost complete binary tree can be numbered so that the root is assigned the number 1, a left son is assigned twice the number assigned its father, and a right son is assigned one more than twice the number assigned its father. Figures 6.1.5(c) and (d) illustrate this numbering technique. Each node in an almost complete binary tree is assigned a unique number that defines the node's position within the tree.

An almost complete strictly binary tree with n leafs has $2n - 1$ nodes, as does any other strictly binary tree with n leafs. An almost complete binary tree with n leafs that is not strictly binary has $2n$ nodes. There are two distinct almost complete binary trees with n leafs, one of which is strictly

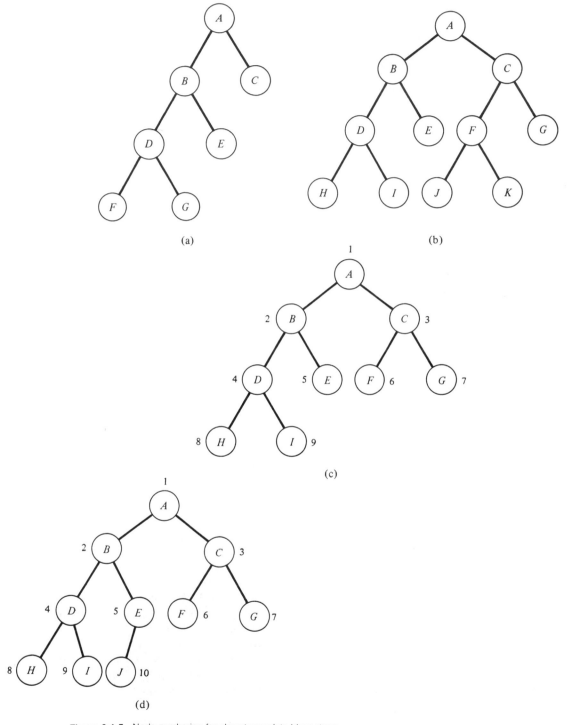

(a)

(b)

(c)

(d)

Figure 6.1.5 Node numbering for almost complete binary trees.

binary and one of which is not. For example, the trees of Figures 6.1.5(c) and (d) are both almost complete and have five leafs; however, the tree of Figure 6.1.5(c) is strictly binary while that of Figure 6.1.5(d) is not.

There is only a single almost complete binary tree with n nodes. This tree is strictly binary if and only if n is odd. Thus the tree of Figure 6.1.5(c) is the only almost complete binary tree with 9 nodes and is strictly binary because 9 is odd, while the tree of Figure 6.1.5(d) is the only almost complete binary tree with 10 nodes and is not strictly binary because 10 is even.

An almost complete binary tree of depth d is intermediate between the complete binary tree of depth $d - 1$, which contains $2^d - 1$ nodes, and the complete binary tree of depth d, which contains $2^{d+1} - 1$ nodes. If tn is the total number of nodes in an almost complete binary tree, then its depth is the largest integer less than or equal to $\log_2 tn$. For example, the almost complete binary trees with 4, 5, 6, and 7 nodes have depth 2, and the almost complete binary trees with 8, 9, 10, 11, 12, 13, 14, and 15 nodes have depth 3.

Operations on Binary Trees

A number of primitive operations can be applied to a binary tree. If p is a pointer to a node nd of a binary tree, then the function $info(p)$ returns the contents of nd. The functions $left(p)$, $right(p)$, $father(p)$, and $brother(p)$ return pointers to the left son of nd, the right son of nd, the father of nd, and the brother of nd, respectively. These functions return the nil pointer if nd has no left son, right son, father, or brother. Finally, the logical functions $isleft(p)$ and $isright(p)$ return the value *true* if nd is a left or right son, respectively, of some other node in the tree and *false* otherwise.

Note that the functions $isleft(p)$, $isright(p)$, and $brother(p)$ can be implemented using the functions $left(p)$, $right(p)$, and $father(p)$. For example, $isleft$ may be implemented as follows:

$q := father(p);$
if $q = nil$
  then $isleft := false$ {p points to the root}
  else if $left(q) = p$
      then $isleft := true$
      else $isleft := false$

$isright$ may be implemented in a similar manner or by calling $isleft$. $brother(p)$ may be implemented using $isleft$ or $isright$ as follows:

if $father(p) = nil$
  then $brother := nil$ {p points to the root}
  else if $isleft(p)$
      then $brother := right(father(p))$
      else $brother := left(father(p))$

In constructing a binary tree, the operations *maketree*, *setleft*, and *setright* are useful. *maketree*(x) creates a new binary tree consisting of a single node with information field x and returns a pointer to that node. *setleft* (p, x) accepts a pointer p to a binary tree node with no left son. It creates a new left son of *node*(p) with information field x. *setright*(p, x) is analogous to *setleft* except that it creates a right son of *node*(p).

Applications of Binary Trees

A binary tree is a useful data structure when two-way decisions must be made at each point in a process. For example, suppose we wanted to find all duplicates in a list of numbers. One way of doing this is to compare each number with all those that precede it. However, this involves a large number of comparisons.

The number of comparisons can be reduced by using a binary tree. The first number in the list is placed in a node that is established as the root of a binary tree with empty left and right subtrees. Each successive number in the list is then compared to the number in the root. If it matches, we have a duplicate. If it is smaller, we examine the left subtree; if it is larger, we examine the right subtree. If the subtree is empty, the number is not a duplicate and is placed into a new node at that position in the tree. If the subtree is nonempty, we compare the number to the contents of the root of the subtree and the entire process is repeated with the subtree. An algorithm for doing this follows:

```
read (number);
tree: = maketree(number); { put the first number in the tree }
while there are numbers left in the input
    do begin
          read(number);
          p: = tree;
          q: = tree;
          while (number <> info(p)) and (q <> nil)
              do begin
                      p: = q;
                      if number < info(p)
                          then q: = left(p)
                          else q: = right(p)
                  end;
          if number = info(p)
              then print(number,' is a duplicate')
              else { insert number to the left or right of p }
                  if number < info(p)
                      then setleft(p, number)
                      else setright(p, number)
    end {while...do begin}
```

Figure 6.1.6 illustrates the tree constructed from the input 14, 15, 4, 9, 7, 18, 3, 5, 16, 4, 20, 17, 9, 14, 5.

Another common operation is to *traverse* a binary tree, that is, to pass through the tree, enumerating each of its nodes once. We may simply wish to print the contents of each node as we enumerate it, or we may wish to process it in some other fashion. In either case, we speak of *visiting* each node as it is enumerated.

The order in which the nodes of a linear list are visited in a traversal is clearly from first to last. However, there is no such "natural" linear order for the nodes of a tree. Thus different orderings are used for traversal in different cases. We shall define three of these traversal methods. In each of these methods, nothing need be done to traverse an empty binary tree. The methods are all defined recursively so that traversing a binary tree involves visiting the root and traversing its left and right subtrees. The only difference among the methods is the order in which these three operations are performed.

To traverse a nonempty binary tree in *preorder* (also known as *depth-first order*), we perform the following three operations:

1. Visit the root.
2. Traverse the left subtree in preorder.
3. Traverse the right subtree in preorder.

To traverse a nonempty binary tree in *inorder* (or *symmetric order*);

1. Traverse the left subtree in inorder.
2. Visit the root.
3. Traverse the right subtree in inorder.

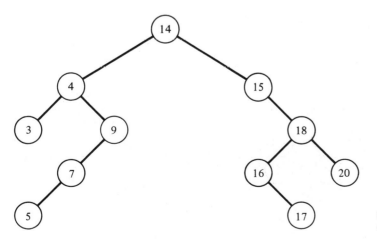

Figure 6.1.6 A binary tree constructed for finding duplicates.

To traverse a nonempty binary tree in *postorder*;

1. Traverse the left subtree in postorder.
2. Traverse the right subtree in postorder.
3. Visit the root.

Figure 6.1.7 illustrates two binary trees and their traversals in preorder, inorder, and postorder.

Many algorithms that use binary trees proceed in two phases. The first phase builds a binary tree and the second traverses the tree. As an example of such an algorithm, consider the following sorting method. Given a list of numbers in an input file, we wish to print them in ascending order. As we read the numbers, they can be inserted into a binary tree such as the one of Figure 6.1.6. However, unlike the previous algorithm used to find

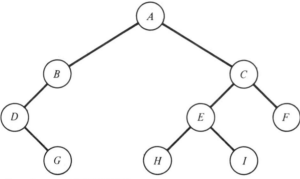

Preorder: *ABDGCEHIF*
Inorder: *DGBAHEICF*
Postorder: *GDBHIEFCA*

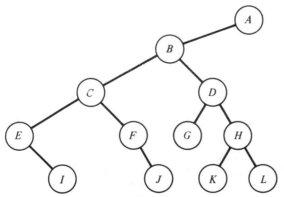

Preorder: *ABCEIFJDGHKL*
Inorder: *EICFJBGDKHLA*
Postorder: *IEJFCGKLHDBA*

Figure 6.1.7 Binary trees and their transversals.

duplicates, duplicate values are also placed in the tree. When a number is compared to the contents of a node in the tree, a left branch is taken if the number is smaller than the contents of the node and a right branch if it is greater or equal to the contents of the node. Thus if the input list is

$$14 \quad 15 \quad 4 \quad 9 \quad 7 \quad 18 \quad 3 \quad 5 \quad 16 \quad 4 \quad 20 \quad 17 \quad 9 \quad 14 \quad 5$$

the binary tree of Figure 6.1.8 is produced.

Such a binary tree has the property that all elements in the left subtree of a node n are less than the contents of n and all elements in the right subtree of n are greater than or equal to the contents of n. A binary tree that has this property is called a *binary search tree*. If a binary search tree is traversed in inorder (left, root, right) and the contents of each node are printed as the node is visited, the numbers are printed in ascending order. Convince yourself that this is the case for the binary search tree of Figure 6.1.8. Binary search trees and their use in sorting and searching are discussed further in Sections 7.3 and 8.2.

As another application of binary trees, consider the following method of representing an expression containing operands and binary operators by a strictly binary tree. The root of the strictly binary tree contains an operator that is to be applied to the results of evaluating the expressions represented

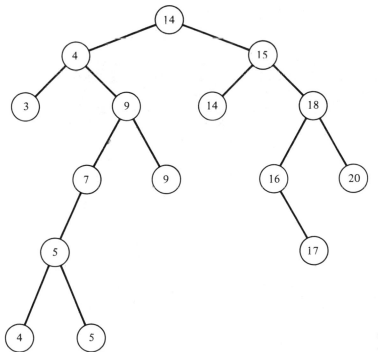

Figure 6.1.8 A binary tree constructed for sorting.

by the left and right subtrees. A node representing an operator is a nonleaf while a node representing an operand is a leaf. Figure 6.1.9 illustrates some expressions and their tree representations. (The character '$' is again used to represent exponentiation.)

Let us see what happens when these binary expression trees are traversed. Traversing such a tree in preorder means that the operator (the root) precedes its two operands (the subtrees). Thus a preorder traversal yields the prefix form of the expression. (For definitions of the prefix and postfix forms of an arithmetic expression, see Sections 2.3 and 3.3.) Traversing the binary trees of Figure 6.1.9 yields the prefix forms

$+A*BC$	(Figure 6.1.9(a))
$*+ABC$	(Figure 6.1.9(b))
$+A*-BC\$D*EF$	(Figure 6.1.9(c))
$\$+A*BC*+ABC$	(Figure 6.1.9(d))

Similarly, traversing a binary expression tree in postorder places an operator after its two operands so that a postorder traversal produces the postfix form of the expression. The postorder traversals of the binary trees of Figure 6.1.9 yield the postfix forms

$ABC*+$	(Figure 6.1.9(a))
$AB+C*$	(Figure 6.1.9(b))
$ABC-DEF*\$*+$	(Figure 6.1.9(c))
$ABC*+AB+C*\$$	(Figure 6.1.9(d))

What happens when a binary expression tree is traversed in inorder? Since the root (operator) is visited after the nodes of the left subtree and before the nodes of the right subtree (the two operands), we might expect an inorder traversal to yield the infix form of the expression. Indeed if the binary tree of Figure 6.1.9(a) is traversed, the infix expression $A + B * C$ is obtained. However, a binary expression tree does not contain parentheses since the ordering of the operations is implied by the structure of the tree. Thus an expression whose infix form requires parentheses to override explicitly the conventional precedence rules cannot be retrieved by a simple inorder traversal. The inorder traversals of the trees of Figure 6.1.9 yield the expressions

$A+B*C$	(Figure 6.1.9(a))
$A+B*C$	(Figure 6.1.9(b))
$A+B-C*D\$E*F$	(Figure 6.1.9(c))
$A+B*C\$A+B*C$	(Figure 6.1.9(d))

which are correct except for parentheses.

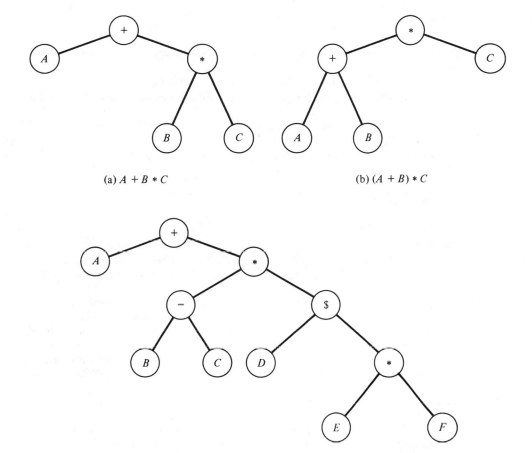

(a) $A + B * C$

(b) $(A + B) * C$

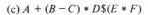

(c) $A + (B - C) * D\$(E * F)$

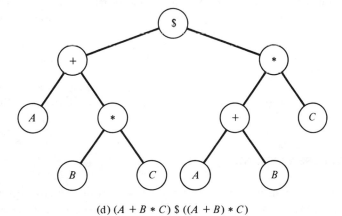

(d) $(A + B * C) \$ ((A + B) * C)$

Figure 6.1.9 Expressions and their binary tree representation.

EXERCISES

1. Prove that the root of a binary tree is an ancestor of every node in the tree except itself.

2. Prove that a node of a binary tree has at most one father.

3. How many ancestors does a node at level n in a binary tree have? Prove your answer.

4. Write recursive and nonrecursive algorithms to determine
   (a) the number of nodes in a binary tree.
   (b) the sum of the contents of all the nodes in a binary tree.
   (c) the depth of a binary tree.

5. Write an algorithm to determine if a binary tree is
   (a) strictly binary.
   (b) complete.
   (c) almost complete.

6. Prove that a strictly binary tree with n leafs contains $2n - 1$ nodes.

7. Given a strictly binary tree with n leafs, let $level(i)$ for i between 1 and n equal the level of the ith leaf. Prove that the sum of $1/(2^{level(i)})$ for all i between 1 and n equals 1.

8. Prove that the nodes of an almost complete strictly binary tree with n leafs can be numbered from 1 to $2n - 1$ in such a way that the number assigned to the left son of the node numbered i is $2i$ and the number assigned to the right son of the node numbered i is $2i + 1$.

9. Two binary trees are *similar* if they are both empty or if they are both nonempty, their left subtrees are similar, and their right subtrees are similar. Write an algorithm to determine if two binary trees are similar.

10. Two binary trees are *mirror similar* if they are both empty or if they are both nonempty and the left subtree of each is mirror similar to the right subtree of the other. Write an algorithm to determine if two binary trees are mirror similar.

11. Write algorithms to determine whether or not one binary tree is similar and mirror similar (see the previous exercises) to some subtree of another.

12. Develop an algorithm to find duplicates in a list of numbers without using a binary tree. If there are n distinct numbers in the list, how many times must two numbers be compared for equality in your algorithm? What if all n numbers are equal?

13. (a) Write an algorithm that accepts a pointer to a binary search tree and deletes the smallest element from the tree.
    (b) Show how to implement an ascending priority queue as a binary search tree. Present algorithms for the operations *pqinsert* and *pqmindelete* on a binary search tree (see Section 4.1).

14. Write an algorithm that accepts a binary tree representing an expression and returns the infix version of the expression that contains only those parentheses that are necessary.

2. BINARY TREE REPRESENTATIONS

In this section we examine various methods of implementing binary trees in Pascal and present routines that build and traverse binary trees. We also present some additional applications of binary trees.

Node Representation of Binary Trees

As is the case with list nodes, tree nodes may be implemented as array elements or as allocations of a dynamic variable. Each node contains *info*, *left*, *right*, and *father* fields. The *left*, *right*, and *father* fields of a node point to the node's left son, right son, and father, respectively. Using the array implementation, we may declare

```
const numnodes = 500;
type  nodeptr = 0..numnodes;
      nodetype = record
                     info: integer;
                     left: nodeptr;
                     right: nodeptr;
                     father: nodeptr
                 end;
var   node: array[1..numnodes] of nodetype;
```

Under this representation, the operations *info*(*p*), *left*(*p*), *right*(*p*), and *father*(*p*) are implemented by references to *node*[*p*].*info*, *node*[*p*].*left*, *node*[*p*].*right*, and *node*[*p*].*father*, respectively. The operations *isleft*(*p*), *isright*(*p*), and *brother*(*p*) can be implemented in terms of the operations *left*(*p*), *right*(*p*), and *father*(*p*), as described in the preceding section.

To implement *isleft* and *isright* more efficiently, we can also include within each node an additional boolean field *isleft*. The value of this field is *true* if the node is a left son and *false* otherwise. The root is uniquely identified by a *nil* value (zero) in its *father* field. The external pointer to a tree usually points to its root.

Alternatively, the type *nodeptr* may be defined to allow positive or negative values, and the sign of the *father* field could be negative if the node is a left son or positive if it is a right son. The pointer to a node's father is then given by the absolute value of the *father* field. The *isleft* or *isright* operations would then need only examine the sign of the *father* field.

To implement *brother*(*p*) more efficiently, we can also include an additional *brother* field in each node.

Once the array of nodes is declared, we could create an available list of nodes by declaring

```
var avail, i: nodeptr;
```

and then executing the following statements:

```
avail := 1;
for i := 1 to numnodes-1
    do node[i].left := i+1;
node[numnodes].left := 0
```

The routines *getnode* and *freenode* are straightforward and are left as exercises. Note that the available list is not a binary tree but a linear list whose nodes are linked together by the *left* field. Each node in a tree is taken from the available pool when needed and returned to the available pool when no longer in use. This representation is called the **linked array representation** of a binary tree.

Alternatively, a node may be defined by

```
type nodeptr = ↑nodetype;
     nodetype = record
                   info:  integer;
                   left:  nodeptr;
                   right: nodeptr;
                   father: nodeptr
                end;
```

The operations *info(p)*, *left(p)*, *right(p)*, and *father(p)* would be implemented by references to *p↑.info*, *p↑.left*, *p↑.right*, and *p↑.father*, respectively. Under this implementation, an explicit available list is not needed. The routines *getnode* and *freenode* simply allocate and free a dynamic variable of type *nodetype* using the system routines *new* and *dispose*. This representation is called the **dynamic node representation** of a binary tree.

Both the linked array representation and the dynamic node representation are implementations of an abstract **linked representation** (also called the **node representation**) in which explicit pointers link together the nodes of a binary tree.

We now present Pascal implementations of the binary tree operations under the dynamic node representation and leave the linked array implementations as simple exercises for the reader. The *maketree* function, which allocates a node and sets it as the root of a single-node binary tree, may be written as follows:

```
function maketree (x: integer): nodeptr;
var p: nodeptr;
begin {function maketree}
     p :=getnode;
     p↑.info:= x;
     p↑.left:= nil;
     p↑.right:= nil;
     p↑.father:= nil;
     maketree:= p
end {function maketree};
```

The routine *setleft(p, x)* sets a node with contents *x* as the left son of *node(p)* which is *p↑* under the dynamic representation).

```
procedure setleft (p: nodeptr; x: integer);
var q: nodeptr;
begin { procedure setleft}
        if p = nil
          then error ('void insertion')
          else if p↑.left <> nil
                  then error ('invalid insertion')
                  else begin
                          q := maketree (x);
                          p↑.left: = q;
                          q↑.father: = p
                        end {else begin}
end { procedure setleft};
```

The routine *setright* (*p*, *x*) to create a right son of *node*(*p*) with contents *x* is similar and is left as an exercise for the reader.

It is not always necessary to use *father*, *left*, and *right* fields. If a tree is always traversed in downward fashion (from the root to the leafs), the *father* operation is never used; in that case, a *father* field is unnecessary. For example, preorder, inorder, and postorder traversal do not use the *father* field. Similarly, if a tree is always traversed in upward fashion (from the leafs to the root), *left* and *right* fields are not needed. The *isleft* and *isright* operations could be implemented even without *left* and *right* fields by using a signed pointer in the *father* field under the linked array representation, as discussed earlier: a right son contains a positive *father* value, and a left son a negative *father* field. Of course, the routines *maketree*, *setleft*, and *setright* must then be suitably modified for these representations. Under the dynamic node representation, an *isleft* boolean field is required in addition to *father* if *left* and *right* fields are not present and it is desired to implement the *isleft* or *isright* operation.

The following program uses a binary search tree to find duplicate numbers in an input file in which each number is on a separate input line. It closely follows the algorithm of Section 6.1. Only top-down links are used, so no *father* field is needed.

```
program dup (input, output);
type nodeptr = ↑nodetype;
     nodetype = record
                    info: integer;
                    left: nodeptr;
                    right: nodeptr
                  end;
var   p, q, tree: nodeptr;
      number: integer;
```

```
begin {program dup}
      readln(number);
      tree := maketree(number);
      while not eof
          do begin
                  readln(number);
                  p := tree;
                  q := tree;
                  while (number <> p↑.info) and (q <> nil)
                      do begin
                              p := q;
                              if number < p↑.info
                                  then q := p↑.left
                                  else q := p↑.right
                          end {while...do begin};
                  if number = p↑.info
                      then writeln(number, 'is a duplicate')
                      else if number < p↑.info
                              then setleft(p, number)
                              else setright(p, number)
          end {while...do begin}
end {program dup}.
```

Internal and External Nodes

By definition, leaf nodes have no sons. Thus, in the linked representation of binary trees, left and right pointers are only needed in nonleaf nodes. Sometimes, two separate sets of nodes are used for nonleafs and leafs. Nonleaf nodes contain *info*, *left*, and *right* fields (often, no information is associated with nonleafs so that an *info* field is unnecessary) and are allocated as dynamic records or as an array of records managed using an available list. Leaf nodes do not contain a *left* or *right* field and are kept as a single *info* array that is allocated sequentially as needed. (This assumes that leafs are never freed, which is often the case.) Alternatively, they can be allocated as dynamic variables containing only an *info* value. This saves a great deal of space, since leafs often represent a majority of the nodes in a binary tree. Each (leaf or nonleaf) node can also contain a *father* field, if necessary.

When this distinction is made between nonleaf and leaf nodes, nonleafs are called *internal nodes* and leafs are called *external nodes*. The terminology is also often used even when only a single type of node is defined. Of course, a son pointer within an internal node must be labeled as pointing to an internal or an external node. This can be done in Pascal in two ways. One technique is to declare two different node types and pointer types and to use a variant record for internal nodes, with each variant containing one of the two pointer types. The other technique is to retain a single pointer type and a single node type, where the node type is a variant record that does (if the node is an internal node) or does not (if an external node) contain *left* and *right* pointer fields. We will see an example of this latter technique at the end of this section.

Implicit Array Representation of Binary Trees

Recall from Section 1 that the n nodes of an almost complete binary tree can be numbered from 1 to n so that the number assigned a left son is twice the number assigned its father and the number assigned a right son is one more than twice the number assigned its father. We can represent an almost complete binary tree without *father*, *left*, or *right* links. Instead, the nodes can be kept in an array *info* of size n. We refer to the node at position p simply as "node p." *info*[p] holds the contents of node p.

The root of the tree is at position 1, so that *tree*, the external pointer to the tree root, always equals 1. The node in position p (that is, node p) is the implicit father of nodes $2p$ and $2p + 1$. The left son of node p is node $2p$ and its right son is node $2p + 1$. Thus the operation *left*(p) is implemented by $2p$ and *right*(p) by $2p + 1$. Given a left son at position p, its right brother is at $p + 1$ and, given a right son at position p, its left brother is at $p - 1$. *father*(p) is implemented by p *div* 2. p points to a left son if and only if p is a multiple of 2. Thus the test for whether node p is a left son (the *isleft* operation) is to check whether p *mod* 2 equals 0 [or whether *odd*(p) is *false*]. Figure 6.2.1 illustrates arrays that represent the almost complete binary trees of Figures 6.1.5(c) and (d).

We can extend this ***implicit array representation*** of almost complete binary trees to an implicit array representation of binary trees generally. We do this by identifying an almost complete binary tree that contains the binary tree being represented. Figure 6.2.2(a) illustrates two (nonalmost-complete) binary trees, and Figure 6.2.2(b) illustrates the smallest almost complete binary trees that contain them. Finally, Figure 6.2.2(c) illustrates the implicit array representations of these almost complete binary trees and, by extension, of the original binary trees. The implicit array representation is also called the ***sequential representation,*** as contrasted with the linked representation presented earlier, because it allows a tree to be implemented in a contiguous block of memory (an array) rather than via pointers connecting widely separated nodes.

Under the sequential representation, an array element is allocated whether or not it serves to contain a node of a tree. We must, therefore, flag unused array elements as nonexistent, or ***nil,*** tree nodes. This may be accomplished by one of two methods. One method is to set *info*[p] to a special value if node p is nil. This special value should be invalid as the information content of a legitimate tree node. For example, in a tree con-

Fig. 6.2.1

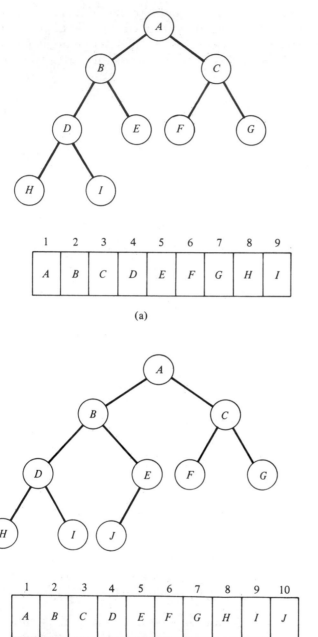

1	2	3	4	5	6	7	8	9
A	B	C	D	E	F	G	H	I

(a)

1	2	3	4	5	6	7	8	9	10
A	B	C	D	E	F	G	H	I	J

(b)

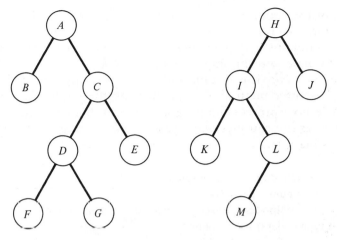

(a) Two binary trees

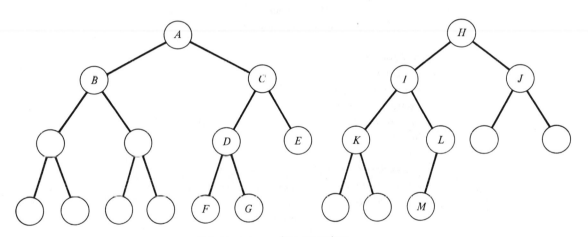

(b) Almost complete extensions

1	2	3	4	5	6	7	8	9	10	11	12	13
A	B	C			D	E					F	G

1	2	3	4	5	6	7	8	9	10
H	I	J	K	L					M

(c) Array representations

Fig. 6.2.2

taining positive numbers, a nil node may be indicated by a negative *info* value. Alternatively, we may add a boolean field, *used*, to each node. Each node then contains two fields: *info* and *used*. The entire structure is contained in an array *node*. *used*(*p*), implemented as *node*[*p*].*used*, is *true* if node *p* is not a nil node and *false* if it is a nil node. *info*(*p*) is implemented by *node*[*p*].*info*. We use this latter method in implementing the sequential representation.

We now present the program to find duplicate numbers in an input list, as well as the routines *maketree* and *setleft*, using the sequential representation of binary trees.

```
program dup2(input, output);
const numnodes = 500;
      dblnodes = 1001;   { twice the number of nodes plus one }
type nodeptr = 1..numnodes;
     nodeptr2 = 1..dblnodes;
     nodetype = record
                    info: integer;
                    used: boolean
                end;
var p: nodeptr;
    q: nodeptr2;
    node: array[1..numnodes] of nodetype;
    number: integer;
{ routines maketree, setleft and setright are inserted here }
begin { program dup2}
    readln(number);
    maketree(number);
    while not eof
        do begin
            readln(number);
            p:= 1;
            q:= 1;
            while (q <= numnodes) and (node[q].used) and
                                (number <> node[p].info)
                do begin
                    p:= q;
                    if number < node[p].info
                        then q:= 2 * p
                        else q:= 2 * p + 1
                    end {while... do begin};
            { if the number is in the tree, it is a }
            {              duplicate               }
            if number = node[p].info
                then writeln(number, ' is a duplicate')
                else {insert the number into the tree}
                    if number < node[p].info
```

```
              then setleft (p, number)
              else setright (p, number)
        end {while not eof do begin}
  end {program dup2}.

  procedure maketree (x: integer);
  var p: nodeptr;
  begin {procedure maketree}
        { the tree consists of node 1 alone }
        {    all other nodes are nil nodes    }
        for p := 2 to numnodes
            do node[p].used := false;
        node[1].info := x;
        node[1].used := true
  end {procedure maketree};

  procedure setleft (p: nodeptr; x: integer);
  var q: nodeptr2;
  begin {procedure setleft}
        q := 2*p;    { q is the position of the left son }
        if q > numnodes
          then error('array overflow')
          else if node[q].used
                  then error('invalid insertion')
                  else begin
                        node[q].info := x;
                        node[q].used := true
                    end {else begin}
  end {procedure setleft};
```

The routine for *setright* is similar.

Note that under this implementation, the routine *maketree* initializes the fields *info* and *used* to represent a tree with a single node. It is no longer necessary for *maketree* to be a function since, under this representation, the single binary tree represented by the *info* and *used* fields is always rooted at node 1. That is the reason that p is initialized to 1 in *dup2* before we move down the tree. It is also necessary to introduce the type *nodeptr2* to represent nonexistent array positions that might be computed in attempting to go to a left son or right son beyond the array bounds. Note also that under this representation, it is always required to check that the bound (*numnodes*) has not been exceeded whenever we move down the tree.

Choosing a Binary Tree Representation

Which representation of binary trees is preferable? There is no general answer to this question. The sequential representation is somewhat simpler, although it is necessary to ensure that all pointers are within the array bounds. The sequential representation clearly saves storage space for trees known to be almost complete, since it eliminates the need for the fields *left*, *right*, and *father* and does not even require a *used* field. It is also space-efficient for trees that are only a few nodes short of being almost complete, or when nodes are successively eliminated from a tree that originates as almost complete, although a *used* field might then be required. However, the sequential representation can only be used in a context in which only a single tree is required, or where the number of trees needed and each of their maximum sizes is fixed in advance.

By contrast, the linked representation requires *left*, *right*, and *father* fields (although we have seen that one or two of these may be eliminated in specific situations) but allows much more flexible use of the collection of nodes. In the linked representation, a particular node may be placed at any location in any tree, whereas in the sequential representation, a node can be utilized only if it is needed at a specific location in a specific tree. In addition, under the dynamic node representation, the total number of trees and nodes is limited only by the amount of available memory. Thus, the linked representation is preferable in the general, dynamic situation of many trees of unpredictable shape.

The duplicate-finding program is a good illustration of the trade-offs involved. The program *dup*, which utilized the linked representation of binary trees, required *left* and *right* fields in addition to *info*. (The *father* field was not necessary in that program.) *dup2*, which utilizes the sequential representation, requires only an additional field *used* (and this too could be eliminated if only positive numbers are allowed in the input so that a nil tree node can be represented by a specific negative *info* value). The sequential representation can be used for this example because only a single tree is required.

However, *dup2* might not work for as many input cases as *dup*. For example, suppose the input is in ascending order. Then the tree formed by either program has all nil left subtress (you are invited to verify that this is the case by simulating the programs for such input). In that case, the only elements of *info* that are occupied in *dup2* are 1, 3, 7, 15, and so on (each position is one more than twice the previous one). If the value of *numnodes* is kept at 500, a maximum of only 16 distinct ascending numbers can be accommodated by *dup2* (the last one will be at position 255). This can be contrasted with *dup*, which permits up to 500 distinct numbers in ascending order before it runs out of space. In the remainder of the text, except as noted otherwise, we assume the linked representation of a binary tree.

Binary Tree Traversals in Pascal

We may implement the traversal of binary trees in Pascal by recursive routines that mirror the traversal definitions. The three Pascal routines *pretrav*, *intrav*, and *posttrav* print the contents of a binary tree in preorder, inorder, and postorder, respectively. The parameter to each routine is a pointer to the root node of a binary tree. We use the dynamic node representation of a binary tree:

```
procedure pretrav (tree: nodeptr);
begin
    if tree <> nil
        then with tree↑
                do begin
                        writeln(info);    { visit the root }
                        pretrav(left);    { traverse left subtree }
                        pretrav(right)    { traverse right subtree }
                    end {with...do begin}
end {procedure pretrav};

procedure intrav (tree: nodeptr);
begin
    if tree <> nil
        then with tree↑
                do begin
                        intrav(left);     { traverse left subtree }
                        writeln(info);    { visit the root }
                        intrav(right)     { traverse right subtree }
                    end {with...do begin}
end {procedure intrav};

procedure posttrav (tree: nodeptr);
begin
    if tree <> nil
        then with tree↑
                do begin
                    posttrav(left);    { traverse left subtree }
                    posttrav(right);   { traverse right subtree }
                    writeln(info)      { visit the root }
                    end {with...do begin}
end {procedure posttrav};
```

The reader is invited to simulate the actions of these routines on the trees of Figures 6.1.7 and 6.1.8.

Of course, the routines could be written nonrecursively to perform the necessary stacking and unstacking explicitly. For example, the following is a nonrecursive routine to traverse a binary tree in inorder:

```
        procedure intrav2 (tree; nodeptr);
        const maxstack = 100;                nodeptr = ^stack;
        type stack = record
                        top: 0..maxstack;
                        item: array [1..maxstack] of nodeptr
                     end;
     var s: stack;
         p: nodeptr;
     { routines pop, push, and empty are inserted here }
     begin {procedure intrav2}
         p: = tree;
         repeat
                { travel down left branches as far as possible }
                {       saving pointers to nodes passed       }
                while p <> nil
                    do begin
                            push (s, p);
                            p: = p↑.left
                        end {while...do begin};
                { check if finished }
                if not empty (s)
                    then begin { at this point the left subtreee is empty }
                            p: = pop (s);
                            writeln (p↑.info);     { visit the root }
                            p: = p↑.right          { traverse right subtree }
                        end {then begin}
            until (empty (s)) and (p = nil)
        end {procedure intrav2};
```

Nonrecursive routines to traverse a binary tree in postorder and preorder as well as nonrecursive traversals of binary trees using the sequential representation are left as exercises for the reader.

intrav and *intrav2* represent an excellent contrast between a recursive routine and its nonrecursive counterpart. If both routines are executed, the recursive *intrav* generally executes much more quickly than does the nonrecursive *intrav2*. This goes against the accepted "folk wisdom" that recursion is slower than iteration. The primary cause of the inefficiency of *intrav2* as written is the calls to *push*, *pop*, and *empty*. Even when the code for these functions is inserted inline into *intrav2*, *intrav2* is still slower than *intrav* because of the often superfluous tests for overflow and underflow included in that code.

Yet, even when the underflow/overflow tests are removed, *intrav* is faster than *intrav2* under a compiler that implements recursion efficiently! For example, under the **IBM PC** Pascal compiler, building a 1001-node almost complete binary tree and traversing it 100 times using *intrav* (with the *writeln* statement removed) required 16.2 seconds. Using *intrav2* (with tests removed and inline code), the same process required 20 seconds. (Turbo Pascal on the IBM PC required 23 seconds for both tests.)

The efficiency of the recursive process in this case is due to a number of factors:

- There is no "extra" recursion, as there is in computing the Fibonacci numbers where $f(n - 2)$ and $f(n - 1)$ are both recomputed separately even though the value of $f(n - 2)$ is used in computing $f(n - 1)$.

- The recursion stack cannot be entirely eliminated, as it can be in computing the factorial function. Thus the automatic stacking and unstacking of built-in recursion is more efficient than the programmed version. (In many systems, stacking can be accomplished by incrementing the value of a register that points to the stack top and moving all parameters into a new data area in a single block move. Program-controlled stacking as we have implemented it requires individual assignments and increments.)

- There are no extraneous parameters and local variables, as there are, for example, in some versions of binary search. The automatic stacking of recursion does not stack any more variables than are necessary.

In cases of recursion that do not involve this excess baggage, such as inorder traversal, the programmer is well advised to use recursion directly.

The traversal routines that we have presented are derived directly from the definitions of the traversal methods. These definitions are in terms of the left and right sons of a node and do not reference a node's father. For that reason, both the recursive and nonrecursive routines do not require a *father* field and do not take advantage of such a field even if it is present. As we shall soon see, the presence of a *father* field allows us to develop nonrecursive traversal algorithms without using a stack. However, we first examine a technique for eliminating the stack in a nonrecursive traversal even if a *father* field is not available.

Threaded Binary Trees

Traversing a binary tree is a common operation, and it would be helpful to find a more efficient method for implementing the traversal. Let us examine the procedure *intrav2* to discover the reason that a stack is needed. The stack is popped when p equals the nil pointer. This happens in one of two cases. In one case, the *while* loop is exited after having been executed one or more times. This implies that the program has traveled down left branches until it reached a nil pointer, stacking a pointer to each node as it was passed. Thus the top element of the stack is the value of p before it became *nil*. If an auxiliary pointer q is kept one step behind p, the value of q can be used directly and need not be popped.

The other case in which p is *nil* is when the *while* loop is skipped entirely. This occurs after reaching a node with an empty right subtree, executing the statement $p := p\uparrow.right$, and returning to repeat the body of the *repeat* loop. At this point, we would have lost our way were it not for the stack whose top points to the node whose left subtree was just traversed. Suppose, however, that instead of containing a nil pointer in its *right* field, a node with an empty right subtree contained in its *right* field a pointer to the node that would be on top of the stack at that point in the algorithm (i.e., a pointer to its inorder successor.) Then there would no longer be a

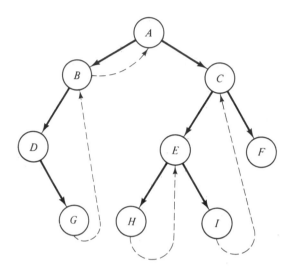

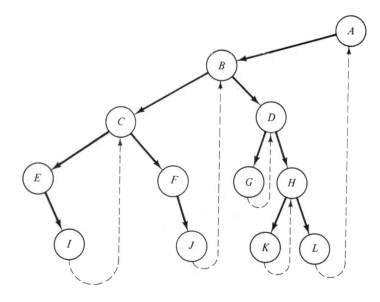

Figure 6.2.3 Right in-threaded binary trees.

need for the stack since the last node visited during a traversal of a left subtree points directly to its inorder successor. Such a pointer is called a **thread** and must be differentiable from a tree pointer that is used to link a node to its left or right subtree.

Figure 6.2.3 shows the binary trees of Figure 6.1.7 with threads replacing nil pointers in nodes with empty right subtrees. The threads are drawn with dashed lines to differentiate them from tree pointers. Note that the rightmost node in each tree still has a nil right pointer since it has no inorder successor. Such trees are called **right-inthreaded** binary trees.

To implement a right-inthreaded binary tree under the dynamic node implementation of a binary tree, an extra boolean field *rthread* is included within each node to indicate whether or not its right pointer is a thread. For consistency, the *rthread* field of the rightmost node of a tree (i.e., the last node in the tree's inorder traversal) is also set to *true* although its *right* field remains *nil*. Thus a node is defined as follows (recall that we are assuming that no *father* field exists):

```
type nodeptr = ↑nodetype;
     nodetype = record
               info:    integer;
               left:    nodeptr;   { pointer to left son }
               right:   nodeptr;   { pointer to right son or a thread }
               rthread: boolean    { rthread is true if right is nil }
                                   { or a non-nil thread }
          end;
```

We present a routine to implement inorder traversal of a right-inthreaded binary tree.

```
procedure intrav3 (tree: nodeptr);
var p, q: nodeptr;
begin
    p: = tree;
    repeat
        q: = nil;
        while p <> nil   { traverse left branch }
           do begin
                  q: = p;
                  p: = p↑.left
              end {while...do begin};
        if q <> nil
           then begin
                  writeln(q↑.info);
                  p: = q↑.right;
```

```
                              while (q↑.rthread) and (p <> nil)
                                 do begin   { backup }
                                          writeln(p↑.info);
                                          q: = p;
                                          p: = q↑.right
                                       end {while...do begin}
                                 end {then begin}
                        until q = nil
                     end {procedure intrav3};
```

In a right-inthreaded binary tree, the inorder successor of any node can be found efficiently. Such a tree can also be constructed in a straightforward manner. The routines *maketree, setleft,* and *setright* are as follows. We assume *info, left, right, rthread,* and *father* fields in each node.

```
            function maketree (x: integer): nodeptr;
            var p: nodeptr;
            begin
                  p: = getnode;
                  p↑.info: = x;
                  p↑.left: = nil;
                  p↑.right: = nil;
                  p↑.rthread: = true;
                  maketree: = p
            end {function maketree};

            procedure setleft (p: nodeptr; x: integer);
            var q: nodeptr;
            begin
               if p = nil
                  then error ('void insertion')
                  else if p↑.left <> nil
                        then error ('invalid insertion')
                        else begin
                                 q: = getnode;
                                 q↑.info: = x;
                                 p↑.left: = q;
                                 q↑.left: = nil;
                        { the inorder successor of node(q) is node(p) }
                                 q↑.right: = p;
                                 q↑.rthread: = true;
                              end {else begin}
            end {procedure setleft};
```

```
procedure setright (p: nodeptr; x: integer);
var q, r: nodeptr;
begin
    if p = nil
        then error('void insertion')
        else if (not p↑.rthread)
                then error('invalid insertion')
                else begin
                        q: = getnode;
                        q↑.info: = x;
                { save the inorder successor of node(p) }
                        r: = p↑.right;
                        p↑.right: = q;
                        p↑.rthread: = false;
                        q↑.left: = nil;
                { the inorder successor of node(q) is the }
                {        previous successor of node(p)       }
                        q↑.right: = r;
                        q↑.rthread: = true
                    end {else begin}
    end {procedure setright};
```

In the linked array implementation, a thread can be represented by a negative value of *node[p].right*. The absolute value of *node[p].right* is the index in the array *node* of the inorder successor of *node[p]*. The sign of *node[p].right* indicates whether its absolute value represents a thread (minus) or a pointer to a nonempty subtree (plus). This requires redefining *nodeptr* to accommodate negative pointers by

```
const numnodes = 500;
      negnodes = -500;
type  nodeptr = negnodes..numnodes;
```

Under this implementation, the following routine traverses a right-inthreaded binary tree in inorder. We leave *maketree*, *setleft*, and *setright* for the linked array representation as exercises for the reader.

```
procedure intrav4 (tree: nodeptr);
var p, q: nodeptr;
begin
    p: = tree;
    repeat
        { travel down left links keeping q behind p }
        q: = 0;
```

```
            while p <> 0
                do begin
                        q: = p;
                        p: = node[p].left
                    end { while...do begin };
                if q <> 0   { check if finished }
                then begin
                        writeln(node[q].info);
                        p: = node[q].right;
                        while p < 0
                            do begin
                                    q: = -p;
                                    writeln(node[q].info);
                                    p: = node[q].right
                                end {while...do begin}
                    end {then begin}
                { traverse right subtree }
            until q = 0
        end {procedure intrav4};
```

Under the sequential representation of binary trees, the *used* field can be redefined to allow it to contain threads by allowing type *nodeptr* to contain negative or positive values and declaring the type of *used* to be *nodeptr* rather than *boolean*. If i represents a node with a right son, $node[i].used$ equals 1 and its right son is at $2*i + 1$. However, if i represents a node with no right son, $node[i].used$ contains the negative of the index of its inorder successor. (Note that use of negative numbers allows us to distinguish a node with a right son from a node whose inorder successor is the root of the tree.) If i is the rightmost node of the tree, so that it has no inorder successor, $node[i].used$ can contain the special value $+2$. If i does not represent a node, then $node[i].used$ is 0. We leave the implementation of traversal algorithms for this representation as an exercise for the reader.

A *left-inthreaded* binary tree may be defined similarly as one in which each nil left pointer is altered to contain a thread to that node's inorder predecessor. An *inthreaded* binary tree may then be defined as a binary tree that is both left-inthreaded and right-inthreaded. However, left-inthreading does not yield the advantages of right-inthreading. We may also define right and left **prethreaded** binary trees in which nil right and left pointers of nodes are replaced by their preorder successors and predecessors, respectively. A right-prethreaded binary tree may be traversed efficiently in preorder without the use of a stack. A right-inthreaded binary tree may also be traversed in preorder without the use of a stack. The traversal algorithms are left as exercises for the reader.

Traversal Using a *father* Field

If each tree node contains a *father* field, neither a stack nor threads are necessary for nonrecursive traversal. Instead, when the traversal process reaches a leaf node, the *father* field can be used to climb back up the tree. When *node(p)* is reached from a left son, its right subtree must still be traversed so the algorithm proceeds to *right(p)*. When *node(p)* is reached from its right son, then both its subtrees have been traversed and the algorithm backs up farther to *father(p)*. The following routine implements this process for inorder traversal:

```
procedure intrav5 (tree: nodeptr);
var p, q: nodeptr;
begin
    q: = nil;
    p: = tree;
    repeat
        while p <> nil
            do begin
                    q: = p;
                    p: = p↑.left
                end {while...do begin};
        if q <> nil
            then begin
                    writeln(q↑.info);
                    p: = q↑.right
                end {then begin};
        while (q <> nil) and (p = nil)
                do begin        { node(q) has no right son  }
                        repeat {   backup until a left son   }
                               {      or the tree root is    }
                               {          encountered        }
                            p: = q;
                            q: = p↑.father
                        until (isleft(p)) or (q = nil);
                        if q <> nil
                            then begin
                                    writeln(q↑.info);
                                    p: = q↑.right
                                end {then begin}
                    end {while...do begin}
    until q = nil
end {procedure intray5};
```

Note that we write *isleft(p)* rather than $p\uparrow.isleft$ because an *isleft* field is unnecessary to determine if *node(p)* is a left or a right son; we can simply check if the node is its father's left son.

In this inorder traversal, a node is visited [*writeln(q↑.info)*] when its left son is recoginzed as **nil** or when it is reached after backing up from its left son. Preorder and postorder traversal are similar except that, in preorder, a node is visited only when it is reached on the way down the tree and, in postorder, a node is visited only when its right son is recognized as **nil** or when it is reached after backing up from its right son. We leave the details as an exercise for the reader.

Traversal using *father* pointers for backing up is less time-efficient than is traversal of a threaded tree. A thread points directly to a node's successor while a whole series of *father* pointers may have to be followed to reach that successor in an unthreaded tree. It is difficult to compare the time efficiencies of stack-based traversal and *father*-based traversal since the former includes the overhead of stacking and unstacking.

This backup traversal algorithm also suggests a stackless nonrecursive traversal technique for unthreaded trees, even if no *father* field exists. This technique is simple: simply reverse the son pointer on the way down the tree so that it can be used to find a way back up. On the way back up, the pointer is restored to its original value.

For example, in *intrav5*, a variable f can be introduced to hold a pointer to the father of *node(q)*. The statements

```
q: = p;
p: = p↑.left
```

in the first **while** loop can be replaced by

```
f: = q;
q: = p;
p: = p↑.left;
if p <> nil
   then q↑.left: = f
```

This modifies the left pointer of *node(q)* to point to the father of *node(q)* when going left on the way down [note that p points to the left son of *node(q)* so that we haven't lost our way]. The statement

```
p: = q↑.right
```

in both of its occurrences can be replaced by

```
p: = q↑.right;
if p <> nil
   then q↑.right: = f
```

similarly to modify the right pointer of *node*(*q*) to point to its father when going right on the way down. Finally, the statements

$$
\begin{aligned}
&p:=q;\\
&q:=p\!\uparrow\!.father
\end{aligned}
$$

in the inner *repeat* loop can be replaced by

```
p: = q;
q: = f;
if q <> nil
    then if isleft(p)
        then begin
                    f: = q↑.left
                    q↑.left: = p
            end
        else begin
                    f: = q↑.right
                    q↑.right: = p
            end
```

to follow a modified pointer back up the tree and restore the pointer's value to point to its left or right son as appropriate.

However, now an *isleft* field is required since the *isleft* operation cannot be implemented using a nonexistent father field. Also, this algorithm cannot be used in a multiuser environment if several users require access to the tree simultaneously. If one user is traversing the tree and is temporarily modifying pointers, another user will be unable to use the tree as a coherent structure. Some sort of lockout mechanism is required to ensure that no one else uses the tree while pointers are reversed.

Heterogeneous Binary Trees

Often, the information contained in different nodes of a binary tree is not all of the same type. For example, in representing a binary expression with constant numerical operands, we may wish to use a binary tree whose leafs contain numbers but whose nonleaf nodes contain characters representing operators. Figure 6.2.4 illustrates such a binary tree.

To implement such a tree in Pascal, we may use variant records to represent the tree nodes. Each tree node also contains a tag field to indicate the type of the data that it contains. Since only operator nodes are nonleafs, only they contain *left* and *right* pointers. This is an example of the internal/ external node dichotomy mentioned at the beginning of this section.

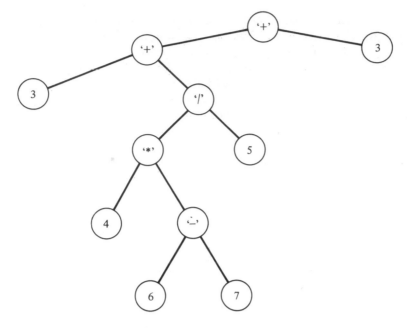

Figure 6.2.4 Binary tree representing 3 + 4 * (6 − 7)/5 + 3.

```
type infotype = (operand, operator);
     nodeptr = ↑nodetype;
     nodetype = record
                   case tag: infotype of
                      operand: (numinfo: real);
                      operator: (chinfo: char;
                                    left, right: nodeptr)
     end;
```

Let us write a Pascal function *evalbintree* that accepts a pointer to such a tree and returns the value of the expression represented by the tree. The function recursiverly evaluates the left and right subtrees and then applies the operator of the root to the two results. We use the auxiliary function *oper(symb, opnd1, opnd2)* introduced in Section 2.3. The first parameter of *oper* is a character representing an operator, and the last two parameters are real numbers that are the two operands. The function *oper* returns the result of applying the operator to the two operands:

```
function evalbintree (tree: nodeptr): real;
var opnd1, opnd2: real;
    symb: char;
```

```
    begin
        case tree↑.tag of
            operand: { the expression is a single operand }
                        evalbintree: = tree↑.numinfo;
            operator: begin
                        { evaluate the left subtree }
                        opnd1: = evalbintree (tree↑.left);
                        { evaluate the right subtree }
                        opnd2: = evalbintree (tree↑.right);
                        symb: = tree↑.chinfo;  { extract the operator }
                        { apply the operator and return }
                        {            the result            }
                        evalbintree: = oper(symb, opnd1, opnd2)
                    end
        end {case}
    end {function evalbintree};
```

Section 10.1 discusses additional methods of implementing linked structures that contain heterogeneous elements. Note also that, in this example, all the operand nodes are leafs and all the operator nodes are nonleafs.

EXERCISES

1. Write a Pascal function that accepts a pointer to a node and returns *true* if that node is the root of a valid binary tree and *false* otherwise.

2. Write a Pascal function that accepts a pointer to a binary tree and a pointer to a node of the tree and returns the level of the node in the tree.

3. Write a Pascal function that accepts a pointer to a binary tree and returns a pointer to a new binary tree that is the mirror image of the first (that is, all left subtrees are now right subtrees, and vice versa).

4. Write Pascal procedures that convert a binary tree implemented using the linked array representation with only a *father* field (in which the left son's *father* field contains the negative of the pointer to its father and a right son's father contains a pointer to its father) to its representation using *left* and *right* fields, and vice versa.

5. Write a Pascal program to perform the following experiment: Generate 100 random numbers. As each number is generated, insert it into an initially empty binary search tree. When all 100 numbers have been inserted, print the level of the leaf with largest level and the level of the leaf with smallest level. Repeat this process 50 times. Print out a table with a count of how many of the 50 runs resulted in a difference between the maximum and minimum leaf level of 0, 1, 2, 3, and so on.

6. Write Pascal routines to traverse a binary tree in preorder and postorder.

7. Implement inorder traversal, *maketree*, *setleft*, and *setright* for right-inthreaded binary trees under the sequential representation.

8. Write Pascal functions to create a binary tree given

    (a) the preorder and inorder traversals of that tree.
    (b) the preorder and postorder traversals of that tree.

    Each function should accept two character strings as parameters. The tree created should contain a single character in each node.

9. The solution to the Towers of Hanoi Problem for n disks (see Section 3.3 and 3.4) can be represented by a complete binary tree of depth $n - 1$ as follows:

    (a) Let the root of the tree represent a move of the top disk on peg *frompeg* to peg *topeg*. (We ignore the identification of the disks being moved, as there is only a single disk—the top one—that can be moved from any peg to any other peg.) If nd is a nonleaf node (at level less than $n - 1$), representing the movement of the top disk from peg x to peg y, let z be the third peg that is neither the source or target of node nd. Then *left*(nd) represents a move of the top disk from peg x to peg z and *right*(nd) represents a move of the top disk from peg z to peg y. Draw sample solution trees as described earlier for $n = 1, 2, 3, 4$, and show that an inorder traversal of such a tree produces the solution to the Towers of Hanoi problem.
    (b) Write a recursive Pascal procedure that accepts a value for n and generates and traverses the tree as was just discussed.
    (c) Because the tree is complete, it can be stored in an array of size $2^n - 1$. Show that the nodes of the tree can be stored in the array so that a sequential traversal of the array produces the inorder traversal of the tree, as follows: The root of the tree is in position 2^{n-1}; for any level j, the first node at that level is in position 2^{n-1-j} and each successive node at level j is 2^{n-j} elements beyond the previous element at that level.
    (d) Write a nonrecursive Pascal program to create the array as described in part (c) and show that a sequential pass through the array does indeed produce the desired solution.
    (e) How could the foregoing programs be extended to include within each node the number of the disk being moved?

10. In Section 4.4, we introduced a method of representing a doubly linked list with only a single pointer field in each node by maintaining its value as the exclusive *or* of pointers to the node's predecessor and successor. A binary tree can be maintained similarly by keeping one field in each node set to the exclusive *or* of pointers to the node's father and left son—call this field *fleft*(p)—and another field in the node set to the exclusive *or* of pointers to the node's father and right son—call this field *fright*(p).

    (a) Given *father*(p) and *fleft*(p), show how to compute *left*(p).
        Given *father*(p) and *fright*(p), show how to compute *right*(p).
    (b) Given *fleft*(p) and *left*(p), show how to compute *father*(p).
        Given *fright*(p) and *right*(p), show how to compute *father*(p).
    (c) Assuming that a node contains only *info*, *fleft*, *fright*, and *isleft* fields, write algorithms for preorder, inorder, and postorder traversal of a binary tree, given an external pointer to the tree root, without using a stack or modifying any fields.
    (d) Can the *isleft* field be eliminated?

11. An index of a textbook consists of major terms, ordered alphabetically. Each major term is accompanied by a set of page numbers and a set of subterms. The subterms are printed on successive lines following the major term and are arranged alphabetically within the major term. Each subterm is accompanied by a set of page numbers.

Design a data structure to represent such an index and write a Pascal program to print an index from data as follows: Each input line begins with an *m* (major term) or an *s* (subterm). An *m* line contains an *m* followed by a major term followed by an integer *n* (possibly zero) followed by *n* page numbers where the major term appears. An *s* line is similar except that it contains a subterm rather than a major term. The input lines appear in no particular order except that each subterm is considered to be a subterm of the major term which last precedes it. There may be many input lines for a single major term or subterm (all page numbers appearing on any line for a particular term should be printed with that term).

The index should be printed with one term on a line followed by all the pages on which the term appears in ascending order. Major terms should be printed in alphabetical order. Subterms should appear in alphabetical order immediately following their major term. Subterms should be indented five columns from the major terms.

The set of major terms should be organized as a binary tree. Each node in the tree contains (in addition to left and right pointers and the major term itself) pointers to two other binary trees. One of these represents the set of page numbers in which the major term occurs, and the other represents the set of subterms of the major term. Each node on a subterm binary tree contains (in addition to left and right pointers and the subterm itself) a pointer to a binary tree representing the set of page numbers in which the subterm occurs.

12. Write a Pascal procedure to implement the sorting method of Section 1 that uses a binary search tree.

13. (a) Implement an ascending priority queue using a binary search tree by writing Pascal implementations of the algorithms *pqinsert* and *pqmindelete*, as in Exercise 6.1.13. Modify the routines to count the number of tree nodes accessed.

    (b) Use a random number generator to test the efficiency of the priority queue implementation as follows: First, create a priority queue with 100 elements by inserting 100 random numbers in an initially empty binary search tree. Then call *pqmindelete* and print the number of tree nodes accessed in finding the minimum element, generate a new random number, and call *pqinsert* to insert the new random number and print the number of tree nodes accessed in the insertion. Note that after calling *pqinsert*, the tree still contains 100 elements. Repeat the delete/print/generate/insert/print process 1000 times. Note that the number of nodes accessed in the deletion tends to decrease while the number of nodes accessed in the insertion tends to increase. Explain this behavior.

3. AN EXAMPLE: THE HUFFMAN ALGORITHM

Suppose we have an alphabet of *n* symbols and a long message consisting of symbols from this alphabet. We wish to encode the message as a long bit string (a bit is either 0 or 1) by assigning a bit string code to each symbol of the alphabet and concatenating the individual codes of the symbols making up the message to produce an encoding for the message. For example, suppose that the alphabet consists of the four symbols *A*, *B*, *C*, and *D* and that codes are assigned to these symbols as follows:

SYMBOL	CODE
A	010
B	100
C	000
D	111

The message *ABACCDA* would then be encoded as 010100010000000111010. Such an encoding is inefficient, since three bits are used for each symbol so that 21 bits are needed to encode the entire message. Suppose that a two-bit code is assigned to each symbol, as follows:

SYMBOL	CODE
A	00
B	01
C	10
D	11

Then the code for the message would be 00010010101100, which requires only 14 bits. We wish to find a code that minimizes the length of the encoded message.

Let us reexamine the preceding example. Each of the letters *B* and *D* appears only once in the message, while the letter *A* appears three times. If a code is chosen so that the letter *A* is assigned a shorter bit string than the letters *B* and *D*, then the length of the encoded message would be small. This is because the short code (representing the letter *A*) would appear more frequently than the long code. Indeed, codes can be assigned as follows:

SYMBOL	CODE
A	0
B	110
C	10
D	111

Using this code, the message *ABACCDA* is encoded 0110010101110, which requires only 13 bits. In very long messages containing symbols that appear very infrequently, the savings are substantial. Ordinarily, codes are not constructed on the basis of the frequency of characters within a single message alone, but on the basis of their frequency within a whole set of messages. The same code set is then used for each message. For example, if messages consist of English words, the known relative frequency of occurrence of the letters of the alphabet in the English language might be used, although the relative frequency of the letters in any single message is not necessarily the same.

If variable-length codes are used, the code for one symbol may not be a prefix of the code for another. To see why, assume that the code for a symbol x, $c(x)$, were a prefix of the code of another symbol y, $c(y)$. Then, when $c(x)$ is encountered in a left-to-right scan, it is unclear whether $c(x)$ represents the symbol x whether it is the first part of $c(y)$.

In our example, decoding proceeds by scanning a bit string from left to right. If a 0 is encountered as the first bit, the symbol is an A; otherwise, it is a B, C, or D, and the next bit is examined. If the second bit is a 0, then the symbol is a C; otherwise, it must be a B or a D, and the third bit must be examined. If the third bit is a 0, the symbol is a B; if it is a 1, the symbol is a D. As soon as the first symbol has been identified, the process is repeated starting at the next bit to find the second symbol.

This suggests a method for developing an optimal encoding scheme, given the frequency of occurrence of each symbol in a message. Find the two symbols that appear least frequently. In our example, these are B and D. The last bit of their codes differentiate between them: 0 for B and 1 for D. Combine these two symbols into the single symbol BD whose code represents the knowledge that a symbol is either a B or a D. The frequency of occurrence of this new symbol is the sum of the frequencies of its two constituent symbols. Thus the frequency of BD is 2. There are now three symbols: A (frequency 3), C (frequency 2), and BD (frequency 2). Again choose the two symbols with smallest frequency: C and BD. The last bit of their codes differentiates between them: 0 for C and 1 for BD. The two symbols are then combined into the single symbol CBD with frequency 4. There are now only two symbols remaining: A and CBD. These are combined into the single symbol $ACBD$. The last bits of the codes for A and CBD differentiate between them: 0 for A and 1 for CBD.

The symbol $ACBD$ contains the entire alphabet; it is assigned the nil bit string of length 0 as its code. At the start of the decoding, before any bits have been examined, it is certain that any symbol is contained in $ACBD$. The two symbols that comprise $ACBD$ (A and CBD) are assigned the codes 0 and 1, respectively. If a 0 is encountered, the encoded symbol is an A; if a 1 is encountered, it is a C, B, or D. Similarly, the two symbols that constitute CBD (C and BD) are assigned the codes 10 and 11, respectively. The first bit indicates that the symbol is one of the constituents of CBD, and the second bit indicates whether it is a C or a BD. The symbols that comprise BD (B and D) are then assigned the codes 110 and 111. By this process, symbols that appear frequently in the message are assigned shorter codes than are symbols that appear infrequently.

The action of combining two symbols into one suggests the use of a binary tree. Each nonleaf node of the tree represents a symbol, and each leaf represents a symbol of the original alphabet. Figure 6.3.1(a) shows the binary tree constructed using the previous example. Each node in the illustration contains a symbol and its frequency. Figure 6.3.1(b) shows the binary tree constructed by this method for the alphabet and frequency table of Figure 6.3.1.(c). Such trees are called *Huffman trees* after the discoverer of this encoding method.

Once the Huffman tree is constructed, the code of any symbol in the alphabet can be constructed by starting at the leaf representing that symbol and climbing up to the root. The code is initialized to nil. Each time that a left branch is climbed, 0 is appended to the beginning of the code; each time that a right branch is climbed, 1 is appended to the beginning of the code.

The Huffman Algorithm

The inputs to the algorithm are n, the number of symbols in the original alphabet, and *frequency*, an array of size at least n such that *frequency*[i] is the relative frequency of the ith symbol. The algorithm assigns values to an array *code* of size at least n so that *code*[i] contains the code assigned to the ith symbol. The algorithm also constructs an array *position* of size at least n such that the *position*[i] points to the node representing the ith symbol. This array is necessary to identify the point in the tree from which to start in constructing the code for a particular symbol in the alphabet. Once the tree has been constructed, the *isleft* operation introduced earlier can be used to determine whether 0 or 1 should be placed at the front of the code as we climb the tree. The *info* portion of a tree node contains the frequency of the occurrence of the symbol represented by that node.

A set *rootnodes* is used to keep pointers to the roots of partial binary trees that are not yet left or right subtrees. Since this set is modified by removing elements with minimum frequency, combining them, and then reinserting the combined element into the set, it is implemented as an ascending priority queue of pointers, ordered by the value of the *info* field of the pointers' target nodes. We use the operations *pqinsert*, to insert a pointer into the priority queue, and *pqmindelete*, to remove the pointer to the node with the smallest *info* value from the priority queue.

```
{      initialize the set of root nodes      }
rootnodes: = the empty ascending priority queue;
{      construct a node for each symbol      }
```

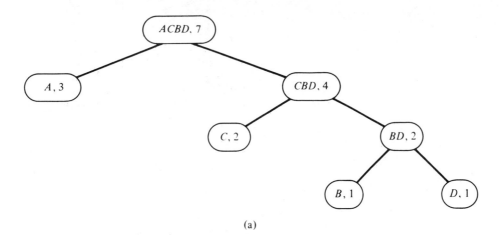

(a)

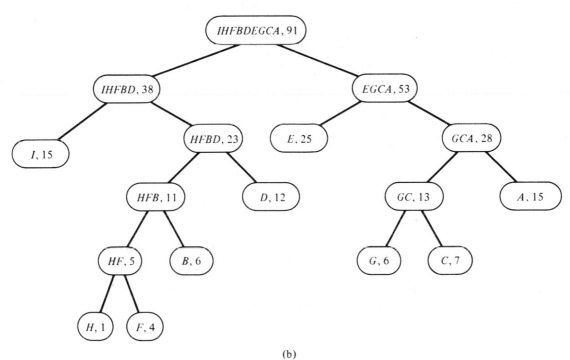

(b)

Symbol	Frequency	Code	Symbol	Frequency	Code	Symbol	Frequency	Code
A	15	111	D	12	011	G	6	1100
B	6	0101	E	25	10	H	1	01000
C	7	1101	F	4	01001	I	15	00

(c)

Figure 6.3.1 Huffman trees.

```
for i: = 1 to n
    do begin
            p: = maketree(frequency[i]);
            position[i] := p;   { a pointer to the leaf containing }
                                {           the ith symbol         }
            pqinsert(rootnodes, p)
        end {for...do begin};
while rootnodes contains more than one item
    do begin
            p1: = pqmindelete(rootnodes);
            p2: = pqmindelete(rootnodes);
            { combine p1 and p2 as branches of a single tree }
            p: = maketree(info(p1) + info(p2));
            setleft(p, p1);
            setright(p, p2);
            pqinsert(rootnodes, p)
        end {while...do begin};
{ the tree is now constructed; use it to find codes }
root: = pqmindelete(rootnodes);
for i: = 1 to n
    do begin
            p: = position[i];
            code[i] : = the nil bit string;
            while p <> root
                do begin
                { travel up the tree }
                        if isleft(p)
                            then code[i] : = 0 followed by code[i]
                            else code[i] : = 1 followed by code[i];
                        p: = father(p)
                    end {while...do begin}
        end {for...do begin}
```

A Pascal Program

Note that the Huffman tree is strictly binary. Thus if there are n symbols in the alphabet, the Huffman tree (which has n leafs) can be represented by an array of nodes of size $2n - 1$. Since the amount of storage needed for the tree is known, it may be allocated in advance in an array *node*.

In constructing the tree and obtaining the codes, it is only necessary to keep a link from each node to its father and an indication of whether each node is a left or right son; *left* and *right* fields are unnecessary. Thus each node contains three fields: *father*, *isleft*, and *freq*. *father* is a pointer to the node's father. If the node is the root, then its *father* field is **nil**. The value of *isleft* is *true* if the node is a left son and *false* otherwise. *freq* (which corresponds to the *info* field of the algorithm) is the frequency of occurrence of the symbol represented by that node.

Unfortunately, Pascal does not permit the size of an array to be determined based on the value of a variable. We must therefore allocate the array *node* based on the maximum possible symbols (a constant *maxsymbs*) rather than on the actual number of symbols, *n*. Thus the array *node*, which should be of size $2n - 1$, must be declared as being of size $2maxsymbs - 1$. This means that some space is wasted. Of course, *n* itself could be made a constant rather than a variable, but then the program must be modified every time that the number of symbols differs. The nodes can also be represented by dynamic variables without wasting space. However, we present a linked array implementation. (Other languages do have the capability of declaring an array dynamically during execution, and in such languages, no space would be wasted using an array implementation.)

In using the linked array implementation, *node*[1] through *node*[*n*] can be reserved for the leafs representing the original *n* symbols of the alphabet, and *node*[*n* + 1] through *node*[2**n* − 1] for the *n* − 1 nonleaf nodes required by the strictly binary tree. This means that the array *position* is not required as a guide to the leaf nodes representing the *n* symbols. If the dynamic node representation were used, the array *position* would be required.

The following program encodes a message using Huffman's algorithm. The input consists of a number *n*, which is the number of symbols in the alphabet, followed by a set of *n* pairs, each of which consists of a symbol and its relative frequency. The program first constructs a string *alph* consisting of all the symbols in the alphabet and an array *code* such that *code*[*i*] is the code assigned to the *i*th symbol in *alph*. The program then prints each character, its relative frequency, and its code.

Since the code is constructed from right to left, we define a type *codetype* as follows:

```
const maxbits = 50;
      maxbitpos = 51;
type bit = '0'..'1';
     codetype = record
                    bits: array [1..maxbits] of bit;
                    startpos: 1..maxbitpos
     end;
```

maxbits is the maximum number of bits allowed in a code. If a code *cd* is nil, then *cd.startpos* equals *maxbitpos*, which is one more than *maxbits*. When a bit *b* is added to *cd* at the left, *cd.startpos* is decremented by 1 and *cd.bits*[*cd.startpos*] is set to *b*. When the code *cd* is completed, the bits of the code are in positions *cd.startpos* through *cd.maxbits* inclusive.

An important issue is how to organize the priority queue of root nodes. In the algorithm, this data structure was represented as a priority queue of node pointers. Implementing the priority queue by a linked list, as in Section 4.2, would require a new set of nodes, each holding a pointer to a root node and a *next* field. Fortunately, the *father* field of a root node is unused, so that it can be used to link together all the root nodes into a list. The pointer *rootnodes* could point to the first root node on the list. The list itself can be ordered or unordered, depending on the implementation of *pqinsert* and *pqmindelete*.

We make use of this technique in the following program that implements the algorithm just presented.

```
program findcode (input, output);
const maxbits = 50;
      maxbitpos = 51;
      maxsymbs = 50;
      maxnodes = 99;  { maxnodes equals 2*maxsymbs-1 }
type  nodeptr = 0..maxnodes;
      bit = '0'..'1';
      codetype = record
                      bits: array[1..maxbits] of bit;
                      startpos: 1..maxbitpos
                 end;
      nodetype = record
                      freq: integer;
                      father: nodeptr;  { if node[p] is not a root node, }
                                        {    father points to the node's }
                                        {    father; if it is, father points }
                                        {    to the next root node in the }
                                        {              priority queue }
                      isleft: boolean
                 end;
var   alph: array[1..maxsymbs] of char;
      code: array[1..maxsymbs] of codetype;
      node: array[1..maxnodes] of nodetype;
      n, i: 0..maxsymbs;
      p, p1, p2, root, rootnodes: nodeptr;
      cd: codetype;
      k: 1..maxbits;
      symb: char;
{ insert routines pqinsert and pqmindelete here }
begin {program findcode}
      for i: = 1 to maxsymbs
          do alph[i] := ' ';
      rootnodes: = 0;
      { input the alphabet and frequencies }
      readln(n);
```

```
for i: = 1 to n
    do begin
            readln(symb, nodes[i].freq);
            pqinsert(rootnodes, i);
            alph[i] := symb
        end {for...do begin};
    { we now build the trees }
    for p: = n + 1 to 2*n - 1
        do begin
            { p points to the next available node. Obtain the }
            {     two root nodes p1 and p2 with smallest       }
            {                  frequencies                     }
            p1: = pqmindelete(rootnodes);
            p2: = pqmindelete(rootnodes);
            { set left(p) to p1 and }
            {    right(p) to p2     }
            node[p1].father: = p;
            node[p1].isleft: = true;
            node[p2].father: = p;
            node[p2].isleft: = false;
            node[p].freq: = node[p1].freq + node[p2].freq;
            pqinsert(rootnodes, p)
        end {for...do begin};
{ there is now only one node left with a nil father field }
root: = pqmindelete(rootnodes);
{ extract the codes from the tree }
    for i: = 1 to n
        do begin  { initialize code[i]  }
                cd.startpos:= maxbitpos;
                { travel up the tree }
                p:= i;
                while p <> root
                    do begin
                            cd.startpos: = cd.startpos - 1;
                            if node[i].isleft
                                then cd.bits[cd.startpos] := 0
                                else cd.bits[cd.startpos] := 1;
                            p: = node[p].father
                        end {while...do begin};
                code[i] := cd
            end {for...do begin};
    { print results }
    for i: = 1 to n
        do begin
            writeln(alph[i], node[i].freq,' ');
```

```
            for k: = code[i].startpos to maxbits
                do write(code[i].bits[k]);
            writeln
        end {for...do begin}
    end {program findcode}.
```

We leave to the reader the coding of the routine *encode(alph, code, msge, bitcode)*. This procedure accepts the string *alph*, the array *code* constructed in the foregoing program, and a message *msge* and sets *bitcode* to the bit string encoding of the message.

Given the encoding of a message and the Huffman tree used in constructing the code, the original message can be recovered as follows: Begin at the root of the tree. Each time that a 0 is encountered, move down a left branch, and each time that a 1 is encountered, move down a right branch. Repeat this process until a leaf is encountered. The next character of the original message is the symbol that corresponds to that leaf. See if you can decode 1110100010111011 using the Huffman tree of Figure 6.3.1(b).

To decode, it is necessary to travel from the root of the tree down to its leafs. This means that, instead of *father* and *isleft* fields, two fields *left* and *right* are needed to hold the left and right sons of a particular node. It is straightforward to compute the fields *left* and *right* from the fields *father* and *isleft*. Alternatively, the values *left* and *right* can be constructed directly from the frequency information for the symbols of the alphabet using an approach similar to that used in assigning the value of *father*. (Of course, if the trees are to be identical, the symbol/frequency pairs must be presented in the same order under the two methods.) We leave these algorithms, as well as the decoding algorithm, as exercises for the reader.

EXERCISES

1. Write a Pascal procedure *encode(alph, code, msge, bitcode)*. The procedure accepts the string *alph* and the array *code* produced by the program *findcode* in the text and a message *msge*. The procedure sets *bitcode* to the Huffman encoding of that message.

2. Write a Pascal procedure *decode(alph, left, right, bitcode, msge)*, where *alph* is the string produced by the program *findcode* in the text, *left* and *right* are arrays used to represent a Huffman tree, and *bitcode* is a bit string. The procedure sets *msge* to the Huffman decoding of *bitcode*.

3. Implement the priority queue *rootnodes* as an ordered list. Write appropriate *pqinsert* and *pqmindelete* routines.

4. Is it possible to have two different Huffman trees for a set of symbols with given frequencies? Either give an example where two such trees exist or prove that there is only a single such tree.

5. Define the **Fibonacci binary tree of order *n*** as follows: If $n = 0$ or $n = 1$, then the tree consists of a single node. If $n > 1$, then the tree consists of a root, with

the Fibonacci tree of order $n - 1$ as the left subtree and the Fibonacci tree of order $n - 2$ as the right subtree.
(a) Write a Pascal function that returns a pointer to the Fibonacci binary tree of order n.
(b) Is such a tree strictly binary?
(c) What is the number of leafs in the Fibonacci tree of order n?
(d) What is the depth of the Fibonacci tree of order n?

6. Given a binary tree T, its **extension** is defined as the binary tree $e(T)$ formed from T by adding a new leaf node at each nil left and right pointer in T. The new leafs are called **external** nodes, and the original nodes (which are now all nonleafs) are called **internal** nodes. $e(T)$ is called an **extended binary tree**.
(a) Prove that an extended binary tree is strictly binary.
(b) If T has n nodes, how many nodes does $e(T)$ have?
(c) Prove that all leafs in an extended binary tree are newly added nodes.
(d) Write a Pascal routine that extends a binary tree T.
(e) Prove that any strictly binary tree with more than one node is an extension of one and only one binary tree.
(f) Write a Pascal function that accepts a pointer to a strictly binary tree $T1$ containing more than one node and deletes nodes from $T1$ creating a binary tree $T2$ such that $T1 = e(T2)$.
(g) Show that the complete binary tree of depth n is the nth extension of the binary tree consisting of a single node.

7. Given a strictly binary tree T in which the n leafs are labeled as nodes 1 through n, let $level(i)$ be the level of node i and let $freq(i)$ be an integer assigned to node i. Define the **weighted path length** of T as the sum of $freq(i)*level(i)$ over all leafs of T.
(a) Write a Pascal routine to compute the weighted path length given fields $freq$ and $father$.
(b) Show that the Huffman tree is the strictly binary tree with minimum weighted path length.

4. REPRESENTING LISTS AS BINARY TREES

Several operations can be performed on a list of elements. Included among these operations are adding a new element to the front or rear of the list, deleting the existing first or last element of the list, retrieving the kth element or the last element of the list, inserting an element following or preceding a given element, deleting a given element, and deleting the predecessor or successor of a given element. Building a list with given elements is an additional operation that is frequently required.

Depending on the representation chosen for a list, some of these operations may or may not be possible with varying degrees of efficiency. For example, a list may be represented by successive elements in an array or as nodes in a linked structure. Inserting an element following a given element is relatively efficient in a linked list (involving modifications to a few pointers aside from the actual insertion) but relatively inefficient in an array (involving moving all subsequent elements in the array one position). However, finding the kth element of a list is far more efficient in an array (involving only the computation of an offset) than in a linked structure (which requires passing through the first $k - 1$ elements). Similarly, it is not possible to delete a specific element in a singly linked linear list given only a pointer to that element, and it is only possible to do so inefficiently in a singly linked circular list (by traversing the entire list to reach the previous element and then performing the deletion). The same operation, however, is quite efficient in a doubly linked (linear or circular) list.

In this section, we introduce a tree representation of a linear list in which the operations of finding the kth element of a list and deleting a specific element are relatively efficient. It is also possible to build a list with given elements using this representation. We also consider briefly the operation of inserting a single new element.

A list may be represented by a binary tree as illustrated in Figure 6.4.1. Figure 6.4.1(a) shows a list in the usual linked format while Figures 6.4.1(b) and (c) show two binary tree representations of the list. Elements of the original list are represented by leafs of the tree (shown as squares in the figure), while nonleaf nodes of the tree (shown as circles in the figure) are present as part of the internal tree structure. Associated with each leaf node are the contents of the corresponding list element. Associated with each nonleaf node is a count representing the number of leafs in the node's left subtree. (Although this count can be computed from the tree structure, it is maintained as a data element to avoid recomputing its value each time that it is needed.) The elements of the list in their original sequence are assigned to the leafs of the tree in the inorder sequence of the leafs. Note from Figure 6.4.1 that several binary trees can represent the same list.

Finding the *k*th Element

To justify using so many extra tree nodes to represent a list, we present an algorithm to find the kth element of a list represented by a tree. Let *tree* point to the root of the tree, and let *lcount*(p) represent the count associated with the nonleaf node pointed to by p. [*lcount*(p) is the number of leafs in the tree rooted at *node*(*left*(p))]. The following algorithm sets the variable *find* to point to the leaf containing the kth element of the list.

The algorithm maintains a variable r containing the number of list elements remaining to be counted. At the beginning of the algorithm, r is initialized to k. At each nonleaf *node*(p), the algorithm determines from the values of r and *lcount*(p) whether the kth element is located in the left or right subtree. If the leaf is in the left subtree, the algorithm proceeds directly to that subtree. If the desired leaf is in the right subtree, the algorithm proceeds to that subtree after reducing the value of r by the value of *lcount*(p). k is assumed to be less than or equal to the number of elements in the list.

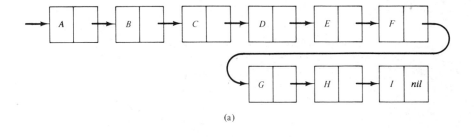

(a)

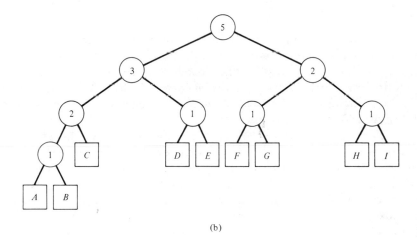

(b)

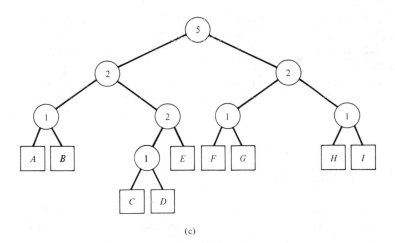

(c)

Figure 6.4.1   A list and two corresponding binary trees.

```
        r:= k;
        p:= tree;
        while p is not a leaf node
             do if r <= lcount(p)
                  then p:= left(p)
                  else begin
                          r:= r - lcount(p);
                          p:= right(p)
                       end {else begin};
        find:= p
```

Figure 6.4.2(a) illustrates finding the fifth element of a list in the tree of Figure 6.4.1(b), while Figure 6.4.2(b) illustrates finding the eighth element in the tree of Figure 6.4.1(c). The dashed line represents the path taken by the algorithm down the tree to the appropriate leaf. We indicate the value of r (the remaining number of elements to be counted) next to each node encountered by the algorithm.

The number of tree nodes examined in finding the kth list element is less than or equal to one more than the depth of the tree (the longest path in the tree from the root to a leaf). Thus, four nodes are examined in Figure 6.4.2(a) in finding the fifth element of the list and also in Figure 6.4.2(b) in finding the eighth element. If a list is represented as a linked structure, four nodes are accessed [that is, the operation $p:= next(p)$ is performed four times] in finding the fifth element of a list, and seven nodes are accessed in finding the eighth element.

Although this is not a very impressive saving, consider a list with 1000 elements. A binary tree of depth 10 is sufficient to represent such a list, since $\log_2 1000$ is less than 10. Thus, finding the kth element (regardless of whether k was 3, 253, 708, or 999) using such a binary tree would require examining no more than 11 nodes. Since the number of leafs of a binary tree increases as 2^d, where d is the depth of the tree, such a tree represents a relatively efficient data structure for finding the kth element of a list. If an almost complete tree is used, the kth element of an n-element list can be found in at most $\log_2 n + 1$ node accesses, while k accesses would be required if a linear linked list were used.

Deleting an Element

How can an element be deleted from a list represented by a tree? The deletion itself is relatively easy. It involves only resetting a left or right pointer in the father of the deleted leaf dl to nil. However, to enable subsequent accesses, the counts in all ancestors of dl may have to be modified. The modification consists of reducing *lcount* by one in each node *nd* of which dl was a left descendant, since the number of leafs in the left subtree of *nd*

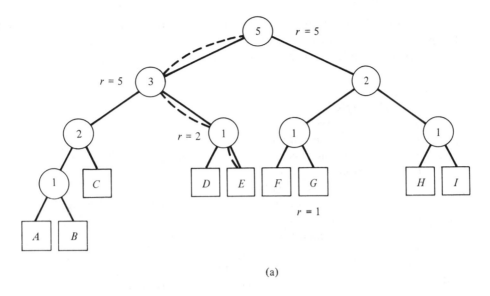

(a)

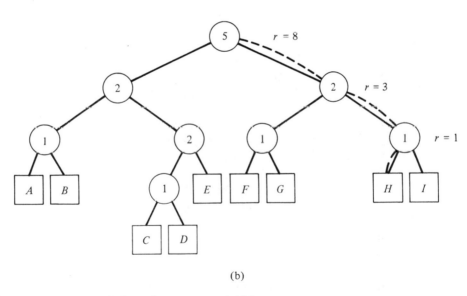

(b)

Figure 6.4.2 Finding the *n*th element in a tree-represented list.

is one fewer. At the same time, if the brother of *dl* is a leaf, it can be moved up the tree to take the place of its father. We can then move that node up even farther if it has no brother in its new position. This may reduce the depth of the resulting tree, making subsequent accesses slightly more efficient.

We may therefore present an algorithm to delete a leaf pointed to by *p* from a tree (and thus an element from a list) as follows. (The line numbers at the left are for future reference.)

```
1    if p = tree
2       then begin
3                    tree := nil;
4                    free node (p)
5              end {then begin}
6       else begin
7                    f := father(p);
8                    { remove node(p) and set b to point to its brother }
9                    if p = left(f)
10                      then begin
11                              left(f) := nil;
12                              b := right(f);
13                              lcount(f) := lcount(f) - 1
14                          end {then begin}
15                      else begin
16                              right(f) := nil;
17                              b := left(f)
18                          end {else begin};
19                   if node(b) is a leaf
20                      then { move the contents of node(b) up to its }
21                           {         father and free node(b)          }
22                      begin
23                              info(f) := info(b);
24                              left(f) := nil;
25                              right(f) := nil;
26                              lcount(f) := 0;
27                              free node(b)
28                          end {then begin};
29                   free node(p);
30                   { climb up the tree }
31                   q := f;
32                   while q <> tree
33                      do begin
34                              f := father(q);
35                              if q = left(f)
36                                  then { the deleted leaf was a left }
37                                       {    descendant of node(f)    }
38                                  begin
39                                          lcount(f) := lcount(f) - 1;
40                                          b := right(f)
41                                      end {then begin}
```

```
42                        else b := left (f);
43                        { node (b) is the brother of node (q) }
44                        if (b = nil) and (node (q) is a leaf)
45                            then { move up the contents of node (q) }
46                                 {   to its father and free node (q)   }
47                            begin
48                                 info (f) := info (q);
49                                 left (f) := nil;
50                                 right (f) := nil;
51                                 lcount (f) := 0;
52                                 free node (q)
53                            end {then begin};
54               q := f
55         end {while...do begin}
```

Figure 6.4.3 illustrates the results of this algorithm for a tree in which the nodes C, D, and B are deleted in that order. Make sure that you follow the actions of the algorithm on these examples. Note that the algorithm maintains a zero count in leaf nodes for consistency, although the count is not required for such nodes. Note also that the algorithm never moves up a nonleaf node even if this could be done. (For example, the father of A and B in Figure 6.4.3(b) has not been moved up.) We can easily modify the algorithm to do this (the modification is left to the reader), but have not done so for reasons that will become apparent shortly.

This deletion algorithm involves inspection of up to two nodes (the ancestor of the node being deleted and that ancestor's brother) at each level. Thus, the operation of deleting the kth element of a list represented by a tree (which involves finding the element and then deleting it) requires a number of node accesses approximately equal to three times the tree depth. While deletion from a linked list requires accesses to only three nodes (the nodes preceding and following the deleted node as well as the deleted node), deleting the kth element requires a total of $k + 2$ accesses ($k - 1$ of which are to locate the node preceding the kth). For large lists, therefore, the tree representation is more efficient.

Similarly we can compare favorably the efficiency of tree-represented lists with array-represented lists. If an n-element list is maintained in the first n elements of an array, finding the kth element involves only a single array access, but deleting it requires shifting the $n - k$ elements that had followed the deleted element. If gaps are allowed in the array so that deletion can be implemented efficiently (by setting a flag in the array position of the deleted element without shifting any subsequent elements), then finding the kth element requires at least k array accesses. The reason is that it is no longer possible to know the array position of the kth element in the list since gaps may exist among the elements in the array. (We should note, however, that if the order of the elements in the list is irrelevant, the kth element in an

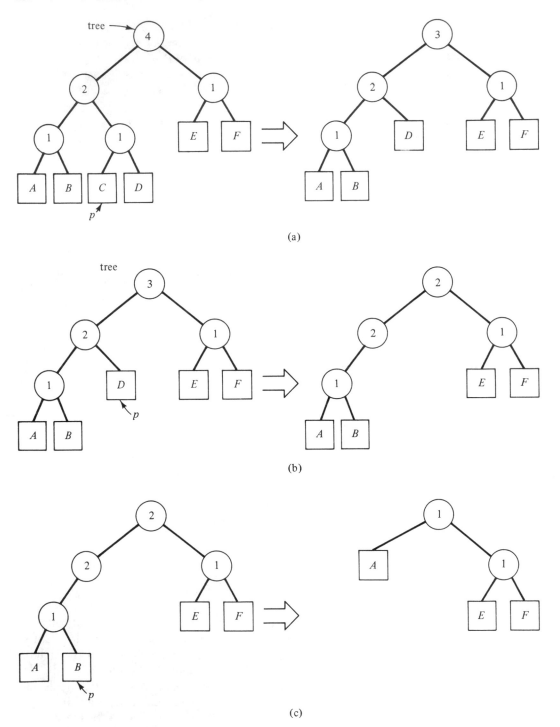

Figure 6.4.3. The deletion algorithm.

array can be deleted efficiently by overwriting it with the element in position n—the last element—and adjusting the count to $n - 1$. However, it is unlikely that we would want to delete the kth element from a list in which the order is irrelevant since there would then be no significance in the kth element over any of the others.)

Inserting a new kth element into a tree-represented list—between the $(k - 1)$st and the previous kth—is also a relatively efficient operation. The insertion consists of locating the kth element, replacing it with a new nonleaf that has a leaf containing the new element as its left son and a leaf containing the old kth element as its right son, and adjusting appropriate counts among its ancestors. We leave the details to the reader. (However, repeatedly adding a new kth element by this method causes the tree to become highly unbalanced since the branch containing the kth element becomes disproportionately long compared to the other branches. This means that the efficiency of finding the kth element is not as great as it would be in a balanced tree in which all paths are approximately the same length. The reader is encouraged to find a "balancing" strategy to alleviate this problem. Nevertheless, if insertions into the tree are made randomly so that it is equally likely for an element to be inserted at any given position, the resulting tree remains fairly balanced, and finding the kth element remains efficient.)

Implementing Tree-Represented Lists in Pascal

The Pascal implementations of the search and deletion algorithms are straightforward using the linked representation of binary trees. However, such a representation requires *info*, *lcount*, *father*, *left*, and *right* fields for each tree node, while a list node requires only *info* and *next* fields. Coupled with the fact that the tree representation requires approximately twice as many nodes as a linked list, this space requirement may make the tree representation impractical. We could, of course, utilize external nodes containing only an *info* field (and perhaps a *father* field) for the leafs, and internal nodes containing *lcount*, *father*, *left*, and *right* fields for the nonleafs. We do not pursue that possibility here.

Under the sequential representation of a binary tree, the space requirements are not nearly so great. If we assume that no insertions are required once the tree is constructed and that the initial list size is known, we can set aside an array to hold an almost complete strictly binary tree representation of the list. Under that representation, *father*, *left*, and *right* fields are unnecessary. As we shall soon show, it is always possible to construct an almost complete binary tree representation of a list.

Once the tree has been constructed, the only fields required are *info* and *lcount* and a field *used* to indicate whether or not an array element represents an existing or a deleted tree node. Also, as we have noted before, *lcount* is only required for nonleaf nodes of the tree so that a variant record could actually be used with either the *lcount* field or the *info* field, depending on whether or not the node is a leaf. We leave this possibility as an exercise for the reader. It is also possible to eliminate the need for the *used* field at some expense to time efficiency (see Exercises 6.4.6 and 6.4.7). We assume the following definitions and declarations (assume 100 elements in the list):

```
const maxelts = 100;    {      maximum number of list elements       }
      numnodes = 199; { number of tree nodes equals 2*maxelts - 1 }
      blanks = '                      '; {         20 blanks        }
type nodeptr = 0..numnodes;
     elementnum = 0..maxelts;
     nodetype = record
                    info: packed array [1..20] of char;
                    lcount: integer;
                    used: boolean
                end;
var node: array [1..numnodes] of nodetype;
```

A nonleaf node can be recognized by an *info* value equal to *blanks*. *father*(p), *left*(p), and *right*(p) can be implemented in the usual way as p **mod** 2, $2*p$, and $2*p + 1$, respectively.

A Pascal routine to find the *k*th element follows:

```
function findelement(k: elementnum): nodeptr;
var p: nodeptr;
    r: elementnum;
begin {function findelement}
    r:= k;
    p:= 1;
    while (node[p].info = blanks)
        do if r <= node[p].lcount
            then p = 2*p
            else begin
                    r:= r - node[p].lcount;
                    p = 2*p + 1
                end {else begin};
    findelement:= p
end {function findelement};
```

The Pascal routine to delete the leaf pointed to by *p* using the sequential representation is somewhat simpler than is the foregoing corresponding algorithm. We can ignore all assignments of *nil* (lines 3, 11, 16, 24, 25, 49, and 50) since pointers are not used. We can also ignore the assignments of zero to an *lcount* field (lines 26 and 51) since such an assignment is part of the conversion of a nonleaf to a leaf and, in our Pascal representation, the *lcount* field in leaf nodes is unused. A node can be recognized as a leaf (lines 19 and 44) by a nonblank *info* value and the pointer *b* as *nil* (line 44) by a *false* value for *node[b].used*. Freeing a node (lines 4, 27, and 52) is accomplished by setting its *used* field to *false*.

```
procedure delete(p: nodeptr);
var b, f, q: nodeptr;
begin {procedure delete}
     if p = 1
          then node[p].used = false { algorithm lines 1-5 }
          else begin
                    f:= p div 2; { algorithm line 7 }
                    if p mod 2 = 0 { algorithm lines 9-18 }
                    then begin
                              b:= 2*f + 1;
                              node[f].lcount:= node[f].lcount - 1
                         end {then begin}
                    else b:= 2*f;
                    if node[b].info <> blanks
                    then begin { algorithm lines 20-28 }
                              node[f].info:= node[b].info;
                              node[b].used:= false
                         end {then begin};
                    node[p].used:= false; { algorithm line 29 }
                    q:= f;                 { algorithm line 31 }
                    while q <> 1
                         do begin
                              f:= q div 2; { algorithm line 34 }
                              if q mod 2 = 0 { algorithm line 35 }
                                   then begin
                                             node[f].lcount:= node[f].lcount - 1;
                                             b:= 2*f + 1
                                        end {then begin}
                                   else b:= 2*f;
                              if (not node[b].used) and (node[q] <> blanks)
                                   then begin { algorithm lines 45-53 }
                                             node[f].info:= node[q].info;
                                             node[q].used:= false
                                        end {then begin};
                              q:= f
                         end {while...do begin}
end {procedure delete};
```

Our use of the sequential representation explains the reason for not moving a nonleaf without a brother farther up in a tree during deletion. Such a moving-up process would involve copying the contents of all nodes in the subtree within the array, whereas it involves modifying only a single pointer if the linked representation is used.

Constructing a Tree-Represented List

We now return to the claim that, given a list of n elements, it is possible to construct an almost complete strictly binary tree representing the list. We have already seen in Section 1 that it is possible to construct an almost complete strictly binary tree with n leafs and $2*n - 1$ nodes. The leafs of such a tree occupy nodes numbered n through $2*n - 1$. If d is the smallest integer such that 2^d is greater than or equal to n [that is, if d equals the smallest integer greater than or equal to $\log_2 n$], then d equals the depth of the tree. 2^d is the number assigned to the first node on the bottom level of the tree. The first elements of the list are assigned to nodes numbered 2^d through $2*n - 1$ and the remainder (if any) to nodes numbered n through $2^d - 1$. In constructing a tree representing a list with n elements, we can assign elements to the *info* fields of tree leafs in this sequence and assign a blank string to the *info* fields of the nonleaf nodes, numbered 1 through $n - 1$. It is also a simple matter to initialize the *used* field to *true* in all nodes numbered 1 to $2*n - 1$.

Initializing the values of the *lcount* array is more difficult. Two methods can be used: one involving more time and a second involving more space. In the first method, all *lcount* fields are initialized to zero. Then the tree is climbed from each leaf to the tree root in turn. Each time a node is reached from its left son, 1 is added to its *lcount* field. After this process is performed for each leaf, all *lcount* values have been properly assigned. The following routine uses this method to construct a tree from a list of input data:

```
procedure buildtree(n: elementnum);
var d, f, i, p, size: nodeptr;
    power: integer;
begin {procedure buildtree}
    { compute the tree depth d and the value of 2ᵈ }
    d:= 0;
    power:= 1;
    while power < n
        do begin
                d:= d + 1;
                power:= power * 2
            end {then begin};
    { assign the elements of the list, initialize the used flags, }
    {     and initialize the lcount field to 0 in all nonleafs    }
    size:= 2*n - 1;
```

```
            for i:= power to size
                do begin
                        readln (node [i]. info);
                        node [i]. used:= true
                    end {for...do begin};
            for i:= n to power-1
                do begin
                        readln (node [i]. info);
                        node [i]. used:= true
                    end {for...do begin};
            for i:= 1 to n-1
                do begin
                        node [i]. used:= true;
                        node [i]. lcount:= 0;
                        node [i]. info:= blanks
                    end {for...do begin};
            { set the lcount fields }
            for i:= n to size  { follow the path from each leaf to the root }
                do begin
                        p: = i
                        while p <> 1
                            do begin
                                    f:= p div 2;
                                    if p mod 2 = 0
                                        then node [f]. lcount:= node [f]. lcount + 1;
                                    p:= f
                                end {while...do begin}
                    end {for...do begin}
        end {procedure buildtree};
```

The second method uses an additional field *rcount* in each node to hold the number of leafs in the right subtree of each nonleaf node. This field as well as the *lcount* field is set to 1 in each nonleaf that is the father of two leafs. If n is odd, so that there is a node (numbered n *div* 2) that is the father of a leaf and a nonleaf, *lcount* in that node is set to 2 and *rcount* is set to 1.

The algorithm then goes through the remaining array elements in reverse order, setting *lcount* in each node to the sum of *lcount* and *rcount* in the node's left son and *rcount* to the sum of *lcount* and *rcount* in the node's right son. We leave to the reader the Pascal implementation of this technique. Note that *rcount* can be implemented as a local array in *buildtree* rather than as a field in every node since its values are unused once the tree is built.

This second method has the advantage that it visits each nonleaf once to calculate directly its *lcount* (and *rcount*) value. The first method visits each nonleaf once for each of its leaf descendants, adding one to *lcount* each time that the leaf is found to be a left descendant. To counterbalance this advantage, the second method requires an extra *rcount* field, while the first method needs no extra fields.

The Josephus Problem Revisited

The Josephus problem of Section 4.4 is a perfect example of the utility of the binary tree representation of a list. In that problem, it was necessary repeatedly to find the *m*th next element of a list and then delete that element. These are operations that can be performed efficiently in a tree-represented list.

If *size* equals the number of elements currently in a list, the position of the *m*th node following the node in position *k* that has just been deleted is given by $1 + (k - 2 + m) \bmod size$. For example, if a list has five elements and the third element is deleted, and we wish to find the fourth element following the deleted element, then $size = 4$, $k = 3$, and $m = 4$. Then $k - 2 + m$ equals 5 and $(k - 2 + m) \bmod size$ is 1, so that the fourth element following the deleted element is in position 2. (After deleting element 3, we count elements 4, 5, 1, and 2.) We can therefore write a Pascal function *follower* to find the *m*th node following a node in position *k* that has just been deleted and to reset *k* to its position. The routine calls the routine *findelement* presented earlier.

```
function follower(size: elementnum; m: integer; var k: elementnum): nodeptr;
var j, d: integer;
begin {function follower}
    j:= k - 2 + m;
    k:= (j mod size) + 1;
    follower:= findelement(k)
end {function follower}
```

The following Pascal program implements the Josephus algorithm using a tree-represented list. The program inputs the number of people in a circle (*n*), an integer count (*m*), and the names of the people in the circle in order, beginning with the person from whom the count starts. The people in the circle are counted in order, and the person at whom the input count is reached leaves the circle. The count then begins again from 1, starting at the next person. The program prints the order in which people leave the circle. Section 4.4 presented a program to do this using a circular list in which $(n - 1) * m$ nodes are accessed once the initial list is constructed. The following algorithm accesses fewer than $(n - 1) * \log_2 n$ nodes once the tree is built.

```
program josephus(input, output);
{ definitions of maxelts, numnodes, blanks, nodeptr, elementnum }
{                    and nodetype go here                        }
var n, size, k: elementnum;
    p: nodeptr;
    m: integer; { the count }
    node: array [1..numnodes] of nodetype;
{   routines buildtree, follower, findelement, and delete go here   }
begin {program josephus}
    readln(n, m);
    buildtree(n);
    k:= n + 1; { initially we have "deleted" the (n + 1) st person }
    for size:= n downto 2 { repeat until one person is left }
        do begin
                p:= follower(size, m, k);
                writeln(node[p].info);
                delete(p)
            end {for...do begin};
    writeln(node[1].info)
end {program josephus}.
```

EXERCISES

1. Prove that the leftmost node at level n in an almost complete strictly binary tree is assigned the number 2^n.

2. Prove that the extension (see Exercise 6.3.5) of an almost complete binary tree is almost complete.

3. For what values of n and m is the solution to the Josephus problem given in this section faster in execution than the solution given in Section 4.4? Why is this so?

4. Explain how we can eliminate the need for a *used* field if we elect not to move up a newly created leaf with no brother during deletion.

5. Explain how we can eliminate the need for a *used* field if we set *lcount* to -1 in a nonleaf that is converted to a leaf node and reset *info* to *blanks* in a deleted node.

6. Write a Pascal routine *buildtree* in which each node is visited only once by using an *rcount* array as described in the text.

7. Show how to represent a linked list as an almost complete binary tree in which each list element is represented by one tree node. Write a Pascal function to return a pointer to the kth element of such a list.

5. TREES AND THEIR APPLICATIONS

In this section we consider general trees and their representations. We also investigate some of their uses in problem solving.

A *tree* is a finite nonempty set of elements in which one element is called the *root* and the remaining elements are partitioned into $m \geq 0$ disjoint subsets, each of which is itself a tree. Each element in a tree is called a *node* of the tree.

Figure 6.5.1 illustrates some trees. Each node may be the root of a tree with zero or more subtrees. A node with no subtrees is a *leaf*. We use the terms *father, son, brother, ancestor, descendent, level,* and *depth* in the same sense that we used them for binary trees. We also define the *degree* of a node in a tree as the number of its sons. Thus in Figure 6.5.1a, node C has degree 0 (and is therefore a leaf), node D has degree 1, node B has degree 2, and node A has degree 3. There is no upper limit on the degree of a node.

Let us compare the trees of Figure 6.5.1a and c. They are equivalent as trees. Each has A as its root and three subtrees. One of those subtrees has root C with no subtrees, another has root D with a single subtree rooted at G, and the third has root B with two subtrees rooted at E and F. The only difference between the two illustrations is the order in which the subtrees are arranged. The definition of a tree made no distinction among subtrees of a general tree as in the case of a binary tree, where a distinction is made between the left and right subtrees. An *ordered tree* is defined as a tree in which the subtrees of each node form an ordered set. Thus, in an ordered tree, we may speak of the first, second, or last son of a particular node. The first son of a node in an ordered tree is often called the *oldest* son of that node, and the last son is called the *youngest*. Although the trees of Figure 6.5.1a and c are equivalent as unordered trees, they are different as ordered trees. In the remainder of this chapter we use the word "tree" to refer to "ordered tree." A *forest* is an ordered set of ordered trees.

The question arises as to whether a binary tree is a tree. Every binary tree except for the empty binary tree is indeed a tree. However, not every tree is binary because a tree node may have more than two sons whereas a binary tree node may not. Even a tree whose nodes have at most two sons is not necessarily a binary tree. This is because an only son in a general tree is not designated as being a "left" or a "right" son, whereas in a binary tree every son must be either a "left" son or a "right" son. In fact, although a nonempty binary tree is a tree, the designations of left and right have no meaning within the context of a tree (except perhaps to order the two subtrees of those nodes with two sons). A nonempty binary tree is a tree each of whose nodes has a maximum of two subtrees, which have the added designation of "left" or "right."

Pascal Representations of Trees

How can an ordered tree be represented in Pascal? Two alternatives immediately come to mind: an array of tree nodes may be declared or a dynamic variable may be allocated for each node created. However, what should the structure of each individual node be? In the representation of a binary tree, each node contains an information field and two pointers to its

Figure 6.5.1 Examples of trees.

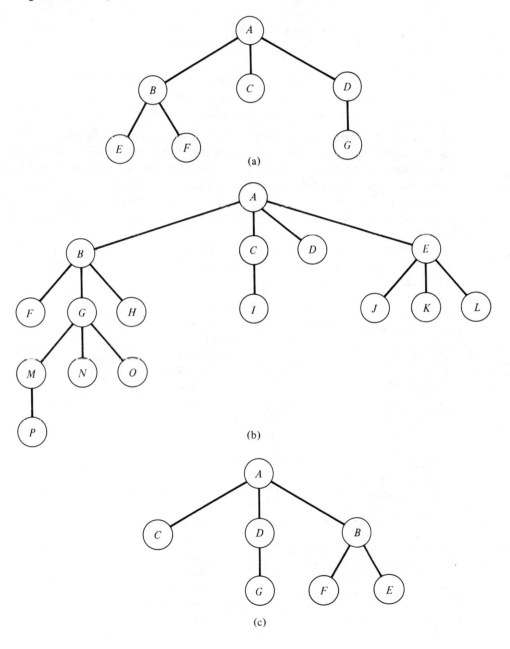

(a)

(b)

(c)

two sons. But how many pointers should a tree node contain? The number of sons of a node is variable and may be as large or as small as desired. If we arbitrarily declare

```
const maxnodes = 500;
      maxsons = 20;
type ndptr = 0..maxnodes;
     treenode = record
                     info: integer;
                     father: ndptr;
                     sons: array[1..maxsons] of ndptr
                end;
var   node: array[1..maxnodes] of treenode;
```

then we are restricting the number of sons a node may have to a maximum of 20. Although it is true that, in most cases, this will be sufficient, it is inadequate when it is necessary to create dynamically a node with 21 or 100 sons. Far worse than this remote possibility is the fact that 20 units of storage are reserved for each node in the tree, even though a node may actually have only one or two (or even zero) sons. This is a tremendous waste of space.

One alternative is to link all the sons of a node together in a linear list. Thus the set of available nodes (using the array implementation) might be declared as follows:

```
const maxnodes = 500;
type  ndptr = 0..maxnodes;
      treenode = record
                     info: integer;
                     father: ndptr;
                     son: ndptr;
                     next: ndptr
                end;
var node: array[1..maxnodes] of treenode;
```

node[*p*].*son* points to the oldest son of *node*[*p*], and *node*[*p*].*next* points to the next younger brother of *node*[*p*].

Alternatively, a node may be declared as a dynamic variable:

```
type ndptr = ↑treenode;
     treenode = record
                     info: integer;
                     father: ndptr;
                     son: ndptr;
                     next: ndptr
                end;
```

If all traversals are from a node to its sons, the *father* field may be omitted. Figure 6.5.2 illustrates the representations of the trees of Figure 6.5.1 under these methods if no *father* field is needed.

Even if it is necessary to access the father of a node, the *father* field can be omitted by placing a pointer to the father in the *next* field of the youngest son instead of leaving it nil. An additional boolean field could then be used to indicate whether the *next* field points to a "real" next son or to the father. Alternatively (in the array of nodes implementation), *ndptr* can be redefined to allow negative as well as positive indices. A negative value would indicate that the *next* field is a pointer to the node's father rather than to its brother, and the absolute value of the *next* field yields the actual pointer. This is similar to the representation of threads in binary trees. Of course, in either of these two latter methods, accessing the father would require a traversal of the remainder of the son list.

If we think of *son* as corresponding to the *left* pointer of a binary tree node and *next* as corresponding to its *right* pointer, this method actually represents a general ordered tree by a binary tree. We may picture this binary tree as the original tree tilted 45 degrees with all father–son links removed except for those between a node and its oldest son, and with links added between each node and its next younger brother. Figure 6.5.3 illustrates the binary trees corresponding to the trees of Figure 6.5.1.

In fact, a binary tree may be used to represent an entire forest since the *next* pointer in the root of a tree can be used to point to the next tree of the forest. Figure 6.5.4 illustrates a forest and its corresponding binary tree.

Tree Traversals

The traversal methods for binary trees induce traversal methods for forests. The preorder, inorder, or postorder traversals of a forest may be defined as the preorder, inorder, or postorder traversals of its corresponding binary tree. If a forest is represented as a set of dynamic variable nodes with *son* and *next* pointers as given above, a Pascal routine to print the contents of its nodes in inorder may be written as follows:

```
procedure intrav (p: ndptr);
begin
    if p <> nil
        then with p↑
            do begin
                    intrav(son);
                    writeln(info);
                    intrav(next)
                end {with...do begin}
end { procedure intrav};
```

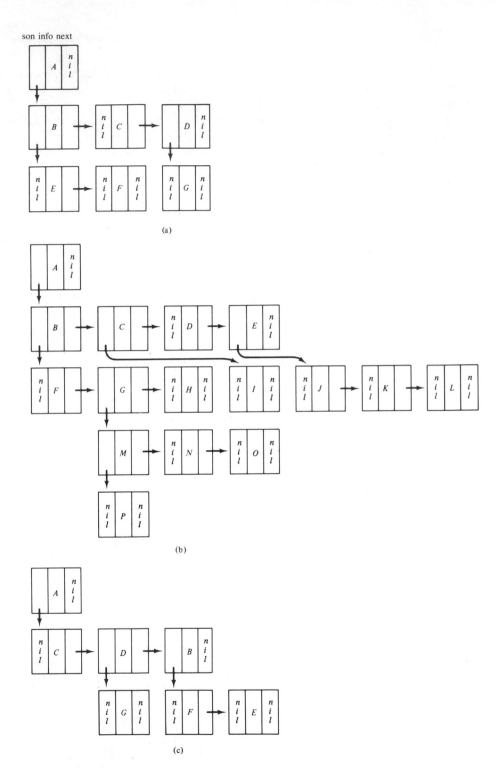

Figure 6.5.2 Tree representations.

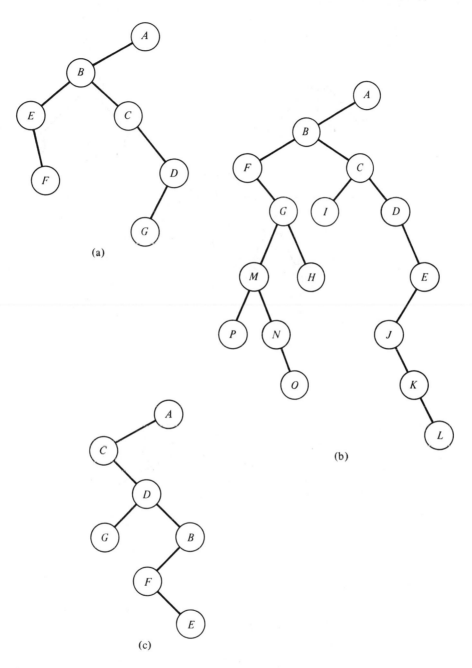

(a)

(b)

(c)

Figure 6.5.3 Binary trees corresponding to trees of Figure 6.5.1.

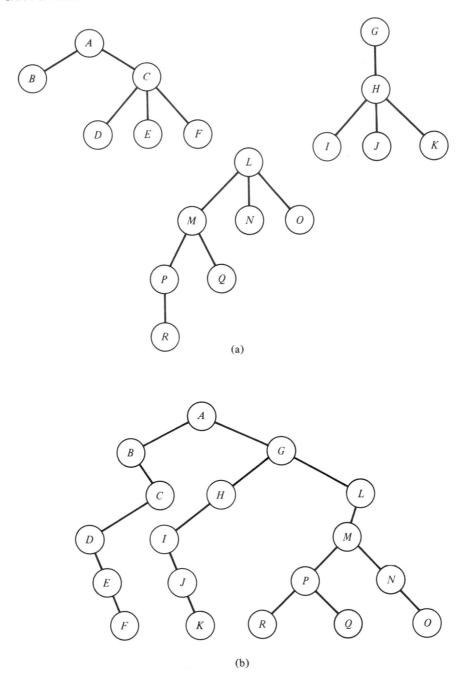

(a)

(b)

Figure 6.5.4 A forest and its corresponding binary tree.

Routines for preorder and postorder traversals are similar.

These traversals of a forest may also be defined directly as follows:

preorder	1. Visit the root of the first tree in the forest.
	2. Traverse in preorder the forest formed by the subtrees of the first tree, if any.
	3. Traverse in preorder the forest formed by the remaining trees in the forest, if any.
inorder	1. Traverse in inorder the forest formed by the subtrees of the first tree in the forest, if any.
	2. Visit the root of the first tree.
	3. Traverse in inorder the forest formed by the remaining trees in the forest, if any.
postorder	1. Traverse in postorder the forest formed by the subtrees of the first tree in the forest, if any.
	2. Traverse in postorder the forest formed by the remaining trees in the forest, if any.
	3. Visit the root of the first tree in the forest.

The nodes of the forest in Figure 6.5.4a may be listed in preorder as *ABCDEFGHIJKLMPRQNO*, in inorder as *BDEFCAIJKHGRPQMNOL*, and in postorder as *FEDCBKJIHRQPONMLGA*. Let us call a traversal of a binary tree a **binary traversal** and a traversal of an ordered general tree a **general traversal**.

General Expressions as Trees

An ordered tree may be used to represent a general expression in much the same way that a binary tree may be used to represent a binary expression. Since a node may have any number of sons, nonleaf nodes need not represent only binary operators but can represent operators with any number of operands. Figure 6.5.5 illustrates two expressions and their tree representations. The symbol '%' is used to represent unary negation to avoid confusing it with binary subtraction, which is represented by a minus sign. A function reference such as $f(G, H, I, J)$ is viewed as the operator f applied to the operands G, H, I, and J.

A general traversal of the trees of Figure 6.5.5 in preorder results in the strings * % + A B − + C log + D ! E f G H I J and q + A B sin C * X + Y Z, respectively. These are the prefix versions of those two expressions. Thus we see that preorder general traversal of an expression tree produces its prefix expression. Inorder general traversal yields the respective strings A B + % C D E ! + log + G H I J f − * and A B + C sin X Y Z + * q, which are the postfix versions of the two expressions.

Figure 6.5.5 Tree representation of an arithmetic expression.

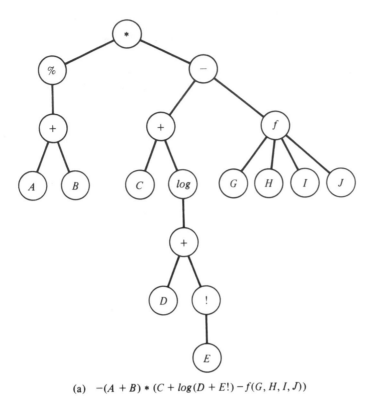

(a) $-(A + B) * (C + log(D + E!) - f(G, H, I, J))$

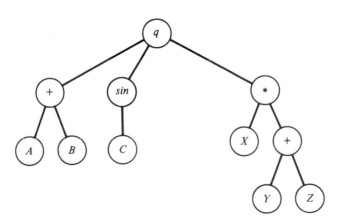

(b) $q(A + B, sin(C), X * (Y + Z))$

The fact that an inorder general traversal yields a postfix expression might be surprising at first glance. However, the reason for it becomes clear upon examination of the transformation that takes place when a general ordered tree is represented by a binary tree. Consider an ordered tree in which each node has zero or two sons. Such a tree is shown in Figure 6.5.6a, and its binary tree equivalent is shown in Figure 6.5.6b. Traversing the binary tree of Figure 6.5.6b is the same as traversing the ordered tree of Figure 6.5.6a. However, a tree such as the one in Figure 6.5.6a may be considered as a binary tree in its own right rather than as an ordered tree. Thus it is possible to perform a binary traversal (rather than a general traversal) directly on the tree of Figure 6.5.6a. Beneath that figure are the binary traversals of that tree; beneath Figure 6.5.6b are the binary traversals of the tree in that figure, which are the same as the traversals of the tree of Figure 6.5.6a if it is considered as an ordered tree.

Note that the preorder traversals of the two binary trees are the same. Thus, if a preorder traversal on a binary tree representing a binary expression yields the prefix of the expression, then that traversal on an ordered tree representing a general expression which happens to have only binary operators yields prefix as well. However, the postorder traversals of the two binary trees are not the same. Instead, the inorder binary traversal of the second (which is the same as the inorder general traversal of the first, if it is considered as an ordered tree) is the same as the postorder binary traversal of the first. Thus, the inorder general traversal of an ordered tree representing a binary expression is equivalent to the postorder binary traversal of the binary tree representing that expression, which yields postfix.

Evaluating an Expression Tree

Suppose that it is desired to evaluate an expression whose operands are all numerical constants. Such an expression can be represented in Pascal by a tree whose nodes are defined by

```
type nodetype = (oprtr, opnd);
     ndptr = ↑treenode;
     treenode = record
                    son: ndptr;
                    next: ndptr;
                    case tag: nodetype of
                        oprtr: (operator: packed array [1..10] of char);
                        opnd: (val: real)
              end;
```

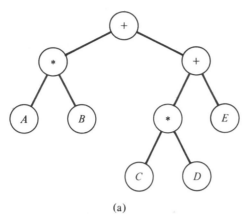

Figure 6.5.6

(a)

Preorder: $+ * AB + * CDE$
Inorder: $A * B + C * D + E$
Postorder: $AB * CD * E + +$

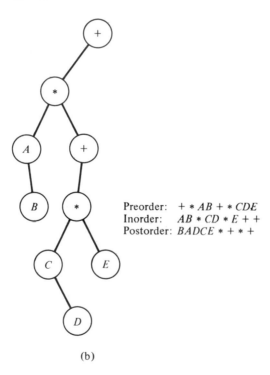

Preorder: $+ * AB + * CDE$
Inorder: $AB * CD * E + +$
Postorder: $BADCE * + * +$

(b)

The *son* and *next* pointers are used to link together the nodes of a tree as previously illustrated. Since a node may contain information that may be either a number (operand) or a character string (operator), the information portion of the node is the variant portion of the record.

We wish to write a Pascal function *evaltree(p)* which accepts a pointer to such a tree and returns the value of the expression represented by that tree. The routine *evalbintree* presented in Section 2 performs a similar function for binary expressions. *evalbintree* utilizes a function *oper* which accepts an operator symbol and two numerical operands and returns the numerical result of applying the operator to the operands. However, in the case of a general expression, we cannot use such a function, since the number of operands (and hence the number of arguments) varies with the operator. We therefore introduce a new function *apply(p)*, which accepts a pointer to an expression tree which contains a single operator and its numerical operands and returns the result of applying the operator to its operands. For example, the result of calling the function *apply* with parameter *p* pointing to the tree in Figure 6.5.7 is 24. Thus if the root of the tree which is passed to *evaltree* represents an operator, each of its subtrees must be replaced by tree nodes representing the numerical results of their evaluation so that the function *apply* may be called. As the expression is evaluated, the tree nodes representing operands must be freed and operator nodes must be converted to operand nodes.

We present a recursive procedure *replace* which accepts a pointer to an expression tree and replaces the tree with a tree node containing the numerical result of the expression's evaluation.

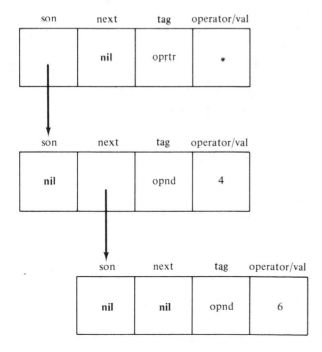

Figure 6.5.7 An expression tree.

```
procedure replace (p: ndptr);
var value: real;
    q, r: ndptr;
begin { procedure replace }
    if p↑.tag = oprtr
        { the tree has an operator }
        {           as its root           }
        then begin
                    q:= p↑.son;
                    while q <> nil
                        do begin
                                    { replace each of its subtrees }
                                    {           by operands           }
                                    replace(q);
                                    q:= q↑.next
                            end {while...do begin};
                    { apply the operator in the root to }
                    {    the operands in the subtrees    }
                    value:= apply(p);
                    { replace the operator by the result }
                    p↑.tag:= opnd;
                    p↑.val:= value;
                    {    free all the subtrees    }
                    q:= p↑.son;
                    p↑.son:= nil;
                    while q <> nil
                        do begin
                                    r:= q;
                                    q:= q↑.next;
                                    dispose(r)
                            end {while...do begin}
            end {then begin}
end { procedure replace };
```

The function *evaltree* may now be written as follows:

```
function evaltree (var p: ndptr): real;
var q: ndptr;
begin
    replace(p);
    evaltree:= p↑.val;
    dispose(p)
end { function evaltree};
```

Note that after calling *evaltree*(*p*) the tree is destroyed and the value of *p* is meaningless. This is a case of a ***dangling pointer*** in which a pointer variable may contain an address of a variable that has been freed (depending on the action taken by *dispose* for a particular implementation). Pascal programmers who use dynamic variables should be very careful to recognize such pointers and not to use them subsequently.

Constructing a Tree

A number of operations are frequently used in constructing a tree. We now present some of these operations and their Pascal implementations. In the Pascal representation, we assume that father pointers are not needed so that the *father* field is not used and the *next* pointer in the youngest node is nil. The routines would be slightly more complex and less efficient if this were not the case.

The first operation that we examine is *setsons*, which accepts a node of a tree that has no sons and a linear list of nodes linked together through the *next* field. *setsons* establishes the nodes in the list as the sons of the node in the tree. The Pascal routine to implement this operation is straightforward (we use the array of nodes implementation).

```
procedure setsons (p, list: ndptr);
      {   p points to a tree node, list to a list   }
      { of nodes linked together through their }
      {               next fields               }
  begin
      if p = 0
         then error('invalid insertion')
         else if treenode[p].son <> 0
                 then error('invalid insertion')
                 else node[p].son:= list
  end { procedure setsons};
```

Another common operation is *addson*(*p*, *x*), where *p* points to a node in a tree and it is desired to add a node containing *x* as the youngest son of *node*(*p*). The Pascal routine to implement *addson* is as follows. The routine calls the auxiliary function *getnode*, which removes a node from the available list and returns a pointer to it.

```
procedure addson (p: ndptr; x: integer);
var q, r: ndptr;
begin
    if p = 0
       then error('invalid insertion')
```

```
    else begin
            { the pointer q traverses the list of sons }
            {      of p.  r is one node behind q        }
            r:= 0;
            q:= node[p].son;
            while q <> 0
                do begin
                        r:= q;
                        q:= node[q].next
                    end;
            { at this point, r points to the youngest }
            {    son of p, or is nil if p has no sons   }
            q: = getnode;
            node[q].info:= x;
            node[q].next:= 0;
            if r = 0        {p has no sons}
                then node[p].son:= q
                else node[r].next:= q
        end {else begin}
    end { procedure addson};
```

Note that in order to add a new son to a node, the list of existing
sons must be traversed. Since adding a son is a common operation, a representation is often used which makes this operation more efficient. Under
this alternative representation, the list of sons is ordered from youngest to
oldest rather than vice versa. Thus *son(p)* points to the youngest son of
node(p), and *next(p)* points to its next older brother. Under this representation
the routine *addson* may be written as follows:

```
    procedure addson (p: ndptr; x: integer);
    var q: ndptr;
    begin
        if p = 0
            then error('invalid insertion')
            else begin
                    q:= getnode;
                    node[q].info:= x;
                    node[q].next:= node[p].son;
                    node[p].son:= q
                end
    end { procedure addson};
```

EXERCISES

1. How many trees exist with n nodes?

2. How many trees exist with n nodes and maximum level m?

3. Prove that if m pointer fields are set aside in each node of a general tree to point to a maximum of m sons, and if the number of nodes in the tree is n, then the number of nil son pointer fields is $n(m - 1) + 1$.

4. If a forest is represented by a binary tree as in the text, show that the number of nil right links is 1 greater than the number of nonleafs of the forest.

5. Define the **breadth-first order** of the nodes of a general tree as the root followed by all nodes on level 1, followed by all nodes on level 2, and so on. Within each level, the nodes should be ordered so that children of the same father appear in the same order as they appear in the tree, and if $n1$ and $n2$ have different fathers, $n1$ appears before $n2$ if the father of $n1$ appears before the father of $n2$. Extend the definition to a forest. Write a Pascal program to traverse a forest represented as a binary tree in breadth-first order.

6. Consider the following method of transforming a general tree gt into a strictly binary tree bt. Each node of gt is represented by a leaf of bt. If gt consists of a single node, then bt consists of a single node. Otherwise, bt consists of a new root node and a left subtree lt and a right subtree rt. lt is the strictly binary tree formed recursively from the oldest subtree of gt, and rt is the strictly binary tree formed recursively from gt without its oldest subtree. Write a Pascal routine to convert a general tree into a strictly binary tree.

7. Write a Pascal function *compute* which accepts a pointer to a tree representing an expression with constant operands and returns the result of evaluating the expression without destroying the tree.

8. Write a Pascal program to convert an infix expression into an expression tree. Assume that all nonbinary operators precede their operands. Let the input expression be represented as follows. An operand is represented by the character 'n' followed by a number, an operator by the character 't' followed by a character string representing the operator, and a function by the character 'f' followed by the name of the function.

9. Consider the definition of an expression, term, and factor given at the end of Section 3.2. Given a string of letters, plus signs, asterisks, and parentheses which form a valid expression, a **parse tree** can be formed for the string. Such a tree is illustrated in Figure 6.5.8 for the string $(A+B)*(C+D)$. Each node in such a tree represents a substring and contains a letter (E for expression, T for term, F for factor, or S for symbol) and two integers. The first is the position within the input string where the substring represented by that node begins and the second is the length of the substring. (The substring represented by each node is shown below that node in the figure.) The leafs are all S nodes and represent single symbols of the original input. The root of the tree must be an E node. The sons of any non-S node n represent the substrings that make up the grammatical object represented by n.

   Write a Pascal routine that accepts such a string and constructs a parse tree for it.

6. AN EXAMPLE: GAME TREES

One application of trees is to game playing by computer. We illustrate this application by writing a Pascal program to determine the "best" move in

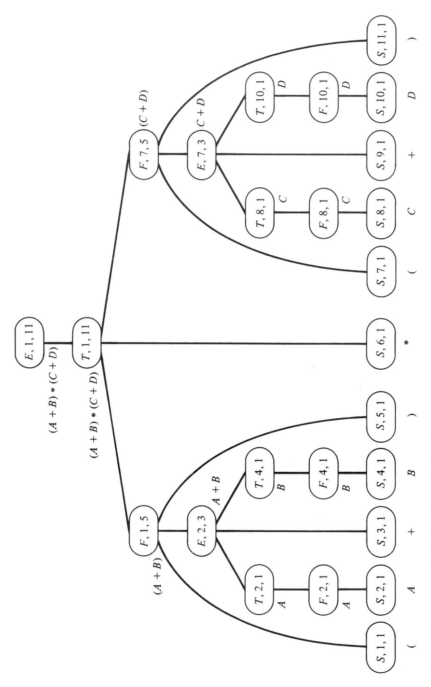

Figure 6.5.8 Parse tree for the string '(A + B) * (C + D)'.

tic-tac-toe from a given board position. Assume that there is a function *evaluate* which accepts a board position and an indication of a player (*X* or *O*) and returns a numerical value which represents how "good" the position seems to be for that player (the larger the value returned by *evaluate*, the better the position). Of course, a winning position yields the largest possible value and a losing position yields the smallest. An example of such an evaluation function for tic-tac-toe is the number of rows, columns, and diagonals remaining open for one player minus the number remaining open for his or her opponent (except that the value 9 would be returned for a position that wins and -9 for a position that loses). This function does not "look ahead" to consider any possible board positions that might result from the current position—it merely evaluates a static board position.

Given a board position, the best next move could be determined by considering all possible moves and resulting positions. That move that results in the board position with the highest evaluation should be selected. However, such an analysis does not necessarily yield the best move, as can be seen from Figure 6.6.1. This figure illustrates a position and the five possible moves which *X* can make from that position. Applying the evaluation function just described to the five resulting positions yields the values shown. Four moves yield the same maximum evaluation although three of them are distinctly inferior to the fourth. (The fourth position yields a certain victory for *X* while the other three can be drawn by *O*.) In fact, the move that yields the smallest evaluation is as good or better than the moves that yield a higher evaluation. The foregoing static evaluation function is not good enough to predict the outcome of the game. Although a better evaluation function could easily be produced for the game of tic-tac-toe (even if it were by the brute-force method of listing all positions and the appropriate response), most games are too complex for static evaluators to determine the best response.

Suppose that it were possible to look ahead several moves. Then the choice of a move could be improved considerably. Define the ***look ahead level*** as the number of future moves to be considered. Starting at any posi-

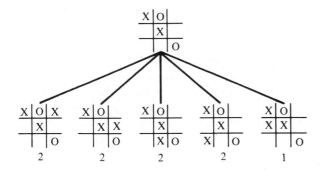

Figure 6.6.1

tion, it is possible to construct a tree of the possible board positions that may result from each move. Such a tree is called a ***game tree***. The game tree for the opening tic-tac-toe position with a look ahead level of 2 is illustrated in Figure 6.6.2. (Actually, other positions do exist but, because of symmetry considerations, these are effectively the same as the positions shown.) Note that the maximum level (called the ***depth***) of the nodes in such a tree is equal to the look-ahead level.

Let us designate the player who must move at the root's game position as *plus* and the opponent as *minus*. We attept to find the best move for plus from the root's game position. The remaining nodes of the tree may be designated as *plus nodes* or *minus nodes* depending upon which player must move from that node's position. Each node of Figure 6.6.2 is marked as a plus or minus node.

Suppose that the game positions of all the sons of a plus node have been evaluated for player plus. Then clearly, plus should choose the move that yields the maximum evaluation. Thus the value of a plus node to player plus is the maximum of the values of its sons. On the other hand, once plus has moved, minus will select the move that yields the minimum evaluation for player plus. Thus the value of a minus node to player plus is the minimum of the values of its sons.

Therefore, to decide the best move for player plus from the root, the positions in the leafs must be evaluated for player plus using a static evaluation function. These values are then moved up the game tree by assigning to each plus node the maximum of its sons' values and to each minus node the minimum of its sons' values on the assumption that minus will select the move that is worst for plus. The value assigned to each node of Figure 6.6.2 by this process is indicated in that figure immediately below the node. The move that plus should select, given the board position in the root node, is the one that maximizes its value. Thus the opening move for *X* should be the middle square, as illustrated in Figure 6.6.2. Figure 6.6.3 illustrates the determination of *O*'s best reply. Note that the designation of ''plus'' and ''minus'' depends on whose move is being calculated. Thus in Figure 6.6.2, *X* is designated as plus, while in Figure 6.6.3, *O* is designated as plus. In applying the static evaluation function to a board position, the value of the position to whichever player is designated as plus is computed. This method is called the ***minimax*** method because, as the tree is climbed, the maximum and minimum functions are applied alternately.

The best move for a player from a given position may be determined by first constructing the game tree and applying a static evaluation function to the leafs. These values are then moved up the tree by applying the minimum and maximum at minus and plus nodes, respectively. Each node of the game tree must include a representation of the board and an indication of whether the node is a plus node or a minus node. An array of nodes is therefore declared by

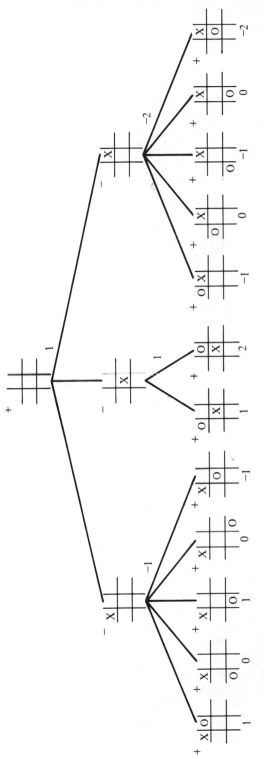

Figure 6.6.2 A game tree for tic-tac-toe.

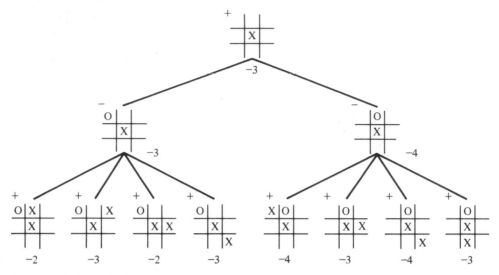

Figure 6.6.3 Computing O's reply.

```
const numnodes = 500;
type  nodeptr = 0..numnodes;
      boxtype = (xval, oval, blank);
      boardtype = array[1..3, 1..3] of boxtype;
      playertype = xval..oval;
      turntype = (plus, minus);
      nodetype = record
                     board: boardtype;
                     turn:  turntype;
                     son:   nodeptr;
                     next:  nodeptr
                 end;
var node: array[1..numnodes] of nodetype;
```

node[*p*].*board*[*i, j*] has the value *xval*, *oval*, or *blank*, depending on whether the square in row *i* and column *j* of *node*[*p*] is occupied by either of the players or is unoccupied. *node*[*p*].*turn* has the value *plus* or *minus*, depending on whether *node*[*p*] is a plus or a minus node, respectively. The remaining two fields of a node are used to position the node within the tree. *node*[*p*].*son* points to the oldest son of *node*[*p*], while *node*[*p*].*next* points to its next younger brother. We assume that the foregoing declaration is global, that an available list of nodes has been established and appropriate *getnode* and *freenode* routines have been written.

The Pascal procedure *nextmove(brd, player, looklevel, newbrd)* computes the best next move. *brd* is a 3 by 3 array representing the current board position; *player* is *xval* or *oval*, depending on whose move is being computed (note that in tic-tac-toe the value of *player* could be computed from *brd*, so that this parameter is not strictly necessary); and *looklevel* is the look-ahead level used in constructing the tree. *newbrd* is an output parameter which represents the best board position that can be achieved by *player* from position *brd*. *nextmove* uses two auxiliary routines, *buildtree* and *bestbranch*. The function *buildtree* builds the game tree and returns a pointer to its root. The procedure *bestbranch* computes the value of two output parameters: *best*, which is a pointer to the tree node representing the best move, and *value*, which is the evaluation of that move using the minimax technique.

```
procedure nextmove (brd: boardtype; looklevel: integer;
                                   player: playertype; var newbrd: boardtype);
var tree, best: nodeptr;
    value: integer;
begin
      tree: = buildtree(brd, looklevel);
      bestbranch(tree, player, best, value);
      newbrd:= node[best].board
end { procedure nextmove };
```

The function *buildtree* returns a pointer to the root of a game tree. It uses the auxiliary function *getnode*, which removes a node from the available list and returns a pointer to it. It also uses a routine *expand(p, plevel, depth)* in which *p* is a pointer to a node in a game tree, *plevel* is its level, and *depth* is the depth of the game tree that is to be constructed. *expand* produces the subtree rooted at *p* to the proper depth.

```
function buildtree (brd: boardtype; looklevel: integer): nodeptr;
var tree: nodeptr;
begin
      {create the root of the tree and initialize it}
      tree:= getnode;
      node[tree].board:= brd;
      {the root is a plus node by definition}
      node[tree].turn:= plus;
      node[tree].son:= 0;
      node[tree].next:= 0;
      {create the rest of the game tree}
      expand(tree, 0, looklevel);
      buildtree:= tree
end { function buildtree };
```

expand may be implemented by generating all board positions that may be obtained from the board position of *node[p]* and establishing them as the sons of *p* in the game tree. *expand* then repeatedly calls itself using each of these sons successively as its first parameter until the desired depth is reached. *expand* uses an auxiliary function *generate*, which accepts a board position *brd* and returns a pointer to a list of nodes containing the board positions that can be obtained from *brd*. This list is linked together by the *next* field. We leave the coding of *generate* as an exercise for the reader.

```
procedure expand (p: nodeptr; plevel, depth: integer);
var q: nodeptr;
begin {procedure expand}
      if plevel < depth
         then begin
                    { p is not at the maximum level }
                    q:= generate(node[p].board);
                    node[p].son:= q;
                    while q <> 0  {traverse the list of nodes}
                       do begin
                              if node[p].turn = plus
                                 then node[q].turn:= minus
                                 else node[q].turn:= plus;
                              node[q].son:= 0;
                              expand(q, plevel+1, depth);
                              q:= node[q].next
                       end {while...do begin}
         end {then begin}
end { procedure expand};
```

Once the game tree has been created, *bestbranch* evaluates the nodes of the tree. When a pointer to a leaf is passed to *bestbranch*, it calls a function *evaluate*, which statically evaluates the board position of that leaf for the player whose move we are determining. The coding of *evaluate* is left as an exercise. When a pointer to a nonleaf is passed to *bestbranch*, the routine calls itself recursively on each of its sons and then assigns the maximum of its sons' values to the nonleaf if it is a plus node and the minimum if it is a minus node. *bestbranch* also keeps track of which son yielded this minimum or maximum value.

If *node[p].turn* is *minus*, then *node[p]* is a minus node and it is to be assigned the minimum of the values assigned to its sons. If, however, *node[p].turn* is *plus*, *node[p]* is a plus node and its value should be the maximum of the values assigned to the sons of *node[p]*. If $min(x, y)$ is the minimum of x and y and $max(x, y)$ is their maximum, then $min(x, y) = -max(-x, -y)$ (you are invited to prove this as a trivial exercise). Thus the correct maximum or minimum can be found as follows. In the case of a plus node, compute the maximum; in the case of a minus node, compute the maximum of the negatives of the values and then reverse the sign of the result. These ideas are incorporated into *bestbranch*. The output parameters *best* and *value* are, respectively, a pointer to that son of the tree's root which maximizes its value and the value of that son which has now been assigned to the root.

```
procedure bestbranch (nd: nodeptr; player: playertype;
                                    var best: nodeptr; var value: integer);
var p, pbest: nodeptr;
    val: integer;
begin { procedure bestbranch}
    if node[nd].son = 0
      then begin { nd is a leaf }
                   value:= evaluate(node[nd].board, player);
                   best:= nd
            end {then begin}
      else begin
            { the node is not a leaf, traverse the list of sons }
                   p:= node[nd].son;
                   bestbranch(p, player, best, value);
                   best:= p;
                   if node[nd].turn = minus
                      then value:= -value;
                   p:= node[p].next;
                   while p <> 0
                      do begin
                              bestbranch(p, player, pbest, val);
                              if node[nd].turn = minus
                                then val:= - val;
                              if val > value
                                then begin
                                           value:= val;
                                           best:= p
                                      end {then begin};
                              p:= node[p].next
                         end {while...do begin};
                   if node[nd].turn = minus
                      then value:= -value
            end {else begin}
end { procedure bestbranch};
```

EXERCISES

1. Examine the routines of this section and determine whether all the parameters are actually necessary. How would you revise the parameter lists?
2. Write the Pascal routines *generate* and *evaluate* as described in the text.

3. Rewrite the programs of this and the preceding sections under the implementation in which each tree node includes a field *father* that contains a pointer to its father. Under which implementation are they more efficient?

4. Write nonrecursive versions of the routines *expand* and *bestbranch* given in the text.

5. Modify the routine *bestbranch* in the text so that the nodes of the tree are freed after they are no longer needed.

6. Combine the processes of building the game tree and evaluating its nodes into a single process so that the entire game tree need not exist at any one time and nodes are freed when no longer necessary.

7. Modify the program of Exercise 6 so that if the evaluation of a minus node is greater than the minimum of the values of its father's older brothers, the program does not bother expanding that minus node's younger brothers, and if the evaluation of a plus node is less than the maximum of the values of its father's older brothers, the program does not bother expanding that plus node's younger brothers. This method is called the **alpha-beta minimax** method. Explain why it is correct.

8. The game of **kalah** is played as follows: Two players each have seven holes, six of which are called **pits** and the seventh a **kalah**. These are arranged according to the following diagram:

Player 1

K P P P P P P
P P P P P P K

Player 2

Initially, there are six stones in each pit and no stones in either kalah, so that the opening position looks like this:

0 6 6 6 6 6 6
6 6 6 6 6 6 0

The players alternate turns, each turn consisting of one or more moves. To make a move, a player chooses one of his or her nonempty pits. The stones are removed from that pit and are distributed counterclockwise into the pits and into that player's kalah (the opponent's kalah is skipped), one stone per hole, until there are no stones remaining. For example, if player 1 moves first, a possible opening might result in the following board position:

1 7 7 7 7 7 0
6 6 6 6 6 6 0

If a player's last stone lands in his or her own kalah, the player gets another move. If the last stone lands in one of his or her own pits which is empty, that stone and the stones in the opponent's pit directly opposite are removed and placed in the player's kalah. The game ends when either player has no stones remaining in his or her pits. At that point, all of the stones in his or her opponent's pits are placed in the opponent's kalah and the game ends. The player with the most stones in his or her kalah is the winner.

Write a program that accepts a kalah board position and an indication of whose turn it is and produces that player's best move.

9. How would you modify the ideas of the tic-tac-toe program to compute the best move in a game that contains an element of chance, such as backgammon?

10. Why have computers been programmed to play perfect tic-tac-toe but not perfect chess or checkers?

11. The game of *nim* is played as follows. Some number of sticks are placed in a pile. Two players alternate in removing either one or two sticks from the pile. The player to remove the last stick is the loser. Write a Pascal procedure to determine the best move in nim.

7

SORTING

Sorting and searching are among the most common programming processes. In the first section of this chapter we discuss some of the overall considerations involved in sorting. In the remainder of the chapter we discuss some of the more common sorting techniques. In Chapter 8 we discuss searching and some applications.

1. GENERAL BACKGROUND

The concept of an ordered set of elements is one that has considerable impact on our daily lives. Consider, for example, the process of finding a telephone number in a telephone directory. This process, called a *search*, is simplified considerably by the fact that the names in the directory are listed in alphabetical order. Consider the trouble you might have in attempting to locate a telephone number if the names were listed in the order in which the customers placed their phone orders with the telephone company. In such a case, the names might as well have been entered in random order. Since the entries are sorted in alphabetical rather than in chronological order, the process of searching is simplified. Or consider the case of someone searching for a book in a library. Because the books are shelved in a specific order (Library of Congress, Dewey Decimal System, etc.), each book is assigned a specific position relative to the others and can be retrieved in a reasonable amount of time (if it is there). Or consider a set of numbers sorted sequentially in a computer's memory. As we shall see in Chapter 8, it is usually easier to find a particular element of that set if the numbers are sorted. In general, a set of items is kept sorted either to produce a report (to simplify manual retrieval of information, as in a telephone book or a library shelf) or to make machine access to data more efficient.

We now present some basic terminology. A *file of size n* is a sequence of n items $r(1)$, $r(2)$, ... , $r(n)$. Each item in the file is called a *record.* (The terms file and record are not being used here as Pascal terminology to refer to specific data structures. Rather, they are being used in a more general sense.) A *key*, $k(i)$, is associated with each record $r(i)$. The key is usually (but not always) a subfield of the entire record. The file is said to be *sorted on the key* if $i < j$ implies that $k(i)$ precedes $k(j)$ in some ordering on the keys. In the example of the telephone book, the file consists of all the entries in the book. Each entry is a record. The key upon which the file is sorted is the name field of the record. Each record also contains fields for an address and a telephone number.

A sort can be classified as being *internal* if the records that it is sorting are in main memory or *external* if some of the records that it is sorting are in auxiliary storage. We restrict our attention to internal sorts.

It is possible for two records in a file to have the same key. A sorting technique is called *stable* if for all records i and j such that $k(i) = k(j)$, if $r(i)$ precedes $r(j)$ in the original file, then $r(i)$ precedes $r(j)$ in the sorted file.

A sort takes place either on the records themselves or on an auxiliary table of pointers (called *sorting by address*). For example, consider Figure 7.1.1a in which a file of five records is shown. If the file is sorted in increasing order on the numeric key shown, the resulting file is as shown in Figure 7.1.1b. In this case the actual records themselves have been sorted.

Suppose, however, that the amount of data stored in each of the records in the file of Figure 7.1.1a is so large that the overhead involved in moving the actual data is prohibitive. In this case an auxiliary table of pointers

	Key	Other fields			
Record 1	4	DDD		1	AAA
Record 2	2	BBB		2	BBB
Record 3	1	AAA		3	CCC
Record 4	5	EEE		4	DDD
Record 5	3	CCC		5	EEE
		File			File

(a) Original file.   (b) Sorted file.   **Figure 7.1.1** Sorting actual records.

may be used so that these pointers are moved instead of the actual data. This is shown in Figure 7.1.2. The table in the center is the file and the table at the left is the initial table of pointers. The entry in position j in the table of pointers points to record j. During the sorting process, the entries in the pointer table are adjusted so that the final table is as shown at the right. Originally, the first pointer was to the first entry in the file; upon completion, the first pointer is to the fourth entry in the table. Note that none of the original file entries is moved. In most of the programs in this chapter we illustrate techniques of sorting actual records. The extension of these techniques to sorting by address is straightforward and will be left as an exercise for the reader.

Because of the relationship between sorting and searching, the first question to ask in any application is whether or not it pays to sort. Sometimes, there is less work involved in searching a set of elements for a particular one than to first sort the entire set and then to extract the desired element. On the other hand, if frequent use of the file is required for the purpose of retrieving specific elements, it might be more efficient to sort the file. This is because the overhead of successive searches may far exceed the overhead involved in first sorting the file and subsequently retrieving elements from the sorted file. Thus it cannot be said that it is more efficient either to sort or not to sort. The programmer must make a decision based on individual circumstances. Once a decision to sort has been made, other decisions must be made, including what is to be sorted and what methods are to be used. There is no one sorting method that is universally superior to all others. The programmer must carefully examine the problem and the desired results before deciding these very important questions.

Efficiency Considerations

As we shall see in this chapter, there are a great number of methods that can be used to sort a file. The programmer must be aware of several

Figure 7.1.2 Sorting by using an auxiliary table of pointers.

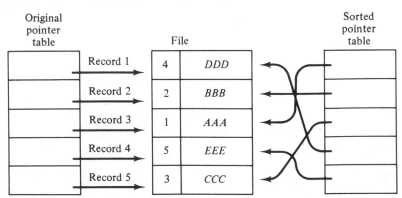

interrelated efficiency considerations to choose intelligently which sorting method is most appropriate to the particular problem. Three of the most important of these considerations include the length of time that must be spent by the programmer in coding a particular sorting program, the amount of machine time necessary for running the program, and the amount of space necessary for the program.

If a file is small, sophisticated sorting techniques designed to minimize space and time requirements are usually worse or only marginally better in achieving efficiencies than are simpler, generally less efficient methods. Similarly, if a particular sorting program is to be run only once and there is sufficient machine time and space in which to run it, it would be ludicrous for a programmer to spend days investigating the best methods of obtaining the last ounce of efficiency. In such cases, the amount of time that must be spent by the programmer is properly the overriding consideration in determining which sorting method to use. However, a strong word of caution must be inserted. Programming time is never a valid excuse for using an incorrect program. A sort that is run only once may be able to afford the luxury of an inefficient technique, but it cannot afford an incorrect one. The presumably sorted data may be used in an application in which the assumption of ordered data is crucial.

A programmer must be able to recognize the fact that a particular sort is inefficient and must be able to justify its use in a particular situation. Too often, programmers take the easy way out and code an inefficient sort which is then incorporated into a larger system in which the sort is a key component. The designers and planners of the system are then surprised at the inadequacy of their creation. To maximize his or her own efficiency, a programmer must be knowledgeable of a wide range of sorting techniques and be cognizant of the advantages and disadvantages of each, so that when the need for a sort arises he or she can supply the one that is most appropriate for the particular situation.

This brings us to the other two efficiency considerations: time and space. As in most computer applications, the programmer must often optimize one of these at the expense of the other. In considering the time necessary to sort a file of size n, we do not concern ourselves with actual time units, as these will vary from one machine to another, from one program to another, and from one set of data to another. Rather, we are interested in the change in the amount of time required to sort a file induced by a change in the file size n. Let us see if we can make this concept more precise. We say that y is **proportional** to x if multiplying x by a constant multiplies y by that same constant. Thus if y is proportional to x, doubling x will double y and multiplying x by 10 multiplies y by 10. Similarly, if y is proportional to x^2, then doubling x multiplies y by 4 and multiplying x by 10 multiplies y by 100.

There are two ways to determine the time requirements of a sort, neither of which yields results that are applicable to all cases. One method is to go through a sometimes intricate and involved mathematical analysis of various cases (e.g., best case, worst case, average case). The result of this analysis is usually a formula giving the average time required for a particular sort as a function of the file size n. Suppose that such a mathematical analysis on a particular sorting program results in the conclusion that the program takes $.01n^2 + 10n$ time units to execute. Figure 7.1.3 shows the time needed by the sort for various values of n. You will notice that for small values of n, the quantity $10n$ overwhelms the quantity $.01n^2$. This is because the difference between n^2 and n is small for small values of n and is more than compensated for by the difference between 10 and .01. Thus for small values of n, an increase in n by a factor of 2 (e.g., from 50 to 100) increases the time needed for sorting by approximately that same factor of 2 (from 525 to 1100). Similarly, an increase in n by a factor of 5 (e.g., from 10 to 50) increases the sorting time by approximately 5 (from 101 to 525).

However, as n becomes larger, the difference between n^2 and n increases so quickly that it eventually more than makes up for the difference between 10 and .01. Thus when n equals 1000, the two terms contribute equally to the amount of time needed by the program. As n becomes even larger, the term $.01n^2$ overwhelms the term $10n$ and the contribution of the term $10n$ becomes almost insignificant. Thus for large values of n, an increase in n by a factor of 2 (e.g., from 50,000 to 100,000) causes an increase in sorting time of approximately 4 (from 25.5 million to 101 million) and an increase in n by a factor of 5 (e.g., from 10,000 to 50,000) increases the sorting time by approximately a factor of 25 (from 1.1 million to 25.5 million). Indeed, as n becomes larger and larger, the sorting time becomes more and more closely proportional to n^2, as is clearly illustrated by the last column of Figure 7.1.3. Thus for large n the time required by the sort is almost proportional to n^2. Of course, for small values of n, the sort may exhibit drastically different behavior (as in Figure 7.1.3), a situation that must be taken into account in analyzing its efficiency.

O Notation

To capture the concept of comparing the growth of one function with that of another, we introduce some terminology and a new notation.

n	$a = 0.01n^2$	$b = 10n$	$a + b$	$\dfrac{(a + b)}{n^2}$
10	1	100	101	1.01
50	25	500	525	0.21
100	100	1,000	1,100	0.11
500	2,500	5,000	7,500	0.03
1,000	10,000	10,000	20,000	0.02
5,000	250,000	50,000	300,000	0.01
10,000	1,000,000	100,000	1,100,000	0.01
50,000	25,000,000	500,000	25,500,000	0.01
100,000	100,000,000	1,000,000	101,000,000	0.01
500,000	2,500,000,000	5,000,000	2,505,000,000	0.01

Figure 7.1.3

In the previous example, the function $.01n^2 + 10n$ is said to be "on the order of" the function n^2 because, as n becomes large, the function becomes more nearly proportional to n^2.

To be precise, given two functions $f(n)$ and $g(n)$, we say that $f(n)$ is **on the order of** $g(n)$ or that $f(n)$ is $O(g(n))$ if there exist positive integers a and b such that $f(n) \leq a * g(n)$ for all $n \geq b$. For example, if $f(n) = n^2 + 100n$ and $g(n) = n^2$, then $f(n)$ is $O(g(n))$ since $n^2 + 100n$ is less than or equal to $2n^2$ for all n greater than or equal to 100. In this case, a equals 2 and b equals 100. This same $f(n)$ is also $O(n^3)$ since $n^2 + 100n$ is less than or equal to $2n^3$ for all n greater than or equal to 8. Given a function $f(n)$, there may be many functions $g(n)$ such that $f(n)$ is $O(g(n))$ and, for each function $g(n)$, there may be many values of a and b that satisfy the above criteria.

If $f(n)$ is $O(g(n))$, then "eventually" (i.e., for $n \geq b$) $f(n)$ becomes permanently smaller or equal to some multiple of $g(n)$. In a sense, we are saying that $f(n)$ is bounded by $g(n)$ from above or that $f(n)$ is a "smaller" function than $g(n)$. Another formal way of saying this is that $f(n)$ is **asymptotically bounded** by $g(n)$. Yet another interpretation is that $f(n)$ grows more slowly than does $g(n)$ since, proportionately (that is, up to a factor of a), $g(n)$ eventually becomes larger.

It is easy to show that if $f(n)$ is $O(g(n))$ and $g(n)$ is $O(h(n))$, then $f(n)$ is $O(h(n))$. For example, $n^2 + 100n$ is $O(n^2)$ and n^2 is $O(n^3)$ (to see this, set a and b both equal to 1), so $n^2 + 100n$ is $O(n^3)$. This is called the **transitive property**.

Note that if $f(n)$ is a constant function, that is, $f(n) = c$ for all n, then $f(n)$ is $O(1)$ since, setting a to c and b to 1, we have that $c \leq c * 1$ for all $n \geq 1$. (In fact, the value of b or n is irrelevant since a constant function's value is independent of n.)

It is also easy to show that the function $c * n^k$ is $O(n^k)$ for any constants c and k. To see this, simply note that $c * n^k$ is less than or equal to $c * n^k$ for any $n \geq 1$ (i.e., set $a = c$ and $b = 1$). It is also obvious that n^k is $O(n^{k+j})$ for any $j \geq 0$ (use $a = 1$, $b = 1$). We can also show that if $f(n)$ and $g(n)$ are both $O(h(n))$, then the new function $f(n) + g(n)$ is also $O(h(n))$. All these facts together can be used to show that if $f(n)$ is any polynomial whose leading power is k—that is, $f(n) = c_1 * n^k + c_2 * n^{k-1} + \ldots + c_k * n + c_{k+1}$ then $f(n)$ is $O(n^k)$. Indeed, $f(n)$ is $O(n^{k+j})$ for any $j \geq 0$.

While a function may be asymptotically bounded by many other functions—as, for example, $10n^2 + 37n + 153$ is $O(n^2), O(10n^2), O(37n^2 + 10n)$ and $O(.05n^3)$—we usually look for an asymptotic bound that is a single term with a leading coefficient of 1 and that is as "close a fit" as possible. Thus we would say that $10n^2 + 37n + 153$ is $O(n^2)$, although it is also asymptotically bounded by many other functions. Ideally, we would like to find a function $g(n)$ such that $f(n)$ is $O(g(n))$ and $g(n)$ is $O(f(n))$. If $f(n)$ is a constant or a polynomial, this can always be done by using its highest term with a coefficient of 1. For more complex functions, however, it is not always possible to find such a tight fit.

An important function in the study of algorithm efficiency is the logarithm function. Recall that $\log_m n$ is the value x such that x^m equals n. m is called the *base* of the logarithm. Consider the functions $\log_m n$ and $\log_k n$. Let xm be $\log_m n$ and xk be $\log_k n$. Then

$$m^{xm} = n \text{ and } k^{xk} = n$$

so that

$$m^{xm} = k^{xk}$$

Taking $\log_m$ of both sides,

$$xm = \log_m (k^{xk})$$

Now it can easily be shown that $\log_z (x^y)$ equals $y * \log_z x$ for any x, y, and z, so that the last equation can be rewritten as (recall that $xm = \log_m n$)

$$\log_m n = xk * \log_m k$$

or as (recall that $xk = \log_k n$)

$$\log_m n = (\log_m k) * \log_k n$$

Thus $\log_m n$ and $\log_k n$ are constant multiples of each other.

It is easy to show that if $f(n) = c * g(n)$, where c is a constant, $f(n)$ is $O(g(n))$; indeed, we have already shown that this is true for the function $g(n) = n^k$. Thus $\log_m n$ is $O(\log_k n)$ and $\log_k n$ is $O(\log_m n)$ for any m and k. Since each logarithm function is on the order of any other, we usually drop the base when speaking of functions of logarithmic order and say that all such functions are $O(\log n)$.

The following facts establish an order hierarchy of functions:

c is $O(1)$ for any constant c.
c is $O(\log n)$ but $\log_k n$ is not $O(1)$.
$c * \log_k n$ is $O(\log n)$ for any constants c, k.
$c * \log_k n$ is $O(n)$ but n is not $O(\log n)$.
$c * n^k$ is $O(n^k)$ for any constants c, k.
$c * n^k$ is $O(n^{k+j})$ but n^{k+j} is not $O(n^k)$.
$c * n * \log_k n$ is $O(n \log n)$ for any constants c, k.
$c * n * \log_k n$ is $O(n^2)$ but n^2 is not $O(n \log n)$.
$c * n^j * \log_k n$ is $O(n^j \log n)$ for any constants c, j, k.
$c * n^j * \log_k n$ is $O(n^{j+1})$ but n^{j+1} is not $O(n^j \log n)$.
$c * n^j * (\log_k n)^l$ is $O(n^j (\log n)^l)$ for any constants c, j, k, l.
$c * n^j * (\log_k n)^l$ is $O(n^{j+1})$ but n^{j+1} is not $O(n^j (\log n)^l)$.
$c * n^j * (\log_k n)^l$ is $O(n^j (\log n)^{l+1})$ but $n^j (\log_k n)^{l+1}$ is not $O(n^j (\log n)^l)$.
$c * n^k$ is $O(d^n)$ but d^n is not $O(n^k)$ for any constants c and k, and $d > 1$.

The hierarchy of functions established by these facts, with each function of lower order than the next, is c, $\log n$, $(\log n)^k$, n, $n(\log n)^k$, n^k, $n^k(\log n)^l$, n^{k+1}, d^n.

Functions that are $O(n^k)$ for some k are said to be of *polynomial order*, whereas functions that are $O(d^n)$ for some $d > 1$ but not $O(n^k)$ for any k are said to be of *exponential order*.

The distinction between polynomial-order functions and exponential-order functions is extremely important. Even a small exponential-order function, such as 2^n, grows far larger than any polynomial-order function, such as n^k regardless of the size of k. As an illustration of the rapidity with which exponential-order functions grow, consider that 2^{10} equals 1024 but that 2^{100} (that is, 1024^{10}) is greater than the number formed by a 1 followed by 30 zeros. The smallest k for which 10^k exceeds 2^{10} is 4, but the smallest k for which 100^k exceeds 2^{100} is 16. As n becomes larger, larger values of k are needed for n^k to keep up with 2^n. For any single k, 2^n eventually becomes permanently larger than n^k.

Because of the incredible rate of growth of exponential-order functions, problems that require exponential time algorithms for solution are considered to be *intractable* on current computing equipment. That is, such problems cannot be practically solved except in the simplest cases.

Efficiency of Sorting

Using this concept of the order of a sort, we can compare various sorting techniques and classify them as being "good" or "bad" in specific cases. One might hope to discover the "optimal" sort, which is $O(n)$ regardless of the contents or order of the input; unfortunately, however, it can be shown that no such sort exists. Most of the classical sorts we shall consider have time requirements that range from $O(n \log n)$ to $O(n^2)$. In the former, multiplying the file size by 100 will multiply the sorting time by less than 200 (if the base of the logarithm is 10); in the latter, multiplying the file size by 100 multiplies the sorting time by a factor of 10,000. Figure 7.1.4 shows

n	$n \log_{10} n$	n^2
1×10^1	1.0×10^1	1.0×10^2
5×10^1	8.5×10^1	2.5×10^3
1×10^2	2.0×10^2	1.0×10^4
5×10^2	1.3×10^3	2.5×10^5
1×10^3	3.0×10^3	1.0×10^6
5×10^3	1.8×10^4	2.5×10^7
1×10^4	4.0×10^4	1.0×10^8
5×10^4	2.3×10^5	2.5×10^9
1×10^5	5.0×10^5	1.0×10^{10}
5×10^5	2.8×10^6	2.5×10^{11}
1×10^6	6.0×10^6	1.0×10^{12}
5×10^6	3.3×10^7	2.5×10^{13}
1×10^7	7.0×10^7	1.0×10^{14}

Figure 7.1.4 A comparison of $n \log n$ and n^2 for various values of n.

the comparison of $n \log n$ with n^2 for a range of values of n. It can be seen from the figure that for large n, as n increases, n^2 increases at a much more rapid rate than does $n \log n$. However, a sort should not be selected simply because it is $O(n \log n)$. The relation of the file size n and the other terms comprising the actual sorting time must be known. In particular, terms that play an insignificant role for large n may play a very dominant role for small n. All these considerations must be taken into account before an intelligent sort selection can be made.

A second method of determining time requirements of a sorting technique is actually to run the program and measure its efficiency (either by measuring absolute time units or the number of operations performed). To use such results, the test must be run on "many" sample files. Even when such statistics have been gathered, the application of that sort to a specific file need not yield results that follow the general pattern. Peculiar attributes of the file in question may make the sorting speed deviate signif- icantly. In the sorts of the subsequent sections we shall give an intuitive explanation as to why a particular sort is classified as $O(n^2)$ or $O(n \log n)$; we leave mathematical analysis and sophisticated testing of empirical data as exercises for the ambitious reader.

In most cases, the time needed by a sort depends upon the original sequence of the data. For some sorts, input data that is almost in sorted order can be completely sorted in time $O(n)$, whereas input data in reverse order needs time $O(n^2)$. For other sorts the time required is $O(n \log n)$ regardless of the original order of the data. Thus, if we have some knowledge about the original data, we can make a more intelligent decision as to which sorting method to select. On the other hand, if we have no such knowledge, we may wish to select a sort based on the worst possible case or based on the "average" case. In any event, the only general comment that can be made about sorting techniques is that there is no "best" general sorting technique. The choice of a sort must, of necessity, depend on the specific circumstances.

Once a particular sorting technique has been selected, the program- mer should try to make the program as efficient as possible. In many pro- gramming applications it is often necessary to sacrifice efficiency for the sake of clarity. With sorting, the situation is usually the opposite. Once a sorting program has been written and tested, the programmer's chief goal is to improve its speed, even if it becomes less readable. The reason for this is that a sort may account for the major part of a program's efficiency, so that any improvement in sorting time significantly affects overall efficiency. An- other reason is that a sort is often used quite frequently, so that a small improvement in its execution speed saves a great deal of computer time. It is usually a good idea to remove subroutine calls, especially from inner loops, and to replace them with the code of the subroutine in line, since the call- return mechanism of a language can be prohibitively expensive in terms of time. In many of the programs we do not do this, so as not to obfuscate the intent of the program with huge blocks of code. But before using the following programs on large files, the reader would do well to replace subroutine calls with code in line.

Space constraints are usually less important than time considerations. One of the reasons for this is that for most sorting programs the amount of space needed is closer to $O(n)$ than to $O(n^2)$. A second reason is that if more space is required, it can almost always be found in auxiliary storage. An ideal sort is an ***inplace sort*** whose additional space requirements are $O(1)$. That is, an inplace sort manipulates the elements to be sorted within the array or list space that contained the original unsorted input. Additional space that is required is in the form of a constant number of locations (such as declared individual program variables) regardless of the size of the set to be sorted.

Usually, the expected relationship between time and space holds for sorting algorithms: those programs that require less time usually require more space, and vice versa. However, there are clever algorithms that utilize both minimum time and minimum space; that is, they are $O(n \log n)$ inplace sorts. These may, however, require more programmer time to develop and verify. They also have higher constants of proportionality than do many sorts that use more space or that have higher time orders and so require more time to sort small sets.

In the remaining sections we investigate some of the more popular sorting techniques and indicate some of their advantages and disadvantages.

EXERCISES

1. Choose any sorting technique with which you are familiar.
   (a) Write a program for the sort.
   (b) Is the sort stable?
   (c) Determine the time requirements of the sort as a function of the file size, both mathematically and empirically.
   (d) What is the order of the sort?
   (e) At what file size does the most dominant term begin to overshadow the others?

2. Show that the function $(\log_m n)^k$ is $O(n)$ for all m and k but that n is not $O((\log n)^k)$ for any k.

3. Suppose that a time requirement is given by the formula $an^2 + bn \log_2 n$, where a and b are constants. Answer the following questions by both proving your results mathematically and writing a program to empirically validate the results.
   (a) For what values of n (expressed in terms of a and b) does the first term dominate the second?
   (b) For what value of n (expressed in terms of a and b) are the two terms equal?
   (c) For what values of n (expressed in terms of a and b) does the second term dominate the first?

4. Show that any process which sorts a file can be extended to find all duplicates in the file.

5. Consider a Pascal subroutine *sort(x, n)* to sort the first n elements of an array x. What are the relative advantages and disadvantages of leaving x as a parameter or of making it a global variable?

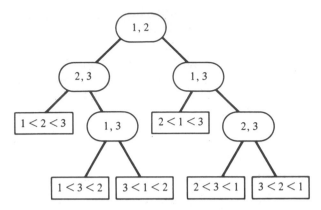

Figure 7.1.5 A decision tree for a file of three elements.

6. A *sort decision tree* is a binary tree that represents a sorting method based on comparisons. Figure 7.1.5 illustrates such a decision tree for a file of three elements. Each nonleaf of such a tree represents a comparison between two elements. Each leaf represents a completely sorted file. A left branch from a nonleaf indicates that the first key was found to be smaller than the second; a right branch indicates that it was larger. (We assume that all the elements in the file have distinct keys.) For example, the tree of Figure 7.1.5 represents a sort on three elements $x[1]$, $x[2]$, $x[3]$, which proceeds as follows:

Compare $x[1]$ to $x[2]$. If $x[1] < x[2]$, then compare $x[2]$ with $x[3]$, and if $x[2] < x[3]$, then the sorted order of the file is $x[1]$, $x[2]$, $x[3]$; otherwise, if $x[1] < x[3]$, the sorted order is $x[1]$, $x[3]$, $x[2]$, and if $x[1] > x[3]$, then the sorted order is $x[3]$, $x[1]$, $x[2]$. If $x[1] > x[2]$, then proceed in a similar fashion down the right subtree.

(a) Show that a sort decision tree which never makes a redundant comparison (i.e., never compares $x[i]$ and $x[j]$ if the relationship between $x[i]$ and $x[j]$ is known) has $n!$ leafs.

(b) Show that the depth of such a decision tree is at least $\log_2(n!)$.

(c) Show that $n! \geqslant (n/2)^{n/2}$, so that the depth of such a tree is $O(n \log n)$.

(d) Explain why this proves that any sorting method which uses comparisons on a file size of n must make at least $O(n \log n)$ comparisons.

7. Given a sort decision tree for a file as in Exercise 6, show that if the file contains some equal elements, the result of applying the tree to the file (where either a left or right branch is taken whenever two elements are equal) is a sorted file.

8. Extend the concept of the binary decision tree of the previous exercises to a ternary tree which includes the possibility of equality. It is desired to determine which elements of the file are equal, in addition to the order of the distinct elements of the file. How many comparisons are necessary?

9. Show that if k is the smallest integer greater than or equal to $n + \log_2 n - 2$, then k comparisons are necessary and sufficient to find the largest and second largest elements of a set of n distinct elements.

10. How many comparisons are necessary to find the largest and smallest of a set of n distinct elements?

11. Show that the function $f(n)$ defined by

$$f(1) = 1$$
$$f(n) = f(n-1) + 1/n \quad \text{for } n > 1$$

is $O(\log n)$.

2. EXCHANGE SORTS

Bubble Sort

The first sort we present is probably the most widely known among beginning students of programming—the *bubble sort*. One of the characteristics of this sort is that it is easy to understand and program. Yet, of all the sorts that we shall consider, it is probably the least efficient.

In each of the subsequent examples, x is an array of integers of which the first n are to be sorted so that $x[i] \leqslant x[j]$ for $1 \leqslant i < j \leqslant n$. It is straightforward to extend this simple format to one that is used in sorting n records, each with a subfield key k.

The basic idea underlying the bubble sort is to pass through the file sequentially several times. Each pass consists of comparing each element in the file with its successor ($x[i]$ with $x[i + 1]$) and interchanging the two elements if they are not in proper order. Consider the following file:

$$25 \quad 57 \quad 48 \quad 37 \quad 12 \quad 92 \quad 86 \quad 33$$

The following comparisons are made on the first pass:

$x[1]$ with $x[2]$	(25 with 57)	no interchange
$x[2]$ with $x[3]$	(57 with 48)	interchange
$x[3]$ with $x[4]$	(57 with 37)	interchange
$x[4]$ with $x[5]$	(57 with 12)	interchange
$x[5]$ with $x[6]$	(57 with 92)	no interchange
$x[6]$ with $x[7]$	(92 with 86)	interchange
$x[7]$ with $x[8]$	(92 with 33)	interchange

Thus, after the first pass, the file is in the order

$$25 \quad 48 \quad 37 \quad 12 \quad 57 \quad 86 \quad 33 \quad 92$$

Notice that after this first pass, the largest element (in this case 92) is in its proper position within the array. In general, $x[n - i + 1]$ will be in its proper position after iteration i. The method is called the bubble sort because each number slowly "bubbles" up to its proper position. After the second pass the file is

$$25 \quad 37 \quad 12 \quad 48 \quad 57 \quad 33 \quad 86 \quad 92$$

Notice that 86 has now found its way to the second highest position. Since each iteration places a new element into its proper position, a file of n elements requires no more than $n - 1$ iterations. The complete set of iterations is illustrated on the top of the next page.

On the basis of this discussion we could proceed to code the bubble sort. However, there are some obvious improvements to the method. First, since all of the elements in positions greater than or equal to $n - i + 1$ are already in proper position after iteration i, they need not be compared in succeeding iterations. Thus on the first pass $n - 1$ comparisons are made, on the second pass $n - 2$ comparisons, and on the $(n - 1)$th pass only one comparison is made (between $x[1]$ and $x[2]$). Therefore, the process speeds up as it proceeds through successive passes.

iteration 0 (original file)	25	57	48	37	12	92	86	33
iteration 1	25	48	37	12	57	86	33	92
iteration 2	25	37	12	48	57	33	86	92
iteration 3	25	12	37	48	33	57	86	92
iteration 4	12	25	37	33	48	57	86	92
iteration 5	12	25	33	37	48	57	86	92
iteration 6	12	25	33	37	48	57	86	92
iteration 7	12	25	33	37	48	57	86	92

We have shown that $n - 1$ passes are sufficient to sort a file of size n. However, in the sample file of eight elements, the file was sorted after five iterations, making the last two iterations unnecessary. To eliminate unnecessary passes, we must be able to detect the fact that the file is already sorted. But this is a simple task since in a sorted file, no interchanges are made on any pass. By keeping a record of whether or not any interchanges are made in a given pass, it can be determined whether any further passes are necessary. Under this method, if the file can be sorted in fewer than $n - 1$ passes, the final pass makes no interchanges.

Using these improvements, we present the routine *bubble*, which accepts two parameters, x and n. We assume the following global declarations:

```
const numelts = 100;
      abovelts = 101; { numelts plus one }
type arraytype = array[1..numelts] of integer;
     aptr = 1..numelts;
     aptr2 = 0..abovelts;
var x: arraytype;
    n: aptr;
```

x is an array of integers and n is an integer representing the number of elements to be sorted. (n may be less than the upper bound of x.) The type *aptr2* is defined because sorting algorithms often need auxiliary variables, whose value can sometimes be 0 or one more than the number of elements being sorted. (For an alternative method of implementing sorting algorithms as Pascal programs, see Section 5 of the Appendix.)

```
procedure bubble(var x: arraytype;n: aptr);
var pass, j: aptr;
    intchnge: boolean;
    hold: integer;
```

```
begin { procedure bubble}
    intchnge:= true;
    pass:= 1;
    while (pass <= n-1) and (intchnge)
        {           outer loop controls the number of passes           }
        do begin
                intchnge:= false;  {   initially no interchanges   }
                                   { have been made on this pass }
                for j:= 1 to n-pass
                    { inner loop governs each individual pass }
                    do if x[j] > x[j+1]  {elements out of order }
                        then begin
                                { an interchange is necessary }
                                intchnge:= true;
                                hold:= x[j];
                                x[j]:= x[j+1];
                                x[j+1]:= hold
                            end {then begin};
                pass:= pass+1
            end {while...do begin}
    end { procedure bubble};
```

What can be said about the efficiency of the bubble sort? In the case of a sort that does not include the two improvements just outlined, the analysis is simple. There are $n - 1$ passes and $n - 1$ comparisons on each pass. Thus the total number of comparisons is $(n - 1) * (n - 1) = n^2 - 2n + 1$, which is $O(n^2)$. Of course, the number of interchanges depends on the original order of the file. However, the number of interchanges cannot be greater than the number of comparisons. It is probable that the number of interchanges rather than the number of comparisons take up the most time in the algorithm's execution.

Let us see how the improvements that we introduced affect the speed of the bubble sort. The number of comparisons on iteration i is $n - i$. Thus, if there are k iterations, the total number of comparisons is $(n - 1) + (n - 2) + (n - 3) + \cdots + (n - k)$, which equals $(2kn - k^2 - k)/2$. It can be shown that the average number of iterations, k, is $O(n)$, so that the entire formula is still $O(n^2)$, although the constant multiplier is smaller than before. However, there is additional overhead involved in testing and intializing the boolean variable *intchange* (once per pass) and setting it to *true* (once for every interchange).

The only redeeming features of the bubble sort are that it requires little additional space (one memory location to hold the temporary value for interchanging) and that it is $O(n)$ in the case that the file is completely sorted (or almost completely sorted). This follows from the observation that only one pass of $n - 1$ comparisons (and no interchanges) is necessary to establish that a sorted file is sorted.

There are some other ways to improve the bubble sort. One of these is to observe that the number of passes necessary before the file is sorted is the largest distance by which a number must move toward the beginning of the array. In our example, for instance, 33 starts at position 8 in the array and ultimately finds its way to position 3 after five iterations. The bubble sort can be speeded up by having successive passes go in opposite directions, so that the number of passes is reduced. This version is left as an exercise.

Quicksort

The next sort we consider is the *partition exchange sort* (or *quicksort*). Let x be an array and n the number of elements in the array to be sorted. Choose an element a from a specific position within the array (e.g., a can be chosen as the first element so that $a = x[1]$). Suppose that the elements of x are partitioned so that a is placed into position j and the following conditions hold:

1. Each of the elements in positions 1 through $j - 1$ is less than or equal to a.
2. Each of the elements in positions $j + 1$ through n is greater than or equal to a.

Notice that if these two conditions hold for a particular a and j, then a remains in position j when the array is completely sorted. (You are asked to prove this fact as an exercise.) If the process is repeated with the subarrays $x[1]$ through $x[j - 1]$ and $x[j + 1]$ through $x[n]$ and any subarrays created by the process in successive iterations, the final result is a sorted file.

Let us illustrate the quicksort with an example. If an initial array is given as

$$25 \quad 57 \quad 48 \quad 37 \quad 12 \quad 92 \quad 86 \quad 33$$

and the first element (25) is placed in its proper position, the resulting array is

$$12 \quad 25 \quad 57 \quad 48 \quad 37 \quad 92 \quad 86 \quad 33$$

At this point, 25 is in its proper position in the array ($x[2]$), each element below that position (12) is less than or equal to 25, and each element above that position (57, 48, 37, 92, 86, and 33) is greater than or equal to 25. Since 25 is in its final position, the original problem has been decomposed into the problem of sorting the two subarrays

$$(12) \quad \text{and} \quad (57 \ 48 \ 37 \ 92 \ 86 \ 33)$$

Nothing need be done to sort the first of these subarrays; a file of one element is already sorted. To sort the second subarray, the process is repeated and the subarray is further subdivided. The entire array may now be viewed as

    12   25   (57   48   37   92   86   33)

where parentheses enclose the subarrays that are yet to be sorted. Repeating the process on the subarray $x[3]$ through $x[8]$ yields

    12   25   (48   37   33)   57   (92   86)

and further repetitions yield

    12   25   (37   33)   48   57   (92   86)
    12   25   (33)   37   48   57   (92   86)
    12   25   33   37   48   57   (92   86)
    12   25   33   37   48   57   (86)   92
    12   25   33   37   48   57   86   92

Note that the final array is sorted.

By this time you should have noticed that the quicksort may be defined most conveniently as a recursive procedure. We may outline an algorithm *quick(lb, ub)* to sort all elements in an array x between $x[lb]$ and $x[ub]$ (*lb* is the lower bound, *ub* the upper bound) as follows:

```
if lb < ub
    then begin        {   if lb ≥ ub, then array is   }
                      {  sorted and return to calling  }
                      {            procedure           }
        partition(lb, ub, j):
                      { partition the elements of the }
                      { subarray such that one of the }
                      {  elements (possibly x[lb]) is  }
                      {  now at x[j] (j is an output  }
                      {        parameter) and:         }
                      {  1.  x[i]≤x[j] for lb≤i<j   }
                      {  2.  x[i]≥x[j] for j<i≤ub  }
                      {    x[j] is now at its final    }
                      {            position            }
        quick(lb, j-1);
                      {  sort the subarray between   }
                      {       x[lb] and x[j-1]       }
        quick(j+1, ub)
                      {  sort the subarray between   }
                      {       x[j+1] and x[ub]       }
    end {then begin}
```

The only remaining problem is to describe a mechanism to implement *partition*, which allows a specific element to find its proper position with respect to the others in the subarray. Note that the way in which this partition is implemented is irrelevant to the sorting method. All that is required by the sort is that the elements are partitioned properly. In the example, the elements in each of the two subfiles remain in the same relative order as they appear in the original file. However, such a partition method is relatively inefficient. (Why?)

One way to effect a partition efficiently is the following. Let $a = x[lb]$ be the element whose final position is sought. (There is no appreciable efficiency gained by selecting the first element of the subarray as the one that is inserted into its proper position; it merely makes some of the programs easier to code.) Two pointers, *up* and *down*, are initialized to the upper and lower bounds of the subarray, respectively. At any point during execution, each element in a position above *up* is greater than or equal to *a*, and each element in a position below *down* is less than or equal to *a*. The two pointers *up* and *down* are moved toward each other in the following fashion.

Step 1: Repeatedly increase the pointer *down* by one position until $x[down] > a$.
Step 2: Repeatedly decrease the pointer *up* by one position until $x[up] \leq a$.
Step 3: If $up > down$, interchange $x[down]$ with $x[up]$.

The process is repeated until the condition in step 3 fails ($up \leq down$), at which point $x[up]$ is interchanged with $x[lb]$ (which equals *a*), whose final position was sought, and *j* is set to *up*.

We illustrate this process on the sample file, showing the positions of *up* and *down* as they are adjusted. The direction of the scan is indicated by an arrow at the pointer being moved. Three asterisks on a line indicates that an interchange is being made.

$a = x[lb] = 25$

down→							*up*
25	57	48	37	12	92	86	33

	down						*up*
25	57	48	37	12	92	86	33

	down						←*up*
25	57	48	37	12	92	86	33

	down					←*up*	
25	57	48	37	12	92	86	33

	down				←*up*		
25	57	48	37	12	92	86	33

	down			*up*			
25	57	48	37	12	92	86	33

	down			*up*				
25	12	48	37	57	92	86	33	***

	down→			*up*				
25	12	48	37	57	92	86	33	

		down		*up*				
25	12	48	37	57	92	86	33	

		down		*←up*				
25	12	48	37	57	92	86	33	

		down	*←up*					
25	12	48	37	57	92	86	33	

		←up, down						
25	12	48	37	57	92	86	33	

	up	*down*						
25	12	48	37	57	92	86	33	

	up	*down*						
12	25	48	37	57	92	86	33	***

At this point 25 is in its proper position (position 2) and every element to its left is less than or equal to 25 and every element to its right is greater than or equal to 25. We could now proceed to sort the two subarrays (12) and (48 37 57 92 86 33) by applying the same method.

This particular algorithm can be implemented by the following procedure. We assume the global definitions of the types *arraytype*, *aptr*, and *aptr2*, as well as the global declarations of the variables x and n, as given.

```
procedure partition (lb, ub: aptr2; var j: aptr);
var     up, down: aptr2;
        a, temp: integer;
        found: boolean;
begin { procedure partition }
        a:= x[lb] ; {a is the element whose final position is sought}
        up:= ub;
        down:= lb;
        while down < up
              do begin
                    while (x[down] <= a) and (down < ub)
                         do down:= down + 1;
                    while x[up] > a
                         do up:= up-1;
```

```
        if down < up
            then begin {interchange x[up] and x[down]}
                    temp:= x[up];
                    x[up]:= x[down];
                    x[down]:= temp
                end {then begin }
        end {while down < up do begin};
        {interchange x[up] with x[lb] = a and set j}
        x[lb]:= x[up];
        x[up]:= a;
        j:= up
    end {procedure partition};
```

Note that the initial inner loop headed by

$$\textbf{while } (x[down] \;<= a) \textbf{ and } (down < ub)$$

can be made much simpler if we could guarantee that *down* never becomes larger than n. In that case, the loop can read simply

$$\textbf{while } x[down] <= a$$
$$\textbf{do } down := down + 1;$$

and the additional test to avoid a possible access to (the possibly nonexistent) $x[n + 1]$ is not necessary. One way of achieving the shorter loop is by ensuring that the initial array is of size at least $n + 1$ and setting $x[n + 1]$ to *maxint*, assuming that none of the other array elements equals *maxint*. In that case, if *down* becomes $n + 1$, the test $x[down] <= a$ will fail (since *maxint* > a) and the loop will exit normally.

We may now code a program to implement the quicksort. As in the case of *bubble*, the parameters are the array x and the number of elements of x we wish to sort, n. Since the algorithm requires the sorting of two subarrays, we write an internal recursive routine *quick* whose parameters are the lower and upper bounds of the array between which we wish to sort.

```
procedure quicksrt(var x:arraytype; n: aptr);
procedure quick(lb, ub: aptr2);
var j: aptr;
            { the procedure partition goes here }
begin {procedure quick}
    if lb < ub
        then begin
                partition(lb, ub, j);
                quick(lb, j-1);
                quick(j+1, ub)
            end {then begin}
end {procedure quick};
```

```
begin {procedure quicksrt}
    quick(1, n)
end {procedure quicksrt};
```

Improving the Program

Although the preceding programs are concise in terms of what they accomplish and how they do it, the overhead of subroutine calls (especially recursive subroutine calls) should be avoided in programs such as sorts in which execution efficiency is a significant consideration. The recursive calls to *quick* can easily be eliminated by using a stack as in Chapter 3. Once *partition* has been executed, the current parameters to *quick* are no longer needed, except in computing the arguments to the two subsequent recursive calls. Thus instead of stacking the current parameters upon each recursive call, we can compute and stack the new parameters for each of the two recursive calls. Under this approach, the stack at any point contains the lower and upper bounds of all subarrays that must yet be sorted. Furthermore, since the second recursive call immediately precedes the return to the calling program (as in the Towers of Hanoi problem), it may be eliminated entirely and replaced with a branch. Finally, since the order in which the two recursive calls are made does not affect the correctness of the algorithm, we elect in each case to stack the larger subarray and process the smaller subarray immediately. As an exercise you are asked to show that this keeps the size of the stack to a minimum. With these improvements in mind, we code the routine *quick* 2:

```
procedure quick2(var x: arraytype; n: aptr);
type stackitem = record
                    lb: aptr2;
                    ub: aptr2
                 end;
     stack = record
                top: 0..numelts;
                item: array[1..numelts] of stackitem
             end;
var s: stack;
    newbnds: stackitem;
    i, j: aptr;
{the routines partition, push, popsub, and empty go here}
begin {procedure quick 2}
    s.top:= 0;
    with newbnds
        do begin
            lb:= 1;
            ub:= n;
            push(s, newbnds);
```

```
                    {     repeat as long as there are     }
                    { unsorted subarrays on the stack  }
                while not empty(s)
                        do begin
                                popsub(s, newbnds);
                                while ub > lb
                                        do begin
                                                { process next subarray }
                                                partition(lb, ub, j);
                                                {     stack the larger     }
                                                {       subarray        }
                                                if j - lb > ub - j
                                                { stack first subarray  }
                                                        then begin
                                                                i:= ub;
                                                                ub:= j - 1;
                                                                push(s, newbnds);
                                                                { process second subarray }
                                                                lb:= j + 1;
                                                                ub:= i
                                                            end {then begin}
                                                { stack second subarray }
                                                else begin
                                                        i:= lb;
                                                        lb:= j + 1;
                                                        push(s, newbnds);
                                                        { process first subarray }
                                                        lb:= i;
                                                        ub:= j - 1
                                                    end {else begin}
                                        end {while ub > lb do begin}
                        end {while not empty(s) do begin}
            end {with...do begin}
    end {procedure quick2};
```

Note that we have chosen to use $x[lb]$ as the element around which to partition each subfile because of programming convenience in the procedure *partition*, but any other element could have been chosen as well. The element around which a file is partitioned is called a ***pivot***. It is not even necessary that the pivot be an element of the subfile; *partition* can be written with the header

```
    procedure partition (lb, ub: aptr2; pivot: integer; var j: aptr);
```

to partition $x[lb]$ through $x[ub]$ so that all elements between $x[lb]$ and $x[j-1]$ are less than *pivot* and all elements between $x[j]$ and $x[ub]$ are greater than or equal to *pivot*. In that case, the element $x[j]$ is itself included in the second subfile (since it is not necessarily in its proper position), so the second recursive call to *quick* is *quick(j, ub)* rather than *quick(j + 1, ub)*.

As we shall see shortly, quicksort is most efficient when the subfiles created by *partition* are as nearly balanced in size as possible. By selecting the pivot value to be the median of the subfile, this condition will be achieved. However, even without making a separate pass to calculate the median, several choices for the pivot value have been found to improve the efficiency of quicksort. The first technique uses the median of the first, last, and middle elements of the subfile to be sorted (that is, the median of $x[lb]$, $x[ub]$, and $x[(lb + ub) \; div \; 2]$) as the pivot value. This median-of-three value is closer to the median of the subfile being partitioned than $x[lb]$, so that the two partitions of the subfile are more nearly equal in size. In this method, the pivot value is an element of the file, so that *quick(j + 1, ub)* can be used for the second recursive call.

A second method, called **meansort**, utilizes $x[lb]$ or the median-of-three as a pivot when partitioning the original file but adds code in *partition* to compute the means (averages) of the two subfiles being created. In subsequent partitions, the mean of each subfile, calculated when the subfile was created, is used as a pivot value. Again, this mean is closer to the median of the subfile than $x[lb]$ and results in more nearly balanced files. The mean is not necessarily an element of the file so that *quick(j, ub)* must be used for the second recursive call. The code to find the mean does not require any additional key comparisons but does add significant extra overhead.

Another technique, called **Bsort,** uses the middle element of a subfile as the pivot. During partition, whenever the pointer *up* is decreased, $x[up]$ is interchanged with $x[up + 1]$ if $x[up] > x[up + 1]$. Whenever the pointer *down* is increased, $x[down]$ is interchanged with $x[down - 1]$ if $x[down] < x[down - 1]$. Whenever $x[up]$ and $x[down]$ are interchanged, $x[up]$ is interchanged with $x[up + 1]$ if $x[up] > x[up + 1]$, and $x[down]$ is interchanged with $x[down - 1]$ if $x[down] < x[down - 1]$. This guarantees that $x[up]$ is always the smallest element in the right subfile (from $x[up]$ to $x[ub]$) and that $x[down]$ is always the largest element in the left subfile (from $x[lb]$ to $x[down]$).

This allows two optimizations: If no interchanges between $x[up]$ and $x[up + 1]$ were required during the partition, then the right subfile is known to be sorted and need not be stacked, and if no interchanges between $x[down]$ and $x[down - 1]$ were required, then the left subfile is known to be sorted and need not be stacked. This is similar to the technique of keeping a flag in bubble sort that detects that no interchanges have taken place during an entire pass so that no additional passes are necessary. Second, a subfile of size 2 is known to be sorted and need not be stacked. A subfile of size 3 can be directly sorted with just a single comparison and possible interchange (between the first two elements in a left subfile and between the last two in a right subfile). Both optimizations in Bsort reduce the number of subfiles that must be processed.

Efficiency of Quicksort

How efficient is the quicksort? Assume that the file size n is a power of 2, say, $n = 2^m$, so that $m = \log_2 n$. Assume also that the proper position for the pivot always turns out to be the exact middle of the subarray. In that case there will be approximately n comparisons (actually $n - 1$) on the first pass, after which the file is split into two subfiles each of size $n/2$ approximately. For each of these two files there are approximately $n/2$ comparisons, and a total of four files each of size $n/4$ are formed. Each of these files requires $n/4$ comparisons, yielding a total of $n/8$ subfiles. After halving the subfiles m times, there are n files of size 1. Thus the total number of comparisons for the entire sort is approximately

$$n + 2(n/2) + 4(n/4) + 8(n/8) + \cdots + n(n/n)$$

or

$$n + n + n + n + \cdots + n \quad (m \text{ terms})$$

comparisons. There are m terms because the file is subdivided m times. Thus the total number of comparisons is $O(nm)$ or $O(n \log n)$ (recall that $m = \log_2 n$). Thus, if these properties describe the file, the quicksort is $O(n \log n)$, which is relatively efficient.

For the unmodified quicksort in which $x[lb]$ is used as the pivot value, this analysis assumes that the original array and all the resulting subarrays are unsorted, so that the pivot value always finds its proper position at the middle of the subarray. Suppose that these conditions do not hold and that the original array is sorted (or almost sorted). If, for example, $x[lb]$ is in its correct position, the original file is split into subfiles of sizes 0 and $n - 1$. If this process continues, a total of $n - 1$ subfiles are sorted, the first of size n, the second of size $n - 1$, the third of size $n - 2$, and so on. Assuming k comparisons for a file of size k, the total number of comparisons to sort the entire file is

$$n + (n - 1) + (n - 2) + \cdots + 2$$

which is $O(n^2)$. Similarly, if the original file is sorted in descending order, the final position of $x[lb]$ is ub and the file is again split into two subfiles, which are heavily unbalanced (sizes $n - 1$ and 0). Thus the unmodified quicksort has the seemingly absurd property that it works best for files that are completely unsorted and worst for files that are completely sorted. The situation is precisely the opposite for the bubble sort, which works best for sorted files and worst for unsorted files.

It is possible to speed up quicksort for sorted files by choosing a random element of each subfile as the pivot value. If a file is known to be nearly sorted, this might be a good strategy (although, in that case, choosing the middle element would be even better). However, if nothing is known about the file, such a strategy does not improve the worst-case behavior since it is possible (although improbable) that the random element chosen each time might consistently be the smallest element of each subfile. As a practical matter, it is more common to encounter sorted files than to encounter a situation in which a good random number generator happens to choose the smallest element repeatedly.

The analysis for the case where the file size is not an integral power of 2 is similar but slightly more complex; the results, however, remain the same. It can be shown, however, that on the average (over all files of size n), the quicksort makes approximately $1.38 \, n \log_2 n$ comparisons for large n even in its unmodified version. In practical situations, quicksort is often the fastest available sort because of its low overhead and its average $O(n \log n)$ behavior.

If the median-of-three technique is used, quicksort can be $O(n \log n)$ even if the file is sorted (assuming that *partition* leaves the subfiles sorted). However, there are pathological files in which the first, last, and middle elements of each subfile are always the three smallest or largest elements. In such cases, quicksort remains $O(n^2)$. Fortunately, these are rare.

Meansort is $O(n \log n)$ as long as the elements of the file are uniformly distributed between the largest and smallest. Again, some rare distributions may make it $O(n^2)$, but this is less likely than the worst case of the other methods. For random files, meansort does not offer any significant reductions in comparisons or interchanges over standard quicksort. Its significant overhead for computing the mean requires far more CPU time than standard quicksort. For a file known to be almost sorted, meansort does provide significant reduction in comparisons and interchanges. However, the mean-finding overhead makes it slower than quicksort unless the file is very close to being completely sorted.

Bsort requires far less time than quicksort or meansort on sorted or nearly sorted input, although it does require more comparisons and interchanges than meansort for nearly sorted input (but meansort has significant overhead in finding the mean). It requires fewer comparisons but more interchanges than meansort and more of both than quicksort for randomly sorted input. However, its CPU requirements are far lower than are meansort's although somewhat greater than quicksort's for random input.

Thus Bsort can be recommended if the input is known to be nearly sorted or if we are willing to forego moderate increases in average sorting time to avoid very large increases in worst-case sorting time. Meansort can be recommended only for input known to be very nearly sorted and standard quicksort for input likely to be random or if average sorting time must be as fast as possible. In Section 5, we present a technique that is faster than either Bsort or meansort on nearly sorted files.

The space requirements for the quicksort depend upon the number of nested recursive calls or on the size of the stack. Clearly, the stack can never grow larger than the number of elements in the original file. How much smaller than n the stack grows depends upon the number of subfiles generated and on their sizes. The size of the stack can be somewhat contained by always stacking the larger of the two subarrays and applying the routine to the smaller of the two. This guarantees that all smaller subarrays are subdivided before larger subarrays, giving the net effect of having fewer elements on the stack at any given time. The reasons for this is that a smaller subarray can be divided fewer times than a larger subarray. Of course, the larger subarray will ultimately be processed and subdivided, but this will occur after the smaller subarrays have been sorted.

Another advantage of quicksort is locality of reference. That is, over a short period of time all array accesses are to one or two relatively small portions of the array (a subfile or portion thereof). This insures efficiency in a virtual memory environment where pages of data are constantly being swapped back and forth between external and internal storage. Locality of reference results in fewer page swaps being required for a particular program. A simulation study has shown that in such an environment, quicksort uses fewer space-time resources than does any other sort considered.

EXERCISES

1. Prove that the number of passes necessary in the bubble sort of the text before the file is in sorted order (not including the last pass, which detects the fact that the file is sorted) equals the largest distance by which an element must move from a larger index to a smaller index.

2. Rewrite the program *bubble* so that successive passes go in opposite directions.

3. Prove that in the sort of Exercise 2, if two elements are not interchanged during two consecutive passes in opposite directions, they are in their final position.

4. Suppose the bubble sort is revised so that each time an element is interchanged with its successor, the entire process is started once again by comparing $x[1]$ with $x[2]$. Show that this revised sort makes $O(n^3)$ comparisons.

5. A sort by *counting* is performed as follows. Declare an array *count* and set $count[i]$ to the number of elements which are less than or equal to $x[i]$. Then place $x[i]$ in position $count[i]$ of an output array. (However, beware of the possibility of equal elements.) Write a routine to sort an array x of size n using this method.

6. Assume that a file contains integers between a and b, with many numbers repeated several times. A *distribution sort* proceeds as follows. Declare *number*: *array*$[a .. b]$ *of integer* and set $number[i]$ to the number of times that integer i appears in the file, and then reset the values in the file appropriately. Write a routine to sort an array x of size n containing integers between a and b by this method.

7. The *odd-even transposition sort* proceeds as follows. Pass through the file several

times. On the first pass, compare $x[i]$ with $x[i + 1]$ for all odd i. On the second pass, compare $x[i]$ with $x[i + 1]$ for all even i. Each time that $x[i] > x[i + 1]$, interchange the two. Continue alternating in this fashion until the file is sorted.

(a) What is the condition for the sort's termination?

(b) Write a Pascal routine to implement the sort.

(c) What is the sort's efficiency on the average?

8. Rewrite the program for the quicksort by starting with the recursive version and applying the methods of Chapter 3 to produce a nonrecursive version.

9. Modify the quicksort program of the text so that if a subarray is small, the bubble sort is used. Determine, by actual computer runs, how small the subarray should be so that this mixed strategy will be more efficient than an ordinary quicksort.

10. Modify *partition* so that the middle value of $x[lb]$, $x[ub]$, and $x[(ub + lb)$ *div* $2]$ is used to partition the array. In what cases is the quicksort using this method more efficient than the version of the text? In what cases is it less efficient?

11. Implement the meansort technique. *partition* should use the mean of the subfile being partitioned (computed when the subfile was created) as the pivot value and should compute the mean of each of the two subfiles that it creates. When the upper and lower bounds of a subfile are stacked, its mean should be stacked as well.

12. Implement the Bsort technique. The middle element of each file should be used as the pivot, the last element of the left subfile being created should be maintained as the largest in the left subfile, and the first element of the right subfile should be maintained as the smallest in the right subfile. Two bits should be used to keep track of whether the two subfiles are sorted at the end of the partition. A sorted subfile need not be processed further. If a subfile has three or fewer elements, sort it directly by a single interchange, at most.

13. (a) Rewrite the routines for the bubble sort and the quicksort as presented in the text and the sorts of the exercises so that a record is kept of the actual number of comparisons and the actual number of interchanges made.

(b) Write a random number generator (or use an existing one if your installation has one) that generates integers between 0 and 9999.

(c) Using the generator of part (b), generate several files of size 10, size 100, and size 1000. Apply the sorting routines of part (a) to measure the time requirements for each of the sorts on each of the files.

(d) Measure the results of part (c) against the theoretical values presented in this section. Do they agree? If not, explain. In particular, rearrange the files so that they are completely sorted and in reverse order and see how the sorts behave with these inputs.

3. SELECTION AND TREE SORTING

A *selection sort* is one in which successive elements are selected in order and placed into their proper sorted positions. The elements of the input may have to be preprocessed to make the ordered selection possible. Any selection sort can be conceptualized as the following general algorithm that uses a descending priority queue:

```
set dpq to the empty descending priority queue;
  { preprocess the elements of the input array }
  { by inserting them into the priority queue }
  for i := 1 to n
    do pqinsert(dpq, x[i]);
```

{ select each successive element in order }
for i: = n *downto* 1
  do x[i] : = *pqmaxdelete*(dpq)

This algorithm is called the ***general selection sort.*** Note that the selection phase is presented as successive deletions from a priority queue, although what is actually required is a traversal of the queue in descending order. As we shall see, such a traversal is sometimes most efficiently implemented directly rather than via successive deletions.

  We now examine several different selection sorts. Two things distinguish specific selection sorts one from the other. One is the data structure used to implement the priority queue. The second is the method used to implement the general algorithm. A particular data structure may allow significant optimization of the general selection sort algorithm.

  Note also that the general algorithm can be modified to use an ascending priority queue *apq* rather than *dpq*. The second loop that implements the selection phase would be modified to

    for i: = 1 *to* n
      do x[i] : = *pqmindelete*(apq)

Straight Selection Sort

  The ***straight selection sort,*** or ***push-down sort,*** implements the descending priority queue as an unordered array. The input array *x* is used to hold the priority queue, thus eliminating the need for additional space. The straight selection sort is, therefore, an inplace sort.

  The input array *x* itself is already an unordered array that can represent the descending priority queue of *n* elements. Since the input is already in the appropriate format, the preprocessing phase is unnecessary.

  Therefore, the straight selection sort consists entirely of a selection phase in which the largest of the remaining elements, *large*, is repeatedly placed in its proper position, *i*, at the end of the array. To do so, *large* is switched with the element x[i]. The initial *n*-element priority queue is reduced by one element after each selection. After $n - 1$ selections, the entire array is sorted. Thus the selection process need be done only from *n* down to 2 rather than down to 1. The following Pascal procedure implements straight selection:

```
procedure select(var x: arraytype; n: aptr);
var i, j, indx: aptr;
    large: integer;
```

```
begin { procedure select}
    for i:= n downto 2
        do begin
                { place the largest number of x[1] through }
                {    x[i] into large and its index into indx    }
                large:= x[1];
                indx:= 1;
                for j:= 2 to i
                    do if x[j] > large
                        then begin
                                large:= x[j];
                                indx:= j
                            end {then begin}
            {           place large into position i            }
                x[indx]:= x[i];
                x[i]:= large
        end { for...do begin}
    end { procedure select};
```

Analysis of the straight selection sort is straightforward. The first pass makes $n - 1$ comparisons, the second pass makes $n - 2$, and so on. Therefore, there is a total of

$$(n - 1) + (n - 2) + (n - 3) + \cdots + 1 = n(n - 1)/2$$

comparisons, which is $O(n^2)$. The number of interchanges is always $n - 1$ (unless a test is added to prevent the interchanging of an element with itself). There is little additional storage required (except to hold a few temporary variables). The sort may therefore be categorized as $O(n^2)$, although it is faster than the bubble sort. There is no improvement if the input file is completely sorted or unsorted because the testing proceeds to completion without regard to the makeup of the file. Despite the fact that it is simple to code, it is unlikely that the straight selection sort would be used on any files except those for which n is small.

It is also possible to implement a sort by representing the descending priority queue by an ordered array. Interestingly, this leads to a sort consisting of a preprocessing phase that forms a sorted array of n elements. The selection phase is, therefore, superfluous. This sort is presented in Section 4 as the *simple insertion sort*; it is not a selection sort since no selection is required.

In the remainder of this section we illustrate several selection sorts that represent a priority queue by a binary tree. The first method is the *binary tree sort* of Section 6.1, which uses a binary search tree.

The method involves scanning each element of the input file and placing it into its proper position in a binary tree. To find the proper position of an element *y*, a left or right branch is taken at each node, depending upon whether *y* is less than the element in the node or greater than or equal to it. Once each input element is in its proper position in the tree, the sorted file can be retrieved by an inorder traversal of the tree. We present the algorithm for this sort, modifying it to accommodate the input as a preexisting array.

```
{ establish the first element as a root }
tree := maketree(x[1]);
{ repeat for each successive element }
for i := 2 to n
    do begin
        y := x[i];
        p := tree;
        { travel down the tree until a leaf is reached }
        while p <> nil
            do begin
                q := p;
                if y < info(p)
                    then p := left(p)
                    else p := right(p)
            end {while...do begin};
        if y < info(q)
            then setleft(q,y)
            else setright(q,y)
    end {for...do begin};
{ the tree is built, traverse it in inorder }
intrav(tree)
```

To convert this algorithm into a procedure to sort an array, it is necessary to revise *intrav* so that visiting a node involves placing the contents of the node into the next position of the original array.

Actually, the binary search tree represents an ascending priority queue, as described in Exercises 6.1.13 and 6.2.13. Constructing the tree represents the preprocessing phase, and the traversal represents the selection phase of the general selection sort algorithm.

Ordinarily, extracting the minimum element (*pqmindelete*) of a priority queue represented by a binary search tree involves traveling down the left side of the tree from the root. Indeed, that is the first step of the inorder traversal process. However, since no new elements are inserted into the tree once the tree is constructed and the minimum element does not actually have to be deleted, the inorder traversal efficiently implements the successive selection process.

The relative efficiency of this method depends on the original order of the data. If the original array is completely sorted (or sorted in reverse order), the resulting tree appears as a sequence of only right (or left) links, as in Figure 7.3.1. In this case the insertion of the first node requires no comparisons, the second node requires two comparisons, the third node three comparisons, and so on. Thus the total number of comparisons is

$$2 + 3 + \cdots + n = n(n + 1)/2 - 1$$

which is $O(n^2)$.

On the other hand, if the data in the original array are organized so that approximately half the numbers following any given number a in the array are less than a and half are greater than a, balanced trees such as those in Figure 7.3.2 result. In such a case, the depth of the resulting binary tree is the smallest integer d greater than or equal to $\log_2(n + 1) - 1$. The number of nodes at any level l (except possibly for the last) is 2^l and the number of comparisons necessary to place a node at level l (except when $l = 0$) is $l + 1$. Thus the total number of comparisons is between

$$d + \sum_{l=1}^{d-1} 2^l(l + 1) \quad \text{and} \quad \sum_{l=1}^{d} 2^l(l + 1)$$

It can be shown (mathematically inclined readers might be interested in proving this fact as an exercise) that the resulting sums are $O(n \log n)$.

Original data:

4   8   12   17   26

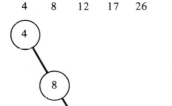

Original data:

26   17   12   8   4

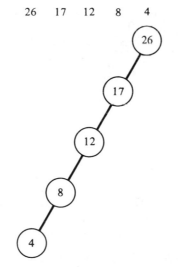

Number of comparisons: 14

(a)

Number of comparisons: 14

(b)   **Figure 7.3.1**

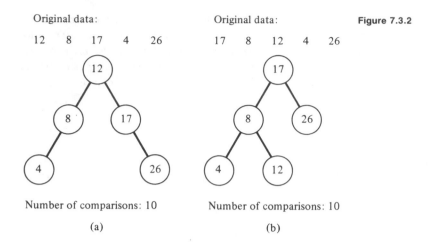

Original data:

12　8　17　4　26

Original data:

17　8　12　4　26

Figure 7.3.2

Number of comparisons: 10

(a)

Number of comparisons: 10

(b)

Fortunately, it can be shown that if every possible ordering of the input is considered equally likely, balanced trees result more often than not. The average sorting time for a binary tree sort is therefore $O(n \log n)$, although the constant of proportionality is larger on the average than in the best case. However, in the worst case (sorted input), the binary tree sort is $O(n^2)$. Of course, once the tree has been created, time is expended in traversing it. If the tree is threaded as it is created, the traversal time is reduced and the need for a stack (implicit in the recursion or explicit in a nonrecursive inorder traversal) is eliminated.

This sort requires that one tree node be reserved for each array element. Depending on the method used to implement the tree, space may be required for tree pointers and threads, if any. This additional space requirement, together with the poor $O(n^2)$ time efficiency for sorted or reverse-order input, represents the primary drawback of the binary tree sort.

Heapsort

The drawbacks of the binary tree sort are remedied by the *heapsort*, an inplace sort that requires only $O(n \log n)$ operations regardless of the order of the input. Define a *descending heap* (also called a *max heap* or a *descending partially ordered tree*) of size n as an almost complete binary tree of n nodes such that the content of each node is less than or equal to the content of its father. If the sequential representation of an almost complete binary tree is used, this condition reduces to the inequality

$$info[j] \leq info[j \ div \ 2] \quad \text{for} \quad 1 \leq (j \ div \ 2) < j \leq n$$

It is clear from this definition of a descending heap that the root of the tree (or the first element of the array) contains the largest element in the heap. Also note that any path from the root to a leaf (or, indeed, any path in the tree that includes no more than one node at any level) is an ordered list in descending order. It is also possible to define an ***ascending heap*** (or a ***min heap***) as an almost complete binary tree such that the content of each node is greater than or equal to the content of its father. In an ascending heap, the root contains the smallest element of the heap, and any path from the root to a leaf is an ascending ordered list.

A heap allows a very efficient implementation of a priority queue. Recall from Section 4.2 that an ordered list containing n elements allows priority queue insertion (*pqinsert*) to be implemented using an average of approximately $n/2$ node accesses and deletion of the minimum or maximum (*pqmindelete* or *pqmaxdelete*) using only one node access. Thus a sequence of n insertions and n deletions from an ordered list such as is required by a selection sort could require $O(n^2)$ operations. While priority queue insertion using a binary search tree could require as few as $\log_2 n$ node accesses, it could require as many as n node accesses if the tree is unbalanced. Thus a selection sort using a binary search tree could also require $O(n^2)$ operations, although on the average only $O(n \log n)$ are needed.

As we shall see, a heap allows both insertion and deletion to be implemented in $O(\log n)$ operations. Thus a selection sort consisting of n insertions and n deletions can be implemented using a heap in $O(n \log n)$ operations, even in the worst case. An additional bonus is that the heap itself can be implemented within the input array x using the sequential implementation of an almost complete binary tree. The only additional space required is for program variables. The heapsort is, therefore, an $O(n \log n)$ inplace sort.

The Heap as a Priority Queue

Let us now implement a descending priority queue using a descending heap. Suppose that *dpq* is an array that implicitly represents a descending heap of size k. Because the priority queue is contained in array elements 1 to k, we add k as a parameter of the insertion and deletion operations. Then the operation *pqinsert* (*dpq*, k, *elt*) can be implemented by simply inserting *elt* into its proper position in the descending list formed by the path from the root of the heap (*dpq*[1]) to the leaf *dpq*[$k + 1$]. Once *pqinsert*(*dpq*, k, *elt*) has been executed, *dpq* becomes a heap of size $k + 1$.

The insertion is done by traversing the path from the empty position $k + 1$ to position 1 (the root), seeking the first element greater than or equal to *elt*. When that element is found, *elt* is inserted immediately preceding it in the path (that is, *elt* is inserted as its son). As each element less than *elt* is passed during the traversal, it is shifted down one level in the tree to make room for *elt*. (This shifting is necessary because we are using the sequential representation rather than a linked representation of the tree. A new element cannot be inserted between two existing elements without shifting some existing elements.)

This heap insertion operation is also called the **siftup** operation because *elt* sifts its way up the tree. The following algorithm implements *pqinsert(dpq, k, elt)*:

$$s := k + 1;$$
$$f := s \ \textbf{div} \ 2; \quad \{ \ f \ \text{is the father of } s \ \}$$
$$\textbf{while} \ (s > 1) \ \textbf{and} \ (dpq[f] < elt)$$
$$\qquad \textbf{do begin}$$
$$\qquad\qquad dpq[s] := dpq[f];$$
$$\qquad\qquad s := f; \quad \{ \ \text{advance up the tree} \ \}$$
$$\qquad\qquad f := s \ \textbf{div} \ 2$$
$$\qquad \textbf{end} \ \{\text{while} \ldots \text{do begin}\};$$
$$dpq[s] := elt$$

Insertion is clearly $O(\log n)$ since an almost complete binary tree with n nodes has $\log_2 n + 1$ levels and at most one node per level is accessed.

In transforming this algorithm into a program, we must ensure that f is nonzero in the **while** condition. This can be done by changing the statement immediately preceding the loop and the last statement in the loop from $f := s \ \textbf{div} \ 2$ to

$$\textbf{if} \ s > 1$$
$$\qquad \textbf{then} \ f := s \ \textbf{div} \ 2$$
$$\qquad \textbf{else} \ f := 1$$

We now examine how to implement *pqmaxdelete (dpq, k)* for a descending heap of size k. First we define *subtree(p, m)*, where m is greater than p, as the subtree (of the descending heap) rooted at position p within the elements $dpq[p]$ through $dpq[m]$. For example, *subtree(3, 10)* consists of the root $dpq[3]$ and its two children $dpq[6]$ and $dpq[7]$. *subtree(3, 14)* consists of $dpq[3]$, $dpq[6]$, $dpq[7]$, $dpq[12]$, $dpq[13]$, and $dpq[14]$. If $dpq[i]$ is included in *subtree(p, m)*, $dpq[2*i]$ is included if and only if $2*i \leq m$ and $dpq[2*i + 1]$ is included if and only if $2*i + 1 \leq m$. If m is less than p, *subtree (p, m)* is defined as the empty tree.

To implement *pqmaxdelete(dpq, k)*, we note that the maximum element is always at the root of a k-element descending heap. When that element is deleted, the remaining $k - 1$ elements in positions 2 through k must be redistributed into positions 1 through $k - 1$ so that the resulting array segment from $dpq[1]$ through $dpq[k - 1]$ remains a descending heap. Let *adjustheap(root, k)* be the operation of rearranging the elements $dpq[root + 1]$ through $dpq[k]$ into $dpq[root]$ through $dpq[k - 1]$ so that *subtree (root, k - 1)* forms a descending heap. Then *pqmaxdelete(dpq, k)* for a k-element descending heap can be implemented by

$$pqmaxdelete := dpq[1];$$
$$adjustheap(1, k)$$

In a descending heap, not only is the root element the largest element in the tree, but an element in *any* position p must be the largest element in $subtree(p, k)$. Now, $subtree(p, k)$ consists of three groups of elements: its root, $dpq[p]$; its left subtree, $subtree(2*p, k)$; and its right subtree, $subtree(2*p + 1, k)$. $dpq[2*p]$, the left son of the root, is the largest element of the left subtree, and $dpq[2*p + 1]$, the right son of the root, is the largest element of the right subtree. When the root $dpq[p]$ is deleted, the larger of these two sons must move up to take its place as the new largest element of $subtree(p, k)$. Then, the subtree rooted at the position of the larger element moved up must be readjusted in turn.

Let us define $largeson(p, m)$ as the larger son of $dpq[p]$ within $subtree(p, m)$. It may be implemented as

```
s := 2*p;  { assume the left son }
if s+1 <= m
   then if x[s] < x[s+1]
           then s := s+1;
   { check if out of bounds }
if s > m
   then larqeson := 0
   else larqeson := s
```

Then $adjustheap(root, k)$ may be implemented recursively by

```
f := root;
s := largeson(f, k - 1);
if (s > 0) and (dpq[k] < dpq[s])
   then begin
           dpq[f] := dpq[s];
           adjustheap(s, k)
        end
   else dpq[f] := dpq[k]
```

Of course, to implement this algorithm in Pascal, it is necessary to avoid a reference to $dpq[s]$ when s equals 0 in the condition of the *if* statement. One way of avoiding the problem is to allocate $dpq[0]$ and initialize it to *maxint* (assuming that the priority queue consists of integers) so that the condition can be executed. The following iterative version of *adjustheap* solves the problem in a slightly different way. The algorithm also uses a temporary variable *kvalue* to hold the value of $dpq[k]$:

```
f: = root;
kvalue: = dpq[k];
s: = larqeson(f, k-1);
if s > 0
    then value: = dpq[s]
    else value: = maxint;
while (s > 0) and (kvalue < value)
    do begin
            dpq[f] : = dpq[s];
            f: = s;
            s: = larqeson(f, k-1);
            if s > 0
                then value: = dpq[s]
                else value: = maxint
    end;
dpq[f] : = kvalue
```

Note that we traverse a path of the tree from the root toward a leaf, shifting up all elements in the path greater than *dpq[k]* and inserting *dpq[k]* in its proper position in the path. Again, the shifting is necessary because we are using the sequential representation rather than a linked implementation of the tree. The adjustment procedure is often called the ***siftdown*** operation because *dpq[k]* sifts its way from the root down the tree.

This heap deletion algorithms is also $O(\log n)$ since there are $\log_2 n + 1$ levels in the tree and at most two nodes are accessed at each level. However, the overhead of shifting and computing *largeson* is significant.

Sorting Using a Heap

Heapsort is simply an implementation of the general selection sort using the input array *x* as a heap representing a descending priority queue. The preprocessing phase creates a heap of size *n* using the siftup operation and the selection phase redistributes the elements of the heap in order as it deletes elements from the priority queue using the siftdown operation. In both phases, the loops need not include the case where *i* equals 1 since *x*[1] is already a one-element priority queue and the array is sorted once *x*[2] through *x*[n] are in proper position.

```
{ Create the priority queue; before each loop iteration  }
{ the priority queue consists of elements x[1] through    }
{    x[i-1]. Each iteration adds x[i] to the queue.       }
for i: = 2 to n
    do pqinsert(x, i-1, x[i]);
{ select each successive element in order }
for i: = n downto 2
    do x[i] : = pqmaxdelete(x, i)
```

Figure 7.3.3 illustrates the creation of a heap of size 8 from the original file

25   57   48   37   12   92   86   33

The dashed lines in that figure indicate an element being shifted down the tree.

Figure 7.3.4 illustrates the adjustment of the heap as $x[1]$ is repeatedly selected and placed into its proper position in the array and the heap is

Figure 7.3.3   Creating a heap of size 8.

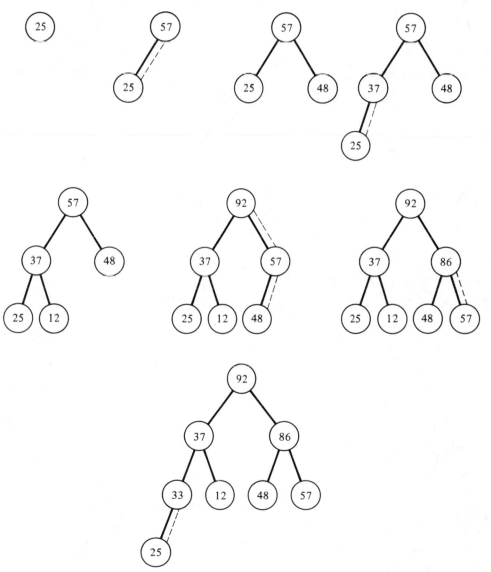

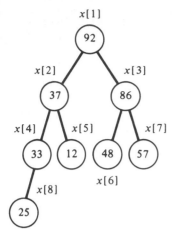

(a) Original tree.

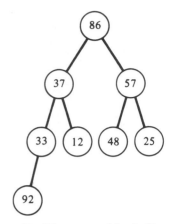

(b) $x[8] := pqmaxdelete(x, 8)$

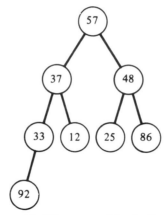

(c) $x[7] := pqmaxdelete(x, 7)$

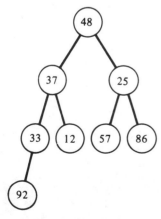

(d) $x[6] := pqmaxdelete(x, 6)$

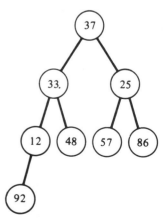

(e) $x[5] := pqmaxdelete(x, 5)$

Figure 7.3.4 Adjusting a heap.

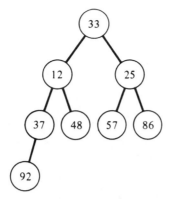

(f) $x[4] := pqmaxdelete (x, 4)$

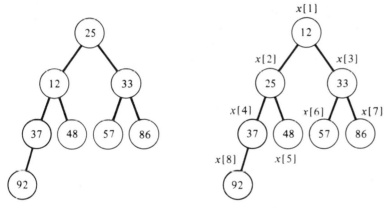

(g) $x[3] := pqmaxdelete (x, 3)$ (h) $x[2] := pqmaxdelete (x, 2)$. The array is sorted.

Figure 7.3.4   (cont.)

readjusted, until all the heap elements are processed. Note that after an element has been "deleted" from the heap, it remains in the array; it is merely ignored in subsequent processing.

The Heapsort Procedure

We now present a heapsort procedure with all subprocedures (*pqinsert*, *pqmaxdelete*, *adjustheap*, and *largeson*) expanded inline and integrated for maximal efficiency. We assume that *numelts*, the size of the array, is greater than or equal to 3.

```
procedure heapsort(var x: arraytype; n: aptr);
var i, elt, s, f, ivalue, value: integer;
begin { procedure heapsort }
        { preprocessing phase; create initial heap }
```

```
for i: = 2 to n
    do begin
            elt: = x[i] ;
            { pqinsert (x, i - 1, elt)  }
            s: = i;
            f: = s div 2;
            while (s > 1) and (x[f] < elt)
                    do begin
                            x[s] : = x[f] ;
                            s: = f;
                            if s > 1
                                then f: = s div 2
                                else f: = 1
                    end {while...do begin};
            x[s] : = elt;
        end {for...do begin};
{selection phase; repeatedly remove x[1] , insert it}
{       in its proper position and adjust the heap     }
for i: = n downto 2
    do begin
            { pqmaxdelete (x, i)  }
            ivalue: = x[i] ;
            x[i] : = x[1] ;
            f: = 1;
            {s: = largeson (1, i - 1)}
            if i = 2
                then s: = 0
                else s: = 2;
            if (i > 3) and (x[3] > x[2] )
                then s: = 3;
                            .
                            .
                            .
            value: = x[s] ;
            while (s > 0) and (ivalue < value)
                    do begin
                            x[f] : = x[s] ;
                            f: = s;
                            { s: = largeson (f, i - 1)  }
                            s: = 2*f;
                            if s+1 <= i-1
                                then if x[s] < x[s+1]
                                            then s: =  s+1;
                            if s < i
                                then value: = x[s]
```

```
                              else begin
                                    s: = 0;
                                    value: = maxint
                              end { else begin }
                        end { while...do begin };
              x[f] : = ivalue
          end { for...do begin }
    end { procedure heapsort };
```

To analyze the heapsort, note that a complete binary tree with n nodes (where n is one less than a power of 2) has $\log_2 (n + 1)$ levels. Thus, if each element in the array were a leaf, requiring it to be filtered through the entire tree both while creating and adjusting the heap, the sort would still be $O(n \log n)$.

In the average case, the heapsort is not as efficient as the quicksort. Experiments indicate that heapsort requires twice as much time as quicksort for randomly sorted input. However, heapsort is far superior to quicksort in the worst case. In fact, heapsort remains $O(n \log n)$ in the worst case. Heapsort is also not very efficient for small n because of the overhead of initial heap creation and computation of the location of fathers and sons.

The space requirement for the heapsort is only one additional variable to hold the temporary for switching, provided that the array implementation of an almost complete binary tree is used.

EXERCISES

1. Explain why the straight selection sort is more efficient than the bubble sort.

2. Consider the following *quadratic selection sort.* Divide the n elements of the file into k groups of k elements each, where $k = \sqrt{n}$. Find the largest element of each group and insert it into an auxiliary array. Find the largest of the elements in the array. This is the largest element of the file. Then replace this element in the array by the next largest element of the group from which it came. Again find the largest element of the array. This is the second largest element of the file. Repeat the process until the file has been sorted. Write a Pascal routine to implement a quadratic selection sort as efficiently as possible.

3. A *tournament* is an almost complete strictly binary tree in which each nonleaf contains the larger of the two elements in its two sons. Thus the contents of a tournament's leafs completely determines the contents of all its nodes. A tournament with n leafs represents a set of n elements.

   (a) Develop an algorithm *pqinsert(t, n, elt)* to add a new element *elt* to a tournament containing n leafs represented implicitly by an array t.

   (b) Develop an algorithm *pqmaxdelete(t, n)* to delete the maximum element from a tournament with n elements by replacing the leaf containing the maximum element with a dummy value smaller than any possible element (e.g., -1 in a tournament of nonnegative integers) and then readjusting all values in the path from that leaf to the root.

   (c) Show how to simplify *pqmaxdelete* by maintaining a pointer to a leaf in the *info* field of each nonleaf rather than an actual element value.

(d) Write a Pascal program to implement a selection sort using a tournament. The preprocessing phase builds the initial tournament from the array x, and the selection phase applies *pqmaxdelete* repeatedly. Such a sort is called a ***tournament sort.***

(e) How does the efficiency of the tournament sort compare with that of the heapsort.

(f) Prove that the tournament sort is $O(n \log n)$ for all input.

4. Use the technique of the tournament sort to merge n input files, each of which is sorted in ascending order, into a single output file, as follows. The tree is maintained so that the key represented by each node is the smaller of the keys of its two sons. Each leaf is designated as an input area for a single file. An auxiliary routine *inp(i)* reads the next input value from the ith input file into the appropriate leaf. When all the elements of file i have been input, *inp(i)* returns *maxint*. An auxiliary routine *writeroot* outputs the element in the tree root into the output file. Each node of the tree contains an element and the input file number from which the element came. An element is contained in only a single node of the tree at any time. When an element is moved from a node *nd* to its father, another element is moved from below to *nd*. When an element is moved up from a leaf, the routine *inp* is called with the appropriate parameter to read a new input value into the leaf.

5. Define an ***almost complete ternary tree*** as a tree in which every node has at most three sons and such that the nodes can be numbered from 1 to n so that the sons of *node[i]* are *node[3 * i − 1]*, *node[3 * i]* and *node[3 * i + 1]*. Define a ***ternary heap*** as an almost complete ternary tree in which the content of each node is greater than or equal to the contents of all its descendants. Write a sorting routine similar to the heapsort except that it uses a ternary heap.

6. Write a routine *combine(x)* that accepts an array x in which the subtrees rooted at $x[2]$ and $x[3]$ are heaps and which modifies the array x so that it represents a single heap.

7. Rewrite the program of Section 6.3 that implements the Huffman algorithm so that the set of root nodes forms a priority queue implemented by an ascending heap.

8. Write a Pascal program that uses an ascending heap to merge n input files, each sorted in ascending order, into a single output file. Each node of the heap contains a file number and a value. The value serves as the key by which the heap is organized. Initially, one value is read from each file and the n values are formed into an ascending heap, with the file number from which each value came kept together with that value in a node. The smallest value is then in the root of the heap and it is output, with the next value of its associated file input to take its place. That value, together with its associated file number, is sifted down to find its proper place in the heap and the new root value is output. This process of output/input/siftdown is repeated until no input remains. (This method is similar to that of Exercise 4, which uses a tournament rather than a heap.)

9. Develop an algorithm using a heap of k elements to find the largest k numbers in a large, unsorted file of numbers.

4. INSERTION SORTS

Simple Insertion Sort

An ***insertion sort*** is one that sorts a set of records by inserting records into an existing sorted file. An example of a simple insertion sort is the following procedure:

```
       procedure insert(var x: arraytype; n: aptr);
       var k: aptr;
           i: aptr2;
           y: integer;
           found: boolean;
begin { procedure insert}
       { Initially x[1] may be thought of as a sorted }
       { file of one element. After each repetition   }
       {   of the following loop, the elements x[1]    }
       {          through x[k] are in order.           }
       for k:= 2 to n
          do begin
                  { insert x[k] into the sorted file }
                  y:= x[k];
                  {   Move down one position all   }
                  {     numbers greater than y.     }
                  i:= k-1;
                  found:= false;
                  while (i >= 1) and (not found)
                      do if y < x[i]
                          then begin
                                  x[i+1]:= x[i];
                                  i:= i-1
                              end
                          else found:= true;
                  {   insert y at proper position   }
                  x[i+1]:= y
           end { for...do begin}
end { procedure insert};
```

As we noted at the beginning of Section 3, the simple insertion sort may be viewed as a general selection sort in which the priority queue is implemented as an ordered array. Only the preprocessing phase of inserting the elements into the priority queue is necessary; once the elements have been inserted, they are already sorted so that no selection is necessary.

If the initial file is sorted, only one comparison is made on each pass so that the sort is $O(n)$. If the file is initially sorted in the reverse order, the sort is $O(n^2)$, since the total number of comparisons is

$$(n - 1) + (n - 2) + \cdots + 3 + 2 + 1 = (n - 1)*n/2$$

which is $O(n^2)$. However, the simple insertion sort is still usually better than the bubble sort. The closer the file is to sorted order, the more efficient the simple insertion sort becomes. The average number of comparisons in the simple insertion sort (by considering all possible permutations of the input array) is also $O(n^2)$. The space requirements for the sort consist of only one temporary variable, y.

The speed of the sort can be improved somewhat by using a binary search (see Sections 3.1, 3.2, and 8.1) to find the proper position for $x[k]$ in the sorted file $x[1], \ldots, x[k-1]$. This reduces the number of comparisons from $O(n^2)$ to $O(n \log n)$. However, even if the correct position i for $x[k]$ is found in $O(\log n)$ steps, each of the elements $x[i+1], \ldots, x[k-1]$ must be moved one position. This latter operation performed n times requires $O(n^2)$ replacements. Unfortunately, therefore, the binary search technique does not significantly improve the overall time requirements of the sort.

Another improvement to the simple insertion sort can be made by using *list insertion*. In this method there is an array *link* of pointers, one for each of the original array elements. Initially, $link[i] = i + 1$ for $1 \le i < n$ and $link[n] = 0$. Thus the array may be thought of as a linear list pointed to by an external pointer *first* initialized to one. To insert the kth element the linked list is traversed until the proper position for $x[k]$ is found or until the end of the list is reached. At that point $x[k]$ can be inserted into the list by merely adjusting the list pointers without shifting any elements in the array. This reduces the time required for insertion but not the time required for searching for the proper position. The space requirements are also increased because of the extra *link* array. The number of comparisons is still $O(n^2)$, although the number of replacements in the *link* array is $O(n)$. The list insertion sort may be viewed as a general selection sort in which the priority queue is represented by an ordered list. Again, no selection is needed because the elements are sorted as soon as the preprocessing, insertion phase is complete. You are asked to code both the binary insertion sort and the list insertion sort as exercises.

Both the straight selection sort and the simple insertion sort are more efficient than bubble sort. Selection sort requires fewer assignments than insertion sort but more comparisons. Thus selection sort is recommended for small files when records are large, so that assignment is expensive, but keys are simple, so that comparison is cheap. If the reverse situation holds, then insertion sort is recommended. If the input is initially in a linked list, then list insertion is recommended even if the records are large since no data movement (as opposed to pointer modification) is required.

Of course, heapsort and quicksort are both more efficient than insertion or selection sort for large n. The break-even point is approximately 20 to 30 for quicksort; for fewer than 30 elements use insertion sort, for more than 30 use quicksort. A useful speedup of quicksort uses insertion sort on any subfile of size less than 20. For heapsort, the break-even point with insertion sort is approximately 60 to 70.

Shell Sort

More significant improvement can be achieved on simple insertion sort than on binary or list insertion can be achieved by using the *Shell sort* (or *diminishing increment sort*), named after its discoverer. This method sorts separate subfiles of the original file. These subfiles contain every kth element of the original file. The value of k is called an **increment**. For example, if k is 5, the subfile consisting of $x[1]$, $x[6]$, $x[11]$, ... is first sorted. Five subfiles, each containing one-fifth of the elements of the original file, are sorted in this manner. These are (reading across):

subfile 1	→	$x[1]$	$x[6]$	$x[11]$ ···
subfile 2	→	$x[2]$	$x[7]$	$x[12]$ ···
subfile 3	→	$x[3]$	$x[8]$	$x[13]$ ···
subfile 4	→	$x[4]$	$x[9]$	$x[14]$ ···
subfile 5	→	$x[5]$	$x[10]$	$x[15]$ ···

In general, the ith element of the jth subfile is $x[(i - 1) * 5 + j]$. If a different increment k is chosen, the k subfiles are divided so that the ith element of the jth subfile is $x[(i - 1) * k + j]$.

After the first k subfiles are sorted (usually by simple insertion), a new smaller value of k is chosen and the file is again partitioned into a new set of subfiles. Each of these larger subfiles is sorted, and the process is repeated yet again with an even smaller value of k. Eventually, the value of k is set to 1 so that the subfile consisting of the entire file is sorted. A decreasing sequence of increments is fixed at the start of the entire process. The last value in this sequence must be 1.

For example, if the original file is

$$25 \quad 57 \quad 48 \quad 37 \quad 12 \quad 92 \quad 86 \quad 33$$

and the sequence (5, 3, 1) is chosen, the following subfiles are sorted on each iteration.

first iteration (increment = 5)
($x[1]$, $x[6]$)
($x[2]$, $x[7]$)
($x[3]$, $x[8]$)
($x[4]$)
($x[5]$)

second iteration (increment = 3)
($x[1]$, $x[4]$, $x[7]$)
($x[2]$, $x[5]$, $x[8]$)
($x[3]$, $x[6]$)

third iteration (increment = 1)
($x[1]$, $x[2]$, $x[3]$, $x[4]$, $x[5]$, $x[6]$, $x[7]$, $x[8]$)

Figure 7.4.1 illustrates the Shell sort on this sample file. The lines underneath each array join individual elements of the separate subfiles. Each of the subfiles is sorted using a simple insertion sort.

Now we present a routine to implement the Shell sort. In addition

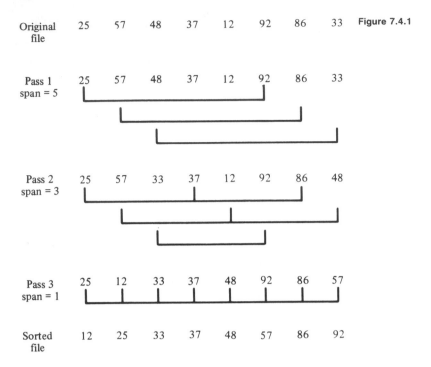

Figure 7.4.1

to the standard parameters *x* and *n*, it requires an array *incrmnts* containing the diminishing increments of the sort. The type definition for the array *incrmnts* is given by

```
type incrarray =
        record
            numinc: 1..numelts;
            incrmnts: array[1..numelts] of aptr
        end;
procedure shell(var x: arraytype; n: aptr; inc: incrarray);
var j, span: aptr;
    incr, y, k: integer;
    found: boolean;
begin { procedure shell}
    for incr:= 1 to inc.numinc
        do begin
            span:= inc.incrmnts[incr];  {  span is the size  }
                                        { of the increment }
            for j:= span+1 to n
                do begin
                    { insert element x[j] into its proper }
                    {      position within its subfile      }
```

```
y:= x[j];
k:= j - span;
found:= false;
while (k >= 1) and (not found)
    do if y < x[k]
        then begin
                x[k+span]:= x[k];
                k:= k-span
        end
        else found:= true;
    x[k+span]:= y
end {for...do begin}
end {for...do begin}
end {procedure shell};
```

Be sure that you can trace the actions of this program on the sample file of Figure 7.4.1. Notice that on the last iteration, where *span* equals 1, the sort reduces to a simple insertion.

The idea behind the Shell sort is a simple one. We have already noted that the the simple insertion sort is highly efficient on a file that is in almost sorted order. It is also important to realize that when the file size n is small, an $O(n^2)$ sort is often more efficient than an $O(n \log n)$ sort. The reason for this is that $O(n^2)$ sorts are generally quite simple to program and involve very few actions other than comparisons and replacements on each pass. Because of this low overhead, the constant of proportionality is rather small. An $O(n \log n)$ sort is generally quite complex and employs a large number of extra operations on each pass in order to reduce the work of subsequent passes. Thus its constant of proportionality is larger. When n is large, n^2 overwhelms $n \log n$ so that the constants of proportionality do not play a major role in determining the faster sort. However, when n is small, n^2 is not much larger than $n \log n$, so that a large difference in those constants often causes an $O(n^2)$ sort to be faster.

Since the first increment used by the Shell sort is large, the individual subfiles are quite small, so that the simple insertion sorts on those subfiles are fairly fast. Each sort of a subfile causes the entire file to be more nearly sorted. Thus, although successive passes of the Shell sort use smaller increments and therefore deal with larger subfiles, those subfiles are almost sorted due to the actions of previous passes. Thus the insertion sorts on those subfiles are also quite efficient. In this connection, it is significant to note that if a file is partially sorted using an increment k and is subsequently partially sorted using an increment j, the file remains partially sorted on the increment k. That is, subsequent partial sorts do not disturb earlier ones.

The efficiency analysis of the Shell sort is mathematically involved and beyond the scope of this book. The actual time requirements for a specific sort depends upon the number of elements in the array *incrmnts* and on their actual values. One requirement that is intuitively clear is that the elements of *incrmnts* should be relatively prime (i.e., have no common divisors other than 1). This guarantees that successive iterations intermingle subfiles so that the entire file is indeed almost sorted when *span* equals 1 on the last iteration.

It has been shown that the order of the Shell sort can be approximated by $O(n(\log n)^2)$ if an appropriate sequence of increments is used. For other series of increments, the running time can be proven to be $O(n^{1.5})$. Empirical data indicate that the running time is of the form $a * n^b$, where a is between 1.1 and 1.7 and b is approximately 1.26, or of the form $c * n * (\ln(n))^2 - d * n * \ln(n)$ where c is approximately .3 and d is between 1.2 and 1.75. In general, the Shell sort is recommended for moderately sized files of several hundred elements.

Knuth recommends choosing increments as follows: Define a function h recursively so that $h(1) = 1$ and $h(i + 1) = 3*h(i) + 1$. Let x be the smallest integer such that $h(x) \geq n$ and set *numinc*, the number of increments, to $x - 2$ and *incrmnts* $[i]$ to $h(numinc - i + 1)$ for i from 1 to *numinc*.

A technique similar to the Shell sort can also be used to improve the bubble sort. In practice, a major source of the bubble sort's inefficiency is not the number of comparisons but the number of interchanges. If a series of increments are used to define subfiles to be sorted individually using the bubble sort (as in the case of the Shell sort), then the initial bubble sorts are applied to small files and the later ones are applied to more nearly sorted files in which few interchanges are necessary. This modified bubble sort, which requires very little overhead, works well in practical situations.

Address Calculation Sort

As a final example of sorting by insertion, consider the following technique, called sorting by *address calculation* (sometimes called sorting by *hashing*). In this method a function f is applied to each key. The result of this function determines into which of several subfiles the record is to be placed. The function should have the property that if $x < y$, then $f(x) < f(y)$. Thus all the records in one subfile will have keys that are less than the keys of the records in another subfile. An item is placed into a subfile in correct sequence by using any sorting method; simple insertion is usually used. After all the items of the original file have been placed into subfiles, the subfiles may be concatenated to produce the sorted result.

For example, consider again the sample file:

25   57   48   37   12   92   86   33

Let us create 10 subfiles, one for each of the 10 possible first digits. Initially, each of these subfiles is empty. An array of pointers $f[0..9]$ is declared, where $f[i]$ points to the first element in the file whose first digit is i. After scanning the first element (25), it is placed into the file headed $f[2]$. Each of the subfiles is maintained as a sorted linked list of the original array elements.

We present a procedure to implement the address calculation sort. The routine assumes an array of two-digit numbers and uses the first digit of each number to assign that number to a subfile. The routine uses the procedure *place*(*list*, *x*) to insert an integer x into its proper position in the ordered list *list*.

```
procedure addr(var x: arraytype; n: aptr);
type nodetype = record
                    info: integer;
                    next: aptr2
                end;
var node: array[1..numelts] of nodetype;
    f: array[0..9] of aptr;
    q: aptr;
    first, i, j, p, avail: aptr2;
    y: integer;
begin { procedure addr}
    { initialize available list }
    avail:= 1;
    for i:= 1 to n-1
        do node[i].next:= i+1;
    node[n].next:= 0;
    for i:= 0 to 9
        do f[i]:= 0; { initialize pointers }
    for i:= 1 to n
        do begin
                { we successively insert each element into its }
                {     respective subfile using list insertion    }
                y:= x[i];
                first:= y div 10; {    find the first digit of    }
                              {    a two-digit number    }
                {         insert into proper linked list          }
                place(f[first] , y)
                {   place inserts y into its proper position   }
                {   in the linked list pointed to by f[first]  }
        end { for...do begin};
    { copy numbers back into the array x }
    i:= 0;
    for j:= 0 to 9
        do begin
                p:= f[j];
```

```
                    while p <> 0
                      do begin
                          i:= i+1;
                          x[i]:= node[p].info;
                          p:= node[p].next
                      end {while...do begin}
                end { for...do begin}
          end { procedure addr};
```

The space requirements of the address calculation sort are approximately 2 * *numelts* (used by the array *node*) plus some header nodes and temporary variables. Note that if the original data are given in the form of a linked list rather than as a sequential array, it is not necessary to maintain both the array *x* and the linked structure *node*.

To evaluate the time requirements for the sort, note the following. If the *n* original elements are approximately uniformly distributed over the *m* subfiles and the value of n/m is approximately 1, the time of the sort is nearly $O(n)$, since the function assigns each element to its proper file and little extra work is required to place the element within the subfile itself. On the other hand, if n/m is much larger than 1, or if the original file is not uniformly distributed over the *m* subfiles, significant work is required to insert an element into its proper subfile and the time is therefore closer to $O(n^2)$.

EXERCISES

1. The *two-way insertion sort* is a modification of the simple insertion sort as follows. A separate output array of size *numelts* is set aside. This output array acts as a circular structure as in Section 4.1. $x[1]$ is placed into the middle element of the array. Once a contiguous group of elements are in the array, room for a new element is made by shifting all smaller elements one step to the left or all larger elements one step to the right. Which of these shifts is performed depends on which would cause the smallest amount of shifting. Write a routine to implement this technique.

2. The *merge insertion sort* proceeds as follows:

    Step 1: For all odd *i* between 1 and $n - 1$, compare $x[i]$ with $x[i + 1]$. Place the larger in the next position of an array *large* and the smaller in the next position of an array *small*. If *n* is odd, place $x[n]$ in the last position of the array *small*. (*large* is of size *n div* 2; *small* is of size *n div* 2 or *n div* 2 + 1, depending on whether *n* is even or odd.)

    Step 2: Sort the array *large* using merge insertion recursively. Whenever an element *large*[*j*] is moved to *large*[*k*], *small*[*j*] is also moved to *small*[*k*]. (At the end of this step, *large*[i] $\leqslant$ *large*[i + 1] for all *i* less than *n div* 2 and *small*[i] $\leqslant$ *large*[i] for all *i* less than or equal to *n div* 2.)

    Step 3: Copy *small*[1] and all the elements of *large* into $x[1]$ through $x[n$ *div* 2 + 1].

    Step 4: Define the integer *int*(*i*) as $(2^{i+1} + (-1)^i)$ *div* 3. Beginning with *i* = 1 and proceeding by 1 while *int*(*i*) $\leqslant$ *n div* 2 + 1, insert the elements *small*[*int*(*i* + 1)] down to *small*[*int*(*i*) + 1] into *x* in turn using binary insertion. (For example, if *n* = 20, then the successive values of *int* are *int*(1) = 1, *int*(2) = 3, *int*(3) = 5, *int*(4) = 11, which equals *n div* 2 + 1. Thus the elments of *small* are inserted in the following order: *small*[3], *small*[2]; then *small*[5], *small*[4]; and then *small*[10], *small*[9], *small*[8], *small*[7], *small*[6]. In this example, there is no *small*[11].)

Write a Pascal procedure to implement this sort.

3. Modify the quicksort of Section 2 so that it uses a simple insertion sort when a subfile is below some size *s*. Determine by experiments what value of *s* should be used for maximum efficiency.

4. Prove that if a file is partially sorted using an increment *j* in the Shell sort, it remains partially sorted on that increment even after it is partially sorted on another increment, *k*.

5. Explain why it is desirable to choose all the increments of the Shell sort so that they are relatively prime.

6. What is the number (in terms of file size *n*) of comparisons and interchanges performed by each of the sorting methods below for the following files?

   (a) A sorted file.
   (b) A file that is sorted in reverse order (i.e., from largest to smallest).
   (c) A file in which the elements $x[1]$, $x[3]$, $x[5]$,... are the smallest elements and are in sorted order and in which the elements $x[2]$, $x[4]$, $x[6]$, ... are the largest elements and are in reverse sorted order (i.e., $x[1]$ is the smallest, $x[2]$ is the largest, $x[3]$ is next to smallest, $x[4]$ is the next to the largest, etc.).
   (d) A file in which $x[1]$ through $x[n \ div \ 2]$ are the smallest elements and are sorted and in which $x[n \ div \ 2 + 1]$ through $x[n]$ are the largest elements and are in reverse-sorted order.
   (e) A file in which $x[1]$, $x[3]$, $x[5]$,... are the smallest elements in sorted order and in which $x[2]$, $x[4]$, $x[6]$,... are the largest elements in sorted order.

   (i) The simple insertion sort.
   (ii) The insertion sort using a binary search.
   (iii) The list insertion sort.
   (iv) The two-way insertion sort of Exercise 1.
   (v) The merge insertion sort of Exercise 2.
   (vi) The Shell sort using increments 2 and 1.
   (vii) The Shell sort using increments 3, 2, and 1.
   (viii) The Shell sort using increments 8, 4, 2, and 1.
   (ix) The Shell sort using increments 7, 5, 3, and 1.
   (x) The address calculation sort presented in the text.

7. Under what circumstances would you recommend the use of each of the following sorts over the others?

   (a) The Shell sort of this section.
   (b) The heapsort of Section 3.
   (c) The quicksort of Section 2.

5. MERGE AND RADIX SORTS

Merge Sorts

Merging is the process of combining two or more sorted files into a third sorted file. An example of a procedure that accepts two sorted arrays *a* and *b* of *an* and *bn* elements, respectively, and merges them into a third array *c* containing *cn* elements is the following:

```
procedure mergearr(a, b: arraytype; var c; arraytype; an, bn: aptr; var cn: aptr);
        {merge arrays a and b into array c}
   var apoint, bpoint, cpoint: aptr2;
   begin {procedure mergearr}
        if an + bn > numelts
           then error('too many elements to be merged')
           else begin
                   cn:= an + bn;
                   {apoint and bpoint are indicators of how}
                   {far we are in arrays a and b, respectively}
                   apoint:= 1;
                   bpoint:= 1;
                   cpoint:= 1;
                   while (apoint <= an) and (bpoint <= bn)
                       do begin
                               if a[apoint] < b[bpoint]
                                   then begin
                                           c[cpoint]:= a[apoint];
                                           apoint:= apoint + 1
                                       end {then begin}
                                   else begin
                                           c[cpoint]:= b[bpoint];
                                           bpoint:= bpoint + 1
                                       end {else begin};
                               cpoint:= cpoint + 1
                           end {while...do begin};
                   {copy any remaining elements}
                   while apoint <= an
                       do begin
                               {copy remaining elements from a}
                               c[cpoint]:= a[apoint];
                               cpoint:= cpoint + 1;
                               apoint:= apoint + 1
                           end {while...do begin};
                   while bpoint <= bn
                       do begin
                               {copy remaining elements from b}
                               c[cpoint]:= b[bpoint];
                               cpoint:= cpoint + 1;
                               bpoint:= bpoint + 1
                           end {while...do begin}
               end {else begin}
   end {procedure mergearr};
```

We can use this technique to sort a file in the following way. Divide the file into *n* subfiles of size 1 and merge adjacent (disjoint) pairs of files. We then have approximately *n*/2 files of size 2. Repeat this process until there is only one file remaining of size *n*. Figure 7.5.1 illustrates how this process operates on a sample file. Each individual file is contained in brackets.

We present a procedure to implement the foregoing description of a ***straight merge sort***. An auxiliary array *aux* of size *numelts* is required to hold the results of merging two subarrays of *x*. The variable *size* is used to control the size of the subarrays being merged. Since at any time the two files being merged are both subarrays of *x*, lower and upper bounds are required to indicate the subfiles of *x* being merged. *lb*1 and *ub*1 represent the lower and upper bounds of the first file and *lb*2 and *ub*2 represent the lower and upper bounds of the second file, respectively. *i* and *j* are used to reference elements of the source files being merged and *k* indexes the destination file. The procedure follows:

```
procedure msort(var x: arraytype; n: aptr);
var aux: arraytype;
    lb2, ub1, ub2: aptr;
    lb1, i, j, k: aptr2;
    size: integer;
begin {procedure msort}
    size:= 1; {merge files of size 1}
    while size < n
        do begin
                lb1:= 1; {initialize lower bound of first file}
                k:= 1;   {  k is index for auxiliary array   }
```

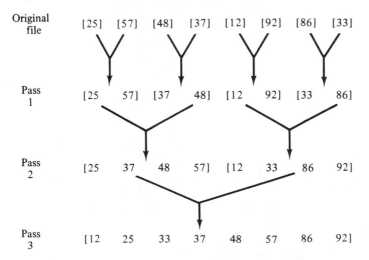

| Original file | [25] | [57] | [48] | [37] | [12] | [92] | [86] | [33] |

| Pass 1 | [25 | 57] | [37 | 48] | [12 | 92] | [33 | 86] |

| Pass 2 | [25 | 37 | 48 | 57] | [12 | 33 | 86 | 92] |

| Pass 3 | [12 | 25 | 33 | 37 | 48 | 57 | 86 | 92] |

Figure 7.5.1 Successive passes of the merge sort.

```
while lb1 + size <= n
        {check if there are two files to merge}
    do begin
            {compute remaining indices}
            lb2:= lb1 + size;
            ub1:= lb2 - 1;
            if lb2 + size-1 > n
                then ub2:= n
                else ub2:= lb2 + size - 1;
            {proceed through the two subfiles}
            i:= lb1;
            j:= lb2;
            while (i <= ub1) and (j <= ub2)
                do begin
                        {enter smaller into}
                        {   the array aux   }
                        if x[i] <= x[j]
                            then begin
                                        aux[k]:= x[i];
                                        i:= i + 1
                                end {then begin}
                            else begin
                                        aux[k]:= x[j];
                                        j:= j + 1
                                end {else begin};
                        k:= k + 1
                    end  {while...do begin};
            {  At this point one of the subfiles  }
            {  has been exhausted.  Insert any   }
            {remaining portions of the other file}
            while i <= ub1
                do begin
                        aux[k]:= x[i];
                        i:= i + 1;
                        k:= k + 1
                    end {while...do begin};
            while j <= ub2
                do begin
                        aux[k]:= x[j];
                        j:= j + 1;
                        k:= k + 1
                    end {while...do begin};
            {advance lb1 to start of next pair}
            {              of files            }
            lb1:= ub2 + 1
    end {while...do begin};
```

```
{copy any remaining single file}
i:= lb1;
while k <= n
      do begin
                aux[k] := x[i];
                k:= k + 1;
                i:= i + 1
            end {while...do begin};
      {adjust x and size}
      for k:= 1 to n
          do x[k] := aux[k];
      size:= size * 2
  end {while...do begin}
end {procedure msort};
```

There is one deficiency in this procedure, which is easily remedied if the program is to be practical for sorting large arrays. Instead of merging each set of files into the auxiliary array *aux* and then recopying the array *aux* into *x*, alternate merges can be performed from *x* to *aux* and from *aux* to *x*. We leave this modification as an exercise for the reader.

There are obviously no more than $\log_2 n$ passes in merge sort, each involving n or fewer comparisons. Thus merge sort requires no more than $n * \log_2 n$ comparisons. In fact, it can be shown that merge sort requires fewer than $n*\log_2 n - n + 1$ comparisons, on the average, compared to $1.386 * n * \log_2 n$ average comparisons for quicksort. In addition, quicksort can require $O(n^2)$ comparisons in the worst case, while merge sort never requires more than $n * \log_2 n$. However, merge sort does require approximately twice as many assignments as quicksort on the average, even if alternating merges go from *x* to *aux* and *aux* to *x*.

Merge sort also requires $O(n)$ additional space for the auxiliary array, while quicksort requires only $O(\log n)$ additional space for the stack. Mannila and Ukkonen have developed an algorithm for an inplace merge of two sorted subarrays in $O(n)$ time. Their algorithm would allow merge sort to become an inplace $O(n \log n)$ sort. However, their method does require a great deal many more assignments and so would not be as practical as finding the $O(n)$ extra space.

There are two modifications of the foregoing procedure which can result in more efficient sorting. The first of these is the **natural merge**. In the straight merge, the files all had the same size (except perhaps for the last file). We can, however, exploit any order that may already exist among the elements and let the files be defined as the longest subarrays of increasing elements. You are asked to code such a procedure as an exercise.

The second modification uses linked allocation instead of sequential allocation. By adding a single pointer field to each record, the need for the second array *aux* can be eliminated. This can be done by explicitly linking together each input and output subfile. The modification can be applied to both the straight merge and the natural merge. You are asked to implement these in the exercises.

Note that using merge sort on a linked list eliminates both of its drawbacks relative to quicksort: it no longer requires significant additional space and does not require significant data element movement. Generally, data elements can be large and complex, so that assignment of data elements requires more work than does the reassignment of pointers that is still required by a list-based merge sort.

Merge sort can also be presented quite naturally as a recursive process in which the two halves of the array are first recursively sorted using merge sort and, once sorted, are joined by merging. For details, see Exercises 1 and 2. Both merge sort and quicksort are methods that involve splitting the file into two parts, sorting the two parts separately, and then joining the two sorted halves together. In merge sort, the splitting is trivial (simply taking two halves), and the joining is hard (merging the two sorted files). In quicksort, the splitting is hard (partitioning), and the joining is trivial (the two halves and the pivot automatically form a sorted array).

Insertion sort may be considered a special case of merge sort in which the two halves consist of a single element and the remainder of the array; selection sort may be considered a special case of quicksort in which the file is partitioned into one half consisting of the largest element alone and a second half consisting of the remainder of the array.

The Cook-Kim Algorithm

Frequently, it is known that a file is almost sorted with only a few elements out of order. Or, it may be known that an input file is likely to be sorted. For small files that are very nearly sorted or for sorted files, simple insertion is the fastest sort (considering both comparisons and assignments) that we have thus far encountered. For large files or files that are slightly less sorted, quicksort using the middle element as a pivot is fastest. (Considering only comparisons, merge sort is fastest.) However, another hybrid algorithm discovered by Cook and Kim is faster than both insertion sort and middle-element quicksort for nearly sorted input.

The Cook-Kim algorithm operates as follows: The input is examined for unordered pairs of elements (e.g., $x[k] > x[k+1]$). The two elements in an unordered pair are removed and added to the end of a new array. The next pair examined after an unordered pair is removed consists of the predecessor and successor of the removed pair. The original array, with the unordered pairs removed, is now in sorted order. The array of unordered pairs is then sorted using middle-element quicksort if it contains more than 30 elements and simple insertion otherwise. The two arrays are then merged.

The Cook-Kim algorithm takes more advantage of the sortedness of the input than do other sorts and is significantly better than middle-element quicksort, insertion sort, merge sort, or Bsort on nearly sorted input. However, for randomly ordered input, Cook-Kim is less efficient than Bsort (and certainly than quicksort or merge sort) so that middle-element quicksort, merge sort, or Bsort is preferable when large, sorted input files are likely but good random input behavior is also required.

Radix Sort

The next sorting method that we consider is called the *radix sort*. This sort is based on the values of the actual digits in the positional representations of the numbers being sorted. For example, the number 235 in decimal notation is written with a 2 in the hundreds position, a 3 in the tens position, and a 5 in the units position. The larger of two such three-digit integers can be determined as follows. Start at the most significant digit and advance through the least significant digits as long as the corresponding digits in the two numbers match. The number with the larger digit in the first position in which the digits of the two numbers do not match is the larger of the two numbers. Of course, if all the digits of both numbers match, the numbers are equal.

We can write a sorting routine based on this method. Using the decimal base, for example, the numbers can be partitioned into 10 groups based on their most significant digit. (For simplicity, we assume that all the numbers have the same number of digits by padding with leading zeros, if necessary.) Thus every element in the "0" group is less than every element in the "1" group which is less than every element in the "2" group, and so on. The elements can be placed directly into an auxiliary array with group i preceding group $i + 1$ by using a preliminary pass through the input array to count the number of elements in each group and then, in a second pass, placing each input element in its appropriate position of the auxiliary array. For example if $num(i)$ is the number of elements with first digit i, and if $n2 = num(0) + num(1) + num(2)$, the first element of the input whose first digit is 3 is placed in position $aux[n2 + 1]$. We can then sort within the individual groups based on the next significant digit. We repeat this process until each subgroup has been subdivided, so that the least significant digits are sorted. At this point the original file is sorted. This method is sometimes called the *radix-exchange sort*; its coding is left as an exercise for the reader.

Note that it is not necessary to limit the number of groups to the radix of the key representations. If the range of keys is from a to b, m groups can be defined, with *key* placed in group i if it is between $a + (i - 1) * ((b - a) \ div \ m)$ and $a + i * ((b - a) \ div \ m)$. Each group can then be partitioned into m subgroups recursively. This is called the *distributive partition sort* and has been found to be quite efficient in practice.

Van der Nat presents a hybrid of the distributive partition sort and merge sort that is very fast on uniformly distributed input. Van der Nat's method operates as follows:

1. Partition the first $n/2$ elements into $m/2$ groups using the distributive partition method.
2. Sort each of the $m/2$ groups, recursively if the number of elements in a group is greater than 10 and using simple insertion if the number is greater than 10.
3. Repeat steps 1 and 2 for the second half of the array. Note that the maximum and minimum (and, therefore, the group range) are different for the two halves of the array.
4. Merge the two sorted halves.

Using $m = n$, experiments indicate that van der Nat's algorithm is significantly superior to quicksort for uniformly distributed data.

Let us now consider an alternative to the radix exchange sort. It is apparent from our discussion that considerable bookkeeping is involved in constantly subdividing files and distributing their contents into subfiles based on particular digits. It would certainly be easier if we could process the entire file as a whole rather than deal with many individual files.

Suppose that we perform the following actions on the file for each digit, beginning with the least significant digit and ending with the most significant digit. Take each number in the order in which it appears in the file and place it into one of 10 queues, depending on the value of the digit currently being processed. Then, starting with the queue of numbers with a 0 digit and ending with the queue of numbers with a 9 digit, return the numbers to the original file in the order in which they were placed onto the queue. When these actions have been performed for each digit, starting with the least significant and ending with the most significant, the file is sorted. This sorting method is called the *radix sort*.

Notice that this scheme sorts on the least significant digit first. This allows processing of the entire file without subdividing the files and keeping track of where each subfile begins and ends. Figure 7.5.2 illustrates this sort on the sample file

$$25 \quad 57 \quad 48 \quad 37 \quad 12 \quad 92 \quad 86 \quad 33$$

Be sure that you can follow the actions depicted in the two passes of Figure 7.5.2.

We can therefore outline an algorithm to sort in the foregoing fashion as follows:

```
for k := least significant digit to most significant digit
    do begin
            for i := 1 to n
                do begin
                        y := x[i];
                        j := kth digit of y;
                        place y at rear of queue[j]
                end {for...do begin};
```

>   *for qu*:= 0 *to* 9
>   *do* place elements of *queue*[*qu*] in next sequential positions of *x*
>   *end* {for...do begin}

We now present a program that implements this sort on four-digit numbers. To save a considerable amount of work in processing the queues (especially in the step where we return the queue elements to the original file), we write the program using linked allocation. If the initial input to the subroutine is an array, that input is first converted into a linear linked list; if the original input is already in linked format, this step is not necessary and, in fact, space is saved. This is the same situation as in the program *addr* (address calculation sort) of Section 4. Again, as in previous programs, we do not make any internal calls to subroutines but rather perform their actions in place.

Original file
      25   57   48   37   12   92   86   33
Queues based on least significant digit.

	Front	Rear
queue [0]		
queue [1]		
queue [2]	12	92
queue [3]	33	
queue [4]		
queue [5]	25	
queue [6]	86	
queue [7]	57	37
queue [8]	48	
queue [9]		

After first pass:
      12   92   33   25   86   57   37   48

Queues based on most significant digit.

	Front	Rear
queue [0]		
queue [1]	12	
queue [2]	25	
queue [3]	33	37
queue [4]	48	
queue [5]	57	
queue [6]		
queue [7]		
queue [8]	86	
queue [9]	92	

Sorted file: 12   25   33   37   48   57   86   92   **Figure 7.5.2** Illustration of the radix sort.

```
procedure radix(var x: arraytype; n: aptr);
const m = 4; {number of digits}
type nodetype = record
                     info: integer;
                     next: aptr2
               end;
var node: array[1..numelts] of nodetype;
    front: array[0..10] of aptr2;
    rear: array[0..9] of aptr2;
    p: aptr;
    first, q, i, j: aptr2;
    y, expon, k: integer;
begin {procedure radix}
    {initialize linked list}
    for i:= 1 to n-1
        do begin
                node[i].info:= x[i];
                node[i].next:= i+1
            end {for...do begin};
    node[n].info:= x[n];
    node[n].next:= 0;
    first:= 1; {first is head of linked list}
    for k:= 1 to m
        {m is the number of digits in the numbers}
        do begin
                for i:= 0 to 9
                    do rear[i]:= 0;
                for i:= 0 to 10
                    do front[i]:= 0; {initialize queues}
                {process each element on the list}
                while first <> 0
                    do begin
                            p:= first;
                            first:= node[first].next;
                            y:= node[p].info;
                            {extract kth digit}
                            expon:= 1;
                            for i:= 1 to k-1
                                do expon:= expon * 10;
                            j:= (y div expon) mod 10;
                            {insert y into queue[j]}
                            q:= rear[j];
                            if q = 0
                                then front[j]:= p
                                else node[q].next:= p;
```

```
                rear[j] := p
            end {while...do begin};
    { At this point each record is in }
    {its proper queue based on digit}
    { k. We now form a single list  }
    { from all the queue elements.  }
    {    Find the first element.     }
    j:= 0;
    while (j <= 9) and (front[j] = 0)
            do j:= j+1;
    first:= front[j] ;
    {    link up remaining queues    }
    while j <= 9
            {check if finished}
            do begin
                    {find next element}
                    i:= j+1;
                    while (i <= 9) and (front[i] = 0)
                            do i:= i + 1;
                    if i <= 9
                        then begin
                                p:= i;
                                node[rear[j]].next:= front[i]
                            end {then begin};
                    j:= i
                end {while...do begin};
            node[rear[p]].next:= 0
        end {for...do begin};
    {copy back to original array}
    for i:= 1 to n
        do begin
                x[i] := node[first].info;
                first:= node[first].next
            end {for...do begin}
end {procedure radix};
```

The time requirements for the radix sorting method clearly depend on the number of digits (m) and the number of elements in the file (n). Since the outer loop *for* $k := 1$ *to* m *do* ... is traversed m times (once for each digit) and the inner loop n times (once for each element in the file), the sort is approximately $O(m*n)$. Thus the sort is reasonably efficient if the number of digits in the keys is not too large. The sort does, however, require space to store pointers to the fronts and rears of the queues in addition to an extra field in each record to be used as a pointer in the linked lists. If the number of digits is large, it is sometimes more efficient to sort the file by first applying the radix sort to the most significant digits and then using simple insertion on the rearranged file. In cases where most of the records in the file have differing most significant digits, this process eliminates wasteful passes on the least significant digits.

EXERCISES

1. Write a routine *merge(x, lb1, ub1, ub2)* which assumes that $x[lb1]$ through $x[ub1]$ and $x[ub1 + 1]$ through $x[ub2]$ are sorted and which merges the two into $x[lb1]$ through $x[ub2]$.

2. Consider the following recursive version of the merge sort, which uses the routine *merge* of Exercise 1. It is called by the statement *msort2(x, 1, n)*. Rewrite the routine by eliminating recursion and simplifying. How does the resulting routine differ from the one given in the text?

```
procedure msort2(var x: arraytype; lb, ub: aptr);
var mid: aptr;
begin
      if lb <> ub
        then begin
                mid := (ub+lb) div 2;
                msort2(x, lb, mid);
                msort2(x, mid+1, ub);
                merge(x, lb, mid, ub)
             end {then begin}
  end {procedure msort2};
```

3. Let $a(l1, l2)$ be the average number of comparisons necessary to merge two sorted arrays of length $l1$ and $l2$, respectively, where the elements of the arrays are chosen at random from among $l1 + l2$ elements.
    (a) What are the values of $a(l1, 0)$ and $a(0, l2)$?
    (b) Show that for $l1 > 0$ and $l2 > 0$, $a(l1, l2)$ is equal to $(l1/(l1 + l2)) * (1 + a(l1 - 1, l2)) + (l2/(l1 + l2)) * (1 + a(l1, l2 - 1))$. (*Hint:* Express the average number of comparisons in terms of the average number of comparisons after the first comparison.)
    (c) Show that $a(l1, l2)$ equals $(l1 * l2 * (l1 + l2 + 2))/((l1 + 1) * (l2 + 1))$.
    (d) Verify the formula in part (c) for two arrays, one of size 2 and one of size 1.

4. Consider the following method of merging two arrays a and b into c. Perform a binary search for $b[1]$ in the array a. If $b[1]$ is between $a[i]$ and $a[i + 1]$, output $a[1]$ through $a[i]$ to the array c, then output $b[1]$ to the array c. Next, perform a binary search for $b[2]$ in the subarray $a[i + 1]$ to $a[la]$ (where la is the number of elements in the array a) and repeat the output process. Repeat this procedure for every element of the array b.
    (a) Write a Pascal routine to implement this method.
    (b) In which cases is this method more efficient than the method given in the text? In which cases is it less efficient?

5. Consider the following method (called *binary merging*) of merging two sorted arrays a and b into c. Let la and lb be the number of elements of a and b respectively, and assume that $la \geqslant lb$. Divide a into $lb + 1$ approximately equal

subarrays. Compare $b[1]$ with the smallest element of the second subarray of a. If $b[1]$ is smaller, then find $a[i]$ such that $a[i] \leqslant b[1] \leqslant a[i + 1]$ by a binary search in the first subarray. Output all elements of the first subarray up to and including $a[i]$ into c, and then output $b[1]$ into c. Repeat this process with $b[2]$, $b[3]$, $\ldots$, $b[j]$, where $b[j]$ is found to be larger than the smallest element of the second subarray. Output all remaining elements of the first subarray and the first element of the second subarray into c. Then compare $b[j]$ to the smallest element of the third subarray of a, and so on.

(a) Write a program to implement the binary merge.

(b) Show that if $la = lb$, the binary merge acts like the merge described in the text.

(c) Show that if $lb = 1$, the binary merge acts like the merge of Exercise 4.

6. Determine the number of comparisons (as a function of n and m) that are performed in merging two ordered files a and b of sizes n and m, respectively, by each of the merge methods listed on each of the following sets of ordered files:

   (i) $m = n$ and $a[i] < b[i] < a[i + 1]$ for all i.
   (ii) $m = n$ and $a[n] < b[1]$.
   (iii) $m = n$ and $a[n \ div \ 2] < b[1] < b[m] < a[(n \ div \ 2) + 1]$.
   (iv) $n = 2m$ and $a[i] < b[i] < a[i + 1]$ for all i between 1 and m.
   (v) $n = 2m$ and $a[m + i] < b[i] < a[m + i + 1]$ for all i between 1 and m.
   (vi) $n = 2m$ and $a[2i] < b[i] < a[2i + 1]$ for all i between 1 and m.
   (vii) $m = 1$ and $b[1] = a[n \ div \ 2]$.
   (viii) $m = 1$ and $b[1] < a[1]$.
   (ix) $m = 1$ and $a[n] < b[1]$.

   (a) The merge method presented in the text.

   (b) The merge of Exercise 4.

   (c) The binary merge of Exercise 5.

7. Generate two random sorted files of size 100 and merge them by each of the methods of Exercise 6, keeping track of the number of comparisons made. Do the same for two files of size 10 and two files of size 1000. Repeat the experiment 10 times. What do the results indicate about the average efficiency of the merge methods?

8. Write a routine that sorts a file by first applying the radix sort to the most significant r digits (where r is a given constant) and then uses simple insertion to sort the entire file. This eliminates excessive passes on low-order digits that may not be necessary.

9. Write a program that prints all sets of six positive integers $a1$, $a2$, $a3$, $a4$, $a5$, and $a6$ such that

$$a1 \leqslant a2 \leqslant a3 \leqslant 20$$

$$a1 < a4 \leqslant a5 \leqslant a6 \leqslant 20$$

and the sum of the squares of $a1$, $a2$, and $a3$ equals the sum of the squares of $a4$, $a5$, and $a6$. (*Hint*: Generate all possible sums of squares, and use a sorting procedure to find duplicates.)

8

SEARCHING

In this chapter we consider various methods of searching through large amounts of data to find a particular piece of information. As we shall see, certain methods of organizing data make the search process more efficient. Since searching is such a common task in computing, a knowledge of these methods goes a long way toward making a good programmer.

1. BASIC SEARCH TECHNIQUES

Before we consider specific search techniques, let us define some terms. A *table* or a *file* is a group of elements, each of which is called a *record*. (We are using the terms "file" and "record" in their general sense. They should not be confused with the same terms as they refer to specific Pascal constructs.) Associated with each record is a *key* which is used to differentiate among different records. The association between a record and its key may be simple or complex. In the simplest form, the key is contained within the record at a specific offset from the start of the record. Such a key is called an *internal key* or an *embedded key*. In other cases, there is a separate table of keys which includes pointers to the records. Such keys are called *external*. For every file there is at least one set of keys (possibly more) that is unique (i.e., no two records have the same key value). Such a key is called a *primary key*. For example, if the file is stored as an array, the index within the array of an element is a unique external key for that element. However, since any field or combination of fields of a record can serve as the key in a particular application, keys need not always be unique. For example, in a file of names and addresses, if the state is used as the key for a particular search, it will probably not be unique, because there may be two records with the same state in the file. Such a key is called a *secondary key*. Some of the algorithms that we present assume unique keys; others allow for multiple keys. When adopting an algorithm for a particular application, the programmer should know whether the keys are unique and make sure that the algorithm selected is appropriate.

A *search algorithm* is an algorithm that accepts an argument *a* and tries to find a record whose key is *a*. The algorithm may return the entire record, or, more commonly, it may return a pointer to that record. It is possible that the search for a particular argument in a table is unsuccessful; that is, there is no record in the table with that argument as its key. In such a case, the algorithm may return a special "nil record" or a nil pointer. Very often, if a search is unsuccessful, it may be desirable to add a new record with the argument as its key. An algorithm that does this is called a *search and insertion algorithm*. A successful search is often called a *retrieval*.

A table of records in which a key is used for retrieval is often called a *search table* or a *dictionary*.

In some cases it is desirable to insert a record with primary key *key* into a file without first searching for another record with the same key. Such a situation could arise if it has already been determined that no such record already exists in the file. In subsequent discussions we investigate and comment upon the relative efficiency of various algorithms. In such cases, the reader should note whether the comments refer to a search, to an insertion, or to a search and insertion.

Note that we have said nothing about the manner in which the table or file is organized. It may be an array of records, a linked list, a tree, or even a graph. Because different search techniques may be suitable for different table organizations, a table is often designed with a specific search technique in mind. The table may be contained completely in memory or completely in auxiliary storage, or it may be divided between the two. Clearly, different search techniques are necessary under these different assumptions. Searches in which the entire table is constantly in main memory are called *internal searches*, while those in which most of the table is kept in auxiliary storage are called *external searches*. In this chapter, we concentrate primarily on internal searching; however, we mention some techniques of external searching when they relate closely to the methods we study.

The Dictionary as an Abstract Data Type

A search table or a dictionary can be presented as an abstract data type. We first assume two type definitions for the key and record type and a function that extracts the key of a record from the record. We also define a nil record to represent a failed search.

const *nilrec*   = ...; { a "nil" record }
type   *keytype* = ...; { type of a key }
          rectype = ...; { type of a record }
function *keyfunct*(*r*: *rectype*): *keytype*;

...

We may then represent the abstract data type *table* as simply a set of records. This is our first example of an ADT defined in terms of a set rather than a sequence.

abstract type *table*(*rectype*) = **set of** *rectype*;

abstract function *member*(*tbl*: *table*, *k*: *keytype*): *boolean*;
postcondition if there exists an *r* in *tbl* such that *keyfunct*(*r*) = *k*
          then *member* = *true*
          else *member* = *false*;

abstract function *search*(*tbl*: *table*; *k*: *keytype*): *rectype*;
postcondition ((**not** *member*(*tbl*, *k*)) **and** (*search* = *nilrec*))
          or ((*member*(*tbl*, *k*)) **and** (*keyfunct*(*search*) = *k*));

abstract procedure *insert*(*tbl*: *table*; *r*: *rectype*);
precondition not *member*(*tbl*, *keyfunct*(*r*))
postcondition *r* **in** *tbl*;
          tbl − [*r*] = *tbl*';

abstract procedure *delete*(*tbl*: *table*; *k*: *keytype*);
postcondition *tbl* = *tbl*' − [*search*(*tbl*, *k*)] ;

Because no relation is presumed to exist among the records or their associated keys, the table that we have specified is called an **unordered table.** Although such a table allows elements to be retrieved based on their key values, the elements cannot be retrieved in a specific order. There are times when, in addition to the facilities provided by an unordered table, it is also necessary to retrieve elements based on some ordering of their keys. Once an ordering among the records is established, it becomes possible to refer to the first element of a table, the last element of a table, and the successor of a given element. A table that supports these additional facilities is called an **ordered table.** The ADT for an ordered table must be specified as a sequence to indicate the ordering of the records rather than as a set. We leave the ADT specification as an exercise for the reader.

Algorithmic Notation

Most of the techniques introduced in this chapter will be presented as algorithms rather than as Pascal programs. The reason for this is that a table may be presented in a wide variety of ways. For example, a table (keys plus records) organized as an array might be declared by

```
const tablesize = 1000;
type keytype = …;
    rectype = …;
    element = record
            k: keytype;
            r: rectype
        end;
var table: array[1..tablesize] of element;
```

or it might be declared as two separate arrays:

```
var k: array[1..tablesize] of keytype;
    r: array[1..tablesize] of rectype;
```

In the first case, the ith key would be referenced as $table[i].k$; in the second case, as $k[i]$:

Similarly, for a table organized as a list, either the array representation of a list or the dynamic representation of a list could be used. In the former case the key of the record pointed to by a pointer p would be referenced as $node[p].k$; in the latter case, as $p\uparrow.k$.

However, the techniques for searching these tables are very similar. Thus to free ourselves from the necessity of choosing a specific representation, we adopt the algorithmic convention of referencing the ith key in an array as $k(i)$ and the key of the record pointed to by p in a linked structure as $k(p)$. Similarly, we reference the corresponding record as $r(i)$ or $r(p)$. In this way we can focus on details of techniques rather than details of implementation.

Sequential Searching

The simplest form of a search is the *sequential search*. This search is applicable to a table that is organized either as an array or as a linked list. Let us assume that k is an array of n keys and r an array of records such that $k(i)$ is the key of $r(i)$. Let us also assume that *key* is a search argument. We wish to set the variable (or function identifier) *search* to the smallest integer i such that $k(i) = key$ if such an i exists and zero otherwise. The algorithm for doing this is as follows:

```
found := false;
i := 1;
while (i ⩽ n) and (not found)
    do if key = k(i)
        then begin
                search := i;
                found := true
            end
        else i := i + 1;
if not found
    then search := 0
```

The algorithm examines each key in turn; upon finding one that matches the search argument, its index (which acts as a pointer to its record) is returned. If no match is found, 0 is returned.

A more efficient algorithm to perform this search requires only one test at the head of the loop:

$$pos := n + 1;$$
$$i := 1$$
while $i <> pos$
  do if $key = k(i)$
    then $pos := i$
    else $i := i + 1;$
if $i > n$
  then $search := 0$
  else $search := pos$

These algorithms can be modified easily to add a record *rec* with key *key* to the table if *key* is not already there. The **then** clause of the last **if** statement in either algorithm is modified to read

then begin
  $n := n + 1;$ { increase the table size }
  $k(n) := key;$ {insert the new key and}
  $r(n) := rec;$ {   record   }
  $search := n$
end

Note that if insertions are made using only the revised algorithm, then no two records can have the same key. When this algorithm is implemented in Pascal, we must ensure that increasing *n* by 1 does not make its value go beyond the upper bound of the array. To use such a *sequential insertion search* on an array, sufficient storage must have been previously allocated for the array.

An even more efficient search method involves inserting the argument key at the end of the array before beginning the search, thus guaranteeing that the key will be found.

$$n1 := n + 1;$$
$$k(n1) := key;$$
$$i := 1;$$
while $key <> k(i)$
    do $i := i + 1;$
if $i < n1$
  then $search := i$
  else $search := 0$

For a search and insertion, the *if* statement is replaced by

$$if \ i = n1$$
$$then \ n := n1;$$
$$search := i$$

The extra key inserted at the end of the array is called a ***sentinel.***

Storing a table as a linked list has the advantage that the size of the table can be increased dynamically as needed. Let us assume that the table is organized as a linear linked list pointed to by *table* and linked by a pointer field *next*. Then assuming *k*, *r*, *key*, and *rec* as before, the sequential insertion search for a linked list may be written as follows:

```
found := false;
q := nil;
p := table;
while (p <> nil) and (not found)
    do if k(p) = key
        then begin
                search := p;
                found := true
            end {then begin}
        else begin
                q := p;
                p := next(p)
            end {else begin};
    if not found
    then begin { insert a new node }
        s := getnode;
        k(s) := key;
        r(s) := rec;
        next(s) := nil;
        if q = nil
            then table := s
            else next(q) := s;
        search := s
    end {then begin}
```

The efficiency of searching a list can be improved by both the techniques just suggested for an array. A pointer variable *pos* can be initialized to *nil* and reset to point to the desired list node, with the loop header modified to *while p <> pos . . .*; or a sentinel node containing the argument key can be added to the end of the list before beginning the search so that the loop is controlled by *while key* $<>$ *k(p)*.... The sentinel method, however, requires maintaining an additional external pointer to the last node in the list.

Deleting a record from a table stored as an unordered array is best implemented by replacing the record to be deleted with the last record in the array and reducing the table size by one. If the array is ordered in some way (even if the ordering is not by key), this method cannot be used, and half the elements in the array must be moved on the average. (Why?) If the table is stored as a linked list, then it is quite efficient to delete an element regardless of the ordering.

Efficiency of Sequential Searching

How efficient is a sequential search? Let us examine the number of comparisons that must be made by a sequential search in searching for a given key. If we assume no insertions or deletions, so that we are searching through a table of constant size n, then the number of comparisons depends on where the record with the argument key appears in the table. If the record is the first one in the table, only one comparison is performed; if the record is the last one in the table, n comparisons are necessary. If it is equally likely for the argument to appear at any given table position, a successful search will take (on the average) $(n + 1)/2$ comparisons, and an unsuccessful search will take n comparisons. In any case, the number of comparisons is $O(n)$.

However, it is usually the case that some arguments are presented to the search algorithm more often than others. For example, in the files of a college registrar, the records of a senior who is applying for transcripts for graduate school or of a freshman whose high school average is being updated are more likely to be called for than are those of the average sophomore and junior. Similarly, the records of scofflaws and tax cheats are more likely to be retrieved from the files of a motor vehicle bureau or the Internal Revenue Service than are those of a law-abiding citizen. (As we shall see later, these examples are unrealistic because it is unlikely that a sequential search would be used for such large files, but for the moment, let us assume that a sequential search is being used.) Then, if frequently accessed records are placed at the beginning of the file, the average number of comparisons is sharply reduced, because the most commonly accessed records take the least amount of time to retrieve.

Let us assume that $p(i)$ is the probability that record i is retrieved. ($p(i)$ is a number between 0 and 1 such that if m retrievals are made from the file, $m*p(i)$ of them will be from $r(i)$.) Let us also assume that $p(1) + p(2) + \cdots + p(n) = 1$, so that there is no possibility that an argument key is missing from the table. Then the average number of comparisons that are made in searching for a record is

$$p(1) + 2p(2) + 3p(3) + \cdots + np(n)$$

Clearly, this number is minimized if

$$p(1) \geqslant p(2) \geqslant p(3) \geqslant \cdots \geqslant p(n)$$

(Why?) Thus, given a large stable file, reordering the file in order of decreasing probability of retrieval achieves a greater degree of efficiency each time the file is searched. Of course, this method implies that an extra field p is kept with each record, which gives the probability of accessing that record, or that p can be computed based on some other information in each record.

Reordering a List for Maximum Search Efficiency

If many insertions and deletions are to be performed on a table, a list structure is preferable to an array. However, even in a list, it would be better to maintain the relationship

$$p(1) \geqslant p(2) \geqslant \cdots \geqslant p(n)$$

to provide for efficient sequential searching. This can be done most easily if a new item is inserted into the list at its proper place. This means that if *prob* is the probability that a record with a given key will be the search argument, that record should be inserted between records $r(i)$ and $r(i + 1)$, where i is such that

$$p(i) \geqslant \text{prob} \geqslant p(i+1)$$

Unfortunately, the probabilities $p(i)$ are rarely known in advance. Although it is usual for certain records to be retrieved more often than others, it is almost impossible to identify those records in advance. Also, the probability that a given record will be retrieved may change over time. To use the example of the college registrar given earlier, a student begins as a freshman (high probability of retrieval) and then becomes a sophomore and a junior (low probability) before becoming a senior (high probability). Thus it would be helpful to have an algorithm which would continually reorder the table so that more frequently accessed records would drift to the front while less frequently accessed records would drift to the back.

There are several search methods that accomplish this. One of them is known as the ***move-to-front*** method and is efficient only for a table that is organized as a list. In this method, whenever a search is successful (i.e., when the argument is found to match the key of a given record), the retrieved record is removed from its current location in the list and is placed at the head of the list. Another method is the ***transposition*** method, in which a successfully retrieved record is interchanged with the record that immediately precedes it. We present an algorithm to implement the transposition method on a table stored as a linked list. The algorithm returns a pointer to the retrieved record, or the nil pointer if the record is not found. As before, *key* is the search argument, and k and r are the tables of keys and records. *table* is a pointer to the first node of the list.

```
found := false;
p := table;
q := nil; { q is one step behind p }
s := nil; { s is two steps behind p }
while (p <> nil) and (not found)
     do if k(p) = key
          then begin { we have found the record. transpose }
                    {  the records pointed to by p and q  }
                    if q <> nil
                      then begin
                                next(q) := next(p);
                                next(p) := q;
                                if s = nil
                                   then table := p
                                   else next(s) := p
                            end {then begin};
                    found := true;
                    search := p
               end {then begin}
          else begin
                    s := q;
                    q := p;
                    p := next(p)
               end {else begin};
     if not found
       then search := nil
```

We leave the implementation of the transposition method for an array and the move-to-front method as exercises for the reader.

Both these methods are based on the observed phenomenon that a record that has been retrieved is likely to be retrieved again. By advancing such records toward the front of the table, subsequent retrievals are more efficient. The rationale behind the move-to-front method is that since the record is likely to be retrieved again, it should be placed at the position within the table at which such retrieval will be most efficient. However, the counterargument for the transposition method is that a single retrieval does not yet imply that the record will be retrieved frequently; placing it at the front of the table reduces search efficiency for all the other records that formerly preceded it. By advancing a record only one position each time that it is retrieved, we ensure that it will advance to the front of the list only if it is retrieved frequently.

It has been shown that, over a large number of search requests with an unchanging probability distribution, the transposition method is more efficient. However, the move-to-front method yields better results for a small to medium number of requests and responds more quickly to a change in probability distribution. It also has better worst-case behavior than does transposition. For this reason, move-to-front is preferred in most practical situations involving sequential search.

If large numbers of searches with an unchanging probability distribution are required, then a mixed strategy may be best: use move-to-front for the first s searches to organize rapidly the list in good sequence and then switch to transposition to obtain even better behavior. The exact value of s to optimize overall efficiency depends on the length of the list and the exact access probability distribution.

One advantage of the transposition method over the move-to-front method is that it can be applied efficiently to tables stored in array form as well as to list structured tables. Transposing two elements in an array is a rather efficient operation, whereas moving an element from the middle of an array to its front involves (on the average) moving half the array. (However, in this case the average number of moves is not as large, because the element to be moved most often comes from the initial portion of the array.)

Searching an Ordered Table

If the table is stored in ascending or descending order of the record keys, several techniques can be used to improve the efficiency of searching. This is especially true if the table is of fixed size. One immediately obvious advantage in searching a sorted file over searching an unsorted file is in the case that the argument key is absent from the file. In the case of an unsorted file, n comparisons are needed to detect this fact. In the case of a sorted file, assuming that the argument keys are uniformly distributed over the range of keys in the file, only $n/2$ comparisons (on the average) are needed. This is because we know that a given key is missing from a file that is sorted in ascending order of keys as soon as we encounter a key in the file which is greater than the argument.

Suppose that it is possible to collect a large number of retrieval requests before any of them is processed. For example, in many applications a response to a request for information may be deferred to the next day. In such a case, all requests on a specific day may be collected and the actual searching may be done overnight, when no new requests are coming in. If both the table and the list of requests are sorted, the sequential search can proceed through both concurrently. Thus it is not necessary to search through the entire table for each retrieval request. In fact, if there are many such requests uniformly distributed over the entire table, each request will require only a few lookups (if the number of requests is less than the number of table entries) or perhaps only a single comparison (if the number of requests is greater than the number of table entries). In such situations sequential searching is probably the best method to use.

Because of the simplicity and efficiency of sequential processing on sorted files, it may be worthwhile to sort a file before searching for keys in it. This is especially true in the situation described in the preceding paragraph, where we are dealing with a "master" file and a large "transaction" file of requests for searches.

The Indexed Sequential Search

There is another technique to improve search efficiency for a sorted file, but it involves an increase in the amount of space required. This method is called the **indexed sequential** search method. An auxiliary table, called an **index**, is set aside in addition to the sorted file itself. Each element in the index consists of a key *kindex* and a pointer to the record in the file that corresponds to *kindex*. The elements in the index, as well as the elements in the file, must be sorted on the key. If the index is one-eighth the size of the file, then every eighth record of the file is represented in the index. This is illustrated by Figure 8.1.1.

The algorithm used for searching an indexed sequential file is straightforward. Let *r*, *k*, and *key* be defined as before; let *kindex* be an array of the keys in the index; and let *pindex* be the array of pointers within the index to the actual records in the file. We assume that the file is stored as an array, that *n* is the size of the file, and that *indxsze* is the size of the index.

$$
\begin{aligned}
&found := false; \\
&i := 1; \\
&\textbf{while } (i \leqslant indxsze) \textbf{ and } (\textbf{not } found) \\
&\qquad \textbf{do if } kindex(i) > key \\
&\qquad\qquad \textbf{then } found := true \\
&\qquad\qquad \textbf{else } i := i + 1; \\
&\textbf{if } i = 1 \\
&\quad \textbf{then } lowlim := 1 \\
&\quad \textbf{else } lowlim := pindex(i - 1); \\
&\textbf{if } found \\
&\quad \textbf{then } hilim := pindex(i) - 1 \\
&\quad \textbf{else } hilim := n; \\
&\{ \text{search the table between positions } lowlim \text{ and } hilim \} \\
&j := lowlim; \\
&found := false; \\
&\textbf{while } (j \leqslant hilim) \textbf{ and } (\textbf{not } found) \\
&\qquad \textbf{do if } k(j) = key \\
&\qquad\qquad \textbf{then } found := true \\
&\qquad\qquad \textbf{else } j := j + 1; \\
&\textbf{if } found \\
&\quad \textbf{then } search := j \\
&\quad \textbf{else } search := 0
\end{aligned}
$$

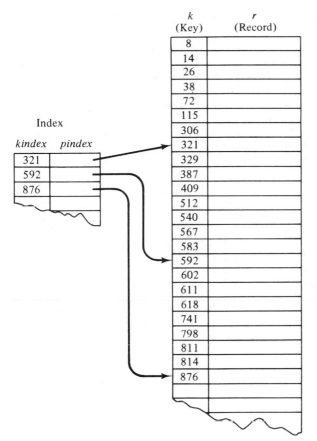

k
(Key)

r
(Record)

Figure 8.1.1 An indexed sequential file.

Index

kindex   *pindex*

Note that in the case of multiple records with the same key, the foregoing algorithm does not necessarily return a pointer to the first such record in the table.

The real advantage of the indexed sequential method is that the items in the table can be examined sequentially if all the records in the file must be accessed, yet the search time for a particular item is sharply reduced. A sequential search is performed on the smaller index rather than on the larger table. Once the correct index has been found, a second sequential search is performed on a small portion of the record table itself.

The use of an index is applicable to a sorted table stored as a linked list, as well as to one stored as an array. Use of a linked list implies a larger space overhead for pointers, although insertions and deletions can be performed much more readily.

If the table is so large that even the use of an index does not achieve sufficient efficiency (either because the index is large in order to reduce sequential searching in the table or because the index is small so that adjacent

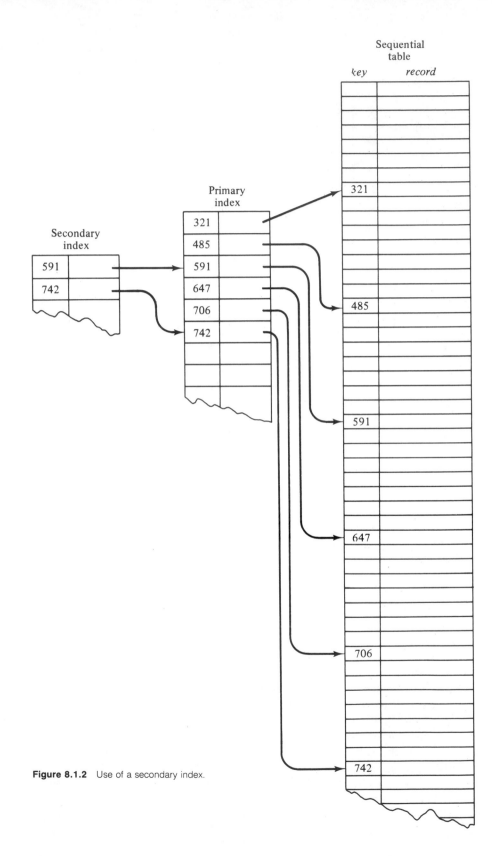

Figure 8.1.2 Use of a secondary index.

keys in the index are far from each other in the table), then a secondary index can be used. The secondary index acts as an index to the primary index, which points to entries in the sequential table. This is illustrated in Figure 8.1.2.

Deletions from an indexed sequential table can be made most easily by flagging deleted entries. In sequential searching through the table, deleted entries are ignored. Note that if an element is deleted, then even if its key is in the index, nothing need be done to the index; only the original table entry is flagged.

Insertion into an indexed sequential table is more difficult because there may not be room between two already existing table entries, thus necessitating a shift in a large number of table elements. However, if a nearby item has been flagged as deleted in the table, only a few items need be shifted, and the deleted item can be overwritten. This may, in turn, neccesitate alteration of the index if an item pointed to by an index element is shifted. An alternative method is to keep an overflow area at some other location and link together any inserted records. However, this would require an extra pointer field in each record of the original table. You are asked to explore these possibilities as an exercise.

The Binary Search

The most efficient method of searching a sequential table without the use of auxiliary indices or tables is the binary search. You should be familiar with this search technique from Sections 3.1 and 3.2. Basically, the argument is compared with the key of the middle element of the table. If they are equal, the search ends successfully; otherwise, either the upper or lower half of the table must be searched in a similar manner.

In Chapter 3 it was noted that the binary search can best be defined recursively. As a result, a recursive definition, a recursive algorithm, and a recursive program were presented for the binary search. However, the large overhead that is associated with recursion makes it inappropriate for use in practical situations in which efficiency is a prime consideration. We therefore present the following nonrecursive version of the binary search algorithm:

```
found := false;
low := 1;
hi := n;
while (low ≤ hi) and (not found)
    do begin
            mid := (low + hi) div 2;
            if key = k(mid)
                then found := true
```

$$\textbf{\textit{else if}} \ key < k(mid)$$
$$\textbf{\textit{then}} \ hi := mid - 1$$
$$\textbf{\textit{else}} \ low := mid + 1$$
$$\textbf{\textit{end}} \ \{\text{while}\ldots\text{do begin}\};$$
$$\textbf{\textit{if found}}$$
$$\textbf{\textit{then}} \ search := mid$$
$$\textbf{\textit{else}} \ search := 0$$

Each comparison in the binary search reduces the number of possible candidates by a factor of 2. Thus the maximum number of key comparisons that will be made is approximately $\log_2 n$. (Actually, it is $2 \log_2 n$, since in Pascal two key comparisons are made each time through the loop: $key = k(mid)$ and $key < k(mid)$. However, in an assembly language or in FORTRAN using an arithmetic IF statement, only one comparison is made. An optimizing Pascal compiler should be able to eliminate the extra comparison.) Thus we may say that the binary search algorithm is $O(\log n)$.

Note that the binary search may be used in conjunction with the indexed sequential table organization mentioned earlier. Instead of searching the index sequentially, a binary search can be used. The binary search can also be used in searching the main table once two boundary records are identified. However, the size of this table segment is likely to be sufficiently small that a binary search is no more advantageous than a sequential search.

Unfortunately, the binary search algorithm can only be used if the table is stored as an array. This is because it makes use of the fact that the indices of array elements are consecutive integers. For this reason the binary search is practically useless in situations where there are many insertions or deletions, so that an array structure is inappropriate.

One method for utilizing binary search in the presence of insertions and deletions if the maximum number of elements is known involves a data structure known as the **_padded list._** The method uses two arrays: an element array and a parallel flag array. The element array contains the sorted keys in the table with "empty" slots initially evenly interspersed among the keys of the table to allow for growth. An empty slot is indicated by a 0 value in the corresponding flag array element. Each empty slot in the element array contains a key value greater than or equal to the key value in the previous full slot and less than the key value in the following full slot. Thus the entire element array is sorted, and a valid binary search can be performed on it.

To search for an element, perform a binary search on the element array. If the argument key is not found, the element does not exist in the table. If it is found and the corresponding flag value is 1, the element has been located. If the corresponding flag value is 0, check if the previous full slot contains the argument key. If it does, the element has been located; if it doesn't, the element does not exist in the table.

To insert an element, first locate its position. If the position is empty, insert the element in the empty position, resetting its flag value to 1, and adjust the contents of all previous contiguous empty positions to equal the contents of the previous full element and of all following contiguous empty positions to the inserted element, leaving their flags at 0. If the position is full, shift forward by one position all the following elements up to the first empty position (overwriting the first empty position and resetting its flag to 1) to make room for the new element. Deletion simply involves locating a key and changing its associated flag value to 0. Of course, the drawbacks of this method are the shifting that must be done at insertion and the limited room for growth. Periodically, it may be desirable to redistribute the empty spaces evenly through the array to improve insertion speed.

Interpolation Search

Another technique for searching an ordered array is called *interpolation search*. If the keys are uniformly distributed between $k(1)$ and $k(n)$, then the method may be even more efficient than binary search.

Initially, as in binary search, *low* is set to 1 and *high* is set to n, and, throughout the algorithm, the argument key *key* is known to be between $k(low)$ and $k(high)$. On the assumption that the keys are uniformly distributed between these two values, *key* would be expected to be at approximately position $mid = low + (high - low) * ((key - k(low)) \ div \ (k(high) - k(low)))$. If *key* is lower than $k(mid)$, then reset *high* to $mid - 1$; if higher, reset *low* to $mid + 1$. Repeat the process until the key has been found or *low* > *high*.

Indeed, if the keys are uniformly distributed through the array, interpolation search requires an average of $\log_2 (\log_2 n)$ comparisons and rarely requires much more, compared to binary search's $\log_2 n$ (again, considering the two comparisons for equality and inequality of *key* and $k(mid)$ as one). However, if the keys are not uniformly distributed, interpolation search can have very poor average behavior. In the worst case, the value of *mid* can consistently equal *low* + 1 or *high* − 1, in which case interpolation search degenerates into sequential search. By contrast, binary search's comparisons are never greater than approximately $\log_2 n$. In practical situations, keys often tend to cluster around certain values and are not uniformly distributed. For example, more names begin with S than with Q, and there are likely to be many SMITHs and very few QUODNOTs. In such situations, binary search is far superior to interpolation search.

A variation of interpolation search, called *robust interpolation search* (or *fast search*), attempts to remedy the poor practical behavior of interpolation search while extending its advantage over binary search to nonuniform key distributions. This is done by establishing a value *gap* so that *mid-low* and *high-mid* are always greater than *gap*. Initially, *gap* is set to $sqrt(high - low + 1)$. *probe* is set to $low + (high - low) * ((key - k(low)) \ div \ (k(high) - k(low)))$, and *mid* is set equal to $min(high - gap, max(probe, low + gap))$ (where *min* and *max* return the minimum and maximum, respectively, of two values). That is, we guarantee that the next position used for comparison is at least *gap* positions from the ends of the interval, where *gap* is at least the square root of the interval. Whenever the argument key is found to lie in the larger portion of the interval between *low* and *high*, the value of *gap* is doubled, but it is never set greater than half the interval size. This guarantees that we will escape from a larger cluster of similar key values. When the key is found to be restricted to the smaller portion of an interval, *gap* is reset to the square root of the new interval size.

The expected number of comparisons for robust interpolation search for a random distribution of keys is $O(\log \log n)$. This is superior to binary search. On a list of approximately 40,000 names, binary search requires an average of approximately 16 key comparisons. Due to clustering of names in practical situations, interpolation search required 134 average comparisons in an actual experiment, while robust interpolation search required only 12.5. On a uniformly distributed list of approximately 40,000 elements—$\log_2$ ($\log_2$ 40,000) is approximately 3.9—robust interpolation search required 6.7 average comparisons. (It should be noted that the extra computation time required for robust interpolation search may be substantial but is ignored in these findings.) The worst case for robust interpolation search is $O((\log n)^2)$, which is higher than that for binary search, but much better than the $O(n)$ of regular interpolation search.

However, on most computers, the computation required by interpolation search are very slow since they involve arithmetic on keys and complex multiplications and divisions. Binary search requires only arithmetic on integer indexes and division by two which can be performed efficiently by shifting one bit to the right. Thus the computational requirements of interpolation search often cause it to perform more slowly than binary search even when it requires fewer comparisons.

EXERCISES

1. Modify the search and insertion algorithms of this section so that they become update algorithms. If an algorithm finds an *i* such that $key = k(i)$, change the value of $r(i)$ to *rec*.

2. Implement the sequential search and the sequential search and insertion algorithms in Pascal for both arrays and linked lists.

3. Compare the efficiency of searching an ordered sequential table of size *n* and searching an unordered table of the same size for the key *key*

   (a) if no record with key *key* is present.
   (b) if one record with key *key* is present and only one is sought.
   (c) if more than one record with key *key* is present and it is desired to find only the first one.
   (d) if more than one record with key *key* is present and it is desired to find them all.

4. Assume that an ordered table is stored as a linked list with two external pointers: *table* and *other*. *table* always points to the node containing the record with the smallest key. *other* is initially equal to *table*, but is reset each time a search is

performed to point to the record that is retrieved. If a search is unsuccessful, *other* is reset to *table*. Write a Pascal function *search(table, other, key)* which implements this method and returns a pointer to a retrieved record or a nil pointer if the search is unsuccessful. Explain how keeping the pointer *other* can reduce the average number of comparisons in a search.

5. Consider an ordered table implemented as an array or as a doubly linked list so that the table can be searched sequentially either backward or forward. Assume that a single pointer p points to the last record successfully retrieved. The search always begins at the record pointed to by p but may proceed in either direction. Write a function *search(table, p, key)* for the case of an array and a doubly linked list to retrieve a record with key *key* and to modify p accordingly. Compare the numbers of key comparisons in both the successful and unsuccessful cases with that of the method of Exercise 4, where the table may be scanned in only one direction but the scanning process may start at one of two points.

6. Consider a programmer who writes the following code:

$$\textbf{if } c_1 \textbf{ then}$$
$$\textbf{if } c_2 \textbf{ then}$$
$$\textbf{if } c_3 \textbf{ then}$$
$$\dots$$
$$\textbf{if } c_n \textbf{ then } \{ statement \}$$

where c_i is a condition that is either true or false. Note that rearranging the conditions in a different order results in an equivalent program, since the {*statement*} is executed only if all the c_i are true. Assume that *time(i)* is the time needed to evaluate condition c_i and that *prob(i)* is the probability that condition c_i is true. In what order should the conditions be arranged to make the program most efficient?

7. Modify the indexed sequential search so that in the case of multiple records with the same key, it returns the first such record in the table.

8. Consider the following Pascal implementation of an indexed sequential file:

```
const indxsize = 100;
      tablesize = 1000;
type  indxtype = record
                    kindex: integer;
                    pindex: 1..tablesize
                 end;
      tabletype = record
                    k: integer;
                    r: integer;
                    flag: boolean
                  end;
var   isfile : record
                    indx: array[1..indxsize] of indxtype;
                    table: array[1..tablesize] of tabletype
               end;
```

Write a Pascal routine *create(isfile)* that initializes such a file from input data. Each input line contains a key and a record. The input is sorted in ascending key order. Each index entry corresponds to 10 table entries. *flag* is set to *true* in an occupied table entry and to *false* in an unoccupied entry. Two of every 10 table entries are left unoccupied, to allow for future growth.

9. Given an indexed sequential file as in Exercise 8, write a Pascal routine *search* (*isfile*, *key*) to print the record in the file with key *key* if it is present and an indication that the record is missing if no record with that key exists. (How can you ensure that an unsuccessful search is as efficient as possible?) Also, write routines *insert*(*isfile*, *key*, *rec*) to insert a record *rec* with key *key* and *delete*(*isfile*, *key*) to delete the record with key *key*.

10. Consider the following version of the binary search, which assumes a special element $k(0)$ which is smaller than every possible key:

```
mid := (n + 1) div 2;
len := n div 2;
finish := false;
while (key <> k(mid)) and (not finish)
      do begin
            if key < k(mid)
               then mid := mid - (len + 1) div 2
               else mid := mid + (len + 1) div 2;
            if len = 1
               then finish := true
               else len := len div 2
         end {while...do begin};
if key = k(mid)
   then search := mid
   else search := 0
```

Prove that this algorithm is correct. What are the advantages and/or disadvantages of this method over the method presented in the text?

11. The following search algorithm on a sorted array is known as the **Fibonaccian search** because of its use of Fibonacci numbers. (For a definition of Fibonacci numbers and the *fib* function, see Section 3.1.)

```
j := 1;
while fib(j) < n + 1
      do j := j + 1;
mid := n - fib(j - 2) + 1;
f1 := fib(j - 2);
f2 := fib(j - 3);
finish := false;
while (key <> k(mid)) and (not finish)
      do if (mid <= 0) or (key > k(mid))
            then if f1 = 1
                    then finish := true
                    else begin
                            mid := mid + f2;
                            f1 := f1 - f2;
                            f2 := f2 - f1
                         end {else begin}
            else if f2 = 0
                    then finish := true
```

$$else \ begin$$
$$mid := mid - f2;$$
$$t := f1 - f2;$$
$$f1 := f2;$$
$$f2 := t$$
$$end \ \{else \ begin\};$$

if finish
  then $search := 0$
  else $search := mid$

Explain how this algorithm works. Compare the number of key comparisons with the number used by the binary search. Modify the initial portion of this algorithm so that it computes the Fibonacci numbers efficiently, rather than looking them up in a table or computing each anew.

12. Modify the binary search of the text so that in the case of an unsuccessful search, it returns the index i such that $k(i) < key < k(i + 1)$. If $key < k(1)$, then it returns 0, and if $key > k(n)$, it returns n. Do the same for the searches of Exercises 10 and 11.

2. TREE SEARCHING

In Section 1 we discussed search operations on a file that is organized either as an array or as a list. In this section we consider several ways of organizing files as trees and some associated searching algorithms.

In Sections 6.1 and 7.3 we presented a method of using a binary tree to store a file to make sorting the file more efficient. In that method, all the left descendants of a node with key *key* have keys that are less than *key*, and all the right descendants have keys that are greater than or equal to *key*. The inorder traversal of such a binary tree yields the file in ascending key order.

Such a tree may also be used as a binary search tree. Using binary tree notation, the algorithm for searching for the key *key* in such a tree is as follows. (We assume that each node contains four fields: k, which holds the record's key value; r, which holds the record itself; and *left* and *right*, which are pointers to the subtrees.)

$$found := false;$$
$$p := tree;$$
while $(p <> nil)$ *and* (*not found*)
  do if $key = k(p)$
    then $found := true$
    else if $key < k(p)$
      then $p := left(p)$
      else $p := right(p);$
if found
  then $search := p$
  else $search := nil$

A more efficient version of this algorithm is the following:

$nd := nil;$
$p := tree;$
while $p <> nd$
    do if $key = k(p)$
       then $nd := p$
       else if $key < k(p)$
          then $p := left(p)$
          else $p := right(p);$
$search := p$

The efficiency of the search process can be improved still further by using a sentinel, as in sequential searching. A sentinel node, with a separate external pointer pointing to it, remains allocated with the tree. All *left* or *right* tree pointers which do not point to another tree node now point to this sentinel node instead of equaling *nil*. When a search is performed, the argument key is first inserted into the sentinel node, thus guaranteeing that it will be located in the tree. This enables the header of the search loop to be written

while $key <> k(p)...$

without the risk of an infinite loop. After leaving the loop, if p equals the external sentinel pointer, then the search was unsuccessful; otherwise, p points to the desired node. We leave the actual algorithm to the reader.

Note that the binary search of Section 1 actually uses a sorted array as an implicit binary search tree. The middle element of the array can be thought of as the root of the tree, the lower half of the array (all of whose elements are less than the middle element) can be considered the left subtree, and the upper half (all of whose elements are greater than the middle element) can be considered the right subtree.

A sorted array can be produced from a binary search tree by traversing the tree in inorder and inserting each element sequentially into the array as it is visited. On the other hand, there are many binary search trees which correspond to a given sorted array. Viewing the middle element of the array as the root of a tree and viewing the remaining elements recursively as left and right subtrees produces a relatively balanced binary search tree (Figure 8.2.1a). Viewing the first element of the array as the root of a tree and each successive element as the right son of its predecessor produces a very unbalanced binary tree (Figure 8.2.1b).

The advantage of using a binary search tree over an array is that a tree enables search, insertion, and deletion operations to be performed efficiently. If an array is used, an insertion or deletion requires that approximately half of the elements of the array be moved. (Why?) Insertion or deletion in a search tree, on the other hand, requires that only a few pointers must be adjusted.

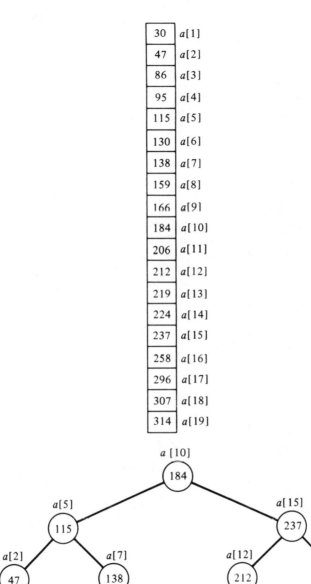

30	$a[1]$
47	$a[2]$
86	$a[3]$
95	$a[4]$
115	$a[5]$
130	$a[6]$
138	$a[7]$
159	$a[8]$
166	$a[9]$
184	$a[10]$
206	$a[11]$
212	$a[12]$
219	$a[13]$
224	$a[14]$
237	$a[15]$
258	$a[16]$
296	$a[17]$
307	$a[18]$
314	$a[19]$

(a)

Figure 8.2.1 A sorted array and two of its binary tree representations.

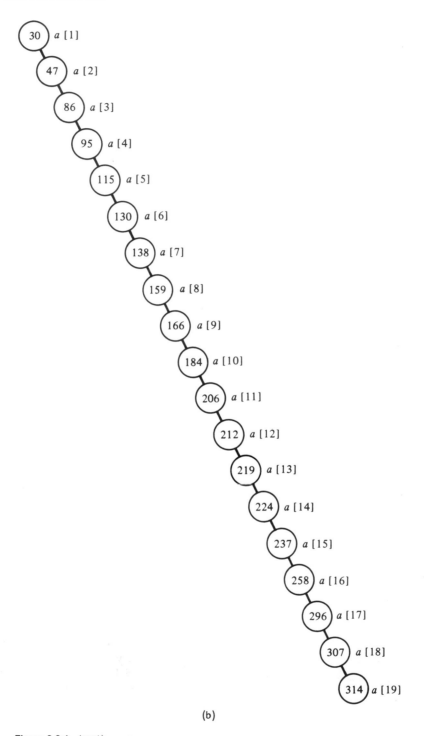

(b)

Figure 8.2.1 *(cont.)*

Inserting into a Binary Search Tree

The following algorithm searches such a binary tree and inserts a new record into the tree if the search is unsuccessful, assuming that no sentinel is used. (We assume the existence of a function *maketree* which constructs a binary tree consisting of a single node whose information field is passed as an argument and returns a pointer to the tree. This function is described in Section 6.1. However, in the version used here, we assume that *maketree* accepts two arguments, a record and a key.)

```
nd := nil;
q := nil;
p := tree;
while p <> nd
    do if key = k(p)
        then nd := p
        else begin
                q := p;
                if key < k(p)
                    then p := left(p)
                    else p := right(p)
            end {else begin};
if p = nil
    then begin
            p := maketree(rec, key);
            if q = nil
                then tree := p
                else if key < k(q)
                        then left(q) := p
                        else right(q) := p
        end {then begin};
search = p
```

Note that after a new record is inserted, the tree retains the property of being sorted in an inorder traversal.

Deleting from a Binary Search Tree

We now present an algorithm that deletes a node with key *key* from a binary search tree and leaves the tree as a binary search tree. There are three cases to consider. If the node to be deleted has no sons, it may be deleted without further adjustment to the tree. This is illustrated in Figure 8.2.2a. If the node to be deleted has only one subtree, its only son can be moved up to take its place. This is illustrated in Figure 8.2.2b. If, however, the node *p* to be deleted has two subtrees, its inorder successor *s* (or pred-

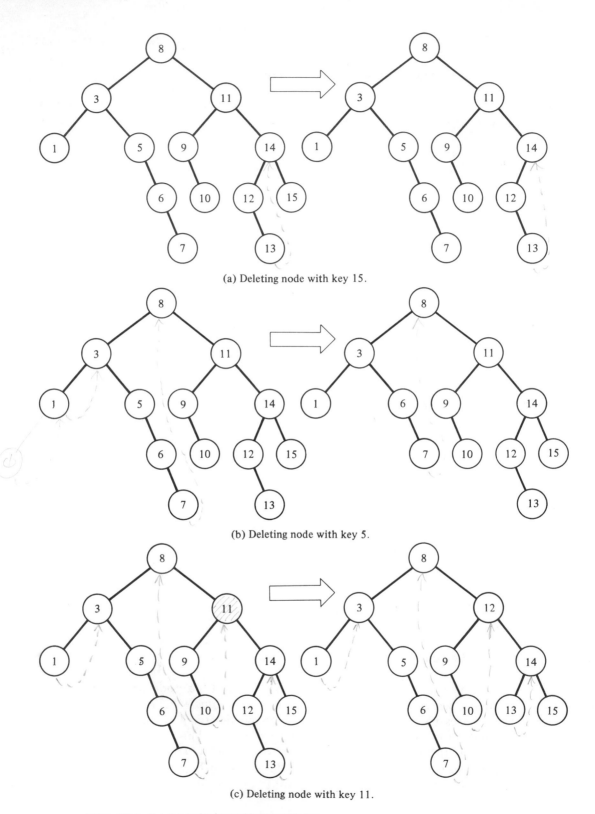

(a) Deleting node with key 15.

(b) Deleting node with key 5.

(c) Deleting node with key 11.

Figure 8.2.2 Deleting nodes from a binary search tree.

ecessor) must take its place. The inorder successor cannot have a left subtree (since a left descendant would be the inorder successor of p). Thus the right son of s can be moved up to take the place of s. This is illustrated in Figure 8.2.2c, where the node with key 12 replaces the node with key 11 and is replaced, in turn, by the node with key 13.

In the following algorithm, if no node with key *key* exists in the tree, the tree is left unchanged.

```
p := tree;
q := nil;
found := false;
{ search for the node with key key. set p to point to }
{        the node and q to its father, if any          }
while (p <> nil) and (not found)
      do if k(p) = key
            then found := true
            else begin
                        q := p;
                        if key < k(p)
                            then p := left(p)
                            else p := right(p)
                  end {else begin};
if found
   then begin { set v to point to the node which will }
              {              replace node(p)           }
        if left(p) = nil
          then v := right(p)
          else if right(p) = nil
                  then v := left(p)
                  else { node(p) has two sons; set v }
                       { to the inorder successor of }
                       { p, and t to the father of v }
                  begin
                     t := p;
                     v := right(p);
                     s := left(v); { s is the left }
                                   {   son of v    }
                     while s <> nil
                        do begin
                              t := v;
                              v := s;
                              s := left(v)
                        end {while...do begin};
                     { at this point, v is the  }
                     { inorder successor of p }
```

```
          if t <> p
             then begin
                              { p is not the father of v }
                              {     and v=left(t)        }
                          left(t):= right(v);
                              { remove node(v) from }
                              {  its current position  }
                              {   to take the place of }
                              {         node(p)        }
                          right(v):= right(p)
                     end {then begin};
               left(v):= left(p)
          end {else begin};
       { insert node(v) into the position formerly occupied }
       {                    by node(p)                      }
     if q = nil
        then {  node(p) was the root of the tree  }
           tree := v
        else if p = left(q)
                then left(q):= v
                else right(q):= v;
     freenode(p)
   end {then begin}
```

Efficiency of Binary Search Tree Operations

As we have already seen in Section 7.3 (see Figures 7.3.1 and 7.3.2), the time required to search a binary search tree varies between $O(n)$ and $O(\log n)$, depending on the structure of the tree. If elements are inserted into the tree by the insertion algorithm just presented, the structure of the tree depends on the order in which the records are inserted. If the records are inserted in sorted (or reverse) order, the resulting tree will contain all nil left (or right) links so that the tree search reduces to a sequential search. If, however, the records are inserted so that half the records inserted after any given record r with key k have keys smaller than k and half have keys greater than k, a balanced tree is achieved in which approximately $\log_2 n$ key comparisons are sufficient to retrieve an element. (Again, it should be noted that examining a node in our insertion algorithm requires two comparisons: one for equality and the other for less than. However, in machine language and in some compilers, these can be combined into a single comparison.)

If the records are presented in random order (i.e., any permutation of the n elements is equally likely), balanced trees will result more often than not, so that on the average, search time will remain $O(\log n)$. To see this, let us define the *internal path length*, I, of a binary tree as the sum of the levels of all the nodes in the tree (note that the level of a node equals the length of the path from the root to the node). In the initial tree of Figure 8.2.2, for example, I equals 30 (1 node at level 0, 2 at level 1, 4 at level 2, 4 at level 3, and 2 at level 4: $1 * 0 + 2 * 1 + 4 * 2 + 4 * 3 + 2 * 4 = 30$). Since the number of comparisons required to access a node in a binary search tree is one greater than the node's level, the average number of comparisons required for a successful search in a binary search tree with n nodes equals $(I + n)/n$, assuming equal likelihood for accessing every node in the tree. Thus, for the initial tree of Figure 8.2.2, $(30 + 13)/13$, or approximately 3.31, comparisons are required for a successful search. Let S_n equal the average number of comparisons required for a successful search in a random binary search tree of n nodes in which the search argument is equally likely to be any of the n keys and let I_n be the average internal path length of a random binary search tree of n nodes. Then S_n equals $(I_n + n)/n$.

   Let U_n be the average number of comparisons required for an unsuccessful search of a random binary search tree of n nodes. There are $n + 1$ possible ways for an unsuccessful search for a key *key* to occur: *key* is less than $k(1)$, *key* is between $k(1)$ and $k(2)$, . . . , *key* is between $k(n - 1)$ and $k(n)$, and *key* is greater than $k(n)$. These correspond to the $n + 1$ nil subtree pointers in any n-node binary search tree. (It can be shown that any binary search tree with n nodes has $n + 1$ nil pointers.)

   Consider the *extension* of a binary search tree formed by replacing each nil left or right pointer with a pointer to a separate, new leaf node, called an *external node*. The extension of a binary tree of n nodes has $n + 1$ external nodes, each corresponding to one of the $n + 1$ key ranges for an unsuccessful search. For example, the initial tree of Figure 8.2.2 contains 13 nodes. Its extension would add two external nodes as sons of each of the leafs containing 1, 7, 10, 13, and 15 and one external node as an additional son of each of the one-son nodes containing 5, 6, 9, and 12, for a total of 14 external nodes. Define the *external path length*, E, of a binary tree as the sum of the levels of all the external nodes of its extension. The extension of the initial tree of Figure 8.2.2 has 4 external nodes at level 3, 6 at level 4, and 4 at level 5, for an external path length of 56. Note that the level of an external node equals the number of comparisons in an unsuccessful search for a key in the range represented by that external node. Then, if E_n is the average external path length of a random binary search tree of n nodes, $U_n = E_n/(n + 1)$. (This assumes that each of the $n + 1$ key ranges is equally likely in an unsuccessful search. In Figure 8.2.2, the average number of comparisons for an unsuccessful search would be 56/14 or 4.0) However, it can be shown that $E = I + 2n$ for any binary tree of n nodes (for example, in Figure 8.2.2, $56 = 30 + 2 * 13$), so that $E_n = I_n + 2n$. Since $S_n = (I_n + n)/n$ and $U_n = E_n/(n + 1)$, this means that $S_n = ((n + 1)/n)U_n - 1$.

   The number of comparisons required to access a key is one more than the number required when the node was inserted. But the number required to insert a key equals the number required in an unsuccessful search for that key before it was inserted. Thus $S_n = 1 + (U_0 + U_1 + \ldots + U_{n-1})/n$. (That is, the average number of comparisons in retrieving an item in an n-node tree equals the average number in accessing each of the first item through the nth, and the number for accessing the ith equals one more than the number for inserting the ith or $1 + U_{i-1}$.) Combining this with the equation $S_n = ((n + 1)/n)U_n - 1$ yields

$$(n + 1)U_n = 2n + U_0 + U_1 + \ldots + U_{n-1}$$

for any n. Replacing n by $n - 1$ yields

$$nU_{n-1} = 2(n - 1) + U_0 + U_1 + \ldots + U_{n-2}$$

and subtracting from the previous equation yields

$$(n + 1)U_n - nU_{n-1} = 2 + U_{n-1}$$

or

$$U_n = U_{n-1} + 2/(n + 1)$$

Since $U_1, = 1$, we have that

$$U_n = 1 + 2/3 + 2/4 + \ldots + 2/(n + 1)$$

and, therefore, since $S_n = ((n + 1)/n) U_n - 1$, that

$$S_n = 2((n + 1)/n)(1 + 1/2 + 1/3 + \ldots + 1/n) - 3$$

As n grows large, $(n + 1)/n$ is approximately 1, and it can be shown that $1 + 1/2 + \ldots + 1/n$ is approximately $\ln(n)$. Thus S_n may be approximated (for large n) by $2 * ln(n)$, which equals $1.386 * \log_2 n$. This means that average search time in a random binary search tree is $O(\log n)$ and requires approximately only 39% more comparisons, on the average, than in a balanced binary tree.

As already noted, insertion in a binary search tree requires the same number of comparisons as does an unsuccessful search for the key. Deletion requires the same number of comparisons as does a search for the key to be deleted, although it does involve additional work in finding the inorder successor or predecessor. It can be shown that the deletion algorithm that we have presented actually improves the subsequent average search cost of the tree! That is, a random n-key tree created by inserting $n + 1$ keys and then deleting a random key has lower internal path length (and therefore lower average search cost) than does a random n-key tree created by inserting n keys. The process of deleting a one-son node by replacing it with its son, regardless of whether that son is a right or left son, yields a better than average tree; a similar deletion algorithm which only replaces a one-son node by its son if it is a left son (that is, if its successor is not contained in its subtree) and otherwise replaces the node with its inorder successor does produce a random tree, assuming no additional insertions. This latter algorithm is called the ***asymmetric deletion algorithm***.

Strangely enough, however, as additional insertions and deletions are made using the asymmetric deletion algorithm, the internal path length and search time initially decrease but then begin to rise rapidly again. For trees containing more than 128 keys, the internal path length eventually becomes worse than that for a random tree, and for trees with more than 2048 keys, the internal path length eventually becomes more than 50% worse than that of a random tree! An alternative ***symmetric deletion algorithm***, which alternates between deleting the inorder predecessor and successor on alternate deletions (but still replaces a one-son node with its son only when the predecessor or successor, respectively, is not contained in its subtree), does eventually produce better than random trees after additional mixed insertions and deletions. Empirical data indicate that path length is reduced after many alternating insertions and symmetric deletions to approximately 88% of its corresponding random value.

All the preceding assumes that it is equally likely for the search argument to equal any key in the table. However, in actual practice it is usually the case that some records are retrieved very often, some moderately often, and some almost never. Suppose that records are inserted into the tree so that a more commonly accessed record precedes one that is not so frequently accessed. Then the most frequently retrieved records will be nearer the root of the tree, so that the average successful search time will be reduced. (Of course, this assumes that reordering the keys in order of reduced frequency of access does not seriously unbalance the binary tree, since if it did, the reduced number of comparisons for the most frequently accessed records might be offset by the increased number of comparisons for the vast majority of records.)

If the elements to be retrieved form a constant set, with no insertions or deletions, it may pay to set up a binary search tree which makes subsequent searches more efficient. For example, consider the binary search trees of Figure 8.2.3. Both the trees of Figures 8.2.3a and b contain three elements $K1$, $K2$ and $K3$ where $K1 < K2 < K3$, and are valid binary search trees for that set. However, a retrieval of $K3$ requires two comparisons in Figure 8.2.3a but only one comparison in Figure 8.2.3b. Of course, there are still other valid binary search trees for this set of keys.

The number of key comparisons necessary to retrieve a record is equal to the level of that record in the binary search tree plus one. Thus a retrieval of $K2$ requires one comparison in the tree of Figure 8.2.3a but requires three comparisons in the tree of Figure 8.2.3b. An unsuccessful search for an argument lying immediately between two keys a and b requires as many key comparisons as the maximum number of comparisons required by successful searches for either a or b. (Why?) This is equal to one plus the maximum of the levels of a or b. For example, a search for a key lying

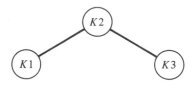

Figure 8.2.3   Two binary search trees.

(a) Expected number of comparisons:
$2p1 + p2 + 2p3 + 2q0 + 2q1 + 2q2 + 2q3$

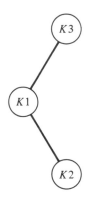

(b) Expected number of comparisons:
$2p1 + 3p2 + p3 + 2q0 + 3q1 + 3q2 + q3$

between $K2$ and $K3$ requires two key comparions in Figure 8.2.3a and three comparisons in Figure 8.2.3b, while a search for a key greater than $K3$ requires two comparisons in Figure 8.2.3a, but only one comparison in Figure 8.2.3b.

Suppose $p1$, $p2$, and $p3$ are the probabilities that the search argument equals $K1$, $K2$, and $K3$, respectively. Suppose also that $q0$ is the probability that the search argument is less than $K1$, $q1$ is the probability that it is between $K1$ and $K2$, $q2$ is the probability that it is between $K2$ and $K3$, and $q3$ is the probability that it is greater than $K3$. Then $p1 + p2 + p3 + q0 + q1 + q2 + q3 = 1$. The *expected number* of comparisons in a search is the sum of the probabilities that the argument has a given value times the number of comparisons required to retrieve that value, where the sum is taken over all possible search argument values. For example, the expected number of comparisons in searching the tree of Figure 8.2.3a is

$$2p1 + p2 + 2p3 + 2q0 + 2q1 + 2q2 + 2q3$$

and the expected number of comparisons in searching the tree of Figure 8.2.3b is

$$2p1 + 3p2 + p3 + 2q0 + 3q1 + 3q2 + q3$$

This expected number of comparisons can be used as a measure of how "good" a particular binary search tree is for a given set of keys and a given set of probabilities. Thus for the probabilities listed next on the left, the tree of Figure 8.2.3a is more efficient; for the probabilities listed on the right, the tree of Figure 8.2.3b is more efficient.

<table>
<tr><td>$p1 = .1$</td><td>$p1 = .1$</td></tr>
<tr><td>$p2 = .3$</td><td>$p2 = .1$</td></tr>
<tr><td>$p3 = .1$</td><td>$p3 = .3$</td></tr>
<tr><td>$q0 = .1$</td><td>$q0 = .1$</td></tr>
<tr><td>$q1 = .2$</td><td>$q1 = .1$</td></tr>
<tr><td>$q2 = .1$</td><td>$q2 = .1$</td></tr>
<tr><td>$q3 = .1$</td><td>$q3 = .2$</td></tr>
</table>

Expected number for 9.2.3a = 1.7   Expected number for 9.2.3a = 1.9
Expected number for 9.2.3b = 2.4   Expected number for 9.2.3b = 1.8

Optimum Search Trees

A binary search tree that minimizes the expected number of comparisons for a given set of keys and probabilities is called **optimum**. The fastest-known algorithm to produce an optimum binary search tree is $O(n^2)$ in the general case. This is too expensive unless the tree will be maintained unchanged over a very large number of searches. In cases where all the $p(i)$ equal zero (that is, the keys act only to define range values with which data are associated, so that all searches are "unsuccessful"), then an $O(n)$ algorithm to create an optimum binary search tree does exist.

However, although an efficient algorithm to construct an optimum tree in the general case does not exist, there are several methods for constructing near-optimum trees in $O(n)$ time. If $p(i)$ is the probability of searching for key $k(i)$, $q(i)$ is the probability of an unsuccessful search between $k(i - 1)$ and $k(i)$ (with $q(0)$ the probability of an unsuccessful search for a key below $k(1)$, and $q(n)$ is the probability of an unsuccessful search for a key above $k(n)$), define $s(i, j)$ as $q(i) + p(i + 1) + \ldots + p(j) + q(j)$. The first method, called the **balancing method**, attempts to find a value i that minimizes the absolute value of $s(0, i - 1) - s(i, n)$ and establishes $k(i)$ as the root of the binary search tree, with $k(1)$ through $k(i - 1)$ in its left subtree and $k(i + 1)$ through $k(n)$ in its right subtree. The process is then applied recursively to build the left and right subtrees. Locating the value i at which $abs(s(0, i - 1) - s(i, n))$ is minimized can be done efficiently as follows. Initially, set up an array $s0[0 \ldots n]$ such that $s[i]$ equals $s(0, i)$. This can be done by initializing $s0[0]$ to $q(0)$ and $s0[j]$ to $s0[j - 1] + p(j) + q(j)$ for j from 1 to n in turn. Once $s0$ has been initialized, $s(i, j)$ can be computed for any i and j as $s0[j] - s0[i - 1] - p[i]$ whenever necessary. We define $si(j)$ as $s(0, j - 1) - s(j, n)$. We wish to minimize $abs(si(i))$.

After $s0$ has been initialized, we begin the process of finding an i to minimize $abs(s(0, i - 1) - s(i, n))$. Note that si is a monotonically increasing function. Note also that $si(0) = q(0) - 1$, which is negative, and $si(n) = 1 - q(n + 1)$, which is positive. Check the values of $si(1)$, $si(n)$, $si(2)$, $si(n - 1)$, $si(4)$, $si(n - 3)$, . . . , $si(2^j)$, $si(n + 1 - 2^j)$, . . . in turn until discovering the first positive $si(2^j)$ or the first negative $si(n + 1 - 2^j)$. If a positive $si(2^j)$ is found first, then the desired i that minimizes $abs(si(i))$ lies within the interval $[2^{j-1}, 2^j]$; if a negative $si(n + 1 - 2^j)$ is found first, then the desired i lies within the interval $[n + 1 - 2^j, n + 1 - 2^{j-1}]$. In either case, i has been narrowed down to an interval of size 2^{j-1}. Within the interval, use a binary search to narrow down on i. The doubling effect in the interval size guarantees that the entire recursive process is $O(n)$, whereas if a binary search were used on the entire interval $[0, n]$ to start, the process would be $O(n \log n)$.

A second method used to construct near-optimum binary search trees is called the **greedy method**. Instead of building the tree from the top down, as in the balancing method, the greedy method builds the tree from the bottom up. The method uses a doubly linked linear list in which each list element contains four pointers, one key value, and three probability values. The four pointers are left and right list pointers used to organize the doubly linked list and left and right subtree pointers used to keep track of binary search subtrees containing keys less than and greater than the key value in the node. The three probability values are the sum of the probabilities in the left subtree, called the **left probability**, the probability $p(i)$ of the node's key value $k(i)$, called the **key probability**, and the sum of the probabilities in the right subtree, called the **right probability**. The **total probability** of a node is defined as the sum of its left, key and right probabilities. Initially, there are n nodes in the list. The key value in the ith node is $k(i)$, its left probability is $q(i - 1)$, its right probability is $q(i)$, its key probability is $p(i)$, and its left and right subtree pointers are *nil*.

Each iteration of the algorithm finds the first node nd on the list whose total probability is less than or equal to its successor's (if no node qualifies, nd is set to the last node in the list) and establishes the key in nd as the root of a binary search subtree whose left and right subtrees are the left and right subtrees of nd. nd is then removed from the list. The left subtree pointer of its successor (if any) and the right subtree pointer of its predecessor (if any) are reset to point to the new subtree, and the left probability of its successor and the right probability of its predecessor are reset to the total probability of nd. This process is repeated until only one node remains on the list. (Note that it is not necessary to begin a full list traversal from the list beginning on each iteration; it is only necessary to begin from the second predecessor of the node removed on the previous iteration.) When only one node remains on the list, its key is placed in the root of the final binary search tree, with the left and right subtree pointers of the node as the left and right subtree pointers of the root.

Another technique of reducing average search time when search probabilities are known is a ***split tree***. Such a tree contains two keys rather than one in each node. The first, called the ***node key***, is tested for equality with the argument key. If they are equal, then the search ends successfuly; if not, the argument key is compared to the second key in the node, called the ***split key***, to determine if the search should continue in the left or right subtree. A particular type of split tree, called a ***median split tree***, sets the node key in each node to the most frequent among the keys in the subtree rooted at that node and sets the split key to the median of the keys in that subtree (that is, the key k such that an equal number of keys in the subtree are less than and greater than k). This has the twin advantage of guaranteeing a balanced tree and assuring that frequent keys are found near the root. Although median split trees require an extra key in each node, they can be constructed as almost complete binary trees which can be implemented in an array, saving space for tree pointers. A median split tree from a given set of keys and frequencies can be built in time $O(n \log n)$, and a search in such a tree always requires fewer than $\log_2 n$ node visits, although each visit does require two separate comparisons.

Balanced Trees

As noted, if the probability of searching for a key in a table is the same for all keys, a balanced binary tree yields the most efficient search. Unfortunately, the search and insertion algorithm presented earlier does not ensure that the tree remains balanced—the degree of balance is dependent on the order in which keys are inserted into the tree. We would like to have an efficient search and insertion algorithm which maintains the search tree as a balanced binary tree.

Let us first define more precisely the notion of a "balanced" tree. The ***height*** of a binary tree is the maximum level of its leafs (this is also sometimes known as the ***depth*** of the tree). For convenience, the height of a nil tree is defined as -1. A ***balanced binary tree*** (sometimes called an ***AVL*** tree) is a binary tree in which the heights of the two subtrees of every node never differ by more than one. The ***balance*** of a node in a binary tree is defined as the height of its left subtree minus the height of its right subtree. Figure 8.2.4a illustrates a balanced binary tree. Each node in a balanced binary tree has a balance of 1, -1, or 0, depending on whether the height of its left subtree is greater than, less than, or equal to the height of its right subtree. The balance of each node is indicated in Figure 8.2.4a.

Suppose that we are given a balanced binary tree and use the search and insertion algorithm to insert a new node p into the tree. Then the resulting tree may or may not remain balanced. Figure 8.2.4b illustrates all possible insertions that may be made to the tree of Figure 8.2.4a. Each insertion that yields a balanced tree is indicated by a B. The unbalanced insertions are indicated by a U and are numbered from 1 to 12. It is easy

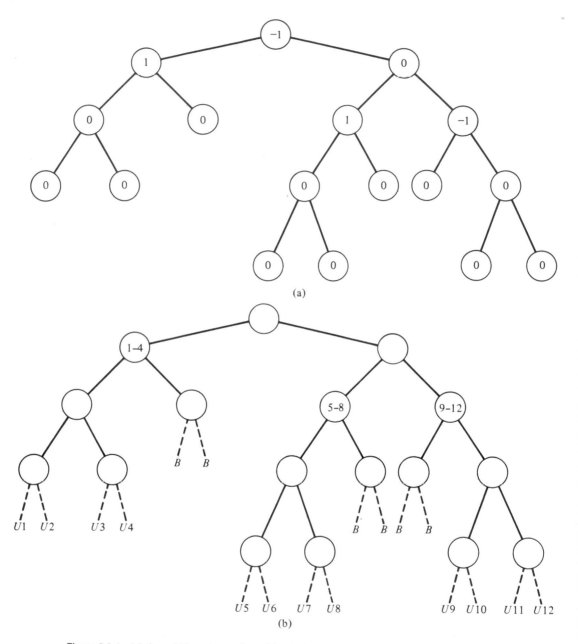

Figure 8.2.4 A balanced binary tree and possible additions.

to see that the tree becomes unbalanced only if the newly inserted node is a left descendant of a node which previously had a balance of 1 (this occurs in cases $U1$ through $U8$ in Figure 8.2.4b) or if it is a right descendant of a node which previously had a balance of -1 (cases $U9$ through $U12$). In

Figure 8.2.4b, the youngest ancestor that becomes unbalanced in each insertion is indicated by the numbers contained in three of the nodes.

Let us examine further the subtree rooted at the youngest ancestor to become unbalanced as a result of an insertion. We illustrate the case where the balance of this subtree was previously 1, leaving the other case to the reader. Figure 8.2.5 illustrates this case. Let us call the unbalanced node A. Since A had a balance of 1, its left subtree was nonnil; we may therefore designate its left son as B. Since A is the youngest ancestor of the new node to become unbalanced, node B must have had a balance of 0. (You are asked to prove this fact as an exercise.) Thus node B must have had (before the insertion) left and right subtrees of equal height n (where possibly $n = -1$). Since the balance of A was 1, the right subtree of A must also have been of height n.

There are now two cases to consider, illustrated by Figure 8.2.5a and b. In Figure 8.2.5a the newly created node is inserted into the left subtree of B, changing the balance of B to 1 and the balance of A to 2. In Figure 8.2.5b the newly created node is inserted into the right subtree of B, changing the balance of B to -1 and the balance of A to 2. To maintain a balanced tree, it is necessary to perform a transformation on the tree so that

1. The inorder traversal of the transformed tree is the same as for the original tree (i.e., the transformed tree remains a binary search tree).
2. The transformed tree is balanced.

Consider the trees of Figure 8.2.6a and b. The tree of Figure 8.2.6b is said to be a **right rotation** of the tree rooted at A of Figure 8.2.6a. Similarly, the tree of Figure 8.2.6c is said to be a **left rotation** of the tree rooted at A of Figure 8.2.6a.

An algorithm to implement a left rotation of a subtree rooted at p is as follows:

```
q := right(p);
hold := left(q);
left(q):= p;
right(p):= hold
```

Let us call this operation *leftrotation(p)*. *rightrotation(p)* may be defined similarly. Of course, in any rotation the value of the pointer to the root of the subtree being rotated must be changed to point to the new root. (In the case of the preceding left rotation, this new root is q.) Note that the order of the nodes in an inorder traversal is preserved under both right and left rotations. It therefore follows that any number of rotations (left or right) can be performed on an unbalanced tree in order to obtain a balanced tree, without disturbing the order of the nodes in an inorder traversal.

Let us now return to the trees of Figure 8.2.5. Suppose that a right rotation is performed on the subtree rooted at A in Figure 8.2.5a. The

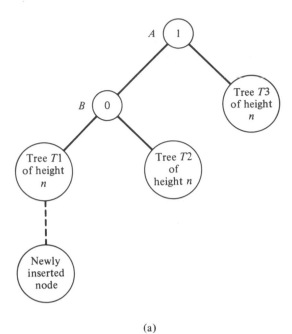

Figure 8.2.5   Initial insertion; all balances are prior to insertion.

(a)

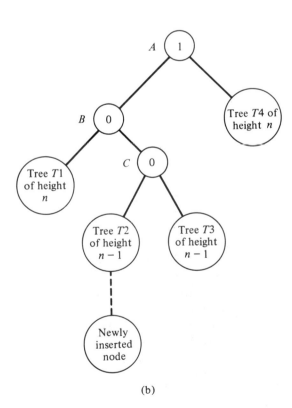

(b)

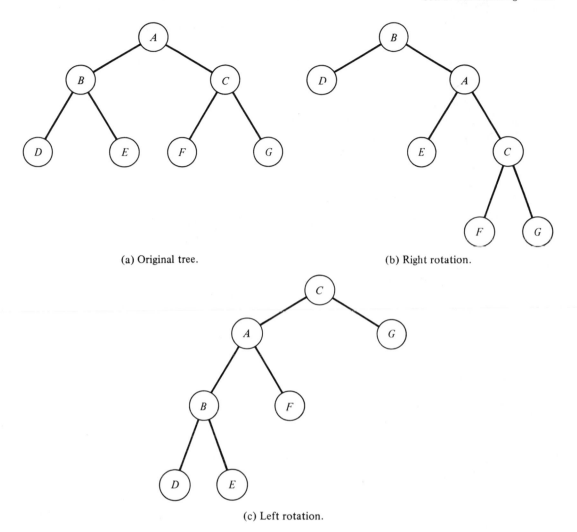

(a) Original tree.   (b) Right rotation.

(c) Left rotation.

Figure 8.2.6   Simple rotation on a tree.

resulting tree is shown in Figure 8.2.7a. Note that the tree of Figure 8.2.7a yields the same inorder traversal as does that of Figure 8.2.5a and is also balanced. Also, since the height of the subtree of Figure 8.2.5a was $n + 2$ before the insertion and the height of the subtree of Figure 8.2.7a is $n + 2$ with the inserted node, the balance of each ancestor of node A remains undisturbed. Thus, replacing the subtree of Figure 8.2.5a with its right rotation of Figure 8.2.7a guarantees that a balanced binary search tree is maintained.

Let us now turn to the tree of Figure 8.2.5b, where the newly created node is inserted into the right subtree of B. Let C be the right son of B.

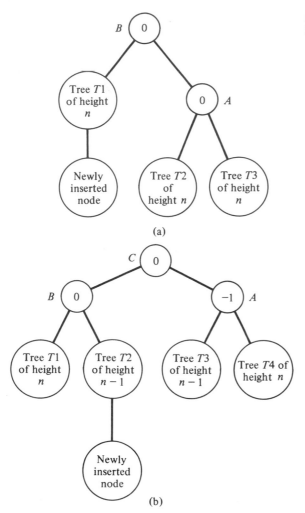

Figure 8.2.7   After rebalancing; all balances are after insertion.

(There are three cases: C may be the newly inserted node in which case $n = -1$, or the newly inserted node may be in the left or right subtree of C. Figure 8.2.5b illustrates the case where it is in the left subtree; the analysis of the other cases is analogous.) Suppose that a left rotation on the subtree rooted at B is followed by a right rotation on the subtree rooted at A. Figure 8.2.7b illustrates the resulting tree. Verify that the inorder traversals of the two trees are the same and that the tree of Figure 8.2.7b is balanced. The height of the tree in Figure 8.2.7b is $n + 2$, which is the same as the height of the tree in Figure 8.2.5b before the insertion, so that the balance in all ancestors of A is unchanged. Therefore, by replacing the tree of Figure 8.2.5b with that of Figure 8.2.7b whenever it occurs after insertion, a balanced search tree is maintained.

Let us now present an algorithm to search and insert into a nonempty balanced binary tree. Each node of the tree contains five fields: k and r, which hold the key and record, respectively; *left* and *right*, which are pointers to the left and right subtrees, respectively; and *bal*, whose value is 1, -1, or 0, depending on the node's balance. In the first part of the algorithm, if the desired key is not already in the tree, a new node is inserted into the binary search tree without regard to balance. This first phase also keeps track of the youngest ancestor, *ya*, which may become unbalanced upon insertion. The algorithm makes use of the function *maketree* described earlier and routines *rightrotation* and *leftrotation*, which accept a pointer to the root of a subtree and perform the desired rotation.

```
{ part 1: search and insert into the binary tree }
s := nil;
p := tree;
v := nil;
ya := p;
        { ya points to the youngest ancestor which may }
        { become unbalanced. v points to the father of }
        {       ya, and s points to the father of p     }
found := false;
while (p <> nil) and (not found)
    do if key = k(p)
        then found := true
        else begin
                if key < k(p)
                    then q := left(p)
                    else q := right(p);
                if q <> nil
                    then if bal(q) <> 0
                            then begin
                                    v := p;
                                    ya := q
                                end {then begin};
                s := p;
                p := q
            end {else begin};
if found
    then search := p
    else begin { insert a new record }
            q := maketree(rec, key);
            bal(q) := 0;
            if key < k(s)
                then left(s) := q
            else right(s) := q;
```

```
                    { the balance in all nodes between node(ya) and }
                    {          node(q) must be changed from 0          }
            if key < k(ya)
               then p := left(ya)
               else p := right(ya);
            s := p;
            while p <> q
                    do if key < k(p)
                          then begin
                                    bal(p):= 1;
                                    p := left(p)
                                end {then begin}
                          else  begin
                                    bal(p):= -1;
                                    p := right(p)
                                end {else begin};


            {    part II:  ascertain whether or not the tree is unbalanced.  }
            {    If it is, q is the newly inserted node, ya is its youngest  }
            {    unbalanced ancestor, v is the father of ya, and s is the    }
            {          son of ya in the direction of the imbalance.          }
        if key < k(ya)
           then imbal := 1
           else imbal := -1;
        if bal(ya) = 0
           then {   Another level has been added to the tree.   }
                {           The tree remains balanced.           }
                bal(ya):= imbal
           else if bal(ya) <> imbal
                   then {   The added node has been placed in   }
                        {        the opposite direction of the        }
                        {   imbalance.  The tree remains balanced.   }
                        bal(ya):= 0
                   else begin


            {    part III:  the additional node has unbalanced the tree.    }
            {       Rebalance it by performing the required rotations        }
            {       and then adjust the balances of the nodes involved.      }
        if bal(s) = imbal
           then begin {   ya and s have been unbalanced in the same       }
                      { direction; see Figure 8.2.5a where ya = A and s = B }
                      p := s;
```

if $imbal = 1$
   then $rightrotation(ya)$
   else $leftrotation(ya)$;
$bal(ya):= 0$;
$bal(s):= 0$
end {then begin}
else *begin* { ya and s are unbalanced in opposite }
        {   directions; see Figure 8.2.5b   }
  if $imbal = 1$
   then begin
         $p:= right(s)$;
         $leftrotation(s)$;
         $left(ya):= p$;
         $rightrotation(ya)$
    end {then begin}
   else *begin*
         $p:= left(s)$;
         $right(ya):= p$;
         $rightrotation(s)$;
         $leftrotation(ya)$
    end {else begin};
  { adjust *bal* field for involved nodes }
  if $bal(p) = 0$
   then begin { p was the inserted node }
        $bal(ya):= 0$;
        $bal(s):= 0$
    end {then begin}
   else if $bal(p) = imbal$
     then begin { see Figures 8.2.5b and 8.2.7b }
          $bal(ya):= -imbal$;
          $bal(s):= 0$
     end {then begin}
     else *begin* { see Figures 8.2.5b and 8.2.7b }
          { but the new node was inserted }
          {   into $T3$ }
          $bal(ya):= 0$;
          $bal(s):= imbal$
     end {else begin};
  $bal(p):= 0$
end {else begin};
{ adjust the pointer to the rotated subtree }
if $v = nil$
  then $tree:= p$

else if $ya = right(v)$
    then $right(v) := p$
    else $left(v) := p$
        end {else begin *part III*};
        $search := q$
end {if *found*...else begin}

It can be shown that the maximum height of a balanced binary search tree is $1.44 \log_2 n$ so that a search in such a tree never requires more than 44% more comparisons that that for a completely balanced tree. In actual practice, balanced binary search trees behave even better, yielding search times of $\log_2 n + .25$ for large n. On the average, a rotation is required in 46.5% of the insertions.

The algorithm to delete a node from a balanced binary search tree while maintaining its balance is even more complex. While insertion requires at most a double rotation, deletion may require one (single or double) rotation at each level of the tree, or $O(\log n)$ rotations. However, in practice, an average of only .214 (single or double) rotations has been found to be required per deletion.

The balanced binary search trees that we have looked at are called *height-balanced trees* because their height is used as the criterion for balancing. There are a number of other ways of defining balanced trees. In one method, the *weight* of a tree is defined as the number of external nodes in the tree (this equals the number of nil pointers in the tree). If the ratio of the weight of the left subtree of every node to the weight of the subtree rooted at the node is between some fraction a and $1 - a$, then the tree is a *weight-balanced tree of ratio a* or is said to be in the class *WB[a]*. When an ordinary insertion or deletion on a tree in class *WB[a]* would remove the tree from the class, rotations are used to restore the weight-balanced property.

Another type of tree, called a *balanced binary tree* by Tarjan, requires that for every node *nd*, the length of the longest path from *nd* to an external node is at most twice the length of the shortest path from *nd* to an external node. (Recall that external nodes are nodes added to the tree at every nil pointer.) Again, rotations are used to maintain balance after insertion or deletion. Tarjan's balanced trees have the property that at most one double and one single rotation restore balance after either insertion or deletion, as opposed to a possible $O(\log n)$ rotations for a deletion in a height-balanced tree.

Balanced trees may also be used for efficient implementation of priority queues (see Sections 3.3 and 7.3). Inserting a new element requires at most $O(\log n)$ steps to find its position and $O(1)$ steps for the insertion, while deleting the minimum element requires $O(\log n)$ steps to access the element (by following left pointers to the leftmost leaf) and $O(\log n)$ or $O(1)$ steps to delete that leaf. Thus, like a priority queue implemented using a heap

(Section 7.3), a priority queue implemented using a balanced tree can perform any sequence of n insertions and minimum deletions in $O(n \log n)$ steps.

EXERCISES

1. Write an efficient insertion algorithm for a binary search tree to insert a new record whose key is known not to exist in the tree.

2. Show that it is possible to obtain a binary search tree in which only a single leaf exists even if the elements of the tree are not inserted in strictly ascending or descending order.

3. Verify by simulation that if records are presented to the binary tree search and insertion algorithm in random order, the number of key comparisons will be $O(\log n)$.

4. Prove that every n-node binary search tree is not equally likely (assuming that items are inserted in random order) and that balanced trees are more probable than are straight-line trees.

5. Write an algorithm to delete a node from a binary tree which replaces the node with its inorder predecessor rather than its inorder successor.

6. Suppose that the node type of a binary search tree is defined as follows:

   type nodetype = **record**

   k, r: integer;

   left, right: nodeptr

   end;

   The k and r fields contain the key and record of the node; *left* and *right* are pointers to the node's sons. Write a Pascal function *sinsert(tree, key, rec)* to search and insert a record *rec* with key *key* into a binary search tree pointed to by *tree*.

7. Write a Pascal function *sdelete(tree, key)* to search and delete a record with key *key* from a binary search tree implemented as in Exercise 6. If such a record is found, the function returns the value of its r field; if it is not found, the function returns 0.

8. Write a Pascal routine *delete(tree, key1, key2)* to delete all records with keys between *key1* and *key2* (inclusive) from a binary search tree whose nodes are declared as in the previous exercises.

9. Consider the search trees of Figure 8.2.8.
   (a) How many permutations of the integers 1 through 7 would produce the binary search trees of Figure 8.2.8a, b, and c, respectively?
   (b) How many permutations of the integers 1 through 7 would produce binary search trees which are similar to the trees of Figure 8.2.8a, b, and c, respectively? (See Exercise 6.1.9.)
   (c) How many permutations of the integers 1 through 7 would produce binary search trees with the same number of nodes at each level as the trees of Figure 8.2.8a, b, and c, respectively?
   (d) Find an assignment of probabilities to the first seven positive integers as search arguments which makes each of the trees of Figure 8.2.8a, b, and c optimum.

10. Show that the Fibonacci tree of order $b + 1$ (see Exercise 6.3.5) is a height-balanced tree of height b and has fewer nodes than does any other height-balanced tree of height b.

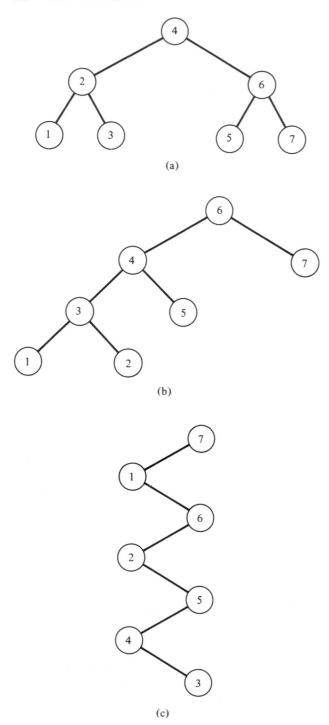

Figure 8.2.8

(a)

(b)

(c)

3. GENERAL SEARCH TREES

General nonbinary trees are also used as search tables, particularly in external storage. There are two broad categories of such trees: multiway search trees and digital search trees. We examine each in turn.

Multiway Search Trees

In binary search tree, each node *nd* contains a single key and points to two subtrees. One of these subtrees contains all the keys in the tree rooted at *nd* that are less than the key in *nd*, and the other subtree contains all the keys in the tree rooted at *nd* that are greater than (or equal to) the key in *nd*. We may extend this concept to a general search tree in which each node contains one or more keys. A *multiway search tree of order n* is a general tree in which each node has *n* or fewer subtrees and contains one fewer key than it has subtrees. That is, if a node has four subtrees, it contains three keys. In addition, if $s_1, s_2, \ldots, s_m$ are the *m* subtrees of a node containing keys $k_1, k_2, \ldots, k_{m-1}$ in ascending order, then all keys in subtree s_1 are less than or equal to k_1, all keys in the subtree s_j (where *j* is between 2 and $m - 1$) are greater than k_{j-1} and less than or equal to k_j, and all keys in the subtree s_m are greater than k_{m-1}. The subtree s_j is called the *left subtree* of key k_j, and its root is called the *left son* of key k_j. Similarly, s_j is called the *right subtree* and its root the *right son* of key k_{j-1}. One or more of the subtrees of a node may be empty. (Sometimes, the term "multiway search tree" is used to refer to any nonbinary tree used for searching, including the digital trees that we introduce at the end of this section in which each node need not contain a complete key. However, we use the term strictly for trees that can contain complete keys in each node.)

Figure 8.3.1 illustrates a number of multiway search trees. Figure 8.3.1a is a multiway search tree of order 4. The eight nodes of that tree have been labeled *A* through *H*. Nodes *A*, *D*, *E*, and *G* contain the maximum number of subtrees, 4, and the maximum number of keys, 3. Such nodes are called *full* nodes. However, some of the subtrees of nodes *D* and *E* and all of the subtrees of node *G* are empty, as indicated by arrows emanating from the appropriate positions in the nodes. Nodes *B*, *C*, *F*, and *H* are not full and also contain some empty subtrees. The first subtree of *A* contains the keys 6 and 10, both smaller than 12, which is the first key of *A*. The second subtree of *A* contains 25 and 37, both greater than 12 (the first key of *A*) and less than 50 (the second key). The third subtree contains 60, 70, 80, 62, 65, and 69, all of which are between 50 (the second key of *A*) and 85 (the third key). Finally, the last subtree of *A* contains 100, 120, 150, and 110, all greater than 85, the last key in node *A*. Similarly, each subtree of any other node contains only keys between the appropriate two keys of

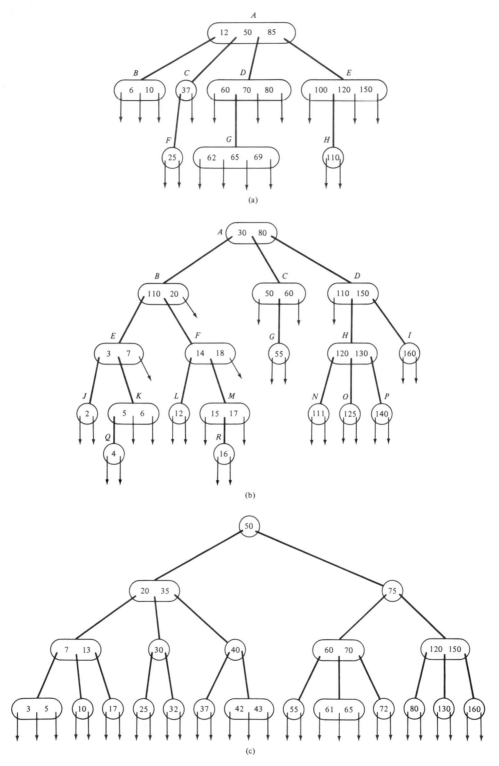

Figure 8.3.1 Multiway search trees.

that node (or, in the case of the first or last subtree of a node, between the first or last key in the node and a key in one of its ancestors).

Figure 8.3.1b illustrates a ***top-down multiway search tree***. Such a tree is characterized by the condition that any nonfull node is a leaf. Note that the tree of Figure 8.3.1a is not top-down since node C is nonfull, yet it contains a nonempty subtree. Define a ***semileaf*** as a node with at least one empty subtree. In Figure 8.3.1a, nodes B through H are all semileafs. In Figure 8.3.1b, nodes B through G and I through R are semileafs. In a top-down multiway tree, a semileaf must be either full or a leaf.

Figure 8.3.1c is yet another multiway search tree of order 3. It is not top-down since there are four nodes with only one key and nonempty subtrees. However, it does have another special property in that it is ***balanced***. That is, all its semileafs are at the same level (3). This implies that all semileafs are leafs. Neither the trees of Figure 8.3.1a (which has leafs at levels 1 and 2) nor of Figure 8.3.1b (leafs at levels 2, 3, and 4) are balanced multiway search trees. (Note that although a binary search tree is a multiway search tree of order 2, a balanced binary search tree as defined at the end of Section 2 is not necessarily balanced as a multiway search tree, since it can have leafs at different levels.)

Searching a Multiway Tree

The algorithm to search a multiway search tree, regardless of whether it is top-down, balanced, or neither, is straightforward. Assume that $node(p)$ contains fields $numtrees(p)$ (whose integer value is less than or equal to the order of the tree, n, and equals the number of subtrees of $node(p)$), $son(p, 1)$ through $son(p, numtrees(p))$ (whose values are pointers to the subtrees of $node(p)$), and $k(p, 1)$ through $k(p, numtrees(p) - 1)$ (whose values are the keys contained in $node(p)$ in ascending order). The subtree to which $son(p, i)$ points (for i between 2 and $numtrees(p) - 1$ inclusive) contains all keys in the tree between $k(p, i - 1)$ and $k(p, i)$. $son(p, 1)$ points to a subtree containing only keys less than $k(p, 1)$, and $son(p, numtrees(p))$ points to a subtree containing only keys greater than $k(p, numtrees(p) - 1)$. We also assume a function $nodesearch(p, key)$ that returns either the smallest integer j such that $key \le k(p, j)$ or $numtrees(p)$ if key is greater than all the keys in $node(p)$. (We will discuss shortly how $nodesearch$ is implemented.) We present the following recursive algorithm for a function $search(tree, key)$ that returns a pointer to the node containing key (or ***nil*** if there is no such node in the tree) and sets the global variable $position$ to the position of key in that node:

```
p := tree
if p = nil
    then begin
            search := nil;
            position := 0
      end {then begin}
```

```
    else begin
        i := nodesearch (p, key);
        if key = k (p, i)
            then begin
                search := p;
                position := i
            end {then begin}
            else search := search (son (p, i), key)
    end {else begin}
```

The following is a nonrecursive version of the foregoing algorithm:

```
p := tree;
found := false;
while (p <> nil) and (not found)
    do begin {search the subtree rooted at p}
        i := nodesearch (p, key);
        if key = k (p, i)
            then found := true
            else p := son (p, i)
    end {while...do begin};
if found
    then begin {key equals k (p, i)}
        search := p;
        position := i
    end {then begin}
    else begin
        search := nil;
        position := 0
    end {else begin}
```

The function *nodesearch* is responsible for locating the smallest key in a node greater than or equal to the search argument. The simplest technique for doing this is a sequential search through the ordered set of keys in the node. If all keys are of the same length, a binary search can also be used to locate the appropriate key. The decision whether to use a sequential or binary search depends on the order of the tree, which determines how many keys must be searched. Another possibility is to organize the keys within the node as a binary search tree.

We should note that if a node is full and *key* is greater than all the keys in the node, *nodesearch* returns n, which is set as the value of i. The subsequent reference to $k(p, i)$ may cause an error if a node contains only $n - 1$ key fields. Thus in implementing the algorithms in Pascal, it is necessary either to add another test for $i = n$ before referencing $k(p, i)$ or to allow n key fields in each node.

Implementing a Multiway Tree

Note that we have implemented a multiway search tree of order n using nodes with up to n sons rather than as a binary tree with *son* and *brother* pointers, as outlined in Section 6.5 for general trees. The reason for this is that in multiway trees, unlike in general trees, there is a limit to the number of sons of a node, and we can expect most nodes to be as full as possible. In a general tree, there was no such limit, and many nodes might contain only one or two items. Therefore, the flexibility of allowing as many or as few items as necessary in a node was worth the overhead of extra brother pointers.

Nevertheless, when nodes are not full, multiway search trees as implemented here do waste considerable storage. Despite this possible waste of storage, multiway trees are frequently used, especially to store data on an external direct-access device, such as a disk. The reason for this is that accessing each new node during a search requires reading a block of storage from the external device. This read operation is relatively expensive in terms of time because of the mechanical work involved in positioning the device properly. However, once the device is positioned, the task of actually reading a large amount of sequential data is relatively fast. This means that the total time for reading a storage block (e.g., a "node") is only minimally affected by its size. Once a node has been read and is contained in internal computer memory, the cost of searching it at electronic internal speeds is minuscule compared to the cost of initially reading it into memory. In addition, external storage is fairly inexpensive so that a technique which improves time efficiency at the expense of external storage space utilization is real cost (e.g., dollars) effective. For this reason, external storage systems based on multiway search trees try to maximize the size of each node, and trees of order 200 or more are not uncommon.

The second factor to consider in implementing multiway search trees is storage of the data records themselves. As in any storage system, the records may be stored with the keys or remotely from the keys. The first technique requires keeping entire records within the tree nodes, while the second requires keeping a pointer to the associated record with each key in a node. (Still another technique involves duplicating keys and keeping records only at the leafs. This mechanism is discussed later in more detail when we discuss B^+-trees.)

In general, we would like to keep as many keys as possible in each node. To see why this is so, consider two top-down trees with 4000 keys and minimum depth, one of order 5 and the other of order 11. The order-5 tree requires 1000 nodes (of 4 keys each) to hold the 4000 keys, while the order-11 tree requires only 400 nodes (of 10 keys each). The depth of the order-5 tree is at least 5 (level 0 contains 1 node, level 1 contains 5, level 2 contains 25, level 3 contains 125, level 4 contains 625, and level 5 contains the remaining 219) while the depth of the order-11 tree can be as low as 3 (level 0 contains 1 node, level 1 contains 11, level 2 contains 121, and level 3 contains the remaining 267). Thus 5 or 6 nodes must be accessed in searching the order-5 tree for most of the keys, but only 3 or 4 nodes must be accessed for the order-11 tree. But as we noted, accessing a node is the most expensive operation in searching external storage where multiway trees are most used. Thus, a tree with a higher order leads to a more efficient search process. The actual storage required by both situations is approximately the same, since, although fewer large nodes are required to hold a file of a given size when the order is high, each node is larger.

Since the size of a node is usually fixed by other external factors (e.g., the amount of storage physically read from the disk in one operation), a higher-order tree is obtained by keeping the records outside the tree nodes. Even if this causes an extra external read to obtain a record after its key has been located, keeping records within a node typically reduces the order by a factor of between 5 and 40 (which is the typical range of the ratio of record size to key size) so the trade-off is not worthwhile.

If a multiway search tree is maintained in external storage, a pointer to a node is an external storage address which specifies the starting point of a storage block. The block of storage which makes up a node must be read into internal storage before any of the fields *numtrees*, *k*, or *son* can be accessed. Assume that the routine *directread*(*p*, *block*) reads a node at external storage address *p* into an internal storage buffer *block*. Assume also that the *numtrees*, *k*, and *son* fields in the buffer are accessed by the Pascal-like notations *block.numtrees*, *block.k*, and *block.son*. Assume also that the function *nodesearch* is modified to accept an (internal) storage block rather than a pointer (i.e., it is invoked by *nodesearch*(*block*, *key*) rather than by *nodesearch* (*p*, *key*)). Then the following is a nonrecursive algorithm for searching an externally stored multiway search tree:

```
p := tree;
found := false;
while (p <> nil) and (not found)
    do begin
            directread(p, block);
            i := nodesearch(block, key);
            if key = block.k(i)
                then found := true
                else p := block.son(i)
        end {while...do begin};
if found
    then begin
            search := p;
            position := i
```

$$else\ begin$$
$$search := nil;$$
$$position := 0$$
$$end\ \{else\ begin\}$$

The algorithm also sets *block* to the node at external address *p*. The record associated with *key* or a pointer to it may be found in *block*. Note that *nil* as used in this algorithm references a nil external storage address rather than the Pascal pointer *nil*. Again, in implementing this algorithm, it is necessary to have *n* key fields in a node or to avoid referencing *k(n)*.

Traversing a Multiway Tree

A common operation on a data structure is traversal—accessing all the elements of the structure in some fixed sequence. The following is a recursive algorithm *traverse(tree)* to traverse a multiway tree and print its keys in ascending order:

$$if\ tree <> nil$$
$$then\ begin$$
$$nt := numtrees(tree);$$
$$for\ i := 1\ to\ nt - 1$$
$$do\ begin$$
$$traverse(son(tree, i));$$
$$writeln(k(tree, i))$$
$$end\ \{for...do\ begin\};$$
$$traverse(son(tree, nt))$$
$$end\ \{then\ begin\}$$

In implementing the recursion, we must keep a stack of pointers to all the nodes in a path beginning with the root of the tree down to the node currently being visited.

If each node is a block of external storage and *tree* is the root node's external storage address, then a node must be read into internal memory before its *son* or *k* fields can be accessed. Thus the algorithm becomes

$$if\ tree <> nil$$
$$then\ begin$$
$$directread(tree, block);$$
$$nt := block.numtrees;$$
$$for\ i := 1\ to\ nt - 1$$
$$do\ begin$$
$$traverse(block.son(i));$$
$$writeln(block.k(i))$$
$$end\ \{for...do\ begin\}$$
$$traverse(block.son(nt))$$
$$end\ \{then\ begin\}$$

where *directread* is a system routine that reads a block of storage at a particular external address (*tree*) into an internal memory buffer (*block*). This requires keeping a stack of buffers as well. If d is the depth of the tree, then $d + 1$ buffers must be kept in memory.

Alternatively, all but one of the buffers can be eliminated if each node contains two additional fields: a *father* field pointing to its father and an *index* field indicating which son of its father the node is. Then, when the last subtree of a node has been traversed, the algorithm uses the *father* field of the node to access its father and its *index* field to determine which key in the father node to output and which subtree of the father to traverse next. However, this would require numerous reads for each node and is probably not worth the savings in buffer space, especially since a high-order tree with a very large number of keys requires very low depth. (As previously illustrated, a tree of order 11 with 4000 keys can be accommodated comfortably with depth 3. A tree of order 100 can accommodate over a million keys with a depth of only 2.)

Another common operation, closely related to traversal, is **direct sequential access**. This refers to accessing the key immediately following a key whose location in the tree is known. Let us assume that we have located a key $k1$ by searching the tree and that it is located at position $k(n1, i1)$. Ordinarily, the successor of $k1$ can be found by executing the following function *next*($n1, i1$) (*nilkey* is a special value indicating that a proper key cannot be found):

$$p := son(n1, i1 + 1);$$
$$q := nil; \ \{q \text{ is one node behind } p\}$$
while $p <> nil$
    do begin
        $q := p;$
        $p := son(p, 1)$
    end {while...do begin};
if $q <> nil$
    then $next := k(q, 1)$
    else if $i1 < numtrees(n1) - 1$
        then $next := k(n1, i1 + 1)$
        else $next := nilkey$

This algorithm relies on the fact that the successor of $k1$ is the first key in the subtree which follows $k1$ in *node*($n1$) or, if that subtree is empty [*son*($n1, i1 + 1$) equals *nil*] and if $k1$ is not the last key in its node [$i1 < numtrees(n1) - 1$], then the successor is the next key in *node*($n1$).

However, if $k1$ is the last key in its node and if the subtree following it is empty, then its successor can only be found by backing up the tree. Assuming *father* and *index* fields in each node as outlined, a complete algorithm *successor*($n1$, $i1$) to find the successor of the key in position $i1$ of the node pointed to by $n1$ may be written as follows:

```
p := son(n1, i1 + 1);
if (p <> nil) or (i1 < numtrees(n1) - 1)
    then successor := next(n1, i1) {use the previous algorithm}
    else begin
            f := father(n1);
            i := index(n1);
            while (i = numtrees(f)) and (f <> nil)
                do begin
                        i := index(f);
                        f := father(f)
                end {while...do begin};
        if f = nil
            then successor := nilkey
            else successor := k(f, i)
    end {else begin}
```

Of course, we would like to avoid backing up the tree whenever possible. Since a traversal beginning at a specific key is quite common, the initial search process is often modified to retain, in internal memory, all nodes in the path from the tree root to the located key. Then, if the tree must be backed up, the path to the root is readily available. As noted, if this is done, the fields *father* and *index* are not needed.

Later in this section we will examine a specialized adaptation of a multiway search tree, called a B^+-tree, that does not require a stack for efficient sequential traversal.

Insertion in a Multiway Search Tree

Now that we have examined how to search and traverse multiway search trees, let us examine insertion techniques for these structures. We examine two insertion techniques for multiway search trees. The first is analogous to binary search tree insertion and results in a top-down multiway search tree. The second technique is new and produces a special kind of balanced multiway search tree. It is this second technique, or a slight variation thereof, that is most commonly used in direct-access external file storage systems.

Both insertion procedures consist of three steps, the first two of which are the same under the two procedures. For convenience, we assume that duplicate keys are not permitted in the tree, so that, if the argument key is found in the tree, no insertion takes place. We also assume that the tree is nonempty. The first step in both insertion procedures is to search for the argument key. If the argument key is found in the tree, then *search* is set to point to the node containing the key, and *position* to its position within the node, just as in the search procedure just presented. However, if the argument key is not found, *search* is set to point to the semileaf which would contain the key if it were present, and *position* is set to the index of the smallest key in *node(search)* which is greater than the argument key (that is, the position of the argument key if it were in the tree). If all the keys in *node(search)* are less than the argument key, *position* is set to *numtrees(search)*. A boolean variable, *found*, is set to *true* or *false* depending on whether the argument key is or is not found in the tree. The header of a Pascal procedure *find* for this search step is the following:

> **procedure** find(tree: nodeptr; key: keytype; **var** search: nodeptr;
>
> **var** position: integer; **var** found: boolean);

Figure 8.3.2 illustrates the result of this procedure for an order-4 top-down balanced multiway search tree and several search arguments. The algorithm for *find* is straightforward:

```
q := nil;
p := tree;
found := false;
while (p <> nil) and (not found)
        do begin
                i := nodesearch(p, key);
                q := p;
                if key = k(p, i)
                    then found := true
                    else p := son(p, i)
            end {while...do begin};
if found
    then search := p  {the key is found in node(p)}
    else search := q;  {p is nil; q points to a semileaf}
position := i
```

In implementing this algorithm, it is important to avoid a reference to $k(p, n)$ if *nodesearch* returns n unless n key fields are maintained in each node.

The second step of the insertion procedure applies only if the key is not found (remember, no duplicate keys are permitted) and if *node(search)* is not full—that is, if *numtrees(search)* $< n$, where n is the order of the tree. In Figure 8.3.2, this applies to cases (d) and (f) only. The second step consists of inserting the new key (and record) into *node(search)*. Note that if the tree

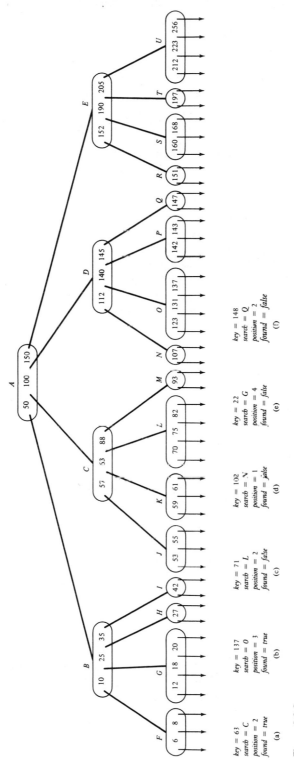

key = 63
search = C
position = 2
found = true

(a)

key = 137
search = O
position = 3
found = true

(b)

key = 71
search = L
position = 2
found = false

(c)

key = 102
search = N
position = 1
found = false

(d)

key = 22
search = G
position = 4
found = false

(e)

key = 148
search = Q
position = 2
found = false

(f)

Figure 8.3.2

is top-down or balanced, a nonfull semileaf discovered by *find* will always be a leaf. Let *insrec*(*p*, *i*, *rec*) be a routine to insert the record *rec* in position *i* of *node*(*p*) as appropriate. Then the second step of the insertion process may be performed as follows:

$$nt := numtrees\,(search);$$
$$numtrees\,(search) := nt + 1;$$
$$\textbf{for } i := nt \textbf{ downto } position + 1$$
$$\quad \textbf{do } k\,(search, i) := k\,(search, i - 1);$$
$$k\,(search, position) := key;$$
$$insrec\,(search, position, rec)$$

We call this procedure *insleaf* (*search*, *position*, *key*, *rec*).

Figure 8.3.3a illustrates the nodes located by the *find* procedure in Figures 8.3.2d and f with the new keys inserted. Note that it is unnecessary to copy the *son* pointers associated with the keys being moved since the node is a leaf so that all pointers are *nil*. We assume that they were initialized to *nil* when the node was initially added to the tree.

If step 2 is appropriate (that is, if a nonfull leaf node where the key can be inserted has been found), then both insertion procedures terminate. The two techniques differ only in the third step which is invoked when the *find* procedure locates a full semileaf.

The first insertion technique, which results in top-down multiway search trees, mimics the actions of the binary search tree insertion algorithm. That is, it allocates a new node, inserts the key and record into the new node, and places the new node as the appropriate son of *node*(*search*). It uses the function *maketree*(*key*, *rec*) to allocate a node and set the *n* pointers in it to *nil*, its *numtrees* field to 2, and its first key field to *key*. *maketree* then calls *insrec* to insert the record as appropriate and finally returns a pointer to the newly allocated node. Using *maketree*, the routine *insfull* to insert the key when the appropriate semileaf is full may be implemented trivially as

$$p := maketree\,(key, rec);$$
$$son\,(search, position) := p$$

If *father* and *index* fields are maintained in each node, the operations

$$father\,(p) := search;$$
$$index\,(p) := position$$

are required as well.

Figure 8.3.3b illustrates the result of inserting keys 71 and 22, respectively, into the nodes located by *find* in Figure 8.3.2c and e. Figure 8.3.3c illustrates subsequent insertions of keys 86, 77, 87, 84, 85, and 73 in that order. Note that the order in which keys are inserted very much affects where the keys are placed. For example, consider what would happen if the keys were inserted in the order 85, 77, 86, 87, 73, 84.

Figure 8.3.3

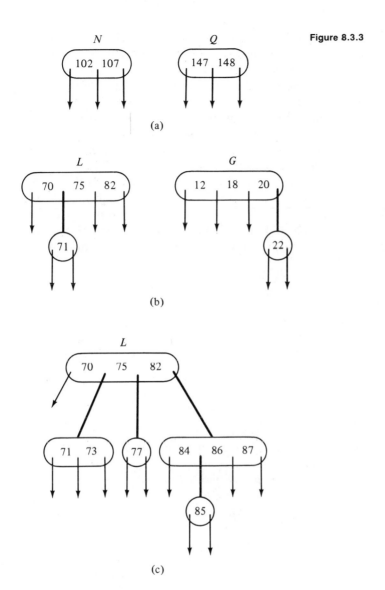

(a)

(b)

(c)

Note also that this insertion technique can transform a leaf into a nonleaf (although it remains a semileaf) and therefore unbalances the multiway tree. It is therefore possible for successive insertions to produce a tree which is heavily unbalanced and in which an inordinate number of nodes must be accessed to locate certain keys. In practical situations, however, multiway search trees created by this insertion technique, while not completely balanced, are not too greatly unbalanced so that too many nodes are not accessed in searching for a key in a leaf. However, the technique does have one major drawback. Since leafs are created containing only one key, and other leafs may be created before previously created leafs are filled, multiway trees created by successive insertions in this manner waste much space with leaf nodes that are nearly empty.

Although this insertion method does not guarantee balanced trees, it does guarantee top-down trees. To see this, note that a new node is not created unless its father is full. Thus any nonfull node has no descendants and is therefore a leaf, which by definition implies that the tree is top-down. The advantage of a top-down tree is that the upper nodes are full so that as many keys as possible are found on short paths.

Before examining the second insertion technique, we put all the pieces of the first technique together to form a complete search and insertion algorithm for top-down multiway search trees. (A cautionary note for Pascal implementors of this algorithm should be added. Do not name the procedure *search* since that would cause attempted recursive invocations at most references to the variable *search*.)

```
if tree = nil
   then begin
           tree := maketree(key, rec);
           search := tree;
           position := 1
        end {then begin}
   else begin
           find(tree, key, search, position, found);
           if not found
             then if numtrees(search) < n
                     then insleaf(search, position, key, rec)
                     else begin
                             p := maketree(key, rec);
                             son(search, position) := p;
                             search := p;
                             position := 1
                          end {else begin}
        end {else begin}
```

B-Trees

The second insertion technique for multiway search trees is more complex. Compensating for this complexity, however, is the fact that it creates balanced trees, so that the maximum number of nodes accessed to find any particular key is kept small. In addition, the technique yields one further bonus, in that all nodes (except for the root) in a tree created by this technique are at least half full, so that very little storage space is wasted. This last advantage is the primary reason that the second insertion technique (or a variation thereof) is used so frequently in actual file systems.

A balanced order-n multiway search tree in which each nonroot node contains at least n **div** 2 keys is called a ***B-tree of order n.*** A B-tree of order n is also called an n-($n - 1$) ***tree*** or an ($n - 1$)-n ***tree.*** (The dash outside the parentheses is a hypen while the dash inside the parentheses is a minus sign.) This reflects the fact that each node in the tree has a maximum of $n - 1$ keys and n sons. Thus, a 4-5 tree is a B-tree of order 5, as is a 5-4 tree. In particular, a **2-3** (or **3-2**) ***tree*** is the most elementary nontrivial (that is, nonbinary) B-tree, with one or two keys per node and two or three sons per node.

(At this point, we should say something about terminology. In discussing B-trees, the word "order" is used differently by different authors. It is common to find the ***order*** of a B-tree defined to mean the minimum number of keys in a nonroot node (i.e., n **div** 2) and the ***degree*** of a B-tree to mean the maximum number of sons (i.e., n). Still other authors use *order* to mean the maximum number of keys in a node (i.e., $n - 1$). We use *order* consistently for all multiway search trees to mean the maximum number of sons.)

The first two steps of the insertion technique are identical for B-trees as for top-down trees. First, use *find* to locate the leaf into which the key should be inserted, and, second, if the located leaf is not full, add the key using *insleaf*. It is in the third step, when the located leaf is found to be full, that the methods differ. Instead of creating a new node with only one key, split the full leaf in two: a left leaf and a right leaf. For simplicity, assume that n is odd. The n keys consisting of the $n - 1$ keys in the full leaf and the new key to be inserted are divided into three groups: the lowest n **div** 2 keys are placed into the left leaf, the highest n **div** 2 keys are placed into the right leaf, and the middle key (there must be a middle key since $2*(n$ **div** 2) equals $n - 1$ if n is odd) is placed into the father node if possible (that is, if the father node is not full). The two pointers on either side of the key inserted into the father are set to the newly created left and right leafs, respectively.

Figure 8.3.4 illustrates this process on a B-tree of order 5. Figure 8.3.4a shows a subtree of a B-tree, and Figure 8.3.4b shows part of the same subtree as it is altered by the insertion of 382. The leftmost leaf was already full so that the five keys 380, 382, 395, 406, and 412 are divided and 380 and 382 are placed in a new left leaf, 406 and 412 are placed in a new right leaf, and the middle key, 395, is advanced to the father node with pointers to the left and right leafs on either side. There is no problem placing 395 in the father node since it contained only two keys and has room for four. Figure 8.3.4c shows the same subtree with first 518 and then 508 inserted. (The same result would be achieved if they were inserted in reverse order.) 518 can be inserted directly in the rightmost leaf since there is room for one additional key. However, when 508 arrives, the leaf is already full. The five keys 493, 506, 508, 511, and 518 are divided so that the lower two (493

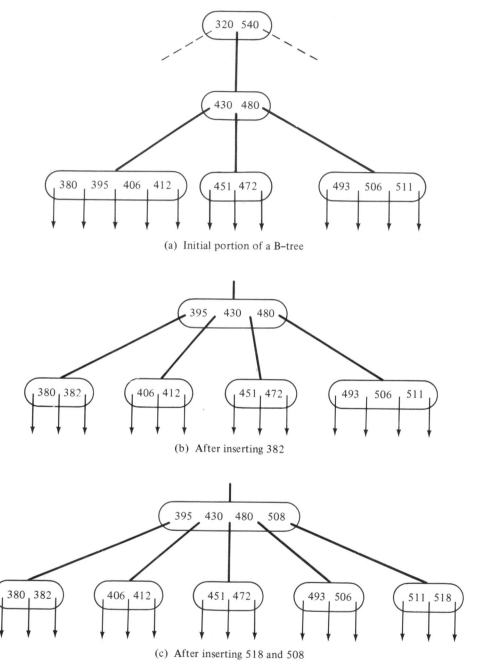

(a) Initial portion of a B–tree

(b) After inserting 382

(c) After inserting 518 and 508

Figure 8.3.4

and 506) are placed in a new left leaf, the higher two (511 and 518) are placed in a new right leaf, and the middle key (508) is advanced to the father which still has room to accommodate it. Note that the key advanced to the father is always the middle key, regardless of whether it arrived before or after the other keys.

If the order of the B-tree is even, then the $n - 1$ keys excluding the middle key must be divided into two unequal-sized groups: one of size n div 2 and the other of size $(n - 1)$ div 2. (The second group is always of size $(n - 1)$ div 2, regardless of whether n is odd or even, since when n is odd, $(n - 1)$ div 2 equals n div 2.) For example, if n equals 10, then 10 div 2 (or 5) keys are in one group, 9 div 2 (or 4) keys are in the other group, and 1 key is advanced, for a total of 10 keys. These may be divided so that the larger group is always in the left leaf or the right leaf, or divisions may be alternated so that on one split, the right leaf contains more keys and on the next split, the left leaf contains more keys. In practice, it makes little difference which technique is used.

Figure 8.3.5 illustrates both left and right biases in a B-tree of order 4. Note that whether a left or right bias is chosen determines which key is to be advanced to the father.

One basis on which the decision can be made as to whether to leave more keys in the left or right leaf is to examine the key ranges under both possibilities. In Figure 8.3.5b, utilizing a left bias, the key range of the left node is 87 to 102, or 15, and the key range of the right node is 102 to 140, or 38. In Figure 8.3.5c, utilizing a right bias, the key ranges are 13 (87 to 100) and 40 (100 to 140). Thus we would select a left bias in this example since it more nearly equalizes the probability of a new key going into the left and right, assuming a uniform distribution of keys.

The entire discussion thus far has assumed that there is room in the father for the middle key to be inserted. What if the father node, too, is full? For example, what happens with the insertion of Figure 8.3.2c, where 71 must be inserted into the full node L, and C, the father of L, is full as well? The solution is quite simple. The father node is also split in the same way, and its middle node is advanced to its father. This process continues until a key is inserted in a node with room or the root node, A, itself is split. When that happens, a new root node NR is created containing the key advanced from the splitting of A, and with the two halves of A as sons.

Figures 8.3.6 and 8.3.7 illustrate this process with the insertions of Figures 8.3.2c and e. In Figure 8.3.6a, node L is split. (We assume a left bias throughout this illustration.) The middle element (75) should be advanced to C, but C is full. Thus, in Figure 8.3.6b, we see C being split as well. The two halves of L are now made sons of the appropriate halves of C. 75, which had been advanced to C, must now be advanced to root node A which also has no room. Thus A itself must be split, as shown in Figure 8.3.6c. Finally, Figure 8.3.6d shows a new root node, NR, established containing the key advanced from A and two pointers to the two halves of A.

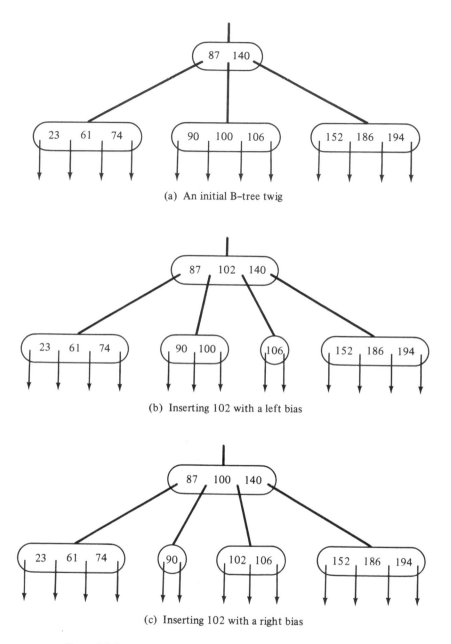

(a) An initial B-tree twig

(b) Inserting 102 with a left bias

(c) Inserting 102 with a right bias

Figure 8.3.5

Figure 8.3.7 illustrates the subsequent insertion of 22, as in Figure
8.3.2e. In that figure, 22 would have caused a split of nodes *G*, *B*, and *A*.
But, in the meantime, *A* has already been split by the insertion of 71, so
the insertion of 22 proceeds as in Figure 8.3.7. First *G* is split and 20 is

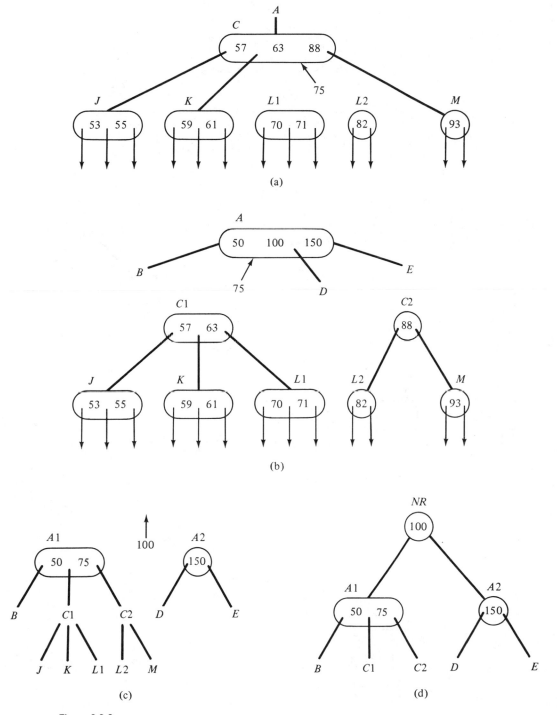

(a)

(b)

(c)

(d)

Figure 8.3.6

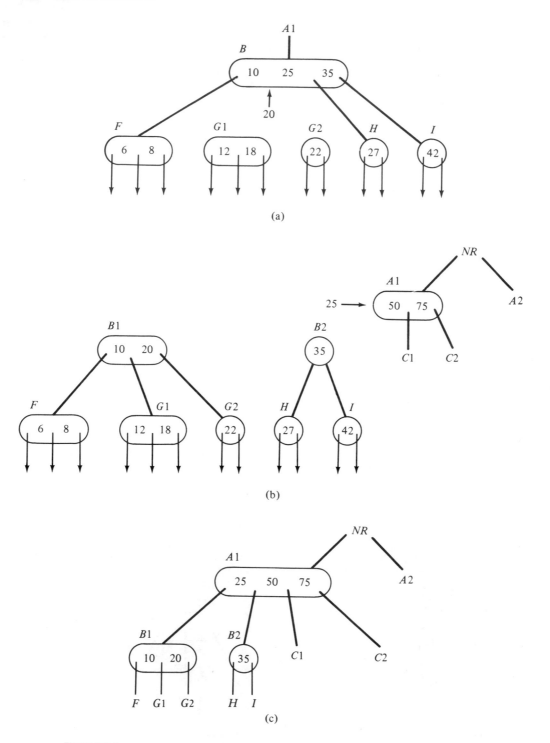

Figure 8.3.7

advanced to B (Figure 8.3.7a), which is split in turn (Figure 8.3.7b). 25 is then advanced to $A1$, which is the new father of B. But since $A1$ has room, no further splits are necessary. 25 is inserted into $A1$, and the insertion is complete (Figure 8.3.7c).

As a final illustration, Figure 8.3.8 shows the insertion of several keys into the order-5 B-tree of Figure 8.3.4c. It would be worthwhile for you to generate a list of keys and insert them continually into an order-5 B-tree to see how it develops.

Note that a B-tree grows in depth through the splitting of the root and the creation of a new root and in width by the splitting of nodes. Thus B-tree insertion into a balanced tree keeps the tree balanced. However, a B-tree is rarely top-down since when a full nonleaf node splits, the two nonleafs created are not full. Thus, while the maximum number of accesses to find a key is low (since the tree is balanced), the average number of such accesses may be higher than in a top-down tree in which the upper levels are always full. (In simulations, the average number of accesses in searching a random top-down tree has indeed been found to be slightly lower than in searching a random B-tree because random top-down trees are generally fairly balanced.) One other point to note in a B-tree is that older keys (those inserted first) tend to be closer to the root than do younger keys since the former have had more opportunity to be advanced. However, it is possible for a key to remain in a leaf forever even if a large number of locally lower and higher keys are subsequently inserted. This is unlike a top-down tree in which a key in an ancestor node must be older than any key in a descendant node.

Algorithms for B-Tree Insertion

As you might imagine, the algorithm for B-tree insertion is fairly involved. To simplify matters temporarily, let us assume that we can access a pointer to the father of $node(nd)$ by referring to $father(nd)$ and the position of the pointer nd in $node(father(nd))$ by $index(nd)$, so that $son(father(nd), index(nd))$ equals nd. (This can be implemented most directly by adding $father$ and $index$ fields to each node, but there are complications to such an approach that we discuss shortly.) We also assume that $r(p, i)$ is a pointer to the record associated with the key $k(p, i)$. Recall that the routine $find$ sets $search$ to point to the leaf in which the key should be inserted and $position$ to the position in $node(search)$ at which the key should be inserted. Recall also that key and rec are the argument key and record to be inserted.

The following is an outline of a routine $insert$ $(key, rec, search, position)$ to insert a record into a B-tree. It is called following a call to $find$, if the output parameter $found$ of that routine is $false$ (i.e., the key is not already in the tree). The routine uses two additional auxiliary routines which will be presented shortly. The first routine, $split$, accepts five input parameters: nd, a pointer to a node to be split; pos, the position in $node(nd)$ where a key and record are to be inserted; $newkey$ and $newrec$, the key and record being

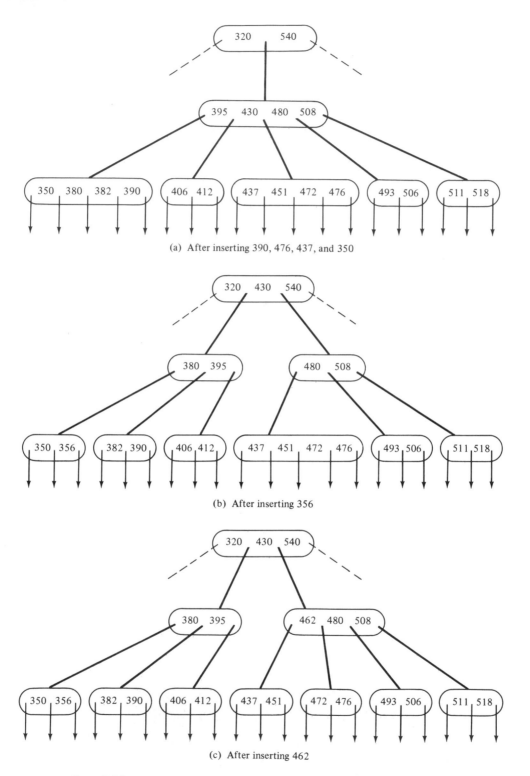

(a) After inserting 390, 476, 437, and 350

(b) After inserting 356

(c) After inserting 462

Figure 8.3.8

inserted (this key and record might be the ones being advanced from a previously split node, or they might be the new key and record being inserted into the tree); and *newnode*, a pointer to the subtree which contains the keys greater than *newkey* (that is, a pointer to the right half of a node previously split which must be inserted into the node currently being split. To maintain the proper number of sons within a node, each time that a new key and record are inserted into a node, a new son pointer must be inserted as well. When a new key and record are inserted into a leaf, the son pointer inserted is *nil*. Because a new key and record are inserted into one of the upper levels only when a node is split at a lower level, the new son pointer to be inserted will be the right half of the node that was split at the lower level. The left half remains intact within the previously allocated lower-level node). *split* arranges *newkey* and the keys of *node(nd)* so that the group of *n* **div** 2 smallest keys remain in *node(nd)*, the middle key and record are assigned to the output parameters *midkey* and *midrec*, and the remaining keys are inserted into a new node, *node(nd2)*, where *nd2* is also an output parameter.

The second routine used by *insert*, *insnode*, inserts key *newkey* and record *newrec* and the subtree pointed to by *newnode* into *node(nd)* at position *pos* if there is room. Recall that the function *maketree(key, rec)* creates a new node containing the single key *key* and record *rec* and all pointers *nil*. *maketree* returns a pointer to the newly created node. We present the algorithm for *insert*:

```
nd := search;
pos := position;
newnode := nil;  {pointer to right half of a split node}
newrec := rec;   {the record to be inserted}
newkey := key;   {the key to be inserted}
f := father(nd);
while (f <> nil) and (numtrees(nd) = n)
    do begin {node(nd) must be split}
            split(nd, pos, newkey, newrec, newnode,
                                    nd2, midkey, midrec);
            newnode := nd2;
            pos := index(nd);
            nd := f;
            f := father(nd);
            newkey := midkey;
            newrec := midrec
        end {while...do begin};
if numtrees(nd) < n
    then insnode(nd, pos, newkey, newrec, newnode)
    else begin { f equals nil and numtrees(nd) equals n so that }
              { nd is a full root; split it and create a new root }
            split(nd, pos, newkey, newrec, newnode,
                                    nd2, midkey, midrec);
            tree := maketree(midkey, midrec);
```

$son(tree, 1) := nd;$
$son(tree, 2) := nd2$
end {else begin}

    The heart of this algorithm is the routine *split* that actually splits a node. *split* itself uses an auxiliary routine *copy(nd1, first, last, nd2)* which sets a local variable *numkeys* to *last* − *first* + 1 and copies fields $k(nd1, first)$ through $k(nd1, last)$ into $k(nd2, 1)$ through $k(nd2, numkeys)$, fields $r(nd1, first)$ through $r(nd1, last)$ (which contains pointers to the actual records) into $r(nd2, 1)$ through $r(nd2, numkeys)$, and fields $son(nd1, first)$ through $son(nd1, last + 1)$ into $son(nd2, 1)$ through $son(nd2, numkeys + 1)$. *copy* also sets *numtrees(nd2)* to *numkeys* + 1. If *last* < *first*, *copy* sets *numtrees(nd2)* to 1 but does not change any k, r, or *son* fields. *split* also uses *getnode* to create a new node and *insnode* to insert a new key in a nonfull node.

    The following is an algorithm for *split*. The n keys contained in *node(nd)* and *newkey* must be distributed so that the smallest n *div* 2 remain in *node(nd)*, the highest $(n − 1)$ *div* 2 (which equals n *div* 2 if n is odd) are placed in a new node, *node(nd2)*, and the middle key is placed in *midkey*. To avoid recomputing n *div* 2 on each occasion, assume that its value has been assigned to the global variable *ndiv2*. The input value *pos* is the position in *node(nd)* in which *newkey* would be placed if there were room.

```
{ create a new node for the right half; }
{     keep the first half in node(nd)    }
nd2 := getnode;
if pos > ndiv2 + 1
   then begin { newkey belongs in node(nd2) }
              copy(nd, ndiv2 + 2, n − 1, nd2);
              insnode(nd2, pos − ndiv2 − 1, newkey, newrec, newnode);
              numtrees(nd) := ndiv2 + 1;
              midkey := k(nd, ndiv2 + 1);
              midrec := r(nd, ndiv2 + 1)
        end {then begin};
if pos = ndiv2 + 1
   then begin { newkey is the middle key }
              copy(nd, ndiv2 + 1, n − 1, nd2);
              numtrees(nd) := ndiv2 + 1;
              son(nd2, 1) := newnode;
              midkey := newkey;
              midrec := newrec
        end {then begin};
if pos < ndiv2 + 1
   then begin { newkey belongs in node(nd) }
              copy(nd, ndiv2 + 1, n − 1), nd2);
              numtrees(nd) := ndiv2;
```

$insnode(nd, pos, newkey, newrec, newnode);$
$midkey := k(nd, ndiv2);$
$midrec := r(nd, ndiv2)$
end {then begin}

The routine *insnode(nd, pos, newkey, newrec, newnode)* inserts a new record *newrec* with key *newkey* into position *pos* of a nonfull node, *node(nd)*. *newnode* points to a subtree to be inserted to the right of the new record. The remaining keys and subtrees in positions *pos* or greater are advanced one position. The value of *numtrees(nd)* is increased by one. An algorithm for *insnode* follows:

for $i := numtrees(nd)$ **downto** $pos + 1$
    do begin
        $son(nd, i + 1) := son(nd, i);$
        $k(nd, i) := k(nd, i - 1);$
        $r(nd, i) := r(nd, i - 1)$
    end {for...do begin}
$son(nd, pos + 1) := newnode;$
$k(nd, pos) := newkey;$
$r(nd, pos) := newrec;$
$numtrees(nd) := numtrees(nd) + 1$

Computing *father* and *index*

Before examining the efficiency of the insertion procedure, we must clear up one outstanding issue: the matter of the *father* and *index* functions. You may have noticed that, although these functions are utilized in the *insert* procedure and we suggested that they could be implemented most directly by adding *father* and *index* fields to each node, those fields are not updated by the insertion algorithm. Let us examine how this update could be achieved and why we chose to omit that operation. We then examine alternative methods of implementing the two functions that do not require the update.

father and *index* fields would have to be updated each time that *copy* or *insnode* were called. In the case of *copy*, both fields in each son whose pointer is copied must be modified. In the case of *insnode*, the *index* field of each son whose pointer is moved must be modified, as well as both fields in the son being inserted. (In addition, the fields must be updated in the two halves of a root node being split in the *insert* routine.) However, this would impact the efficiency of the insertion algorithm in an unacceptable manner, especially when dealing with nodes in external storage. In the entire B-tree search and insertion process (excluding the update of *father* and *index* fields), at most two nodes at each level of the tree are accessed. In most cases, when a split does not occur on a level, only one node at the level is accessed. The *copy* and *insnode* operations, although they move nodes from one subtree to another, do so by moving pointers within one or two father nodes and thus do not actually require access to the son nodes being moved. Requiring an update to *father* and *index* fields in those sons would require accessing and modifying all the son nodes themselves. But reading and writing a node from and to external storage are the most expensive operations in the entire B-tree management process. When one considers that, in a practical information storage system, a node can have several hundred sons, it becomes apparent that maintaining *father* and *index* fields could result in 100-fold decrease in system efficiency.

How then can we obtain the *father* and *index* data required for the insertion process without maintaining separate fields? First recall that the function *nodesearch(p, key)* returns the position of the smallest key in *node(p)* greater than or equal to *key*, so that *index(nd)* equals *nodesearch(father(nd), key)*. Therefore, once *father* is available, *index* can be obtained without a separate field.

To understand how we can obtain *father*, let us look at a related problem. No B-tree insertion can take place without a prior search to locate the leaf where the new key must be inserted. This search proceeds from the root and accesses one node at each level until it reaches the appropriate leaf. That is, it proceeds along a single path from the root to a leaf. The insertion then backs up along that same path, splitting all full nodes in a path from the leaf toward the root, until it reaches a nonfull node into which it can insert a key without splitting. Once that insertion is performed, the insertion process terminates.

The insertion process accesses the same nodes as the search process. Since we have seen that accessing a node from external storage is quite expensive, it would make sense for the search process to store the nodes on its path together with their external addresses in internal memory, where the insertion process can access them without an expensive second read operation. But once all the nodes in a path are stored in internal memory, a node's father can be located by simply examining the previous node in the path. Thus there is no need to maintain and update a *father* field.

Let us then present modified versions of *find* and *insert* to locate and insert a key in a B-tree. Let *pathnode(i)* be a copy of the *i*th node in the path from the root to a leaf, let *location(i)* be its location (either a pointer if the tree is in internal memory or an external storage address if it is in external storage), and let *index(i)* be the position of the node among the sons of its father (note that *index* can be determined during the search process and retained for use during insertion). We refer to *son(i, j)*, *k(i, j)*, and *r(i, j)* as the *j*th son, key, and record field, respectively, in *pathnode(i)*. Similarly, *numtrees(i)* is the *numtrees* field in *pathnode(i)*.

The following *find* algorithm utilizes the operation *access(i, loc)* to copy a node from location *loc* (either from internal or external memory) into *pathnode(i)* and *loc* itself into *location(i)*. If the tree is stored internally, this operation consists of

$$pathnode\,(i) := node\,(loc);$$
$$location\,(i) := loc$$

If the tree is stored externally, the operation consists of

$$directread\,(loc, pathnode\,(i));$$
$$location\,(i) := loc$$

where *directread* reads a block of storage at a particular external address (*loc*) into an internal memory buffer (*pathnode(i)*). We also assume that *nodesearch* (*i*, *key*) searches *pathnode(i)* rather than *node(i)*. We present the algorithm *find*:

```
q := nil;
p := tree;
j := 0;
i := 0;
found := false;
while (p <> nil) and (not found)
        do begin
                j := j + 1;
                index(j) := i;
                access(j, p);
                i := nodesearch(j, key);
                q := p;
                if key = k(j, i)
                    then found := true
                    else p := son(j, i)
            end {while...do begin};
    search := j; {key is in pathnode(j) or belongs there}
    position := i
```

Again, it is necessary to avoid referencing $k(j, n)$ if *nodesearch* returns n or to establish n key fields in each node.

The insertion process is modified in several places. First, *insnode* and *copy* access *pathnode(nd)* rather than *node(nd)*. That is, *nd* is now an array index rather than a pointer so that all references to k, *son*, r, and *numtrees* are to fields within an element of *pathnode*. The algorithms for *insnode* and *copy* do not have to be changed.

Second, *split* must be modified to write out the two halves of a split node. It assumes a routine *replace(i)* which replaces the node at *location(i)* with the contents of *pathnode(i)*. This routine is the reverse of *access*. If the tree is stored internally, it may be implemented by

$$node\,(location\,(i)) := pathnode\,(i)$$

and, if externally, by

$$directwrite\,(location\,(i),\ pathnode\,(i))$$

where *directwrite* writes a buffer in memory (*pathnode(i)*) into a block of external storage at a particular external address (*location(i)*). *split* also uses a function *makenode(i)* that obtains a new block of storage at location *x*, places *pathnode(i)* in that block, and returns *x*. The following is a revised version of *split*:

> *if pos* $>$ *ndiv2* + 1
>> *then begin*
>>> *copy(nd, ndiv2* + 2, *n* − 1, *nd* + 1);
>>> *insnode (nd* + 1, *pos* − *ndiv2* − 1, *newkey, newrec, newnode*);
>>> *numtrees (nd)* := *ndiv2* + 1;
>>> *midkey* := *k (nd, ndiv2* + 1);
>>> *midrec* := *r(nd, ndiv2* + 1)
>> *end* {then begin};
> *if pos* = *ndiv2* + 1
>> *then begin*
>>> *copy(nd, ndiv2* + 1, *n* − 1, *nd* + 1);
>>> *numtrees (nd)* := *ndiv2* + 1;
>>> *son(nd* + 1), 1) := *newnode*;
>>> *midkey* := *newkey*;
>>> *midrec* := *newrec*
>> *end* {then begin};
> *if pos* $<$ *ndiv2* + 1
>> *then begin*
>>> *copy (nd, ndiv2* + 1, *n* − 1, *nd* + 1);
>>> *numtrees (nd)* := *ndiv2*;
>>> *insnode (nd, pos, newkey, newrec, newnode*);
>>> *midkey* := *k (nd, ndiv2)*;
>>> *midrec* := *r(nd, ndiv2)*
>> *end* {then begin};
> *replace (nd)*;
> *nd2* := *makenode (nd* + 1);

Notice that *nd* is now a position in *pathnode* rather than a node pointer and that *pathnode(nd* + 1) rather than *node(nd2)* is used to build the second half of the split node. This can be done since the node at level *nd* + 1 (if any) of the path has already been updated by the time *split* is called on *nd*, so that *pathnode(nd* + 1) can be reused. *nd2* remains the actual location of the new node (allocated by *makenode*). (We should note that it may be desirable to retain a path to the newly inserted key in *pathnode*, as, for example, if we wish to perform a sequential traversal or sequential insertions beginning at that point. In that case, the algorithm must be suitably adjusted to place the appropriate left or right half of the split node at the appropriate position in *pathnode*. We could not then use *pathnode*(*i* + 1) to build the right half but must use an additional auxiliary internal memory node instead. We leave the details to the reader.)

The routine *insert* itself is also modified in that it uses *nd* − 1 rather than *father*(*nd*). It also calls upon *replace* and *makenode*. When the root must be split, *maketree* builds a new tree root node in internal storage. This node is placed in *pathnode*(1) (which is no longer needed since the old root node has been updated by *split*) and written out using *makenode*. The following is the revised algorithm for *insert*:

```
nd := search;
pos := position;
newnode := nil;
newrec := rec;
newkey := key;
while (nd <> 1) and (numtrees(nd) = n)
    do begin
            split(nd, pos, newkey, newrec, newnode, nd2, midkey, midrec);
            newnode := nd2;
            pos := index(nd);
            nd := nd - 1;
            newkey := midkey;
            newrec := midrec
        end {while...do begin};
if numtrees(nd) < n
    then begin
            insnode(nd, pos, newkey, newrec, newnode);
            replace(nd)
        end {then begin}
    else begin
            split(nd, pos, newkey, newrec, newnode, nd2, midkey, midrec);
            pathnode(1) := maketree(midkey, midrec);
            son(1, 1) := nd;
            son(1, 2) := nd2;
            tree := makenode(1)
        end {else begin}
```

Deletion in Multiway Search Trees

The simplest method for deleting a record from a multiway search tree is to retain the key in the tree but mark it in some way as representing a deleted record. This could be accomplished by setting the pointer to the record corresponding to the key to *nil* or by allocating an extra flag field for each key to indicate whether or not it has been deleted. The space which the record itself occupies can, of course, be reclaimed. In this way, the key remains in the tree as a guidepost to the subtrees but does not represent a record within the file.

The disadvantage of this approach is that the space occupied by the key itself is wasted, possibly leading to unnecessary nodes in the tree when a large number of records have been deleted. Extra "deleted" bits require still more space.

Of course, if a record with a deleted key is subsequently inserted, the space for the key can be recycled. In a nonleaf node, only the same key would be able to reuse the space since it is too difficult to determine dynamically that the newly inserted key is between the predecessor and successor of the deleted key. However, in a leaf node (or, in certain situations, in a semileaf), the deleted key's space can be reused by a neighboring key since it is relatively easy to determine proximity. Since a large portion of keys are in leafs or semileafs, if insertions and deletions occur with equal frequency (or if there are more insertions than deletions) and are uniformly distributed (that is, the deletions are not bunched together to reduce significantly the total number of keys in the tree temporarily), the space penalty is tolerable in exchange for the advantage of ease of deletion. There is also a small time penalty in subsequent searches since some keys will require more nodes to be examined than if the deleted key had never been inserted in the first place.

If we are unwilling to pay the space/search time penalty of simplified deletion, then there are more expensive deletion techniques which eliminate the penalty. In an unrestricted multiway search tree, a technique similar to deletion from a binary search tree can be employed:

1. If the key to be deleted has empty left or right subtree, simply delete the key and compact the node. If it was the only key in the node, free the node.
2. If the key to be deleted has nonempty left and right subtrees, find its successor key (which must have an empty left subtree); let the successor key take its place and compact the node which had contained that successor. If the successor was the only key in the node, free the node.

We leave the development of a detailed algorithm and program to the reader.

However, this procedure may result in a tree that does not satisfy the requirements for either a top-down tree or a B-tree, even if the initial tree did satisfy those requirements. In a top-down tree, if the key being deleted is from a semileaf that is not a leaf and the key has empty right and left subtrees, the semileaf will be left with fewer than $n - 1$ keys even though it is not a leaf. This violates the top-down requirement. In that case, it is necessary to choose a random nonempty subtree of the node and move the largest or smallest key from that subtree into the semileaf from which the key was deleted. This process must be repeated until the semileaf from which a key is taken is a leaf. This leaf can then be compacted or freed. In the worst case, this might require rewriting one node at each level of the tree.

In a strict B-tree, we must preserve the requirement that each node contains at least *n div* 2 keys. As noted, if a key is being deleted from a nonleaf node, its successor (which must be in a leaf) is moved to the deleted position and the deletion proceeds as if the successor were deleted from the leaf node. When a key (either the key to be deleted or its successor) is removed from a leaf node and the number of keys in the node drops below *n div* 2, remedial action must be taken. This situation is called an ***underflow***. When an underflow occurs, the simplest solution is to examine the leaf's younger or older brother. If the brother contains more than *n div* 2 keys, then the key *ks* in the father node which separates between the two brothers can be added to the underflow node and the last or first key of the brother (last if the brother is older; first if younger) added to the father in place of *ks*. Figure 8.3.9a illustrates this process on an order-5 B-tree. (We should note that once a brother is being accessed, we could distribute the keys evenly between the two brothers rather than simply shifting one key. For example, if the underflow node *n*1 contains 106 and 112, the separating key in the father *f* is 120, and the brother *n*2 contains 123, 128, 134, 139, 142, and 146 in an order-7 B-tree, we can rearrange them so that *n*1 contains 106, 112, 120, and 123; 128 moves up to *f* as the separator; and 134, 139, 142, and 146 remain in *n*2.)

If both brothers contain exactly *n div* 2 keys, no keys can be shifted. In that case, the underflow node and one of its brothers are ***concatenated***, or ***consolidated***, into a single node which also contains the separator key from their father. This is illustrated in Figure 8.3.9b, where we combine the underflow node with its younger brother.

Of course, it is possible that the father contained only *n div* 2 keys so that it also has no extra key to spare. In that case, it can borrow from its father and brother as in Figure 8.3.10a. In the worst case, when the father's brothers also have no spare keys, the father and its brother may also be consolidated and a key taken from the grandfather. This is illustrated in Figure 8.3.10b. Potentially, if all nonroot ancestors of a node and their brothers contain exactly *n div* 2 keys, a key will be taken from the root, as consolidations take place at each level from the leafs to the level just below the root. If the root had more than one key, this ends the process since the root of a B-tree need have only one key. If, however, the root contained only a single key, that key is used in the consolidation of the two nodes below the root, the root is freed, the consolidated node becomes the new root of the tree, and the depth of the B-tree is reduced. We leave to the reader the development of an actual algorithm for B-tree deletion from this description.

You should note, however, that it is foolish to form a consolidated node with *n* − 1 keys if a subsequent insertion will immediately split the node in two. In a B-tree of large order, it may make sense to leave an underflow node with fewer than *n div* 2 keys (even though this violates the formal B-tree requirements) so that future insertions can take place without splitting. Typically a minimum number, *min* less than *n div* 2, of keys is

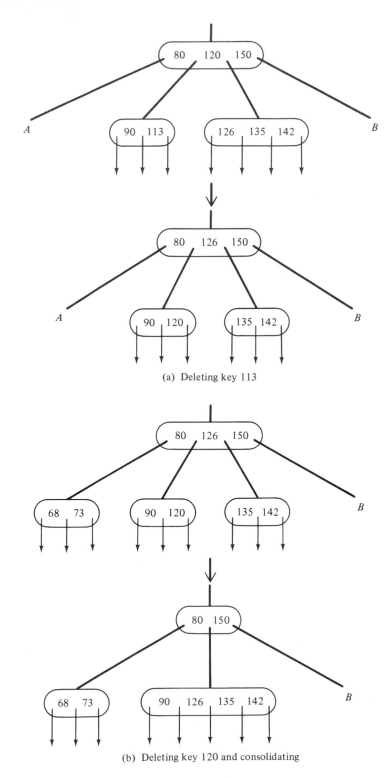

(a) Deleting key 113

(b) Deleting key 120 and consolidating

Figure 8.3.9

504

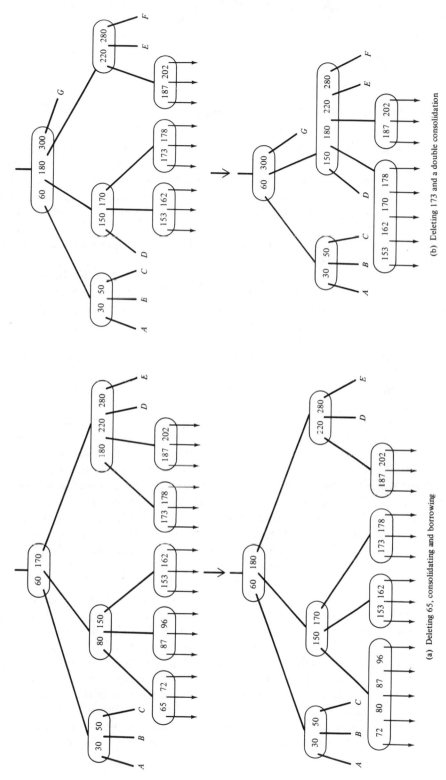

(a) Deleting 65, consolidating and borrowing

(b) Deleting 173 and a double consolidation

Figure 8.3.10

defined so that consolidation takes place only if fewer than *min* keys remain in a leaf node.

Efficiency of Multiway Search Trees

The primary considerations in evaluating the efficiency of multiway search trees, as for all data structures, are time and space. Time is measured by the number of nodes accessed or modified in an operation rather than by the number of key comparisons. The reason for this, as mentioned earlier, is that accessing a node usually involves reading from external storage and modifying a node involves writing to external storage. These operations are far more time consuming than are internal memory operations and therefore dominate the time required.

Similarly, space is measured by the number of nodes in the tree and the size of the nodes rather than by the number of keys actually contained in the nodes, since the same space is allocated for a node regardless of the number of keys it actually contains. Of course, if the records themselves are stored outside the tree nodes, the space requirements for the records will be determined by how the record storage is organized rather than by how the tree itself is organized. The storage requirements for the records generally overwhelm the requirements for the key tree so that the actual tree space may not be significant.

First, let us examine top-down multiway search trees. Assuming an order-*m* tree and *n* records, there are two extreme possibilities. In the worst case for search time, the tree is totally unbalanced. Every node except one is a semileaf with one son and contains $m - 1$ keys. The single leaf node contains $((n - 1) \bmod ((m - 1)) + 1$ keys. The tree contains $((n - 1) \mathbf{\textit{div}} (m - 1)) + 1$ nodes, one on each level. A search or an insertion accesses half that many nodes on the average and every node in the worst case. An insertion also requires writing one or two nodes (one if the key is inserted in the leaf, two if a new leaf must be created). A deletion always accesses every node and can modify as few as one node, but can potentially modify every node (unless a key can be simply marked as deleted).

In the best case for search time, the tree is almost balanced, each node except one contains $m - 1$ keys, and each nonleaf except one has m sons. There are still $((n - 1) \mathbf{\textit{div}} (m - 1)) + 1$ nodes, but there are fewer than $\log_m (n - 1) + 1$ levels. Thus the number of nodes accessed in a search, insertion, or deletion is less than this number. (In such a tree, more than half the keys are in a semileaf or leaf so that the average search time is not much better than the maximum.) Fortunately, as is the case for binary trees, fairly balanced trees occur far more frequently than do unbalanced trees, so that the average search time using multiway search trees is $O(\log n)$.

However, a general multiway tree, and even a top-down multiway tree, uses an inordinate amount of storage. To see why this is so, see Figure 8.3.11, which illustrates a typical top-down multiway search tree of order 11 with 100 keys. The tree is fairly balanced, and average search cost is approximately 2.19 (10 keys at level 0 require accessing one node, 61 at level 1 require accessing two nodes, and 29 at level 2 require accessing three nodes: (10 * 1 + 61 * 2 + 29 * 3)/100 = 2.19), which is reasonable. However, to accommodate the 100 keys, the tree uses 23 nodes or 4.35 keys per node, representing a space utilization of only 43.5%. The reason for this is that many leafs contain only one or two keys and the vast majority of the nodes are leafs. As the order and the number of keys increase, the utilization becomes worse, so that an order-11 tree with thousands of keys can expect 27% utilization and an order-21 tree can expect only 17% utilization. As the order grows even larger, the utilization drops toward zero. Since high orders are required to produce reasonable search costs for large numbers of keys, top-down multiway trees are an unreasonable alternative for data storage.

Every B-tree is balanced and each node contains at least $(m - 1)$ *div* 2 keys. Figure 8.3.12 illustrates the minimum and maximum number of nodes and keys at levels 0, 1, 2, and an arbitrary level i, as well as the minimum and maximum number of total nodes and keys in a B-tree of order m and maximum level d. In that figure, q equals $(m - 1)$ *div* 2. Note that the maximum level is one less than the number of levels (since the root is at level 0) so that $d + 1$ equals the maximum number of node accesses needed to find an element. From the minimum total number of keys in Figure 8.3.12, we can deduce that the maximum number of node accesses for one of n keys in an order m B-tree is $1 + \log_{q+1}(n/2)$. Thus, unlike top-down multiway trees, the maximum number of node accesses grows only logarithmically as the number of keys. Nevertheless, as we pointed out earlier, average search time is competitive between top-down multiway trees and B-trees since top-down trees are usually fairly balanced.

Insertion into a B-tree requires reading one node per level and writing one node at minimum plus two nodes for every split that occurs. If s splits occur, $2s + 1$ nodes are written (two halves of each split plus the father of the last node split). Deletion requires reading one node per level to find a leaf, writing one node if the deleted key is in a leaf and the deletion does not cause an underflow, and writing two nodes if the deleted key is in a nonleaf and removing the replacement key from a leaf does not cause that leaf to underflow. If an underflow does occur, one additional read (of the brother of each underflowed node) per underflow, one additional write for every consolidation except the last, and three additional writes for the final underflow if no consolidation is necessary (the underflow node, its brother and its father) or two additional writes if a consolidation is necessary (the consolidated node and its father) are required. All these operations are $O(\log n)$.

As is the case with a heap (Section 7.3) and a balanced binary tree

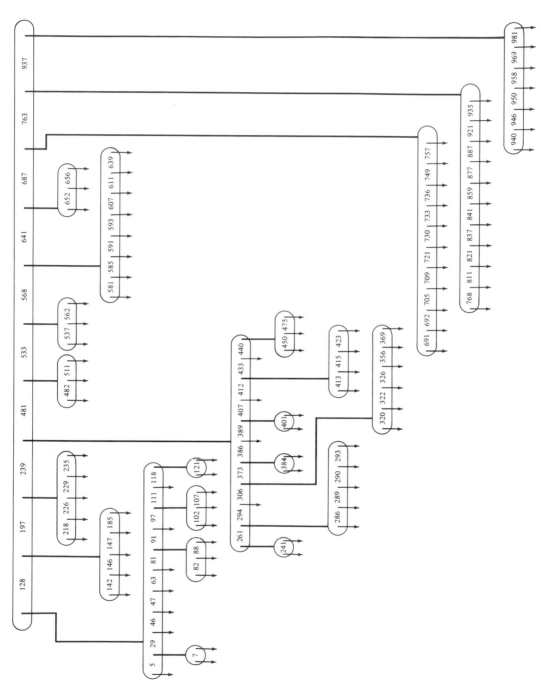

Figure 8.3.11

Level	Minimum		Maximum	
	Nodes	Keys	Nodes	Keys
0	1	1	1	$m-1$
1	2	$2q$	m	$(m-1)m$
2	$2(q+1)$	$2q(q+1)$	m^2	$(m-1)m^2$
I	$2(q+1)^{i-1}$	$2q(q+1)^{i-1}$	m^i	$(m-1)m^i$
Total	$1 + \dfrac{2(q+1)^d - 1)}{q}$	$2(q+1)^d$	$\dfrac{m^{d+1}-1}{m-1}$	$m^{d+1}-1$

Figure 8.3.12

(Section 8.2), insertion and deletion of the minimum or maximum element are both $O(\log n)$ in a B-tree, so the structure can be used to implement an (ascending or descending) priority queue efficiently. In fact a 3-2 tree (a B-tree of order 3) is probably the most efficient practical method for implementing a priority queue in internal memory.

Since each node in a B-tree (except the root) must be at least approximately half full, its worst-case storage utilization approaches 50%. In practice, average storage utilization in a B-tree approaches 69%. For example, Figure 8.3.13 illustrates a B-tree of order 11 with the same 100 keys as the multiway tree of Figure 8.3.11. Average search time is 2.88 (1 key requiring one node access, 10 keys requiring two accesses, and 89 keys requiring two accesses), which is greater than the corresponding multiway tree. Indeed, a fairly balanced top-down multiway tree will have lower search cost than will a B-tree, since all its upper nodes are always completely full. However, the B-tree contains only 15 nodes, yielding a storage utilization of 66.7%, far higher than the 43.5% utilization of the multiway tree.

Improving the B-Tree

There are a number of ways to improve the storage utilization of a B-tree. One method is to delay splitting a node when it overflows. Instead, the keys in the node and one of its adjacent brothers, as well as the key in the father which separates between the two nodes, are redistributed evenly. When both a node and its brother are full, the two nodes are split into 3. This guarantees a minimum storage utilization of almost 67%, and the storage utilization is higher in actual practice. Such a tree is called a **B*-tree**.

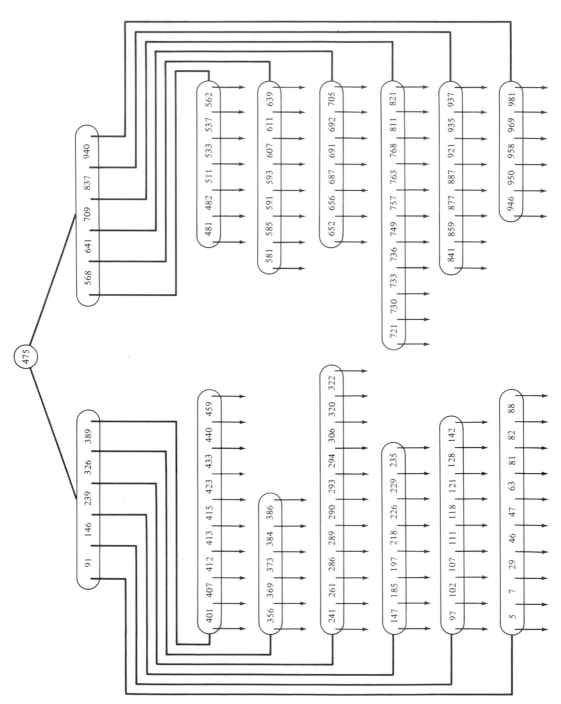

Figure 8.3.13

510

Indeed, this technique can be extended even farther by redistributing keys among all the brothers and the father of a full node. Unfortunately, this method exacts its own price since it requires expensive additional accesses upon overflow insertions while the marginal additional space utilization achieved by considering each extra brother becomes smaller and smaller.

Another technique is to use a *compact B-tree*. Such a B-tree has maximum storage utilization for a given order and number of keys. It can be shown that this maximum storage utilization for a B-tree of a given order and a given number of keys is attained when nodes toward the bottom of the tree contain as many keys as possible. Figure 8.3.14 illustrates a compact B-tree for the 100 keys of Figures 8.3.11 and 8.3.13. It can be shown that the average search cost for a compact B-tree is never more than one more than the minimum average search cost among all B-trees with the given order and number of keys. Thus, although a compact B-tree achieves a maximum storage utilization, it also achieves reasonable search cost. For example, the search cost for the tree of Figure 8.3.14 is only 1.91 (19 keys at level 1 and 91 at level 2: $9 * 1 + 91 * 2 = 191/100 = 1.91$), which is very close to optimal. Yet the tree uses only 11 nodes, for a storage utilization of 90.9%. With more keys, storage utilization in compact B-trees reaches 98% or even 99%.

Unfortunately, there is no efficient algorithm to insert a key into a compact B-tree and maintain compactness. Instead, insertion proceeds as in an ordinary B-tree and compactness is not retained. Periodically (for example, at night when the file is not used), a compact B-tree can be constructed from the noncompact tree. However, a compact B-tree degrades so rapidly with insertions that, for high orders, storage utilization drops below that of a random B-tree after fewer than 2% additional keys have been inserted. Also, the number of splits required for an insertion is higher on the average than is that for a random B-tree. Thus a compact B-tree should only be used when the set of keys is highly stable. Huang presents techniques for dynamically maintaining parameterized B-trees, which he calls *H-trees*, to balance storage, search, and update efficiencies. The reader is referred to the Bibliography for additional information.

A widely used technique for reducing both space and time requirements in a B-tree is to use various compression techniques on the keys. Since all keys in a given node are fairly close to each other, the initial bits of those keys are likely to be the same. Thus those initial bits can be stored once for the entire node (or they can be determined as part of the search process from the root of the tree by noticing that, if two adjacent keys in a node have the same prefix, then all keys in the subtree between the two keys also have the same prefix). In addition, all bits preceding the first bit that distinguishes a key from its preceding neighbor need not be retained (although an indication of its position must be). This is called *front compression*. A second technique, called *rear compression*, maintains only enough of the rear of the key to distinguish between a key and its successor.

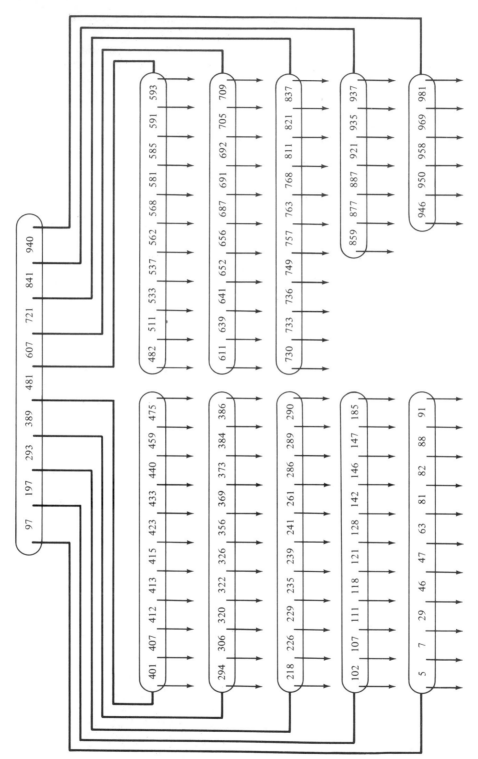

Figure 8.3.14

For example, if three keys are *anchor*, *andrew*, and *antoin*, *andrew* can be encoded as 2*d*, indicating that the first two characters are the same as its predecessor and that the next character, *d*, distinguishes among it and its predecessor and successor. If the sucessors of *andrew* within the node were *andule*, *antoin*, *append*, and *apples*, then *andrew* would be encoded as 2*d*, *andule* as 3*u*, *antoin* as simply 2, and *append* as 1*ppe*.

If rear compression is used, it is necessary to access the record itself to determine if a key is present in a file since the entire key cannot be reconstructed from the encoding. Also, under both methods, the key code that is retained is of variable length so that the maximum number of keys in a node is no longer fixed. Another disadvantage of variable-length key encoding is that binary search can no longer be used to locate a key in a node. In addition, the key code for some existing keys may have to be changed when a new key is inserted. The advantage of compression is that it enables more keys to be retained in a node so that the depth of the tree and the number of nodes required can be reduced.

B⁺-Trees

One of the major drawbacks of the B-tree is the difficulty of traversing the keys sequentially. A variation of the basic B-tree structure, the **B⁺-*tree***, retains the rapid random access property of the B-tree while also allowing rapid sequential access. In the B⁺-tree, all keys are maintained in leafs, and keys are replicated in nonleaf nodes to define paths for locating individual records. The leafs are linked together to provide a sequential path for traversing the keys in the tree.

Figure 8.3.15 illustrates a B⁺-tree. To locate the record associated with key 53 (random access), the key is first compared with 98 (the first key in the root). Since it is less, proceed to node *B*. 53 is then compared with 36 and then 53 in node *B*. Since it is less than or equal to 53, proceed to node *E*.

Note that the search does not halt when the key is found (as is the case in a B-tree). In a B-tree, a pointer to the record corresponding to a key is contained with each key in the tree, whether in a leaf or a nonleaf node. Thus once the key is found, the record can be accessed. In a B⁺-tree, pointers to records are only associated with keys in leaf nodes, so the search is not complete until the key is located in a leaf. Therefore, when equality is obtained in a nonleaf, the search continues. In node *E* (a leaf), key 53 is located, and from it, the record associated with that key. If we now wish to traverse the keys in the tree sequentially beginning with key 53, we need only follow the pointers in the leaf nodes.

The linked list of leafs is called a ***sequence set***. In actual implementations, the nodes of the sequence set frequently do not contain all the keys in the file. Rather, each sequence set node serves as an index to a large data area where a large number of records are kept. A search involves traversing

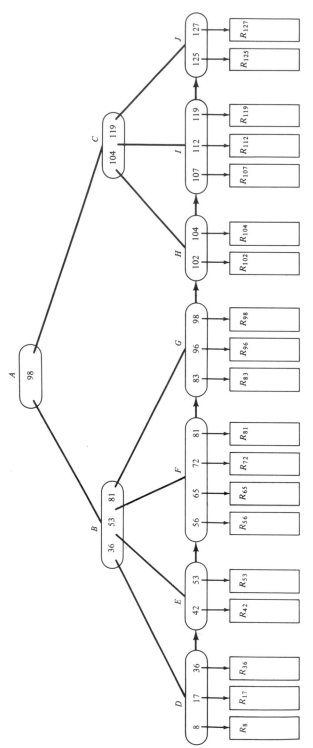

Figure 8.3.15

a path in the B^+-tree, reading a block from the data area associated with the leaf node that is finally accessed, and then searching the block sequentially for the required record.

The B^+-tree may be considered to be a natural extension of the indexed sequential file of Section 1. Each level of the tree is an index to the succeeding level, and the lowest level, the sequence set, is an index to the file itself.

Insertion into a B^+-tree proceeds much like in a B-tree except that when a node is split, the middle key is retained in the left half-node as well as being promoted to the father. When a key is deleted from a leaf, it can be retained in the nonleafs since it is still a valid separator between the keys in the nodes below.

The B^+-tree retains the search and insertion efficiencies of the B-tree but increases the efficiency of finding the next record in the tree from $O(\log n)$ (in a B-tree where finding the successor involves climbing up or down the tree) to $O(1)$ (in a B^+-tree where it involves accessing one additional leaf at most). An additional advantage of the B^+-tree is that no record pointers need be kept in the nonleaf nodes, which increases the potential order of the tree.

Digital Search Trees

Another method of using trees to expedite searching is to form a general tree based on the symbols of which the keys are comprised. For example, if the keys are integers, each digit position determines 1 of 10 possible sons of a given node. A forest representing one such set of keys is illustrated in Figure 8.3.16. If the keys consist of alphabetic characters, each letter of the alphabet determines a branch in the tree. Note that every leaf node contains the special symbol *eok*, which represents the end of a key. Such a leaf node must also contain a pointer to the record that is being stored.

If a forest is represented by a binary tree, as in Section 6.5, each node of the binary tree contains three fields: *symbol*, which contains a symbol of the key; *son*, which is a pointer to the node's oldest son in the original tree; and *brother*, which is a pointer to the node's next younger brother in the original tree. The first tree in the forest is pointed to by an external pointer *tree*, and the roots of the other trees in the forest are linked together in a linear list by the *brother* field. The *son* field of a leaf in the original forest points to a record; the concatenation of all the *symbols* in the path of nodes from root to the leaf is the key of the record. We make two further stipulations that speed up the search and insertion process for such a tree: each list of brothers is arranged in the binary tree in ascending order of the *symbol* field, and the symbol *eok* is considered to be larger than any other.

Using this binary tree representation, we may present an algorithm to search and insert into such a nonempty ***digital tree.*** As usual, *key* is the

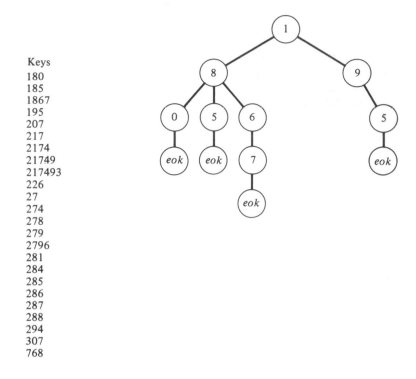

Keys
180
185
1867
195
207
217
2174
21749
217493
226
27
274
278
279
2796
281
284
285
286
287
288
294
307
768

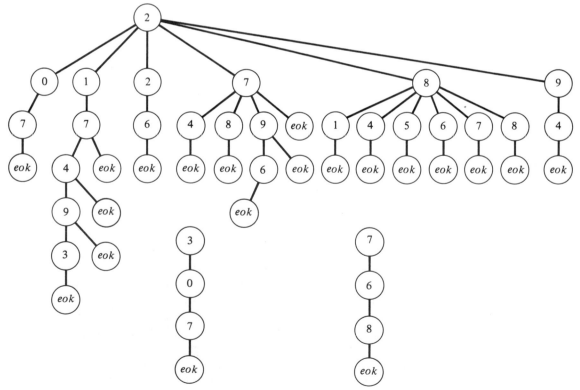

Figure 8.3.16 A forest representing a table of keys.

516

key for which we are searching, and *rec* is the record that we wish to insert if *key* is not found. We also let *key(i)* be the *i*th symbol of the key. If the key has *n* symbols, we assume that *key(n* + 1) equals *eok*. The algorithm uses the *getnode* operation to allocate a new tree node when necessary. We assume that *recptr* is a pointer to the record *rec* to be inserted. The algorithm sets *search* to the pointer to the record that is being sought and uses an auxiliary function *insert*, whose algorithm is also given.

```
p: = tree;
father: = nil;   { father is the father of p }
found: = false;
i: = 1;
while not found
      do begin   { search for the ith symbol in the key }
            q: = nil;   { q points to the older brother of p }
            past: = false;
            while (p <> nil) and (not past)
                  do if symbol(p) > = key(i)
                        then past: = true
                        else begin
                                    q: = p;
                                    p: = brother(p)
                              end {else begin};
            found: = true;
            if(p = nil) or (symbol(p) > key(i))
               then search: = insert   { insert the record }
               else if key(i) = eok
                        then search: = son(p) {found the record}
                        else begin {continue searching for}
                                    {   the next symbol   }
                                    father: = p;
                                    p: = son(p);
                                    found: = false;
                                    i: = i + 1
                              end {else begin}
      end {while...do begin}
```

The algorithm for *insert* is as follows:

```
{ insert the ith symbol of the key }
s: = getnode;
symbol(s): = key(i);
brother(s): = p;
if tree = nil
   then tree: = s
   else if q <> nil
            then brother(q): = s
```

```
                          else if father = nil
                              then tree:= s
                              else son(father):= s;
                     { insert the remaining symbols of the key }
                     j: = i;
                     while key(j) <> eok
                         do begin
                                 father:= s;
                                 s:= getnode;
                                 symbol(s):= key(j + 1);
                                 son(father):= s;
                                 brother(s):= nil;
                                 j:= j + 1
                             end {while...do begin};
                 son(s):= recptr;
                 insert:= recptr
```

Note that by keeping the table of keys as a general tree, we need search only a small list of sons to find whether a given symbol appears at a given position within the keys of the table. However, it is possible to make the tree even smaller by eliminating those nodes from which only a single leaf can be reached. For example, in the keys of Figure 8.3.16, once the symbol '7' is recognized, the only key that can possibly match is 768. Similarly, upon recognizing the two symbols '1' and '9', the only matching key is 195. Thus the forest of Figure 8.3.16 can be abbreviated to the one of Figure 8.3.17. In that figure, a box indicates a key, and a circle indicates a tree node. A dashed line is used to indicate a pointer from a tree node to a key.

There are some significant differences between the trees of Figures 8.3.16 and 8.3.17. In Figure 8.3.16, a path from a root to a leaf represents an entire key; thus there is no need to repeat the key itself. In Figure 8.3.17, however, a key may be recognized only by its first few symbols. In those cases where the search is made for a key that is known to be in the table, then upon finding a leaf the record corresponding to that key can be accessed. If, however, as is more likely, it is not known whether the key is present in the table, it must be confirmed that the key is indeed correct. Thus the entire key must be kept in the record as well. Furthermore, a leaf node in the tree of Figure 8.3.16 can be recognized because its contents are *eok*. Thus its *son* pointer can be used to point to the record which that leaf represents. However, a leaf node of Figure 8.3.17 may contain any symbol. Thus to use the *son* pointer of a leaf to point to the record, an extra boolean field is required in each node to indicate whether or not the node is a leaf. We leave the representation of the forest of Figure 8.3.17 and the implementation of a search-and-insert algorithm for it as an exercise for the reader.

The binary tree representation of a digital search tree is efficient when

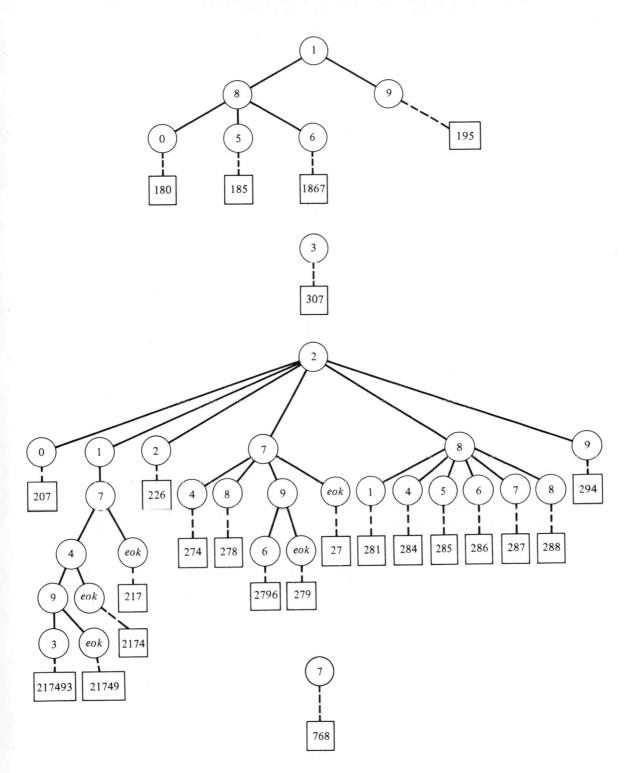

Figure 8.3.17 A condensed forest representing a table of keys.

each node has relatively few sons. For example, in Figure 8.3.17 only one node has as many as 6 (out of a possible 10) sons, whereas most nodes have only 1, 2, or 3 sons. Thus the process of searching through the list of sons to match the next symbol in the key is relatively efficient. However, if the set of keys is dense within the set of all possible keys (i.e., if almost any possible combination of symbols actually appears as a key), most nodes will have a large number of sons, and the cost of the search process becomes prohibitive.

Tries

A digital search tree need not be implemented as a binary tree. Instead, each node in the tree can contain m pointers, corresponding to the m possible symbols in each position of the key. Thus, if the keys were numeric, there would be 10 pointers in a node, and, if strictly alphabetic, there would be 26. (There might also be an extra pointer corresponding to *eok* or a flag with each pointer indicating that it pointed to a record rather than to a tree node.) A pointer in a node is associated with a particular symbol value based on its position in the node; that is, the first pointer corresponds to the lowest symbol value, the second pointer to the second lowest, and so on. It is therefore unnecessary to keep the symbol values themselves in the tree. The number of nodes that must be accessed to find a particular key is $\log_m n$. A digital search tree implemented in this way is called a *trie* (from the word re*trie*val).

A trie is useful when the set of keys is dense so that most of the pointers in each node are used. When the key set is sparse, a trie wastes a large amount of space with large nodes which are mostly empty. If the set of keys in a trie is known in advance and does not change, there are a number of techniques for minimizing the space requirements. One technique is to establish a different order in which the symbols of a key are used for searching (so that, for example, the third symbol of the argument key might be used to access the appropriate pointer in the trie root, the first symbol in level 1 nodes, etc.). Another technique is to allow trie nodes to overlap each other so that occupied pointers of one node overlay empty pointers of another.

EXERCISES

1. Show how a B-tree and a B^+-tree can be used to implement a priority queue (see Section 3.3 and 7.3). Show that any sequence of n insertion and minimum-deletion operations can be performed in $O(n \log n)$ steps. Write Pascal routines to insert and delete from a priority queue implemented by a 2-3 tree.

2. Choose any large paragraph from a book. Insert each word of the paragraph, in order, into an initially empty top-down multiway search tree of order 5, omitting any duplicates. Do the same for a B-tree of order 5, a B^+-tree of order 5, and a digital search tree. For each of these trees, determine the total number of nodes and the level of the tree.

3. Write Pascal routines to implement the B-tree successor and insertion operations if the B-tree is maintained

    (a) in internal memory.

    (b) in external direct-access storage.

4. Write an algorithm and a Pascal routine to delete a record from a top-down multiway search tree of order n.

5. Write an algorithm and a Pascal routine to delete a record from a B-tree of order n.

6. Write an algorithm to create a compact B-tree from input in sorted order. Use the algorithm to write a Pascal routine to produce a compact B-tree from an ordinary B-tree.

7. Write an algorithm and a Pascal routine to search in a B^+-tree.

8. Write an algorithm and a Pascal routine to

    (a) insert into a B^+-tree.

    (b) insert into a B^*-tree.

    (c) delete from a B^+-tree.

    (d) delete from a B^*-tree.

9. How many different 2-3 trees containing the integers 1 through 10 can you construct? How many permutations of these integers result in each tree if they are inserted into an initially empty tree in permutation order?

10. Develop algorithms to search and insert into a B-tree that uses front and rear compression.

11. Write a search and insert algorithm and Pascal routine for the digital search forest of Figure 8.3.17.

12. Show how to implement a trie in external storage. Write a Pascal search and insert routine for a trie.

4. HASHING

In the preceding two sections we assumed that the record being sought is stored in a table and that it is necessary to pass through some number of keys before finding the desired one. The organization of the file (sequential, indexed sequential, binary tree, etc.) and the order in which the keys are inserted affect the number of keys that must be inspected before obtaining the desired one. Obviously, the efficient search techniques are those that minimize the number of these comparisons. Optimally, we would like to have a table organization in which there are no unnecessary comparisons. Let us see if such a table organization is feasible.

    If each key is to be retrieved in a single access, the location of the record within the table can depend only upon the key; it may not depend upon the locations of other keys as in a tree. The most efficient way to organize such a table is as an array (i.e., each record is stored at a specific offset from the base address of the table). If the record keys are integers, the keys themselves can serve as indices to the array.

    Let us consider an example of such a system. Suppose that a manufacturing company has an inventory file consisting of 100 parts, each part having a unique two-digit part number. Then the obvious way to store this file is to declare an array

$$\textbf{var } part: \textbf{array}[0..99] \textbf{ of } parttype;$$

where *part[i]* represents the record whose part number is *i*. In this situation, the part numbers are keys which are used as indices to the array. Even if the company stocks fewer than 100 parts, the same structure can be used to maintain the inventory file (provided that the keys are still two-digit integers). Although many locations in *part* may correspond to nonexistent keys, this waste is offset by the advantage of direct access to each of the existent parts.

Unfortunately, however, such a system is not always practical. For example, suppose that the company has an inventory file of more than 100 items and that the key to each record is a seven-digit part number. To employ direct indexing using the entire seven-digit key, an array of 10 million elements would be required. This clearly wastes an unacceptably large amount of space because it is extremely unlikely that a company stocks more than a few thousand parts.

What is necessary is some method of converting a key into an integer within a limited range. Ideally, no two keys should be converted into the same integer. Unfortunately, such an ideal method usually does not exist. Let us attempt to develop methods that come close to the ideal and determine what action to take when the ideal is not achieved.

Let us reconsider the examples of a company with an inventory file in which each record is keyed by a seven-digit part number. Suppose that the company has fewer than 1000 parts and that there is only a single record for each part. Then an array of 1000 elements is sufficient to contain the entire file. The array is indexed by an integer between 0 and 999 inclusive. The last three digits of the part number are used as the index for the part's record in the array. This is illustrated in Figure 8.4.1. Note that two keys which are relatively close to each other numerically, such as 4618396 and 4618996, may be farther from each other in the table than two keys that are widely separated numerically, such as 0000991 and 9846995. This is because only the last three digits of the key are used in determining the position of a record.

A function that transforms a key into a table index is called a *hash function*. If *h* is a hash function and *key* is a key, then *h(key)* is called the *hash* of *key* and is the index at which a record with key *key* should be placed. If *r* is a record whose key hashes into *hr*, then *hr* is called the *hash key* of *r*. The hash function in this example is $h(k) = key \bmod 1000$. The values that *h* produces should cover the entire set of indices in the table. For example, the function $x \bmod 1000$ can produce any integer between 0 and 999, depending upon the value of *x*. As we shall see shortly, it is a good idea for the table size to be somewhat larger than the number of records

Position	key	record
0	4967000	
1		
2	8421002	
3		
⋮	⋮	
395		
396	4618396	
397	4957397	
398		
399	1286399	
400		
401		
⋮	⋮	
990	0000990	
991	0000991	
992	1200992	
993	0047993	
994		
995	9846995	
996	4618996	
997	4967997	
998		
999	0001999	

Figure 8.4.1

that are to be inserted. This is illustrated in Figure 8.4.1, where several positions in the table are unused.

The foregoing method has one flaw. Suppose that two keys $k1$ and $k2$ are such that $b(k1) = b(k2)$. Then when a record with key $k1$ is entered into the table, it is inserted at position $b(k1)$. But when $k2$ is hashed, because its hash key is the same as that of $k2$, an attempt may be made to insert the record into the same position where the record with key $k1$ is stored. Clearly, two records cannot occupy the same position. Such a situation is called a *bash collision* or a *bash clash*. A hash clash occurs in the inventory example of Figure 8.4.1 if a record with key 0596397 is added to the table. There are two basic methods of dealing with a hash clash. We will explore both in detail in the remainder of this section. Briefly, the first technique, called *rebashing*, involves using a secondary hash function, called a *rebash function*, on the hash key of the item. When the hash position of the item is found to be occupied by a different item during a search, the rehash function is used to locate the item. This rehash function is applied successively until an empty position is found where the item can be inserted. The second technique, called *chaining*, builds a linked list of all items whose keys hash to the same value. During search, this short linked list is traversed sequentially for the desired key. This technique involves adding an extra link field to each table position.

However, it should be noted that a good hash function is one that minimizes collisions and spreads the records uniformly throughout the table. That is why it is desirable to have the array size larger than the number of actual records. The larger the range of the hash function, the less likely it is that two keys yield the same hash value. Of course, this involves a space/ time trade-off. Leaving empty spaces in the array is inefficient in terms of space, but it reduces the necessity of resolving hash clashes and is therefore more efficient in terms of time.

Although hashing allows direct access to a table and may therefore be preferable to other techniques when searching for a specific key, the method has one limitation. Items in a hash table are not stored sequentially by key, nor is there any generally practical method for traversing the items in key sequence. *Order-preserving hash functions*, in which $h(key1) > h(key2)$ whenever $key1 > key2$, are usually nonuniform; that is, they do not minimize hash collisions and so do not serve the basic purpose of hashing—rapid access to any record directly from its key.

Resolving Hash Clashes by Open Addressing

Let us consider what would happen if it were desired to enter a new part number 0596397 into the table of Figure 8.4.1. Using the hash function *key mod* 1000, we find that $h(0596397) = 397$ and that the record for that part belongs in position 397 of the array. However, position 397 is already occupied because the record with key 4957397 is in that position. Therefore, the record with key 0596397 must be inserted elsewhere in the table.

The simplest method of resolving hash clashes is to place the record in the next available position in the array. In Figure 8.4.1, for example, since position 397 is already occupied, the record with key 0596397 may be placed in location 398, which is still open. Once that record has been inserted, another record, which hashes to either 397 (such as 8764397) or 398 (such as 2194398), is inserted at the next available position, which is 400.

This technique is called *linear probing* and is an example of a general method for resolving hash clashes called *rehashing* or *open addressing*. In general, a *rehash function*, *rh*, accepts one array index and produces another. If array location $h(key)$ is already occupied by a record with a different key, *rh* is applied to the value of $h(key)$ to find another location where the record may be placed. If position $rh(h(key))$ is also occupied, it, too, is rehashed to see if $rh(rh(h(key)))$ is available. This process continues until an empty location is found. Thus we may write a search and insertion function using hashing as follows. We assume the following declarations:

```
const maxtable = ...;  {one less than the table size}
type keytype = ...;    {      type of a key       }
     rectype = ...;    {      type of a record    }
     entry = record
               k: keytype;
               r: rectype
             end;
     index = 0..maxtable;
var table: array [index] of entry;
```

We also assume a hash function h(key: *keytype*): *index* and a rehash function rh(i: *index*): *index*. The special value *nilkey* is used to indicate an empty record.

```
function search (key: keytype; rec: rectype): index;
var i: index;
begin
    i: = h (key);  { hash the key }
    while (table [i] .k <> key) and (table [i] .k <> nilkey)
        do i: = rh (i);  { rehash }
    if table [i] .k = nilkey
        then begin {insert the record into the empty position}
                 table [i] .k: = key;
                 table [i] .r: = rec
             end   { then begin };
    search: = i
end   { function search };
```

In the example of Figure 8.4.1, $h(key)$ is the function *key mod* 1000, and $rh(i)$ is the function $(i + 1)$ *mod* 1000 (i.e., the rehash of any index is the next sequential position in the array, except that the rehash of 999 is 0).

Let us examine the algorithm more closely to see if we can determine the properties of a "good" rehash function. In particular, we focus our attention on the loop, because the number of iterations determines the efficiency of the search. The loop can be exited in one of two ways: either i is set to a value such that $table[i].k$ equals *key* (in which case the record is found) or i is set to a value such that $table[i].k$ equals *nilkey* (in which case an empty position is found and the record may be inserted).

It may happen, however, that the loop executes forever. There are two possible reasons for this. First, the table may be full, so that it is impossible to insert any new records. This situation can be detected by keeping a count of the number of records in the table. When the count is equal to the table size, no additional insertions are attempted.

However, it is possible for the algorithm to loop indefinitely even if there are some (or even many) empty positions. Suppose, for example, that the function $rh(i) = (i + 2)$ *mod* 1000 is used as a rehash function. Then any key that hashes into an odd integer rehashes into successive odd integers, and any key that hashes into an even integer rehashes into successive even integers. Consider the situation in which all the odd positions of the table are occupied and all the even ones are empty. Despite the fact that half the positions of the array are empty, it is impossible to insert a new record whose key hashes into an odd integer. Of course, it is unlikely that all the odd positions are occupied while none of the even positions are. However, if the rehash function $rh(i) = (i + 200)$ *mod* 1000 is used, each key can be placed in only one of five places [since x *mod* $1000 = (x + 1000)$ *mod* 1000], and it is quite possible for these five positions to be full while much of the table is empty.

One property of a good rehash function is that for any index i, the successive rehashes $rh(i)$, $rh(rh(i))$, . . . cover as many of the integers between 0 and *maxtable* as possible (ideally, all of them). The rehash function $rh(i) = (i + 1)$ *mod* 1000 has this property. In fact, any function $rh(i) = (i + c)$ *mod* m, where m is the number of elements in the table (note that $m = maxtable + 1$) and c is a constant value such that c and m are relatively prime (i.e., they cannot both be divided evenly by a single integer other than 1), produces successive values which cover the entire table. You are invited to confirm this fact by choosing some examples; the proof is left as an exercise. In general, however, there is no reason to choose a value of c other than 1. If the hash table is stored in external storage, it is desirable to have successive references as close to each other as possible (this minimizes seek delay on disks and may eliminate an I/O if the two references are on the same page).

There is another measure of the suitability of a rehash function. Consider the case of the linear rehash. Assuming that the hash function produces indices which are uniformly distributed over the interval 0 through *maxtable* (i.e., it is equally likely that $h(key)$ is any particular integer in that range), then initially, when the entire array is empty, it is equally likely that a random record will be placed at any given (empty) position within the array. However, once entries have been inserted and several hash clashes have been resolved, this is no longer true. For example, in Figure 8.4.1 it is five times as likely for a record to be inserted at position 994 than at position 401. This is because any record whose key hashes into 990, 991, 992, 993, or 994 will be placed in 994, while only a record whose key hashes into 401 will be placed in that location. This phenomenon, where two keys that hash into different values compete with each other in successive rehashes, is called *primary clustering*.

The same phenomenon occurs in the case of the rehash function $rh(i) = (i + c)$ *mod* (*maxtable* + 1). For example, if *maxtable* = 999, $c = 21$, and positions 10, 31, 52, 73, and 94 are all occupied, any record whose key is any one of these five integers will be placed at location 115. In fact, any rehash function that depends solely upon the index to be rehashed causes primary clustering.

One way of eliminating primary clustering is to allow the rehash function to depend on the number of times that the function is applied to a particular hash value. In this approach, the function rh is a function of two arguments. $rh(i, j)$ yields the rehash of the integer i if the key is being rehashed for the jth time. One example is $rh(i, j) = (i + j) \bmod (maxtable + 1)$. The first rehash yields $rh1 = rh(h(key), 1) = (h(key) + 1) \bmod (maxtable + 1)$, the second yields $rh2 = (rh1 + 2) \bmod (maxtable + 1)$, the third yields $rh3 = (rh2 + 3) \bmod (maxtable + 1)$, and so on.

Another approach is to use a random permutation of the numbers between 1 and *maxtable*, $p_1, p_2, \ldots, p$, and to let the jth rehash of $h(key)$ be $(h(key) + p_1) \bmod (maxtable + 1)$. This has the advantage of ensuring that no two rehashes of the same key conflict. Still a third approach is to let the jth rehash of $h(key)$ be $(h(key) + sqr(j)) \bmod (maxtable + 1)$. This is called the **quadratic rehash**. Yet another method of eliminating primary clustering is to allow the rehash to depend on the hash value, as in $rh(i, key) = (i + hkey) \bmod (maxtable + 1)$ where $hkey = 1 + h(key) \bmod maxtable$. (We cannot use $hkey$ equal to $h(key)$, which might be 0, or to $h(key) + 1$, which might be $maxtable + 1$. Either of these cases would result in $rh(i, key)$ equaling i, which is unacceptable.) All these methods allow keys that hash into different locations to follow separate rehash paths.

However, while these methods eliminate primary clustering, they do not eliminate the phenomenon known as **secondary clustering**, in which different keys which hash to the same value follow the same rehash path. One way to eliminate all clustering is to use **double hashing**, which involves the use of two hash functions, $h1(key)$ and $h2(key)$. $h1$, which is known as the **primary** hash function, is first used to determine the position at which the record should be placed. If that position is occupied, the rehash function $rh(i, key) = (i + h2(key)) \bmod (maxtable + 1)$ is used successively until an empty location is found. As long as $h2(key1)$ does not equal $h2(key2)$, records with keys $key1$ and $key2$ do not compete for the same set of locations. This is true despite the possibility that $h1(key1)$ may indeed equal $h1(key2)$. The rehash function depends not only on the index to be rehashed but also on the original key. Note that the value $h2(key)$ does not have to be recomputed for each rehash—it need be computed only once for each key that must be rehashed. Optimally, one should choose functions $h1$ and $h2$ which distribute the hashes and rehashes uniformly over the interval 0 to *maxtable* and also minimize clustering. Such functions are not always easy to find.

Examples of double hashing functions are $h1(key) = key \bmod (maxtable + 1)$ and $h2(key) = 1 + key \bmod (maxtable - 1)$, where *maxtable* + 1 is a prime number. Another example is $h1(key)$ as above and $h2(key) = 1 + (key \ div \ (maxtable + 1)) \bmod (maxtable - 1)$.

Deleting Items from a Hash Table

Unfortunately, it is difficult to delete items from a hash table which uses rehashing for search and insertion. For example, suppose that record $r1$

is at position p. To add a record $r2$ whose key $k2$ hashes into p, it must be inserted into the first free position from among $rh(p)$, $rh(rh(p))$, ... Suppose that $r1$ is then deleted, so that position p becomes empty. A subsequent search for record $r2$ begins at position $h(k2)$, which is p. But since that position is now empty, the search process may erroneously conclude that record $r2$ is absent from the table.

One possible solution to this problem is to mark a deleted record as "deleted" rather than as "empty" and to continue searching whenever a "deleted" position is encountered in the course of a search. But this is possible only if the number of deletions is small; otherwise, an unsuccessful search would require a search through the entire table because most positions will be marked "deleted" rather than "empty." Ideally, we would prefer a deletion mechanism in which retrieval time is the same whenever n records are in the table, regardless of whether the n records are a result of n insertions, or w insertions and $w - n$ subsequent deletions. Later in this section, we examine alternatives to rehashing which allow us to accomplish this.

Efficiency of Rehashing Methods

The efficiency of a hashing method is usually measured by the average number of table positions that must be examined in searching for a particular item. This is called the number of **probes** required by the method. Note that in the algorithms we have presented, the number of key comparisons equals twice the number of probes since the key at each probe position is compared to both the search argument and *nilkey*. However, the comparison to *nilkey* may be less expensive than the general key comparison. An additional bit can also be used in each table position to indicate whether it is empty to avoid an extra key comparison.

Under rehashing, the average number of probes depends on both the hash function and the rehash method. The hash function is assumed to be **uniform**. That is, it is assumed that an arbitrary key is equally likely to hash into any table index as any other. Mathematical analysis of the average number of probes required to find an element in a hash table if the table had been constructed using a particular hash and rehash method can be quite involved. Let n be the number of items currently in the hash table, and let m be the number of positions in the table ($m = maxtable + 1$). Then for large m, it has been proved that the average number of probes required for a successful retrieval in a table organized using linear rehashing is approximately $(2m - n + 1)/(2m - 2n + 2)$. If we set $x = (n - 1)/m$, this equals $(2 - x)/(2 - 2x)$. Define the **load factor** of a hash table, lf, as n/m, the fraction of the table which is occupied. Since lf is approximately equal to x for large m, we may approximate the number of probes for a successful search under linear rehashing by $(2 - lf)/(2 - 2 * lf)$ or $.5/(1 - lf) + .5$. When lf approximates 1 (that is, when the table is almost full), this formula is not useful. Instead, the average number of key comparisons for a successful search may be approximated by $sqrt(\pi\ m/8)\ +\ .33$.

For an unsuccessful search, the average number of probes in a table organized using linear rehashing is approximately equal to $.5/(1\ -\ lf)^2\ +\ .5$ for large m. When the table is full (that is, when $n\ =\ m\ -\ 1$, since one position must be left open to detect that the key is not present), the average number of probes for an unsuccessful comparison under linear rehashing is $(m\ +\ 1)/2$, which is the same as the average number of comparisons required to find a single empty slot among m slots by sequential search.

For tables with low load factors, this performance is not unreasonable, but for high load factors, it can be improved considerably. Eliminating primary clustering by setting $rh(i,\ key)$ to $(i\ +\ hkey)\ \textbf{\textit{mod}}\ m$ or by using quadratic rehashing sets the average number of probes to approximately $1\ -\ ln(1\ -\ lf)\ -\ lf/2$ for successful retrievals and $1/(1\ -\ lf)\ -\ lf\ -\ ln(1\ -\ lf)$ for unsuccessful searches. For full tables, successful search time approximates $ln(m\ +\ 1)$ and unsuccessful search time remains at $(m\ +\ 1)/2$.

Double hashing improves efficiency even further by eliminating both primary and secondary clustering. Let us define **uniform hashing** as any hashing scheme in which any newly inserted element is equally likely to be placed at any of the empty positions of the hash table. For such a theoretical scheme, it can be proved that successful search time is approximately $-ln(1\ -\ lf)/lf$ for large m and that unsuccessful searching requires $(m\ +\ 1)/(m\ +\ 1\ -\ n)$, or approximately $1/(1\ -\ lf)$, probes for large m. Experience with good double hashing functions shows that the average number of comparisons equal these theoretical values. For full tables, successful search time is approximately $ln(m\ +\ 1)\ -\ .5$ and unsuccessful search time is again $(m\ +\ 1)/2$.

The following table lists approximate number of probes for each of the three methods for various load factors. Recall that these approximations are generally valid only for large table sizes.

LOAD FACTOR	SUCCESSFUL			UNSUCCESSFUL		
	LINEAR	$i + hkey$	DOUBLE	LINEAR	$i+hkey$	DOUBLE
25%	1.17	1.16	1.15	1.39	1.37	1.33
50%	1.50	1.44	1.39	2.50	2.19	2.00
75%	2.50	2.01	1.85	8.50	4.64	4.00
90%	5.50	2.85	2.56	50.50	11.40	10.00
95%	10.50	3.52	3.15	200.50	22.04	20.00

For full tables (in the successful case, where $n\ =\ m$; in the unsuccessful case, where $n\ =\ m\ -\ 1$), the following are some approximations of the average number of probes. We have also included the value of $\log_2 m$ for comparison with binary search and tree searching.

TABLE SIZE(m)	SUCCESSFUL			UNSUCCESSFUL	LOG$_2$ m
	LINEAR	$i+hkey$	DOUBLE		
100	6.60	4.62	4.12	50.50	6.64
500	14.35	6.22	5.72	250.50	8.97
1000	20.15	6.91	6.41	500.50	9.97
5000	44.64	8.52	8.02	2500.50	12.29
10000	63.00	9.21	8.71	5000.50	13.29

These data indicate that linear rehashing should be strongly avoided for tables that will become more than 75% full, especially if unsuccessful searches are common, since primary clustering does have a significant effect on search time for large load factors. The effects of secondary clustering, however, never add more than .5 probes to the average number required. Given the fact that double hashing requires an expensive additional computation to determine $h2(key)$, it may be preferable to accept the extra half probe and use $rh(i, key) = (i + hkey) \bmod (maxtable + 1)$.

One technique that can be used to improve the performance of linear rehashing is *split sequence linear rehashing*. Under this technique, when $h(key)$ is found to be occupied, we compare *key* with the key *kh* located in position $h(key)$. If $kh < h(key)$, then the rehash function $i + c1$ is used; if $kh > h(key)$, then another rehash function $i + c2$ is used. This splits the rehashes from a particular slot into two separate sequences and reduces clustering without requiring additional space or reordering the hash table. For tables with a load factor of 95%, the split sequence technique reduces the number of probes in a successful search by more than 50% and the number of probes in an unsuccessful search by more than 80%! However, nonlinear rehash methods were still better. A similar technique yields some, but not significant, improvement for the nonlinear rehash methods.

Another point to note regarding efficiency is that, in the context of rehashing, the *mod* function should not be obtained by using the system *mod* operator which involves division, but rather by a comparison and possibly a subtraction. Thus $rh(i, key) = (i + hkey) \bmod (maxtable + 1)$ should be computed as follows, assuming that m holds the value $maxtable + 1$

```
x:= i + hkey;
if x < m
    then rh:= x
    else rh:= x - m
```

The foregoing tables also indicate the great expense of an unsuccessful search in a nearly full table. Insertion also requires the same number of comparisons as unsuccessful search. When the table is nearly full, the insertion efficiency of hashing approaches that of sequential search and is far worse than tree insertion.

Hash Table Reordering

When a hash table is nearly full, many items in the table are not at the locations given by their hash keys. Many key comparisons must be made before finding some items. If an item is not in the table, then an entire list of rehash positions must be examined before that fact is determined. There are several techniques for remedying this situation.

In the first technique, discovered by Amble and Knuth, the set of items that hash into the same location are maintained in descending order of the key. (We assume that *nilkey* is less than any key possibly occupying the table.) When searching for an item, it is not necessary to rehash repeatedly until an empty slot is found; as soon as an item in the table whose key is less than the search key is found, we know that the search key is not in the table. When inserting a key *key*, if a rehash accesses a key smaller than *key*, *key* and its associated record replace the smaller key in the table and the insertion process continues with the displaced key. A hash table organized in this way is called an ***ordered hash table***. The following is a search and insertion function for an ordered hash table.

```
function search(key: keytype; rec: rectype): index;
var i, j: index;
    newentry, tempentry: entry;
    tk: keytype;
    finished, first: boolean;
begin
    i:= h(key);
    newentry.k:= key;
    newentry.r:= rec;
    finished:= false;
    first:= true;
    while not finished
        do begin
            while (table[i].k > newentry.k)
                do i:= rh(i);
            tk := table[i].k;
            if (tk <> nilkey) and (tk <> newentry.k)
                then begin {insert newentry and }
                           {displace the entry   }
                           {    at position i     }
                    tempentry:= table[i];
```

```
                                      table[i]:= newentry;
                                      newentry:= tempentry;
                                      if first
                                         then begin
                                                    j:= i;
                                                    first:= false
                                                 end {then begin}
                                end { then begin }
                             else begin
                                      if tk = nilkey
                                         then table[i]:= newentry;
                                      finished:= true;
                                      if first
                                         then j:= i
                                 end { else begin }
                       end { while not finished do begin };
              search:= j
    end { function search };
```

The ordered hash table method can be used with any rehashing technique in which a rehash depends only on the index and the key; it cannot be used with a rehash function that depends on the number of times the item is rehashed (unless that number is kept in the table).

Using an ordered hash table does not change the average number of key comparisons required to find a key that is in the table, but it reduces significantly the number of key comparisons necessary to determine that a key does not exist in the table. It can be shown that unsuccessful search in an ordered hash table requires the same average number of probes as does successful search (in an ordered or unordered table). This is a significant improvement. Unfortunately, however, the average number of probes for insertion is not reduced in an ordered hash table and equals the number required for an unsuccessful search in an unordered table. Ordered hash table insertions also require a significant number of hash table modifications.

Brent's Method

A different reordering scheme, due to Brent, can be used to improve the average search time for successful retrievals when double hashing is used. The technique involves rehashing the search argument until an empty slot is found. Then each of the keys in the rehash path is itself rehashed to determine if placing one of those keys in an empty slot would require fewer rehashes. (Recall that, under double hashing, the rehash paths for two keys that rehash to the same slot will diverge.) If this is the case, then the search argument replaces the existing key in the table, and the existing key is inserted in its empty rehash slot. The following is a routine to implement Brent's search and insertion algorithm. It uses auxiliary routines *setempty*, which initializes a queue of table indexes to empty, *insert*, which inserts an index onto a queue, *remove*, which returns an index removed from a queue, and *freequeue*, which frees all nodes of a queue.

```
function search(key: keytype; rec: rectype): index;
var qq: queue; { of table indexes }
    i, j, jj, minoldpos, minnewpos: index;
    count, mincount, rehashcount, displacecount: integer;
    displacekey: keytype;
begin
    setempty(qq);
    {      rehash repeatedly, placing each successive index     }
    {      in the queue and keeping a count of the number       }
    {                 of rehashes required                      }
    count:= 0;
    i:= h1(key);
    while (table[i].k <> key) and (table[i].k <> nilkey)
        do begin
            insert(qq, i);
            i:= rh(i, key);
            count:= count + 1
        end { while...do begin };
    {  minoldpos and minnewpos hold the initial and final   }
    {   indexes of the key on the rehash path of key that   }
    {    can be displaced with a minimum of rehashing.       }
    {    Initially, assume no displacement and set them      }
    {          both to i, the first empty index for key.     }
    minoldpos:= i;
    minnewpos:= i;
    {  mincount is the minimum number of rehashes of key    }
    {     plus rehashes of the displaced key, displacekey.   }
    {     rehashcount is the number of rehashes of key       }
    {        needed to reach the index of the key being      }
    {        displaced. Initially, assume no displacement.    }
    mincount:= count;
    rehashcount:= 0;
    {  The following loop determines if displacement of      }
    {      the key at the next rehash of key will yield a    }
    {   lower total number of rehashes. If key was found     }
    {             in the table, then skip the loop.          }
```

```
            if table[i].k = nilkey
              then while (not empty(qq)) and (rehashcount + 1 < mincount)
                    do begin
                        j:= remove(qq);
                        displacekey:= table[j].k;  {the candidate key}
                                                    {for displacement }
                        jj:= rh(j, displacekey);
                        {displacecount is the number of rehashes}
                        {    required to displace displacekey      }
                        displacecount:= 1;
                        while table[jj].k <> nilkey
                            do begin
                                jj:= rh(jj, displacekey);
                                displacecount:= displacecount + 1
                              end { while...do begin };
                        if rehashcount + displacecount < mincount
                            then begin
                                mincount:= rehashcount + displacecount;
                                minoldpos:= j;
                                minnewpos:= jj
                              end { then begin };
                        rehashcount:= rehashcount + 1
                      end { then while...do begin };
            { free any extra items on the queue }
            freequeue(qq);
            {      At this point, if no displacement is necessary      }
            {      minoldpos equals minnewpos. minoldpos is the        }
            {   position where key was found or should be inserted.    }
            { minnewpos (if not equal to minoldpos) is the position    }
            {    where the key displaced from minoldpos should be      }
            {                         placed.                          }
            if minoldpos <> minnewpos
              then table[minnewpos]:= table[minoldpos];
            if (minoldpos <> minnewpos) or (table[minoldpos].k = nilkey)
              then begin
                    table[minoldpos].k:= key;
                    table[minoldpos].r:= rec
                  end { then begin };
            search:= minoldpos
          end { function search };
```

Brent's method has been found to reduce the average number of comparisons for successful retrievals but to have no effect on the number of comparisons for unsuccessful searches. Also, the effort required to insert a new item is increased substantially. An extension of Brent's method that yields even greater improvements in retrieval times at the expense of correspondingly greater insertion time involves recursive insertion of items displaced in the table. That is, in determining the minimum number of rehashes required to displace an item on a rehash path, all the items on that item's subsequent rehash path are considered for displacement as well, and so on. However, the recursion cannot be allowed to proceed to its natural conclusion since insertion time would become so large as to become impractical, even though insertion is infrequent. A maximum recursion depth of 4, plus an additional modification by which tentative rehash paths longer than 5 are penalized excessively, has been found to yield average retrievals very close to optimal with reasonable efficiency.

The following table shows the average number of probes required for retrieval and insertion under the unmodified Brent algorithm. The last column shows the number of retrievals per item required to make Brent's algorithm worthwhile (that is, so the cumulative advantage on retrievals outweighs the disadvantage on insertion compared to using an ordered hash table).

LOAD FACTOR	PROBES/ RETRIEVAL	PROBES/ INSERTION	BREAK-EVEN NO. RETRIEVALS/ITEM
20%	1.10	1.15	2.85
60%	1.37	1.92	2.48
80%	1.60	2.97	2.32
90%	1.80	4.27	2.26
95%	1.97	5.84	2.26

As the table becomes full, approximately 2.5 probes per retrieval are required on the average, regardless of the table size. This compares very favorably with ordinary double hashing in which retrieval from a full table requires $O(\log n)$ probes.

Binary Tree Hashing

Another method of improving Brent's algorithm is due to Gonnet and Munro and is called *binary tree hashing*. Again, we assume the use of double hashing. When a key is to be inserted into the table, an almost complete binary tree is constructed. Figure 8.4.2 illustrates such a tree, in which the nodes are numbered according to the array representation of an almost complete binary tree, as outlined in Section 6.2 (that is, *node*(1) is the root, and *node*($2 * i$) and *node*($2 * i + 1$) are the left and right sons of *node*(i)). (The details of that figure will be explained shortly.) Each node of the tree contains an index into the hash table. For purposes of this discussion, the hash table index contained in *node*(i) will be referred to as *index*(i) and

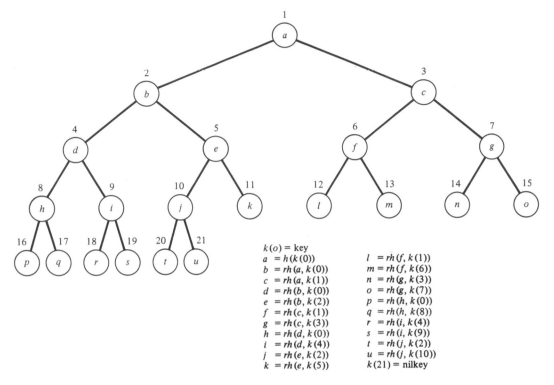

$$k(o) = \text{key}$$

$a = h(k(0))$	$l = rh(f, k(1))$
$b = rh(a, k(0))$	$m = rh(f, k(6))$
$c = rh(a, k(1))$	$n = rh(g, k(3))$
$d = rh(b, k(0))$	$o = rh(g, k(7))$
$e = rh(b, k(2))$	$p = rh(h, k(0))$
$f = rh(c, k(1))$	$q = rh(h, k(8))$
$g = rh(c, k(3))$	$r = rh(i, k(4))$
$h = rh(d, k(0))$	$s = rh(i, k(9))$
$i = rh(d, k(4))$	$t = rh(j, k(2))$
$j = rh(e, k(2))$	$u = rh(j, k(10))$
$k = rh(e, k(5))$	$k(21) = \text{nilkey}$

Figure 8.4.2

the key at that position (that is, *table*[*index*(*i*)].*k*) as $k(i)$. *key* is referred to as $k(0)$.

To explain how the tree is constructed, we first define the *youngest right ancestor* of *node*(*i*), or *yra*(*i*), as the node number of the father of the youngest ancestor of *node*(*i*) that is a right son. For example, in Figure 8.4.2, *yra*(12) is 1, since *node*(12) (containing *l*) is a left son and its father *node*(6) (containing *f*) is also a left son. Thus the youngest ancestor of *node*(12) which is a right son is *node*(3) (containing *c*) and its father is *node*(1). Similarly, *yra*(20) is 2 and *yra*(18) is 4. If *node*(*i*) is a right son, then *yra*(*i*) is defined as the node number of its father, *i div* 2. Thus, *yra*(15) in Figure 8.4.2 is 7. If *node*(*i*) has no ancestor which is a right son (as, for example, do nodes 1, 2, 4, 8, and 16 of Figure 8.4.2), then *yra*(*i*) is defined as zero.

The binary tree is constructed in node number order. *index*(1) is set to *h*(*key*). *index*(*i*), for each subsequent *i*, is set to *rh* (*index*(*i div* 2), *k*(*yra*(*i*))). This process continues until *k*(*i*) (that is, *table*[*index*(*i*)].*k*) equals *nilkey* and an empty position is found in the table.

For example, in Figure 8.4.2, *key* is hashed to obtain $a = h(key)$ which is established as the index in the root node. Its left son is $b =$

$rh(a, key)$, and its right son is $c = rh(a, k(1))$. Similarly, the left son of b is $d = rh(b, key)$, the right son of b is $e = rh(b, k(2))$, the left son of c is $f = rh(c, k(1))$, and the right son of c is $g = rh(c, k(3))$. This continues until $t = rh(j, k(2))$ is placed in $node(20)$ and $u = rh(j, k(10))$ is placed in $node(21)$. Since $table[u].k$ (which is $k(21)$) is $nilkey$, an empty position in the hash table has been found, and the tree construction is completed. Note that any path following a series of left pointers through the tree consists of successive rehashes of a particular key and that a right pointer indicates that a new key is being rehashed.

Once the tree has been constructed, the keys along the path from the root to the last node are reordered in the hash table. Let i be initialized to the position of the last node of the tree. Then, if $yra(i)$ is nonzero, $k(yra(i))$ and its associated record are moved from $table[index(yra(i))]$ to $table[index(i)]$, and i is reset to $yra(i)$. This process is repeated until $yra(i)$ is zero, at which point key and rec are inserted into $table[index(i)]$ and the insertion is complete. For example, in Figure 8.4.2, $yra(21) = 10$ and $index(10) = j$, so the key and record from position j of the hash table are moved to the previously empty position u. Then, since $yra(10) = 2$ and $index(2) = b$, the key and record from position b are moved to position j. Finally, since $yra(2) = 0$, key is inserted into position b.

When subsequently searching for key, two table positions are probed: a and b. When searching for the former $table[b].k$ (now at $table[j]$), two additional probes will be required. When searching for the former $table[j].k$ (now at $table[u]$), one additional probe is required. Thus a total of five extra positions over the entire hash table contents must be probed as a result of the insertion of key, while at least six would have been required had key been inserted directly along its rehash path (consisting of a, b, d, h, and p and at least one more position). Similarly, under Brent's method, no path shorter than length 6 would have been found (considering paths $abejt$, $abdir$, $abdhq$, and $abdhp$, representing attempts to relocate b, d, h, and p, the values on the initial rehash path of a. Each of these paths requires one more position before an empty table element is found.).

Note also that if key had previously been inserted in the table using the Gonnet and Munro insertion algorithm, it would have been found along the leftmost path of the tree (in Figure 8.4.2, $abdhp$) before an empty table position would have been found at a different node. Thus the tree-building process can be initiated, in preparation for a possible insertion, as part of the search process. However, if insertions are infrequent, it may be desirable to construct the full left path of the tree until an empty position is found (that is, to perform a straight search for key) before building the remainder of the tree.

Of course, the entire algorithm depends on the function $yra(i)$. Fortunately, $yra(i)$ may be computed quite easily. The binary representation of $yra(i)$ can be derived directly from the binary representation of i by deleting any trailing zero bits and the one bit preceding them. For example, the binary representation of 12 is 1100. Removing the trailing 100 yields 1, which is the binary representation of 1. Thus $yra(12) = 1$. Similarly, 18 in binary is 10010, which yields 100 or 4 so that $yra(18) = 4$, 15 in binary is 1111, which yields 111 or 7 so that $yra(15) = 7$, and 16 in binary is 1000 (or 01000), which yields 0 so that $yra(16) = 0$. You may confirm this in Figure 8.4.2.

Gonnet and Munro's method yields results even closer to optimal than Brent's. However, they are not quite optimal since the hash table can only be rearranged by moving elements to later positions in their hash sequence, never to earlier positions. At 90% loading, binary tree hashing requires 1.75 probes per retrieval (compared to Brent's 1.80) and, at 95%, requires 1.88 (compared to 1.97). For a full table, 2.13 probes are required on average compared to Brent's 2.5. The maximum number of probes required to access an element under Brent's method is $O(sqrt(n))$, while under binary hashing it is $O(\log n)$. Note that the queue of Brent's method and the tree of Gonnet and Munro's can be reused for each insertion. If all insertions take place initially, and the table is subsequently required only for searches, the space for these data structures may be freed.

If the hash table is static, that is, if elements are initially inserted and the table remains unchanged for a long series of searches, then another reordering strategy is to perform all the insertions initially and then to rearrange the elements of the table to minimize the expected retrieval costs. Experiments show that the minimum expected retrieval cost is 1.4 probes per retrieval with a load factor of .5, 1.5 for a load factor of .8, 1.7 for a load factor of .95, and 1.83 for a full table. Unfortunately, algorithms to reorder a table optimally to achieve this minimum are $O(n * m^2)$ and are therefore impractical for large numbers of keys.

Improvements with Additional Memory

Thus far, we have assumed that no additional memory is available in each table element. If additional memory is available, we can maintain some information in each entry to reduce the number of probes required to find a record or to determine that the desired record is absent.

Before looking at specific techniques, we should make one observation. The most obvious use to which additional memory can be put is to expand the size of the hash table. This would reduce the load factor and immediately improve efficiency. Therefore, in evaluating any efficiency improvements caused by adding more information to each table entry, one must consider whether the improvement outweighs utilizing the memory to expand the table. On the other hand, the benefit of expanding each table entry by one or two bytes may indeed be worthwhile. Each table item (including space for the key and record) may require 10, 50, 100, or even

1000 bytes, so that utilizing the space to expand the table may not buy as much as utilizing the space in small increments in each table element. (In reality, long records would not be kept within a hash table, since empty table entries would waste too much space. Instead, each table entry would contain the key and a pointer to the record. This could still require 30 or 40 bytes if the key were large and 10 to 15 bytes for typical key sizes.) In addition, for technical reasons (e.g., word size), not all the space in a table entry may actually be used, so there may be some extra space available that could not be used for additional table entries. In that case, whatever use can be made of the storage is beneficial.

The first improvement that we consider reduces the time required for an unsuccessful search, but not that for a retrieval. It involves keeping with each table element a one-bit field whose value is initialized to 0 and is set to 1 whenever a key to be inserted hashes or rehashes to that position but the position is found occupied. When hashing or rehashing a key during a search and finding the bit still set to 0, we immediately know that the key is not in the table, since if it were, it would either be found in that position or the bit would have been reset to 1 when it or some other key had been inserted. Use of this technique, together with the ordered hash table algorithm of Amble and Knuth, reduces the average number of probes for an unsuccessful search in a table with a load factor of 95% from 10.5 to 10.3 using linear rehashing and from 3.15 to 2.2 using double hashing. This method is called the ***pass-bit method*** since the additional bit indicates whether a table element has been passed over while inserting an item.

The next method can be used with both linear rehashing and quadratic rehashing. In both cases we can define a function $prb(j, key)$ which directly computes the position of the jth rehash of key, which is the position of the jth probe in searching for key. $prb(0, key)$ is defined as $h(key)$. For linear rehashing ($rh(i) = (i + c)$ *mod* $(maxtable + 1)$ where c is a constant), $prb(j, key)$ is defined as $(h(key) + j * c)$ *mod* $(maxtable + 1)$. For quadratic rehashing, $prb(j, key)$ is defined as $(h(key) + sqr(j))$ *mod* $(maxtable + 1)$. Note that no such function can be defined for double hashing, so the method is not applicable to that technique.

The method uses an additional integer field, called a ***predictor***, in each table position. Let $prd(i)$ be the predictor field in table position i. Initially, all predictor fields are zero. Under linear rehashing, the predictor field is reset as follows. Suppose that key $k1$ is being inserted and j is the smallest integer such that $prb(j, k1)$ is a probe position whose predictor field $prd(prb(j, k1))$ is zero. Then, after $k1$ is rehashed several more times and is inserted in position $prb(p, k1)$, $prd(prb(j, k1))$ is reset from zero to $p - j$. Then, during a search, when position $prb(j, k1)$ is found not to contain $k1$, the next position examined is $prb(j + prd(prb(j, k1)), k1)$ or $prb(p, k1)$ rather than $prb(j + 1, k1)$. This eliminates $p - j - 1$ probes.

An advantage of this approach is that it can be adapted quite easily when only a few extra bits are available in each table position. Since the predictor field contains only the number of additional rehashes needed, in most cases this number will be low and can fit in the available space. It would be very rare for a predictor value to be greater than the largest integer expressible in four or five bits. If only b bits are available for the prd field and the predictor field cannot fit, the field value can be set to $2^b - 1$ (the largest integer representable by b bits). Then we would skip at least $2^b - 2$ probes after reaching such a position.

Under linear rehashing, suppose two keys, $k1$ and $k2$, hash into different values but the mth probe of one equals the nth probe of the other. (That is, $prb(n, k1) = prb(m, k2)$ where n and m are unequal.) Suppose $k1$ is inserted first into position $i = prb(n, k1)$. Then when $k2$ is placed in position $prb(m + x, k2)$, $prd(i)$ is set to x. This presents no problem since $prb(n + x, k1)$ and $prb(m + x, k2)$ both equal $(i + x * c) \bmod (maxtable + 1)$. Thus anything that hashes into either $b(k1)$ or $b(k2)$ and rehashes into i can be referred to $i + prd(i)$ for the next probe. This reflects the fact that linear rehashing involves primary clustering in which keys hashing into different locations follow the same rehash paths once those paths intersect.

Under quadratic rehashing, however, primary clustering is eliminated. Thus, the paths followed by $k1$ and $k2$ differ if $b(k1) <> b(k2)$ even after those paths intersect. Thus $prb(n + x, k1) = (b(k1) + sqr(n + x)) \bmod (maxtable + 1)$ does not equal $prb(m + x, k2) = (b(k2) + sqr(m + x)) \bmod (maxtable + 1)$ even though $prb(n, k1)$ does happen to equal $prb(m, k2)$. Thus, if $prd(prb(i, k1))$ is set to x, and if we are searching for $k2$ at $prb(j, k2)$, which happens to equal $prb(i, k1)$, we cannot directly go to $prb(j + x, k2)$ unless $b(k1)$ equals $b(k2)$ (that is, $k1$ and $k2$ are in the same secondary cluster) and $i = j$. Therefore, under quadratic rehashing or any other rehashing method which involves only secondary clustering, we must ensure that $b(k(i)) = b(key)$ before using or setting $prd(i)$ during a search or insertion of key. If the two hash values are unequal, then rehashing continues in the usual fashion until a location j is reached where $b(k(j)) = b(key)$, where use of the prd field can be resumed.

Unfortunately, the predictor method cannot be used at all under double hashing. The reason for this is that even secondary clustering is eliminated so there is no guarantee that $prb(n + x, k1)$ equals $prb(n + x, k2)$ even if $b(k1)$ equals $b(k2)$ and $prb(n, k1)$ equals $prb(n, k2)$.

An extension of the predictor method is the ***multiple predictor method***. Under this technique, np predictor fields are maintained in each table position. A ***predictor hash function*** $ph(key)$ whose value is between 1 and np determines which predictor is used for a particular key. The jth predictor in table position i is referenced as $prd(i, j)$. When a key probes an occupied slot $i = prb(j, key)$, such that $ph(k(i)) = ph(key)$, the next position probed is $prb(j + prd(i, ph(key)), key)$. Similarly, if $ph(k(i)) = ph(key)$ and $prd(i, ph(key))$ is zero, then we know that key is not in the table. If key is inserted at $prb(i + x, key)$, then $prd(i, ph(key))$ is set to x.

The advantage of the multiple predictor method is similar to the advantages of double hashing; it eliminates the effects of secondary clustering by dividing the list of elements that hash or rehash into a particular location into *np* separate and shorter lists.

Simulation results of a slightly modified version of the predictor method using the quadratic rehash method are shown in the following table, which lists the average number of probes required for a successful search under various load factors, with various numbers of predictor fields, and numbers of bits in each predictor. By comparison, recall that quadratic hashing without predictors required 1.44 average probes for a 50% load factor and 2.85 for 90% and that double hashing required 1.39 and 2.56, respectively.

NUMBER OF PREDICTORS	LOAD FACTOR	BITS IN EACH PREDICTOR		
		3	4	5
1	50%	1.25	1.25	1.25
	70%	1.39	1.35	1.35
	90%	1.83	1.55	1.46
2	50%	1.24	1.23	1.23
	70%	1.35	1.32	1.31
	90%	1.79	1.50	1.41
4	50%	1.23	1.23	1.23
	70%	1.33	1.30	1.30
	90%	1.74	1.47	1.38
8	50%	1.22	1.22	1.22
	70%	1.32	1.29	1.29
	90%	1.72	1.46	1.37

As the number of bits in each predictor and the number of predictors grow very large, the average number of probes required for a successful search with a load factor lf becomes $2 \quad (1 \quad exp(-lf))/lf$. For a single full-integer predictor, the average number of probes is $1 + lf/2$. The predictor method also reduces the average number of probes for unsuccessful searches.

Coalesced Hashing

Perhaps the simplest use of additional memory to reduce retrieval time is to add a link field to each table entry. This field contains the next position of the table to examine in searching for a particular item. In fact, under this method, a rehash function is not required at all, so the technique is our first example of the second major method of collision resolution, called *chaining*. This method uses links rather than a rehash function to resolve hash clashes.

The simplest of the chaining methods is called *standard coalesced hashing*. A search and insertion algorithm for this method can be presented as follows. Assume that each table entry contains a *next* field initialized to −1. The algorithm uses an auxiliary function *getempty* that returns the index of an empty table location.

```
i:= h(key);
while (k(i) <> key) and (next(i) >= 0)
      do i:= next(i);
if k(i) = key
  then search:= i
  else begin
              { set j to the position where the new record }
              {              is to be inserted              }
              if k(i) = nilkey
                  then {the hash position is empty}
                      j:= i
                  else begin
                          j := getempty;
                          next(i):= j
                      end {else begin};
              k(j):= key;
              r(j):= rec;
              search:= j
      end { else begin }
```

The function *getempty* can use any technique to locate an empty position. The simplest method is to use an index variable *avail* initialized to *maxtable* and to execute

```
while k(avail) <> nilkey
      do avail:= avail − 1;
getempty:= avail
```

each time that *getempty* is called. When *getempty* is called, all table positions between *avail* and *maxtable* have been already allocated. *getempty* sequentially examines positions less than *avail* to locate the first empty position. *avail* is reset to that position which is then allocated. Of course, it may be desirable to avoid the *nilkey* comparisons in *getempty*. This can be done in a number of ways. An additional one-bit *empty* field can be added to each table position, or the *next* fields can be initialized to −2 and modified to −1 when keys are inserted in the table. An alternative solution is to link the free positions together in a list that acts as a stack.

Figure 8.4.3 illustrates a table of 10 elements that has been filled using standard coalesced hashing using the hash function *key mod* 10. The keys were inserted in the order 14, 29, 34, 28, 42, 39, 84, and 38. Note that items hashing into both 4 and 8 have coalesced into a single list (in

	K	next
0	nilkey	−1
1	nilkey	−1
2	42	−1
3	38	−1
4	14	8
5	84	3
6	39	−1
7	28	5
8	34	7
9	29	6

AVAIL =

Figure 8.4.3

positions 4, 8, 7, 5, 3, containing items 14, 34, 28, 84, 38). This is how the method gets its name.

There are several advantages to standard coalesced hashing. First, it reduces the average number of probes to approximately $exp\ (2 * lf)/4 - lf/2 + .75$ for an unsuccessful search and to approximately $(exp\ (2 * lf) - 1)/(8 * lf) + lf/4 + .75$ for a successful search. This compares favorably with all previous methods other than the predictor method. A full table requires only an average of 1.8 probes to locate an item and a fraction of approximately $1 - lf/2$ can be found on the first probe.

Another major advantage of chaining methods is that they permit efficient deletion without penalizing the efficiency of subsequent retrievals. An item being deleted can be removed from its list, its position in the table freed, and *avail* reset to the following position (unless *avail* already points to a position later in the table). This may slow down the second subsequent insertion somewhat by forcing *avail* to be repeatedly decremented through a long series of occupied positions, but that is not very significant. If the free table positions are kept in a linked list, then this penalty disappears.

A variation of standard coalesced hashing inserts a new element into its chain immediately following the item at its hash location rather than at the end of the chain. This technique, called *early insertion standard coalesced hashing*, requires approximately 5% fewer probes—approximately $(exp\ (lf) - 1)/lf$—for a successful search in a full table and the same number for an unsuccessful search.

A generalization of the standard coalesced hashing method, which we call *general coalesced hashing*, adds extra positions to the hash table which can be used for list nodes in the case of collisions, but not for initial hash locations. Thus the table would consist of t entries (numbered 0 to $t - 1$), but keys would hash only into one of $m < t$ values (0 to $m - 1$). The extra $t - m$ positions are called the *cellar* and are available for storing items whose hash positions are full. Using the cellar results in less conflict between lists of items with different hash values and therefore reduces the lengths of the lists. However, a cellar that is too large could increase list lengths relative to what they might be if the cellar positions were permitted as hash locations.

For full tables, lowest average successful search time is achieved if the ratio m/t is .853 (that is, approximately 15% of the table is used as a cellar). In that case, the average number of probes is only 1.69. Lowest average unsuccessful search time is attained if the ratio is equal to .782, in which case only 1.79 probes are required for the average unsuccessful search. Higher values of m/t produce lowest successful and unsuccessful search times for lower load factors (when the table is not full).

Unlike the situation with standard coalesced hashing, the early insertion method yields worse retrieval times than if elements are added at the end of the chain in general coalesced hashing. A combination of the two techniques, called *varied insertion coalesced hashing*, seems to yield the best results. Under this method, a colliding element is ordinarily inserted in the list immediately following its hash position, as in the early insertion method, unless three conditions are met: the cellar is full, there is at least one cellar position in the chain, and the hash position of the colliding element is occupied by an element that hashed directly into that position. When these three conditions occur, the varied insertion method inserts the collider directly following the last cellar position in the chain.

Separate Chaining

Both rehashing and coalesced hashing assume fixed table sizes determined in advance. If the number of records grows beyond the number of table positions, it is impossible to insert them without allocating a larger table and recomputing the hash values of the keys of all records already in the table using a new hash function. (In general coalesced hashing, the old table can be copied into the first half of the new table and the remaining portion of the new table used to enlarge the cellar so items do not have to be rehashed.) To avoid the possibility of running out of room, too many locations may be initially allocated for a hash table, resulting in much wasted space.

Another method of resolving hash clashes is called *separate chaining* and involves keeping a distinct linked list for all records whose keys hash into the same value. Suppose that the hash function produces values between 0 and $m - 1$. Then an array *bucket* of header nodes of size m is declared. This array is called the *hash table*. *bucket*[i] points to the list of all records whose keys hash into i. In searching for a record, the list head *bucket*[i] is accessed and the list that it initiates is traversed. If the record is not found, it is inserted at the end of the list. Figure 8.4.4 illustrates separate chaining. We assume a 10-element array and the hash function *key mod* 10. The keys in that figure are presented in the order

75   66   42   192   91   40   49   87   67   16   417   130   372   227

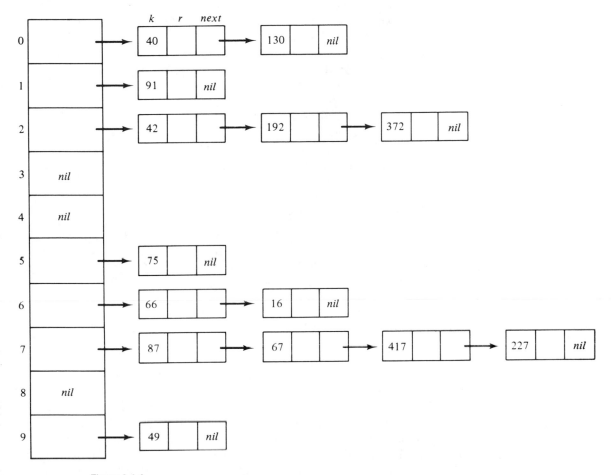

Figure 8.4.4

We may write a search and insertion function for separate chaining using a hash function h, an array *bucket*, and nodes which contain three fields: k for the key, r for the record, and *next* as a pointer to the next node in the list. *getnode* is used to allocate a new list node.

```
function search(key: keytype; rec: rectype): nodeptr;
var i: index;
    p, q, s: nodeptr;
    found: boolean;
begin
    found:= false;
    i:= h(key);
    q:= nil;
    p:= bucket[i];
```

```
            while (p <> nil) and (not found)
                do if p↑.k = key
                        then found := true
                        else begin
                                    q := p;
                                    q := p↑.next
                              end {else begin};
        if found
            then search := p
            else begin { insert a new record }
                        s := getnode;
                        s↑.k := key;
                        s↑.r := rec;
                        s↑.next := nil;
                        if q = nil;
                            then bucket[i] := s
                            else q↑.next := s;
                        search := s
                  end {else begin}
        end {function search};
```

Note that the lists may be reordered dynamically for more efficient searching by the methods of Section 1. The time for unsuccessful searches can be reduced by keeping each of the lists ordered by key. Then only half the list need be traversed on the average to determine that an item is missing.

The primary disadvantage of chaining is the extra space that is required for the hash table and pointers. However, the initial array is usually smaller in schemes that use separate chaining than in those that use rehashing or coalesced hashing. This is because under separate chaining it is less catastrophic if the entire array becomes full—it is always possible to allocate more nodes and make them available to the various lists. Of course, if the lists become very long, the whole purpose of hashing—direct addressing and resultant search efficiency—is defeated. One advantage of separate chaining is that the list items need not be in contiguous storage. Another advantage over all other hashing methods is that separate chaining allows traversal of the items in hash key order, although not in sequential key order.

There is a technique which might be used to save some space in separate chaining. Consider the hash function $h(key) = key \bmod (maxtable + 1)$. Then if we define $p(key) = key \text{ div } (maxtable + 1)$, we can store $p(key)$ rather than key in the k field of each list node. When searching for key, we compute $h(key)$, and since key equals $p(key) * (maxtable + 1) + h(key)$, we can recompute the key value in each list node from the value of $p(key)$ stored in the k field. Since $p(key)$ requires less space than key, space may be saved in each list node. The technique can be used for separate chaining but not for any of the other hashing methods because only in separate chaining is the value of $h(key)$ for the key stored in a particular position being probed always known with certainty during the search process. However, this technique is not of much use for integer keys in a language like Pascal in which the size of an integer is fixed by the computer implementation.

Another space efficiency decision that must be made is whether the hash table should be simply list headers (as we have presented it) or whether each list header should itself also contain a key and a record (or record pointer). Space would be wasted for empty array items but gained for full ones.

The average number of probes required to locate an existing item under the separate chaining technique is approximately $1 + lf/2$. The average number required for an unsuccessful search is approximately $exp(-lf) + lf$ if the lists are not kept ordered and approximately $1 + lf/2 - (1 - exp(-lf))/lf + exp(-lf)$ if they are kept ordered. If there are m keys and m elements in the hash table (for a load factor of 1), this translates to 1.5 average probes per successful search, 1.27 probes for an unsuccessful search if unordered lists are used, and 1.05 probes for an unsuccessful search if ordered lists are used. Note that the average for an unsuccessful search may actually be lower than for a successful search since, when an array element is empty, an unsuccessful search to that element involves zero probes while a successful search requires at least one probe. (This assumes that a key is not kept in each element, since an unsuccessful search to an empty element would then require a key comparison with *nilkey*.)

One technique that can be used to reduce the number of probes in separate chaining is to maintain the records that hash into the same value as a binary search tree emanating from the hash bucket rather than as a linked list. However, this requires two pointers to be kept with each record. Since chains are usually small (otherwise, the initial bucket table should be larger), the added space and programming complexity do not seem to be warranted.

Although the average number of probes for separate chaining appears to be quite low, the numbers are deceiving. The reason for this is that the load factor is defined as the number of keys in the table divided by the number of positions in the table. But, in separate chaining, the number of positions in the hash table is not a valid measure of space utilization since the keys are not stored in the hash table but in the list nodes. Indeed, the formulas for search time remain valid even if lf is greater than one. For example, if there are five times as many keys as buckets, $lf = 5$, and the average number of probes for a successful search is $1 + lf/2$ or 3.5. Thus the total space allocated to the hash table should be adjusted to include the list nodes. When this is done, coalesced hashing is quite competitive with separate chaining. Note also that rehashing with multiple predictors also performs better than does separate chaining.

Hashing in External Storage

If a hash table is maintained in external storage on a disk or some other direct-access device, then time rather than space is the critical factor. Most systems will have sufficient external storage to allow the luxury of unused allocated space for growth but cannot afford the time needed to perform an I/O operation for every element on a linked list. In such a situation, the table in external storage is divided into a number of blocks called *buckets*. Each bucket consists of a useful physical segment of external storage such as a page or a disk track or track fraction. The buckets are usually contiguous and can be accessed by bucket offsets from 0 to *maxtable* that serve as hash values, much like indexes of an array in internal storage.

Alternatively, one or more contiguous storage blocks can be used as a hash table containing pointers to buckets distributed noncontiguously. In that situation, the hash table is most likely read into memory as soon as the file is opened (or upon the first record read) and remains in memory until the file is closed. When a record is requested, its key is hashed and the hash table (now in internal memory) is used to locate the external storage address of the appropriate bucket. Such a hash table is often called an *index* (not to be confused with the term "index" as used to refer to a particular table position).

Each external memory bucket contains room for a moderate number of records (in practical situations, from 10 to 100). An entire bucket is read into memory at once and is searched sequentially for the appropriate record. (Of course, a binary search or some other appropriate search mechanism based on the internal organization of the records within the bucket can be used, but the number of records in a bucket is usually small enough that no significant advantage is gained.)

We should note that, when dealing with external storage, the computational efficiency of a hash function is not as important as its success at avoiding hash clashes. It is more efficient to spend microseconds computing a complex hash function at internal CPU speeds than milliseconds or longer accessing additional buckets at I/O speeds when a bucket overflows. We also note that external storage space is usually inexpensive. Thus the number of contiguous initial buckets or the size of the hash table should be chosen so that it is unlikely that any of the buckets becomes full, even though this entails allocating unused space. Then, when a new record must be inserted, there usually will be room in the appropriate bucket, and an additional expensive I/O will not be required.

If a bucket is full and a record must be inserted, any of the rehash or chaining techniques discussed earlier can be used. Of course, additional I/O operations will be required when searching for records that are not in the buckets directly corresponding to the hash value. Thus the size of the hash table (which equals the number of buckets that are accessible in one

I/O operation) is crucial. A hash table that is too large implies that most buckets will be empty and a great deal of space is wasted. A hash table that is too small implies that buckets will be full and large numbers of I/O operations will be required to access many records. If a file is very volatile, growing and shrinking rapidly and unpredictably, this simple hashing technique will be inefficient in either space or time. We will see how to deal with this situation shortly.

The following table indicates the expected number of external storage accesses per successful search under linear rehashing, double rehashing, and separate chaining for various bucket sizes and load factors (the load factor is defined as the number of records in the file divided by the product of the number of buckets and the bucket size).

BUCKET SIZE	LOAD FACTOR	LINEAR REHASH	DOUBLE HASHING	SEPARATE CHAINING
1	.5	1.500	1.386	1.250
	.8	3.000	2.012	1.400
	.95	10.5	3.153	1.5
5	.5	1.031	1.028	1.036
	.8	1.289	1.184	1.186
	.95	2.7	1.529	1.3
10	.5	1.005	1.005	1.007
	.8	1.110	1.079	1.115
	.95	1.8	1.292	1.3
50	.5	1.000	1.000	1.000
	.8	1.005	1.005	1.015
	.95	1.1	1.067	1.2

This table would indicate that double hashing is the preferred method for moderate or large bucket sizes.

However, when dealing with external storage such as a disk, the number of buckets that have to be read from external storage is not the only determinant of access efficiency. Another important factor is the *dispersal* of the buckets accessed, that is, how far apart the buckets accessed are from each other. In general, a major factor in the time it takes to read a block from a disk is the *seek time*. This is the time it takes for the disk head to move to the location of the desired data on the disk. Thus if two buckets accessed one after the other are far apart, more time will be required than if they are close together. Given this fact, it would seem that linear rehashing is the most effective technique because, although it may require accessing more buckets, the buckets it accesses are contiguous (we are assuming that $c = 1$ in the linear rehash so that if a record is not in a full bucket, the next sequential bucket is checked). Surprisingly, the table indicates that fewer buckets are accessed under linear rehashing than under separate chaining for large bucket sizes.

If separate chaining is used, it is desirable to reserve an overflow area in each cylinder of the file so that full buckets in that cylinder can link to overflow records in the same cylinder, thus minimizing seek time and essentially eliminating the dispersal penalty. It should be noted that the overflow area need not be organized into buckets and should be organized as individual records with links. The reason is that, in general, few records will overflow, and the likelihood that sufficiently many will overflow from a single bucket to fill an additional complete bucket is unlikely. Thus, by keeping individual overflow records, more buckets can overflow into the same cylinder. Since space is being reserved within the file for overflow records, the load factor does not represent a true picture of storage utilization for this version of separate chaining. The number of accesses in separate chaining is therefore even higher for a given amount of external storage than the numbers in the table would indicate.

Although double hashing requires fewer accesses than does linear rehashing, it will disperse the buckets that must be accessed to a degree that may overwhelm this advantage. However, in systems where dispersal is not a factor, double hashing is preferred. This is true of modern large multiuser systems in which many users may be requesting access to a disk simultaneously, and the requests are scheduled by the operating system based on the way the data are arranged on the disk. In such situations, waiting time for disk access is required in any case so that dispersal is not a significant factor.

The major drawback in using hashing for external file storage is that sequential access (in ascending key order) is not possible since a good hash function disperses keys without regard to order. Access to records in key sequential order is particularly important in external file systems.

The Separator Method

One technique for reducing access time in external hash tables at the expense of increasing insertion time is due to Gonnet and Larson. We will call the technique the *separator method*. The method uses rehashing (either linear rehashing or double hashing) to resolve collisions but also uses an additional hash function, s, called the *signature function*. Given a key *key*, let $h(key, i)$ be the ith rehash of *key* and let $s(key, i)$ be the ith **signature** of *key*. If a record with key *key* is stored in bucket number $h(key, j)$, then the *current signature* of the record and the key, $sig(key)$, is defined as $s(key, j)$. That is, if a record is placed in a bucket corresponding to its key's jth rehash, then its current signature is its key's jth signature.

A *separator table*, *sep*, is maintained in internal memory. If b is a bucket number, then $sep(b)$ contains a signature value greater than the current signature of every record in $bucket(b)$. To access the record with key *key*, repeatedly hash *key* until obtaining a value j such that $sep(h(key, j)) > s(key, j)$.

At that point, if the record is in the file, if must be in $bucket(b(key, j))$. This ensures the ability to access any record in the file with only a single external memory access.

If m is the number of bits allowed in each item of the separator table (so that it can hold values between 0 and $2^m - 1$), then the signature function, s, is restricted to producing values between 0 and $2^m - 2$. Initially, before any overflows have occurred in bucket b, the value of $sep(b)$ is set to $2^m - 1$ so that any record whose key hashes to b can be inserted directly into $bucket(b)$ regardless of its signature. Now, suppose $bucket(b)$ is full and a new record to be inserted hashes into b. (That is, $h(key, j) = b$ and j is the smallest integer such that $sep(b(key, j)) > s(key, j)$.) Then the records in b with the largest current signature lcs must be removed from $bucket(b)$ to make room for the new record. The new record is then inserted into $bucket(b)$, and the old records that had current signature lcs and were removed from bucket b are rehashed and relocated into new buckets (with new current signatures, of course). $sep(b)$ is then reset to lcs since the current signatures of all records in $bucket(b)$ are less than lcs. Future keys will be directed to $bucket(b)$ only if their signatures are less than lcs. Notice that more than one record may have to be removed from a bucket if they have equal maximal current signature values. This may leave a bucket with some remaining space after an insertion causes it to overflow.

Records that overflow from a bucket during an insertion may cause cascading overflows in other buckets when attempting to relocate them. This means that an insertion may cause an indefinite number of additional external storage reads and writes. In practice, a limit is placed on the number of such cascading overflows beyond which the insertion fails. If the insertion does fail, it is necessary to restore the file to the status it was in before inserting the new record that caused the original overflow. This is usually done by delaying writing modified buckets to external storage, keeping the modified versions in internal memory until it is determined that the insertion can be completed successfully. If the insertion is aborted because the cascade limit is reached, then no writes are done, leaving the file in its original state.

With 40 buckets per record, four-bit signature values, and a load factor of 90%, an average of no more than two pages need to modified per insertion under this method. However, the number of modified pages per insertion rises rapidly as the load factor is increased so that the technique is impractical with a load factor greater than 95%. Larger signature values and larger bucket sizes permit the method to be used with larger load factors.

Dynamic Hashing and Extendible Hashing

One of the most serious drawbacks of hashing for external storage is that it is insufficiently flexible. Unlike internal data structures, files and data bases are semipermanent structures that are not usually created and destroyed within the lifetime of a single program. Further, the contents of an external storage structure tend to grow and shrink unpredictably. All the hash table structuring methods that we have examined have a sharp space/time trade-off. Either the table uses a large amount of space for efficient access, resulting in much wasted space when the structure shrinks, or it uses a small amount of space and accommodates growth very poorly by sharply increasing the access time for overflow elements. We would like to develop a scheme that does not utilize too much extra space when a file is small but that permits efficient access when it grows larger. Two such schemes are called *dynamic hashing*, due to Larson, and *extendible hashing*, due to Fagin, Nievergelt, Pippenger, and Strong.

The basic concept under both methods is the same. Initially, m buckets and a hash table (or index) of size m are allocated. Assume that m equals 2^b, and assume a hash function h that produces hash values that are $w > b$ bits in length. Let $h_b(key)$ be the integer between 0 and m represented by the first b fits of $h(key)$. Then, initially, h_b is used as the hash function, and records are inserted into the m buckets as in ordinary external storage hashing. When a bucket overflows, the bucket is split in two and its records are assigned to the two new buckets based on the $(b + 1)$st bit of $h(key)$. If the bit is 0, the record is assigned to the first (or left) new bucket; if the bit is 1, the record is assigned to the second (or right) bucket. (Of course, the original bucket can be reused as one of the two new buckets.) The records in each of the two new buckets now all have the same first $b + 1$ bits in their hash keys, $h(key)$. Similarly, when a bucket representing i bits overflows (where $b \leq i \leq w$), the bucket is split and the $(i + 1)$st bit of $h(key)$ for each record in the bucket is used to place the record in the left or right new bucket. Both new buckets then represent $i + 1$ bits of the hash key. We call the bucket whose keys have 0 in their $(i + 1)$st bit the **0 *bucket*** and the other bucket the **1 *bucket***.

Dynamic hashing and extendible hashing differ as to how the index is modified when a bucket splits. Under dynamic hashing, each of the m original index entries represents the root of a binary tree each of whose leafs contains a pointer to a bucket. Initially, each tree consists of only one node (a leaf node) that points to one of the m initially allocated buckets. When a bucket splits, two new leaf nodes are created to point to the two new buckets. The former leaf that had pointed to the bucket being split is transformed into a nonleaf node whose left son is the leaf pointing to the 0 bucket and whose right son is the leaf pointing to the 1 bucket. Dynamic hashing with $b = 2$ ($m = 4$) is illustrated in Figure 8.4.5.

To locate a record under dynamic hashing, compute $h(key)$ and use the first b bits to locate a root node in the original index. Then, use each successive bit of $h(key)$ to move down the tree, going left if the bit is 0 and right if the bit is 1, until a leaf is reached. Then use the pointer in the leaf to locate the bucket which contains the desired record, if it exists.

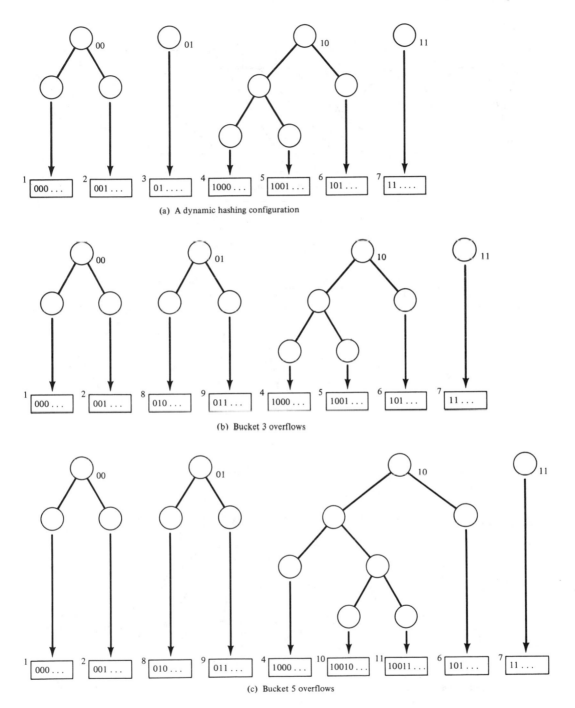

(a) A dynamic hashing configuration

(b) Bucket 3 overflows

(c) Bucket 5 overflows

Figure 8.4.5 Dynamic hashing with $b = 2$.

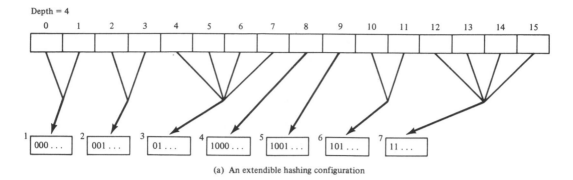

(a) An extendible hashing configuration

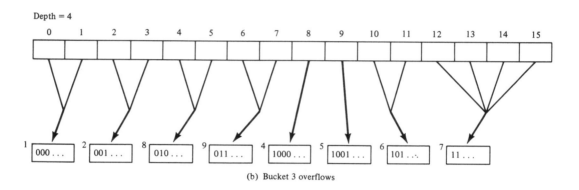

(b) Bucket 3 overflows

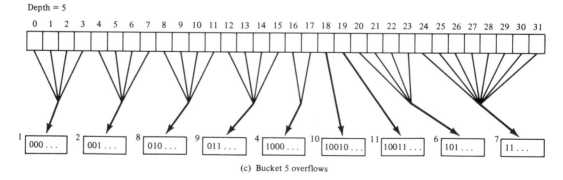

(c) Bucket 5 overflows

Figure 8.4.6   Extendible hashing.

In extendible hashing, each bucket contains an indication of the number of bits of $h(key)$ that determine which records are in that bucket. This number is called the **bucket depth**. Initially, this number is b for all bucket entries; it is increased by one each time a bucket splits. Associated with the index is the **index depth**, d, which is the maximum of all the bucket depths. The size of the index is always 2^d (initially, 2^b). Suppose a bucket of depth i is to be split. Let $a_1a_2\ldots a_i$ (where each a_i is either 0 or 1) be the first i bits of $h(key)$ for the records in the bucket being split. There are two cases to consider: $i < d$ and $i = d$. If $i < d$ (so that the bucket depth is being increased to $i + 1$ but the index remains at d), then all index positions with bit values $a_1a_2\ldots a_i00\ldots0$ (up to a bit size of d) through $a_1a_2\ldots a_i01\ldots1$ of the index (that is, all positions starting with $a_1\ldots a_i0$) are reset to point to the 0 bucket and index positions with bit values $a_1a_2\ldots a_i10\ldots0$ through $a_1a_2\ldots a_i11\ldots1$ (that is, all positions starting with $a_1\ldots a_i1$) arc rcsct to point to the 1 bucket. If $i = d$ (so that the bucket depth and the index depth are both being increased to $d + 1$), the index is doubled in size from 2^d to 2^{d+1}; the old contents of all index positions $x_1\ldots x_d$ are copied into the new positions $x_1\ldots x_d0$ and $x_1\ldots x_d1$; and the contents of index position $a_1\ldots a_d0$ are set to point to the new 0 bucket and the contents of index position $a_1\ldots a_d1$ to point to the new 1 bucket. Extendible hashing is illustrated in Figure 8.4.6. Figure 8.4.6a illustrates a configuration with index depth 1, Figure 8.4.6b illustrates an overflow which does not increase the index depth, and Figure 8.4.6c illustrates an overflow which does.

To locate a record under extendible hashing, we compute $h(key)$ and use the first d bits (where d is the index depth) to obtain a position in the index. The contents of this position point to the bucket containing the desired record, if it exists.

Under both dynamic and extendible hashing, if the entire index is maintained in internal storage, only one I/O operation is required to locate a record regardless of how large the file grows. When a file shrinks, buckets can be combined and freed and the index size can be reduced. Thus these methods achieve our twin goals of efficient space ultilization and efficient access. Both schemes also allow effective sequential traversal of records in hash key order. However, they do not permit traversal in key order, and this often prevents the practical use of the techniques for file implementation. (Of course, one could use the key itself as a hash value or some other order-preserving hash function, although such functions are usually nonuniform. The lack of uniformity is not as serious an obstacle under these methods since any number of bits can be used. The more bits used, the less likely that two keys clash. While too large a number of bits can result in too large an index for practical use, dynamic hashing, which does not use as large an index as extendible hashing, may indeed be practical with a nonuniform hash function.)

A simple variation of extendible hashing, in which the last bits of the hash key rather than the first are used to locate a bucket, is also possible. Such a variation would simplify doubling the index since it would allow merely copying the first half of the new index into the second and only modifying the two entries pointing to the two new buckets. However, such a scheme would not permit traversal in hash key sequence.

One suggestion for a hashing technique for use with these methods is to use a random number generator to produce an arbitrarily long sequence of 0s and 1s as needed, with the key or some function thereof as the seed. This has the advantage of allowing the file to grow arbitrarily large and, in the case of dynamic hashing, to ensure balanced trees.

In comparing dynamic and extendible hashing, we note that extendible hashing is more time efficient since a tree path need not be traversed as in dynamic hashing. However, if the entire index is kept in memory, the time spent in traversing the tree path does not involve any I/Os. Traversal time is therefore likely to be negligible compared to the time for accessing the bucket. The maximum number of tree nodes required in dynamic hashing is $2n - 1$, assuming n buckets, while there may be an many as 2^{n-1} index entries required under extendible hashing. However, usually fewer than twice as many extendible hashing index entries as dynamic hashing tree nodes are required, and the tree nodes require two pointer fields compared to one for each extendible hashing index entry. Thus the two methods are comparable in average internal space utilization.

It is also possible to compress very large extendible hashing indexes by keeping only one copy of each bucket pointer and maintaining from/to indicators. Another point to note is that extendible hashing performs the same way regardless of the value of m, the initial number of index entries, whereas dynamic hashing will require longer tree paths if m is smaller. In fact, there is no reason not to initialize m to 0 (that is, $b = 0$) with a single empty bucket in extendible hashing, other than for contiguity of the buckets in external storage.

External storage utilization of both dynamic and balanced hashing is approximately 69% on the average, which is the same as is achieved with B-trees. However, the storage utilization of the hashing methods oscillates far more sharply and persists longer than for B-trees, so that there is a period of low utilization (approximately 50%) after buckets are split as they begin filling up. This is followed by a period of high utilization (approaching 90–100%) as new records are uniformly distributed into the buckets and they all become full more or less simultaneously. Finally, a short period of intensive splitting is observed, after which utilization is again low.

The reason for this oscillation is that the hash function is expected to be uniform so that all buckets will be filled at approximately the same time. It may be desirable to minimize this oscillation by purposely introducing some nonuniformity in the hash function. However, if this is done in extendible hashing, the nonuniformity could cause extremely large indexes.

This problem can be solved by keeping a compressed version of the index as noted.

To achieve storage utilization higher than 69%, it is possible to utilize overflow buckets. When a bucket becomes full and an additional record is to be inserted, an overflow bucket is allocated and is linked to the full bucket. Only when the overflow bucket fills up are both buckets' contents redistributed into two nonoverflow buckets, with an overflow bucket linked to the new bucket with more than half of the records. This results in more than two full buckets of data being distributed into three buckets (two regular, one overflow), yielding a minimum utilization of 67%, rather than 50%, once the initial buckets are filled. Of course, it is also possible to use overflow buckets that are smaller than regular buckets (in which case not every split would result in an overflow bucket remaining allocated), as well as to allow an overflow bucket to contain records that have overflowed from more than one bucket. This latter technique, however, complicates traversal in hash key order.

Another method of increasing space utilization is to allow overflow records to be placed in a full bucket's brother (under extendible hashing, the brother of a 0 bucket is its corresponding 1 bucket, and vice versa). This method also complicates traversal in hash key order. Both the use of overflow buckets and the use of a brother bucket for overflow records increase the average number of accesses required for a search. However, if brother buckets are kept contiguous, this penalty may not be great.

Linear Hashing

One drawback of dynamic and extendible hashing is the need for an index. While the index may be kept in internal storage once the file is opened, this is not always possible if the index becomes very large. Also, the index does require external storage when the file is not in use. In addition, the external copy of the index may have to be constantly updated to guard against power failure or other interruption that would prevent rewriting the index when the file is closed.

Another technique, *linear hashing* (not to be confused with linear rehashing), proposed by Litwin and modified by Larson, permits a hash table to expand and shrink dynamically without requiring an index. However, the basic technique does require the use of overflow buckets, unlike dynamic and extendible hashing. The version that we present is called "linear hashing with two partial expansions," or LH2P.

Under LH2P, the initial file consists of m buckets, where m is even, numbered 0 to $m - 1$. The file is considered divided into ng groups of buckets, numbered 0 to $ng - 1$. Initially, there are m *div* 2 groups of buckets ($ng = m$ *div* 2), each consisting of two buckets. Group i initially consists of buckets i and $i + ng$. For example, if m equals 6, the file initially contains six buckets, numbered 0 to 5. There are three groups: group 0 contains buckets 0 and 3, group 1 contains buckets 1 and 4, and group 2 contains buckets 2 and 5.

The file grows in two ways: overflow growth and regular growth. Unlike B-trees, dynamic hashing, or extendible hashing, a bucket is not split when it overflows. Instead, an overflow mechanism is used to contain the overflowing records from a particular bucket. This mechanism can be any of the techniques discussed earlier.

Regular growth takes place by expanding the size of the file by one bucket at a time. Expansion of the file by one bucket is called a *simple expansion*. A simple expansion takes place whenever the load factor (defined as the total number of records in the file divided by the number of records that fit into regular, nonoverflow buckets) exceeds a threshold percentage. When a simple expansion takes place, the number of regular buckets in the file, *nb*, increases by one. At any time, the file consists of buckets 0 through *nb* plus any overflow buckets or records. Initially, *nb* equals *m*.

Regular growth under LH2P takes place in a series of simple expansions, grouped into *partial expansions* and *full expansions*. Each full expansion doubles the number of regular buckets in the file and consists of two partial expansions. The first partial expansion increases the number of regular buckets by 50%, and the second increases the number by the same amount. Thus, after the first partial expansion, *nb* equals 3 * (*m div* 2); after the first full expansion, *nb* equals 2 * *m*; and, after the second full expansion, *nb* equals 4 * *m*.

Each simple expansion increases the size of a particular group of buckets by one bucket. The variable *nextgroup* always holds the number of the next group to be expanded (initially, *nextgroup* is zero). During the first partial expansion, two-bucket groups are expanded to three buckets by moving some records from buckets *nextgroup* and *nextgroup* + *ng* (and some of their associated overflow records) into bucket *nextgroup* + 2 * *ng*. (Exactly which records are moved to the new bucket and which remain in place will be discussed shortly.) Note that the buckets are numbered from 0 to *nb* − 1, so that *nb* is always the number of the next bucket added to the file. During the first partial expansion, *nb* always equals *nextgroup* + 2 * *ng*. (Initially, *nextgroup* = 0 and *ng* = *m div* 2, so *nb* = *m*.) After a group has been expanded, *nextgroup* and *nb* are both increased by one, and the next group is ready for expansion.

After the first partial expansion, all *ng* groups have been expanded and *nextgroup* is reset to zero. Each group now contains three regular buckets rather than two, and the file size (in number of buckets) has grown by 50%.

During the second expansion, *nb* always equals *nextgroup* + 3 * *ng*. (At the start of a second partial expansion, *nextgroup* is zero and *nb* equals 3 * *ng*.) Three-bucket groups are expanded to four by moving some records from buckets *nextgroup*, *nextgroup* + *ng*, and *nextgroup* + 2 * *ng* (and some of their associated overflow records) into bucket *nextgroup* $+$ $3 * ng$ (which equals *nb* during the second partial expansion). Any overflow records not moved to bucket *nb* during an expansion are moved back into their home bucket, if there is room.

After the second partial expansion, the file size has doubled and a full expansion has taken place. In preparation for the next full expansion, the number of groups (*ng*) is doubled and the size of each group is halved, from four to two. That is, group *i*, consisting of buckets $i, i + j, i + 2 * j$, and $i + 3 * j$ (where *j* is the old value of *ng*), is now viewed as two separate groups: group *i* consisting of buckets i and $i + 2 * j$ and group $i + j$ consisting of buckets $i + j$ and $i + 3 * j$. The first partial expansion of the next full expansion then begins.

Note that the group that is expanded is always the next sequential group and is independent of whether or not overflow has taken place in that group. Overflow is handled by a separate mechanism from expansion.

A key question is how a hash function is used to access a record directly. When the file contains *nb* buckets, the hash function must produce a value between 0 and $nb - 1$, but when the file size is increased by one bucket, it must produce a value between 0 and *nb*. Further, a record moved from bucket *i* to bucket *j* must have previously hashed into *i* and must henceforth hash into *j*. The hash function must also be used to determine whether or not a record should be moved during an expansion. The following technique allows direct access to a record's bucket. Although it does involve many CPU operations, it only requires one I/O operation to obtain the appropriate bucket for a nonoverflow record.

A function $h1(key)$ that produces values in the range 0 to $m - 1$ is used as a direct hashing function initially, before any expansions have taken place. The value $h1(key)$ is called the ***initial hash*** of *key*. We also assume a function $h2(key, i)$ for $i > 0$ that uniformly produces values in the range 1 to 4. The value of $h2(key, i)$ determines whether the record with key *key* is moved during the *i*th full expansion and, if so, whether it is moved to the first or the second expansion bucket of its group. If $h2(key, i)$ is 1 or 2, then the record is not moved during the *i*th full expansion; if $h2(key, i) = 3$, then it is moved to the first expansion bucket of its group in the *i*th full expansion; if $h2(key, i) = 4$, then it is moved to the second expansion bucket. Thus a random record has a 50% chance of being moved during a full expansion and a 25% chance of being moved to either of the two expansion buckets.

During the first partial expansion of the *i*th full expansion, the hashing algorithm examines the values $h2(key, i)$, $h2(key, i + 1)$, $h2(key, i + 2)$, and so on, seeking the first value less than 4. If that value is 1 or 2, then the record is not moved; if it is 3, it is moved to the single expansion bucket. It will stay there after the second partial expansion if $h2(key, i)$ is 3; it will be moved to the second partial expansion bucket by the second partial expansion if $h2(key, i)$ is 4. Thus a random record has a one-third chance of being moved to the third bucket of a group in a first partial expansion and a one-quarter chance of being moved to the fourth bucket in a second partial expansion. This guarantees that the records are distributed uniformly throughout the file.

Let us define the *level* of an LH2P file as the number of full expansions that have taken place and let the variable *level* contain the level of the file. If *pe* is the number of the current partial expansion (either 1 or 2), then *pe* + 1 is the number of buckets in a group that has not yet been expanded in the current partial expansion and *pe* + 2 is the number of buckets in a group that has been expanded. At all times,

$$ng = m * 2^{level - 1}$$

and

$$nb = nextgroup + (pe + 1) * ng$$

The values *m*, *level*, *nextgroup*, and *pe* therefore define the state of an LH2P file and must be kept with the file at all times.

To locate the address of a record, it is necessary to follow its relocations through the *level* full expansions, the *pe* − 1 completed partial expansions, and the *nextgroup* completed simple expansions of the current partial expansion. The hash of a key, *h(key)*, is therefore computed by the following algorithm:

```
h:= h1(key);                { initial hash }
numgroups:= m div 2;        { initial number of groups }
for i:= 1 to level
    do begin
        { trace the movement of the record }
        {     through level full expansions }
        bucketnum:= h2(key, i);
        if bucketnum > 2
            then begin          { record was moved in ith full expansion }
                groupnum:= h mod numgroups;
                h:= groupnum + (bucketnum - 1) * numgroups
            end { then begin };
        numgroups:= 2 * numgroups   { number of groups after }
                                    {   i full expansions    }
    end { for...do begin };
{ At this point, h holds the key's hash after level full expansions }
{ and no partial expansions. Now, compute the record's current     }
{ location after possible movement in the current full expansion.  }
groupnum:= h mod numgroups;   { current group number }
i:= level + 1;
```

```
bucketnum: = b2(key, i);          { eventual bucket number at end }
                                  {    of current full expansion  }
  {          compute the size of the current group.          }
  { pe holds the number of the current partial expansion }
if groupnum < nextgroup
   then groupsize: = pe + 2
   else groupsize: = pe + 1;
  { if the eventual bucket number is larger than the current group size, }
  {    then continue hashing until the current bucket number is found   }
while bucketnum > groupsize
     do begin
             i: = i + 1;
             bucketnum: = b2(key, i)
        end [ while...do begin ];
if bucketnum > 2
   then   { the record was already moved in }
          {     the current full expansion      }
        b: = groupnum + (bucketnum - 1) * numgroups
```

The following example illustrates LH2P. Consider an LH2P file that initially contains six buckets, 0 through 5, consisting of three groups: (0, 3), (1, 4), and (2, 5). In this case, m is 6 and nb is initially 6. Consider six records $r0$ through $r5$ with keys $k0$ through $k5$ that initially hash into 0 through 5, respectively (i.e., $b1(ki) = i$). Then $r0$ through $r5$ are placed in buckets 0 through 5 initially.

Assume that the following are the values of $b2(key, i)$ for key equal to $k0$ through $k5$ and i from 1 to 4

key	$b2(key, 1)$	$b2(key, 2)$	$b2(key, 3)$	$b2(key, 4)$
$k0$	1	4	2	3
$k1$	4	2	1	2
$k2$	3	1	2	1
$k3$	4	4	3	1
$k4$	1	2	1	2
$k5$	2	4	4	3

The following table illustrates the expansion of this LH2P file. Each simple expansion is specified in the first column by a status triple consisting of the number of full expansions that have taken place (*level*), the number of the current partial expansion (*pe*), and the number of the group currently being expanded (*nextgroup*). Initially, there are three groups ($ng = 3$), six buckets ($nb = 6$), and two buckets per group. The second column shows the existing buckets of the current group in parentheses, followed by the bucket being added to the group in the current expansion step. We use the notation bi to indicate bucket i. Below the buckets of the group in each second-column entry are the records contained in that group. The third column indicates the results of the simple expansion.

status	group and records	result of expansion
(0, 1, 0)	$(b0, b3)$; $b6$ $(r0, r3)$	$h2(k0, 1) = 1$, so $r0$ remains in $b0$. $h2(k3, 1) = 4$, $h2(r3, 2) = 4$, $\quad h2(k3, 3) = 3$, so $r3$ moves to $b6$.
(0, 1, 1)	$(b1, b4)$; $b7$ $(r1, r4)$	$h2(k1, 1) = 4$, $h2(k1, 2) = 2$, $\quad$ so $r1$ remains in $b1$. $h2(k4, 1) = 1$, so $r4$ remains in $b4$.
(0, 1, 2)	$(b2, b5)$; $b8$ $(r2, r5)$	$h2(k2, 1) = 3$, so $r2$ moves to $b8$. $h2(k5, 1) = 2$, so $r5$ remains in $b5$.

This ends the first partial expansion. There are still three groups, but each now contains three buckets, so $nb = 9$. The second partial expansion then begins:

status	group and records	result of expansion
(0, 2, 0)	$(b0, b3, b6)$; $b9$ $(r0, r3)$	$h2(k0, 1) = 1$, so $r0$ remains in $b0$. $h2(k3, 1) = 4$, so $r3$ moves to $b9$.
(0, 2, 1)	$(b1, b4, b7)$; $b10$ $(r1, r4)$	$h2(k1, 1) = 4$, so $r1$ moves to $b10$. $h2(k4, 1) = 1$, so $r4$ remains in $b4$.
(0, 2, 2)	$(b2, b5, b8)$; $b11$ $(r2, r5)$	$h2(k2, 1) = 3$, so $r2$ remains in $b8$. $h2(k5, 1) = 2$, so $r5$ remains in $b5$.

This ends the first full expansion. There are now three groups, and each contains four buckets, so $nb = 12$. To start the second full expansion, the number of groups is doubled ($ng = 6$), and the number of buckets in each is reset to 2. The second full expansion proceeds:

status	group and records	result of expansion
(1, 1, 0)	$(b0, b6)$; $b12$ $(r0)$	$h2(k0, 2) = 4$; $h2(k0, 3) = 2$, $\quad$ so $r0$ remains in $b0$.
(1, 1, 1)	$(b1, b7)$; $b13$	No records in this group.
(1, 1, 2)	$(b2, b8)$; $b14$ $(r2)$	$h2(k2, 2) = 1$, so $r2$ remains in $b8$.
(1, 1, 3)	$(b3, b9)$; $b15$ $(r3)$	$h2(k3, 2) = 4$, $h2(k3, 3) = 3$, $\quad$ so $r3$ moves to $b15$.
(1, 1, 4)	$(b4, b10)$; $b16$ $(r1, r4)$	$h2(k1, 2) = 2$, so $r1$ remains in $b10$. $h2(k4, 2) = 2$, so $r4$ remains in $b4$.
(1, 1, 5)	$(b5, b11)$; $b17$ $(r5)$	$h2(k5, 2) = 4$; $h2(k5, 3) = 4$; $h2(k5, 4) = 3$, $\quad$ so $r5$ moves to $b17$.

This ends the first partial expansion.

$(1, 2, 0)$	$(b0, b6, b12); b18$ $(r0)$	$h2(k0, 2) = 4$, so $r0$ moves to $b18$.
$(1, 2, 1)$	$(b1, b7, b13); b19$	No records in this group.
$(1, 2, 2)$	$(b2, b8, b14); b20$ $(r2)$	$h2(k2, 2) = 1$, so $r2$ remains in $b8$.
$(1, 2, 3)$	$(b3, b9, b15); b21$ $(r3)$	$h2(k3, 2) = 4$, so $r3$ moves to $b21$.
$(1, 2, 4)$	$(b4, b10, b16); b22$ $(r1, r4)$	$h2(k1, 2) = 2$, so $r1$ remains in $b10$. $h2(k4, 2) = 2$, so $r4$ remains in $b4$.
$(1, 2, 5)$	$(b5, b11, b17); b23$ $(r5)$	$h2(k5, 2) = 4$, so $r5$ moves to $b23$.

This ends the second full expansion.

The techniques of LH2P can be generalized to allow n partial expansions in each full expansion. Such a scheme is called LHnP. Each partial expansion increases the file size by the fraction $1/n$. While higher values of n reduce the average number of overflow records (since records hashing to a particular bucket are redistributed more frequently) and therefore the number of accesses for both search and insertion, more partial expansions require more frequent allocations of storage and more complex hash value computations. Thus practical insertion costs and expansion costs are higher. The value $n = 2$, leading to the scheme LH2P, is a practical compromise.

Overflow can be handled by a variety of methods under linear hashing. Use of overflow buckets is the simplest technique but may require varying-sized buckets for efficiency. Such variation would complicate storage management. Ramamohanarao and Sacks-Davis suggest recursive linear hashing in which records that overflow the prime area are placed in a second linear hashing file, records that overflow that area are placed in a third, and so on. More than three areas are rarely needed.

There are several techniques that eliminate the need for separate, dedicated overflow areas. Mullin suggests using chaining within the linear hashing file, in which the most recently expanded group is used to contain overflow records (since that group is most likely to have empty space). Larson suggests that every kth bucket in the primary area be reserved for overflow records, with the hash function suitably modified to avoid the overflow buckets.

Larson also suggests the possibility of using linear rehashing to locate overflow records. When linear rehashing is used, it is more efficient to implement each partial expansion in several sweeps of step size $s > 1$ and to go backward among the groups. Thus, if there are ng groups, the first sweep would expand groups $ng - 1$, $ng - 1 - s$, $ng - 1 - 2 * s$, and so on; the second sweep would expand groups $ng - 2$, $ng - 2 - s$, $ng - 2$

- 2 * s, and so on; and so on. Linear rehashing can also be combined with the separator method of Gonnet and Larson to allow one-access retrieval and eliminate the overhead of overflow.

Choosing a Hash Function

Let us now turn to the question of how to choose a good hash function. Clearly, the function should produce as few hash clashes as possible; that is, it should spread the keys uniformly over the possible array indices. Of course, unless the keys are known in advance, it cannot be determined whether a particular hash function will disperse them properly. However, although it is rare to know the keys before selecting a hash function, it is fairly common to know some properties of the keys that affect their dispersal.

In general, a hash function should depend on every single bit of the key, so that two keys which differ in only one bit or one group of bits (regardless of whether the group is at the beginning, end, or middle of the key or strewn throughout the key) hash into different values. Thus a hash function which simply extracts a portion of a key is not suitable. Similarly, if two keys are simply digit or character permutations of each other (such as 139 and 319 or *MEAL* and *LAME*), they should also hash into different values. The reason for this is that key sets frequently have clusters or permutations which might otherwise result in collisions.

For example, the most common hash function (which we have used in the examples of this section) uses the *division method*, in which an integer key is divided by the table size and the remainder is taken as the hash value. This is the hash function $h(key) = key \bmod (maxtable + 1)$. Suppose, however, that $maxtable + 1$ equals 1000 and that all the keys end in the same three digits (e.g., the last three digits of a part number might represent a plant number, and the program is being written for that plant). Then the remainder on dividing by 1000 will yield the same values for all the keys, so that a hash clash will occur for each record except the first. Clearly, given such a collection of keys, a different hash function should be used.

It has been found that the best results with the division method are achieved when the table size m (which equals $maxtable + 1$) is prime (i.e., m is not divisible by any positive integer other than 1 and m). However, even if m is prime, an additional restriction is called for. If r is the number of possible character codes on a particular computer (assuming an 8-bit byte, r is 256), then if m is a prime such that $r \bmod m$ equals 1, the hash function $key \bmod m$ is simply the sum of the binary representation of the characters in the key modulo m. For example, suppose r equals 256 and m equals 17, in which case $r \bmod m = 1$. Then the key 37956 which equals $148 \times 256 + 68$ (so that the first byte of its representation is 148 and the second byte is 68) hashes into 37956 $\bmod$ 17 which equals 12 which equals $(148 + 68)$ $\bmod$ 17. Thus two keys which are simply character permutations (such as

STEAM and *MATES*) will hash into the same value. This may promote collisions and should be avoided. Similar problems occur if m is chosen so that r^k *mod m* is very small or very close to m for some small value of k.

Another hash method is the ***multiplicative method***. In this method, a real number c between 0 and 1 is selected. $h(key)$ is defined as $trunc(m * frac(c * key))$, where $frac(x)$ is the fractional part of the real number x (note that $frac(x) = x - trunc(x)$). That is, multiply the key by a real number between 0 and 1, take the fractional part of the product yielding a random number between 0 and 1 dependent on every bit of the key, and multiply by m to yield an index between 0 and $m - 1$. If the word size of the computer is b bits, c should be chosen so that $2^b * c$ is an integer relatively prime to 2^b, and c should not be too close to either 0 or 1. Also if r, as before, is the number of possible character codes, avoid values c such that $frac(r^k * c)$ is too close to 0 or 1 for some small value of k (these values yield similar hashes for keys with the same last k characters) and values c of the form $i/(r - 1)$ or $i/(r^2 - 1)$ (these values yield similar hashes for keys which are character permutations). Values of c that yield good theoretical properties are .6180339887, which equals $(sqrt(5) - 1)/2$, or .3819660113, which equals $1 - (sqrt(5) - 1)/2$. If m is chosen as a power of 2 such as 2^p, the computation of $h(key)$ can be done quite efficiently by multiplying the one-word integer *key* by the one-word integer $c * 2^b$ to yield a two-word product. The integer represented by the most significant p bits of the integer in the second word of this product is then equal to the value of $h(key)$. However, such a computation would most likely have to be implemented in assembler language rather than in Pascal.

In another hash function, known as the ***midsquare method***, the key is multiplied by itself and the middle few digits (the exact number depends on the number of digits allowed in the index) of the square are used as the index. If the square is considered as a decimal number, the table size must be a power of 10, whereas if it is considered as a binary number, the table size must be a power of 2. Alternatively, the number represented by the middle digits can be divided by the table size and the remainder used as the hash value. Unfortunately, the midsquare method does not yield uniform hash value and does not perform as well as do the previous two techniques.

The ***folding method*** breaks up a key into several segments which are added or exclusive *or*ed together to form a hash value. For example, suppose that the internal bit string representation of a key is 010111001010110 and that 5 bits are allowed in the index. The three bit strings 01011, 10010, and 10110 are exclusive *or*ed to produce 01111, which is 15 as a binary integer. (The ***exclusive or*** of two bits is 0 if the two bits are the same and 1 otherwise. This is the same as the binary sum of the bits, ignoring the carry.) The disadvantage of the folding method is that two keys which are k-bit permutations of each other (that is, where both keys consist of the same groups of k bits in a different order) will hash into the same k-bit value. Still another technique is to apply a multiplicative hash function to each segment individually before folding.

There are many other hash functions, each with its own advantages and disadvantages, depending on the set of keys to be hashed. One consideration in choosing a hash function is efficiency of calculation; it does no good to be able to find an object on the first try if that try takes longer than several tries in an alternative method.

If the keys are not integers, they must be converted into integers before applying one of the foregoing hash functions. There are several ways to do this. For example, for a character string the internal bit representation of each character can be interpreted as a binary number. One disadvantage of this is that the bit representations of all the letters or digits tend to be very similar on most computers. If the keys consist of letters alone, the index of each letter in the alphabet can be used to create an integer. Thus the first letter of the alphabet (*a*) is represented by the digits 01 and the fourteenth (*n*) is represented by the digits 14. The key '*hello*' is represented by the integer 0805121215. Once an integer representation of a character string exists, the folding method can be used to reduce it to manageable size. However, here too, every other digit is a 0, 1, or 2, which may result in nonuniform hashes. Another possibility is to view each letter as a digit in base-26 notation so that '*hello*' is viewed as the integer $8 \times 26^4 + 5 \times 26^3 + 12 \times 26^2 + 12 \times 26 + 15$.

One of the drawbacks of all these hash functions is that they are not *order preserving;* that is, the hash value of the two keys are not necessarily in the same order as the keys themselves. It is therefore not possible to traverse the hash table in sequential order by key. An example of a hash function that is order preserving is $h(key) = key \ div \ c$, where c is some constant chosen so that the highest possible key divided by c equals *maxtable*. Unfortunately, order preserving hash functions usually are severely nonuniform, leading to many hash clashes and a larger average number of probes to access an element. Note also that, to enable sequential access to keys, the separate chaining method of resolving collisions must be used.

Perfect Hash Functions

Given a set of keys $k = \{k_1, k_2, \ldots, k_n\}$, a *perfect hash function* is a hash function h such that $h(k_i) <> h(k_1)$ for all distinct i and j. That is, no hash clashes occur under a perfect hash function. In general, it is difficult to find a perfect hash function for a particular set of keys. Further, once a few more keys are added to the set for which a perfect hash function has been found, the hash function generally ceases to be perfect for the expanded set. Thus although it is desirable to find a perfect hash function to ensure immediate retrieval, it is not practical to do so unless the set of keys is static and is frequently searched. The most obvious example of such a situation is a compiler in which the set of reserved words of the programming language being compiled does not change and must be accessed repeatedly. In such a situation, the effort required to find a perfect hashing function is worthwhile because, once the function is determined, it can save a great deal of time in repeated applications.

Of course, the larger the hash table, the easier it is to find a perfect hash function for a given set of keys. If 10 keys must be placed in a table of 100 elements, 63% of the possible hash functions are perfect (although as soon as the number of keys reaches 13 in a 100-item table, the majority are no longer perfect). In the example given earlier, if the compiler symbol table is to contain all symbols used in any program so that a large table must be allocated to allow for a large number of user-declared identifiers, a hash function which is perfect can easily be found for the reserved symbols of the language. The table can be initialized with the reserved symbols already in the positions determined by that function, with the user-defined symbols inserted as they are encountered. While hash clashes may occur for user symbols, we are guaranteed immediate lookup for the reserved symbols.

In general, it would be desirable to have a perfect hash function for a set of n keys in a table of only n positions. Such a perfect hash function is called **minimal**. In practice, this is difficult to achieve. Sprugnoli has developed a number of perfect hash function determination algorithms. The algorithms are fairly complex and will not be presented here. One technique finds perfect hash functions of the form $h(key) = (key + s)$ **div** d for some integers s and d. These are called **quotient reduction** perfect hash functions and, once found, are quite easy to compute. For the key set $\{17, 138, 173, 294, 306, 472, 540, 551, 618\}$, Sprugnoli's algorithm find the quotient reduction hash function $(key + 25)/64$, which yields the hash values 0, 2, 3, 4, 5, 7, 8, 9, 10. The function is not minimal since it distributes the nine keys to a table of 11 positions. Sprugnoli's algorithm does, however, find the quotient reduction perfect hash function with the smallest table size. An improvement to the algorithm yields a minimal perfect hash function of the form

$$h(key) = (key + s) \textbf{ div } d \qquad \text{if } key <= t$$
$$h(key) = (key + s + r) \textbf{ div } d \quad \text{if } key > t$$

where the values s, d, t, and r are determined by the algorithm. However, the algorithm to discover such a minimal perfect hash function is $O(n^3)$ with a large constant of proportionality so that it is not practical even for very small key sets. A slight modification yields a more efficient algorithm that produces a near-minimal perfect hashing function of this form for small key sets. In the example, such a function is

$$h(key) = (key - 7) \textbf{ div } 72 \quad \text{if } key <= 306$$
$$h(key) = (key - 42) \textbf{ div } 72 \quad \text{if } key > 306$$

which yields the hash values 0, 1, 2, 3, 4, 5, 6, 7, and 8 and happens to be minimal. A major advantage of quotient reduction hash functions and their variants is that they are order preserving.

Sprugnoli also presents another group of hashing functions, called *remainder reduction* perfect hash functions, which are of the form

$$h(key) = ((r + s * key) \bmod x) \ div \ d$$

and an algorithm to produce values r, s, x, and d which yield such a perfect hash function for a given key set and a desired minimum load factor. If the minimum load factor is set to 1, a minimal perfect hash function results. Unfortunately, the algorithm does not guarantee that a perfect remainder reduction hash function can be found in reasonable time for high load factors. Nevertheless, the algorithm can often be used to find minimal perfect hash functions for small key sets in reasonable time.

Unfortunately, Sprugnoli's algorithms are all at least $O(n^2)$ and are therefore only practical for small sets of keys (12 or fewer). Given a larger set of keys, K, a perfect hash function can be developed by a technique called *segmentation*. This technique involves dividing K into a number of small sets, K_0, K_2, ... , K_p, and finding a perfect hash function h_i for each small set K_i. Assume a grouping function *set* such that *key* is in the set $K_{set(key)}$. If m_i is the maximum value of h_i on K_i and b_i is defined as $i + m_0 + m_1 + ... + m_{i-1}$, we can define the segmented hash function h as $h(key) = b_{set(key)} + h_{set(key)} (key)$. Of course, the function *set* which determines the grouping must be chosen with care to disperse the keys reasonably.

Jaeschke presents a method for generating minimal perfect hash functions using a technique called *reciprocal hashing*. The reciprocal hash functions generated by Jaeschke's algorithm are of the form

$$h(key) = (c \ div \ (d * key + e)) \bmod (maxtable + 1)$$

for some constants c, d, and e and *maxtable* equal to one less than the number of keys. Indeed, if the keys are all relatively prime, then a constant c can be found which yields a minimal perfect hash function of the form

$$(c \ div \ key) \bmod (maxtable + 1)$$

by the following algorithm. Assume that the keys are initially in a sorted array $k[1]$ through $k[n]$ and that $f(c, key)$ is the function $(c \ div \ key) \bmod n$.

```
found := false; {has c been found ?}
c := ((n - 2) * k[1] * k[n]) div (k[n] - k[1]);
while not found
      do begin {check if c yields a perfect hash function}
            bigi := 0; {    these will be set to the    }
```

```
bigj:= 0; {    largest values such that    }
           { f(c, k [bigi]) = f(c, k [bigj]) }
for i:= 1 to n
    do val[i]:= f(c, k [i]);
i:= n;
while (bigi = 0) and (i > 0)
       do begin
                vi:= val[i];
                j:= i - 1;
                while (bigi = 0) and (j > 0)
                    do if vi = val[ j]
                           then begin
                                    bigi:= i;
                                    bigj:= j
                               end {then begin}
                           else j:= j - 1;
                i:= i - 1
       end {while...do begin};
    if bigi = 0
       then found:= true
       else begin {increment c}
                x:= k [bigj] - (c mod k [bigj]);
                y:= k [bigi] - (c mod k [bigi]);
                if x < y
                   then c:= c + x
                   else c:= c + y
           end {else...begin}
   end {while...do begin}
```

Applying this algorithm to the key set $\{3, 5, 11, 14\}$ yields $c = 11$ and the minimal perfect hash function $(11 \ div \ key) \ mod \ 4$. For the key set $\{3, 5, 11, 13, 14\}$, the algorithm produces $c = 66$. In practice, one would set an upper limit on the value of c to ensure that the algorithm does not go on indefinitely.

If the keys are not relatively prime, Jaeschke presents another algorithm to compute values d and e so that the values of $d * k[i] + e$ are relatively prime.

For low values of n, approximately 1.82^n values of c must be examined by this algorithm, which is tolerable for $n \le 20$. For values of n up to 40, we can divide the keys into two sets $S1$ and $S2$ of size $n1$ and $n2$, where all keys in $S1$ are smaller than those of $S2$. Then we can find values $c1, d1, e1$ and $c2, d2, e2$ for each of the sets individually and use

$$h(key) = (c1 \ div \ (d1 * key + e1)) \ mod \ n1$$

for keys in $S1$ and

$$h(key) = n1 + (c2 \ \textbf{div} \ (d2 * key + e2)) \ \textbf{mod} \ n2$$

for keys in $S2$. For larger key sets, the segmentation technique of Sprugnoli can be used.

Chang presents an order-preserving minimal perfect hash function that depends on the existence of a ***prime number function***, $p(key)$, for the set of keys. Such a function always produces a prime number corresponding to a given key and has the additional property that if $key1$ is less than $key2$ then $p(key1)$ is less than $p(key2)$. An example of such a prime number function is

$$p(x) = x^2 - x + 41 \quad \text{for} \quad 1 <= x <= 40$$

If such a prime number function has been found, Chang presents an algorithm to produce a value c such that the function $h(key) = c \ \textbf{mod} \ p(key)$ is an order-preserving minimal hash function. Unfortunately, prime number functions are not easy to find, and the value c is too large to be practically useful.

Cichelli presents a very simple method that often produces a minimal or near-minimal perfect hash function for a set of character strings. The hash function produced is of the form

$$h(key) = val(key[1]) + val(key[length(key)]) + length(key)$$

That is, add integer values associated with the first and last characters of the key to the length of the key. The integer values associated with particular characters are determined in two steps as follows.

The first step is to order the keys so that the sum of the occurrence frequencies of the first and last characters of the keys are in decreasing order. Thus if E occurs 10 times as a last or first character, G occurs 6 times, T occurs 9 times, and O occurs 4 times, then the keys *GATE*, *GOAT*, and *EGO* have occurrence frequencies 16 (6 + 10), 15 (6 + 9), and 14 (10 + 4), respectively, and are therefore ordered properly.

Once the keys have been ordered, we attempt to assign integer values. Each key is examined in turn. If the key's first or last character has not been assigned a value, attempt to assign one or two values between zero and some predetermined limit. If appropriate values can be assigned to produce a hash value which does not conflict with the hash value of a previous key, then tentatively assign those values. If not, or if both characters have been assigned values which result in a conflicting hash value, then it is necessary to backtrack to modify tentative assignments made for a previous key. To find a minimal perfect hash function, the predetermined limit for each character is set to the number of distinct first and last character occurrences.

Cichelli perfect hash functions may not exist for some key sets. For example, if two keys of the same length have the same or reversed first and last characters, no such hash function can exist. In that case, different character positions may be used to develop the hash function. However, in other cases no such hash function can be found regardless of what character positions are used. In practice, it is often useful to attempt to find a Cichelli perfect hash function before trying other methods. If the predetermined limit is set high enough, so that minimality is not required, Cichelli's algorithm can be quite practical for up to 50 keys. Cook and Oldehoeft present several improvements on the basic Cichelli method.

Sager presents an important generalization and extension of Cichelli's method that efficiently finds perfect hash functions for as many as 512 keys. The method is fairly complex and is not presented here; the interested reader is referred to Sager's paper listed in the Bibliography.

An additional technique for generating minimal perfect hash functions is due to Du, Hsieh, Jea, and Shieh. The technique uses a number of nonperfect random hash functions $h_1, \ldots, h_j$ and a separate **hash indicator table** (or **hit**) of size n. The table is initialized as follows. First, set all its entries to zero. Next, apply h_1 to all the keys. For all values x between 1 and n such that only one key hashes to x using h_1, reset $hit[x]$ from 0 to 1. Remove all keys that hash to unique values using h_1 from the key set and apply h_2 to the remaining keys. For all values x between 1 and n such that $hit[x] = 0$ and only one key hashes to x using h_2, reset $hit[x]$ from 0 to 2. This process continues until either the key set is empty (in which case hit has been initialized and any remaining unused hash functions are unnecessary) or until all the hash functions have been applied (in which case, if there are remaining keys, a perfect hash function cannot be found using this method and the given random hash functions).

Once hit has been fully initialized, the hashing algorithm is as follows

```
found := false;
i := 1;
while not found
    do begin
            x := h_i(key);
            if hit[x] = i
                then begin
                        hash := x;
                        found := true
                    end {then begin};
            i := i + 1
    end {while...do begin}
```

Unfortunately, the probability that a perfect hash function will result rises very slowly as additional random hash functions are added. Therefore, a segmentation technique, with distinct *bit* tables, should be used for large sets of keys.

Universal Classes of Hash Functions

As we have seen, it is very difficult to obtain a perfect hash function for a large set of keys. It is also not possible to guarantee that a specific hash function will minimize collisions without knowing the precise set of keys to be hashed. If a particular hash function is found not to work well in practice in a particular application, it is very difficult to come up with another hash function that will do better.

Carter and Wegman have introduced the concept of a ***universal class of bash functions***. Such a class consists of a set of hash functions $\{b_i(key)\}$. While an individual function in the class may work poorly on a particular input key set, enough of the functions work well for any random input set that if one function is chosen randomly from the class, it is likely to perform well on any input set that is actually presented.

Given a hash table of size m, and a set A of possible keys, a class of nb hash functions H is ***universal$_2$*** if there are no two keys in A on which more than nb/m of the functions in H result in collision. This means that no pair of distinct keys clash under more than $1/m$th of the functions. It can be shown that if k items have been inserted into a hash table of size m using a random member of a universal$_2$ class of hash functions with separate chaining, the expected number of probes for an unsuccessful search is less than $1 + k/m$ (the number for a successful search will be even lower).

Carter and Wegman present several examples of such universal$_2$ classes. One example of such a class is for keys that can be represented as positive integers between 0 and $w - 1$ ($w - 1$ is usually the maximum value that fits into one computer word). Let p be a prime number larger than w, let s be an integer between 1 and $p - 1$, and let t be an integer between 0 and $p - 1$. Then define $b_{s,t}(key)$ as $((s * key + t) \bmod p) \bmod m$. The set of all such functions $b_{s,t}$ for given w and p is universal$_2$. A second example is for keys consisting of i bits and a table size $m = 2^j$ for some j. Let a be an i-element array of table indexes (between 0 and $m - 1$). Then define $b_a(key)$ as the exclusive *or* of the indexes $a[k]$ such that the kth bit of *key* is 1. For example, if $m = 128$, $i = 16$, a is an array containing the values 47, 91, 35, 42, 16, 81, 113, 91, 12, 6, 47, 31, 106, 87, 95, and 11, and *key* is 15381 (which is 0011110000010101 as a 16-bit number), then $b_a(key)$ is the exclusive *or* of $a[3]$, $a[4]$, $a[5]$, $a[6]$, $a[12]$, $a[14]$, and $a[16]$ (these are 35, 42, 16, 47, 31, 87, and 11), which is 01110101 or 117. The set of functions b_a for all such array values a is universal$_2$.

If the hash table is being maintained internally and is not required between program runs (as in a compiler, for example), then the hash function used may be generated by the program from a universal$_2$ class to guarantee reasonable average running time (although any particular run may be slow). In the foregoing examples, a random number generator might be used to select *s*, *t*, and the elements of *a*. If the hash table remains between program runs, as in a file or data base, then a random hash function from the universal$_2$ class might be selected initially, and if poor program behavior is observed (although this is unlikely), a new random function could be selected and the entire hash table reorganized at a convenient time.

Sarwate has introduced an even better category of hash functions classes, called ***optimally universal$_2$ (OU$_2$)*** classes. If there are *nk* possible keys and *m* table entries, a set *H* containing *nb* hash functions is OU$_2$ if any two keys collide under exactly $nb * (nk - m)/(m * (nk - 1))$ functions in OU$_2$ and if, for any function *b* in *H*, every key collides with exactly $nk/m - 1$ other keys. Sarwate provides several examples of such OU$_2$ classes. Unfortunately, hash functions in OU$_2$ classes are very difficult to compute and may not be practically useful.

EXERCISES

1. Write a Pascal function *search(table, key)* which searches a hash table for a record with key *key*. The function accepts an integer key and a table declared by

    type elemtype = **record**
               k: keytype;
               r: rectype;
               flag: boolean
          end;
    var table: **array**[0..maxtable] **of** elemtype;

    table[i].k and *table[i].r* are the *i*th key and record, respectively. *table[i].flag* equals *false* if the *i*th table position is empty and *true* if it is occupied. The function returns an integer in the range 0.. *maxtable* if a record with key *key* is present in the table. If no such record exists, the function returns −1. Assume the existence of a hashing routine, *b(key)*, and a rehashing routine, *rb(index)*, which both produce integers in the range 0.. *maxtable*.

2. Write a Pascal function *sinsert(table, key, rec)* to search and insert into a hash table as in Exercise 1.

3. Develop a mechanism for detecting when all possible rehash positions of a given key have been searched. Incorporate this method into the Pascal routines *search* and *sinsert* of the previous exercises.

4. Consider a double hashing method using primary hash function *b1(key)* and rehash function $rb(index) = m \bmod(index + b2(key))$. Assume that *b2(key)* is relatively prime to *m* for any key *key*. Develop a search algorithm and an algorithm to insert a record whose key is known not to exist in the table so that the keys at successive rehashes of a single key are in ascending order. The insertion algorithm may rearrange records previously inserted into the table. Can you combine these algorithms into a search and insertion algorithm?

5. Suppose that a key is equally likely to be any integer between *a* and *b*. Suppose

that the midsquare hash method is used to produce an integer between 0 and 2^{k-1}
Is the result equally likely to be any integer within that range? Why?

6. Given a hash function $h(key)$ for a table of size m, write a Pascal simulation program
   to determine each of the following quantities after $.8m$ random keys have been
   generated. The keys should be random six-digit integers.

   (i)   The percentage of integers between 0 and $m - 1$ that do not equal $h(key)$ for
         any generated key.
   (ii) The percentage of integers between 0 and $m - 1$ that equal $h(key)$ for more
         than one generated key.
   (iii) The maximum number of keys that hash into a single value between 0 and
         $m - 1$.
   (iv) The average number of keys that hash into values between 0 and $m - 1$, not
         including those values into which no key hashes.

   Run the program to test the uniformity of each of the following hash functions:

   (a) $h(key) = key \bmod m$ for m a prime.
   (b) $h(key) = key \bmod m$ for m a power of 2.
   (c) The folding method, using exclusive *or* to produce five-bit indices, where m
       $= 32$.
   (d) The midsquare method, using decimal arithmetic to produce four-digit indices,
       where $m = 10,000$.

7. If a hash table contains m positions and n records currently occupy the table, the
   load factor is defined as n/m. Show that if a hash function uniformly distributes
   keys over the m positions of the table and if lf is the load factor of the table, then
   $(n - 1) * lf/2$ of the n keys in the table collided upon insertion with a previously
   entered key.

8. Assume that n random positions of an m-element hash table are occupied, using
   hash and rehash functions which are equally likely to produce any index in the
   table. What is the average number of comparisons needed to insert a new element
   in terms of m and n? Explain why linear probing does not satisfy this condition.

9

![shaded banner]

GRAPHS AND THEIR APPLICATIONS

In this chapter we consider a new data structure, the graph. We define some of the terms associated with graphs and show how to implement them in Pascal. We also present several applications of graphs.

1. GRAPHS

A *graph* consists of a set of *nodes* (or *vertices*) and a set of *arcs* (or *edges*). Each arc in a graph is specified by a pair of nodes. Figure 9.1.1a illustrates a graph. The set of nodes is $\{A, B, C, D, E, F, G, H\}$ and the set of arcs is $\{(A, B), (A, D), (A, C), (C, D), (C, F), (E, G), (A, A)\}$. If the pairs of nodes that make up the arcs are ordered pairs, the graph is said to be a *directed graph* (or *digraph*). Figures 9.1.1b, c, and d illustrate three digraphs. The arrows between nodes represent arcs. The head of each arrow represents the second node in the ordered pair of nodes making up an arc, while the tail of each arrow represents the first node in the pair. The set of arcs for the graph of Figure 9.1.1b is $\{\langle A, B \rangle, \langle A, C \rangle, \langle A, D \rangle, \langle C, D \rangle, \langle F, C \rangle, \langle E, G \rangle, \langle A, A \rangle\}$. We use parentheses to indicate an unordered pair and angled brackets to indicate an ordered pair. In the first three sections of this chapter, we restrict our attention to digraphs. We consider undirected graphs again in Section 4.

Note that a graph need not be a tree (Figure 9.1.1a, b, and d) but that a tree must be a graph (Figure 9.1.1c). Note also that a node need not have any arcs associated with it (node H in Figure 9.1.1a and b).

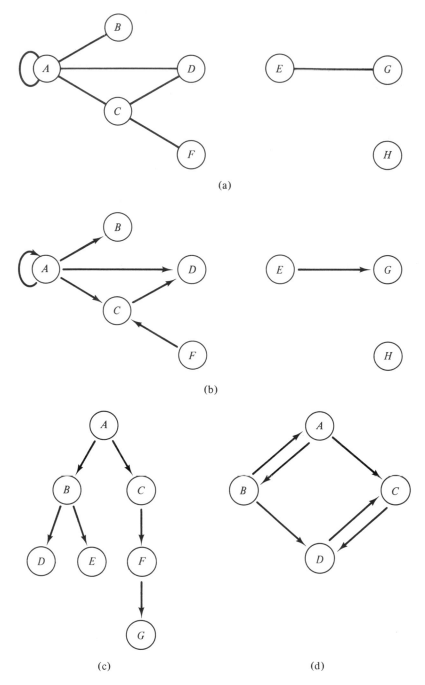

Figure 9.1.1   Examples of graphs.

A node n is *incident* to an arc x if n is one of the two nodes in the ordered pair of nodes that comprise x. (We also say that x is incident to n.) The *degree* of a node is the number of arcs incident to it. The *indegree* of a node n is the number of arcs that have n as the head and the *outdegree* of n is the number of arcs that have n as the tail. For example, node A in Figure 9.1.1d has indegree 1, outdegree 2, and degree 3. A node n is *adjacent* to a node m if there is an arc from m to n. If n is adjacent to m, then n is called the *successor* of m, and m a *predecessor* of n.

A *relation R* on a set A is a set of ordered pairs of elements of A. If $\langle x, y \rangle$ is a member of a relation R, then x is said to be *related* to y in R. For example, if $A = \{3, 5, 6, 8, 10, 17\}$, then the set $R = \{\langle 3, 10 \rangle, \langle 5, 6 \rangle, \langle 5, 8 \rangle, \langle 6, 17 \rangle, \langle 8, 17 \rangle, \langle 10, 17 \rangle\}$ is a relation on A. The relation R may be described by saying that x is related to y if x is less than y and the remainder obtained by dividing y by x is odd. $\langle 8, 17 \rangle$ is a member of this relation since 8 is smaller than 17 and the remainder on dividing 17 by 8 is 1, which is odd. A relation may be represented by a graph in which the nodes represent the underlying set and the arcs represent the ordered pairs of the relation. Figure 9.1.2a illustrates the graph representing the foregoing relation. A number may be associated with each arc of a graph as in Figure 9.1.2b. In that figure, the number associated with each arc is the remainder obtained by dividing the integer at the head of the arc by the integer at the tail. Such a graph, in which a number is associated with each arc, is called a *weighted graph* or a *network*. The number associated with an arc is called its *weight*.

We identify several primitive operations which are useful in dealing with graphs. The operation *join* (a, b) adds an arc from node a to node b if one does not already exist. *joinwt* (a, b, x) adds an arc from a to b with weight x in a weighted graph. *remv* (a, b) and *remvwt* (a, b, x) remove an arc from a to b if one exists (*remvwt* also sets x to its weight). Although we may also want to add or delete nodes from a graph, we postpone a discussion of these possibilities until a later section. The function *adjacent* (a, b) returns *true* if b is adjacent to a, and *false* otherwise.

A *path of length k* from node a to node b is defined as a sequence of $k + 1$ nodes $n_1, n_2, \ldots, n_{k+1}$ such that $n_1 = a$, $n_{k+1} = b$, and *adjacent* (n_i, n_{i+1}) is *true* for all i between 1 and k. If for some integer k, a path of length k exists between a and b, there is a *path* from a to b. A path from a node to itself is called a *cycle*. If a graph contains a cycle, it is *cyclic*; otherwise it is *acyclic*. A *d*irected *a*cyclic *g*raph is called a *dag* from its acronym.

Consider the graph of Figure 9.1.3. There is a path of length 1 from A to C, two paths of length 2 from B to G, and a path of length 3 from A to F. There is no path from B to C. There are cycles from B to B, from F to F, and from H to H. Be sure that you can find all paths of length less than 9 and all cycles in the figure.

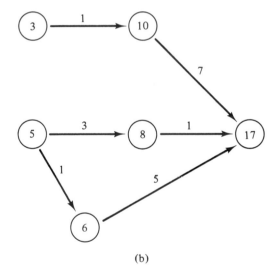

Figure 9.1.2   Relations and graphs.

An Application of Graphs

We now consider an example. We wish to read one input line containing four integers, followed by any number of input lines with two integers each. The first integer on the first line, n, represents a number of cities which for simplicity are numbered from 1 to n. The second and third integers on that line are between 1 and n and represent two cities, A and B. It is desired

Figure 9.1.3

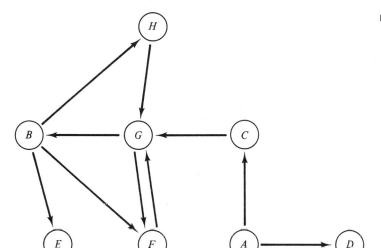

to travel from city *A* to city *B* using exactly *nr* roads, where *nr* is the fourth integer on the first input line. Each subsequent input line contains two integers representing two cities. This indicates that there is a road from the first city to the second. The problem is to determine whether there is a path of required length by which one can travel from city *A* to city *B*.

A plan for solution is the following. Create a graph with the cities as nodes and the roads as arcs. To find a path of length *nr* from node *A* to node *B*, look for a node *C* such that an arc exists from *A* to *C* and a path of length *nr* — 1 exists from *C* to *B*. If these conditions are satisfied for some node *C*, the desired path exists. If the conditions are not satisfied for any node *C*, the desired path does not exist. The algorithm uses an auxiliary recursive function *findpath*(*k*, *a*, *b*). This function returns *true* if there is a path of length *k* from *A* to *B* and *false* otherwise. The algorithms for the program and the function follow:

```
read (n);      {number of cities}
create n nodes and label them from 1 to n;
read (a, b);       {     seek path from a to b      }
read (nr);       {desired number of roads to take}
while there is more input
    do begin
            readln (city1, city2);
            join (city1, city2)
        end {while...do begin};
if findpath (nr, a, b)
    then write ('a path exists from ', a, ' to ', b, ' in ', nr, ' steps')
    else write ('no path exists from ', a, ' to ', b, ' in ', nr, ' steps')
```

The algorithm for the function *findpath*(k, a, b) follows:

```
if k=1
   then {search for a path of length 1}
        if adjacent (a, b)
           then findpath := true
           else findpath := false
   else begin
               findpath := false; {assume that no path exists}
               for c := 1 to n
                   do if adjacent (a, c)
                         then if findpath (k - 1, c, b)
                                    then findpath := true
        end {else begin}
```

Although the foregoing algorithm is a solution to the problem, it has several deficiencies. Many paths are investigated several times during the recursive process. Also, although the algorithm must actually check each possible path, the final result merely ascertains whether a desired path exists; it does not produce the path itself. More likely than not, it is desirable to find the arcs of the path in addition to knowing whether or not a path exists. Also, the algorithm does not test for the existence of a path regardless of length; it only tests for a path of specific length. We explore solutions to some of these problems later in this chapter and in the exercises.

Pascal Representation of Graphs

Let us now turn to the question of representing graphs in Pascal. Suppose that the number of nodes in the graph is constant (i.e., arcs may be added or deleted but nodes may not). A graph with 50 nodes could then be declared as follows:

```
const maxnodes = 50;
type  nodeptr = 1..maxnodes;
      arc = record
              adj: boolean;
              { information associated with each arc }
            end;
      node = record
               {information associated with each node}
             end;
      graph = record
                nodes: array [nodeptr] of node;
                arcs: array [nodeptr, nodeptr] of arc
              end;
var   g: graph;
```

Each node of the graph is represented by an integer between 1 and
maxnodes, and the array field *nodes* represents the appropriate information
assigned to each node. The array field *arcs* is a two-dimensional array representing every possible ordered pair of nodes. The value of $g.\,arcs\,[i,\,j].\,adj$
is either *true* or *false*, depending upon whether or not node j is adjacent to
node i. The two-dimensional array $g.\,arcs\,[nodeptr,\ nodeptr].\,adj$ is called an
adjacency matrix. In the case of a weighted graph, information can also be
assigned to each arc.

Frequently, the nodes of a graph are numbered from 1 to *maxnodes*
and no information is assigned to them. Also, we may be interested in the
existence of arcs but not in any weights or other information about them.
In such cases the graph could be declared simply by

```
const maxnodes = 50;
type  nodeptr = 1..maxnodes;
      adjmatrix = array[nodeptr, nodeptr] of boolean;
var   adj: adjmatrix;
```

In effect, the graph is totally described by its adjacency matrix. We present
the code for the primitive operations just described in the case where a graph
is described by its adjacency matrix.

```
procedure join (var adj: adjmatrix; node1, node2: nodeptr);
begin {add an arc from node1 to node2}
    adj[node1, node2] := true
end {procedure join};

procedure remv (var adj: adjmatrix; node1, node2: nodeptr);
begin {delete arc from node1 to node2 if one exists}
    adj[node1, node2] := false
end {procedure remv};

function adjacent (adj: adjmatrix; node1, node2: nodeptr): boolean;
begin {test whether there is an arc from node1 to node2}
    if adj[node1, node2]
        then adjacent := true
        else adjacent := false
end {function adjacent};
```

A weighted graph with a fixed number of nodes may be declared by

```
type arc = record
              adj: boolean;
              weight: integer
           end;
     arcs = array[nodeptr, nodeptr] of arc;
var  g: arcs;
```

The routine *joinwt*, which adds an arc from *node*1 to *node*2 with a given weight *wt*, may be coded as follows:

```
procedure joinwt (var g: arcs; node1, node2: nodeptr; wt: integer);
begin
      g[node1, node2].adj:= true;
      g[node1, node2].weight:= wt
end {procedure joinwt};
```

The routine *remvwt* is left to the reader as an exercise.

Transitive Closure

Let us assume that a graph is completely described by its adjacency matrix, *adj* (i.e., no data are associated with the nodes, and the graph is not weighted). Consider the logical expression $adj[i, k]$ *and* $adj[k, j]$. Its value is *true* if and only if the values of both $adj[i, k]$ and $adj[k, j]$ are *true*, which implies that there is an arc from node i to node k and an arc from node k to node j. Thus $adj[i, k]$ *and* $adj[k, j]$ equal *true* if and only if there is a path of length 2 from i to j passing through k.

Now consider the expression

$$(adj[i, 1] \text{ } \textbf{and} \text{ } adj[1, j]) \text{ } \textbf{or} \text{ } (adj[i, 2] \text{ } \textbf{and} \text{ } adj[2, j])$$
$$\textbf{or}\dots\textbf{or} \text{ } (adj[i, maxnodes] \text{ } \textbf{and} \text{ } adj[maxnodes, j])$$

The value of this expression is *true* only if there is a path of length 2 from node i to node j either through node 1 or through node 2, ... , or through node *maxnodes*. This is the same as saying that the expression evaluates to *true* if and only if there is some path of length 2 from node i to node j. Consider an array adj_2 such that $adj_2[i, j]$ is the value of the foregoing expression. adj_2 is called the **path matrix of length** 2. $adj_2[i, j]$ indicates whether or not there is a path of length 2 between i and j. [If you are familiar with matrix multiplication, you should realize that adj_2 is the product of adj with itself, with numerical multiplication replaced by conjunction (the **and** operation) and addition replaced by disjunction (the **or** operation).] adj_2 is said to be the **boolean product** of adj with itself.

Figure 9.1.4 illustrates this process. Figure 9.1.4a depicts a graph and its adjacency matrix in which *true* is represented by 1 and *false* is represented by 0. Figure 9.1.4b is the boolean product of that matrix with itself and thus is the path matrix of length 2 for the graph. Convince yourself that a 1 appears in row i, column j of the matrix of Figure 9.1.4b if and only if there is a path of length 2 from node i to node j in the graph.

Similarly, define adj_3, the path matrix of length 3, as the boolean product of adj_2 with adj. $adj_3[i, j]$ equals *true* if and only if there is a path of length 3 from i to j. In general, to compute the path matrix of length l, form the boolean product of the path matrix of length $l - 1$ with the

Figure 9.1.4

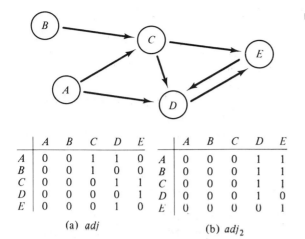

	A	B	C	D	E			A	B	C	D	E
A	0	0	1	1	0		A	0	0	0	1	1
B	0	0	1	0	0		B	0	0	0	1	1
C	0	0	0	1	1		C	0	0	0	1	1
D	0	0	0	0	1		D	0	0	0	0	1
E	0	0	0	1	0		E	0	0	0	0	1

(a) *adj*   (b) *adj*$_2$

adjacency matrix. Figure 9.1.5 illustrates the matrices *adj*$_3$ and *adj*$_4$ of the graph in Figure 9.1.4a.

     Assume that we want to know whether a path of length 3 or less exists between two nodes of a graph. If such a path exists between nodes i and j, it must be of length 1, 2, or 3. If there is a path of length 3 or less between nodes i and j, the value of

$$adj\,[i, j] \ or \ adj_2\,[i, j] \ or \ adj_3\,[i, j]$$

must be *true*. Figure 9.1.6 shows the matrix formed by *or*ing the matrices *adj*, *adj*$_2$, and *adj*$_3$. This matrix contains the value *true* (represented by the value 1 in the figure) in row i, column j, if and only if there is a path of length 3 or less from node i to node j.

     Suppose that we wish to construct a matrix *path* such that *path*[i, j] equals *true* if and only if there is some path from node i to node j (of any length). Clearly,

$$path\,[i, j] \ = adj\,[i, j] \ or \ adj_2\,[i, j] \ or \dots$$

	A	B	C	D	E			A	B	C	D	E
A	0	0	0	1	1		A	0	0	0	1	1
B	0	0	0	1	1		B	0	0	0	1	1
C	0	0	0	1	1		C	0	0	0	1	1
D	0	0	0	0	1		D	0	0	0	1	0
E	0	0	0	1	0		E	0	0	0	0	1

(a) *adj*$_3$ (b) *adj*$_4$ **Figure 9.1.5**

	A	B	C	D	E
A	0	0	1	1	1
B	0	0	1	1	1
C	0	0	0	1	1
D	0	0	0	1	1
E	0	0	0	1	1

Figure 9.1.6

Unfortunately, this equation cannot be used in computing *path*, since the process that it describes is an infinite one. However, if the graph has n nodes, it must be true that

$$path\,[i, j] = adj\,[i, j] \ or \ adj_2\,[i, j] \ or...or \ adj_n\,[i, j].$$

This is because if there is a path of length $m > n$ from i to j such as i, i_2, i_3, ... , i_m, j, there must be another path from i to j of length less than or equal to n. To see this, note that since there are only n nodes in the graph, at least one node k must appear in the path twice. The path from i to j can be shortened by removing the cycle from k to k. This process is repeated until no two nodes in the path (except possibly i and j) are equal and therefore the path is of length n or less. Figure 9.1.7 illustrates the matrix *path* for the graph of Figure 9.1.4a. The matrix *path* is often called the **transitive closure** of the matrix *adj*.

We may write a Pascal routine that accepts an adjacency matrix *adj* and computes its transitive closure *path*. This routine uses an auxiliary routine *prod(a, b, c)*, which sets the array c equal to the boolean product of a and b.

```
procedure transclose (adj: adjmatrix; var path: adjmatrix);
var i, j, k: nodeptr;
    newprod, adjprod: adjmatrix;
begin
    adjprod:= adj;
    path:= adj;
    for i:= 1 to maxnodes - 1
        {i represents the number of times adj has}
        {  been multiplied by itself to obtain    }
        { adjprod. At this point path represents }
        {       all paths of length i or less        }
    do begin
            prod(adjprod, adj, newprod);
            for j := 1 to maxnodes
                do for k := 1 to maxnodes
                    do path[j, k] := path[j, k] or newprod[j, k];
            adjprod:= newprod
        end {for...do begin}
end {procedure transclose};
```

	A	B	C	D	E
A	0	0	1	1	1
B	0	0	1	1	1
C	0	0	0	1	1
D	0	0	0	1	1
E	0	0	0	1	1

Figure 9.1.7 *path = adj or adj$_2$ or adj$_3$ or adj$_4$ or adj$_5$.*

The routine *prod* may be written as follows:

```
procedure prod (a, b: adjmatrix; var c: adjmatrix);
var val: boolean;
    i, j, k: integer;
begin
    for i:= 1 to maxnodes {pass through rows}
        do for j:= 1 to maxnodes {pass through columns}
            do begin {compute c[i, j]}
                val := false;
                for k := 1 to maxnodes
                    do val := val or (a[i, k] and b[k, j]);
                c[i, j] := val
            end {for...do begin}
    end {procedure prod};
```

To analyze the efficiency (or inefficiency) of this procedure, note that finding the boolean product by the method we have presented is $O(n^3)$, where n is the number of graph nodes (i.e., *maxnodes*). In *transclose*, this process (the call to *prod*) is embedded in a loop which is repeated $n - 1$ times, so the entire transitive closure procedure is $O(n^4)$.

Warshall's Algorithm

The method just described is quite inefficient. Let us see if a more efficient method to compute *path* can be produced. Let us define the matrix *path$_k$* such that *path$_k$*[i, j] equals *true* if and only if there is a path from node i to node j which does not pass through any nodes numbered higher than k (except, possibly, for i and j themselves). How can the value of *path$_{k+1}$*[i, j] be obtained from *path$_k$*? Clearly, for any i and j such that *path$_k$*[i, j] = *true*, *path$_{k+1}$*[i, j] must equal *true* (why?). The only situation in which *path$_{k+1}$*[i, j] can equal *true* while *path$_k$*[i, j] equals *false* is if there is a path from i to j passing through node $k + 1$ but there is no path from i to j passing through only nodes 1 through k. But this means that there must be a path from i to $k + 1$ passing through only nodes 1 through k and a similar path from $k + 1$ to j. Thus *path$_{k+1}$*[i, j] = *true* if and only if one of the following two conditions holds:

1. *path$_k$*[i, j] = *true*   or
2. *path$_k$*[i, k + 1] = *true* and *path$_k$*[k + 1, j] = *true*.

This means that $path_{k+1}[i, j]$ equals $path_k[i, j]$ *or* ($path_k[i, k + 1]$ *and* $path_k[k + 1, j]$). An algorithm to obtain the matrix $path_k$ from the matrix $path_{k-1}$ based on this observation follows:

> *for* $i := 1$ *to maxnodes*
>> *do for* $j := 1$ *to maxnodes*
>>> *do* $path_k[i, j] := path_{k-1}[i, j]$ *or* ($path_{k-1}[i, k]$ *and* $path_{k-1}[k, j]$)

This may be logically simplified and made more efficient as follows:

> $path_k := path_{k-1}$;
> *for* $i := 1$ *to maxnodes*
>> *do if* $path_{k-1}(i, k)$
>>> *then for* $j := 1$ *to maxnodes*
>>>> *do* $path_k[i, j] := path_{k-1}[i, j]$ *or* $path_{k-1}[k, j]$

Clearly, $path_0[i, j] = adj$ since the only way to go from node i to node j without passing through any other nodes is to go directly from i to j. Further, $path_{maxnodes}[i, j] = path[i, j]$ since if a path may pass through any nodes numbered from 1 to *maxnodes*, then any path from node i to node j may be selected. The following Pascal routine may therefore be used to compute the transitive closure.

```
procedure transclose (adj: adjmatrix; var path: adjmatrix);
var i, j, k: nodeptr;
begin
      path := adj; {path starts off as adj}
      for k := 1 to maxnodes
         do for i := 1 to maxnodes
            do if path[i, k]
               then for j := 1 to maxnodes
                  do path[i, j] := path[i, j] or path[k, j]
   end {procedure transclose};
```

This technique increases the efficiency of finding the transitive closure to $O(n^3)$. The method is often called **Warshall's algorithm**, after its discoverer.

A Shortest Path Algorithm

In a weighted graph, or network, it is frequently desired to find the shortest path between two nodes, s and t. The **shortest path** is defined as a path from s to t such that the sum of the weights of the arcs on the path is minimized. To represent the network, we assume a *weight* function, such that $weight(i, j)$ is the weight of the arc from i to j. If there is no arc from i to j, then $weight(i, j)$ is set to an arbitrarily large value (such as *maxint*) to indicate the infinite cost (i.e., the impossibility) of going directly from i to j.

If all weights are positive, the following algorithm, due to Dijkstra, determines the shortest path from *s* to *t*. *distance*[*i*] keeps the cost of the shortest path known thus far from *s* to *i*. Initially, *distance*[*s*] is 0 and *distance*[*i*] equals *maxint* for all *i* not equal to *s*. A set *perm* contains all nodes whose minimal distance from *s* is known: that is, those nodes whose *distance* value is permanent and will not change. If a node *i* is in *perm*, then *distance*[*i*] is the minimal distance from *s* to *i*. Initially, *perm* equals [*s*]. Once *t* becomes a member of *perm*, *distance*[*t*] is known to be the shortest distance from *s* to *t*, and the algorithm terminates.

The algorithm maintains a variable, *current*, that is the node that has been added to *perm* most recently. Initially, *current* equals *s*. For every successor *i* of *current*, if *distance*[*current*] + *weight*(*current*, *i*) is less than *distance*[*i*], the distance from *s* to *i* through *current* is smaller than any other distance from *s* to *i* thus far found. Thus *distance*[*i*] must be reset to this smaller value.

Once *distance* has been recomputed for every successor of *current*, then *distance*[*j*] (for any *j*) represents the shortest path from *s* to *j* that includes only members of *perm* (except for *j* itself). This means that for the node *k*, not in *perm*, for which *distance*[*k*] is smallest, there is no path from *s* to *k* whose length is shorter than *distance*[*k*]. (*distance*[*k*] is already the shortest path to *k* that includes only nodes in *perm*, and any path to *k* that includes a node *nd* as its first node not in *perm* must be longer, since *distance*[*nd*] is greater than *distance*[*k*].) Thus *k* can be added to *perm*. *current* is then reset to *k* and the process is repeated.

The following is a Pascal procedure to implement this algorithm. In addition to calculating distances, the program finds the shortest path itself by maintaining an array *precede* such that *precede*[*i*] is the node that precedes node *i* on the shortest path found thus far. The procedure accepts a weight matrix (with nonadjacent arcs having a weight of *maxint*) and two nodes, *s* and *t*, and calculates the minimum distance *d* from *s* to *t* as well as the *precede* array to define the path. The procedure uses the Pascal set manipulation operations and assumes the following definitions and declarations:

```
const  maxnodes = ... ;
type   nodeptr = 1..maxnodes;
       weightmatrix = array [nodeptr, nodeptr] of integer;
       nodeset = set of nodeptr;
       nodearray = array [nodeptr] of nodeptr;

procedure shortpath (var weight: weightmatrix; s, t: nodeptr;
                                    var d: integer; var precede: nodearray;

var distance: array [nodeptr] of integer;
    current i, k: nodeptr;
    perm: nodeset;
    smalldist, newdist: integer;
```

```
begin {procedure shortpath}
    {initialization}
    perm := [s] ;
    for i := 1 to maxnodes
        do distance[i] := maxint;
    distance[s] := 0;
    current := s;
    while (current <> t)
        do begin
                smalldist := maxint;
                dc := distance[current] ;
                for i := 1 to maxnodes
                    do if not (i in perm)
                        then begin
                                newdist := dc + weight[current, i] ;
                                if newdist < distance[i]
                                    then begin
                                            { distance from s to i }
                                            {  through current is  }
                                            {    smaller than      }
                                            {      distance[i]      }
                                            distance[i] := newdist;
                                            precede[i] := current
                                        end {then begin};
                                { determine the smallest distance }
                                if distance[i] < smalldist
                                    then begin
                                            smalldist := distance[i] ;
                                            k := i
                                        end {then begin}
                            end {then begin};
                current := k;
                perm := perm + [current]
            end {while...do begin};
    d := distance[t]
end {procedure shortpath};
```

This program will not work if *maxnodes* exceeds the maximum set size in a particular Pascal implementation. An alternative implementation that maintains the set of "permanent" nodes as a linked list instead of as the set *perm* is left as an exercise for the reader. Note that Dijkstra's algorithm can be modified to find the shortest path from a node *s* to every other node in the graph by modifying the **while** header to

```
while (perm <> [1..maxnodes])
```

To analyze the efficiency of this implementation of Dijkstra's algorithm, note that one node is added to *perm* in each iteration of the *while* loop so that, potentially, the loop must be repeated *n* times (where *n* equals *maxnodes*, the number of nodes in the graph). Each iteration involves examining every node (*for i := 1 to maxnodes...*), so the entire algorithm is $O(n^2)$. We will examine a more efficient implementation of Dijkstra's algorithm in Section 3.

EXERCISES

1. For the graph of Figure 9.1.1b;
   (a) find its adjacency matrix.
   (b) find its path matrix using powers of the adjacency matrix.
   (c) find its path matrix using Warshall's algorithm.
2. Draw a digraph to correspond to each of the following relations on the integers from 1 to 12:
   (a) x is related to y if $x - y$ is evenly divisible by 3.
   (b) x is related to y if $x + 10 * y < x * y$.
   (c) x is related to y if the remainder on division of x by y is 2.
   Compute the adjacency and path matrices for these relations.
3. A node $n1$ is **reachable** from a node $n2$ in a graph if $n1$ equals $n2$ or there is a path from $n2$ to $n1$. Write a Pascal function *reach(adj, i, j)* which accepts an adjacency matrix and two integers and determines if the *j*th node in the digraph is reachable from the *i*th node.
4. Write Pascal routines which, given an adjacency matrix and two nodes of a graph, compute:
   (a) the number of paths of a given length existing between them.
   (b) the total number of paths existing between them.
5. A relation on a set S (and its corresponding digraph) is **symmetric** if for any two elements x and y in S such that x is related to y, y is also related to x.
   (a) What must be true of a digraph if it represents a symmetric relation?
   (b) Give an example of a symmetric relation and draw its digraph.
   (c) What must be true of the adjacency matrix of a symmetric digraph?
   (d) Write a Pascal routine that accepts an adjacency matrix and determines if the digraph it represents is symmetric.
6. A relation on a set S (and its corresponding digraph and adjacency matrix) is **transitive** if for any three elements x, y, and z in S, if x is related to y and y is related to z, then x is related to z.
   (a) What must be true of a digraph if it represents a transitive relation?
   (b) Give an example of a transitive relation and draw its digraph.
   (c) What must be true of the boolean product of the adjacency matrix of a transitive digraph with itself?
   (d) Write a Pascal routine that accepts an adjacency matrix and determines if the digraph it represents is transitive.
   (e) Prove that the transitive closure of any digraph is transitive.
   (f) Prove that the smallest transitive digraph which includes all nodes and arcs of a given digraph is the transitive closure of that digraph.

7. Given a digraph, prove that it is possible to renumber its nodes so that the resultant adjacency matrix is lower triangular (see Exercise 1.2.8) if and only if the digraph is acyclic. Write a Pascal program *lowtri(adj, ltadj, perm)* which accepts an adjacency matrix *adj* of an acyclic graph and creates a lower triangular adjacency matrix *ltadj* which represents the same graph. *perm* is a one-dimensional array such that *perm*[*i*] is set to the new number assigned to the node that was numbered *i* in the matrix *adj*.

8. Rewrite the routine *shortpath* to implement the set of "permanent" nodes as a linked list. Show that the efficiency of the method remains $O(n^2)$.

2. A FLOW PROBLEM

In this section we consider a real-world problem and illustrate a solution that uses a weighted graph. There are a number of formulations of this problem whose solutions carry over to a wide range of applications. We present one such formulation here and refer the reader to the literature for alternative versions.

Assume a water pipe system as in Figure 9.2.1a. Each arc represents a pipe and the number above each arc represents the capacity of that pipe in gallons per minute. The nodes represent points at which pipes are joined and water is transferred from one pipe to another. Two nodes, S and T, are designated as a *source* of water and a *user* of water (or a *sink*), respectively. This means that water originating at S must be carried through the pipe system to T. Water may flow through a pipe in only one direction (pressure-sensitive valves may be used to prevent water from flowing backward), and there are no pipes entering S or leaving T. Thus a weighted directed graph, as in Figure 9.2.1a, is an ideal data structure to model the situation.

We would like to maximize the amount of water flowing from the source to the sink. Although the source may be able to produce water at a prodigious rate and the sink may be able to consume water at a comparable rate, the pipe system may not have the capacity to carry it all from the source to the sink. Thus the limiting factor of the entire system is the pipe capacity. Many other real-world problems are similar in nature. The system could be an electrical network, a railway system, a communications network, or any other distribution system in which one wants to maximize the amount of an item being delivered from one point to another.

Define a *capacity function*, $c(a, b)$, where a and b are nodes, as follows. If *adjacent*(a, b) (i.e., if there is a pipe from a to b), then $c(a, b)$ is the capacity of the pipe from a to b. If there is no pipe from a to b, then $c(a, b) = 0$. At any point in the operation of the system, a given amount of water (possibly 0) flows through each pipe. Define a *flow function*, $f(a, b)$, where a and b are nodes, as 0 if b is not adjacent to a and as the amount of water flowing through the pipe from a to b otherwise. Clearly, $f(a, b) \geq 0$ for all nodes a and b. Furthermore, $f(a, b) \leq c(a, b)$ for all nodes a and b since a

Figure 9.2.1

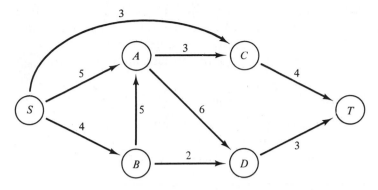

(a) A flow problem.

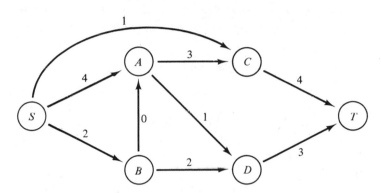

(b) A flow function.

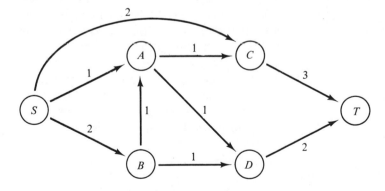

(c) A flow function.

pipe may not carry more water than its capacity. Let v be the amount of water that flows through the system from S to T. Then the amount of water leaving S through all pipes equals the amount of water entering T through all pipes, and both these amounts equal v. This can be stated by the equality

$$\sum_{x \in nodes} f(S, x) = v = \sum_{x \in nodes} f(x, T)$$

No node other than S can produce water, and no node other than T can absorb water. Thus the amount of water leaving any node other than S or T is equal to the amount of water entering that node. This can be stated by

$$\sum_{y \in nodes} f(x, y) = \sum_{y \in nodes} f(y, x) \quad \text{for all nodes } x \neq S, T$$

Define the *inflow* of a node x as the total flow entering x and the *outflow* as the total flow leaving x. The foregoing conditions may be rewritten as

$$outflow(S) = inflow(T) = v$$
$$inflow(x) \quad = outflow(x) \quad \text{for all } x \neq S, T$$

Several flow functions may exist for a given graph and capacity function. Figures 9.2.1b and c illustrate two possible flow functions for the graph of Figure 9.2.1a. Make sure that you understand why both of them are valid flow functions and why both satisfy the foregoing equations and inequalities.

We wish to find a flow function that maximizes the value of v, the amount of water going from S to T. Such a flow function is called *optimal*. Clearly, the flow function of Figure 9.2.1b is better than the one of Figure 9.2.1c, since v equals 7 in the former but only 5 in the latter. See if you can find a flow function that is better than the one of Figure 9.2.1b.

One valid flow function can be achieved by setting $f(a, b)$ to 0 for all nodes a and b. Of course, this flow function is least optimal since no water flows from S to T. Given a flow function, it can be improved so that the flow from S to T is increased. However, the improved version must satisfy all the conditions for a valid flow function. In particular, if the flow entering any node (except for S or T) is increased or decreased, the flow leaving that node must be increased or decreased correspondingly. The strategy for producing an optimal flow function is to begin with the zero flow function and to improve successively upon it until an optimal flow function is produced.

Improving a Flow Function

Given a flow function f, there are two ways to improve upon it. One way consists of finding a path $S = x_1, x_2, \ldots, x_n = T$ from S to T such that the flow along each arc in the path is strictly less than the capacity:

that is, $f(x_{k-1}, x_k) < c(x_{k-1}, x_k)$ for all k between 2 and n. The flow can be increased on each arc in such a path by the minimum value of $c(x_{k-1}, x_k) - f(x_{k-1}, x_k)$ for all k between 2 and n—so that when the flow has been increased along the entire path there is at least one arc $\langle x_{k-1}, x_k \rangle$ in the path for which $f(x_{k-1}, x_k) = c(x_{k-1}, x_k)$ and through which the flow may not be increased.

This may be illustrated by the graph of Figure 9.2.2a, which gives the capacity and the current flow, respectively, for each arc. There are two paths from S to T with positive flow [(S, A, C, T) and (S, B, D, T)]. However, each of these paths contains one arc ($\langle A, C \rangle$ and $\langle B, D \rangle$) in which the flow equals the capacity. Thus the flow along these paths may not be improved. However, the path (S, A, D, T) is such that the capacity of each arc in the path is greater than its current flow. The maximum amount by which the flow can be increased along this path is 1, since the flow along arc $\langle D, T \rangle$ cannot exceed 3. The resulting flow function is shown in Figure 9.2.2b. The total flow from S to T has been increased from 5 to 6. To see that the result is still a valid flow function, note that for each node (except T) whose inflow is increased, the outflow is increased by the same amount.

Are there any other paths whose flow can be improved? In this example, you should satisfy yourself that there are not. However, given the graph of Figure 9.2.2a, we could have chosen to improve the path (S, B, A, D, T). The resulting flow function is illustrated in Figure 9.2.2c. This function also provides for a net flow of 6 from S to T and is therefore neither better nor worse than the flow function of Figure 9.2.2b.

Even if there is no path whose flow may be improved, there may be another method of improving the net flow from the source to the sink. This is illustrated by Figure 9.2.3. In Figure 9.2.3a there is no path from S to T whose flow may be improved. But if the flow from X to Y is reduced, the flow from X to T can be increased. To compensate for the decrease in the inflow of Y, the flow from S to Y could be increased, thereby increasing the net flow from S to T. The flow from X to Y can be redirected to T as shown in Figure 9.2.3b, and the net flow from S to T can thereby be increased from 4 to 7.

We may generalize this second method as follows. Suppose that there is a path from S to some node y, a path from some node x to T, and a path from x to y with positive flow. Then the flow along the path from x to y may be reduced and the flows from x to T and from S to y may be increased by the same amount. This amount is the minimum of the flow from x to y and the differences between capacity and flow in the paths from S to y and x to T.

These two methods may be combined by proceeding through the graph from S to T as follows. The amount of water emanating from S toward T can be increased by any amount (since we have assumed no limit on the amount that can be produced by the source) only if the pipes from S to T

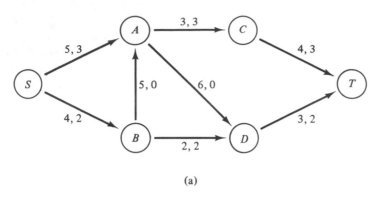

(a)

Figure 9.2.2   Increasing the flow in a
graph.

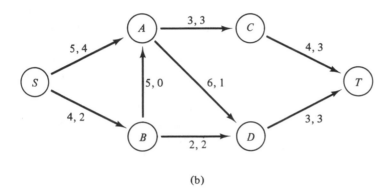

(b)

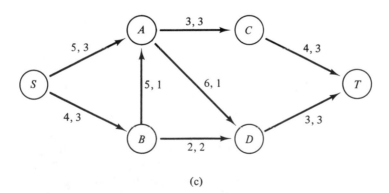

(c)

can carry the increase. Suppose that the pipe capacity from S to x allows
the amount of water entering x to be increased by an amount a. If the pipe
capacity to carry the increase from x to T exists, then the increase can be
made. Then if a node y is adjacent to x (i.e., there is an arc $\langle x, y \rangle$), the

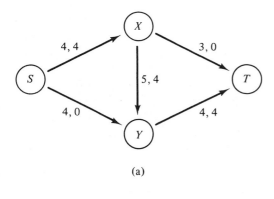

Figure 9.2.3 Increasing the flow in a graph.

(a)

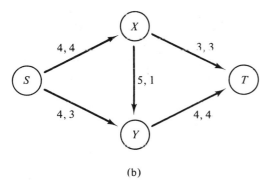

(b)

amount of water emanating from y toward T can be increased by the minimum of a and the unused capacity of arc $\langle x, y \rangle$. This is an application of the first method. Similarly, if node x is adjacent to some node y (i.e., there is an arc $\langle y, x \rangle$), then the amount of water emanating from y toward T can be increased by the minimum of a and the existing flow from y to x. This can be done by reducing the flow from y to x, as in the second method. Proceeding in this fashion from S to T, the amount by which the flow to T may be increased can be determined.

Define a *semipath* from S to T as a sequence of nodes $S = x_1, x_2, \ldots,$ $x_n = T$ such that, for all $1 < i \le n$, either $\langle x_{i-1}, x_i \rangle$ or $\langle x_i, x_{i-1} \rangle$ is an arc. Using the foregoing technique, we may describe an algorithm to discover a semipath from S to T such that the flow to each node in the semipath may be increased. This is done by building upon already discovered partial semipaths from S. If the last node in a discovered partial semipath from S is a, the algorithm considers extending it to any node b such that either $\langle a, b \rangle$ or $\langle b, a \rangle$ is an arc. The partial semipath is extended to b only if the extension can be made in such a way that the inflow to b can be increased. Once a partial semipath has been extended to a node b, that node is removed from consideration as an extension of some other partial semipath. (This is because at this point we are trying to discover a single semipath from S to T). The algorithm, of course, keeps track of the amount by which the inflow to b may be increased and whether its increase is due to consideration of the arc $\langle a, b \rangle$ or $\langle b, a \rangle$.

This process continues until some partial semipath from S has been completed by extending it to T. The algorithm then proceeds backward along the semipath, adjusting all flows until S is reached. (This will be illustrated shortly with an example.) The entire process is then repeated in an attempt to discover yet another such semipath from S to T. When no partial semipath may be successfully extended, the flow cannot be increased and the existing flow is optimal. (You are asked to prove this as an exercise.)

An Example Let us illustrate this process with an example. Consider the arcs and capacities of the weighted graph of Figure 9.2.4. We begin by assuming a flow of 0 and attempt to discover an optimal flow. Figure 9.2.4a illustrates the initial situation. The two numbers next to each arc represent the capacity and current flow, respectively. We may extend a semipath from S to (S, X) and (S, Z), respectively. The flow from S to X may be increased by 4, and the flow from S to Z may be increased by 6. The semipath (S, X) may be extended to (S, X, W) and (S, X, Y) with corresponding increases of flow to W and Y of 3 and 4, respectively. The semipath (S, X, Y) may be extended to (S, X, Y, T) with an increase of flow to T of 4. (Note that at this point we could have chosen to extend (S, X, W) to (S, X, W, T). Similarly, we could have extended (S, Z) to (S, Z, Y) rather than (S, X) to (S, X, W) and (S, X, Y). These decisions are arbitrary.)

Since we have reached T by the semipath (S, X, Y, T) with a net increase of 4, we increase the flow along each forward arc of the semipath by this amount. The results are depicted in Figure 9.2.4b.

We now repeat the foregoing process with the flow of Figure 9.2.4b. (S) may be extended to (S, Z) only since the flow in arc $\langle S, X \rangle$ is already at capacity. The net increase to Z through this semipath is 6. (S, Z) may be extended to (S, Z, Y), yielding a net increase of 4 to Y. (S, Z, Y) cannot be extended to (S, Z, Y, T) since the flow in arc $\langle Y, T \rangle$ is at capacity. However, it can be extended to (S, Z, Y, X) with a net increase to node X of 4. Note that since this semipath includes a backward arc $\langle Y, X \rangle$ it implies a reduction in the flow from X to Y of 4. The semipath (S, Z, Y, X) may be extended to (S, Z, Y, X, W) with a net increase of 3 (the unused capacity of $\langle X, W \rangle$) to W. This semipath may then be extended to (S, Z, Y, X, W, T) with a net increase of 3 in the flow to T. Since we have reached T with an increase of 3, we proceed backward along this semipath. Since $\langle W, T \rangle$ and $\langle X, W \rangle$ are forward arcs, their flow may each be increased by 3. Since $\langle Y, X \rangle$ is a backward arc, the flow along $\langle X, Y \rangle$ is reduced by 3. Since $\langle Z, Y \rangle$ and $\langle S, Z \rangle$ are forward arcs, their flow may be increased by 3. This results in the flow shown in Figure 9.2.4c

We then attempt to repeat the process. (S) may be extended to

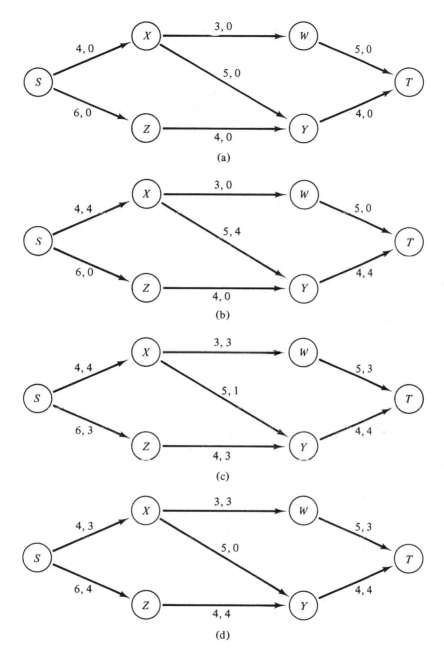

Figure 9.2.4 Producing an optimum flow.

$(S,\ Z)$ with an increase of 3 to Z, $(S,\ Z)$ may be extended to $(S,\ Z,\ Y)$ with an increase of 1 to Y, and $(S,\ Z,\ Y)$ may be extended to $(S,\ Z,\ Y,\ X)$ with an increase of 1 to X. However, since arcs $\langle S,\ X \rangle$, $\langle Y,\ T \rangle$, and $\langle X, W \rangle$ are at capacity, no semipath may be extended further and an optimum flow has been found. Note that this optimum flow need not be unique. Figure 9.2.4d illustrates another optimum flow for the same graph, which was obtained from Figure 9.2.4a by considering the semipaths (S, X, W, T) and (S, Z, Y, T).

The Algorithm and Program

Given a weighted graph (an adjacency matrix and a capacity matrix) with a source S and a sink T, the algorithm to produce an optimum flow function for that graph may be outlined as follows:

1. initialize the flow function to 0 at each arc;
2. *cannotimprove*:= *false*;
3. *repeat*
4.   attempt to find a semipath from S to T which increases the flow to T by $x > 0$;
5.   *if* a semipath cannot be found
        then *cannotimprove*:= *true*
6.   *else* increase the flow to each node (except S) in the semipath by x
7. *until cannotimprove*

Of course, the heart of the algorithm lies in line 4. Once a node has been placed on a partial semipath, it can no longer be used to extend a different semipath. Thus the algorithm uses a boolean array *onpath* such that *onpath*[*node*] indicates whether or not *node* is on some semipath. It also needs an indication of which nodes are at the ends of partial semipaths so that such partial semipaths can be extended by adding adjacent nodes. *endpath*[*node*] indicates whether or not *node* is at the end of a partial semipath. For each node on a semipath, the algorithm must keep track of what node precedes it on that semipath and the direction of the arc. *precede*[*node*] points to the node that precedes *node* on its semipath, and *forward*[*node*] has the value *true* if and only if the arc is from *precede*[*node*] to *node*. *improve*[*node*] indicates the amount by which the flow to *node* may be increased along its semipath. The algorithm that attempts to find a semipath from S to T along which the flow may be increased may be written as follows. (We assume that $c[a, b]$ is the capacity of the pipe from a to b and that $f[a, b]$ is the current flow from a to b.)

```
set endpath[node], onpath[node] to false for all nodes;
endpath[S]:= true;
onpath[S]:= true;
  { compute maximum flow from S which pipes can carry }
improve[S] := sum of c[S, node] over all nodes node;
while (not onpath[T]) and (there exists a node nd such that endpath[nd])
    do begin
            endpath[nd]:= false;
```

```
while there exists a node i such that
            (not onpath[i]) and (f[nd, i] < c[nd, i]) and (adjacent(nd, i))
{ the flow from nd to i may be increased }
{           place i on the semipath           }
      do begin
              onpath[i]:= true;
              endpath[i]:= true;
              precede[i]:= nd;
              forward[i]:= true;
              x:= c[nd, i] - f[nd, i];
              if improve[nd] < x
                then improve[i]:= improve[nd]
                else improve[i]:= x
      end {while there exists...do begin};

while there exists a node i such that
            (not onpath[i]) and (f[i, nd] > 0) and (adjacent(i, nd))
{ the flow from i to nd may be decreased }
{           place i on the semipath           }
      do begin
              onpath[i]:= true;
              endpath[i]:= true;
              precede[i]:= nd;
              forward[i]:= false;
              if improve[nd] < f[i, nd]
                then improve[i]:= improve[nd]
                else improve[i]:= f[i, nd]
      end {while there exists...do begin}
end {while (not onpath[T])...do begin};
if onpath[T] then we have found a semipath from S to T
      else the flow is already optimum;
```

Once a semipath from S to T has been found, the flow may be increased along that semipath (line 6) by the following algorithm:

```
x:= improve[T];
nd:= T;
while nd <> S
  do begin
          pred:= precede[nd];
          if forward[nd] then f[pred, nd]:= f[pred, nd] + x
                         else f[nd, pred]:= f[nd, pred] - x;
          nd:= pred
  end {while ..do begin}
```

This method of solving the flow problem is known as the **Ford-Fulkerson algorithm** after its discoverers.

Let us now convert these algorithms into a Pascal procedure *maxflow(cap, s, t, flow, totflow)*. *cap* is an input parameter representing a capacity function defined on a weighted graph whose type *capfunct* is defined by

```
const maxnodes = 50;
type  nodeptr = 1..maxnodes;
      capfunct = array[nodeptr, nodeptr] of integer;
```

s and *t* are input parameters representing the source and sink, *flow* is an output parameter representing the maximum flow function, and *totflow* is the amount of flow from *s* to *t* under the flow function *flow*.

The previous algorithms may be converted easily into Pascal programs. Three boolean arrays—*endpath*, *forward*, and *onpath*; one integer array—*improve*; and an array *precede* of *nodeptr*s are required. (In some nonstandard Pascal implementations, *forward* is a reserved word and may not be used as a variable identifier.) The question of whether *j* is adjacent to *i* can be answered by checking whether or not *cap*[*i*, *j*] = 0.

We present the routine here as a straightforward implementation of the algorithms. *any* is a function that accepts a boolean array and returns *true* if any element of the array is *true*. If none of the elements of the array is *true*, then *any* returns *false*. We leave its coding as an exercise.

```
procedure maxflow (cap: capfunct; s, t: nodeptr; var flow: capfunct; var totflow: integer);
var pred, nd, i: nodeptr;
    x: integer;
    precede: array[nodeptr] of nodeptr;
    improve: array[nodeptr] of integer;
    endpath, forward, onpath: array[nodeptr] of boolean;
    {insert the function any here}
begin {procedure maxflow}
  for nd:= 1 to maxnodes
      do for i:= 1 to maxnodes
             do flow[nd, i]:= 0;
  totflow:= 0;
  repeat
      {attempt to find a semipath from s to t}
      for nd:= 1 to maxnodes
          do begin
                  endpath[nd]:= false;
                  onpath[nd]:= false
             end {for...do begin};
      endpath[s]:= true;
      onpath[s]:= true;
      improve[s]:= maxint;
      {we assume that s can provide infinite flow}
```

```
while (not onpath[t] ) and (any(endpath))
      do begin
                  {attempt to extend an existing path}
                  nd:= 1;
                  while not endpath[nd]
                        do nd:= nd + 1;
                  endpath[nd]:= false;
                  for i:= 1 to maxnodes
                      do begin
                              if (flow[nd, i] < cap[nd, i] ) and (not onpath[i] )
                                  then begin
                                              onpath[i]:= true;
                                              endpath[i]:= true;
                                              precede[i]:= nd;
                                              forward[nd]:= true;
                                              x:= cap[nd, i] - flow[nd, i];
                                              if improve[nd] < x
                                                  then improve[i]:= improve[nd]
                                                  else improve[i]:= x
                                          end {then begin};
                              if (flow[i, nd] > 0) and (not onpath[i] )
                                  then begin
                                              onpath[i]:= true;
                                              endpath[i]:= true;
                                              precede[i]:= nd;
                                              forward[nd]:= false;
                                              if improve[nd] < flow[i, nd]
                                                  then improve[i]:= improve[nd]
                                                  else improve[i]:= flow[i, nd]
                                          end {then begin}
                          end { for...do begin}
            end {while...do begin};
if onpath[t]
    then { flow on semipath to t can be increased }
        begin
                x:= improve[t];
                totflow:= totflow + x;
                nd:= t;
                while nd <> s
                    do begin { travel back along path }
                            pred:= precede[nd];
                            if forward[pred]
                                then { increase flow from pred }
                                    flow[pred, nd]:= flow[pred, nd]  + x
```

```
                        else  { decrease flow to pred }
                            flow[nd, pred]:= flow[nd, pred] – x;
                    nd:= pred
                end {while...do begin}
            end {then begin}
        until not onpath[t]
end { procedure maxflow};
```

For large graphs with many nodes, the arrays *improve* and *endpath* may be prohibitively expensive in terms of space. Furthermore, a search through all nodes to find one such that *endpath[nd]* = *true* may be very inefficient in terms of time. An alternative solution might be to note that the value of *improve* is required only for those nodes *nd* such that *endpath[nd]* = *true*. Those graph nodes which are at the end of semipaths may be kept in a list whose nodes are defined by

```
const maxnodes = 100;
type  nodeptr = 0..maxnodes;
      listnode = record
                     graphnode: nodeptr;
                     improve: integer;
                     next: nodeptr
                 end;
```

When a node that is at the end of a semipath is required, remove the first element from the list. We can similarly dispense with the array *precede* by maintaining a separate list of nodes for each semipath. However, this suggestion is of dubious value since almost all nodes will be on some semipath. You are invited to write the routine *maxflow* as an exercise using these suggestions to save time and space.

EXERCISES

1. Find the maximum flows for the graphs in Figure 9.2.1 using the Ford-Fulkerson method (the capacities are shown next to the arcs).
2. Given a graph and a capacity function as in this section, define a *cut* as any set of nodes *x* containing *S* but not *T*. Define the *capacity of the cut x* as the sum of the capacities of all the arcs leaving the set *x* minus the sum of the capacities of all the arcs entering *x*.
   (a) Show that for any flow function *f*, the value of the total flow *v* is less than or equal to the capacity of any cut.
   (b) Show that equality in part (a) is achieved when the flow is maximum and the cut has minimum capacity.
3. Prove that the Ford-Fulkerson algorithm produces an optimum flow function.
4. Rewrite the routine *maxflow* using a linked list to contain nodes at the end of semipaths, as suggested in the text.

5. Assume that in addition to a capacity function, there is also a cost function, *cost*. *cost(a, b)* is the cost of each unit of flow from node *a* to node *b*. Modify the program of the text to produce the flow function that maximizes the total flow from source to sink at the lowest cost (i.e., if there are two flow functions, both of which produce the same maximum flow, choose the one with the least cost).

6. Assuming a cost function as in Exercise 5, write a program to produce the maximum cheapest flow, that is, a flow function such that the total flow divided by the cost of the flow is greatest.

7. A *probabilistic* directed graph is one in which a probability function associates a probability with each arc. The sum of the probabilities of all arcs emanating from any node is 1. Consider an acyclic probabilistic digraph representing a tunnel system. A person is placed at one node in the tunnel. At each node, the person chooses to take a particular arc to another node with probability given by the probability function. Write a program to compute the probability that the person passes through each node of the graph. What if the graph were cyclic?

8. Write a Pascal program that reads the following information about an electrical network:

   (a) *n*, the number of wires in the network.
   (b) the amount of current entering through the first wire and leaving through the *n*th.
   (c) the resistance of each of the wires 2 through $n - 1$.
   (d) a set of ordered pairs $\langle i, j \rangle$ indicating that wire *i* is connected to wire *j* and that electricity flows through wire *i* to wire *j*.

   The program should compute the amount of current flowing though each of wires 2 through $n - 1$ by applying Kirchoff's law and Ohm's law. Kirchoff's law states that the amount of current flowing into a junction equals the amount leaving a junction. Ohm's law states that if two paths exist between two junctions, the sums of the currents times the resistances over all wires in each of the two paths are equal.

3. THE LINKED REPRESENTATION OF GRAPHS

The adjacency matrix representation of a graph is frequently inadequate because it requires advance knowledge of the number of nodes. If a graph must be constructed in the course of solving a problem, or if it must be dynamically updated as the program proceeds, a new matrix must be created for each addition or deletion of a node. This is prohibitively inefficient, especially in a real-world situation where a graph may have 100 or more nodes. Further, even if a graph has very few arcs so that the adjacency matrix (and the weight matrix for a weighted graph) is sparse, space must be reserved for every possible arc between two nodes, whether or not such an arc exists. If the graph contains *n* nodes, a total of n^2 locations must be used.

As you might expect, the remedy is to use a linked structure, allocating and freeing nodes from an available pool. This is similar to the methods used to represent dynamic binary and general trees. In the linked representation of trees, each allocated node corresponds to a tree node. This is possible because each tree node is the son of only one other tree node and is therefore contained in only a single list of sons. However, in a graph, an arc may exist between any two graph nodes. It is possible to keep an adjacency list for every node in a graph (such a list contains all nodes adjacent to a given node), and a node might find itself on many different adjacency lists (one for each node to which it is adjacent). But this requires that each allocated node contain a variable number of pointers, depending on the number of nodes to which it is adjacent. This solution is clearly impractical, as we saw in attempting to represent general trees with nodes containing pointers to each of its sons.

An alternative is to construct a multilinked structure in the following way. The nodes of the graph (hereafter referred to as **graph nodes**) are represented by a linked list of **header nodes**. Each such header node contains three fields: *info*, *nextnode*, and *arcptr*. If *p* points to a header node representing a graph node *a*, then *info(p)* contains any information associated with graph node *a*. *nextnode(p)* is a pointer to the header node representing the next graph node, if any. Each header node is at the head of a list of nodes of a second type called **list nodes**. This list is called the **adjacency list**. Each node on an adjacency list represents an arc of the graph. *arcptr(p)* points to the adjacency list of nodes representing the arcs emanating from the graph node *a*.

Each adjacency list node contains two fields: *ndptr* and *nextarc*. If *q* points to a list node representing an arc ⟨*A*, *B*⟩, *ndptr(q)* is a pointer to the header node representing the graph node *B*. *nextarc(q)* points to a list node representing the next arc emanating from graph node *A*, if any. Each list node is contained in a single adjacency list representing all arcs emanating from a given graph node. The term **allocated nodes** is used to refer to both header and list nodes of a multilinked structure representing a graph. We also refer to an adjacency list node as an **arc node**.

Figure 9.3.1 illustrates this representation. If each graph node carries some information but (since the graph is not weighted) the arcs do not, then two types of allocated nodes are needed: one for header nodes (graph nodes) and the other for adjacency list nodes (arcs). These are illustrated in Figure 9.3.1a. Each header node contains an *info* field and two pointers. The first of these is to the adjacency list of arcs emanating from the graph node, and the second is to the next header node in the graph. Each arc node contains two pointers, one to the next arc node in the adjacency list and the other to the header node representing the graph node that terminates the arc. Figure 9.3.1b depicts a graph and 9.3.1c its linked representation.

Note that header nodes and list nodes have different formats and must be represented by different Pascal types. This necessitates either keeping two distinct available lists or defining a single variant type. Even in the case of a weighted graph in which each list node contains an *info* field to hold the weight of an arc, two different types may be necessary if the information in the header nodes is not an integer. However, for simplicity we make the assumption that both header and list nodes have the same format and contain

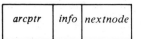 

arcptr	info	nextnode

A sample header node representing a graph node.

ndptr	nextarc

A sample list node representing an arc.

(a)

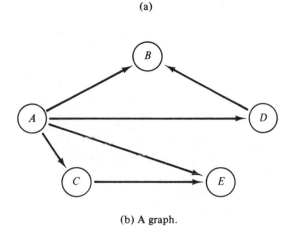

(b) A graph.

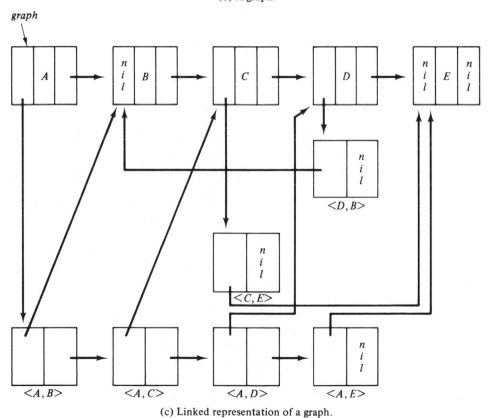

(c) Linked representation of a graph.

Figure 9.3.1 Linked representation of a graph.

two pointers and a single-integer information field. These nodes are declared using the array implementation by

```
const maxnodes = 500;
type  nodeptr = 0..maxnodes;
      nodetype = record
                     info: integer;
                     point: nodeptr;
                     next: nodeptr
                 end;
var   node: array[1..maxnodes] of nodetype;
```

In the case of a header node, *node*[*p*] represents a graph node *A*, *node*[*p*].*info* represents the information associated with the graph node *A*, *node*[*p*].*next* points to the next graph node, and *node*[*p*].*point* points to the first list node representing an arc emanating from *A*. In the case of a list node, *node*[*p*] represents an arc ⟨*A*, *B*⟩, *node*[*p*].*info* represents the weight of the arc, *node*[*p*].*next* points to the next arc emanating from *A*, and *node*[*p*].*point* points to the header node representing the graph node *B*.

Using the dynamic implementation, the nodes may be defined by

```
type nodeptr = ↑nodetype;
     nodetype = record
                    info: integer;
                    point: nodeptr;
                    next: nodeptr
                end;
```

We use the array implementation in the remainder of this section and assume the existence of routines *getnode* and *freenode*.

We now present the implementation of the primitive graph operations using the linked representation. The operation *joinwt*(*p*, *q*, *wt*) accepts two pointers *p* and *q* to two header nodes and creates an arc between them with weight *wt*. If an arc already exists between them, that arc's weight is set to *wt*.

```
procedure joinwt (p, q: nodeptr; wt: integer);
var r, r2: nodeptr;
    found: boolean;
begin
    {search the list of arcs emanating from node[p] }
    {            for an arc to node[q]              }
    found:= false;
    r2:= 0;
    r:= node[p].point;
```

```
        while (r <> 0) and (not found)
          do if node[r].point = q
              then begin {node[r] represents an arc from}
                       {     node[p] to node[q]     }
                     node[r].info := wt;
                     found := true
                   end {then begin}
              else {keep looking}
                 begin
                       r2 := r;
                       r := node[r].next
                   end {else begin};
        if not found
          then {an arc from node[p] to node[q] does not}
              {    exist; such an arc must be created.    }
             begin
                 r := getnode;
                 node[r].point := q;
                 node[r].next := 0;
                 node[r].info := wt;
                 if r2 = 0
                     then node[p].point := r
                     else node[r2].next := r
             end {then begin}
    end {procedure join.wt};
```

We leave the implementation of the operation *join* for an unweighted graph as an exercise for the reader. The operation *remv(p, q)* accepts pointers to two header nodes and removes the arc between them, if one exists.

```
        procedure remv (p, q: nodeptr);
        var r, r2: nodeptr;
            deleted: boolean;
        begin {procedure remv}
            deleted := false;
            r2 := 0;
            r := node[p].point;
            while (r <> 0) and (not deleted)
              do if node[r].point = q
                  then {r points to an arc from node[p]}
                      {         to node[q]         }
                     begin
                         if r2 = 0
                             then node[p].point := node[r].next
```

```
                    else  node[r2].next:= node[r].next;
                        freenode(r);
                        deleted:= true
                    end {then begin}
                else {continue searching}
                    begin
                        r2:= r;
                        r:= node[r].next
                    end {else begin}
            {if no arc has been found, then no action}
            {            need be taken            }
        end {procedure remv};
```

We leave the implementation of the operation *remvwt*(*p*, *q*, *x*), which sets *x* to the weight of the arc ⟨*p*, *q*⟩ in a weighted graph and then removes the arc from the graph as an exercise for the reader.

The function *adjacent*(*p*, *q*) accepts pointers to two header nodes and determines whether *node*(*q*) is adjacent to *node*(*p*).

```
        function adjacent (p, q: nodeptr): boolean;
        var r: nodeptr;
            found: boolean;
        begin
            r:= node[p].point;
            found:= false; {assume no arc exits}
            while (r <> 0) and (not found)
                do if node[r].point = q
                    then found:= true {an arc is found}
                    else r:= node[r].next;
            adjacent:= found
        end {function adjacent};
```

Another useful function is *findnode*(*graph*, *x*), which returns a pointer to a header node with information field *x* if such a header node exists and returns the nil pointer otherwise.

```
        function findnode (graph: nodeptr; x: integer): nodeptr;
        var p: nodeptr;
            found: boolean;
        begin
            p:= graph;
            found:= false;
            while (p <> 0) and (not found)
                do begin
```

```
            if node[p].info = x
                then begin
                            findnode:= p;
                            found:= true
                    end {then begin}
                else  p:= node[p].next
            end {while...do begin};
        if not found
            then findnode:= 0
    end {function findnode};
```

The function *addnode(graph, x)* adds a node with information field *x* to a graph and returns a pointer to that node.

```
    function addnode (var graph: nodeptr; x: integer): nodeptr;
    var p: nodeptr;
    begin
        p:= getnode;
        node[p].info:= x;
        node[p].point:= 0;
        node[p].next:= graph;
        graph:= p;
        addnode:= p
    end {function addnode};
```

The reader should be aware of another important difference between the adjacency matrix representation and the linked representation of graphs. Implicit in the matrix representation is the ability to traverse a row or column of the matrix. Traversing a row is equivalent to identifying all arcs emanating from a given node. This can be done efficiently in the linked representation by traversing the list of arc nodes starting at a given header node. Traversing a column of an adjacency matrix, however, is equivalent to identifying all arcs that terminate at a given node; there is no corresponding method for accomplishing this under the linked representation. Of course, the linked representation could be modified to include two lists emanating from each header node: one for the arcs emanating from the graph node and the other for the arcs terminating at the graph node. However, this would require allocating two nodes for each arc, thus increasing the complexity of adding or deleting an arc.

Alternatively, each arc node could be placed on two lists. In this case, an arc node would contain four pointers: one to the next arc emanating from the same node, one to the next arc terminating at the same node, one to the header node at which it terminates, and one to the header node from which it emanates. A header node would contain three pointers: one to the next header node, one to the list of arcs emanating from it, and one to the list of arcs terminating at it. The programmer must, of course, choose from among these representations by examining the needs of the specific problem and considering both time and storage efficiency.

We invite the reader to write a routine *remvnode(graph, p)* which removes a header node pointed to by *p* from a graph pointed to by *graph* using the various graph representations that we have just outlined. Of course, when a node is removed from a graph, all arcs emanating and terminating at that node must also be removed. In the linked representation that we have presented there is no easy way of removing a node from a graph since the arcs terminating at the node cannot be obtained directly.

It would also be instructive for the reader to compare and contrast the methods outlined for representing a graph with the methods outlined in Section 5.3 for representing a sparse matrix.

Dijkstra's Algorithm Revisited

In Section 1, we presented an implementation of Dijkstra's algorithm for finding the shortest path between two nodes in a weighted graph represented by a weight matrix. That implementation was $O(n^2)$, where n is the number of nodes in the graph. We now show how the algorithm can be implemented more efficiently in most cases if the graph is implemented using adjacency lists.

We suggest review of the algorithm described in Section 1. This algorithm may be outlined as follows. We seek a shortest path from *s* to *t*. *d* is to be set to the shortest distance, *precede*[*i*] to the node preceding node *i* in the shortest path:

```
1       for all nodes i
2          do distance[i] := maxint;
3       distance[s] := 0;
4       current := s;
5       perm := [s] ;
6       while current <> t
7          do begin
8                 dc := distance[current] ;
9                 for all nodes i that are successors of current
10                   do begin
11                       newdist := dc + weight(current, i);
12                       if newdist < distance[i]
13                          then begin
14                              distance[i] := newdist;
15                              precede[i] := current
16                          end {then begin}
17                   end {for...do begin};
```

```
18                      k: = the node not in perm such that distance [k]
                                                        is smallest;
19                      current: = k;
20                      add k to perm
21               end {while...do begin};
22      d: = distance [t]
```

Review how this algorithm is implemented in Section 1. Note especially how finding the minimum distance (line 18) is incorporated into the *for* loop and how that loop is implemented.

The keys to an efficient implementation are lines 9 and 18. In Section 1, where we had access only to a weight matrix, there is no way to limit the access to the successors of *current* as specified in line 9. It is necessary to traverse all n nodes of the graph each time the inner loop is repeated. We are able to increase efficiency by only looking at elements not in *perm*, but that cannot speed things up by more than a constant factor. Once an $O(n)$ inner loop is required, we may as well use it to compute the minimum as well (line 18).

However, given an adjacency list representation of the graph, it is possible to traverse directly all nodes adjacent to *current* without examining all graph nodes. Therefore, the total number of nodes i examined in the loop headed by line 9 is $O(e)$, where e is the number of edges in the graph. (Note that we are not saying that each execution of the inner loop is $O(e)$ but that the total of all repetitions of the inner loop is $O(e)$.) In most graphs, e is far smaller than n^2, so this is quite an improvement.

However, we are not yet done. Since we are eliminating a traversal through all nodes, we must find an alternative way of implementing line 18 to find the node with the smallest distance. If the best we can do in finding this minimum distance is $O(n)$, then the entire process remains $O(n^2)$.

Fortunately, there is a solution. Suppose that, instead of maintaining the set *perm*, we maintained its complement, *notperm*. Then line 5 would become

```
5               notperm: = all nodes except s;
```

line 18 would become

```
18              k: = the node in notperm such that distance (k) is smallest;
```

and line 20 would become

```
20              remove k from notperm
```

The operations performed on the set *notperm* are creation (line 5; this may be $O(n)$ but it is outside the *while* loop and therefore does not hurt the overall efficiency), finding the minimum element (line 18), and deleting the minimum element (line 20). But these latter two operations can be combined into the single *pqmindelete* operation of an ascending priority queue, and, by now, we have a number of ways of implementing that operation in less than $O(n)$. In fact, we can implement *pqmindelete* in $O(\log n)$ by using an ascending heap, a balanced binary tree, or a 2-3 tree. If the set *notperm* is implemented as a priority queue using one of these techniques, the efficiency of *n* such operations is $O(n \log n)$. If a priority queue ordered by the value of *distance* is used to implement *notperm*, the position of *i* must be adjusted in the priority queue whenever *distance*[i] is modified in line 14. Fortunately, this can also be done in $O(\log n)$ steps.

Thus Dijkstra's algorithm can be implemented using $O((e + n) \log n)$ operations, which is significantly better than $O(n^2)$ for sparse graphs (that is, graphs with very few edges as opposed to dense graphs that have an edge between almost every pair of nodes). We leave an actual Pascal implementation as an exercise for the reader.

Organizing the Set of Graph Nodes

In many applications, the set of graph nodes (as implemented by header nodes) need not be organized as a simple linked list. The linked list organization is suitable only when the entire set of graph nodes must be traversed and when graph nodes are being dynamically inserted. Both these operations are highly efficient on a linked list.

If graph nodes must also be deleted, then the list must be doubly linked. In addition, as noted earlier, there is the need to ensure that no arcs emanate or terminate at a deleted node or that all such arcs are deleted as part of the node deletion procedure. If we choose merely to ensure that no arcs terminate in a node being deleted rather than to delete any such arcs, it is not necessary to keep with each node a list of arcs terminating at the node. It is only necessary to maintain a *count* field in the node to hold the number of arcs terminating in the node; when *count* becomes 0 (and no arcs emanate from the node), the node may be deleted.

If graph nodes are not being added or deleted, then the nodes can be kept in a simple array, where each array element contains any necessary information about the node plus a pointer to an adjacency list of arcs. Each arc need contain only an array index to indicate the position of its terminating node in the array.

In many applications, graph nodes must be accessed by their contents. For example, in a graph whose nodes represent cities, an application must find the appropriate node given the name of the city. If a linked list is used to represent the graph nodes, then the entire list must be traversed to find the node associated with a particular name.

The problem of finding a particular element in a set based on its contents, or value, is one that we have already studied in great detail: it is simply the searching problem. And we know a great many possible solutions:

binary search trees, multiway search trees, and hash tables are all ways of organizing sets to permit rapid searching.

The set of graph nodes can be organized in any of these ways. The particular organization chosen depends on the detailed needs of the application. In Dijkstra's algorithm, for example, we have just seen an illustration where the set of graph nodes could be organized as an array that implements an ascending heap used as a priority queue. Let us now look at a different application. We introduce it with a frivolous example, but the application itself is quite important.

An Application to Scheduling

Suppose a chef in a diner receives an order for a fried egg. The job of frying an egg can be decomposed into a number of distinct subtasks:

Get egg	Crack egg	Get grease
Grease pan	Heat grease	Pour egg into pan
Wait until egg is done		Remove egg

Some of these tasks must precede others (e.g., "get egg" must precede "crack egg"). Others may be done simultaneously (e.g., "get egg" and "heat grease"). The chef wishes to provide the quickest service possible and is assumed to have an unlimited number of assistants. The problem is to assign tasks to the assistants so as to complete the job in the least possible time.

Although this example may seem frivolous, it is typical of many real-world scheduling problems. A computer system may wish to schedule jobs to minimize turnaround time, a compiler may wish to schedule machine language operations to minimize execution time, a plant manager may wish to organize an assembly line to minimize production time, and so on. All these problems are closely related and can be solved by the use of graphs.

Let us represent this problem as a graph. Each node of the graph represents a subtask, and each arc $\langle x, y \rangle$ represents the requirement that subtask y cannot be performed until subtask x has been completed. This graph G is shown in Figure 9.3.2.

Consider the transitive closure of G. The transitive closure is the graph T such that $\langle x, y \rangle$ is an arc of T if and only if there is a path from x to y in G. This transitive closure is shown in Figure 9.3.3.

In the graph T, an arc exists from node x to node y if and only if subtask x must be performed before subtask y. Note that neither G nor T can contain a cycle, since if a cycle from node x to itself existed, then subtask x could not be performed until after subtask x had been completed. This is clearly an impossible situation in the context of the problem. Thus G is a dag, a *d*irected *a*cyclic *g*raph.

Since G does not contain a cycle, there must be at least one node in

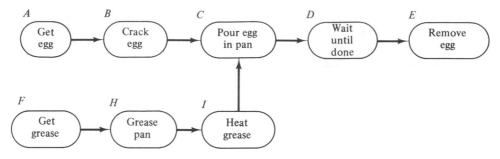

Figure 9.3.2 The graph G.

G which has no predecessors. To see this, suppose that every node in the graph did have a predecessor. In particular, let us choose a node z that has a predecessor y. y cannot equal z or the graph would have a cycle from z to itself. Since every node has a predecessor, y must also have a predecessor x which is not equal to either y or z. Continuing in this fashion, a sequence of distinct nodes

$$z, y, x, w, v, u, \ldots$$

is obtained. If any two nodes in this sequence were equal, a cycle would exist from that node to itself. However, the graph contains only a finite number of nodes, so that eventually, two of the nodes must be equal. This

Figure 9.3.3 The graph T.

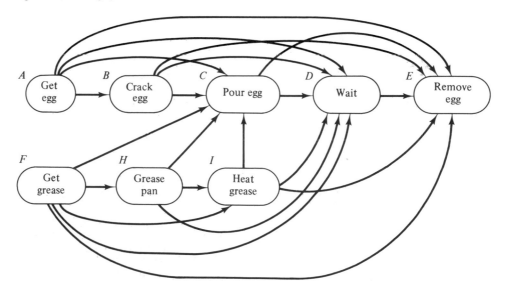

is a contradiction. Thus there must be at least one node without a predecessor.

In the graphs of Figures 9.3.2 and 9.3.3, the nodes A and F do not have predecessors. Since they have no predecessors, the subtasks which they represent may be performed immediately and simultaneously without waiting for any other subtasks to be completed. Every other subtask must wait until at least one of these is completed. Once these two subtasks have been performed, their nodes and incident arcs can be removed from the graph. Note that the resulting graph does not contain any cycles since nodes and arcs have been removed from a graph that originally contained no cycles. Therefore, the resulting graph must also contain at least one node with no predecessors. In the example, B and H are two such nodes. Thus the subtasks B and H may be performed simultaneously in the second time period.

Continuing in this fashion we find that the minimum time in which the egg can be fried is six time periods (assuming that every subtask takes exactly one time period) and that a maximum of two assistants need be employed, as follows:

Time period	Assistant 1	Assistant 2
1	Get egg	Get grease
2	Crack egg	Grease pan
3	Heat grease	
4	Pour egg into pan	
5	Wait until done	
6	Remove egg	

This process can be outlined as follows:

1. Read the precedences and construct the graph.
2. Use the graph to determine the subtasks that can be done simultaneously.

Let us refine each of these two steps. Two crucial decisions must be made in refining step 1. The first is to decide the format of the input; the second is to decide on the representation of the graph. Clearly the input must contain indications of which subtasks must precede others. The most convenient way to represent these requirements is by ordered pairs of subtasks; each input line contains the names of two subtasks, where the first subtask on a line must precede the second. Of course, the data must be valid in the sense that no subtask may precede itself (no cycles are permitted in the graph). Only those precedences that are implied by the data and the transitive closure of the resulting graph are assumed to hold. A subtask may be represented by a character string such as '*get egg*' or by a number. We choose to represent subtasks by character strings in order that the input data reflect the real-world situation as closely as possible.

What information should be kept with each node of the graph? Clearly, the name of the subtask that the node represents is needed to locate the node associated with a particular task and for output purposes. This name will be kept as a packed array of characters. The remaining information depends on how the graph is used. This will become apparent only after step 2 is refined. Here is a good example of how the various parts of a program outline interact with each other to produce a single unit.

Step 2 can be refined into the following algorithm:

while the graph is not empty
   do begin
            determine which nodes have no predecessors;
            output this group of nodes with an indication that
                   they can be performed simultaneously in the next time period;
            remove these nodes and their incident arcs from the graph
   end;

How can it be determined which nodes have no predecessors? One method is to maintain a *count* field in each node containing the number of nodes that precede it. Note that we are not interested in which nodes precede a given node—only in how many.

Initially, after the graph has been constructed, we examine all the graph nodes and place those with zero *count* on an output list. Then, during each simulated time period, the output list is traversed, each graph node on the list is output, and the adjacency list of arcs emanating from that graph node is traversed. For each arc, *count* in the graph node that terminates the arc is reduced by one and, if the *count* thereby becomes zero, that terminating graph node is placed on the output list of the next time period. At the same time, the arc node is freed.

The refinement of step 2 may then be rewritten as follows:

```
      { traverse the set of graph nodes and place all those nodes with }
      {              zero count on the initial output list             }
1     outp:= nil;
2     for all node(p) in the graph
3        do if count(p) = 0
4           then begin
5                    remove node(p) from the graph;
6                    place node(p) on the output list
7                end {for...do if...then begin};
      { simulate the time periods }
8     period:= 0;
9     while outp <> nil
10        do begin
11                period:= period + 1;
```

```
12              print (period);
                { initialize the next period's output list }
13              nextout: = nil;
                { traverse the output list }
14              p: = outp;
15              while p <> nil
16                  do begin
17                      print (info (p));
18                      for all arcs a emanating from node (p)
19                          do begin
                              { reduce count in terminating }
                              {            node            }
20                          t: - the pointer to the node
                                  which terminates a;
21                          count (t): = count (t) - 1;
22                          if count (t) = 0
23                              then begin
24                                  remove node (t)
                                      from the graph;
25                                  add node (t) to
                                      the nextout list
26                              end { then begin };
27                          free arc a
28                          end { for...do begin };
29                      q: - next (p);
30                      free node (p);
31                      p: = q
32                  end { while p <> nil do begin };
33              outp: = nextout
34          end {while outp <> nil do begin };
35  if any nodes remain in the graph
36      then error - there is a cycle in the graph
```

We have been purposely vague in this algorithm about how the graph is implemented. Clearly, to process efficiently all arcs emanating from a node (lines 18–28), an adjacency list implementation is desired. But what of the set of graph nodes? Only a single traversal is required (lines 3–8) to initialize the output list. Thus the efficiency of this operation is not very crucial to the efficiency of the program.

It is necessary in step 1 to be able to access each graph node from the character string that specifies the task the node represents. For this reason, it makes sense to organize the set of graph nodes in a hash table. While the initial traversal will require accessing some extra table positions, this is more than offset by the ability to access a node directly from its task name. The only impediment is the need (in line 24) to delete nodes from the graph.

However, further analysis reveals that the only reason to delete a node is to be able to check whether any nodes remain when the output list is empty (line 35) so that a cycle may be detected. If we maintain a counter of the number of nodes and implement the deletion by reducing this counter by 1, we can check for remaining nodes by comparing the counter with zero. (This is similar to using a *count* field rather than requiring a list of arcs terminating in a given node.) Having determined the data structures required, we are ready to transform the algorithm into a Pascal program.

The Pascal Program

At this point, we can indicate the structure of nodes that we shall need. The header nodes which represent graph nodes contain the following fields:

info	the name of the subtask represented by this node.
count	the number of predecessors of this graph node.
arcptr	a pointer to the list of arcs emanating from this node.
nextnode	a pointer to the next node in the output list

Each list node representing an arc contains two pointers:

nodeptr	a pointer to its terminating node.
nextarc	a pointer to the next arc in the adjacency list.

Thus two types of nodes are required—one to represent graph nodes and one to represent arcs. These may be declared by

```pascal
const maxgraph = 500;
      maxarc = 500;
type  graphpointer = 0..maxgraph;
      arcpointer = 0..maxarc;
      task = packed array[1..20] of char;
      graphtype = record
                     info: task;
                     count: integer;
                     arcptr: arcpointer;
                     nextnode: graphpointer
                  end;
      arctype = record
                   nodeptr: graphpointer;
                   nextarc: arcpointer
                end;
var   graphnode: array[0..maxgraph] of graphtype;
      arc: array[1..maxarc] of arctype;
```

The array *graphnode* is a hash table, with rehashing used to resolve collisions. The array *arc* is a list of available arc nodes allocated by a routine *getarc* and freed by *freearc*. These manipulate an available pointer *availarc*

We also assume the existence of a function *find(inf)* that searches *graphnode* for the presence of an element *nd* (i.e., a graph node) such that *graphnode[nd].info* equals *inf*. If no such graph node exists, *find* allocates a previously empty position *nd*, sets *graphnode[nd].info* to *inf*, *graphnode[nd].count* to 0 and *graphnode[nd].arcptr* to 0, and increases the count of nodes in the graph (which is maintained in a variable *numnodes*) by one. In either case, *find* returns *nd*. Of course, *nd* is determined within *find* via functions *hash* and *rehash* applied to *inf*.

A routine *join* is also used. This routine accepts pointers to two graph nodes, *n1* and *n2*, and allocates an arc node (using *getarc*) that is established as an arc from *graphnode[n1]* to *graphnode[n2]*. *join* is responsible for adding the arc node to the list of arcs emanating from *graphnode[n1]* as well as for increasing *graphnode[n2].count* by one. Finally, a procedure *readstr* is used to read a character string.

We may now write a Pascal scheduling program:

```
program schedule(input, output);
const maxgraph = 499;
      maxarc = 500;
      niltask = '
type  graphpointer = 0..maxgraph;
      arcpointer = 0..maxarc;
      task = packed array[1..20] of char;
      graphtype = record
                       info task;
                       count: integer;
                       arcptr: arcpointer;
                       nextnode: graphpointer
                  end;
      arctype  =  record
                       nodeptr: graphpointer;
                       nextarc: arcpointer
                  end;
var   graphnode: array[0..maxgraph] of graphtype;
      arc: array[1..maxarc] of arctype;
      p, q, t, outp, nextout: graphpointer;
      availarc, r, s: arcpointer;
      period: integer;
      inf1, inf2: task;
      numnodes: integer;  { number of graph nodes }
```

```
                    {  insert routines readstr, find, getarc, hash, rehash  }
                    {                  join, freearc here                    }
        begin {program schedule}
            for p: = 0 to maxgraph
                do begin
                        graphnode[p] .info: = niltask;
                        graphnode[p] .count: = 0
                    end {for...do begin};
            for s: = 1 to maxarc - 1
                do arc[s] .nextarc: = s + 1;
            arc[maxarc] .nextarc: = 0;
            availarc: = 1;
            numnodes: = 0;
            while not eof
                    do begin
                            readstr(inf1);
                            readstr(inf2);
                            readln;
                            p: = find(inf1);
                            q: = find(inf2);
                            join(p, q)
                        end {while...do begin};
            {  The graph has been constructed. Traverse the hash table and  }
            {     place all graph nodes with zero count on the output list.  }
                    outp: = 0;
            for p: = 0 to maxgraph
                do if graphnode[p] .info <> niltask
                    then if graphnode[p] .count = 0
                            then begin
                                    graphnode[p] .nextnode: = outp;
                                    outp: = p
                                end {then begin};
            { simulate the time periods }
            period: = 0;
            while outp <> 0
                    do begin
                            period: = period + 1;
                            writeln ('period:', period);
                            {initialize output list for next period}
                            nextout: = 0;
                            {traverse the output list}
                            p: = outp;
```

```
            while p <> 0
            do begin
                    writeln(graphnode[p].info);
                    r: = graphnode[p].arcptr;
                    {traverse the list of arcs}
                    while r <> 0
                        do begin
                    s: = arc[r].nextarc;
                    t: = arc[r].nodeptr;
                    graphnode[t].count: = graphnode[t].count - 1;
                    if graphnode[t].count = 0
                        then begin
                                {place graphnode[t] on the next}
                                {      period's output list      }
                                graphnode[t].nextnode: = nextout;
                                nextout: = t
                            end {then begin};
                    freearc(r);
                    r: = s
                        end {while r <> 0 do begin};
                    {delete the graph node}
                    numnodes: = numnodes - 1;
                    {continue traversing the output list}
                    p: = graphnode[p].nextnode
                end {while p <> 0 do begin};
            {reset output list for the next period}
            outp: = nextout
        end {while outp <> 0 do begin};
        if numnodes <> 0
            then error ('error in input - graph contains a cycle')
end {program schedule}.
```

EXERCISES

1. Implement a graph using linked lists so that each header node heads two lists: one containing the arcs emanating from the graph node and the other containing the arcs terminating at the graph node.

2. Implement a graph so that the lists of header nodes and arc nodes are circular.

3. Implement a graph using an adjacency matrix represented by the sparse matrix techniques of Section 5.3.

4. Implement a graph using an array of adjacency lists. Under this representation, a graph of n nodes consists of n header nodes, each containing an integer from 1 to n and a pointer. The pointer is to a list of list nodes each of which contains the node number of a node adjacent to the node represented by the header node.

Implement Dijkstra's algorithm using this graph representation with the array formed into an ascending heap.

5. There may be more than one way to organize a set of subtasks in a minimum number of time periods. For example, the subtasks in Figure 9.3.2 may be completed in six time periods by one of three different methods:

Period	Method 1	Method 2	Method 3
1	A, F	F	A, F
2	B, H	A, H	H
3	I	B, I	B, I
4	C	C	C
5	D	D	D
6	E	E	E

Write a program which will generate all possible methods of organizing the subtasks in the minimum number of time periods.

6. Consider the graph of Figure 9.3.4. The program *schedule* outputs the following organization of tasks:

Time	Subtasks
1	A, B, C
2	D, E
3	F
4	G

This requires three assistants (for time period 1). Can you find a method of organizing the subtasks so that only two assistants are required at any time period, yet the entire job can be accomplished in the same four time periods? Write a program which organizes subtasks so that a minimum number of assistants are needed to complete the entire job in the minimum number of time periods.

7. If there is only one worker available, it will take k time periods to complete the entire job, where k is the number of subtasks. Write a program to list a valid

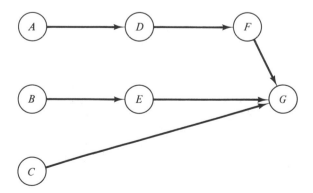

Figure 9.3.4

order in which the worker can perform the tasks. Note that this program is simpler than *schedule*, since an output list is not needed; as soon as the *count* field reaches 0, the task may be output. The process of converting a set of precedences into a single linear list in which no later element precedes an earlier one is called a *topological sort*.

8. A *PERT network* is a weighted acyclic directed graph in which each arc represents an activity and its weight represents the time needed to perform that activity. If arcs $\langle a, b \rangle$ and $\langle b, c \rangle$ exist in the network, then the activity represented by arc $\langle a, b \rangle$ must be completed before the activity represented by $\langle b, c \rangle$ can be started. Each node x of the network represents a time at which all activities represented by arcs terminating at x can be completed.

   (a) Write a Pascal routine that accepts a representation of such a network and assigns to each node x the earliest time that all activities terminating in that node can be completed. Call this quantity $et(x)$. (*Hint:* Assign time 0 to all nodes with no predecessors. If all predecessors of a node x have been assigned times, then $et(x)$ is the maximum over all predecessors of the sum of the time assigned to a predecessor and the weight of the arc from that predecessor to x.)

   (b) Given the assignment of times in part (a), write a Pascal routine that assigns to each node x the latest time that all activities terminating in x can be completed without delaying the completion of all the activities. Call this quantity $lt(x)$. (*Hint:* Assign time $et(x)$ to all nodes x with no successors. If all successors of a node x have been assigned times, then $lt(x)$ is the minimum over all successors of the difference between the time assigned to a successor and the weight of the arc from x to the successor.)

   (c) Prove that there is at least one path in the graph from a node with no predecessors to a node with no successors such that $et(x) = lt(x)$ for every node x on the path. Such a path is called a *critical path*.

   (d) Explain the significance of a critical path by showing that reducing the time of the activities along every critical path reduces the earliest time by which the entire job can be completed.

   (e) Write a Pascal routine to find all critical paths in a PERT network.

   (f) Find the critical paths in the networks of Figure 9.3.5.

9. Write a Pascal program that accepts a representation of a PERT network as given in Exercise 8 and computes the earliest time in which the entire job can be finished if as many activities as possible may be performed in parallel. The program should also print the starting and ending time of each activity in the network. Write another Pascal program to schedule the activities so that the entire job can be completed at the earliest possible time subject to the constraint that at most m activities can be performed in parallel.

4. GRAPH TRAVERSAL AND SPANNING FORESTS

A great many algorithms depend on being able to traverse a graph. In this section, we examine techniques for systematically accessing all the nodes of a graph and present several useful algorithms that implement and use those traversal techniques. We also look at ways of creating subgraphs that are also general forests.

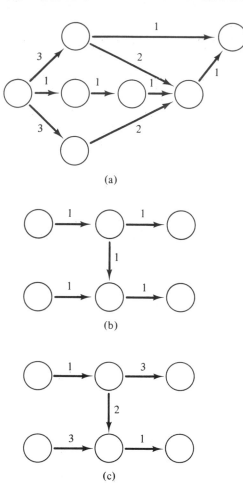

Figure 9.3.5 Some PERT networks.

Traversal Methods for Graphs

It is often desirable to *traverse* a data structure, that is, to visit each of its elements in a systematic manner. We have already seen traversal techniques for lists and trees; we now examine traversal techniques for graphs.

The elements of the graph to be visited are usually the graph nodes. It is always possible to traverse a graph efficiently by visiting the graph nodes in an implementation-dependent manner. For example, if a graph with n nodes is represented by an adjacency matrix or an array of adjacency lists, simply listing the integers from 1 to n "traverses" the graph. Similarly, if the graph nodes are maintained as a linked list, a search tree, a hash table, or some other structure, traversing the underlying structure might be considered a "traversal" of the graph. However, of greater interest is a traversal that corresponds to the graph structure of the object, not one for the underlying implementation structure. That is, the sequence in which the nodes are visited should relate to the adjacency structure of the graph.

Defining a traversal that relates to the structure of a graph is more complex than is that for a list or a tree for three reasons:

1. In general, there is no natural "first" node in a graph from which the traversal should start, as there is a first node in a list or a root in a tree. Further, once a starting node has been determined and all nodes reachable from that node have been visited, there may remain other nodes in the graph that have not been visited because they are not reachable from the starting node. This is again unlike a list or tree where every node is reachable from the header or the root. Thus, once all reachable nodes in a graph have been visited, the traversal algorithm again faces the problem of selecting another starting node.

2. There is no natural order among the successors of a particular node. Thus there is no a priori order in which the successors of a particular node should be visited.

3. Unlike a node of a list or a tree, a node of a graph may have more than one predecessor. If node x is a successor of both nodes y and z, then x may be visited after y but before z. It is therefore possible for a node to be visited before one of its predecessors. In fact, if a graph is cyclic, every possible traversal must include some node that is visited before one of its predecessors.

To deal with these three complications, any graph traversal method incorporates the following three features:

1. The algorithm is either presented with a starting node for the traversal or chooses a random node at which to start. The same traversal algorithm produces a different ordering of the nodes depending on the node at which it starts. In the following discussion, s denotes the starting node.

   We also assume a function *select* with no parameters that chooses an arbitrary unvisited node. The *select* operation is usually dependent on the graph representation. If the graph nodes are represented by the intergers 1 to n, *select* maintains a global variable *last* (initialized to 0) that keeps track of the last node selected by *select* and utilizes a flag *visited*(i) that is *true* only if *node*(i) has been visited:

   ```
   i:= last + 1;
   found:= false;
   while (not found) and (i <= n)
       do if visited(i)
           then i:= i + 1
           else found:= true;
   last:= i;
   if found
       then select:= i
       else select:= 0
   ```

A similar *select* routine can be implemented if the graph nodes are organized as a linked list, with *last* being a pointer to the last header node selected.

2. Generally, the implementation of the graph determines the order in which the successors of a node are visited. For example, if the adjacency matrix implementation is used, the node numbering (from 1 to *n*) determines the order; if the adjacency list implementation is used, the order of the arcs on the adjacency list determines the order in which the successors are visited. Alternatively, and much less commonly, the algorithm may choose a random ordering among the successors of a node. We consider two operations: *first*(*x*), which returns a pointer to the "first" successor of *node*(*x*); and *nextsucc*(*x*, *y*), where *node*(*y*) is a successor of *node*(*x*), which returns a pointer to the "next" successor of *node*(*x*) following *node*(*y*). Let us examine how to implement these functions under both the adjacency matrix and linked representations of a graph.

In the adjacency matrix representation, if *x* and *y* are indices such that *node*(*y*) is a successor of *node*(*x*), the next successor of *x* following *y* can be computed as the lowest index *i* greater than *y* such that *adj*(*x*, *i*) is *true*. Unfortunately, things are not so simple for the linked representation. If *x* and *y* represent two graph nodes in a graph representation that uses adjacency lists (*x* and *y* can be either array indices or pointers to header nodes), there is no way to access the "next" successor of *node*(*x*) following *node*(*y*). This is because, in the adjacency list representation, the ordering of successors is based on the ordering of arc nodes. It is therefore necessary to locate the arc node following the arc node that points to *node*(*y*). But there is no reference from *node*(*y*) to the arc node that points to it, and therefore no way to get to the next arc node. It is therefore necessary for *y* to point to an arc node rather than a graph node, although it actually represents the graph node terminating arc (that is, *node*(*ndptr*(*y*))). The next successor of *node*(*x*) following that graph node can then be found as *node*(*ndptr*(*nextarc*(*y*))), that is, the node that terminates the arc that follows the arc node *node*(*y*) on the adjacency list emanating from *node*(*x*).

To employ a uniform calling technique for *first* and *nextsucc* under all graph implementations, we present them as procedures rather than functions:

first(*x*, *yptr*, *ynode*) sets both *yptr* and *ynode* to the index of the first successor of *node*(*x*) under the adjacency matrix representation. Under the linked representation, *ynode* is set to a pointer to the header node (or a node number) of the first successor of *node*(*x*), and *yptr* is set to point to the arc node representing the arc from *node*(*x*) to *node*(*ynode*).

nextsucc(*x*, *yptr*, *ynode*) accepts two array indices (*x* and *yptr*) in the adjacency matrix representation and sets both *yptr* and *ynode* to the array index of the successor of *node*(*x*) that follows *node*(*yptr*). In the linked representation, *x* is an array index or a pointer to a header node, *yptr* is a pointer to an arc node and is reset to point to the arc node that follows *node*(*yptr*) on the adjacency list, and *ynode* is set to point to the header node that terminates the arc node pointed to by the modified value of *yptr*.

Given these conventions, an algorithm to visit all successors of *node*(*x*) can be written as follows:

> *first*(*x*, *yptr*, *ynode*);
> **repeat**
>> *visit*(*ynode*);
>> *nextsucc*(*x*, *yptr*, *ynode*)
>
> **until** *yptr* = *nil*

This algorithm will operate correctly under both implementations.

Let us now present algorithms for *first* and *nextsucc*. If the adjacency matrix implementation is used, *nextsucc*(*x*, *yptr*, *ynode*) is implemented as follows:

> *i*:= *yptr*;
> *finished*:= *false*;
> **repeat**
>> *i*:= *i* + 1;
>> **if** *i* > *n*
>>> **then begin**
>>>> *finished*:= *true*;
>>>> *yptr*:= 0;
>>>> *ynode*:= 0
>>>
>>> **end** {then begin}
>>> **else if** *adj*(*x*, *i*)
>>>> **then begin**
>>>>> *finished*:= *true*;
>>>>> *yptr*:= *i*;
>>>>> *ynode*:= *i*
>>>>
>>>> **end** {then begin}
>
> **until** *finished*

first(*x*, *yptr*, *ynode*) is implemented by

> *nextsucc*(*x*, 0, *ynode*);
> *yptr*:= *ynode*

Note that traversing all of a node's successors in a graph of *n* nodes is $O(n)$ using the adjacency matrix representation.

If the linked representation is used, *nextsucc* is implemented quite simply as follows. (We assume an *arcptr* field in each header node and *ndptr* and *nextarc* fields in each arc node.)

> *yptr*:= *nextarc*(*yptr*);
> **if** *yptr* = *nil*
>> **then** *ynode*:= *nil*
>> **else** *ynode*:= *ndptr*(*yptr*)

first is implemented by

> *yptr*:= *arcptr*(*x*);
> **if** *yptr* = *nil*
>> **then** *ynode*:= *nil*
>> **else** *ynode*:= *ndptr*(*yptr*)

Note that if e is the number of edges (arcs) in the graph and n the number of graph nodes, e/n is the average number of arcs emanating from a given node. Traversing the successors of a particular node by this method is therefore $O(e/n)$ on the average. If the graph is sparse (i.e., very few of the n^2 possible edges exist), this is a significant advantage of the adjacency list representation.

3. If a node has more than one predecessor, it is necessarily encountered more than once during a traversal. Therefore, to ensure termination and to ensure that each node is visited only once, a traversal algorithm must check that a node being encountered has not been visited previously. There are two ways to do this. One is to maintain a set of visited nodes. The set would be maintained for efficient lookup and insertion as a search tree or a hash table and whenever a node is encountered, the table is searched to see if the node has already been visited. If it has, the node is ignored; if it has not, the node is visited and added to the table. Of course, the lookup and insertion add to the traversal overhead.

The second technique is to keep a flag $visited(nd)$ in each node. Initially, all flags are set off (*false*) via a quick nongraph traversal through the list of graph nodes. The *visit* procedure turns the flag on (*true*) in the nodes being visited. When a node is encountered, its flag is examined. If it is on, the node is ignored; if it is off, the node is visited and the flag is set on. The flagging technique is used more commonly, since the flag initialization overhead is less than the table lookup and maintenance overhead.

Spanning Forests

A *forest* may be defined as an acyclic graph in which every node has one or no predecessors. A *tree* may be defined as a forest in which only a single node (called the *root*) has no predecessors. Any forest consists of a collection of trees. An *ordered forest* is one whose component trees are ordered. Given a graph G, F is a *spanning forest* of G if

1. F is a subgraph of G containing all the nodes of G.
2. F is an ordered forest containing trees $T_1, T_2, \ldots, T_n$.
3. T_i contains all nodes that are reachable in G from the root of T_i and are not contained in T_j for some $j < i$.

F is a *spanning tree* of G if it is a spanning forest of G and consists of a single tree.

Figure 9.4.1 illustrates four spanning forests for the graph of Figure 9.1.3. In each forest, the arcs of the graph that are not included in the forest are shown as dash-tailed arrows, while the arcs included in the forest are solid-tailed arrows. The spanning forests of Figures 9.4.1a and b are spanning trees, while those of Figures 9.4.1c and d are not.

Any spanning tree divides the edges (arcs) of a graph into four distinct

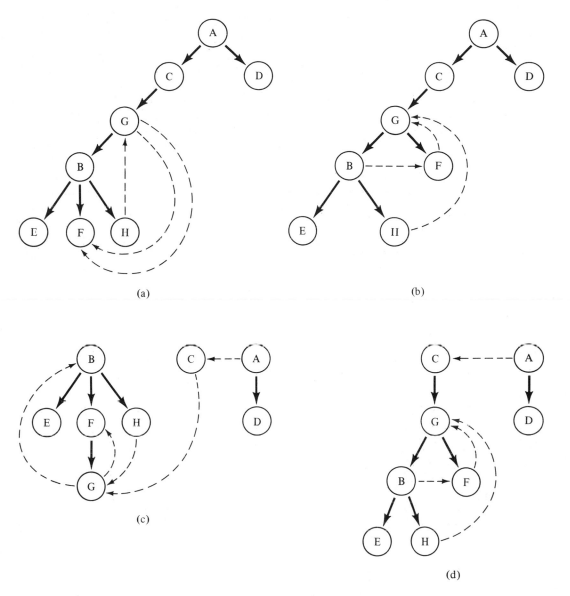

(a)   (b)

(c)   (d)

Figure 9.4.1

groups: *tree edges*, *forward edges*, *cross edges*, and *back edges*. Tree edges are arcs of the graph that are included in the spanning forest. Forward edges are arcs of the graph from a node to a spanning forest non-son descendant. A cross edge is an arc from one node to another node that is not the first node's descendant or ancestor in the spanning forest. Back edges are arcs from a node to a spanning forest ancestor. The following table classifies the arcs of the graph of Figure 9.1.3 in relation to each of the spanning trees of Figure 9.4.1:

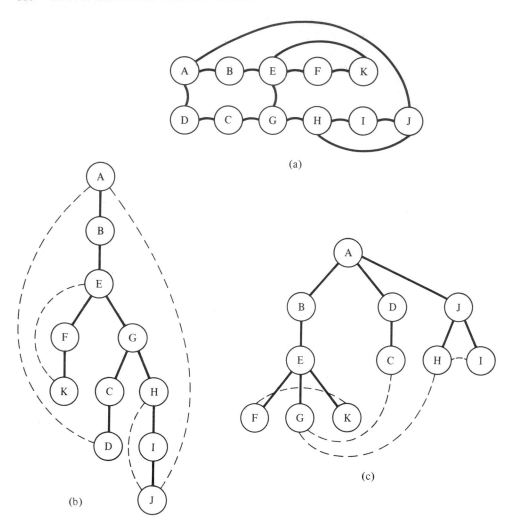

(a)

(b)

(c)

Figure 9.4.2

arc	(a)	(b)	(c)	(d)
$\langle A, C \rangle$	tree	tree	cross	cross
$\langle A, D \rangle$	tree	tree	tree	tree
$\langle B, E \rangle$	tree	tree	tree	tree
$\langle B, F \rangle$	tree	cross	tree	cross
$\langle B, H \rangle$	tree	tree	tree	tree
$\langle C, G \rangle$	tree	tree	cross	tree
$\langle F, G \rangle$	back	back	tree	back
$\langle G, B \rangle$	tree	tree	back	tree
$\langle G, F \rangle$	forward	tree	back	tree
$\langle H, G \rangle$	back	back	cross	back

Consider a traversal method that visits all nodes reachable from a previously visited node before visiting any node not reachable from a previously visited node. In such a traversal, a node is visited either arbitrarily or as the successor of a previously visited node. The traversal defines a spanning forest in which an arbitrarily selected node is the root of a tree in the spanning forest and in which a node $n1$ selected as the successor of $n2$ is a son of $n2$ in the spanning forest. For example, the traversal *ACGBEFHD* defines the forest of Figure 9.4.1a while the traversal *BEFGHCAD* defines that of Figure 9.4.1c. While a particular traversal defines a single spanning forest, a number of traversals may define the same forest. For example *ACDGBEFH* also defines the spanning forest of Figure 9.4.1a.

Undirected Graphs and Their Traversals

Thus far, we have been concerned exclusively with directed graphs. An undirected graph may be considered a ***symmetric*** directed graph, that is, one in which an arc $\langle B, A \rangle$ must exist whenever an arc $\langle A, B \rangle$ exists. The undirected arc (A, B) represents the two directed arcs $\langle A, B \rangle$ and $\langle B, A \rangle$.

An undirected graph may therefore be represented as a directed graph using either the adjacency matrix or adjacency list method. An adjacency matrix representing an undirected graph must be symmetric; the values in row i, column j and in row j, column i must be either both *false* (i.e., the arc (i, j) does not exist in the graph) or both *true* (the arc (i, j) does exist). In the adjacency list representation, if (i, j) is an undirected arc, the arc list emanating from *node*(i) contains a list node representing directed arc $\langle i, j \rangle$ and the list emanating from *node*(j) contains a list node representing directed arc $\langle j, i \rangle$. In an undirected graph, if a node x is reachable from a node y (that is, there is a path from y to x), then y is reachable from x as well along the reversed path.

Since an undirected graph is represented by a directed graph, any traversal method for directed graphs induces a traversal method for undirected graphs as well. Figure 9.4.2 illustrates an undirected graph and two spanning trees for that graph. The tree in Figure 9.4.2b is created by either of the traversals *ABEFKGCDHIJ* or *ABEFGKCHDIJ*, among others. The tree in Figure 9.4.2c is created by the traversal *ABEFGKDCJHI* or *ABDJECHIFGK*, among others. Note that the edges included and excluded from the spanning tree are all bidirectional.

Spanning forests constructed by undirected graph traversals have several special properties. First, there is no distinction between forward edges (or tree edges) and back edges. Since an edge in an undirected graph is bidirectional, such a distinction is meaningless. In an undirected graph, any arc between a node and its non-son descendant is called a back edge.

Second, in an undirected graph, all cross edges are within a single tree. Cross edges between trees arise in a directed graph traversal when there is an arc $\langle x, y \rangle$ such that y is visited before x and there is no path from y to x. Therefore, the arc $\langle x, y \rangle$ is a cross edge. In an undirected graph containing an arc (x, y), x and y must be part of the same tree since each is reachable from the other via that arc at least. A cross edge in an undirected graph is only possible if three nodes x, y, and z are part of a cycle and y and z are in separate subtrees of a subtree whose root is x. The path between y and z must then include a cross edge between the two subtrees. Confirm that this is the case with all cross edges of Figure 9.4.2c.

Because undirected graphs have "double" the edges of directed graphs, their spanning forests tend to have fewer, but larger, trees.

An undirected graph is termed **connected** if every node in it is reachable from every other. Pictorially, a connected graph has only one segment. For example, the graph of Figure 9.4.2a is a connected graph. The graph of Figure 9.1.1a is not connected since node E is not reachable from node C, for example. A **connected component** of an undirected graph is a connected subgraph containing all arcs incident to any of its nodes such that no graph node outside the subgraph is reachable from any node in the subgraph. For example, the subgraph of Figure 9.1.1a has three connected components: nodes A, B, C, D, F; nodes E and G; and node H. A connected graph has a single connected component.

The spanning forest of a connected graph is a spanning tree. Each tree in the spanning forest of an undirected graph contains all the nodes in a single connected component of the graph. Thus any traversal method that creates a spanning forest (that is, one that visits all nodes reachable from visited nodes before visiting any other nodes) can be used to determine whether an undirected graph is connected and to identify an undirected graph's connected components.

In traversing an undirected graph, it is not very important which node s is used as the starting node or how *select* chooses an arbitrary node (except perhaps in terms of the efficiency of *select*). This is because all nodes of a connected component will wind up in the same tree regardless of the choice of s or how *select* operates. This is not true in traversing a directed graph. For example, the traversal of Figures 9.4.1a and b used $s = A$. Since all nodes are reachable from A, the spanning forest is a tree, and *select* is never needed to choose an arbitrary node once that tree is built. In Figure 9.4.1c, however, B is the starting node, so only nodes reachable from B are included in the first tree. *select* then chooses C. Since only visited nodes are reachable from C, it is alone in its tree. *select* is then required again to choose A, whose tree completes the traversal. In Figure 9.4.1d, s equals C and *select* is required only once, when it returns A. Thus, if it is desired to create as large and as few trees as possible, s should be a node with as few predecessors as possible (preferably none) and *select* should choose such a node as well. This may make *select* less efficient.

We now examine two traversal methods and their applications to both directed and undirected graphs.

Depth-First Traversal

The ***depth-first traversal*** technique is best defined using a routine *dftraverse(s)* that visits all nodes reachable from *s*. This routine is presented shortly. We assume a procedure *visit(nd)* that visits a node *nd* and a function *visited(nd)* that returns *true* if *nd* has already been visited and *false* otherwise. This is best implemented by a boolean field in each node. *visit* sets the field to *true*. To execute the traversal, the field is first set *false* for all nodes. The traversal algorithm also assumes the function *select* with no parameters to select an arbitrary unvisited node. *select* returns *nil* if all nodes have been visited.

```
for every node nd
        do visited(nd) := false;
s:= a pointer to the starting node for the traversal;
while s <> nil
        do begin
                dftraverse(s);
                s:= select
        end  {while...do begin}
```

Note that a starting node *s* is specified for the traversal. This node becomes the root of the first tree in the spanning forest. The following is a recursive algorithm for *dftraverse(s)*, using the routines *first* and *nextsucc* presented earlier:

```
{visit all nodes reachable from s}
visit(s);
{traverse all unvisited successors of s}
first(s, yptr, nd);
repeat
        if not visited(nd)
                then dftraverse(nd);
        nextsucc(s, yptr, nd)
until yptr = nil;
```

If it is known that every node in the graph is reachable from the starting node *s* (as in the case of the graph of Figure 9.1.3 starting from node *A* or in the case of a connected undirected graph such as that of Figure 9.4.2a), then the spanning forest is a single spanning tree and the ***while*** loop and *select* are not required since every node is visited in a single call to *dftraverse*.

A depth-first traversal, as its name indicates, traverses a single path of the graph as far as it can go (that is, until it visits a node with no successors or a node all of whose successors have already been visited). It then resumes at the last node on the path just traversed that has an unvisited successor and begins traversing a new path emanating from that node. Spanning trees created by a depth-first traversal tend to be very deep. Depth-first traversal is also sometimes called *depth-first search*.

Figures 9.4.1a and c are both depth-first spanning trees of the graph of Figure 9.1.3. In Figure 9.4.1a, the traversal started at *A* and proceeded as follows: *ACGBEFHD*. Note that this is the preorder traversal of the spanning tree. In fact, the depth-first traversal of a tree is its preorder traversal. In Figure 9.4.1c, the traversal starts at *B* and proceeds as follows: *BEFGH*. At that point, all nodes reachable from *B* have been enumerated, so *select* is called to find an arbitrary unvisited node. Figure 9.4.1c assumes that *select* returned a pointer to *C*. But no unvisited nodes are successors of *C* (*G* has already been visited), so *select* is called again and returns *A*. *D* is an unvisited successor of *A* and is visited to complete the traversal. Thus Figure 9.4.1c corresponds to the complete depth-first traversal *BEFGHCAD*.

This illustrates that there may be several depth-first traversals and depth-first spanning trees for a particular directed graph. The traversal depends very much on how the graph is represented (adjacency matrix or adjacency list; how the nodes are numbered), the starting node, and on how the basic depth-first traversal is implemented (in particular, the implementation of *first*, *nextsucc*, and *select*). The essential feature of a depth-first traversal is that, after a node is visited, all descendants of the node are visited before its unvisited brothers. Figure 9.4.2b represents the depth-first traversal *ABEFKGCDHIJ* of the undirected graph of Figure 9.4.2a.

As usual, a stack can be used to eliminate the recursion in depth-first traversal. The following is a complete nonrecursive depth-first traversal algorithm:

```
for every node nd
do visited(nd) := false;
s := a pointer to the starting node for the traversal;
ndstack := the empty stack;
while s <> nil
    do begin
            visit(s);
            {find first unvisited successor}
            first(s, yptr, nd);
            while (nd <> nil) and (visited(nd))
                do nextsucc(s, yptr, nd);
            {  if no unvisited successors, simulate return  }
            {             from recursive call              }
            while (nd = nil) and (not empty(ndstack))
                do begin
                        popsub(ndstack, s, yptr);
                        {find next unvisited successor}
                        nextsucc(s, yptr, nd);
```

$$\textbf{while } (nd <> nil) \textbf{ and } (visited(nd))$$
$$\textbf{do } nextsucc(s, yptr, nd)$$
$$\textbf{end } \{\text{while}\ldots\text{do begin}\};$$
$$\textbf{if } nd <> nil$$
$$\textbf{then begin } \{\text{simulate the recursive call}\}$$
$$push(ndstack, s, yptr);$$
$$s := nd$$
$$\textbf{end } \{ \text{ then begin } \}$$
$$\textbf{else } s := select$$
$$\textbf{end } \{\text{while}\ldots\text{do begin}\}$$

Note that each stack element contains pointers to both a father node (*s*) and an incident arc or its son (*yptr*) to allow continuation of the traversal of the successors.

To use this algorithm to construct a spanning tree, it is necessary to keep track of a node's father when it is visited, as follows. First, change the *if* statement at the end of the algorithm to

$$\textbf{if } nd <> nil$$
$$\textbf{then begin } \{\text{simulate the recursive call}\}$$
$$push(ndstack, s, yptr);$$
$$f := s; \{\text{this statement is added}\}$$
$$s := nd$$
$$\textbf{end } \{\text{then begin}\}$$
$$\textbf{else begin}$$
$$s := select;$$
$$f := nil \{\text{this statement is added}\}$$
$$\textbf{end } \{\text{else begin}\}$$

Second, initialize *f* to *nil* at the beginning of the algorithm. Third, change *visit(s)* to *addson(f, s)*; *visited(s)* := *true*, where *addson* adds *node(s)* to the tree as the next son of *node(f)*. If *f* is *nil*, *addson(f, s)* adds *node(s)* as a new tree in the forest (e.g., it calls *maketree*; it is assumed that the tree roots are kept in a linked list managed by *maketree* using two global variables pointing to the first and last trees in the forest).

You are invited to apply this modified algorithm to the graph of Figure 9.1.3, with *s* initialized to *A* and the successors of any node ordered alphabetically, to obtain the spanning tree of Figure 9.4.1a. Similarly, applying the modified algorithm to the same graph, with *s* initialized to *B*, and assuming that *select* chooses *C* before *A* and *D*, and *A* before *D*, yields the spanning forest of Figure 9.4.1c. Applying the algorithm to the graph of Figure 9.4.2a produces the tree of Figure 9.4.2b.

As illustrated by Figure 9.4.2b, a depth-first spanning forest of an undirected graph may contain tree edges and back edges but cannot contain any cross edges. To see why, assume that (x, y) is an edge in the graph and that x is visited before y. In a depth-first traversal, y must be visited as a descendant of x before any nodes that are not reachable from x. Thus the arc (x, y) is either a tree edge or a back edge. The same is true in reverse if y is visited first since the undirected arc (x, y) is equivalent to (y, x). In a directed graph, however, the arc $\langle x, y \rangle$ but not $\langle y, x \rangle$ may be in the graph. If y is visited first, then, since x may not be reachable from y, x may not be in a subtree rooted at y, so the arc $\langle x, y \rangle$ may be a cross edge even in a depth-first spanning tree. This is illustrated by the arcs $\langle A, C \rangle$ and $\langle C, G \rangle$ in Figure 9.4.1c.

Applications of Depth-First Traversal

Depth-first traversal, like any other traversal method that creates a spanning forest, can be used to determine if an undirected graph is connected and to identify the connected components of an undirected graph. Whenever *select* is called, a new connected component of the graph is being traversed. If *select* is never called, the graph is connected.

Depth-first traversal can also be used to determine if a graph is acyclic. In both directed and undirected graphs, a cycle exists if and only if a back edge exists in a depth-first spanning forest. It is obvious that if a back edge exists, the graph contains a cycle formed by the back edge itself and the tree path starting at the ancestor head of the back edge and ending at the descendant tail of the back edge. To prove that a back edge must exist in a cyclic graph, consider the node *nd* of a cycle that is the first node in its cycle visited by a depth-first traversal. There must exist a node x such that the arc (x, nd) or $\langle x, nd \rangle$ is in the cycle. Since x is in the cycle, it is reachable from *nd* so that x must be a descendant of *nd* in the spanning forest. Thus the arc (x, nd) or $\langle x, nd \rangle$ is a back edge by definition.

Therefore, to determine if a graph is acyclic, it is only necessary to determine that an edge encountered during a depth-first traversal is not a back edge. When considering an edge (s, nd) or $\langle s, nd \rangle$ in the depth-first traversal algorithm, the edge can be a back edge only if *visited(nd)* is *true*. In an undirected graph, where there are no cross edges in a depth-first traversal, (s, nd) is a back edge if and only if *visited(nd)* is *true* and *nd* $\langle \rangle$ *father(s)* in the spanning forest.

In a directed graph, $\langle s, nd \rangle$ can be a back edge even if *nd* equals *father(s)* since $\langle s, nd \rangle$ and $\langle nd, s \rangle$ are distinct arcs. Thus, in a directed graph, a cycle may consist of only two nodes (such as s and *nd*), whereas in an undirected graph, at least three are required. However, since a directed graph's spanning tree may contain cross edges as well as back edges, *visited(nd)* equaling *true* is not enough to detect a cycle. For example, cross edges $\langle A, C \rangle$, $\langle H, G \rangle$, and $\langle C, G \rangle$ in Figure 9.4.1c are not part of a cycle, although C has been visited by the time $\langle A, C \rangle$ is considered and G has been visited by the time $\langle H, G \rangle$ and $\langle C, G \rangle$ are considered. To determine that an arc $\langle s, nd \rangle$ is not a back edge when *visited(nd)* is *true*, it is necessary to consider each ancestor of s in turn to ensure that it does not equal nd. We leave the details of an algorithm to determine if a directed graph is acyclic (that is, a dag) as an exercise for the reader.

In the previous section, we examined an algorithm to schedule tasks given a series of required precedences among those tasks. We saw that the precedence relations among the tasks can be represented by a dag. The algorithm presented in that section can be used to specify a linear ordering of the nodes in which no node comes before a preceding node. Such a linear ordering is called a ***topological sort*** of the nodes.

A depth-first traversal can be used to produce a reverse topological ordering of the nodes. Consider the inorder traversal of the spanning forest formed by a depth-first traversal of a dag. We claim that such an inorder traversal produces a reverse topological ordering. To repeat the recursive definition of inorder traversal of a forest from Section 6.5,

1. Traverse the forest formed by the subtrees of the first tree in the forest, if any.
2. Visit the root of the first tree.
3. Traverse the forest formed by the remaining trees of the forest, if any.

To differentiate in the following discussion between the depth-first traversal that creates the forest and the inorder traversal of the forest, we refer to DF-visits (and a DF-traversal) and IO-visits (and an IO-traversal), respectively.

An IO-traversal of the depth-first spanning tree of a dag must be in reverse topological order. That is, if x precedes y, then x is IO-visited after y. To see why this is so, consider the arc $\langle x, y \rangle$. We show that y is IO-visited before x. Since the graph is acyclic, $\langle x, y \rangle$ cannot be a back arc. If it is a tree arc or a forward arc, so that y is a descendant of x in the spanning forest, then y is IO-visited before x because an inorder traversal IO-visits the root of a subtree after traversing all its subtrees. If $\langle x, y \rangle$ is a cross edge, then y must have been IO-visited before x (otherwise, y would have been a descendant of x). Consider the smallest subtrees, $S(x)$ and $S(y)$, containing x and y, respectively, whose roots are brothers. (Roots of trees of the spanning forest are also considered brothers in this context.) Then since y was DF-visited before x, $S(y)$ precedes $S(x)$ in their subtree ordering. Thus $S(y)$ is IO-traversed before $S(X)$, which means that y is IO-visited before x.

Thus an algorithm to determine a reverse topological ordering of the nodes of a dag consists of a depth-first search of the dag followed by an inorder traversal of the resulting spanning forest. Fortunately, it is unnecessary to make a separate traversal of the spanning tree since an inorder traversal can be incorporated directly into the recursive depth-first traversal algorithm. To do this, simply push a node onto a stack when it is DF-visited. Whenever *dftraverse* returns, pop the stack and IO-visit the popped node.

Since *dftraverse* depth-first traverses all the subtrees of a tree before completing the tree's DF-traversal and traverses the first subtree of a set of brothers before depth-first traversing the others, this procedure yields an inorder traversal. The reader is invited to implement this algorithm nonrecursively.

Efficiency of Depth-First Traversal

The depth-first traversal procedure visits every node of a graph and traverses all the successors of each node. We have already seen that, for the adjacency matrix implementation, traversing all successors of a node using *first* and *nextsucc* is $O(n)$, where n is the number of graph nodes. Thus traversing the successors of all the nodes is $O(n^2)$. For this reason, depth-first search using the adjacency matrix representation is $O(n + n^2)$ (n node visits and n^2 possible successor examinations), which is the same as $O(n^2)$.

If the adjacency list representation is used, then traversing all successors of all nodes is $O(e)$, where e is the number of edges in the graph. Assuming that the graph nodes are organized as an array or a linked list, visiting all n nodes is $O(n)$, so that the efficiency of depth-first traversal using adjacency lists is $O(n + e)$. Since e is usually much smaller than n^2, the adjacency list representation yields more efficient traversals. (The difference, however, is somewhat offset by the fact that in an adjacency matrix, traversal of successors involves merely counting from 1 to n, while in an adjacency list, it involves successively accessing fields in nodes.) Depth-first traversal is often considered $O(e)$ since e is usually larger than n.

Breadth-First Traversal

An alternative traversal method, **breadth-first traversal** (or **breadth-first search**) visits all successors of a visited node before visiting any successors of any of those successors. This is in contradistinction to depth-first traversal, which visits the successors of a visited node before visiting any of its "brothers." Whereas depth-first traversal tends to create very long, narrow trees, breadth-first traversal tends to create very wide, short trees. Figure 9.4.1b represents the breadth-first traversal of the graph of Figure 9.1.3, and Figure 9.4.2c represents the breadth-first traversal of the graph of Figure 9.4.2a.

In implementing depth-first traversal, each visited node is placed on a stack (either implicitly via recursion or explicitly), reflecting the fact that the last node visited is the first node whose successors will be visited. Breadth-first traversal is implemented using a queue, representing the fact that the first node visited is the first node whose successors are visited. The following is an algorithm *bftraverse(s)* to traverse a graph using breadth-first traversal beginning at *node(s)*:

```
ndqueue:= the empty queue;
while s <> nil
    do begin
            visit (s);
            insert(ndqueue, s);
            while not empty (ndqueue)
                do begin
                        x:= remove(ndqueue);
                        { visit all successors of x }
                        first(x, yptr, nd);
                        while (nd <> nil)
                            do begin
                                    if not visited (nd)
                                    then begin
                                            visit (nd);
                                            insert (ndqueue, nd)
                                    end {then, begin};
                                    nextsucc(x, yptr, nd)
                            end {while...do begin}
                end {while...do begin};
        s:= select
    end {while...do begin}
```

We leave modification of the algorithm to produce a breadth-first spanning forest as an exercise for the reader. Figure 9.4.1b illustrates a breadth-first spanning tree for the graph of Figure 9.1.3, representing the breadth-first traversal *ACDGBFEH*. Note that while the traversal differs significantly from the depth-first traversal *ACGBEFHD* that produced the spanning tree of Figure 9.4.1a, the two spanning trees themselves do not differ except for the position of node *F*. This reflects the fact that the graph of Figure 9.1.3 has relatively few arcs (10) compared to the total number of potential arcs ($n^2 = 64$). In a graph with more arcs, the difference in spanning forests is more pronounced.

A breadth-first spanning tree does not have any forward edges since all nodes adjacent to a visited node *nd* have already been visited or are spanning tree sons of *nd*. For the same reason, for a directed graph, all cross edges within the same tree are to nodes on the same or higher levels of the tree. For an undirected graph, a breadth-first spanning forest contains no back edges, since every back edge is also a forward edge.

Breadth-first traversal can be used for some of the same applications as depth-first traversal. In particular, breadth-first traversal can be used to determine if an undirected graph is connected and to identify the graph's connected components. Breadth-first traversal can also be used to determine if a graph is cyclic. For a directed graph, this is detected when a back edge is found; for an undirected graph, it is detected when a cross edge within the same tree is found.

For an unweighted graph, breadth-first traversal can also be used to find the shortest path (fewest arcs) from one node to another. Simply begin the traversal at the first node and stop when the target node has been reached. The breadth-first spanning tree path from the root to the target is the shortest path between the two nodes.

The efficiency of breadth-first traversal is the same as that of depth-first traversal: each node is visited once, and all arcs emanating from every node are considered. Thus its efficiency is $O(n^2)$ for the adjacency matrix graph representation and $O(n + e)$ for the adjacency list graph representation.

Minimum Spanning Trees

Given a connected weighted graph G, it is often desired to create a spanning tree T for G such that the sum of the weights of the tree edges in T is as small as possible. Such a tree is called a *minimum spanning tree* and represents the "cheapest" way of connecting all the nodes in G.

There are a number of techniques for creating a minimum spanning tree for a weighted graph. The first of these, *Prim's algorithm,* discovered independently by Prim and Dijkstra, is very much like Dijkstra's algorithm for finding shortest paths. An arbitrary node is chosen initially as the tree root (note that in an undirected graph and its spanning tree, any node can be considered the tree root and the nodes adjacent to it as its sons). The nodes of the graph are then appended to the tree one at a time until all nodes of the graph are included.

The node of the graph added to the tree at each point is that node adjacent to a node of the tree by an arc of minimum weight. The arc of minimum weight becomes a tree arc connecting the new node to the tree. When all the nodes of the graph have been added to the tree, a minimum spanning tree has been constructed for the graph.

To see that this technique creates a minimum spanning tree, consider a minimum spanning tree T for the graph and consider the partial tree PT built by Prim's algorithm at any point. Suppose that (a, b) is the minimum-cost arc from nodes in PT to nodes not in PT and suppose that (a, b) is not in T. Then, since there is a path between any two graph nodes in a spanning tree, there must be an alternate path between a and b in T that does not include arc (a, b). This alternate path P must include an arc (x, y) from a node in PT to a node outside of PT. Let us assume that P contains subpaths between a and x and between y and b.

Now, consider what would happen if we replaced arc (x, y) in T with (a, b) to create NT. We claim that NT is also a spanning tree. To prove this, we need to show two things: that any two nodes of the graph are connected in *NT* and that *NT* does not contain a cycle—that is, that there is only one path between any two nodes in *NT*.

Since *T* is a spanning tree, any two nodes, *m* and *n*, are connected in *T*. If the path between them in *T* does not contain (*x*, *y*), then the same path connects them in *NT*. If the path between them in *T* does contain (*x*, *y*), then consider the path in *NT* formed by the subpath in *T* from *m* to *x*, the subpath in *P* (which is in *T*) from *x* to *a*, the arc (*a*, *b*), the subpath in *P* from *b* to *y*, and the subpath in *T* from *y* to *n*. This is a path from *m* to *n* in *NT*. Thus any two nodes of the graph are connected in *NT*.

To show that *NT* does not contain a cycle, suppose it did. If the cycle does not contain (*a*, *b*), then the same cycle would exist in *T*. But that is impossible since *T* is a spanning tree. Thus the cycle must contain (*a*, *b*). Now consider the same cycle with arc (*a*, *b*) replaced with the subpath of *P* between *a* and *x*, the arc (*x*, *y*), and the subpath in *P* between *y* and *b*. The resulting path must also be a cycle and is a path entirely in *T*. But, again, *T* cannot contain a cycle. Therefore *NT* also does not contain a cycle.

NT has been shown to be a spanning tree. But *NT* must have lower cost than *T* since (*a*, *b*) was chosen to have lower cost than (*x*, *y*). Thus *T* is not a minimum spanning tree unless it includes the lowest-weight arc from *PT* to nodes outside *PT*. Therefore any arc added by Prim's algorithm must be made part of a minimum spanning tree.

The crux of the algorithm is a method for efficient determination of the "closest" node to a partial spanning tree. Initially, when the partial tree consists of a single node *root*, the distance of any other node *nd* from the tree, *distance[nd]*, equals *weight(root, nd)*. When a new node, *current*, is added to the tree, *distance[nd]* is modified to the minimum of *distance[nd]* and *weight(current, nd)*. The node added to the tree at each point is the node whose *distance* is lowest. For nodes *tnd* in the tree, *distance[tnd]* is set to *maxint* so that a node outside the tree is chosen as closest. An additional array *closest[nd]* points to the node in the tree such that *distance[nd]* = *weight(closest[nd], nd)*, that is, the node in the tree closest to *nd*.

Prim's algorithm may therefore be implemented as follows:

```
root:= an arbitrary node chosen as root;
for every node nd in the graph
    do begin
            distance[nd]:= weight(root, nd);
            closest[nd]:= root
        end;
distance[root]:= maxint;
current:= root;
for i:= 2 to the number of nodes in the graph
    do begin
            { find the node closest to the tree }
            mindist:= maxint;
```

```
            for every node nd in the graph
               do if distance[nd] < mindist
                  then begin
                              current := nd;
                              mindist := distance[nd]
                     end {for...if...then begin};
               {add the closest node to the tree and adjust distances}
               addson(closest[current], current);
               distance[current] := maxint;
               for every node nd adjacent to current
                  do if (distance[nd] < maxint)
                              and (weight(current, nd) < distance[nd])
                     then begin
                              distance[nd] := weight(current, nd);
                              closest[nd] := current
                        end {for...if...then begin}
         end {for...do begin}
```

If the graph is represented by an adjacency matrix, then each *for* loop in Prim's algorithm must examine $O(n)$ nodes. Since the algorithm contains a nested *for* loop, it is $O(n^2)$.

However, just as in Dijkstra's algorithm, Prim's algorithm can be made more efficient by maintaining the graph using adjacency lists and keeping a priority queue of the nodes not in the partial tree. The first inner loop (*for every node* nd *in the graph*...) can then be replaced by removing the minimum-distance node from the priority queue and adjusting the priority queue. The second inner loop simply traverses an adjacency list and adjusts the position of any nodes whose distance is modified in the priority queue. Under this implementation, Prim's algorithm is $O((n + e) \log n)$.

Kruskal's Algorithm

Another algorithm to create a minimum spanning tree is due to Kruskal. The nodes of the graph are initially considered as n distinct partial trees with one node each. At each step of the algorithm, two distinct partial trees are connected into a single partial tree by an edge of the graph. When only one partial tree exists (after $n - 1$ such steps), it is a minimum spanning tree.

The issue of course is what connecting arc to use at each step. The answer is to use the arc of minimum cost that connects two distinct trees. To do this, the arcs can be placed in a priority queue based on weight. The arc of lowest weight is then examined to see if it connects two distinct trees.

To determine if an arc (x, y) connects distinct trees, we can implement the trees with a *father* field in each node. Then we can traverse all ancestors of x and y to obtain the roots of the trees containing them. If the roots of the two trees are the same node, then x and y are already in the same tree, arc (x, y) is discarded, and the arc of next lowest weight is examined. Combining two trees simply involves setting the *father* of the root of one to the root of the other.

We leave the actual algorithm and its Pascal implementation for the reader. Forming the initial priority queue is $O(e \log e)$. Removing the minimum-weight arc and adjusting the priority queue is $O(\log e)$. Locating the root of a tree is $O(\log n)$. Initial formation of the n trees is $O(n)$. Thus, assuming that $n < e$, as is true of most graphs, Kruskal's algorithm is $O(e \log e)$.

The Round-Robin Algorithm

Still another algorithm, due to Tarjan and Cheriton, provides even better performance when the number of edges is low. The algorithm is similar to Kruskal's except that there is a priority queue of arcs associated with each partial tree, rather than one global priority queue of all unexamined arcs.

All partial trees are maintained in a queue, Q. Associated with each partial tree, T, is a priority queue, $P(T)$, of all arcs with exactly one incident node in the tree, ordered by the weights of the arcs. Initially, as in Kruskal's algorithm, each node is a partial tree. A priority queue of all arcs incident to nd is created for each node nd, and the single-node trees are inserted into Q in arbitrary order. The algorithm proceeds by removing a partial tree, $T1$, from the front of Q; finding the minimum-weight arc a in $P(T1)$; deleting from Q the tree, $T2$, at the other end of arc a; combining $T1$ and $T2$ into a single new tree $T3$ (and at the same time combining $P(T1)$ and $P(T2)$, with a deleted, into $P(T3)$); and adding $T3$ to the rear of Q. This continues until Q contains a single tree: the minimum spanning tree.

It can be shown that this **round-robin algorithm** requires only $O(e \log \log n)$ operations if an appropriate implementation of the priority queues is used.

EXERCISES

1. Consider the following nonrecursive depth-first traversal algorithm:

```
for every node nd
    do visited(i) := false;
s:= a pointer to the starting node of the traversal;
ndstack:= the empty stack;
```

```
while s <> nil
    do begin
            push(ndstack, s);
            while(not empty(ndstack))
                do begin
                        x:= pop(ndstack);
                        if not visited(x)
                        then begin
                                visit(x);
                                first(x, yptr, nd);
                                while(nd <> nil)
                                    do begin
                                            if not visited(nd)
                                            then push(ndstack, nd);
                                            nextsucc(x, yptr, nd)
                                    end {while...do begin}
                        end {then begin}
                end {while...do begin};
            s:= select
    end {while...do begin}
```

(a) Apply the algorithm to the graphs of Figures 9.1.3 and 9.4.2a to determine the order in which the nodes are visited, if the successors of a node are assumed ordered in alphabetical order.

(b) Draw the spanning trees induced by the traversal on each of the graphs. Modify the algorithm to construct a depth-first spanning forest.

(c) Would a modified ordering of successors produce the spanning trees of Figures 9.4.1a and 9.4.2b using this algorithm? Would a modified ordering produce the spanning trees in (b) using the algorithm of the text?

(d) Is either algorithm preferable?

2. Write an algorithm and a Pascal program to determine if a directed graph is a dag.

3. Write a recursive Pascal program to print the nodes of a dag in reverse topological order.

4. Write a nonrecursive Pascal program to print the nodes of a dag in reverse topological order.

5. A node *nd* in a connected graph is an **articulation point** if removing *nd* and all arcs adjacent to *nd* results in an unconnected graph. Thus the "connectedness" of the graph depends on *nd*. A graph with no articulation points is called **biconnected**.

(a) Show that the root of the depth-first spanning tree of a biconnected graph has only a single son.

(b) Show that if *nd* is not the root of a depth-first spanning tree *T*, then *nd* is an articulation point if and only if *T* does not contain a back edge from a descendant of *nd* to an ancestor of *nd*.

(c) Modify the recursive depth-first traversal algorithm to determine if a connected graph is biconnected.

6. Write a Pascal routine to create a breadth-first spanning forest of a graph.

7. Write Pascal routines that use a breadth-first traversal to determine if a directed and an undirected graph are cyclic.

8. Write a Pascal routine to produce the shortest path from node x to node y in an unweighted graph, if a path exists, or an indication that no path exists between the two nodes.

9. Show that the algorithms to find a cycle using depth-first or breadth-first search must be $O(n)$.

10. Implement Prim's algorithm using an adjacency matrix and using adjacency lists and a priority queue.

11. Implement Kruskal's algorithm as a Pascal procedure.

10

STORAGE MANAGEMENT

A programming language that incorporates a large number of data structures must contain mechanisms for managing those structures, and for controlling how storage is assigned to them. The previous chapters of this book illustrated some of those management techniques. As data structures become more complex and provide greater capabilities to the user, the management techniques grow in complexity as well.

In this chapter, we look at several techniques for implementing dynamic allocation and freeing of storage. Most of these methods are used in some form by operating systems to grant or deny user program requests. Others are used directly by individual language processors. We begin by expanding the concept of a list.

1. GENERAL LISTS

In Chapters 4 and 5 and in Section 8.1, we examined linked lists as a concrete data structure and as a method of implementation for such abstract data types as the stack, queue, priority queue, and table. In those implementations, a list always contained elements of the same type.

It is also possible to view a list as an abstract data type in its own right. As an abstract data type, a list is simply a sequence of objects called *elements*. Associated with each list element is a *value*. We make a very specific distinction between an *element*, which is an object as part of a list, and the element's *value*, which is the object considered individually. For example, the number 5 may appear on a list twice. Each appearance is a distinct element of the list, but the values of the two elements—the number

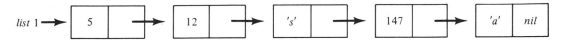

Figure 10.1.1   A list of integers and characters.

5—are the same. An element may be viewed as corresponding to a node in the implementation of a linked list, while a value corresponds to the node's contents. Note that the phrase "linked list" refers to the linked implementation of the abstract data type "list."

There is also no reason to assume that the elements of a list must be of the same type. Figure 10.1.1 illustrates a linked list implementation of an abstract list *list*1 that contains both integers and characters. The elements of that list are 5, 12, 's,' 147, and 'a.' The pointer *list*1 is called an ***external pointer*** to the list (because it is not contained within a list node), whereas the other pointers in the list are ***internal pointers*** (because they are contained within list nodes). We often reference a linked list by an external pointer to it.

It is also not necessary that a list contain only "simple" elements (e.g., integers or characters); it is possible for one or more of the elements of a list to themselves be lists. The simplest way to implement a list element *e* whose value is itself a list, *l*, is by representing the element by a node containing a pointer to the linked list implementation of *l*.

For example, consider the list *list*2 of Figure 10.1.2. This list contains four elements. Two of these are integers (the first element is the integer 5; the third element is the integer 2), and the other two are lists. The list that is the second element of *list*2 contains five elements, three of which are integers (the first, second, and fifth elements) and two of which are lists [the third element is a list containing the integers 14, 9, and 3 and the fourth element is the nil list (the list with no elements)]. The fourth element of *list*2 is a list containing the three integers 6, 3, and 10.

Figure 10.1.2

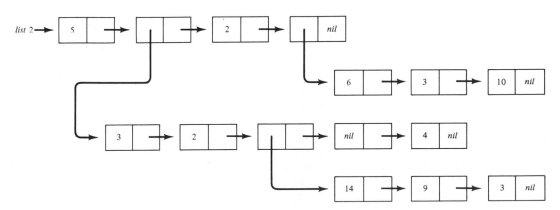

There is a convenient notation for specifying abstract general lists. A list may be denoted by a parenthesized enumeration of its elements separated by commas. For example, the abstract list represented by Figure 10.1.1 may be denoted by

$$list1 = (5, 12, \text{‘s’}, 147, \text{‘a’})$$

The nil list is denoted by an empty parenthesis pair [such as ( )]. Thus the list of Figure 10.1.2 may be denoted by

$$list2 = (5, (3, 2, (14, 9, 3), (\ ), 4), 2, (6, 3, 10))$$

We now define a number of abstract operations on lists. (For now, we are concerned only with the definition and logical properties of the operations; we consider methods of implementing the operations later in this section.) If *list* is a list, then *head*(*list*) is defined as the value of the first element of *list*. If *list* is a nonempty list, *tail*(*list*) is defined as the list obtained by removing the first element of *list*. If *list* is the empty list, *tail*(*list*) is not defined. For a general list, *head*(*list*) may be either a list (if the value of the first list element is itself a list) or a simple data item; *tail*(*list*) must be a (possibly nil) list.

For example, if *list*1 and *list*2 are as in Figures 10.1.1 and 10.1.2, then

```
list1 = (5, 12, ‘s’, 147, ‘a’)
head(list1) = 5
tail(list1) = (12, ‘s’, 147, ‘a’)
head(tail(list1)) = 12
tail(tail(list1)) = (‘s’, 147, ‘a’)
list2 = (5, (3, 2, (14, 9, 3), (  ), 4), 2, (6, 3, 10))
tail(list2) = ((3, 2, (14, 9, 3), (  ), 4), 2, (6, 3, 10))
head(tail(list2)) = (3, 2, (14, 9, 3), (  ), 4)
head(head(tail(list2))) = 3
```

The *head* and *tail* operations are not defined if their argument is not a list. A **sublist** of a list *l* is a list that results from the application of zero or more *tail* operations to *l*.

The operation *first*(*list*) returns the first element of list *list*. (If *list* is empty, *first*(*list*) is a special **nil element**, which we denote by *nilelm*.) The operation *info*(*elt*) returns the value of the list element *elt*. The *head* operation produces a value, while the *first* operation produces an element. In fact, *head*(*list*) equals *info*(*first*(*list*)). Finally, the operation *next*(*elt*) returns the element that follows the element *elt* on its list. This definition presupposes that an element can have only one follower.

The operation *nodetype*(*elt*) accepts a list element *elt* and returns an indication of the type of the element's value. Recall that, in the linked list implementation, an element is represented by a node. Thus if the enumerated constants *ch*, *int*, and *lst* represent the types character, integer and list, respectively, then *nodetype*(*first*(*list* 1)) equals *int*, *nodetype*(*first*(*tail*(*tail*(*list* 1)))) equals *ch* and *nodetype*(*first*(*tail*(*list* 2))) equals *lst*.

Operations That Modify a List

head, *tail*, *first*, *info*, *next*, and *nodetype* extract information from lists already in existence. We now consider operations that build and modify lists.

Recall the *push* operation of Chapter 2 and its list implementation in Section 4.2. If *list* points to a list, the operation *push*(*list*, *x*) adds an element with value *x* to the front of the list. To illustrate the use of the *push* operation in constructing lists, consider the list (5, 10, 8), which can be constructed by the operations

$$list:= nil;$$
$$push(list, 8);$$
$$push(list, 10);$$
$$push(list, 5)$$

Note that the abstract *push* operation changes the value of its first parameter to the newly created list. We introduce as a new operation the function

$$addon(list, x)$$

which returns a new list that has *x* as its head and *list* as its tail. For example, if *l*1 equals (3, 4, 7), then the operation

$$l2:= addon(l1, 5)$$

creates a new list *l*2 equal to (5, 3, 4, 7). The crucial difference between *push* and *addon* is that *push* changes the value of its first parameter while *addon* does not. Thus, in the example, *l*1 retains the value (3, 4, 7). The operation *push*(*list*, *x*) is equivalent to *list*:= *addon*(*list*, *x*). Since *addon* is more flexible than *push*, and since *push* is usually used only in connection with stacks, we henceforth use *addon* exclusively.

Two other operations used to modify lists are *setinfo* and *setnext*. *setinfo*(*elt*, *x*) changes the value of a list element *elt* to the value *x*. Thus we may write *setinfo*(*first*(*list*), *x*) to reset the value of the first element of the list *list* to *x*. This operation is often abbreviated *sethead*(*list*, *x*). For example, if *list* equals (5, 10, 8), then the operation

$$sethead(list, 18)$$

changes *list* to (18, 10, 8) and the operation *sethead*(*list*, (5, 7, 3, 4)) changes *list* to ((5, 7, 3, 4), 10, 8) *sethead* is called the "inverse *head* operation" for an obvious reason. After performing the operation *sethead*(*list*, *x*), the value of *head*(*list*) is *x*. Note that *sethead*(*list*, *x*) is equivalent to

$$list := addon(tail(list), x)$$

The operation *setnext*(*elt*1, *elt*2) is somewhat more complex. It modifies the list containing *elt*1 so that *next*(*elt*1) = *elt*2. *elt*1 cannot be the nil element. *next*(*elt*2) is unchanged. Also if *next*(*elt*3) had equaled *elt*2 before execution of *setnext*(*elt*1, *elt*2), *next*(*elt*3) still equals *elt*2 after its execution, so that both *next*(*elt*1) and *next*(*elt*3) equal *elt*2. In effect, *elt*2 has become an element of two lists. The operation *settail*(*list*1, *list*2) is defined as *setnext*(*first*(*list*1), *first*(*list*2)) and sets the tail of *list*1 to *list*2. *settail* is sometimes called the inverse *tail* operation.

For example, if *list* equals (5, 9, 3, 7, 8, 6), then *settail*(*list*, (8)) changes the value of *list* to (5, 8) and *settail*(*list*, (4, 2, 7)) changes its value to (5, 4, 2, 7). Note that the operation *settail*(*list*, *l*) is equivalent to *list* := *addon*(*l*, *head*(*list*)).

Examples   Let us look at some examples of algorithms that use these operations.

The first example is an algorithm to add 1 to every integer that is an element of a list *list*. Character or list elements remain unchanged.

```
p := first(list);
while p <> nilelt
    do begin
            if nodetype(p) = int
                then setinfo(p, info(p) + 1);
            p := next(p)
        end  { while...do begin }
```

The second example involves deletions. We wish to delete from a list *list* any character element whose value is 'w'. (Compare this example with the routine of Section 4.2.) One possible solution is as follows:

```
q := nilelt;
p := first(list);
while p <> nilelt
    do if info(p) = 'w'
            then begin  { remove node(p) from the list }
                    p := next(p);
                    if q = nilelt
                        then list := tail(list)
                        else setnext(q, p)
                end  { then begin }
```

```
    else begin
        q := p;
        p := next(p)
    end { else begin }
```

Before looking at a more complex example, we define a new term. An element (or a node) *n* is **accessible** from a list (or an external pointer) *l* if there is a sequence of *head* and *tail* operations which, if applied to *l*, yields a list with *n* as its first element. For example, in Figure 10.1.2 the node containing 14 is accessible from *list 2* since it is the first element of *tail(tail(head(tail(list 2))))*. In fact, all the nodes shown in that figure are accessible from *list 2*. When a node is removed from a list, it becomes inaccessible from the external pointer to that list.

Now, suppose we wish to increase by 1 the value in every integer node accessible from a given list pointer *list*. We cannot simply traverse *list* since it is also necessary to traverse all lists that are elements of *list*, as well as all lists that may be elements of elements of *list*, and so on. One tentative solution is the following recursive algorithm *addone2(list)*:

```
    p := first(list);
    while p <> nilelt
        do begin
            if nodetype(p) = int
                then setinfo(p, info(p) + 1)
                else if nodetype(p) = lst
                        then addone2(info(p));
            p := next(p)
        end { while...do begin }
```

It is simple to remove the recursion and use a stack explicitly.

The Linked List Representation of a List

As previously noted, the abstract concept of a list is usually implemented by a linked list of nodes, each containing an *info* and *next* field. Each element of the abstract list corresponds to a node of the linked list. Each node contains fields *info* and *next*, whose contents correspond to the abstract list operations *info* and *next*. The abstract concepts of a "list" and an "element" are both represented by a pointer: a list by an external pointer to the first node of a linked list and an element by a pointer to a node. Thus, a pointer to a node *nd* in a list, which represents a list element, also represents the sublist formed by the elements represented by the nodes from *nd* to the end of the list. The value of an element corresponds to the contents of the *info* field of a node.

Under this implementation, the abstract operation *first(list)*, which returns the first element of a list, is meaningless. If *list* is a pointer that represents a list, then it points to the first node of a linked list. That pointer therefore also represents the first element of the list. Since *first*(*list*) and *list* are equivalent, *head*(*list*), which is equivalent to *info*(*first*(*list*)), is equivalent to *info*(*list*). *sethead*(*list*, *x*), defined as *setinfo*(*first*(*list*), *x*), is equivalent to *setinfo*(*list*, *x*). Similarly, *settail*(*list*1, *list*2), defined as *setnext*(*first*(*list*1), *first*(*list*2)), is equivalent to *setnext*(*list*1, *list*2) under the linked list representation.

The operation *setinfo*(*elt*, *x*) is implemented by the assignment statement *info*(*elt*):= *x*, where *elt* is a pointer to a node and the operation *setnext*(*elt*1, *elt*2) by the assignment *next*(*elt*1):= *elt*2. Since a list is represented by a pointer to its first node, an element of a list that is itself a list is represented by a pointer to the list in the *info* field of the node representing the element.

We defer a discussion of the implementation of *nodetype* until we present the Pascal implementation of general lists later in this section.

There are two methods of implementing the *addon* and *tail* operations. Consider the list *l*1 = (3, 4, 7) and the operation *l*2:= *addon*(*l*1, 5). The two possible ways of implementing this operation are illustrated in Figures 10.1.3a and b. In the first method, called the **pointer method**, the list (3, 4, 7) is represented by a pointer to it, *l*1. To create the list *l*2, a node containing 5 is allocated, and the value of *l*1 is placed in its *next* field. Thus the list *l*1 becomes a sublist of *l*2. The nodes of list *l*1 are used in two contexts: as part of list *l*1 and of list *l*2. In the second method, called the **copy method**, the list (3, 4, 7) is copied before the new list element is added to it. *l*1 still points to the original version, while the new copy is

Figure 10.1.3

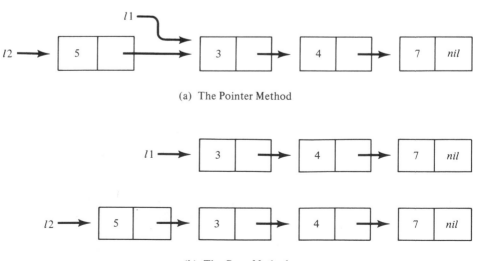

(a) The Pointer Method

(b) The Copy Method

made a sublist of *l*2. The copy method ensures that a node appears in only one context.

The difference between these methods becomes apparent when we attempt to perform the operation

$$sethead\,(l1,\ 7)$$

The resulting lists are shown in Figures 10.1.4a and b. If the copy method is used, then a change in list *l*1 does not affect list *l*2 (Figures 10.1.3b and 10.1.4b). If the pointer method is used, any subsequent change in list *l*1 also modifies *l*2 (Figures 10.1.3a and 10.1.4a).

The *tail* operation can also be implemented by either the pointer method or the copy method. Under the pointer method, *tail*(*list*) returns a pointer to the second node in the input list. After a statement such as *l*:=*tail*(*list*), the pointer *list* still points to the first node, and all nodes from the second on are on both list *list* and list *l*. Under a strict copy method, a new list would be created containing copies of all nodes from the second list node onward, and *l* would point to that new list. Here, too, if the pointer method is used, then a subsequent change in either the input list (*list*) or the output list (*l*) causes a change in the other list. If the copy method is used, the two lists are independent. Note that, under the pointer method, the operation *tail*(*list*) is equivalent to *next*(*list*): both return the pointer in the *next* field of the node pointed to by the pointer *list*. Under the copy method, however, an entirely new list is created by the *tail* operation.

The operation of the copy method is similar to the operation of the assignment statement *a*:= *b* so that a subsequent change in *b* does not change

Figure 10.1.4

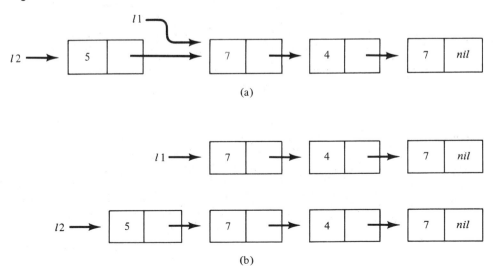

(a)

(b)

a. This is because the assignment statement copies the contents of location *b* (the "value of *b*") into location *a*. A change in the value of *b* changes only the copy in location *b*. Similarly, in the copy method, although *l*1 is a pointer, it really refers to the abstract list being represented. When a new list is formed from the old, the value of the old list is copied. The two lists are then entirely independent. In the pointer method, *l*1 refers to the nodes themselves rather than to the list that they collectively represent. A change in one list modifies the contents of nodes that are also part of another.

For reasons of efficiency, most list processing systems use the pointer method rather than the copy method. Imagine a 100-element list to which nodes are constantly being added (using *addon*) and from which nodes are being deleted (using *tail*). The overhead involved in both time and space in allocating and copying 100 list nodes (not to mention any list nodes on lists that appear as elements) each time that an operation is performed is prohibitive. Under the pointer method, the number of operations involved in adding or deleting an element is independent of the list size, since it involves only modification of a few pointers. However, in exchange for this efficiency, the user must be aware of possible changes to other lists. When the pointer method is used, it is common for list nodes to be used in more than one context.

In list processing systems that use the pointer method, an explicit copy operation is provided. The function

$$copy(list)$$

copies the list pointed to by *list* (including all list elements) and returns a pointer to the new copy. The user can use this operation to ensure that a subsequent modification to one list does not affect another.

Representation of Lists

So far, we have ignored a number of important implementation questions: When may list nodes be freed? When must new list nodes be allocated? How are list nodes allocated and freed? For example, *settail* appends a new list to the first element of a list. But what happens to the previous tail of the list that was replaced?

These questions are related to another question: What happens when a node (or a list) is an element or a sublist of more than one list? For example, suppose the list (4, 5, 3, 8) occurs twice as an element of a list (i.e., it is the information field of two separate nodes of the list). One possibility is to maintain two copies of the list, as in Figure 10.1.5a. Or suppose a list appears at the end of two lists as does (43, 28) in Figure 10.1.5b. Although it is possible to duplicate each element whenever it appears, this often results in a needless waste of space. An alternative is to maintain the lists as in Figure 10.1.6. In this representation, a list appears only once, with all appropriate

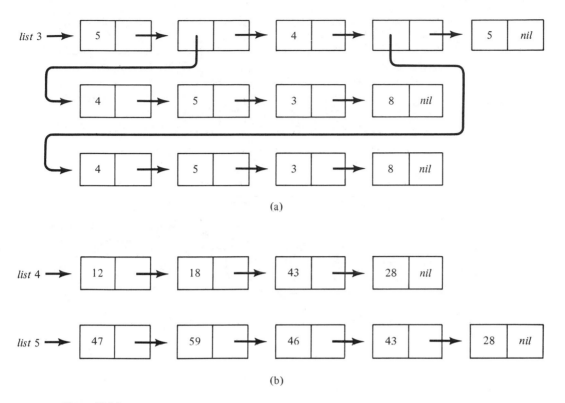

(a)

(b)

Figure 10.1.5

pointers pointing to the head of the single list. Under this method, a node is pointed to by more than one pointer.

If this possibility is allowed, then the routine *addone2* does not work correctly. For example, if *addone2* is applied to *list 6* in Figure 10.1.6a, when 1 is added to the integer 4 as the first element of the second element of *list 6*, the contents of that node are changed to 5. But the routine again adds 1 to that node since the node is pointed to by the information field of another list element as well. Thus the final value in the node becomes 6 rather than 5. Similarly, the values of the nodes containing 5, 3, and 8 are changed to 7, 5, and 10, respectively. (Why?) This is clearly incorrect.

In general, modifying the contents of a node from 4 to 5 is equivalent to replacing the node containing 4 by a new node containing 5 and then freeing the node containing 4. But this assumes, possibly erroneously, that the node containing 4 is no longer needed. Whenever the contents of a node are changed or a node is deleted, it is first necessary to ensure that the old value is no longer required.

In Figure 10.1.6b, the list (43, 28) appears as a sublist of both *list 7*, which is (12, 18, 43, 28), and *list 8*, which is (47, 59, 16, 43, 28). Imagine

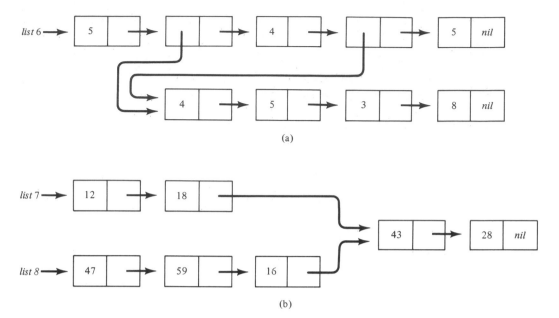

(a)

(b)

Figure 10.1.6

the chaos that would result if an attempt were made to remove the third element of *list7*.

One solution to this problem is to disallow use of the same node in more than one context. That is, lists should be constructed as in Figure 10.1.5a rather then as in Figure 10.1.6a. Then, when a node is no longer needed in a particular context, it can be freed since no other internal pointers point to it.

The *crlist* Operation

Suppose that we wanted to create the list of Figure 10.1.6a. The following sequence of operations accomplishes this:

$$l := nil;$$
$$l := addon(l, 8);$$
$$l := addon(l, 3);$$
$$l := addon(l, 5);$$
$$l := addon(l, 4);$$
$$list6 := nil;$$
$$list6 := addon(list6, 5);$$
$$list6 := addon(list6, l);$$
$$list6 := addon(list6, 4);$$
$$list6 := addon(list6, l);$$
$$list6 := addon(list6, 5)$$

Let us introduce the operation $l := crlist(a_1, a_2, \ldots, a_n)$, where each parameter is either a simple data item or a list pointer. This operation is defined as the sequence of statements:

$$l := nil;$$
$$l := addon(l, a_n);$$
$$\cdots$$
$$l := addon(l, a_2);$$
$$l := addon(l, a_1)$$

That is, $crlist(a_1, a_2, \ldots, a_n)$ creates the list $(a_1, a_2, \ldots, a_n)$. Then the sequence of operations can be rewritten as

$$l := crlist(4, 5, 3, 8);$$
$$list6 := crlist(5, l, 4, l, 5)$$

Notice that this is not the same as the single operation

$$list6 := (5, crlist(4, 5, 3, 8), 4, crlist(4, 5, 3, 8), 5)$$

which creates two distinct copies of the list $(4, 5, 3, 8)$: one as its second element and one as its fourth.

We leave as an exercise for the reader the task of finding a sequence of list operations that create the lists *list*7 and *list*8 of Figure 10.1.6b.

If the pointer method is used to implement list operations, it is possible to create **recursive lists**. These are lists that contain themselves as elements. For example, suppose the following operations are performed:

$$l := crlist(2, crlist(9, 7), 6, 4);$$
$$l1 := tail(tail(l));$$
$$sethead(l1, l);$$
$$l2 := head(tail(l));$$
$$l2 := tail(l2);$$
$$sethead(l2, l)$$

Figure 10.1.7 illustrates the effect of each of these operations. At the end of the sequence (Figure 10.1.7e), the list l contains itself as its third element. In addition, the second element of l is a list whose second element is l itself.

The Use of List Headers

In Chapter 4, list headers were introduced as a place to store global information about an entire list. In many general list processing systems, header nodes are used for other purposes as well. We have already seen two ways of implementing general lists—the pointer method and the copy method. There is a third alternative, called the **header method**, that is widely used in list processing systems. Under this method, a header node is always placed at the beginning of any group of nodes that is to be considered a list. In particular, an external pointer always points to a header node. Similarly, if

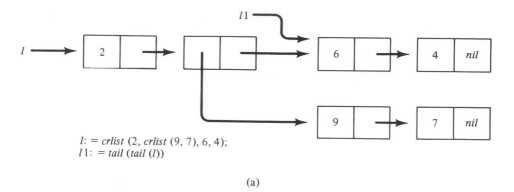

l: = crlist (2, crlist (9, 7), 6, 4);
l1: = tail (tail (l))

(a)

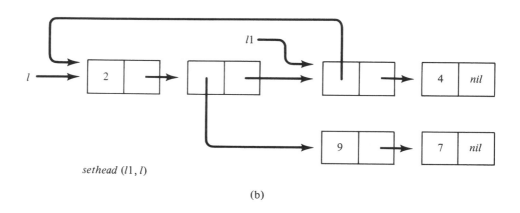

sethead (l1, l)

(b)

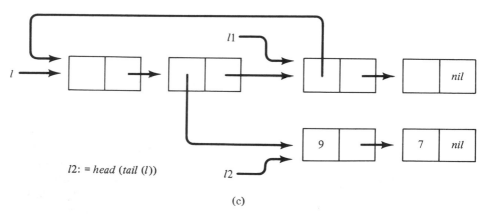

l2: = head (tail (l))

(c)

Figure 10.1.7

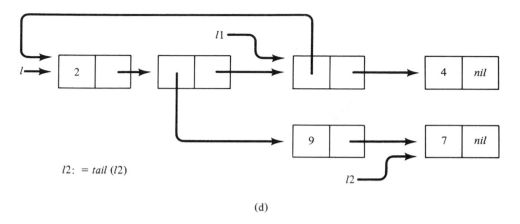

$l2: = tail(l2)$

(d)

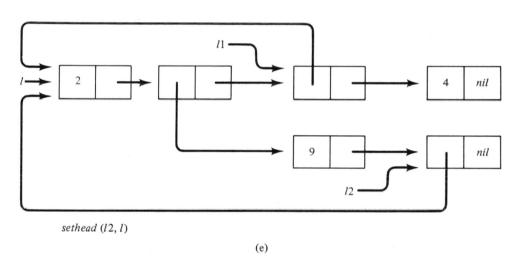

sethead $(l2, l)$

(e)

Figure 10.1.7 *(cont.)*

a list l is an element of another list, there is a header node at the front of l. Figure 10.1.8 illustrates the list of Figure 10.1.2 using the header method. The information portion of a header node holds global information about the list (such as the number of nodes in it or a pointer to its last node). In the figure, this field is shaded. Note that a nil list is now represented by a pointer to a header node containing a nil pointer in its *next* field rather than by the nil pointer itself.

Any parameter that represents a list must now be a pointer to a header node for that list. Any function that returns a pointer to a list must return a pointer to a header node.

The header method is similar to the pointer method in that a list is represented by a pointer to it. However, the presence of the header node

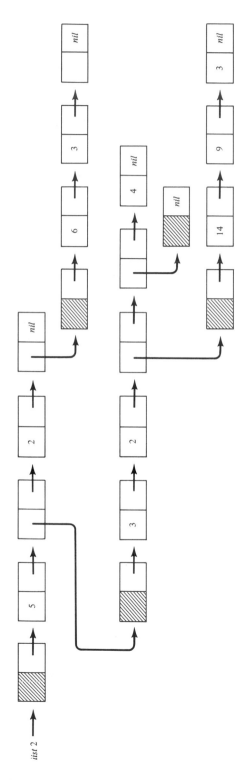

Figure 10.1.8

causes significant differences (as we noted earlier in Chapter 5 when we discussed linear, circular, and doubly linked lists with headers). For example, we made a distinction between the *push* and the *addon* operations. If *l* is a list pointer, the function *addon*(*l*, *x*) adds a node containing *x* to the list pointed to by *l*, without changing the value of *l*, and returns a pointer to the new node. *push*(*l*, *x*) changes the value of its parameter *l* to point to the new node. Under the header method, adding an element to a list involves inserting a node between the header and the first list node. Thus despite the fact that the value of the pointer *l* is not changed, the list that *l* represents has been altered.

Freeing List Nodes

Earlier in this section, we saw that a set of nodes could be an element and/or a sublist of one or several lists. In such cases, there is difficulty in determining when such a node can be modified or freed. Define a *simple node* as a node containing a simple data item (so that its *info* field does not contain a pointer). Generally, multiple use of simple nodes is not permitted. That is, operations on simple nodes are performed by the copy method rather than by the pointer method. Thus any simple node deleted from a list can be freed immediately.

However, the copy method is highly inefficient when applied to list nodes, and the pointer method is the more commonly used technique. Thus whenever a list is modified or deleted as an element or a sublist, it is necessary to consider the implications of the modification or freeing of the list on other lists that may contain it. The question of how to free a deleted list is compounded by the fact that lists may contain other lists as elements. If a particular list is freed, it may also be necessary to free all the lists that are elements of it; however, if these lists are also elements of other lists, they cannot be freed.

As an illustration of the complexity of the problem, consider *list9* of Figure 10.1.9. The nodes in that figure are numbered arbitrarily so that we may refer to them easily in the text.

Consider the operation

$$list9 := nil$$

Which nodes can be freed and which must be retained? Clearly, the list nodes of *list9* (nodes 1, 2, 3, 4) can be freed since no other pointers reference them. Freeing node 1 allows us to free nodes 11 and 12, since they too are accessed by no other pointers. Once node 11 is freed, can nodes 7 and 8 also be freed? Node 7 can be freed because each of the nodes containing a pointer to it (nodes 11 and 4) can be freed. However, node 8 cannot be freed since *list11* points to it. *list11* is an external pointer and therefore the node to which it points may still be needed elsewhere in the program. Since node 8 is kept, nodes 9 and 10 must also be kept (even though node 12 is

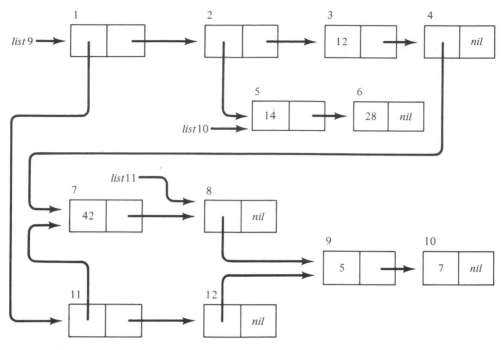

Figure 10.1.9

being freed). Finally nodes 5 and 6 must be kept because of the external pointer *list*10.

The problem to be addressed in the next section is how to determine algorithmically which nodes are to be kept and which are to be freed. However, before considering possible solutions, let us consider how lists can be implemented in Pascal and make some comments about list processing languages and their design.

General Lists in Pascal

Because general list nodes can contain simple data elements of any type or pointers to other lists, the most direct way to declare list nodes is by using variant records. One possible implementation is as follows:

```
type infotag = (ch, int, lst);
     nodeptr = ↑nodetype;
     infotype = record
                    case tag: infotag of
                        ch: (chinfo: char);
                        int: (intinfo: integer);
                        lst: (lstinfo: nodeptr)
                end;
```

```
nodetype = record
              info: infotype;
              next: nodeptr
        end;
```

Each list node has three elementary fields: a tag field to indicate the type of the information field, the actual information field, and a pointer to the next node in the list. The operation *nodetype(p)* is implemented by simply referencing $p\uparrow.info.tag$.

The actual implementation of any list operation depends upon whether the system in question is implemented using the pointer method, the copy method, or the header method. We consider the pointer method. The *tail* operation always produces a pointer to a list (possibly the *nil* pointer), assuming that its argument points to a valid list. Thus this operation may be implemented as a simple Pascal function:

```
function tail(list: nodeptr): nodeptr;
begin
    if list = nil
        then error ('illegal tail operation')
        else tail: = list↑.next
end {procedure tail};
```

We might be tempted to implement the *head* operation in similar fashion, by simply returning the value in the *info* field of the node to which the parameter points. However, because standard Pascal does not allow a function to return a variant record (or even a nonvariant record), we implement the *head* operation as a procedure with two parameters: an input parameter that holds a pointer to the input list and an output parameter that is set to the first data item of the input list. Because the Pascal version of *head* yields an object of type *infotype* rather than the actual data value (the integer, the character or the list pointer), we call the procedure *headinfo* rather than *head*. The procedure is implemented as follows:

```
procedure headinfo(list: nodeptr; var item: infotype);
begin
    if list = nil
        then error ('illegal head operation')
        else item: = list↑.info
end {procedure headinfo};
```

The procedure *headinfo* is invoked by a statement such as *headinfo(list1, item1)*. When *item1* (of type *infotype*) is declared, the actual variant it will assume is unknown, and space for the largest variant must be allocated. This is often a waste of space, as the actual variants of *infotype* may range from a single integer to a large array of records (although in our example, the variation in size among a character, an integer, and a pointer is minimal or nonexistent). Allocation of space for the largest of these records for all invocations of the *headinfo* procedure would be wasteful of storage.

An alternative implementation of *head* (which we call *headptr*) allows us to overcome this problem. Instead of returning the actual data itself in a second output parameter, the function *headptr* returns a pointer to a variant record containing the information. Because the variant record containing the information field is allocated within the function *headptr* when its type is already known, space need be allocated only for the size of the actual variant. Unnecessary space will not be allocated.

Let us assume that a pointer type is defined by

$$\textbf{type} \ \text{infoptr} = \uparrow \text{infotype};$$

The function *headptr* may be written as follows:

```
function headptr (list: nodeptr): infoptr;
var tempptr: infoptr;
begin
    if list = nil
        then error ('illegal head operation')
        else begin
                new(tempptr, list↑.info.tag);
                tempptr↑.tag:= list↑.info.tag;
                case tempptr↑.tag of
                    ch: tempptr↑chinfo:= list↑.info.chinfo;
                    int: tempptr↑.intinfo:= list↑.info.intinfo;
                    lst: tempptr↑.lstinfo:= list↑.info.lstinfo
                end {case};
                headptr:= tempptr
            end {else begin}
end {function headptr};
```

The statement *new(tempptr, list↑ .info.tag)* allocates a new object of type *infotype* of the particular variant corresponding to the tag of *list↑ .info*. Note that the assignment to *tempptr↑.tag* and the *case* statement could not be replaced by the single assignment *tempptr:= list↑ .info* because, under standard Pascal, a variant record variable whose value was dynamically allocated by a call to *new* with more than one parameter (that is, whose value is restricted to a single variant) may not appear in an assignment statement. (Of course, any of its fields may appear.) Given a variable *p: infoptr*, the function *headptr* may be invoked by *p:= headptr(list1)*.

In some applications, it may not be necessary to return the value of the contents of the information portion of the node; it may be sufficient to identify a pointer to the desired node. In such a case, the value of the pointer variable traversing the list may be used instead of the *headinfo* or *headptr* procedures. Note that neither the *head* nor *tail* operations change the original list in any way. All fields retain the same values that they had before the routines were called.

Once the basic forms of *head* and *tail* have been implemented, other list operations can be implemented either in terms of these operations or by accessing list nodes directly. For example, the *addon* operation may be implemented as follows:

```
function addon(list: nodeptr; item: infotype): nodeptr;
var newptr: nodeptr;
    begin
         new(newptr);
         newptr↑.info: = item;
         newptr↑.next: = list;
         addon: = newptr
    end { function addon };
```

Note that, in this implementation of *addon*, the second parameter is of type *infotype*, rather than simply the data item itself.

Now that *addon* has been implemented, *sethead(list, item)* can be implemented either by the statement *list:= addon(tail(list), item)*, as we mentioned earlier, or directly by *list↑ .info:= item*. The *settail* operation may be implemented similarly as follows, using an auxiliary routine *freelist* to free the previous tail of *list*:

```
procedure settail(var list: nodeptr; tl: nodeptr);
var  p : nodeptr
    begin
         p: = list↑.next;
         list↑.next: = tl;
         freelist(p)
    end { procedure settail };
```

Despite the fact that we are using the pointer method, more likely than not, there is no need for the previous tail of *list*. If some other pointer points to this portion of the list, then the call to *freelist* should be omitted.

The implementation of *settail* highlights the problem of automatic list management and how to determine when a node should be freed if it may indeed appear in more than one context (as in the pointer method or if recursive lists are permitted). As mentioned, we examine these issues in Section 2.

Programming Languages and Lists

Throughout this text, we have been treating a list as a compound data structure (a collection of nodes) rather than as a native data type (an elementary item such as *integer*, *char*, etc.). The reason for this is that we have been working closely with the Pascal language. In Pascal, one cannot make a declaration such as

var x: list;

and apply such functions as *head* and *tail* to *x* directly. Rather, the programmer must implement lists by writing the necessary procedures and functions for their manipulation. Other languages, however, do contain lists as elementary data structures with the operations *crlist*, *head*, *tail*, *addon*, *sethead*, and *settail* already built into the language. An example of such a language is LISP.

One consequence of the fact that Pascal does not include list manipulation capabilities is that if a programmer programs a list manipulation application, it is the programmer's responsibility to allocate and free the necessary list nodes. As we have seen in this section, that problem is not at all trivial if lists are allowed in all their generality. However, any given application can usually be designed more easily using a specific type of list, tree, or graph, as we have seen in Chapters 4, 5, 6, and 9. Indeed, general list manipulation techniques are more expensive in terms of both time and space than are techniques designed specifically for a particular application. (This is a corollary to the axiom that a price is always paid for generality.) Thus the Pascal programmer will rarely have occasion to use general list manipulation techniques.

However, a general list processing system, in which the list is a native data type and list operations are built in, must be able to deal with lists in all their generality. Since the fundamental objects are lists and data items rather than nodes, the programmer cannot be responsible for allocating and freeing individual nodes. Rather, when a program issues a statement such as

$l1 := crlist(3, 4, 7)$

the system is responsible for allocating sufficient list nodes and initializing the proper pointers. When the program later issues the command

$l1 := nil$

the system is responsible for identifying and freeing those nodes previously on list $l1$ that now become inaccessible. If such nodes are not freed, available space would rapidly become exhausted.

In some sense, languages that include lists as native data types are of "higher level" than is Pascal because the programmer is freed from so much of the bookkeeping activity associated with storage management. Pascal may be thought of as a language of higher level than FORTRAN in that Pascal includes data structures such as records and enumerated data types, whereas

FORTRAN does not. So too, a list processing system is of higher level than is Pascal in that it includes lists whereas Pascal does not.

Another point that should be made concerns the implementation of lists. The implementation of lists as presented in this section is oriented toward Pascal. Because Pascal permits the use of variant records, it was possible to define a type *infotype* to contain any of the legal data types in our list system. Some languages (e.g., PL/I) do not support variant records. In such languages, the type of a node (with certain limited exceptions) is fixed in advance. In such languages it would be necessary to separate a list system into **list nodes** and **atomic nodes**. An atomic node is a node that contains no pointers—only a simple data item. Several different types of atomic nodes would exist, each with a single data item corresponding to one of the legal data types. A list node contains a pointer to an atomic node and a type indicator indicating the type of atomic node to which it points (as well as a pointer to the next node on the list, of course). When it is necessary to place a new node on a list, an atomic node of the appropriate type must be allocated, its value must be assigned, the list node information field must be set to point to the new atomic node and the type field in the list node must be set to the proper type.

To understand how clumsy this situation is, suppose there are 10 different types of atomic nodes (there is no reason that an atomic node may not be an array or a stack or a queue or a program label, etc.). Each of these must have a unique typecode. Further there must be a separate variable declared for each type of atomic node. Let us suppose that the typecodes used for the 10 types are $t1, t2, \ldots, t10$ and that the atomic node variables are *node*1, *node*2, . . . , *node*10. Then each time that an atomic node is processed, we would need codes such as

```
case typecode of
    t1:   {do something with node1}
    t2:   {do something with node2}
        . . .
    t10:  {do something with node10}
end {case}
```

This is a cumbersome organization and one that we can avoid by using variant records.

In the next section of this chapter, we examine techniques incorporated into list processing systems to recover storage that is no longer needed. We retain the list structure conventions of this section but it should be understood that they are not absolute.

EXERCISES

1. How would you implement a general stack and queue in Pascal? Write all the routines necessary for doing so.

2. Implement the routines *addon*, *sethead*, *settail*, and *crlist* in Pascal.

3. Write a Pascal procedure *freelist(list)* that frees all nodes accessible from a pointer *list*. If your solution is recursive, rewrite it nonrecursively.

4. Rewrite *addone2* so that it is nonrecursive.

5. Write a Pascal routine *dlt(list, n)* that deletes the *n*th element of a *list*. If this *n*th element is itself a list, all nodes accessible through that list should be freed. Assume that a list can appear in only one position.

6. Implement the function *copy(list)* in Pascal. This routine accepts a pointer *list* to a general list and returns a pointer to a copy of that list. What if the list is recursive?

7. Write a Pascal procedure that accepts a list pointer and prints the parenthesized notation for that list. Assume that list nodes can appear only on a single list and that recursive lists are prohibited.

8. What are the advantages and disadvantages of languages in which the type of variables need not be declared, as compared to languages such as Pascal?

9. Write two sets of list operations to create the lists of Figures 10.1.4b and 10.1.9.

10. Redraw all the lists of this section that do not include header nodes so that they are now included.

11. Implement the routines *addon*, *head*, *tail*, *sethead*, and *settail* in Pascal for lists using the following methods:
    (a) the copy method.
    (b) the header method.

12. Implement the list operations for a system that uses doubly linked lists.

2. AUTOMATIC LIST MANAGEMENT

In the last section, we presented the need for algorithms to determine when a given list node is no longer accessible. In this section we investigate such algorithms. The philosophy behind incorporating such an algorithm into a programming system is that the programmer should not have to decide when a node should be allocated or freed. Instead, the programmer should code the solution to the problem with the assurance that the system will automatically allocate any list nodes that are necessary for the lists being created and that the system will make available for reuse any nodes that are no longer accessible.

There are two principal methods used in automatic list management: the *reference count* method and the *garbage collection* method. We proceed to a discussion of each.

The Reference Count Method

Under this method, each node has an additional *count* field which keeps a count (called the *reference count*) of the number of pointers (both internal and external) to that node. Each time that the value of some pointer is set to point to a node, the reference count in that node is increased by 1; each time that the value of some pointer that had been pointing to a node is changed, the reference count in that node is decreased by 1. When the reference count in any node becomes 0, that node can be returned to the available list of free nodes.

Each list operation of a system using the reference count method must make provision for updating the reference count of each node that it accesses and for freeing any node whose count becomes 0. For example, to execute the statement

$$l := tail(l)$$

the following operations must be performed:

$$p := l;$$
$$l := next(l);$$
$$next(p) := nil;$$
$$reduce(p)$$

where the operation *reduce(p)* is defined recursively as follows:

if $p <> nil$
    then begin
        $count(p) := count(p) - 1;$
        if $count(p) = 0$
          then begin
            $r := next(p);$
            $reduce(r);$
            if $nodetype(p) = lst$
              then $reduce(head(p));$
            freenode(p)
          end {then begin}
    end {then begin}

reduce must be invoked whenever the value of a pointer to a list node is changed. Similarly, whenever a pointer variable is set to point to a list node, the *count* field of that node must be increased by 1. The count field of a free node is 0.

To illustrate the reference count method, consider again the list of Figure 10.1.9. The following set of statements creates that list:

$$list10 := crlist(14, 28);$$
$$list11 := crlist(crlist(5, 7));$$
$$l1 := addon(list11, 42);$$
$$m := crlist(l1, head(list11));$$
$$list9 := crlist(m, list10, 12, l1);$$
$$m := nil;$$
$$l1 := nil$$

Figure 10.2.1 illustrates the creation of the list using the reference count method. Each part of that figure shows the list after an additional group of the foregoing statements has been executed. The reference count is shown as the leftmost field of each list node. Each node in that figure is numbered according to the numbering of the nodes in Figure 10.1.9. Make sure that you understand how each statement alters the reference count in each node.

Let us now see what happens when we execute the statement

$$list9 := nil$$

The results are illustrated in Figure 10.2.2, where freed nodes are illustrated using dashed lines. The following sequence of events may take place:

	count of node 1 is set to 0
	Node 1 is freed
	*count*s of nodes 2 and 11 are set to 0
	Nodes 2 and 11 are freed
	*count*s of nodes 5 and 7 are set to 1
(Figure 10.2.2a)	*count*s of nodes 3 and 12 are set to 0
	Nodes 3 and 12 are freed
	count of node 4 is set to 0
	Node 4 is freed
	count of node 9 is set to 1
	count of node 7 is set to 0
	Node 7 is freed
(Figure 10.2.2b)	*count* of node 8 is set to 1

Only those nodes accessible from the external pointers *list*10 and *list*11 remain allocated—all others are freed.

One drawback of the reference count method is illustrated by the preceding example. The amount of work that must be performed by the system each time that a list manipulation statement is executed can be considerable. Each time that the value of a pointer is changed, all nodes previously accessible from that pointer can potentially be freed. Often, the work involved in identifying the nodes to be freed is not worth the reclaimed space, since there may be ample space for the program to run to completion without reusing any nodes. After the program has terminated, a single pass through all its lists reclaims all its storage without having to worry about reference count values.

One solution to this problem can be illustrated by a different approach to the previous example. When the statement

$$list9 := nil$$

is executed, the reference count in node 1 is reduced to 0, and node 1 is freed—that is, it is placed on the available list. However, the fields of this

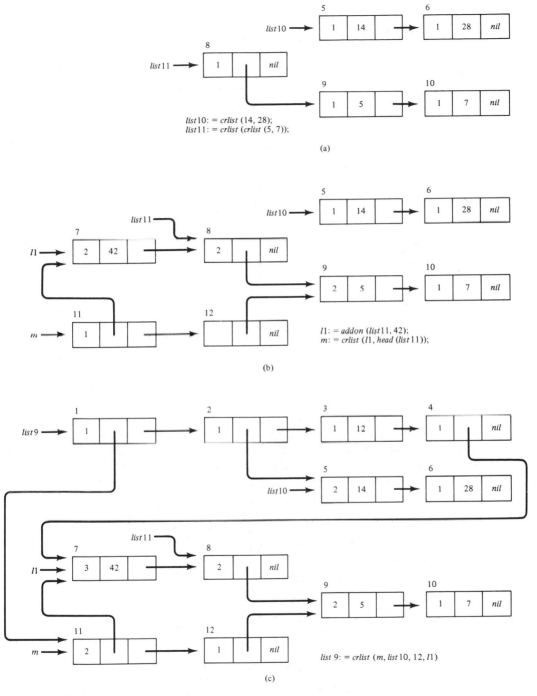

$list10: = crlist (14, 28);$
$list11: = crlist (crlist (5, 7));$

(a)

$l1: = addon (list11, 42);$
$m: = crlist (l1, head (list 11));$

(b)

$list 9: = crlist (m, list 10, 12, l1)$

(c)

Figure 10.2.1

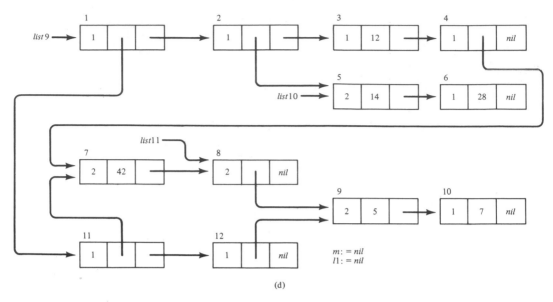

(d)

Figure 10.2.1   (cont.)

node retain their original values, so that it still points to nodes 2 and 11. (This means that an additional pointer field is necessary to link such nodes on the available list. An alternative is to reuse the reference count field for this purpose.) The reference count values in these two nodes remain unchanged. When additional space is needed and node 1 is reallocated for some other use, the reference counts in nodes 2 and 11 are reduced to zero, and they are then placed on the available list. This removes much of the work from the deallocation process and adds it to the allocation process. If node 1 is never reused because enough space is available, then nodes 2, 11, 3, 4, 7, and 12 are not freed during program execution. For this scheme to work best, however, the available list should be kept as a queue rather than as a stack, so that freed nodes are never allocated before nodes that have not been used for the first time. (Of course, once a system has been running for some time so that all nodes have been used at least once, this advantage no longer exists.)

There are two additional disadvantages to the reference count method. The first is the additional space required in each node for the count. This is not usually an overriding consideration, however. The problem can be somewhat alleviated if each list is required to contain a header node and a reference count is kept only in the header. However, then only a header node could be referenced by more than one pointer (i.e., a list such as in Figure 10.2.3b would be prohibited). The lists of Figure 10.2.3 are analogous to those of Figure 10.1.4 except that they include header nodes. The counts are kept in the second field of the header node. When the count in a header node reaches 0, all the nodes on its list are freed, and the counts in header nodes pointed to by *lstinfo* fields in the list nodes are reduced.

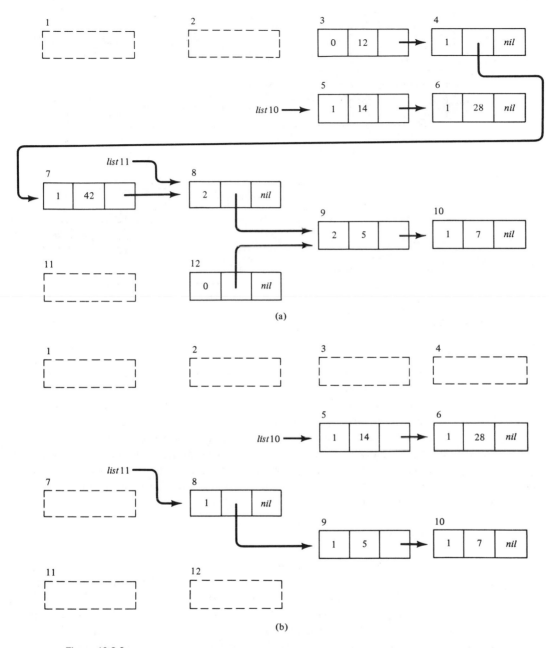

Figure 10.2.2

If counts are to be retained in header nodes only, then certain operations may have to be modified. For example, the *settail* operation must be modified so that the situation of Figure 10.2.3b does not occur. One method of modification is to use the copy method in implementing these operations. Another method is to differentiate somehow between external

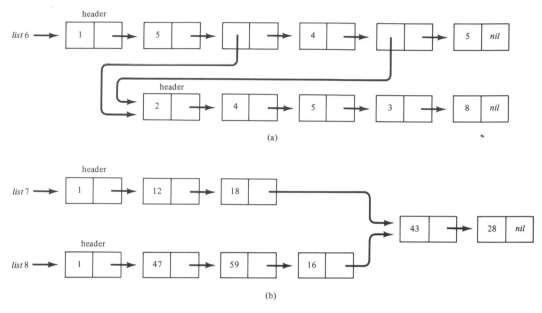

Figure 10.2.3

pointers, which represent lists (and therefore must point to a header node), and "temporary" external pointers, which are used for traversal (and can point directly to list nodes). When the count in a header node becomes 0, references to its list nodes through temporary pointers become illegal.

The other disadvantage of the reference count method is that the count in the first node of a recursive or circular list will never be reduced to zero. Of course, whenever a pointer within a list is set to point to a node on that list, the reference count can be maintained rather than increased, but detecting when this is so is often a difficult task.

Garbage Collection

Under the reference count method, nodes are reclaimed when they become available for reuse (or under one version when they are needed). The other principal method of detecting and reclaiming free nodes is called *garbage collection*. Under this method, nodes no longer in use remain allocated and undetected until all available storage has been allocated. A subsequent request for allocation cannot be satisfied until nodes which had been allocated but are no longer in use are recovered. When a request is made for additional nodes and there are none available, a system routine called the *garbage collector* is called. This routine searches through all the nodes in the system, identifies those that are no longer accessible from an external pointer, and restores the inaccessible nodes to the available pool. The request for additional nodes is then fulfilled with some of the reclaimed nodes, and the system continues processing user requests for more space. When available space is used up again, the garbage collector is called once more.

Garbage collection is usually done in two phases. The first phase, called the ***marking phase***, involves marking all nodes that are accessible from an external pointer. The second phase, called the ***collection phase***, involves proceeding sequentially through memory and freeing all nodes that have not been marked. We examine the marking phase first, and then turn our attention to the collection phase.

One field must be set aside in each node to indicate whether a node has or has not been marked. The marking phase sets the mark field to *true* in each accessible node. As the collection phase proceeds, the mark field in each accessible node is reset to *false*. Thus, at the start and end of garbage collection, all mark fields are *false*. User programs do not affect the mark fields.

It is sometimes inconvenient to reserve one field in each node solely for the purpose of marking. In that case, a separate area in memory can be reserved to hold a long array of mark bits, one bit for each node that may be allocated.

One aspect of garbage collection is that it must run when there is very little space available. This means that auxiliary tables and stacks needed by the garbage collector must be kept to a minimum since there is little space available for them. An alternative is to reserve a specific pecentage of memory for the exclusive use of the garbage collector. However, this effectively reduces the amount of memory available to the user and means that the garbage collector will be called more frequently.

Whenever the garbage collector is called, all user processing comes to a halt while the algorithm examines all allocated nodes in memory. For this reason, it is desirable that the garbage collector be called as infrequently as possible. For real-time applications, in which a computer must respond to a user request within a specific short time span, garbage collection has generally been considered an unsatisfactory method of storage management. We can picture a spaceship drifting off into the infinite as it waits for directions from a computer occupied with garbage collection. However, methods have recently been developed whereby garbage collection can be performed simultaneously with user processing. This means that the garbage collector must be called before all space has been exhausted so that user processing can continue in whatever space is left, while the garbage collector recovers additional space.

Another important consideration is that users must be careful to ensure that all lists are well formed and that all pointers are correct. Usually, the operations of a list processing system are carefully implemented so that if garbage collection does occur in the middle of one of them, the entire system will work correctly. However, some users try to outsmart the system and implement their own pointer manipulations. This requires great care so that garbage collection will work properly. In a real-time garbage collection system, not only must we ensure that user operations do not upset list structures that the garbage collector must have, but also that the garbage collection algorithm itself does not unduly disturb the list structures that are being used concurrently by the user. As we shall see, some marking algorithms do disturb (temporarily) list structures and are therefore unsuitable for real-time use.

It is possible that, at the time the garbage collection program is called, users are actually using almost all the nodes that are allocated. Thus, almost all nodes are accessible and the garbage collector recovers very little additional space. After the system runs for a short time, it will again be out of space; the garbage collector will again be called only to recover very few additional nodes, and the vicious cycle starts again. This phenomenon, in which system storage management routines, such as garbage collection, are executing almost all the time, is called *thrashing*.

Clearly, thrashing is a situation to be avoided. One drastic solution is to impose the following condition. If the garbage collector is run and does not recover a specific percentage of the total space, then the user who requested the extra space is terminated and removed from the system. All that user's space is then recovered and is made available to other users.

Algorithms for Garbage Collection

The simplest method for marking all accessible nodes is to mark initially all nodes that are immediately accessible (i.e., those pointed to by external pointers) and then repeatedly pass through all of memory sequentially. On each sequential pass, whenever a marked node *nd* is encountered, all nodes pointed to by a pointer within *nd* are marked. These sequential passes continue until no new nodes have been marked in an entire pass. Unfortunately, this method is as inefficient as it is simple. The number of sequential passes necessary is equal to the maximum path length to any accessible node (why?), and on each pass every list node in memory must be examined. However, this method requires almost no additional space.

A somewhat more efficient variation is the following: Suppose that a node $n1$ in the sequential pass has been previously marked and that $n1$ includes a pointer to an unmarked node, $n2$. Then node $n2$ is marked and the sequential pass would ordinarily continue with the node that follows $n1$ sequentially in memory. However, if the address of $n2$ is less than the address of $n1$, the sequential pass resumes from $n2$ rather than from $n1$. Under this modified technique, when the last node in memory is reached, all accessible nodes have been marked.

Let us present this method as an algorithm. Assume that all list nodes in memory are viewed as a sequential array.

```
const maxnodes = ...;
type infotype = (ch, int, lst);
     nodeptr = 0..maxnodes;
```

```
nodetype = record
              mark: boolean;
              next: nodeptr;
              case tag: infotype of
                   ch: (chinfo: char);
                   int: (intinfo: integer);
                   lst: (lstinfo: nodeptr)
          end;
var node: array[nodeptr] of nodetype;
```

An array *node* is used to convey the notion that we can step through all nodes sequentially. We also include a node called *node*[0]. This is not a real node (since 0 represents the *nil* pointer), but it is used as a dummy node so that a reference to *node*[0].*lstinfo* (for example) does not generate an error. We assume that *node*[0].*lstinfo* and *node*[0].*next* are initialized to 0, *node*[0].*mark* to *true*, and *node*[0].*tag* to *lst* and that these values are never changed throughout the system's execution. The *mark* field in each node is initially *false* and is set to *true* by the marking algorithm when a node is found to be accessible.

Now that we have defined the format of our nodes, we turn to the actual algorithm. Assume that *acc* is an array containing external pointers to immediately accessible nodes, declared by

```
const numacc = ...;
var acc: array[1..numacc] of nodeptr;
```

The marking algorithm is as follows:

```
            { mark all immediately accesible nodes }
for i := 1 to numacc
    do node[acc[i]].mark := true;
               { begin a sequential pass through the array of nodes }
               {   i points to the node currently being examined     }
    i := 1;
while i <= maxnodes
    do begin
         j := i + 1; { j points to the node to be examined next }
       if node[i].mark
         then begin { mark nodes to which i points }
              if (node[i].tag = lst) and (not node[node[i].lstinfo].mark)
                    { the information portion of i }
                    { points to an unmarked node   }
              then begin
                     node[node[i].lstinfo].mark := true;
                     if node[i].lstinfo < j
                       then j := node[i].lstinfo
                   end {then begin};
```

```
            if not node [node [i] . next] . mark
                {       the list node following      }
                { node [i] is an unmarked node }
            then begin
                        node [node [i] . next] . mark := true;
                        if node [i] . next < j
                            then j := node [i] . next
                    end {then begin}
            end {if node[i].mark then begin};
        i := j
    end {while...do begin}
```

In the exercises you are asked to trace the execution of this algorithm on a list distributed throughout memory such as *list*9 in Figure 10.1.9.

Although this method is better than successive sequential passes, it is still inefficient. Consider how many nodes must be examined if *node*[1] is immediately accessible and points to *node*[999] which points to *node*[2], and so on. Thus it is usually too slow to use in an actual system.

A more desirable method is one that is not based on traversing memory sequentially, but rather traverses all accessible lists. Thus it examines only those nodes that are accessible rather than all nodes.

The most obvious way to accomplish this is by use of an auxiliary stack and is very similar to depth-first traversal of a graph. As each list is traversed through the *next* fields of its constituent nodes, the *tag* field of each node is examined. If the *tag* field of a node is *lst*, then the value of the *lstinfo* field of that node is placed on the stack. When the end of a list or a marked node is reached, the stack is popped and the list headed by the node at the top of the stack is traversed. In the algorithm that follows, we again assume that *node*[0].*mark* equals *true*.

```
    for i := 1 to numacc
        do begin
                { mark the next immediately accessible }
                {     node and place it on the stack       }
            node [acc [i]] . mark := true;
            push (stack, acc [i]);
            while not empty (stack)
                do begin
                        p := pop (stack)
                        while p <> 0
                        do begin
                            if (node [ p] .tag = lst) and
                                    (not node [node [p] .lstinfo] . mark)
                            then begin
                                    node [node [p] . lstinfo] . mark := true;
                                    push (stack, node [p] . lstinfo)
                                end {then begin};
```

$$\textbf{if } node\,[node\,[p]\,.next]\,.mark$$
$$\quad\textbf{then } p := 0$$
$$\quad\textbf{else begin}$$
$$\qquad p := node\,[p]\,.next;$$
$$\qquad node\,[p]\,.mark := true$$
$$\quad\textbf{end } \{\text{else begin}\}$$
$$\textbf{end } \{\text{while } p <> 0 \text{ do begin}\}$$
$$\textbf{end } \{\text{while not empty}\dots\text{do begin}\}$$
$$\textbf{end } \{\text{for}\dots\text{do begin}\}$$

This algorithm is as efficient as we can hope for in terms of time, since each node to be marked is visited only once. However, it has a significant weakness because of its dependence on an auxiliary stack. A garbage collection algorithm is called when there is no extra space available, so where is the stack to be kept? Since the size of the stack is never greater than the depth of list nesting and lists are rarely nested beyond some reasonable limit (such as 100), a specific number of nodes reserved for the garbage collection stack would suffice in most cases. However, there is always the possibility that some user would want to nest nodes more deeply.

One solution is to use a stack limited to some maximum size. If the stack is about to overflow, we can revert to the sequential method given in the previous algorithm. We ask the reader to work out the details in an exercise.

Another solution is to use the allocated list nodes themselves as the stack. Clearly, we do not want to add an additional field to each list node to hold a pointer to the next node on the stack, since the extra space could be better used for other purposes. Thus either the *lstinfo* field or *next* field of the list nodes must be used to link together the stack. But this means that the list structure is temporarily disturbed. Provision must be made for the lists to be restored properly.

In the foregoing algorithm, each list is traversed using the *next* fields of its nodes, and the value of each pointer *lstinfo* to a list node is pushed onto a stack. When either the end of a list or a section of the list which had already been marked is reached, the stack is popped and a new list is traversed. Therefore, when a pointer to a node *nd* is popped, there is no need to restore any of the fields within *nd*.

However, suppose the stack is kept as a list, linked by the *next* fields. Then when a node is pushed onto the stack, its *next* field must be changed to point to the top node in the stack. This implies that the field must be restored to its original value when the node is popped. But that original value has not been saved anywhere. (It cannot be saved on the stack, since there is no extra storage available for it.)

A solution to this problem can be described by the following scheme. Let us first assume a list with no elements that are themselves lists. As each node in the list is visited, it is pushed onto the stack and its *next* field is used to link it onto the stack. Since each node preceding the current node on the list is also present on the stack (the top of the stack is the last encountered element on the list), the list can be reconstructed easily by simply popping the stack and restoring the *next* fields.

The situation is only slightly different in the case where one list is an element of another. Suppose that *nd*1 is a node on *list*1 and *nd*2 is a node on *list*2 and that *node*[*nd*1].*lstinfo* equals *nd*2. This is, *nd*2 is the first node of *list*2 where *list*2 is an element of *list*1. The algorithm has been traversing *list*1 and is now about to begin traversing *list*2. In this case, *node*[*nd*1].*next* cannot be used as a stack pointer because it is needed to link *nd*1 to the remainder of *list*1. However, the *lstinfo* field of *nd*1 can be used to link *nd*1 onto the stack since it is currently being used to link to *nd*2.

In general, when a node *nd* is pushed onto the stack, either its *lstinfo* field or its *next* field is used to point to the previous top element. If the next node to be examined is pointed to by *node*[*nd*].*lstinfo*, then the *lstinfo* field is used to link *nd* onto the stack, while if the node is pointed to by *node*[*nd*].*next*, then the *next* field is used to link *nd* onto the stack. The remaining problem is how to determine for a given node on the stack whether the *lstinfo* or *next* field is used to link the stack.

If the *tag* field of a node indicates that the node is a simple node, then its *next* field must be in use as a stack pointer. (This is because the node has no *lstinfo* field that must be traversed.) However, a node with a *tag* field of *lst* is not so easily handled. Suppose that each time the *lstinfo* field is used to advance to the next node, the *tag* field in the list node is changed from *lst* to some new code (say, *stk* for stack) which is neither *lst* nor any of the codes that denote simple elements. Then when a node is popped from the stack, if its *tag* field is not *stk*, its *next* field must be restored, and if its *tag* field is *stk*, its *lstinfo* field must be restored and the *tag* field restored to *lst*.

Figure 10.2.4 illustrates how this stacking mechanism works. Figure 10.2.4a shows a list before the marking algorithm begins. The pointer *p* points to the node currently being processed, *top* points to the stack top and *q* is an auxiliary pointer. The mark field is shown as the first field in each node. Figure 10.2.4b shows the same list immediately after node 4 has been marked. The path taken to node 4 is through the *next* fields of nodes 1, 2, and 3. This path can be retraced in reverse order, beginning at *top* and following along the *next* fields. Figure 10.2.4c shows the list after node 7 has been marked. The path to node 7 from the beginning of the list was from node 1, through *node*[1].*next* to node 2, through *node*[2].*lstinfo* to node 5, through *node*[5].*next* to node 6, and then from *node*[6].*next* to node 7. The same fields that link together the stack are used to restore the list to its original form. Note that the *tag* field in node 2 is *stk* rather than *lst*, to indicate that its *lstinfo* field, not its *next* field, is being used as a stack pointer. The algorithm that incorporates these ideas is known as the Schorr-Waite algorithm, after its discoverers.

Now that we have described the temporary distortions that are made in the list structure by the Schorr-Waite algorithm, we present the algorithm

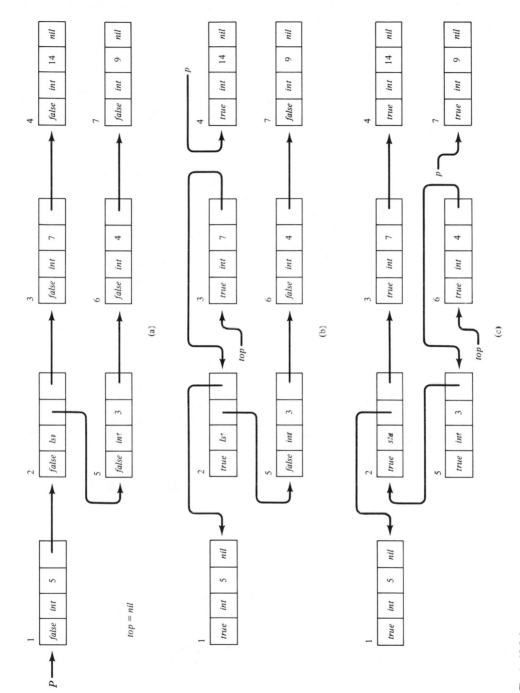

Figure 10.2.4

itself. We invite the reader to trace through the effects of the algorithm on the lists of Figure 10.2.4a and 10.1.9.

```
        for i := 1 to numacc
            do begin
                    { for each immediately accessible node, }
                    {         trace through its list          }
                    p := acc(i);
                    {      initialize the stack to empty       }
                    top := 0;
10:             { Traverse the list through its next fields, marking each node }
                { and placing it on the stack until a marked node or the end }
                {    of the list is reached. Assume node[0].mark = true      }
                while not node[p].mark
                    do begin
                            node[p].mark := true;
                                { place node[p] on the stack, saving a pointer }
                                {              to the next node                }
                            q := node[p].next;
                            node[p].next := top;
                            top := p;
                                {            advance to the next node           }
                            p := q
                    end {while...do begin};
                { at this point trace the way back through the list, }
                { popping the stack until a node is reached whose    }
                { lstinfo field points to an unmarked node, or until }
                {              the list is empty                      }
                while top <> 0
                    do begin
                            { restore lstinfo or next to p and pop the }
                            {                  stack                    }
                            p := top;
                            { restore the proper field of node[p] }
                            if node[p].tag = stk
                                then begin
                                        { lstinfo was used as the stack }
                                        {  link. Restore the tag field  }
                                        node[p].tag := lst;
                                        {     pop the stack      }
                                        top := node[top].lstinfo;
                                        { restore the lstinfo field }
                                        node[p].lstinfo := q;
                                        q := p
                                end {then begin}
```

```
          else begin
                       {    next was used as the stack    }
                       {        link. Pop the stack.        }
                  top := node[top].next;
                       {      restore the next field        }
                  node[p].next := q;
                  q := p;
                  { check if we must travel down }
                  {        node[p].lstinfo            }
                  if node[p].tag = lst
                       then begin
                                   {     indicate that lstinfo is    }
                                   {        used as the stack link    }
                                   node[p].tag := stk;
                                   { push node[p] on the stack }
                                   node[p].lstinfo := top;
                                   top := p;
                                   {    advance to next node      }
                                   p := q;
                                   go to 10
                            end {then begin}
                 end {else begin}
          end {while...do begin}
   end {for...do begin}
```

Although this algorithm is advantageous in terms of space since no auxiliary stack is necessary, it is disadvantageous in terms of time because each list must be traversed twice: once in pushing each node in the list on the stack and once in popping the stack. This can be contrasted with the relatively few nodes that must be stacked when an auxiliary stack is available.

Of course, several methods of garbage collection can be combined into a single algorithm. For example, an auxiliary stack of fixed size can be set aside for garbage collection, and when the stack is about to overflow, the algorithm can switch to the Schorr-Waite method. We leave the details as an exercise.

Collection and Compaction

Once the memory locations of a given system have been marked appropriately, the collection phase may begin. The purpose of this phase is to return to available memory all those locations that were previously garbage (not used by any program but unavailable to any user). Based on the mechanism used to maintain the available list, it should not be too difficult a task to pass through memory sequentially, examining each node in turn and returning unmarked nodes to available storage. For example, given the type definitions and declarations just presented, the following algorithm could be used to return the unmarked nodes to an available list headed by *avail*:

```
for p := 1 to maxnodes
    do begin
        if not node[p].mark
            then begin
                    node[p].next := avail;
                    avail := p
                end {then begin};
        node[p].mark = false
    end {for...do begin}
```

After this algorithm has been completed, all nodes that were previously garbage will be on the available list, and all nodes that are in use by programs will have their *mark* fields turned off (for the next call to garbage collection). Note that this algorithm places nodes on the available list in opposite order of their memory location. If it were desired to return nodes to available memory in the order of increasing memory location, the *for* loop could be reversed to read

$$for\ p := maxnodes\ \textbf{downto}\ 1$$

Although at this point (following the marking and collection phases of the system) all nodes that are not in use are on the available list, the memory of the system may not be in an optimal state for future use. This is because the interleaving of the occupied nodes with available nodes may make much of the memory on the available list unusable. For example, memory is often required in blocks (groups of contiguous nodes) rather than as single discrete nodes one at a time. The memory request by a compiler for space in which to store an array would require the allocation of such a block. If, for example, all the odd locations in memory were occupied and all the even locations were on the available list, then a request for even an array of size 2 could not be honored, despite the fact that half of memory is on the available list. Although this example is probably not very realistic, there certainly exist situations in which a request for a contiguous block of memory could not be honored, despite the fact that sufficient memory does indeed exist.

There are several approaches to this problem. Some methods allocate and free portions of memory in blocks (groups of contiguous nodes) rather than in units of individual nodes. This guarantees that when a block of storage is freed (returned to the available pool), a block will be available for subsequent allocation requests. The size of these blocks and the manner in which they are stored, allocated, and freed are discussed in the next section.

However, even if storage is maintained as units of individual nodes rather than as blocks, it is still possible to provide the user with blocks of contiguous storage. The process of moving all used (marked) nodes to one end of memory and all the available memory to the other end is called *compaction*, and an algorithm that performs such a process is called a *compaction* (or *compacting*) *algorithm*.

The basic problem in developing an algorithm that moves portions of memory from one location to another is to preserve the integrity of pointer values to the nodes being moved. For example, if *node(p)* in memory contains a pointer to *node(q)*, then when *node(p)* and *node(q)* are moved, not only must the addresses of *node(p)* and *node(q)* be modified, but the contents of *node(p)* (which contained the pointer *q*) must be modified to point to the new address of *node(q)*. In addition to being able to change addresses of nodes, we must have a method of determining whether the contents of any node contains a pointer to some other node (in which case its value may have to be changed) or whether it contains some other data type (so that no change is necessary).

A number of compaction techniques have been developed. As in the case of a marking algorithm, because the process is required at precisely the time that little additional space is available, methods that require substantial additional storage (e.g., a stack) are not practical. Let us examine one compaction algorithm that does not need additional memory when it runs.

The compaction algorithm is executed after the marking phase and traverses memory sequentially. Each marked node, as it is encountered in the sequential traversal, is assigned to the next available memory location starting from the beginning of available memory. When examining a marked node *nd1* that points to a node *nd2*, the pointer in *nd1* that now points to *nd2* must be updated to the new location where *nd2* will be moved. That location may not yet be known because *nd2* might be at a later address than *nd1*. *nd1* is therefore placed on a list emanating from *nd2* of all nodes that contain pointers to *nd2*, so that when the new location of *nd2* is determined, *nd1* can be accessed and the pointer to *nd2* contained in it modified.

For now, let us assume that a new field *header* in each node *nd2* points to the list of nodes that contain pointers to *nd2*. Let us call this list the *adjustment list* of *nd2*. We can reuse the field that pointed to *nd2* (either *next* or *lstinfo*) as the link field for the adjustment list of *nd2*; we know that its "real" value is *nd2* because the node is on the list emanating from *header(nd2)*. Thus once its adjustment list has been formed, when *nd2* is reached in a sequential traversal, that adjustment list can be traversed, and the values in the fields used to link that list can be changed to the new location assigned to *nd2*. Then, once all nodes that point to *nd2* have had their pointers adjusted, *nd2* itself can be moved.

However, there is one additional piece of information that is required. The adjustment list of nodes pointing to *nd2* can be linked via either the *next* pointer of a node *nd1* (if *next(nd1)* = *nd2*) or the *lstinfo* pointer (if *lstinfo(nd1)* = *nd2*). How can we tell which it is? For this purpose, three additional fields in each node are necessary. The values of these fields can be *none*, which indicates that a node is not on an adjustment list; *info*, which indicates that a node is linked onto the adjustment list using *lstinfo*; or *link*, which indicates that it is linked onto the adjustment list using *next*. The three fields are *headptr*, *infoptr*, and *nextptr*. *headptr(nd)* defines the link field in the node pointed to by *header(nd)*; *infoptr(nd)* defines the link field in the node pointed to by *lstinfo(nd)*; and *nextptr(nd)* defines the link field in the node pointed to by *next(nd)*.

Thus, we assume the following format for the nodes:

```
type  fieldtype = (info, link, none);
type  nodetype = record
            mark:    boolean;
            header:  nodeptr;
            next:    nodeptr;
            headptr: fieldtype
            infoptr: fieldtype;
            nextptr: fieldtype;
            case tag: infotype of
                ch: (chinfo: char);
                int: (intinfo: integer);
                lst: (lstinfo: nodeptr)
      end;
```

Now consider a single sequential pass of the algorithm. If a node *nd*1 points to a node *nd*2 that appears later in memory, by the time the algorithm reaches *nd*2 sequentially, *nd*1 will have already been placed on the adjustment list of *nd*2. When the algorithm reaches *nd*2, therefore, the pointers in *nd*1 can be modified. But if *nd*1 points to *nd*2 that appears earlier in memory, then when *nd*2 is reached, it is not yet known that *nd*1 points to it so the pointer in *nd*1 cannot be adjusted. For this reason, the algorithm requires two sequential passes. The first places nodes on adjustment lists and modifies pointers in nodes that it finds on adjustment lists. The second clears away adjustment lists remaining from the first pass and actually moves the nodes to their new locations. The first pass may be outlined as follows:

> update the memory location to be assigned to the next marked node, *nd*.
> traverse the list of nodes pointed to by *header(nd)* and change the appropriate pointer fields to point to the new location of *nd*.
> if the *tag* field of *nd* is *lst* and *lstinfo(nd)* is not *nil*, then place *nd* on the list of the nodes headed by *header(lstinfo(nd))*.
> if *next(nd)* is not *nil*, then place *nd* on the list of the nodes headed by the *header(next(nd))*.

Once this process has been completed for each marked node, a second pass through memory will perform the actual compaction. During the second pass we perform the following operations:

update the memory location to be assigned to the next marked node, *nd*.
traverse the list of nodes pointed to by *header(nd)* and change the appropriate
    pointer fields to point to the new location of *nd*.
move *nd* to its new location.

    The following algorithm performs the actual compaction. (We assume an auxiliary variable *source* of type *fieldtype* for use in traversing the lists.)

```
{ initialize fields for compaction algorithm }
for i := 0 to maxnodes
    do begin
            node[i].header := 0;
            node[i].headptr := none;
            node[i].infoptr := none;
            node[i].nextptr := none
        end {for...do begin};
{                           Pass 1                           }
{ Scan nodes sequentially. As each node nd is encountered    }
{ perform the following operations:                          }
{ 1.  Determine the new location of the node                 }
{ 2.  For all nodes that were previously encountered on      }
{      this pass that point to nd, adjust the appropriate    }
{      pointer to point to the new location of nd.           }
{ 3.  If any of the fields of nd point to some other node,   }
{      p, place nd on the list headed by node[p].header      }
newadd := 0;
for nd := 1 to maxnodes
    do if node[nd].mark
        then begin { nodes that are not marked are }
                  {        to be ignored.         }
              newadd := newadd + 1; { operation 1 }
              { operation 2 }
              p := node[nd].header;
              source := node[nd].headptr;
              while p <> 0
                  do {  traverse the list of nodes  }
                     {  encountered thus far that  }
                     {        point to nd          }
                  if source = info
                      then begin
                              q := node[p].lstinfo;
                              source := node[p].infoptr;
                              node[p].lstinfo := newadd;
```

```
                              node[p].infoptr := none;
                              p := q
                        end {then begin}
                  else begin
                              q := node[p].next;
                              source := node[p].nextptr;
                              node[p].next := newadd;
                              node[p].nextptr := none;
                              p := q
                        end {else begin};
            node[nd].headptr := none;
            node[nd].header := 0;
            { operation 3 }
            if (node[nd].tag = lst) and
                              (node[nd].lstinfo <> 0)
                  then begin {    place node[nd] on a list    }
                              { linked by node[nd].lstinfo  }
                              p := node[nd].lstinfo;
                              node[nd].lstinfo := node[p].header;
                              node[nd].infoptr := node[p].headptr
                              node[p].header := nd;
                              node[p].headptr := info
                  end {then begin};
            { place node[nd] on a list linked by }
            {           node[nd].next             }
            p := node[nd].next;
            node[nd].next := node[p].header;
            node[nd].nextptr := node[p].headptr;
            if p <> 0
                  then begin
                              node[p].header := nd;
                              node[p].headptr := link
                  end {then begin}
            end {if node[nd].mark then begin};
      {   Pass 2: This pass examines each node nd in turn,   }
      { updates all nodes on the adjustment list of nd, and  }
      { then moves the contents of nd to its new location.   }
      newadd := 0;
      for nd := 1 to maxnodes
            do if node[nd].mark
                  then begin
                              newadd := newadd + 1
                              p := node[nd].header;
                              source := node[nd].headptr;
```

```
while p <> 0
    do if source = info
        then begin
                    q := node[p].lstinfo;
                    source := node[p].infoptr;
                    node[p].lstinfo := newadd;
                    node[p].infoptr := none;
                    p := q
            end {then begin}
        else begin
                    q := node[p].next;
                    source := node[p].nextptr;
                    node[p].next := newadd;
                    node[p].nextptr := none;
                    p := q
            end {else begin};
        node[nd].headptr := none;
        node[nd].header := 0;
        node[nd].mark := false;
        node[newadd] := node[nd]
end {if node[nd].mark then begin}
```

Several points should be noted with respect to this algorithm. First, a special node, *node*[0], is suitably initialized so that the algorithm need not test for special cases. Second, the process of adjusting the pointers of all nodes on the list headed by the header field of a particular node is performed twice: once during the first pass and once during the second. This process could not be deferred entirely to the second pass, when all the pointers to a particular node are known. The reason for this is that when a field in a node *nd2* in the adjustment list of node *nd* is changed to *nd*, it must be changed before *nd2* is moved to a new location, since no record of the new location is maintained in *nd2*. Thus nodes on the adjustment list of *nd* that precede *nd1* sequentially must have their fields modified before they have been moved. But since they are moved before we reach *nd* in the second pass, and they have already been placed on the adjustment list by the time we reach *nd* in the first pass, we must clear the adjustment lists and modify the pointer fields at that point. We also must modify pointer fields in the second pass for nodes on the adjustment list of *nd* that are sequentially after *nd* and were put on the adjustment list of *nd* during the first pass after having already passed *nd*.

The algorithm seems to require several additional fields for each node. In reality, these additional fields are not required. Most systems have at least one field in each node that cannot take on a pointer value during the ordinary course of processing. This field can be used to hold the *header* pointer to the adjustment list, so that an additional *header* field is not necessary. The value that was held in this field can be moved to the last node in the adjustment list and placed in either the *next* or *lstinfo* field, depending on which of the two held the pointer to the target node. We assume that it is possible to distinguish between a pointer and a nonpointer value so that we can detect when we reach the end of the adjustment list by the presence of a nonpointer value in the last node.

In addition, we used the fields *headptr*, *nextptr*, and *infoptr* to indicate which field (*next* or *lstinfo*) in the node pointed to by *header*, *next*, or *lstinfo*, respectively, held the target pointer. But if *header*, *next*, and *lstinfo* could contain actual addresses, rather than just a pointer to a node, they could hold the address of the specific field that held the target pointer rather than just the address of the node. Thus an additional field to identify the particular field within the node is unnecessary, and we can eliminate *headptr*, *nextptr*, and *infoptr* from the nodes. In machine language, it is possible to keep actual addresses in the fields, although it is not possible to do so in standard Pascal.

We therefore see that our compaction algorithm can be modified so that it does not require any additional storage in the nodes. Such an algorithm is called a ***bounded workspace algorithm.***

The time requirements of the algorithm are easy to analyze. There are two linear passes throughout the complete array of memory. Each pass through memory scans each node once and adjusts any pointer fields to which the nodes point. The time requirements are obviously $O(n)$.

With respect to the actual compaction itself, it is not necessary to invoke the compaction routine each time the garbage collection routine is called. The garbage collection routine is called when there is little (or no) space available. The amount of space that is reclaimed by the algorithm may or may not provide sufficient contiguous blocks. It is the compaction algorithm that assures that the space that is reclaimed is contiguous at one end of memory. It may be that the memory that is returned by the garbage collection algorithm is not sufficiently fragmented to warrant a call to the compaction routine and that only after several calls to the collection routine is it necessary to call the compaction algorithm. On the other hand, if the compaction routine is not called sufficiently often, then the system may indicate that insufficient space is available when in fact there is sufficient space but that space is not contiguous. Failure to invoke the compaction routine may then result in additional calls to the garbage collection routine. The decision of when to invoke the compaction algorithm in conjunction with the garbage collection algorithm is a difficult one. Yet, because compaction is usually more efficient than garbage collection, it is usually not too inefficient to invoke them at the same time.

Variations of Garbage Collection

There are a number of recently discovered variations of the garbage collection systems just presented. In the traditional schemes we have considered, the applications programs function as long as space availability of the system satisfies certain criteria. (These criteria may relate to the total amount of free space available, the number and size of contiguous memory locations available, the amount of memory requested since the last garbage collection phase, etc.) When these criteria are no longer met, then all applications programs halt, and the system directs its resources to garbage collection. Once the collection has been completed, the applications programs may resume execution from the point at which they were interrupted.

In some situations, however, this is not satisfactory. Applications that are executing in real time (e.g., computing the trajectory of a spaceship, or monitoring a chemical reaction) cannot be halted while the system is performing garbage collection. In these circumstances, it is usually necessary to dedicate a separate processor devoted exclusively to the job of garbage collection. When the system signals that garbage collection must be performed, the separate processor begins executing concurrently with the applications program. Because of this simultaneous execution, it is necessary to guarantee that nodes that are in the process of being acquired for use by an application program are not mistakenly returned to the available pool by the collector. Avoiding such problems is not a trivial process. Systems that allow the collection process to proceed simultaneously with the applications program use "on-the-fly" garbage collection.

Another subject of interest deals with minimizing the cost of reclaiming unused space. In the methods we have discussed, the cost of reclaiming any portion of storage is the same as the cost of reclaiming any other portion (of the same size). Recent attention has been directed toward designing a system in which the cost of reclaiming a portion of storage is proportional to its lifetime. It has been shown empirically that some portions of memory are required for smaller time intervals than are others and that requests for portions of memory with smaller lifetimes occur more frequently than do requests for portions of memory with longer lifetimes. Thus, by reducing the cost of retrieving portions of memory required for short time periods at the expense of the cost of retrieving portions of memory with longer lifespans, the overall cost of the garbage collection process will be reduced. Exactly how one classifies the lifetimes of portions of memory and algorithms for retrieving such portions of memory will not be considered further. The interested reader is referred to the references.

The process of garbage collection is also applied to reclaiming unused space in secondary devices (e.g., a disk). While the concept of allocation and freeing space is the same (i.e., space may be requested or released by a program), algorithms that manage space on such devices often cannot be translated efficiently from their counterparts that manipulate main memory. The reason for this is that the cost of accessing any location in main memory is the same as that of accessing any other location in main memory. In secondary storage, on the other hand, the cost depends on the location of storage that is currently being accessed as well as the location we desire to access. It is very efficient to access a portion of secondary storage that is in the same block that is now being accessed; to access a location in a different block may involve expensive disk seeks. For this reason, device management systems for off-line storage try to minimize the number of such accesses. The interested reader is referred to the literature for a discussion of the relevant techniques.

EXERCISES

1. Implement each of the following list operations of Section 1 in Pascal, assuming that the reference count method of list management is used.

   (a) *head*   (b) *tail*   (c) *addon*   (d) *sethead*   (e)*settail*

2. Rewrite the routines of the previous exercise under the system in which the reference counter in a node *nd*1 is decremented when a node *nd*2 pointing to *nd*1 is reallocated rather than when *nd*2 is freed.

3. Implement the list operations of Exercise 1 in Pascal assuming the use of list headers, with reference counts in header nodes only. Ensure that illegal lists are never formed.

4. Write an algorithm to detect recursion in a list; that is, whether or not there is a path from some node on the list back to itself.

5. Write an algorithm to restore all nodes on a list *list* to the available list. Do the same using no additional storage.

6. In a multiuser environment where several users are running concurrently, it may be possible for one user to ask for additional storage and thus invoke the garbage collector while another user is in the middle of list manipulation. If garbage collection is allowed to proceed at that point (before the lists of the second user have been restored to legal form), the second user will find that many list nodes have been freed. Assume that there exist two system routines, *nogarbage* amd *okgarbage*. A call to the first inhibits the invocation of garbage collection until after the same user calls the second. Implement the list operations of Exercise 1, using calls to these two routines to ensure that garbage collection is not invoked at inopportune moments.

7. Trace the actions of the three garbage collection algorithms of the text on the lists of Figures 10.2.4a and 10.1.9, assuming that the integer above each list node is the index of that node in the array *node*. Trace through the algorithms on the list of Figure 10.1.9, after executing the statement.

$$list9 := nil$$

8. Given pointers p and q to two list nodes, write an algorithm to determine if *node*(q) is accessible from *node*(p).

9. Assume that each node contains an arbitrary number of pointers to other nodes rather than just two so that the lists now become graphs. Revise each of the marking algorithms presented in this section under this possibility.

10. Revise each of the marking algorithms presented in this section under the assumption that the lists are doubly linked, so that each list node contains a *prevptr* field to the previous node on the same list. How do each of the algorithms increase in efficiency? What restriction on the list structure does the presence of such a field imply?

11. Do the same as in Exercise 10, under the assumption that each list node has a field *father* pointing to its containing node (i.e., *node*[*node*[p].*father*].*lstinfo* = p).

12. Write two marking algorithms that use a finite, auxiliary stack of size *stksize*. The algorithms operate like the second marking algorithm presented in the text until the stack becomes full. At that point, the first of the two algorithms operates like the sequential algorithm presented in the text, and the second operates like the Schorr-Waite algorithm.

13. Can you rewrite the Schorr-Waite algorithm to eliminate the **goto** statement?

3. DYNAMIC MEMORY MANAGEMENT

In the previous sections, we assumed that storage is allocated and is freed one node at a time. There are two characteristics of nodes that make the previous methods suitable. The first is that each node of a given type is of fixed size, and the second is that the size of each node is fairly small. In some applications, however, these characteristics do not apply. For example, a particular program might require a large amount of contiguous storage (e.g., a large array). It would be impractical to attempt to obtain such a block one node at a time. Similarly, a program may require storage blocks in a large variety of sizes. In such cases, a memory management system must be able to process requests for variable-length blocks. In this section we discuss some systems of this type.

As an example of this situation, consider a small memory of 1024 words. Suppose that a request is made for three blocks of storage of 348, 110, and 212 words, respectively. Let us further suppose that these blocks are allocated sequentially, as shown in Figure 10.3.1a. Now suppose that the second block of size 110 is freed, resulting in the situation depicted in Figure 10.3.1b. There are now 464 words of free space; yet, because the free space is divided into noncontiguous blocks, a request for a block of 400 words could not be satisfied.

Suppose that block 3 were now freed. Clearly, it is not desirable to retain three free blocks of 110, 212, and 354 words. Rather, the blocks should be combined into a single large block of 676 words so that further large requests can be satisfied. After combination, memory will appear as in Figure 10.3.1c.

This example illustrates that the necessity to keep track of the space that is available, to allocate portions of that space when allocation requests are presented, and to combine contiguous free spaces when a block is freed.

Compaction of Blocks of Storage

One scheme sometimes used involves compaction of storage as follows: Initially memory is one large block of available storage. As requests for storage arrive, blocks of memory are allocated sequentially starting from the first location in memory. This is illustrated in Figure 10.3.2a. A variable *freepoint* contains the address of the first location following the last block allocated. In Figure 10.3.2a, *freepoint* equals 950. Note that all memory locations between *freepoint* and the highest address in memory are free. When

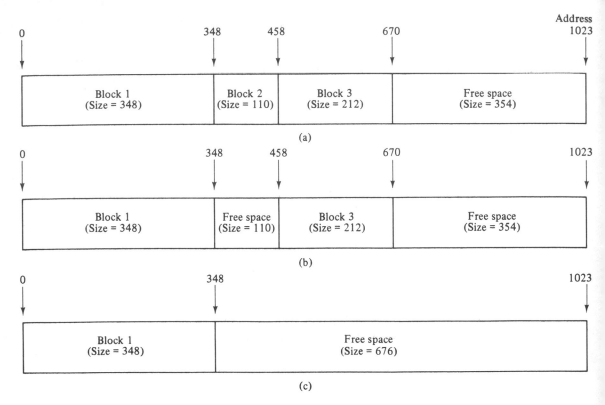

Figure 10.3.1

a block is freed, *freepoint* remains unchanged, and no combinations of free spaces take place. When a block of size n is allocated, *freepoint* is increased by n. This continues until a block of size n is requested and *freepoint* + $n - 1$ is larger than the highest address in memory. The request cannot be satisfied without further action being taken.

At that point, user routines come to a halt and a system compaction routine is called. Although the algorithm of the previous section was designed to address uniform nodes, it could be modified to compact memory consisting of blocks of storage as well. Such a routine copies all allocated blocks into sequential memory locations starting from the lowest address in memory. Thus all free blocks that were interspersed with allocated blocks are eliminated, and *freepoint* is reset to the sum of the sizes of all the allocated blocks. One large free block is created at the upper end of memory, and the user request may be filled if there is sufficient storage available. This process is illustrated in Figure 10.3.2 on a memory of 1024 words.

When allocated blocks are copied into lower portions of memory, special care must be taken so that pointer values remain correct. For example, the contents of memory location 420 in allocated block 2 of Figure 10.3.2a might contain the address 340. After block 2 is moved to locations 125

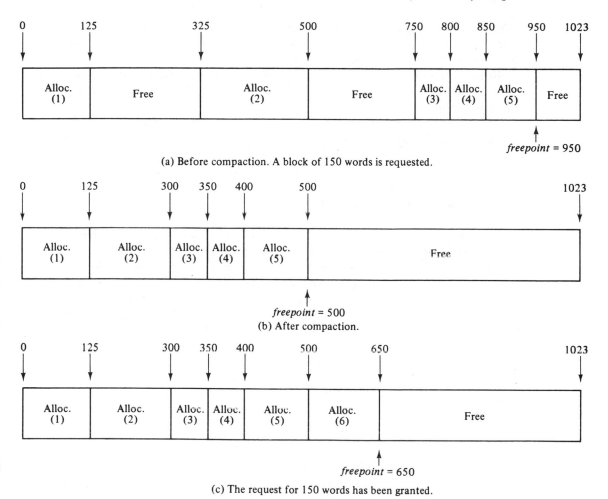

(a) Before compaction. A block of 150 words is requested.

freepoint = 950

(b) After compaction.

freepoint = 500

(c) The request for 150 words has been granted.

freepoint = 650

Figure 10.3.2

through 299, location 140 contains the previous contents of location 340. In moving the contents of 420 to 220, those contents must be changed to 140. Thus, for compaction to be successful, there must be a method to determine if the contents of a given location is an address.

An alternative is a system which computes addresses as offsets from some base register. In that case, only the contents of the base register must be changed while the offset in memory need not be altered. For example, in the previous instances, location 420 would contain the offset 15 before compaction rather than the address 340. Since the base address of the block is 325, the address 340 would be computed as the base address 325 plus the offset 15. When the block is moved, its base address is changed to 125, while the offset 15 is moved from location 420 to location 220. Adding the new base address 125 to the offset 15 yields 140, which is the address to which the contents of 340 have been moved. Note that the offset 15 contained in memory has not been changed at all. However, such a technique is useful only for intrablock references; interblock references to locations in a different block must still be modified. A compaction routine requires a method by which the size of a block and its status (allocated or free) could be determined.

Compaction is similar to garbage collection in that all user processing must stop as the system takes time to clean up its storage. For this reason, and because of the pointer problem just discussed, compaction is not used as frequently as the more complicated schemes presented next.

First Fit, Best Fit, and Worst Fit

If it is not desirable to move blocks of allocated storage from one area of memory to another, then it must be possible to reallocate memory blocks that have been freed dynamically as user processing continues. For example, if memory is fragmented as shown in Figure 10.3.1b and a request is made for a block of 250 words of storage, locations 670 through 919 would be used. The result is shown in Figure 10.3.3a. If memory is as shown in Figure 10.3.1b, then a request for a block of 50 words could be satisfied

Figure 10.3.3

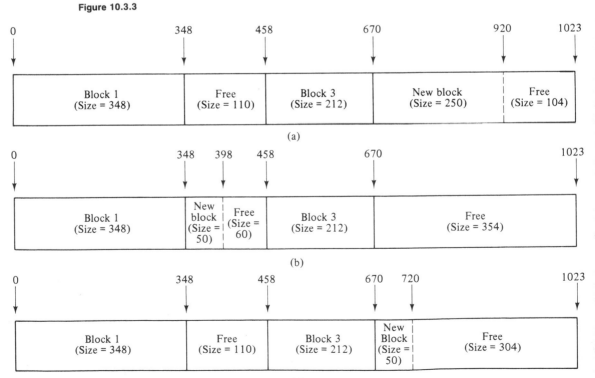

by either words 348 through 397 or words 670 through 719 (see Figures 10.3.3b and c. In each case, part of a free block becomes allocated, leaving the remaining portion free.

Each time that a request is made for storage, a free area large enough to accommodate the size requested must be located. The most obvious method for keeping track of the free blocks is to use a linear linked list. Each free block contains a field containing the size of the block and a field containing a pointer to the next free block. These fields are in some uniform location (say, the first two words) in the block. If p is the address of a free block, the expressions $size(p)$ and $next(p)$ are used to refer to these two quantities. A global pointer *freeblock* points to the first free block on this list. Let us see how blocks are removed from the free list when storage is requested. We will then examine how blocks are added onto this list when they are freed.

Consider the situation of Figure 10.3.1b, reproduced in Figure 10.3.4a to show the free list. There are several principal methods of selecting the free block to use when requesting storage. In the *first-fit* method, the free list is traversed sequentially to find the first free block whose size is larger than or equal to the amount requested. Once the block is found, it is removed from the list (if it is equal in size to the amount requested), or it is split into two portions (if it is greater than the amount requested). The first of these portions remains on the list and the second is allocated. The reason for allocating the second portion rather than the first is that the free list *next* pointer is at the beginning of each free block. By leaving the first portion of the block on the free list, this pointer need not be copied into some other location, and the *next* field of the previous block in the list need not be changed.

Before presenting an allocation algorithm using the first-fit method, we examine some general issues that are raised in implementing dynamic allocation algorithms. As noted, the blocks of storage being manipulated are of variable length. There is often a need to locate a word that is a specific number of words past the location designated by a pointer p. For example, when a free block of size s beginning at location p is split into two to provide a block B of size n, the location of B is at $p + s - n$. Thus we must have the ability to perform arithmetic operations on addresses. For these reasons, it is cumbersome to implement these algorithms in Pascal. Also it is often necessary to interpret information within the computer's memory in different data formats. For example, if the size of a free block is contained in the first word of that block and the list *next* pointer is contained in its second word, and if p is the location of a free block, then $size(p)$ refers to the information stored at location p interpreted as an integer, while $next(p)$ refers to the information stored at location $p + 1$ interpreted as an address. In the exercises, there is a scheme by which the algorithms of this section can be implemented in Pascal. For the sake of clarity and ease of expression, we present storage management methods as algorithms rather than as Pascal programs.

The first-fit allocation algorithm returns the address of a free block of storage of size n in the variable *alloc* if one is available and sets *alloc* to the nil address if no such block is available.

```
p := freeblock;
alloc := nil;
q := nil;
while (p <> nil) and (size(p) < n)
    do begin
            q := p;
            p := next(p)
        end {while...do begin};
if p <> nil   { there is a block large enough }
    then begin
            s := size(p);
            alloc := p + s - n;   { alloc contains the address }
                                  {     of the desired block    }
            if s = n
                then { remove the block from the free list }
                    if q = nil
                        then freeblock := next(p)
                        else next(q) := next(p)
                else { adjust the size of the remaining }
                     {            free block            }
                    size(p) := s - n
        end {then begin}
```

The **best-fit** method obtains the smallest free block whose size is greater than or equal to n. An algorithm to obtain such a block by traversing the entire free list follows. We assume that *memsize* is the total number of words in memory.

```
p := freeblock;      { p is used to traverse the free list }
q := nil;            {      q is one block behind p         }
r := nil;            {   r points to the desired block      }
rq := nil;           {      rq is one block behind r        }
rsize := memsize + 1; {     rsize is the size of r          }
alloc := nil;        {  alloc will point to the block       }
                     {              selected                }
while p <> nil
    do begin
        if(size(p) >= n) and (size(p) < rsize)
            then begin { we have found a free block closer in size }
                    r := p;
                    rq := q;
                    rsize := size(p)
                end {then begin};
```

```
                    { continue traversing the free list }
                q:= p;
                p:= next(p)
            end {while...do begin};
        if r <> nil
            then begin { there is a block of sufficient size }
                    alloc:= r + rsize - n;
                    if rsize = n
                        then { remove the block from the free list }
                            if rq = nil
                                then freeblock:= next(r)
                                else next(rq):= next(r)
                        else
                            size(r):= rsize - n
                end {then begin}
```

To see the difference between the first-fit and best-fit methods, consider the following examples. We begin with memory fragmented as in Figure 10.3.4a. There are two blocks of free storage, of sizes 110 and 354. If a request is made for a block of 300 words, the block of 354 is split as shown in Figure 10.3.4b under both the first-fit and best-fit methods. Suppose a block of size 25 is then requested. Under first-fit, the block of size 110 is split (Figure 10.3.4c), while under best-fit, the block of size 54 is split (Figure 10.3.4d). If a block of size 100 is then requested, the request can be fulfilled under best-fit since the block of size 110 is available (Figure 10.3.4e), but it cannot be fulfilled under first-fit. This illustrates an advantage of the best-fit method in that very large free blocks remain unsplit so that requests for large blocks can be satisfied. In the first-fit method, a very large block of free storage at the beginning of the free list is nibbled away by small requests so that it is severely shrunken by the time a large request arrives.

However, it is also possible for the first-fit method to succeed where the best-fit method fails. As an example, consider the case in which the system begins with free blocks of size 110 and 54 and then makes successive requests for 25, 70, and 50 words. Figure 10.3.5 illustrates that the first-fit method succeeds in fulfilling these requests, while the best-fit method does not. The reason is that remaining unallocated portions of blocks are smaller under best-fit than under first-fit.

Yet another method of allocating blocks of storage is the **worst-fit method**. In this method, the system will always allocate a portion of the largest free block in memory. The philosophy behind this method is that by using a small number of very large blocks repeatedly to satisfy the majority of requests, many moderately sized blocks will be left unfragmented. Thus, this method is likely to satisfy a larger number of requests than the other methods, unless most of the requests are for very large portions of memory. For example, if memory consists initially of blocks of sizes 200, 300, and 100, then the sequence of requests 150, 100, 125, 100, and 100 can be

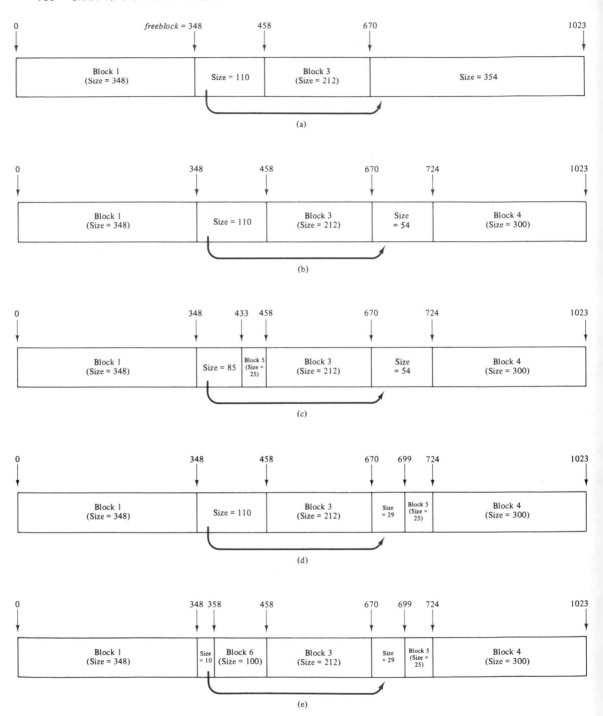

Figure 10.3.4

Figure 10.3.5

| | Blocks remaining using | |
Request	First-fit	Best-fit
Initially	110, 54	110, 54
25	85, 54	110, 29
70	15, 54	40, 29
50	15, 4	cannot be fulfilled

satisfied by the worst-fit method but not by either the first-fit or best-fit methods. (Convince yourself that this is the case.)

The major reason for choosing one method over the other is efficiency. In each of the methods, the search can be made more efficient. For example, a true first-fit method, which allocates the block at the lowest memory address first, will be most efficient if the available list is maintained in the order of increasing memory address (as it should be for reasons to be discussed shortly). On the other hand, if the available list is maintained in the order of increasing size, then a best-fit search for a block becomes more efficient. And, finally, if the list is maintained in the order of decreasing size, then a worst-fit request requires no searching, as the largest-size block is always the first on the list. However, for reasons we shall discuss shortly, it is not always practical to maintain the list of available blocks ordered by size.

Each of the methods has certain characteristics that make it either desirable or undesirable for various request patterns. In the absence of any specific consideration to the contrary, the first-fit method is usually preferred.

Improvements in the First-Fit Method

Several improvements can be made in the first-fit method. If the size of a free block is only slightly larger than the size of the block to be allocated, the portion of the free block that remains free is very small. Very often, this remaining portion is so small that there is little likelihood of its being used before the allocated portion is freed and the two portions are recombined. Thus little benefit is achieved by leaving that small portion on the free list. Also recall that any free block must be of some minimum size (in our case, two words) so that it may contain *size* and *next* fields. What if the smaller portion of a free block is below this minimum size after the larger portion has been allocated?

The solution to these problems is to insist that no block may remain free if its size is below some reasonable minimum. If a free block is about to be split and the remaining portion is below this minimum size, the block is not split. Instead, the entire free block is allocated as though it were exactly the right size. This allows the system to remove the entire block from the free list and does not clutter up the list with very small blocks.

The phenomenon in which there are many small noncontiguous free blocks is called **external fragmentation** because free space is wasted outside allocated blocks. This contrasts with **internal fragmentation** in which free space is wasted within allocated blocks. The preceding solution transforms external fragmentation into internal fragmentation. The choice of what minimum size to use depends on the pattern of allocation requests in the particular system. It is reasonable to use a minimum size such that only a small percentage (say, 5%) of the allocation requests are less than or equal to that size. Note that the possibility of small slivers remaining is even greater under the best-fit method than under first-fit, so that the establishment of such a minimum size is of correspondingly greater importance under that method.

Another significant improvement in the first-fit method can be made. As time goes on, smaller free blocks will tend to accumulate near the front of the free list. This is because a large block near the front of the list is reduced in size before a large block near the back of the list. Thus, in searching for a large- or even a moderate-size block, the small blocks near the front are skipped. The algorithm would be more efficient if the free list were organized as a circular list whose first element varies dynamically as blocks are allocated.

Two ways of implementing this dynamic variance suggest themselves. In the first, *freeblock* (which is the pointer to the first free block on the list) is set to *next(freeblock)*, so that the front of the list advances one block each time that a block is allocated. In the second, *freeblock* is set to *next(alloc)*, where *alloc* points to the block just chosen for allocation. Thus all blocks that were too small for this allocation request are in effect moved to the back of the list. The reader is invited to investigate the advantages and disadvantages of both techniques.

Freeing Storage Blocks

Thus far, nothing has been said about how allocated blocks of storage are freed and how they are combined with contiguous free blocks to form larger blocks of free storage. Specifically, three questions arise:

1. When a block of storage is freed, where is it placed on the free list? The answer to this question determines how the free list is ordered.
2. When a block of storage is freed, how can it be determined whether the blocks of storage on either side of it are free (in which case the newly freed block should be combined with an already existing free block)?
3. What is the mechanism for combining a newly freed block with a previously free contiguous block?

The term *liberation* is used for the process of freeing an allocated block of storage; an algorithm to implement this process is called a *liberation algorithm*. The free list should be organized to facilitate efficient allocation and liberation.

Suppose that the free list is organized arbitrarily, so that when a block is freed, it is placed at the front of the list. It may be that the block just freed is adjacent to a previously free block. To create a single large free block, the newly freed block should be combined with the adjacent free block. There is no way, short of traversing the entire free list, to determine if such an adjacent free block exists. Thus each liberation would involve a traversal of the free list. For this reason it is inefficient to maintain the free list this way.

An alternative is to keep the free list sorted in order of increasing memory location. Then, when a block is freed, the free list is traversed in a search for the first free block *fb* whose starting address is greater than the starting address of the block being freed. If a contiguous free block is not found in this search, no such contiguous block exists and the newly freed block can be inserted into the free list immediately before *fb*. If *fb* or the free block immediately preceding *fb* on the free list is contiguous to the newly freed block, it can be combined with that newly freed block. Under this method, the entire free list need not be traversed. Instead, only half of the list must be traversed on the average.

The following liberation algorithm implements this scheme, assuming that the free list is linear (not circular) and that *freeblock* points to the free block with the smallest address. The algorithm frees a block of size n beginning at address *alloc*.

```
q:= nil;
p:= freeblock;
    { p traverses the free list. q remains one step behind p }
while (p <> nil) and (p < alloc)
    do begin
            q:= p;
            p:= next(p)
        end {while...do begin};
    {   At this point, either q = nil or q < alloc and either p = nil   }
    {   or alloc < p. Thus if p and q are not nil, the block must      }
    {   be combined with the blocks beginning at p or q or both, or    }
    {       must be inserted in the list between the two blocks.        }

if q = nil
    then freeblock:= alloc
    else if q + size(q) = alloc
            then begin { combine with previous block }
                    alloc:= q;
                    n:= size(q) + n
                end {then begin}
```

$$\textbf{\textit{else}} \; next(q) := alloc;$$
$$\textbf{\textit{if}} (p <> nil) \; \textbf{\textit{and}} \; (alloc + n = p)$$
$$\qquad \textbf{\textit{then begin}} \; \{ \text{ combine with subsequent block } \}$$
$$\qquad\qquad size(alloc) := n + size(p);$$
$$\qquad\qquad next(alloc) := next(p)$$
$$\qquad \textbf{\textit{end}} \; \{\text{then begin}\}$$
$$\qquad \textbf{\textit{else begin}}$$
$$\qquad\qquad size(alloc) := n;$$
$$\qquad\qquad next(alloc) := p$$
$$\qquad \textbf{\textit{end}} \; \{\text{else begin}\}$$

If the free list is organized as a circular list, the first-fit allocation algorithm begins traversing the list from varying locations. However, to traverse the list from the lowest location during liberation, an additional external pointer, *lowblock*, to the free block with the lowest location is required. Ordinarily, traversal starts at *lowblock* during liberation. However, if it is found that *freeblock* < *alloc* when the block that starts at *alloc* is about to be freed, traversal starts at *freeblock* so that even less search time is used during liberation. The reader is urged to implement this variation as an exercise.

The Boundary Tag Method

It is desirable to eliminate all searching during liberation to make the process more efficient. One method of doing this comes at the expense of keeping extra information in all blocks (both free and allocated).

A search is necessary during liberation to determine if the newly freed block may be combined with some existing free block. There is no way of detecting whether such a block exists or which block it is without a search. However, if such a block exists, it must immediately precede or succeed the block being freed. The first address of the block that follows a block of size n at *alloc* is $alloc + n$. Suppose every block contains a field *flag* which is *true* if the block is allocated and *false* if the block is free. Then by examining *flag*($alloc + n$), it can be determined whether or not the block immediately following the block at *alloc* is free.

It is more difficult to determine the status of the block immediately preceding the block at *alloc*. The address of the last location of that preceding block is, of course, $alloc - 1$. But there is no way of finding the address of its first location without knowing its size. Suppose, however, that each block contains two flags—*fflag* and *bflag*—both of which are *true* if the block is allocated and *false* otherwise. *fflag* is at a specific offset from the front of the block, and *bflag* is at a specific negative offset from the back of the block.

Thus, to access *fflag*, the first location of the block must be known; to access *bflag*, the last location of the block must be known. The status of the block following the block at *alloc* can be determined from the value of *fflag*($alloc + n$), and the status of the block preceding the block at *alloc* can be determined from the value of *bflag*($alloc - 1$). Then, when a block is to be freed, it can be determined immediately whether it must be combined with either of its two neighboring blocks.

A list of free blocks is still needed for the allocation process. When a block is freed, its neighbors are examined. If both blocks are allocated, the block can simply be appended to the front of the free list. If one (or both) of its neighbors is free, the neighbor(s) can be removed from the free list and combined with the newly freed block, and the newly created large block can be placed at the head of the free list. Note that this would tend to reduce search times under first-fit allocation as well, since a previously allocated block (especially if it has been combined with other blocks) is likely to be large enough to satisfy the next allocation request. Since it is placed at the head of the free list, the search time is reduced sharply.

To remove an arbitrary block from the free list (to combine it with a newly freed block) without traversing the entire list, the free list must be doubly linked. Thus each free block must contain two pointers, *next* and *prev*, to the next and previous free blocks on the free list. It is also necessary to be able to access these two pointers from the last location of a free block. (This is needed when combining a newly freed block with a free block that immediately precedes it in memory.) Thus the front of a free block must be

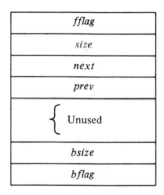

Free block

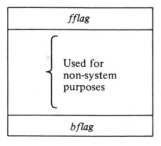

Allocated block   **Figure 10.3.6**

accessible from its rear. One way to do this is to introduce a *bsize* field at a given negative offset from the last location of each free block. This field contains the same value as the *size* field at the front of the block. Figure 10.3.6 illustrates the structure of free and allocated blocks under this method, which is called the **boundary tag method**. Each of the control fields, *fflag*, *size*, *next*, *prev*, *bsize*, and *bflag* is shown as occupying a complete word, although in practice they may be packed together, several fields to a word.

      We now present the liberation algorithm using the boundary tag method. For clarity, we assume that *fflag* and *bflag* are boolean variables and that *true* indicates an allocated block and *false* indicates a free block. (We assume that *bflag*(0) and *fflag*(m + 1), where m is the size of memory, are both *true*.) The algorithm frees a block of size n at location *alloc*. It makes use of an auxiliary routine *remove* that removes a block from the doubly linked list. The details of that routine are left as an exercise for the reader.

```
{ check the preceding block }
if not bflag(alloc - 1)
  then begin { the block must be combined with the preceding block }
            start: = alloc - bsize(alloc - 1);   { find the initial address of }
                                                 {          the block          }
            remove(start);   { remove the block from the free list }
            { increase the size and combine the blocks }
            n: = n + size(start);
            alloc: = start
        end {then begin};
{ check the following block }
if not fflag(alloc + n)
  then begin { the block must be combined with the following block }
            start: = alloc + n;
            n: = n + size(start);
            remove(start);
        end {then begin}
{ add the newly free, possibly combined block to the free list }
next(alloc): = freeblock;
prev(freeblock): = alloc;
prev(alloc): = nil;
freeblock: = alloc;
{ adjust the fields in the new block }
fflag(alloc): = false;
bflag(alloc + n - 1): = false;
size(alloc): = n;
bsize(alloc + n - 1): = n
```

Of course, the newly freed block can be inserted into the list based on its size, so that one of the other methods (e.g., best fit, worst fit) can also be used.

The Buddy System

An alternative method of handling the storage management problem without frequent list traversals is to keep separate free lists for blocks of different sizes. Each list contains free blocks of only one specific size. For example, if memory contains 1024 words, it might be divided into 15 blocks: 1 block of 256 words, 2 blocks of 128 words, 4 blocks of 64 words, and 8 blocks of 32 words. Whenever storage is requested, the smallest block whose size is greater than or equal to the size needed is reserved. For example, a request for a block of 97 words is filled by a block of size 128. There are several drawbacks to this scheme. First, space is wasted due to internal fragmentation. (In the example, 31 words of the block are totally unusable.) Second, and more serious, is that a request for a block of size 300 cannot be filled since the largest size maintained is 256. Also, if two blocks of size 150 are needed, the requests cannot be filled even if sufficient contiguous space is available. Thus, the solution is impractical. The source of the impracticality is that free spaces are never combined. However, there is a variation of this scheme that is quite useful. This variation is called the ***buddy system***.

Several free lists consisting of various sized blocks are maintained. Adjacent free blocks of smaller size may be removed from their lists, combined into free blocks of larger size and placed on the larger size free list. These larger blocks can then be used intact to satisfy a request for a large amount of memory or they can be split once more into their smaller constituent blocks to satisfy several smaller requests.

The method outlined next works best on binary computers in which the memory size is an integral power of 2 and in which multiplication and division by two can be performed very efficiently by shifting. Initially, the entire memory of size 2^m is viewed as a single free block. For each power of two between 1 (which equals 2^0) and 2^m, a free list containing blocks of that size is maintained. A block of size 2^i is called an ***i-block***, and the free list containing i-blocks is called the ***i-list***. (In practice, it may be unreasonable to keep free blocks of sizes 1, 2, and 4 so that 8 is the smallest free block size allowed; we will ignore the possibility.) However, it may be (and usually is) the case that some of these free lists are empty. Indeed, initially all the lists except the m-list are empty.

Blocks may be allocated only in sizes 2^k for some integer k between 0 and m. If a request for a block of size n is made, an i-block is reserved where i is the smallest integer such that $n \leq 2^i$. If no i-block is available (the i-list is empty), an $(i + 1)$-block is removed from the $(i + 1)$-list and is split into two equal size ***buddies***. Each of these buddies is an i-block. One of the buddies is allocated and the other remains free and is placed on the i-list. If an $(i + 1)$-block is also unavailable, an $(i + 2)$-block is split into two $(i + 1)$-block buddies, one of which is placed on the $(i + 1)$-list and the other of which is split into two i-blocks. One of these i-blocks is allocated, and the other is placed onto the i-list. If no $(i + 2)$-block is free, this process continues until either an i-block has been allocated or an m-block is found to be unavailable. In the former case, the allocation attempt is successful; in the latter case, a block of proper size is not available.

The buddy system allocation process can best be described as a recursive function $getblock(n)$ that returns the address of the block to be allocated, or the nil pointer if no block of size n is available. An outline of this function follows:

> find the smallest integer i such that $2^i >= n$;
> *if* the i-list is not empty
>   *then begin*
> p: = the address of the first block on the i-list;
> $getblock$: = p;
>   remove the first block from the i-list
>   *end* {then begin}
>   *else* {the i-list is empty}
>   *if* $i = m$
>   *then* $getblock$: = nil
>   *else begin*
> p: = $getblock(2^{i+1})$;
>   *if* $p = nil$
>   *then* $getblock$: = nil
>   *else begin*
>   put the i-block starting at location p
>   on the i-list;
> $getblock$: = $p + 2^i$
>   *end* {else begin}
>   *end* {else begin}

In this outline, if an $(i + 1)$-block starts at location p, then the two i-blocks into which it is split start at locations p and $p + 2^i$. The first of these remains on the free list, and the second is allocated. Each block is created by splitting a block of one size higher. If an $(i + 1)$-block is split into two i-blocks $B1$ and $B2$, then $B1$ and $B2$ are **buddies** of each other. The buddy of an i-block at location p is called the **i-buddy** of p. Note that a block at location p can have several buddies but only one i-buddy.

If an i-block is freed and its i-buddy is already free, the two buddies are combined into the $(i + 1)$-block from which they were initially created. In this way, a larger free block of storage is created to satisfy large requests. If the i-buddy of a newly freed i-block is not free, then the newly freed block is placed directly on the i-list.

Suppose a newly freed i-block has been combined with its previously free i-buddy into an $(i + 1)$-block. It is possible that the $(i + 1)$-buddy of this recombined $(i + 1)$-block is also free. In that case, the two $(i + 1)$-blocks can be recombined further into an $(i + 2)$-block. This process continues until a recombined block is created whose buddy is not free or until the entire memory is combined into a single m-block.

The liberation algorithm can be outlined as a recursive procedure *liberate(alloc, i)* that frees an i-block at location *alloc*.

> *if* ($i = m$) *or* (the i-buddy of alloc is not free)
>> *then* add the i-block at alloc to the i-list
>> *else begin*
>>> remove the i-buddy of *alloc* from the i-list;
>>> combine the i-block at *alloc* with its i-buddy;
>>> $p :=$ the address of the newly formed $(i + 1)$-block;
>>> *liberate*$(p, i + 1)$;
>> *end* {else begin}

Let us refine the outline of *liberate*; we leave the refinement of *getblock* as an exercise for the reader.

There is one obvious question that must be answered. How can the free status of the i-buddy of *alloc* be established? Indeed, how can it be determined whether an i-buddy of *alloc* exists at all? It is quite possible that the i-buddy of *alloc* has been split and part (or all) of it is allocated. Additionally, how can the starting address of the i-buddy of *alloc* be determined? If the i-block at *alloc* is the first half of its containing $(i + 1)$-block, then its i-buddy is at *alloc* $+ 2^i$; if the i-block is the second half of its containing block then its i-buddy is at *alloc* $- 2^i$. How can we determine which is the case?

At this point, it would be instructive to look at some examples. For illustrative purposes, consider an absurdly small memory of 1024 $(= 2^{10})$ words. Figure 10.3.7a illustrates this memory after a request for a block of 100 words has been filled. The smallest power of 2 greater than 100 is 128 $(= 2^7)$. Thus, the entire memory is split into two blocks of size 512; the first is placed on the 9-list and the second is split into two blocks of size 256. The first of these is placed on the 8-list, and the second is split into two blocks of size 128, one of which is placed on the 7-list and the second of which is allocated (block $B1$). At the bottom of the figure, the starting addresses of the blocks on each nonempty i-list are indicated. Make sure that you follow the execution of the functions *getblock* and *liberate* on this and succeeding examples.

Figure 10.3.7b illustrates the sample memory after filling an additional request for 50 words. There is no free 6-block, so the free 7-block at location 768 is split into two 6-blocks. The first 6-block remains free, and the second is allocated as block $B2$. In Figure 10.3.7c three additional 6-blocks have been allocated in the order $B3$, $B4$, and $B5$. When the first request is made, a 6-block at location 768 is free so that no splitting is necessary. The second request forces the 8-block at 512 to be split into two 7-blocks and the second 7-block at 640 to be split into two 6-blocks. The second of these is allocated as $B4$, and when the next request for a 6-block is made, the first is also allocated as $B5$.

Note that in Figure 10.3.7a the block beginning at 768 is a 7-block, while in Figure 10.3.7b, it is a 6-block. Similarly, the block at 512 is an 8-block in Figures 10.3.7a and b, but a 7-block in Figure 10.3.7c. This illustrates that the size of a block cannot be determined from its starting address.

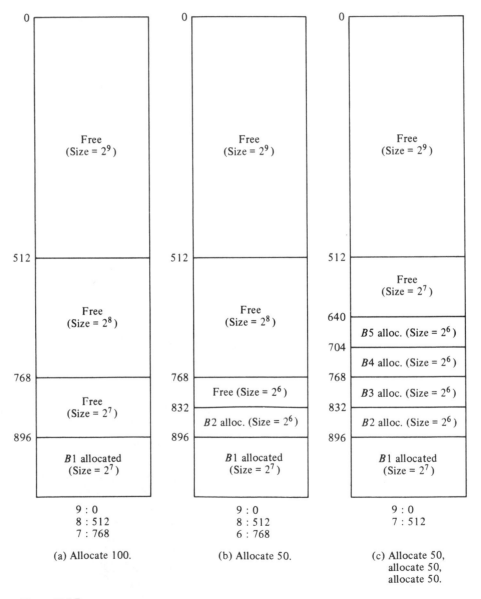

(a) Allocate 100.

(b) Allocate 50.

(c) Allocate 50, allocate 50, allocate 50.

Figure 10.3.7

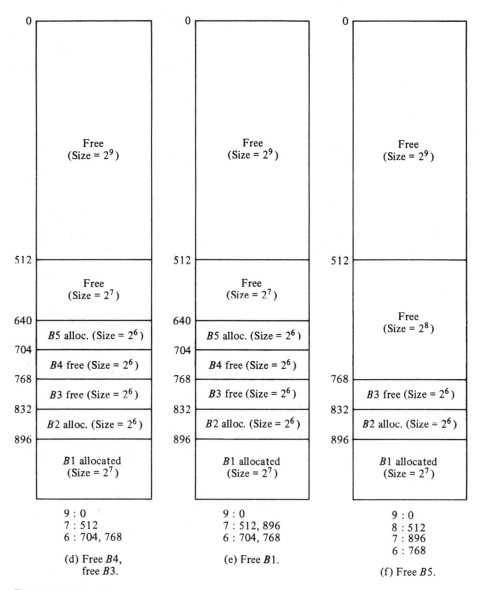

9 : 0
7 : 512
6 : 704, 768

(d) Free $B4$,
   free $B3$.

9 : 0
7 : 512, 896
6 : 704, 768

(e) Free $B1$.

9 : 0
8 : 512
7 : 896
6 : 768

(f) Free $B5$.

Figure 10.3.7 (cont.)

However, as we shall soon see, a block of a given size can start only at certain addresses.

Figure 10.3.7d illustrates the situation after blocks $B4$ and $B3$ have been freed. When block $B4$ at location 704 is freed, its buddy is examined. Since $B4$ is a 6-block that is the second half of the 7-block from which it was split, its buddy is at location $704 - 2^6 = 640$. However, the 6-block at location 640 (which is $B5$) is not free so no combination can take place. When $B3$ is freed, since it is a 6-block and was the first half of its containing 7-block, its 6-buddy at $768 + 2^6 = 832$ must be examined. However, that 6-buddy is allocated so, again, no combination can take place. Notice that two adjacent blocks of the same size (6-blocks $B4$ and $B3$ at 704 and 768) are free but are not combined into a single 7-block. This is because they are not buddies; that is, they were not originally split from the same 7-block. $B4$ can be combined only with its buddy $B5$, and $B3$ can be combined only with its buddy $B2$.

In Figure 10.3.7e, the 7-block $B1$ has been freed. $B1$ is the second half of its 8-block, so its 7-buddy is at $896 - 2^7 = 768$. Although block $B3$ which starts at that location is free, no combination can take place. This is because block $B3$ is not a 7-block, but only a 6-block. This means that the 7-block starting at 768 is split and therefore partially allocated. We see that it is not yet ready for combination. Both the address and the size of a given free block must be considered when making a decision as to whether or not to combine buddies.

In Figure 10.3.7f, the 6-block $B5$ at location 640 is freed. $B5$ is the first half of its containing 7-block so its 6-block is at $640 + 2^6 = 704$. That 6-block (block $B4$) is already free so the two can be combined into a single 7-block at 640. That 7-block is the second half of its containing 8-block, so its 7-buddy is at $640 - 2^7 = 512$. The 7-block at that location is free so that the two 7-blocks can be combined into an 8-block at 512. That 8-block is the first half of its containing 9-block, so its 8-buddy is at $512 + 2^8 = 768$. But the block at location 768 is a 6-block rather than an 8-block, so no further combination can take place.

These examples illustrate that it is necessary to be able to determine whether a given i-block is the first or second half of its containing $(i + 1)$-block in order to compute the location of its i-buddy.

Clearly, there is only one m-block in memory and its starting location is 0. When this block is split, it produces two $(m - 1)$-blocks starting at location 0 and 2^{m-1}. These split into four $(m - 2)$-blocks at locations 0, 2^{m-2}, 2^{m-1}, and $3 * 2^{m-2}$. In general, there are 2^{m-i} i-blocks starting at locations that are integer multiples of 2^i. For example, if $m = 10$ (memory size is 1024), there are $2^{10-6} = 16$ 6-blocks starting at locations 0, 64, 128, 192, 256, 320, 384, 448, 512, 576, 640, 704, 768, 832, 896, and 960. Each of these addresses is an integral multiple of 64 (which is 2^6), from $0 * 64$ to $15 * 64$.

Notice that any address that is the starting location of an i-block is also the starting location of a k-block for all $0 \le k < i$. This is because the i-block can be split into two $(i - 1)$-blocks, the first of which begins at the same location as the i-block. This is consistent with the observation that an integral multiple of 2^i is also an integral multiple of 2^{i-1}. However, the reverse is not necessarily true. A location that is the starting address of an i-block is the starting address of an $(i + 1)$-block only if the i-block is the first half of the $(i + 1)$-block, but not if it is the second half. For example, in

Figure 10.3.7, addresses 640 and 768 begin 7-blocks as well as 6-blocks and 768 begins an 8-block as well. However, addresses 704 and 832 begin 6-blocks but not 7-blocks.

After making these observations, it is easy to determine whether a given i-block is the first or second half of the $(i + 1)$-block from which it was split. If the starting address p of the i-block is evenly divisible by 2^{i+1}, then the block is the first half of an $(i + 1)$-block and its i-buddy is at $p + 2^i$; otherwise, it is the second half of an $(i + 1)$-block, and its buddy is at $p - 2^i$.

We can therefore introduce a function $buddy(p, i)$ that returns the address of the i-buddy of p (we use an auxiliary function $expon(a, b)$ that computes a^b):

if p **mod** $\text{expon}(2, i + 1) = 0$
   then $buddy := p + expon(2, i)$
   else $buddy := p - expon(2, i)$

Now that the address of a newly freed block's i-buddy can be found, how can we determine whether or not that buddy is free? One way of making that determination is to traverse the i-list to see if a block at the desired address is present. If it is, then it can be removed and combined with its buddy. If it is not, then the newly freed i-block can be added to the i-list. Since each i-list is generally quite small (because as soon as two i-buddies are free they are combined into an $(i + 1)$-buddy and removed from the i-list), this traversal is fairly efficient. Furthermore, to implement this scheme, each i-list need not be doubly linked since a block is removed from the i-list only after the list is traversed so that its predecessor is known.

An alternative method that avoids list traversal is to have each block contain a boolean field to indicate whether or not it is allocated. Then when an i-block is freed, it is possible to determine directly whether or not the block beginning at the address of its buddy is already free. However, this flag alone is insufficient. For example, in Figure 10.3.7e, when 7-block $B1$ at location 896 is freed, its buddy's starting address is calculated as 768. The block at 768 is free and its flag would indicate that fact. Yet the two blocks at 768 and 896 cannot be combined because the block at 768 is not a 7-block, but a 6-block whose 6-buddy is allocated. Thus an additional *power* field is necessary in each block. The value of this integer field is the base-2 logarithm of its size (e.g., if the block is of size 2^i, the value of *power* is i). When an i-block is freed, its buddy's address is calculated. If the *power* field at that address is i and if the flag indicates that the buddy is free, the two blocks are combined.

Under this method, the i-lists are required only for the allocation algorithm so that a block of proper size can be found efficiently. However, because blocks are removed from the i-lists without traversing them, the lists must be doubly linked. Thus each free block must contain four fields: *free*, *power*, *prev*, and *next*. The last two are pointers to the previous and next blocks on the i-list. An allocated block need contain only the *flag* field.

We present the second method of liberation, leaving the first to the reader as an exercise. We assume an array of pointers $list[0..m]$ where $list[i]$ points to the first block on the i-list. We also replace the recursive call to *liberate* by a loop in which successively larger blocks are combined with their buddies until a block is formed whose buddy is not free. The algorithm *liberate(alloc, i)* frees an i-block at location *alloc*. For completeness, let us establish that *buddy(p, m)* equals 0. The flag *free* is *true* if the block is free and *false* otherwise.

```
p: = alloc;
bud: = buddy (p, i);
while (i < m) and (free(bud)) and (power(bud) = i)
    do begin  { remove i-buddy of p from the i-list }
            q: = prev(bud);
            if q = nil
              then list [i] : = next(bud)
              else next(q): = next(bud);
            if next(bud) <> nil
              then prev(next(bud)): = q;
            { combine the i-block at p with its buddy }
            if p div expon(2, i + 1) <> 0
              then { the combined block begins at bud }
                  p: = bud;
            i: = i + 1;
            bud: = buddy(p, i)
              { attempt to combine the larger block with its buddy }
        end {while...do begin};
    { add the i-block at p to the i-list }
    q: = list[i] ;
    prev(p): = nil;
    next(p): = q;
    list [i] : = p;
    if q <> nil
      then prev(q): = p;
    { adjust the fields on the i-block }
    power(p): = i;
    free(p) = true
```

Other Buddy Systems

The buddy system that we have just considered is called the **binary buddy system** based on the rule that when an i-block (of size 2^i) is split, two equal sized $(i - 1)$-blocks are created. Similarly, two i-blocks that are buddies can be joined into a single $(i + 1)$-block.

There are, however, other buddy systems in which a large block is not necessarily split into two equal-sized smaller blocks. One such system is called the *Fibonacci buddy system*. The sizes of the blocks in this system are based on the Fibonacci numbers first introduced in Section 3.1. Instead of blocks of size 1, 2, 4, 8, 16, ... as in the case of the binary buddy system, the Fibonacci buddy system uses blocks of size 1, 2, 3, 5, 8, 13, ... When an i-block (the size of an i-block in this system is the ith Fibonacci number) is split into two blocks, one of the blocks is an $(i - 1)$-block, and the other is an $(i - 2)$-block. Thus, for example, a 9-block (of size 34) may split into an 8-block (size 21) and a 7-block (size 13). Similarly, the buddy of an i-block may be either an $(i + 1)$-block or an $(i - 1)$-block. In the former case, recombination produces an $(i + 2)$-block, while in the latter case, an $(i + 1)$-block is produced.

Another alternative buddy system is the *weighted buddy system*. In this scheme, a block of size 2^k is split into two blocks, one of size 2^{k-2} and the other of size $3 * 2^{k-2}$. For example, a block of size 64 splits into two buddies of sizes 16 and 48. Rules for recombination are similar.

The philosophy behind such schemes, in which blocks are split into unequal subblocks, is that requests for storage are usually not for sizes that match those of the blocks in the system. Thus, the next larger size block must be used, with the result that space is wasted within the block. For example, in the binary buddy system, when a request is made for a block of size 10, a block of size 16 will be allocated (resulting in six wasted bytes); in the Fibonacci buddy system, however, a block of size 13 may be allocated (resulting in only three wasted bytes); while in the weighted buddy system, a block of size 12 will be sufficient (resulting in only two wasted bytes). It is not always the case that the Fibonacci system results in less wasted space than the binary system (e.g., a request for a block of size 15), but, in general, allowing blocks of varying sizes will more likely produce a closer fit than will requiring groups of blocks to be of uniform size.

An alternative to the foregoing approach is to combine smaller blocks into larger ones only when necessary. In such a scheme, called a *recombination delaying buddy system*, when a block is freed, it is returned to the list of blocks of its size. When a block of a particular size is required, the list of blocks of that size is searched. If a block of the required size is found, then the search halts successfully; otherwise, a search is made for a pair of blocks of the next smaller size that are buddies. If such a pair exists, then the two blocks are combined to form a single block of the required size. If no such pair exists, then this process is repeated recursively with successively smaller blocks until either a block of the required size can be formed from smaller blocks, so that the search is successful, or until it is determined that the required block cannot be formed from smaller blocks. Blocks of larger sizes will also be searched to determine if a split is feasible. If a block of the desired size cannot be found either by splitting larger blocks or by combining smaller blocks, then the search ends in failure.

The philosophy behind this type of scheme is that smaller blocks are often returned to the available pool only to be called for again. Instead of recombining the smaller blocks into a larger block only to decompose it again, the smaller blocks are retained and are recombined into larger blocks only when blocks of the larger size are necessary. The disadvantage of this approach is that blocks of larger sizes may not be available when there is, in fact, enough memory to satisfy their requests. For example, there may be three i-blocks available, two of which are buddies. If a request for an i-block arrives and one of the i-buddies is used to satisfy this request, then a subsequent request for an $(i + 1)$-block cannot be satisfied. If, on the other hand, the two i-blocks were recombined into an $(i + 1)$-block first, then the request for an i-block would be satisfied from the isolated i-block before an attempt would be made to break up an $(i + 1)$-block. (Of course, it is possible to place the i-block on the i-list in such a way that i-buddies are always at the rear of the list. This prevents the allocation of one of a pair of buddies before an isolated block of the required size is allocated. However, when it is necessary to allocate one of several pairs of buddies, it may be difficult to select the pair that will allow subsequently larger recombinations.)

Yet another variation of the buddy system is the *tailored list buddy system*. In this system, instead of maintaining the lists in blocks as large as possible (the standard system) and instead of not combining buddies until blocks of a larger size are necessary (the recombination delaying system), the blocks are distributed on the various lists in preassigned proportions.

If the relative frequency of requests for blocks of the possible block sizes are known, then memory may be divided initially into blocks of the different sizes according to the given distribution. As blocks are called for and returned to the pool, a record is kept of the actual number of blocks of each block size. When a block is returned to the pool and the number of blocks of that size is as or greater than the number specified by the distribution, then an attempt is made to combine the block into a block of the next larger size. This process is repeated successively until no such recombination is possible or until the number of blocks of each size is not exceeded.

When a block of a particular size is requested and there is no block of the required size, then a block may be formed either by splitting a block of larger size or by recombining several blocks of smaller size. Various allocation strategies can be used in this case. Very often the distribution of requests is not known in advance. In such a case, it is possible to allow the distribution of blocks to stabilize slowly, by maintaining a record of the actual distribution of requests as they arrive. The desired distribution will probably never be achieved exactly, but it can be used as a guide in determining whether and when to recombine blocks.

There are two primary disadvantages to buddy systems. The first is internal fragmentation. For example, in the binary buddy system, only blocks whose sizes are integral powers of 2 can be allocated without waste. This means that a little less than half the storage in each block could be wasted. The other disadvantage is that adjacent free blocks are not combined if they are not buddies. However, simulations have shown that the buddy system

does work well and that once the pattern of memory allocations and liber-
ations stabilizes, splitting and combinations take place infrequently.

EXERCISES

1. Let s be the average size of an allocated block in a system that uses compaction. Let r be the average number of time units between block allocations. Let m be the memory size, f the average percentage of free space, and c the average number of time units between calls on the compaction algorithm. If the memory system is in equilibrium (over a period of time, equal numbers of blocks are allocated as are freed), derive a formula for c in terms of s, r, m, and f.

2. Implement the first-fit, best-fit, and worst-fit methods of storage allocation in Pascal as follows: Write a function *getblock(n)* that returns the address of a block of size n that is available for allocation and modifies the free list appropriately. The function should utilize the following variables:

memsize	the largest address in memory.
memory[0..*memsize*]	an array of integers representing the memory.
freeblock	a pointer to the first location of the first free block on the list.

   The value of *size(p)* may be obtained by the expression *memory*[*p*] and the value of *next(p)* by the expression *memory*[*p* + 1].

3. Revise the first-fit and best-fit algorithms so that if a block on the free list is less than x units larger than a request, the entire block is allocated as is, unsplit. Revise the Pascal implementations of Exercise 2 in a similar manner.

4. Revise the first-fit algorithm and its implementation (see Exercise 2) so that the free list is circular and is modified in each of the following ways:
   (i) The front of the free list is moved up one block after each allocation request.
   (ii) The front of the free list is reset to the block following the block that satisfied the last allocation request.
   (iii) If a block is split in meeting an allocation request, the remaining portion of that block is placed at the rear of the free list.
   What are the advantages and disadvantages of these methods over the method presented in the text? Which of the three methods yields the smallest average search time? Why?

5. Design two liberation algorithms in which a newly freed block is placed on the front of the free list when no combinations can be made. Do not use any additional fields other than *next* and *size*. In the first algorithm, when two blocks are combined, the combined block is moved to the front of the free list; in the second, the combined block remains at the same position in the free list as its free portion was before the combination. What are the relative merits of the two methods?

6. Implement the liberation algorithm presented in the text in which the free list is ordered by increasing memory location. Write a Pascal procedure *liberate(alloc, n)* that uses the variables presented in Exercise 2, where *alloc* is the address of the block to be freed and n is its size. The procedure should modify the free list appropriately.

7. Implement a storage management system by writing a Pascal program that accepts inputs of two types: an allocation request containing an 'A', the amount of memory

requested, and an integer that becomes the identifier of the block being allocated (block 1, block 2, block 3, etc.); and a liberation request containing an 'L' and the integer identifying the block to be liberated. The program should call the routines *getblock* and *liberate* programmed in Exercises 2 and 6.

8. Implement the boundary tag method of liberation as a Pascal procedure, as in Exercise 2 and 6. The values of $size(p)$ and $bsize(p)$ should be obtained by the expression $abs(memory[p])$, $fflag(p)$ and $bflag(p)$ by $(memory[p] > 0)$, $next(p)$ by $memory[p + 1]$, and $prev(p)$ by $memory[p + 2]$.

9. How could the free list be organized to reduce the search time in the best-fit method? What liberation algorithm would be used for such a free list?

10. A storage management system is in *equilibrium* if as many blocks are allocated as are liberated in any given time period. Prove the following about a system in equilibrium.
   (a) The fraction of total storage that is allocated is fairly constant.
   (b) If adjacent free blocks are always combined, then the number of allocated blocks is half the number of free blocks.
   (c) If adjacent free blocks are always combined, and the average size of an allocated block is greater than some multiple of the average size of a free block, then the fraction of memory that is free is greater than $k/(k + 2)$.

11. Present allocation and liberation algorithms for the following systems:
   (a) Fibonacci buddy system.
   (b) weighted buddy system.
   (c) recombination delaying buddy system.
   (d) tailored list buddy system.

12. Refine the outline of *getblock*, which is responsible for allocation in the buddy system, into a nonrecursive algorithm that explicitly manipulates free lists.

13. Prove formally (using mathematical induction) that in the binary buddy system:
   (a) there are 2^{m-i} possible i-blocks.
   (b) the starting address of an i-block is an integer multiple of 2^i.

14. Implement the binary buddy system as a set of Pascal programs.

APPENDIX

This appendix is a compendium of information on Pascal that students may not have seen in an introductory course and which is important in a data structures context. These topics were originally included in the text (primarily in Chapter 1). In the interest of identifying these topics and allowing the familiar or rushed reader to skip them on a first reading, we have placed them in this appendix. The topics are not related to one another and can be covered individually in any order, or assigned as independent reading when convenient.

1. SCALAR DATA TYPES IN PASCAL

The Pascal language contains four basic data types: *integer*, *real*, *boolean*, and *char*. In most computers, these four types are native to the machine's hardware. Section 1.1 describes how integers, reals, and characters can be implemented in hardware. A boolean variable can be implemented by a single bit which has the value 1 to represent *true* and 0 to represent *false*.

There are two other kinds of scalar types in Pascal. (A *scalar* type is a type whose variables each contain only a single value, as opposed to arrays, records, or sets, which are composed of several values.) The first is the *enumeration type*, in which the programmer specifies a set of identifiers as the possible values of objects of the type being defined. For example, the declaration

type fruittype = (apple, orange, pear, banana);

defines an enumeration type *fruittype*. An object of this type can have one of the four constant values *apple*, *orange*, *pear*, *banana*. If we then declare

$$\textbf{var } fruit:\ fruittype;$$

then *fruit* is an object of this type and the assignment statement

$$fruit:=\ pear$$

sets *fruit* to one of the four allowable values. The statement

$$\textbf{if } fruit = orange \textbf{ then}...$$

tests whether the value of *fruit* is another of these allowable values. An object of an enumeration type has one of several specifically defined values. Enumeration types are useful for representing any of a myriad of real-world concepts (such as colors, days of the week, job titles, etc.) using names that are meaningful in the context (such as "red," "Tuesday," "supervisor") instead of representing them by some artificial construct (such as using the integer 1 to represent red, 2 to represent blue, etc.).

Because enumeration types are not native to the hardware of any computer, a set of routines must exist to implement these types and the Pascal operations defined on them. These routines are already present in the software of the Pascal system, so that the Pascal programmer need understand only the Pascal definitions of such data types and need not worry about implementation details. It is, nevertheless, instructive to consider the subject of implementation.

How are enumeration data types implemented? The simplest method is by assigning consecutive integers, beginning with 0, to each value of an enumeration type. For example, in the case of *fruittype*, *apple* is represented by 0, *orange* by 1, *pear* by 2, and *banana* by 3. Thus the assignment statement

$$fruit:=\ pear$$

places the integer value 2 into the storage location named *fruit*, and the statement

$$\textbf{if } fruit = orange \textbf{ then}...$$

tests whether the contents of that storage location represent the integer 1.

However, the programmer need not be concerned with these implementation details. As far as he or she is concerned, the value of the variable *fruit* can only be *apple*, *orange*, *pear*, or *banana*.

The second Pascal scalar type that is not one of the four basic types is the **subrange type**. For any scalar type *t* except *real*, it is possible to define a new type as a subrange of the values of *t*. For example, consider the following subrange-type definitions

$$\begin{aligned}\textbf{type } digit &= 0..9;\\ grade &= \text{'a'..'f'};\\ newfruit &= apple..pear;\end{aligned}$$

Each of these types represents a subset of the values of its parent type. Thus *digit* represents the set of *integer* values 0, 1, 2, 3, 4, 5, 6, 7, 8, and 9; *grade* represents the set of *char* values 'a', 'b', 'c', 'd', 'e', and 'f' (assuming that no other characters exist between 'a' and 'f' in the character representation of the particular computer being used; this is true of almost every computer in existence); and *newfruit* represents the set of *fruittype* values *apple*, *orange*, and *pear*.

A subrange type may be used for two reasons. The first is that the programmer may know that a certain variable can assume values only from a given range. By declaring this range explicitly using a subrange type, the machine can check that all values assigned to the variable are indeed within the specified range. In this way, the computer is able to detect a very common programming error.

The second reason for using a subrange type is to save space. A variable of type *integer* uses as many bits as is necessary to represent the largest integer under that particular Pascal implementation. (This largest integer is the value of the standard constant identifier *maxint*.) However, a variable whose range of possible values is smaller need not use as many bits.

The scalar types, excluding the type *real*, are known as **ordinal types**. For any ordinal type, the standard function *ord* yields the position of a value within the set of values allowed by the type. For example, *ord(pear)* is 2, while *ord(banana)* is 3, since the first value of an enumeration type is considered to be at position 0. If x is a character, *ord(x)* is an integer representation of that character. One of the rules of Pascal is that the characters '0' through '9' must be represented by successive integers, so that *ord(x)* − *ord('0')* for any digit character x yields the numeric value of that digit. However, the values of *ord('a')*, *ord('b')*, and so on need not be successive integers, although it must be true that *ord('a')* < *ord('b')* < *ord('c')*, and so on. The function *chr(x)*, where x is an integer, yields the character c such that $x = ord(c)$. If x is an integer, *ord(x)* equals x. If a value is a member of a subrange type, applying the *ord* function to it yields its position within the host type rather than the subrange type.

Two other functions defined on ordinal types are *pred* and *succ. pred(x)* is the predecessor of x within its host type, and *succ(x)* is the successor of x. These functions are not applicable to extreme values of a given type, so that *succ(maxint)* or *pred(apple)* are undefined.

2. USING ONE-DIMENSIONAL ARRAYS

Beginning students often have difficulty in determining when a one-dimensional array is required. In general, a one-dimensional array is used when it is necessary to keep a large number of items in memory and reference all the items in a uniform manner. Let us see how these two requirements apply to practical situations.

Suppose that we wish to read 100 integers, find their average, and determine by how much each integer deviates from the average. The following program accomplishes this:

```
program aver(input, output);
const numelts = 100;
type index = 1..numelts;
var num: array [index] of integer;        {array of numbers}
    i: index;
    total: integer;              {  sum of the numbers  }
    avg: real;                   {average of the numbers }
    diff: real;                  {difference between each}
                                 {number and the average}
begin
    total:= 0;
    for i:= 1 to numelts
        do begin {read the numbers into the array and add them}
                read(num[i]);
                total:= total + num[i]
            end {for...do begin};
        {compute the average}
        avg:= total/numelts;
        {print heading}
        writeln('number ', ' difference');
        {print each number and its difference}
        for i:= 1 to numelts
            do begin
                    diff:= num[i] - avg;
                    writeln(num[i], diff)
                end {for...do begin};
        writeln('average is: ', avg)
end {program aver}.
```

This program uses two groups of 100 numbers. The first group is the set of input integers and is represented by the array *num*; the second group is the set of differences that are the successive values assigned to the variable *diff* in the second loop. The question arises as to why an array is used to hold all the values of the first group simultaneously, but only a single variable is used to hold one value of the second group at a time.

The answer is quite simple. Each difference is computed and printed and is never needed again. Thus the variable *diff* can be reused for the difference of the next integer and the average. However, the original integers which are the values of the array *num* must all be kept in memory. Although each can be added into *total* as it is input, it must be retained until after the average is computed in order for the program to compute the difference between it and the average. Therefore, an array is used.

Of course, 100 separate variables could have been used to hold the integers. The advantage of an array, however, is that it allows the programmer to declare only a single identifier and yet obtain a large amount of space. Furthermore, in conjunction with the *for* loop, it also allows the programmer to reference each element of the group in a uniform manner instead of forcing him to code a statement such as

read(num1, num2, num3, ..., num99, num100)

A particular element of an array may be retrieved through its index. For example, suppose that a company is using a program in which an array is declared by

var sales: **array** [1960..1979] **of** real;

The array will hold sales figures for a 20-year period. Suppose that each line input to the program contains a year and a sales figure for that year and it is desired to read the sales figure into the appropriate element of the array. This can be accomplished by executing the statement

read(yr, sales[yr])

within a loop. In this statement, a particular element of the array is accessed directly by using its index. Consider the situation if 20 variables $s1960$, $s1961$, ... , $s1979$ had been declared. Then even after executing *read(yr)* to set *yr* to the integer representing the year, the sales figure could not be read into the proper variable without coding something like

if yr = 1960 **then** read(s1960);
if yr = 1961 **then** read(s1961);

.
.
.

if yr = 1979 **then** read(s1979)

This is bad enough with 20 elements—imagine the inconvenience if there were a hundred or a thousand.

3. PACKED ARRAYS

The usual implementation of arrays often leads to a large waste of storage space. For example, consider an array of characters implemented on a computer whose byte size is 8 and whose word size is 32. That is, a single character is represented by 8 bits, but the unit of storage most commonly accessed by the set of hardware instructions on the machine is 32 bits. A Pascal character variable on such a machine is often implemented by reserving an entire 32-bit word, although only the last 8-bit byte of the word is used to contain the character. The reason for doing this is that on this machine it is faster and simpler to manipulate an entire word than a single byte. Thus we are willing to forgo some space efficiency in the interests of time efficiency.

But consider what happens when an array of 100 characters is declared. Instead of reserving 100 bytes, 100 words or 400 bytes are reserved. Although we might have been willing to put up with 3 bytes of unused space in implementing a single character, we may not be willing to waste 300 bytes. The situation is even worse in the case of an array of booleans. Only a single bit is required to hold the value *true* or *false*, but an entire word might be reserved for each element of the array, leading to a waste of over 95% of the storage used.

For this reason, Pascal permits the declaration of a *packed array*. For example, a 100-element character array may be declared by

var ch: **packed array**[1..100] **of** char;

In implementing this array on our sample computer, Pascal may pack four elements into each word. Thus the entire array will occupy 25, rather than 100, words. Similarly, an array declared by

var b: **packed array**[1..256] **of** boolean;

might occupy only eight words, rather than 256. Of course, a price is paid for the space efficiency obtained by the packing process. Each access to an element of an array now involves locating the word containing the element and extracting the element from that word. If every element of an array is accessed in turn, this can be a very expensive time overhead. For example, $ch[1]$, $ch[2]$, $ch[3]$, and $ch[4]$ might all be kept in the same computer word. When $ch[1]$ is accessed, that word is located, and the first byte is extracted. Then $ch[2]$ is accessed, so the same word is located again and the second byte is extracted. The process is repeated for $ch[3]$ and $ch[4]$. It would be much more economical if the word were "unpacked" all at once; that is, the single word is located and its four bytes extracted and saved for later use in a single operation.

To realize this time savings for accessing consecutive elements of an array, Pascal provides two standard procedures: *pack* and *unpack*. Let t be a type identifier, let a be an array declared by

var a: **array**[m..n] **of** t;

and let b be a packed array declared by

var b: **packed array**[p..q] **of** t;

where m, n, p, and q are integer constants such that $n - m \geq q - p$. Then $pack(a, i, b)$ is equivalent to the statement

for j:= p **to** q
    do a[j] := a[j - p + i]

and *unpack*(*b*, *a*, *i*) is equivalent to the statement

> **for** j := p **to** q
>> **do** a[j − p + i] := b[j]

That is, *pack*(*a*, *i*, *b*) sets the elements of the packed array *b* to consecutive elements of the unpacked array *a* beginning with the *i*th element of *a*. Similarly, *unpack*(*b*, *a*, *i*) sets the elements of the unpacked array *a* beginning with *a*'s *i*th element to the consecutive elements of the packed array *b* until the elements of *b* are exhausted.

Packed arrays can be used in the same way as unpacked arrays. Whether or not a given array is packed does not affect the meaning of a program; it affects only its efficiency. The only restriction is that an element of a packed array cannot be passed as a variable parameter to a function or procedure. Note that this means that if *a* is a packed array of characters, the call *read*(*a*[*i*]) may be invalid since it involves passing an element of a packed array as a variable parameter. You should check whether this is true for your Pascal compiler. If it is, you can use the two statements *read*(*cb*); *a*[*i*] := *cb* instead.

Many versions of Pascal implement any array of characters or booleans as a packed array to save space. For example, in a machine in which a byte can be accessed as easily as a word, there is no advantage to keeping one character per word. Several characters can be packed in a word, and each can be accessed quickly. In such a version, there is no advantage to the Pascal programmer in explicitly declaring a character array to be packed. Other versions of Pascal ignore any packed declarations completely and implement all arrays as unpacked. The option of using unpacked and packed arrays to implement time-efficient and space-efficient alternative methods of representing arrays is available to any Pascal implementor as part of the language. However, the compiler designer is free to ignore the option as long as the meaning of Pascal programs is preserved. Thus it is important for the programmer to determine exactly how the compiler treats packed and unpacked arrays and to program accordingly. Some nonstandard versions of Pascal that do not differentiate between the implementations of packed and unpacked arrays or that automatically convert betwen packed and unpacked representations do not include the procedures *pack* and *unpack*. Examples of such versions are UCSD Pascal and Turbo Pascal.

4. ARRAYS AS PARAMETERS

A parameter of a Pascal procedure or function must be declared with a type identifier. This type identifier can be a basic type (such as *integer* or *char*) or it may have been previously defined. For example, the following procedure headings are invalid:

> **procedure** proc(i: 1..10);
>
> **procedure** proc2(a: **array**[1..10] **of** integer);

Instead, we can define

```
type index = 1..10;
    atype = array [index] of integer;
```

and write

```
procedure proc(i: index);

procedure proc2(a: atype);
```

In Pascal, the upper and lower bounds of an array are part of its type and must be specified at the time the program is written. An array parameter must have its type explicitly declared, so that a procedure can accept only one type of array with fixed upper and lower bounds. For example, consider the following function to compute the average of the elements of an array:

```
const alength = 100;
type atype = array [1..alength] of real;

function avg(a: atype): real;
var i: 1..alength;
    sum: real;
begin
    sum:= 0;
    for i:= 1 to alength
        do sum:= sum + a[i];
    avg:= sum/alength
end {function avg};
```

The function can compute only the average of 100 numbers; a different function is needed to compute the average of a 10- or 50-element array. Of course, since we used the constant *alength* consistently for the array size, it is easy to modify the program to work on a smaller or larger array by simply modifying the constant definition. However, the same function can never be applied to arrays of different sizes in the same program. This is considered to be one of the major drawbacks of the Pascal language. (One version of the Pascal standard allows this restriction to be relaxed.) See the end of Section 5 for a discussion of this feature.) Other languages allow the size of an array parameter to be determined at the time a procedure is called, and that size can vary from one call to another. The reason for this restriction in Pascal is efficiency. It is easier to implement the parameter passing and access mechanism if the size of the array is known at the time the program is compiled.

What, then, should the Pascal programmer do if he or she requires a procedure to accept different-sized groups of elements at different points in the program? One solution is to write several versions of the procedure, one for each size needed. This is highly impractical, for several reasons. First, the work of writing the different versions and compiling a longer program is excessive. Second, each size array will have its own type. Therefore, a separate array variable must be declared for each group of elements to be passed. This wastes an unacceptable amount of storage.

A far better solution is to reserve an array large enough to hold the largest group of elements and include an additional parameter to indicate the number of elements being passed in this particular call. For example, the following function averages a varying-sized group of elements. A type identifier for the array's index type is defined by

type index = 1..alength;

The function itself can be written as follows:

```
function avg2(a: atype; n: index): real;
var i: index;
    sum: real;
begin
    sum:= 0;
    for i:= 1 to n
        do sum:= sum + a[i];
    avg2:= sum/n
end {function avg2};
```

The second parameter, n, specifies the number of elements of the array to be averaged. Another proposed solution to this problem is discussed at the end of Section 5.

If the number of elements needed in a particular situation depends on the input, the Pascal programmer must estimate the maximum number that will ever be required and declare an array of that size. If the program is used repetitively in a production environment, it will eventually be presented with input for which the estimate is not large enough and will fail. On the other hand, in most cases the estimate is a gross exaggeration and all the extra space in the array is wasted. Unfortunately, there is no remedy for this situation in standard Pascal, which does not allow the size of an array to be determined dynamically during execution. In such a case, a programmer should use a linked list (as presented in Chapters 4 and 5) instead of an array. Some Pascal implementations do allow nonstandard dynamic arrays.

5. VALUE AND VARIABLE PARAMETERS

When one procedure calls another, information is passed between the two through parameters. The parameters that appear in the calling procedure are called *actual parameters* or *arguments*; those that appear in the heading of the called procedure are called *formal parameters*, or simply *parameters*. There are two methods of passing data as parameters in Pascal: as *value parameters* or as *variable parameters*. An argument to a value parameter may be any expression, including a constant, a variable, an arithmetic expression, an array, or an array element. The argument is evaluated before the procedure is called, and the resulting value is used by the called procedure as the initial value of the formal parameter. Any change in the value of the formal parameter within the called procedure does not affect the value of any other variable in the program. Thus a value parameter is a local variable of the called procedure. Its purpose is to input a value to the procedure.

A variable parameter is identified by the keyword *var* preceding its declaration in the procedure heading. An argument passed to a variable parameter must be a variable; it cannot be constant or an arithmetic expression. However, the argument may be an array variable or an element of an unpacked array. (As previously noted, an element of a packed array may not be passed as a variable parameter.) The formal parameter references the same memory location as the argument. Thus any change in the formal parameter in the called procedure represents a change in the variable argument being passed. A variable parameter may serve to input a value to the called procedure (e.g., if its value is used but never changed), or to output a value from the called procedure to the calling procedure (e.g., if its value is set by the called procedure), or to both input and output a value (e.g., if its value is used by the called procedure and then changed by it). Note that an argument passed to a variable parameter need not have been initialized before the procedure is called if the purpose of the procedure is simply to set the value of its variable parameter. However, an argument passed to a value parameter must have been initialized before the call.

Generally, a value parameter is used when it is desired to simply input a value to a procedure. The benefit of using a value parameter rather than a variable parameter in such a situation is that the argument being passed is protected against change by the called procedure. If some fact is known about the value of the argument before the call (e.g., that its value is positive), that fact remains true after the call, regardless of the actions of the called routine.

If a routine computes a single scalar value, the routine can be written as a function returning that value rather than as a procedure that places the value in a variable parameter. However, if a routine computes more than one value, it is stylistically preferable to pass two variable parameters and code the routine as a procedure rather than to use a function returning one value and assigning the other value to a variable parameter.

Since an array cannot be returned as the value of a function, it should be passed as a variable parameter to a procedure if it is being initialized or modified. Even when an array is not being modified but serves only as input to a computation, it is often a good idea to pass it as a variable rather than a value parameter. The reason for this is efficiency. To ensure that the value of the argument to a value parameter is not changed, that value is copied into a new portion of memory reserved for the value parameter. In the case of a scalar value, the time needed for the copying and the extra space needed for the copy are negligible. In addition, access to a value parameter is usually faster than is access to a variable parameter. (This is because the address of the copy used to access a value parameter can be determined at compile time or load time, whereas the address of the variable passed to a variable parameter varies from call to call and must be determined at execution time.) However, copying an entire array may take quite a bit of time, and the extra space needed for another copy of an array may be considerable. Therefore, in the interest of efficiency, it is often a good idea to pass an array as a variable parameter.

In standardizing Pascal, two standard versions of Pascal were defined. *Level* **0** Pascal, the version we have been using in this book, requires the size of an array parameter to be fixed. *Level* **1** Pascal introduces a new kind of variable array parameter that allows a function or procedure to operate on arrays of different sizes. The new kind of parameter, called a *conformant array parameter*, is best illustrated by an example. The following function returns the average of any integer array whose index type is a subrange of the type *integer*.

```
function avg3 (var a: array [low..high: integer] of integer): real;
var i: integer;
    sum: real;
begin
    sum:=0;
    for i:= low to high
        do sum:= sum + a[i];
    avg3 := sum/(high - low + 1)
end {function avg3};
```

Suppose the main program contained the declaration

```
var x: array [1..10] of integer;
    y: array [1..100] of integer;
    z: array [-100..100] of integer;
    i: integer;
    xav, yav, zav: real;
```

and the statements

```
for i:= 1 to 10
    do read (x[i]);
for i:= 1 to 100
    do read (y[i]);
for i:= -100 to 100
    do read (z[i]);
xav:= avg3 (x);
yav:= avg3 (y);
zav:= avg3 (z);
writeln (xav, yav, zav)
```

The first three statements read 10 numbers into the array *x*, 100 numbers into the array *y*, and 201 numbers into the array *z*. When *avg3* is called with argument *x*, the identifiers *low* and *high* denote the lower and upper bounds of the array *x*. That is, *low* equals 1 and *high* equals 10. Thus the *for* loop in the function adds the 10 values of the array *x*. When *avg3* is called with the argument *y*, the identifiers *low* and *high* denote the bounds of the array *y* and, therefore, equal 1 and 100, respectively. *avg3* returns the average of the 100 elements of *y*. Similarly, when *avg3* is called with argument *z*, *low* equals −100, *high* equals 100 and *avg3* returns the average of the 201 elements of *z*.

The programs of the text that could best take advantage of this feature are the sorting routines of Chapter 7. In Section 7.2, we introduced conventions for the sorting routines of that chapter. The constant *numelts* was the size of the largest array to be sorted. An array passed to a sorting routine was declared to be of type *array* [1..*numelts*] *of integer*. A smaller group of elements could be sorted by specifying a parameter *n* between 1 and *numelts* to the sorting routine which would sort the elements in positions 1 through *n*. The disadvantages of this approach are obvious. If an array is logically of size *n*, there should be no reason that it must be declared to be of size *numelts* or copied into the first *n* elements of a different array. Using a conformant array parameter, we can eliminate *n* as a parameter. For example, the bubble sort of Section 7.2 could be coded as follows:

```
procedure bubble (var x: array [low..high: integer] of integer);
var pass, j, hold: integer;
    intchange: boolean;
begin {procedure bubble}
    intchange:= true;
    pass:= low;
    while (pass < high) and (intchange)
        do begin
            intchange:= false;
            for j:= low to high − pass + low − 1
                do if x[j] > x[j + 1]
                    then begin
                        intchange:= true;
                        hold:= x[j];
                        x[j]:= x[j + 1];
                        x[j + 1]:= hold
                    end {then begin};
            pass:= pass + 1
        end {while...do begin}
end {procedure bubble};
```

A conformant array parameter may not be a value parameter even if the array is not modified by the calleded routine.

Many Pascal compilers, particularly compilers on personal computers, do not implement the conformant array parameters of level 1 Pascal but instead incorporate one of several different, nonstandard, methods of allowing a procedure to accept array parameters of varying size.

6. RECORDS IN PASCAL

In this section we review some highlights of records in Pascal. A record is a group of items in which each item is identified by its own *field identifier*. For example, consider the following type definition:

          type nametype = **record**
                first: **packed array**[1..10] **of** char;
                midinit: char;
                last: **packed array**[1..20] **of** char
          end;

This definition creates a record type *nametype* containing three fields of different types: *first*, *midinit*, and *last*. Two of the fields are arrays of characters; the third is a single character.

Once a record type has been defined, a variable of that type may be declared. For example, we may declare

        var sname, ename: nametype;

sname and *ename* are both variables of type *nametype*. Each consists of an array of characters representing a first name, a single character representing a middle initial, and an array of characters representing a last name. We could have specified the record type directly in the variable declaration as follows:

        var sname, ename: **record**
                first: **packed array**[1..10] **of** char;
                midinit: char;
                last: **packed array**[1..20] **of** char
        end;

However, it is recommended that a type identifier be declared for each record type. This simplifies the declaration of several variables with the same record type. It also enables a record type to appear in the parameter list of a function or procedure, where only a type identifier is permitted.

Once a variable has been declared as a record, each item (or *field*) within that variable may be accessed by specifying the variable name and the item's field identifier separated by a period. Thus the statement

        write(sname.first)

can be used to print the first name in the record *sname*, while the statement

        ename.midinit:= 'm'

can be used to set the middle initial in the record *ename* to the letter *m*. If a field of a record is an array, a subscript may be used to access a particular element of the array, as in

for i:= 1 **to** 20
    do sname.last[i] := ename.last[i]

Note that this statement is equivalent to the statement

sname.last:= ename.last

Two records of the same type may participate in an assignment, as in

sname:= ename

which is equivalent to

sname.first:= ename.first;
sname.midinit:= ename.midinit;
sname.last:= ename.last

However, a record (as a whole) may not participate in any other operation. Thus, if a record type *r* consisted of three integer fields, it is not possible to add the three fields of one variable of that type to the corresponding fields of another variable of that type in a single statement. Instead, each field of the two variables must be added separately.

A record type may be a (value or variable) parameter to a procedure or function. For example, the following function prints a name in a neat format and returns the number of characters printed.

```
function writename(name: nametype): integer;
var count, i: integer;
begin
    writeln;
    count:= 0;
    for i:= 1 to 10
        do if name.first[i] <> ' '
            then begin
                    write(name.first[i] );
                    count:= count + 1
                end {then begin};
    write(' ');
    count:= count + 1;
    if name.midinit <> ' '
        then begin
                write(name.midinit, '.', ' ');
                count:= count + 3
            end {then begin};
```

```
        for i:= 1 to 20
            do if name.last[i] <> ' '
                then begin
                        write(name.last[i]);
                        count:= count + 1
                    end {then begin};
        writename:= count
    end {function writename};
```

The following table illustrates the effects of the statement $x := $ *writename(sname)* on two different values of *sname*:

value of *sname.first*:	'allen '	'carl '
value of *sname.midinit*:	'j'	' '
value of *sname.last*:	'schreier '	'markowitz '
printed output:	allen j. schreier	carl markowitz
value of x:	17	14

Similarly, the statement $x := $ *writename(ename)* would print the values of *ename*'s fields and assign the number of characters printed to x.

Although a record type may appear as the type of a parameter, it may not appear as the type of the value returned by a function. Thus a function header such as

function transname(name: nametype): nametype;

is invalid. Instead, the function should be transformed into a procedure with a variable parameter, as in

procedure transname(inname: nametype; **var** outname: nametype);

A field of a record type may be declared using any other type, including another record type. For example, given the foregoing definition of *nametype* and the following type definition of *addrtype*.

```
type addrtype = record
            straddr: packed array[1..40] of char;
            city: packed array[1..10] of char;
            state: packed array[1..2] of char;
            zip: packed array[1..5] of '0'..'9'
        end;
```

we may define a new type *nmadtype* by

```
type nmadtype = record
            name: nametype;
            address: addrtype
        end;
```

If we declare two variables

> **var** nmad1, nmad2: nmadtype;

then the following are examples of valid statements:

> nmad1:= nmad2;
> nmad1.name:= nmad2.name;
> nmad1.address.zip:= nmad2.address.zip;
> nmad1.name.first:= nmad2.name.city

As a further example, we may define two record types, describing an employee and a student, respectively:

```
type employee = record
            nameaddr: nmadtype;
            position: record
                    deptno: packed array[1..3] of '0'..'9';
                    jobtitle: packed array[1..20] of char
                end;
            salary: real;
            numdep: integer; {number of dependents}
            hplan: boolean;   { is employee a health }
                              {    plan member?      }
            datehired: record
                    month: 1..12;
                    day: 1..31;
                    year: 1900..2000
                end
        end;
    student = record
            nmad: nmadtype;
            gpindx: real;      {    grade point index    }
            credits: integer;  {number of credits earned}
            dateadm: record    {    date admitted      }
                    month: 1..12;
                    day: 1..31;
                    year: 1900..2000
                end
        end;
var e: employee;
    s: student;
```

A statement to give a 10% raise to an employee if his grade-point index as a student is above 3.0 is the following:

```
if (e.nameaddr.name.first = s.nmad.name.first) and
    (e.nameaddr.name.midinit = s.nmad.name.midinit) and
    (e.nameaddr.name.last = s.nmad.name.last)
then if s.gpindx > 3.0
        then e.salary:= 1.10 * e.salary
```

This statement first ensures that the employee record and the student record refer to the same person by comparing their names. Note that we cannot simply write

> if e.nmaddr.name = s.nmad.name
>   **then**...

since two records cannot be compared for equality in a single operation in Pascal.

Note the redefinition of a date record as a subrecord of both the student and employee record types. As previously mentioned, if we had earlier defined a date type by

> **type** datetype = **record**
>   month: 1..12;
>   day: 1..31;
>   year: 1900..2000
>   **end**;

both the fields *datehired* and *dateadm* could have been declared as being of type *datetype*.

You may have noticed that we used two different type identifiers *nameaddr* and *nmad* for the name/address fields of the *employee* and *student* records, respectively. It is not necessary to do so and the same identifiers can be reused, as we shall see in Section 8. In fact, the identifiers *month*, *day*, and *year* are used in two contexts, within the field *datehired* of *employee* and *dateadm* of *student*.

7. ARRAYS OF RECORDS

We have already seen that a field of a record may be an array or another record. Similarly, a record type may serve as the base type of an array.

For example, if the types *employee* and *student* are defined as earlier, we can declare two arrays of employee and student records as follows:

> **var** e: **array**[1..100] **of** employee;
>   s: **array**[1..100] **of** student;

The salary of the fourteenth employee is referenced by e[14].*salary*, and his last name is referenced by e[14].*nameaddr.name.last*. Similarly, the admission year of the first student is s[1].*dateadm.year*.

As a further example, we present a procedure used at the start of a new year to give a 10% raise to all employees with more than 10 years seniority and a 5% raise to all others. First, we must define a new type:

> **type** empset = **array**[1..100] **of** employee;

The procedure now follows:

```
procedure raise(var e: empset);
const thisyear = ... ;
var i: 1..100;
begin
     for i:= 1 to 100
          do if e[i].datehired.year < thisyear – 10
               then e[i].salary:= 1.10 * e[i].salary
               else  e[i].salary:= 1.05 * e[i].salary
end {procedure raise};
```

As another example, suppose that we add an additional field, *sindex*, to the definition of the *employee* record type. This field contains an integer between 1 and 100 and indicates the student record (in the array *s*) of the particular employee. Let us declare *sindex* (within the *employee* record) as follows:

```
type employee = record
                    nameaddr: nmadtype;
                             ...
                    datehired: ... ;
                    sindex: 1..100
               end;
```

The number of credits earned by employee *i* when he was a student can then be referenced by *s[e[i].sindex].credits*.

The following function can be used to give a 10% raise to all employees whose grade-point index was above 3.0 as a student and to return the number of such employees. Note that we no longer have to compare an employee name to a student name to ascertain that their records represent the same person (although those names should be equal if they do). Instead, the field *sindex* can be used directly to access the appropriate student record for an employee. We assume the two type definitions that precede the function:

```
type empset = array[1..100] of employee;
     stset = array[1..100] of student;
function raise2(var e: empset; s: stset): integer;
var j, i, count: 0..100;
begin
     count:= 0;
     for i:= 1 to 100
          do begin
                    j:= e[i].sindex;
                    if s[j].gpindx > 3.0
                         then begin
                                   count:= count + 1;
                                   e[i].salary:= 1.10 * e[i].salary
                              end {then begin}
               end {for...do begin};
     raise2:= count
end {function raise2};
```

Very often, a large array of records is used to contain an important data table for a particular application. There is generally only one table for each such array-of-record type. The student table *s* and the employee table *e* of the previous discussion are good examples of such data tables. In such cases, the unique tables are often used as global variables rather than as parameters, with a large number of procedures and functions accessing them. This increases efficiency by eliminating the overhead of parameter passing, especially if the tables are value parameters. We could easily rewrite the function *raise2* to access *s* and *e* as global variables rather than as parameters by simply changing the function header to

function raise2: integer;

The body of the function need not be changed, assuming that the tables *s* and *e* are declared in the outer program.

8. SCOPE OF IDENTIFIERS

There are many different kinds of identifiers in Pascal. Constant identifiers and type identifiers are defined by constant and type definitions beginning with the keywords ***const*** and ***type***, respectively. Variable identifiers, procedure identifiers, and function identifiers are declared by variable procedure, and function declarations beginning with the keywords ***var***, ***procedure***, and ***function***, respectively. Labels are declared by label declarations beginning with the keyword ***label***. Parameter identifiers are declared in a function or procedure heading.

The *scope* of a definition or declaration (sometimes called the scope of an identifier or label) is that part of the program text in which an occurrence of the identifier (or label) refers to the same object as in the definition or declaration. The scope of all the identifiers listed is the block in which the identifier (or label) was defined or declared. (By a *block*, we mean a program, function, or procedure.) However, if the identifier (or label) is redefined or redeclared in an inner block, the inner block is excluded from the scope of the definition or declaration in the outer block. An identifier defined or declared in a block is called *local* to that block. An identifier defined or declared in an outer block and not redefined or redeclared in an inner block is called *global* to the inner block. (Note that a procedure or function name is considered to be declared in the surrounding block, whereas parameter identifiers are considered to be declared in the procedure or function block. The type identifiers used to declare parameters and the returned value of a function are occurrences of identifiers that must have been defined in a surrounding block.) An identifier used as a constant, type, variable, parameter, function, or procedure may not be defined or declared twice within a single block.

To illustrate these rules, consider the following program.

```
1  program sample;
2  var i: integer;
3  procedure proc1;
4  var i: integer;
5  procedure proc2;
        {no declaration of i in proc2}
6  begin {procedure proc2}
7      i:= i + 2
8  end {procedure proc2};

9  begin {procedure proc1}
10      i:= 0;
11      proc2;
12      writeln(i)
13 end {procedure proc1};

14 procedure proc3;
        {no declaration of i in proc3}
15 procedure proc4;
16 var i: integer;
17 begin {procedure proc4}
18      i:= 4
19 end {procedure proc4};

20 begin {procedure proc3}
21      i:= i + 3;
22      writeln(i);
23      proc4;
24      writeln(i)
25 end {procedure proc3};
26 begin {program sample}
27      i:= 12;
28      proc1;
29      writeln(i);
30      proc3;
31      writeln(i)
32 end {program sample}.
```

The identifier *i* is declared in three places in this program: once in the main program *sample*, once in the procedure *proc*1, and once in the procedure *proc*4. Since the identifier is not declared twice in the same block, the declarations are valid.

Let us determine the scope of each of the three declarations. The *i* declared in the program *sample* (line 2) includes the heading and body of that program (lines 1–2, 26–32) in its scope. Since *i* is redeclared in procedure *proc*1 (line 4), all of that procedure (lines 3–13) is excluded from the scope of the first declaration. Since *proc3* does not include a redeclaration of *i*, and *sample* includes *proc3* between its opening and closing statements, the header and body of *proc3* (lines 14, 20–25) are included in the scope of the first declaration. *proc4*, however, does include a declaration of *i* (line 16), so that it (lines 15–19) is excluded from the scope of the first declaration. Thus the scope of *i* declared in line 2 is lines 1–2, 14, 20–25, and 26–32.

The scope of the second *i*, declared in line 4, may similarly be determined as the entire *proc1* (lines 3–13). The scope of the third *i*, declared in line 16, is all of *proc4* (lines 15–19).

Let us see what happens when *sample* is executed. Execution begins with line 27, where the *i* declared in line 2 is initialized to 12. In line 28, *proc1* is called. This transfers execution to the body of *proc1* at line 10. However, before the body of *proc1* is executed, the local variables of the procedure are **allocated.** By this we mean that new memory space is set aside for variables declared in *proc1* (such as *i* in line 4). Any references to *i* are now to the local variable declared in line 4 rather than the variable declared in line 2. Since memory has been allocated to this variable, it must be initialized. This is done in line 10, where *i* is set to 0. Note that it would be illegal to use the value of *i* in line 10 without initializing it. Note, also, that the assignment of line 10 does not change the value of the *i* declared in line 2, which retains the value 12. There is no way to reference this value within the body of *proc1* since *i* is redeclared.

In line 11, *proc2* is called. *i* is not redeclared in *proc2*, so that any references to *i* in the body of *proc2* are to the *i* declared in the surrounding block (*proc1*). Thus line 7 increases the value of that *i* from 0 to 2. Line 12 then prints the value 2. *proc1* then returns and line 29 is executed next. The *i* in that line is the *i* declared in line 2 whose value is 12 (from line 27). Thus line 29 prints 12. Line 30 calls *proc3*. *i* is not redeclared in *proc3*, so that the *i* in line 21 is the *i* declared in the surrounding block (*sample*) whose value was 12. Line 21 changes this value to 15 and line 22 prints this value.

Line 24 calls *proc4*. Since *i* is redeclared in this procedure (line 16), a new memory location is allocated and must be initialized before it can be used. This is done in line 18, but the value assigned is never used, since *proc4* returns immediately. At line 24, the value of *i* declared in line 2 is printed. This value is 15. Line 31 prints this value once again.

Note that *proc2* and *proc4* cannot be called from the body of the main program (lines 26–32). This is because *proc2* is declared by its appearance in line 5, which is interior to *proc1*. Thus the identifier *proc2* is local to *proc1* and cannot be referenced outside *proc1*. Similarly, *proc4* is declared inside *proc3* and cannot be referenced outside *proc3*. Note that it would be legal for *proc1* to call *proc3* (or vice versa) because the identifier *proc3* is declared in *sample* and so is global to *proc1*.

Field identifiers of a record, however, have different scope rules from other kinds of identifiers. A field identifier *f* may only appear following a variable of the record type in which the field identifier was declared.

For example, suppose that we define two record types and declare a variable as follows:

```
type date = record
              month: 1..12;
              day: 1..31;
              year: 1900..2000
           end;
     person = record
                name: packed array[1..30] of char;
                birthday: date
              end;
var x: person;
```

A reference to *x.name* is valid because *x* was declared as a *person* and *name* is declared within the type definition of *person*. Similarly, a reference to *x.birthday.day* is valid because *birthday* is declared within the type definition of *person*, *birthday* is declared with the type identifier *date*, and *day* is declared in the type definition of *date*. A reference to *x.month* is invalid because *month* was not declared within the definition of *person* (which is the type of *x*). A reference to *name* alone is invalid because a reference to a field identifier must be preceded by a record variable. Similarly, references to *x.date* and *person.name* are invalid.

Because a field indentifier must be preceded by a variable of the proper type, no ambiguity can arise from the multiple declaration of a field identifier within the same block. For example, consider the following series of definitions and declarations:

```
type date = record
              month: 1..12;
              day: 1..31;
              year: 1900..2000
           end;
     person = record
                name: packed array[1..30] of char;
                birthday: date;
                mother: record
                          name: packed array[1..30] of char;
                          birthday: date
                        end
              end;
     daytype = (sun, mon, tues, wed, thurs, fri, sat);
     monthtype = (jan, feb, mar, apr, may, jun, jul, aug, sep, oct, nov, dec);
     newdate = record
                 day: daytype;
                 month: monthtype;
                 mday: 1..31
               end;
```

var day: daytype;
     month: monthtype;
     x: person;
     d: date;
     dd: newdate;

These type definitions and variable declarations are perfectly valid. This is true despite the fact that four identifiers (*month, day, name, birthday*) are declared more than once. The reason for this is that in any occurrence of these identifiers, it is clear which declaration is applicable. Let us see why this is true.

     month and *day* are each declared three times, once as a field identifier in the record type *date*, once as a field identifier in the record type *newdate*, and once as a variable. When either identifier is used, it is clear from the context which one of these three is meant. If *month* or *day* appears by itself, it is a variable identifier, since a field identifier may appear only after a variable of the appropriate record type. In a reference to *d.month* or *d.day*, the identifier *month* or *day* is a field identifier and the reference is to a field of type 1..12 or 1..31, respectively, within the record variable *d* of type *date*. In a reference to *dd.month* or *dd.day*, the identifier is also a field identifier, but the reference is now to a field of type *daytype* and *monthtype*, respectively, within the record variable *dd* of type *newdate*. Note that it would be invalid to name both the first and third fields of the record type *newdate* with the identifier *day*, since there would then be no way to distinguish between those fields of a record variable of type *newdate*, such as *dd*. Therefore, the third field of *newdate* is named *mday*.

     name and *birthday* are both declared twice as field identifiers. Again, no ambiguity can arise. If either *name* or *birthday* appears immediately following a record variable of type *person* (as in *x.name*), it references the first or second field of that record variable. However, if it appears after the field identifier *mother* (as in *x.mother.name*), it refers to the first or second subfield of the third field of the record variable.

     Make sure that you can identify each of the following references: *x.birthday.day, d.month, x.mother.birthday.month.*

9. THE *with* STATEMENT

It is often tedious for a Pascal programmer to specify the record variable each time that he or she wishes to select a field of that record. Often, a programmer is working with a specific record and is selecting several fields within that record in several different statements. To make such references shorter, Pascal contains a *with* statement. The form of this statement is

with *rv* **do** *s*

where *rv* is a record variable and *s* is any Pascal statement. *s* is usually a compound statement. Within *s*, a field identifier declared in the record type of *rv* can be used as a variable identifier as though it were preceded by *rv*. For example, given the set of declarations presented in Section 8, the statement

> **with** x.birthday
> **do** read (month, day, year)

is equivalent to

> read (x.birthday.month, x.birthday.day, x.birthday.year)

and is also equivalent to

> **with** x
> **do** read (birthday.month, birthday.day, birthday.year)

As another example, if we wish to initialize *x* (of type *person*) with the name John Smith, birthday May 13, 1950, and mother named Jean Smith, with birthday June 15, 1925, we can use the following **with** statement:

> **with** x
> **do begin**
> > name:= 'john smith';
> > **with** birthday
> > **do begin**
> > > month:= 5;
> > > day:= 13;
> > > year:= 1950
> > **end** {*with* birthday *do begin*};
> > **with** mother
> > **do begin**
> > > name:= 'jean smith';
> > > birthday.month:= 6;
> > > birthday.day:= 15;
> > > birthday.year:= 1925
> > **end** {*with* mother *do begin*}
> **end** {*with* x *do begin*}

This last example illustrates an important point about **with** statements and the scope of field identifiers. As previously noted, the scope of a field identifier of a record type *rt* is restricted to the positions in the program text which immediately follow a variable of type *rt*. The effect of a **with** statement is to broaden this scope to include the entire substatement following the symbol **do** in the **with** statement. Thus it is legal to reference the field identifiers *name*, *birthday*, and *mother* within the scope of **with x do**... without preceding them with the name of the record variable *x*. It is understood that the reference to *name* is *x.name*. Similarly, the statement **with birthday do**... is equivalent to **with x.birthday do**.... Within this statement, references to *month*, *day*, and *year* are to *x.birthday.month*, *x.birthday.day*, and *x.birthday.year*. This is true despite the fact that *month* and *day* may have been also declared as variables within the same block. The reason for this is simple. Although a reference to *day* or *month* outside the **with** statement is to the variable identifier, the **with** statement opens a new scope for these identifiers (because they appear as field identifiers within the record type, *date*, of the record variable *x.birthday*) in much the same way that a function or procedure block opens a new scope for identifiers declared within that block. The innermost scope for an identifier is always the effective scope for a reference within that scope.

Within the **with** statement **with mother do**..., the identifier *name* refers to *x.mother.name*, while outside that statement (but within **with x do**...), *name* refers to *x.name*. Again, the inner **with** statement opens a new scope for *name* which overrides the scope opened by the outer **with**.

Of course, it is valid to include variables which are not fields of the record variable *rv* within the scope of a **with** statement. For example, assume the following type definition and variable declarations:

```
type pair = record
              first: integer;
              second: integer
            end;
  var x, y: pair;
      i: integer;
```

The following **with** statement can be used to switch the fields of *x* and set the fields of *y* to the sum and product of the fields of *x*.

```
with x
  do begin
        i:= first;
        first:= second;
        second:= i;
        y.first:= first + second;
        y.second:= first * second
     end
```

The **with** statement

$$\text{with } rv1, rv2 \text{ do } s$$

is equivalent to

$$\text{with } rv1 \text{ do with } rv2 \text{ do } s$$

As many record variables as you wish may appear after the keyword *with*, and each succeeding variable opens a new scope. For example, given the earlier declarations, the statement

```
with d, dd
    do begin
            year:= 1980;
            mday:= 20
    end
```

is equivalent to the statement

```
begin
        d.year:= 1980;
        dd.mday:= 20
end
```

It is also equivalent to

```
with d, dd
    do begin
            mday:= 20;
            year:= 1980
    end
```

However, the following two statements are not equivalent and one of them is invalid. Make sure that you understand why.

```
with d,dd                       with dd,d
    do begin                        do begin
            month:= 6;                      month:= 6;
            day:= 13;                       day:= 13;
            year:= 1936;                    year:= 1936;
            mday:= 14                       mday:= 14
    end                             end
```

Caution should be used in dealing with the scoping rules of *with* statements. Some nonstandard Pascal implementations do not follow these scoping rules faithfully, and users of such implementations should be alert for violations.

There is one restriction on the use of *with* statements, which we illustrate with the following example. Assume the following declarations:

```
type pair = record
                first: integer;
                second: integer
            end;
var a: array [1..10] of pair;
    i, x: integer;
```

Assume that the array *a* and integer *x* have been initialized and that we wish to print the *second* field of every array element whose *first* field equals *x*. A correct way to do this is

```
for i:= 1 to 10
    do with a[i]
        do if x = first
            then writeln(second)
```

An incorrect way is the following:

```
i:= 1;
with a[i]
    do while i <= 10
        do begin
            if x = first
                then writeln(second);
            i:= i + 1
        end
```

The record variable in the **with** header is determined at the time that the **with** statement is entered and cannot be changed during its execution. In the second example, *i* equals 1 when the **with** statement is entered, so that the record variable of the **with** statement is *a*[1]. Despite the fact that *i* is changed within the statement, all references to *first* and *second* are to *a*[1].*first* and *a*[1].*second*, not to *a*[*i*].*first* and *a*[*i*].*second*. However, in the first example, execution of the entire **with** statement is repeated 10 times. After each execution, control leaves the **with** statement and reenters it with a new value of *i*. Thus the record variable *a*[*i*] is redetermined using the current value of *i* each time that the **with** statement is executed.

10. EFFICIENCY OF RECORD ACCESS

The **with** statement can be used to make references to record components more efficient. For example, consider the following definition and declaration

```
type rectype = record
                field1: integer;
                field2: real;
                field3: packed array[1..10] of char
            end;
var rr: array[1..20] of rectype;
```

Suppose that we wish to set the characters in the array *rr*[10].*field3* to the last 10 characters of an array *a* declared by

```
var a: array[1..100] of char;
```

One way of doing this is to use the *for* statement

```
for i:= 1 to 10
    do rr[10].field3[i]:= a[90+i]
```

The address of *rr*[10] must be computed 10 times. However, if we use a **with** statement

```
          with rr[10]
             do for i:= 1 to 10
                do field3[i]:= a[90+i]
```

the address of *rr*[10] need be computed only once. As another example of
using the *with* statement to promote efficiency, consider the following program segment:

```
type string = record
                 length: 0..100;
                 ch: packed array[1..100] of char
              end;
     student = record
                  name: string;
                  address: string
               end;
var s: student;
    i: integer;
    c: char;
begin
    read(c);
    i:= 1;
    while (c <> ' ') and (i <= 100)
        do begin
               s.name.ch[i]:= c;
               read(c);
               i:= i + 1
           end {while...do begin};
    s.name.length:= i - 1;
    ...
```

This segment reads the characters of a student's name until a terminating
blank is read. The statements in the body of the segment can be rewritten
as a *with* statement:

```
begin
    with s.name
        do begin
               read(c);
               i:= 1;
               while (c <> ' ') and (i <= 100)
                   do begin
                          ch[i]:= c;
                          read(c);
                          i:= i + 1
                      end {while...do begin};
               length:= i - 1
           end {with...do begin};
    ...
```

In the latter version, the address of *s.name* need be computed only once, whereas in the previous version it must be recomputed each time that a statement involving *s.name* is executed.

(More advanced students may note, however, that the address of *s.name* can actually be computed at compile time rather than at execution time. If this is done by the compiler, the first version involves two compile-time address computations for the two textual appearances of *s.name*, whereas the latter version involves only one such computation. This is hardly a major savings. Similarly, in the previous example, a "smart" compiler might compute the address of *rr*[10] only once at compile time, even if the **with** statement were not used. If, however, *rr*[10] were replaced by *rr*[*j*], the address of *rr*[*j*] would have to be computed at execution time. But even then, a "supersmart" compiler could recognize that since *j* is not changed in the *for* loop, the address of *rr*[*j*] need be computed only once for each execution of the entire loop. However, it should be recognized that one of the primary advantages of Pascal over other languages is that it permits the programmer to write efficient programs, even without the benefit of "supersmart" compilers.

Note also that the **with** statement improves efficiency even when an array of records or a record of records is not being used. Even in a statement such as

> **for** i:= 1 to 10
> > **do** r.field3[i]:= a[i]

the computation of the base address of *r.field3* is done by loading the base address of *r* into a register and adding the constant offset of *field3* to the contents of that register. The load and add are performed 10 times. However, if the statement were rewritten as

> **with** r
> > **do for** i:= 1 to 10
> > > **do** field3[i]:= a[i]

then the base address of *r* can be loaded into a register once and only the addition need be performed 10 times. Nine load operations are eliminated.)

11. PACKED RECORDS

Another method of increasing efficiency is to decrease the space requirements of a record. A record type may be defined as packed in much the same way as an array. Defining a type as a packed record means that the Pascal system should attempt to minimize the space requirements for that record. For example, a packed record type and variable may be defined and declared by

> **type** packrec = **packed record**
> > field1: char;

```
                    field2: char;
                    field3: char
                  end;
        var r: packrec;
```

Ordinarily, if the record were not packed, *r* would consist of enough space to hold three *char* variables. Although a character can be represented by a single byte, a character variable may cause an entire word to be allocated. (Recall that a word is a group of bytes.) Thus, if the record were not packed, three words would be used for *r*. However, since the record is packed, the three characters in *r* may be packed into a single word.

There are several points to be noted about packed records. First, the space efficiency that may result from declaring a record packed may come at the expense of time efficiency in accessing a component. In the preceding example, a reference to *r.field2* involves extracting the relevant byte from the packed word, whereas if the record were not packed, the extraction would be unnecessary.

Second, a compiler may or may not implement a space savings for a packed record. The packed declaration merely allows the compiler to make such a saving (even at the expense of lowering access time) if it can. It does not guarantee that such a saving is realizable. Some compilers may already implement a space saving for all records, even without the *packed* prefix, so the use of the prefix is irrelevant.

Third, the presence or absence of the prefix *packed* does not alter the meaning of a program. Its only effect is on the program's efficiency. The only exception to this rule is that a component of a packed type may not appear in a function or procedure call as the actual parameter corresponding to a *var* formal parameter.

12. FILES OF RECORDS

One extremely important application of records is to input/output. Much computing revolves around the use of sequential external files. These files contain a sequence of records on some external storage medium, such as a disk or a tape. The records in the file are usually ordered on some field. For example, a school may maintain a file of student records ordered by student name or ID number, and a company might maintain a file of employee records ordered by employee number. If *rt* is a record type, a file of records of type *rt* may be declared by a declaration such as

```
        var f: file of rt;
```

A file is used as an input or an output file. An input file is one that is read by the program, whereas an output file is written by the program. Initially, an input file must be positioned to its beginning by a call to the standard procedure *reset(f)*. Once an input file *f* of type ***file of** rt* has been reset, it can be read by the statement

read (f, r)

where *r* is type *rt*. Each such statement sets *r* to the value of the next record of the file and advances the file one record. Several records may be read from a file in a single statement such as

read(f, r1, r2, r3)

which is equivalent to

read(f, r1);
read(f, r2);
read(f, r3)

After the last record of an input file has been read, the value of the standard boolean function *eof(f)* becomes *true* and a call on the procedure *read* produces an error. Before all the records of *f* have been read, *eof(f)* is *false*.

   An output file must be initialized as a new file by a call to the standard procedure *rewrite(f)*. Once an output file *f* of type ***file of** rt* has been initialized, a record *r* of type *rt* can be added to the end of file *f* by the statement

write (f, r)

Several records may be written to a file in a single statement such as

write(f, r1, r2, r3)

   If a program references an external file, the name of the file must appear in the program header. For example, the header

program merge (f, g, h);

would be used if the program accesses files *f*, *g*, and *h*. Of course, *f*, *g*, and *h* must be declared as files within the program.

   There are two standard files *input* and *output*, which are the system input and output files, respectively. Both of these are text files, that is, files of characters divided into lines. If a call to *read* does not include a file name as an argument, it references the file *input* by default. If a call to *write* does not include a file name as an argument, it references the file *output* by default. These two files should not be declared in the program, but must appear in the program header. These files need not be initialized by *reset* and *rewrite*. More information on these files, as well as text files in general, may be found in an introductory Pascal text.

   As an example of the use of external sequential files, consider the following situation. A student grade record at a college consists of a nine-digit student number, the student's numerical high school average and the number of credits of As, Bs, Cs, Ds, and Fs that the student has earned. The grade-point index for a student is defined as 4 times the number of A credits the student has earned plus 3 times the number of B credits plus 2 times the number of C credits plus the number of D credits, all divided by the total number of credits (including the F credits). Thus the grade-point index is a real number between 0 and 4.

The college maintains a file of student records, one per student, ordered by increasing student number. This file is updated periodically, using a nonempty group of input transactions. There are three types of transactions, types *A*, *G*, and *D*. Each input line contains a letter ('*a*', '*g*', or '*d*') in its first column and a student number in columns 2 through 10. An *A* line indicates an admission. Columns 11 through 15 of an *A* line contain the student's high school average, and all columns past 16 are blank. A *G* line indicates a new grade. Column 11 of a *G* line contains the letter grade ('*a*', '*b*', '*c*', '*d*', or '*f*'), columns 12 through 15 contain the number of credits, and all columns past 16 are blank. A *D* line indicates a discharge and contains blanks from columns 11 on. The lines in the transaction input are also ordered by increasing student number. Only one type of transaction may appear for any one student. If the transaction type is *A* or *D*, only a single input line may appear for the student, but many *G* transactions may appear.

We would like to read the student file and the transaction input, produce an updated student file reflecting the transactions, and print an appropriate message for each student whose record has been updated. The following program does this. The input student file is called *stin*, and the output student file is called *stout*. We use three procedures, *updatea*, *updateg*, and *updated*, to perform the updates and output required for each of three types of transaction. We assume the minor Pascal extension which allows a packed array of a character subrange as an argument to the *writeln* procedure.

```
program update(stin, stout, input, output);
type grade = (f, d, c, b, a);
     gradelett = 'a'..'f';
     digit = '0'..'9';
     numtype = packed array[1..9] of digit;
     strec = record
                 stnum: numtype;
                 hsavg: real;
                 numcr: array[grade] of real
             end;
var i: integer;
    student: strec;
    trnum: numtype;
    trans: char;
    stin,stout: file of strec;
    dig: digit;
    lastdel: boolean { indicates if the last element }
                     { of the file has been deleted }
```

```
function gpi(st: strec): real;
{ this function computes the grade point index of a student }
var totcr, total: real;
    gr: grade;
begin
    totcr:= 0;
    total:= 0;
    for gr:= f to a
        do begin
                totcr:= totcr + st.numcr[gr];
                total:= total + ord(gr) * st.numcr[gr]
            end { for...do begin};
        if totcr:= 0
          then writeln('error in gpi, no credits earned')
          elsc gpi:= total/totcr
end { function gpi};
```

```
procedure updatea;
var st: strec;
begin
    if trnum = student.stnum
      then writeln('admission error ', trnum, ' already a student');
    if trnum < student.stnum
      then with st
              do begin
                    stnum:= trnum;
                    read(hsavg);
                    for gr:= f to a
                      do numcr[gr]:= 0;
                    write(stout, st);
                    writeln(trnum, ' admitted with average ', hsavg)
                end {with...do begin};
    if (trnum > student.stnum) and (eof(stin))
      then with student
              do begin
                    write(stout, student);
                    stnum:= trnum;
                    read(hsavg);
                    for gr:= f to a
                      do numcr[gr]:= 0;
                    writeln(trnum, ' admitted with average ', hsavg)
                end {with...do begin}
end { procedure updatea};
```

```
    procedure updateg;
var lett: gradelett;
    i: integer;
    cr: real;
    gr: grade;
begin
    if trnum <> student.stnum
        then writeln('error grade, no student ', trnum)
        else begin
                    read(lett, cr);
                    case lett of
                        'a': gr:= a;
                        'b': gr:= b;
                        'c': gr:= c;
                        'd': gr:= d;
                        'f': gr:= f
                    end {case};
                    with student
                        do numcr[gr]:= numcr[gr] + cr;
                    writeln(trnum, ' now has a grade point index of ', gpi(student))
            end {else begin}
end { procedure updateg};

procedure updated;
begin
    if trnum = student.stnum
        then begin
                    writeln('discharging ',trnum, ' with grade point index ', gpi(student));
                    if not eof(stin)
                        then read(stin, student)
                        else lastdel:= true
            end {then begin}
        else writeln('discharge error, no student ',trnum)
end { procedure updated};

begin { program update}
    reset(stin);
    rewrite(stout);
    read(stin, student);
    repeat
        lastdel:= false;
        read(trans):
        for i:= 1 to 9
            do begin
                    read(dig);
                    trnum[i]:= dig
                end { for...do begin};
```

```
        while (trnum > student.stnum) and (not eof(stin))
            do begin
                    write(stout, student);
                    read(stin, student)
                end {while...do begin};
        case trans of
            'a': updatea;
            'g': updateg;
            'd': updated
        end {case};
        readln
    until eof(input);

    while (not eof(stin))
        do begin
                write(stout, student);
                read(stin, student)
            end {while...do begin};
    if not lastdel
        then write(stout, student)
end { program update}.
```

This program is quite complex, particularly in the way it deals with the last student record, once *eof(stin)* becomes *true*. Mimic its actions using sample student files and transaction input to understand it better.

We have merely touched on the topic of files in Pascal, since the study and use of files deserves an entire book in itself. For more details, see other Pascal texts and manuals. The actual use and implementation of files vary from installation to installation.

BIBLIOGRAPHY AND REFERENCES

The following bibliography is in no way complete. However, it is an attempt to list a large number of sources and references for further reading. Following each entry is a list of the sections of this book to which the entry applies. If the letter A appears in this list, then the entry is a general reference to the topic of algorithms and their development and efficiency; if the letter D appears, then the entry is a general reference to the topic of data structures, their implementations and applications. Such entries are relevant to most of the topics discussed in this book and are, therefore, not categorized further. If the letter P appears after an entry, then the entry is a general reference to the Pascal language. Other entries contain either an integer, in which case they are relevant to an entire chapter, or a section number (of the form X.X), in which case they are relevant to a particular section.

ACKERMAN, A. F.: "Quadratic Search for Hash Tables of Size p^n," *Comm. ACM*, **17** (3), Mar. 1974. **(8.4)**

ADELSON-VELSKII, G. M. and E. M. LANDIS: "An Algorithm for the Organization of Information," *Dokl. Akad. Nauk SSSR, Mathemat*, **146** (2): 263–66, 1962. **(8.2)**

AHO, A. V., J. E. HOPCROFT and J. D. ULLMAN: *Data Structures and Algorithms*, Addison-Wesley, Reading, Mass., 1983. **(D)**

AHO, A., J. HOPCROFT and J. ULLMAN: *The Design and Analysis of Computer Algorithms*, Addison-Wesley, Reading, Mass., 1974. **(A)**

AHO, A. V., J. E. HOPCROFT, and J. D. ULLMAN: "On Finding Lowest Common Ancestors in Trees," *SIAM J. COMP.*, **5** (1), Mar. 1976. **(6)**

AI-SUWAIYEL, M. and E. HOROWITZ: "Algorithms for Trie Compaction," *ACM Trans. on Database Sys.*, **9** (2): 243–263, June 1984. **(8.3)**

ALAGIC, S. and M. A. ARBIB: *The Design of Well-Structured and Correct Programs*, Springer-Verlag, New York, 1978. **(P, A)**

ALANKO, T. O., H. H. ERKIO and I. J. HAIKALA: "Virtual Memory Behavior of Some Sorting Algorithms," *IEEE Trans. Software Eng.*, **10** (4), July 1984. **(7.2)**

AMBLE, O. and D. E. KNUTH: "Ordered Hash Tables," *Computer J.*, **18**: 135–42, 1975. **(8.4)**

AMSBURY, W.: *Data Structures From Arrays to Priority Queues*, Wadsworth, Belmont, Ca., 1985.   **(D)**

ANDERSON, M. R. and M. G. ANDERSON: "Comments on Perfect Hashing Functions: A Single Probe Retrieving Method for Static Sets," *Comm. ACM*, **22** (2), Feb. 1979.   **(8.4)**

AUGENSTEIN, M. and A. TENENBAUM: "A Lesson in Recursion and Structured Programming," *SIGCSE Bulletin*, **8** (1): 17–23, Feb. 1976.   **(3.4)**

AUGENSTEIN, M. and A. TENENBAUM: "Program Efficiency and Data Structures," *SIGCSE Bulletin*, **9** (3): 21–37, Aug. 1977.   **(4.4, 6.4)**

AUGENSTEIN, M. J. and A. M. TENENBAUM: *Data Structures and PL/I Programming*, Prentice-Hall, Englewood Cliffs, N. J., 1979.   **(D)**

AUSLANDER, M. A. and H. R. STRONG: "Systematic Recursion Removal," *Comm. ACM*, **21** (2), Feb. 1978.   **(3.4)**

BAASE, S.: *Computer Algorithms: Introduction to Design and Analysis*, Addison-Wesley, Reading, Mass., 1978.   **(A)**

BAER, J. L. and B. SCHWAB: "A Comparison of Tree-Balancing Algorithms," *Comm. ACM*, **20** (5), May 1977.   **(8.2)**

BARRON, D. W.: *Recursive Techniques in Programming*, American-Elsevier, New York, 1968.   **(3)**

BATAGELJ, V.: "The Quadratic Hash Method When the Table Size is Not a Prime Number," *Comm. ACM*, **18** (4), Apr. 1975.   **(8.4)**

BAYER, R.: "Binary B-trees for Virtual Memory," *Proc. 1971 ACM SIGFIDET Workshop:* 219–35. ACM, New York.   **(8.3)**

BAYER, R.: "Symmetric Binary B-Trees: Data Structure and Maintenance Algorithms," *Acta Informatica*, **1** (4): 290–306, 1972.   **(8.3)**

BAYER, R. and C. McCREIGHT: "Organization and Maintenance of Large Ordered Indexes," *Acta Informatica*, **1** (3): 173–89, 1972.   **(8.3)**

BAYER, R. and J. METZGER: "On Encipherment of Search Trees and Random Access Files," *ACM Trans. Database Syst.*, **1** (1): 37–52, Mar. 1976.   **(8.2)**

BAYER, R. and K. UNTERAUER: "Prefix B-trees," *ACM Trans. Database Syst.*, **2** (1): 11–26, Mar. 1977.   **(8.3)**

BAYS, C.: "A Note on When to Chain Overflow Items Within a Direct-Access Table," *Comm. ACM*, **16** (1), Jan. 1973.   **(8.4)**

BECHTOLD, U. and K. KUSPERT: "On the Use of Extendible Hashing Without Hashing," *Info. Proc. Lett.*, **19** (1), July 1984.   **(8.4)**

BELL, J. R.: "The Quadratic Quotient Method: A Hash Code Eliminating Secondary Clustering," *Comm. ACM*, **13** (2), Feb. 1970.   **(8.4)**

BELL, J. R. and C. H. KAMAN: "The Linear Quotient Hash Code," *Comm. ACM*, **13** (11), Nov. 1970.   **(8.4)**

BELL, R. C. and B. FLOYD: "A Monte Carlo Study of Cichelli Hash-Function Solvability," *Comm. ACM*, **26** (11), Nov. 1983.   **(8.4)**

BELLMAN, R.: *Dynamic Programming*, Princeton University Press, Princeton, N. J., 1957.   **(A)**

BENTLEY, J. L.: "Multidimensional Binary Search Trees Used for Associative Searching," *Comm. ACM*, **18** (9), Sept. 1975.   **(8.2)**

BENTLEY, J. L.: "Decomposable Searching Problems," *Inf. Proc. Letters*, **8** (5), Jun. 1979.   **(8)**

BENTLEY, J. L.: "Multidimensional Divide and Conquer," *Comm. ACM*, **23** (4), Apr. 1980.   **(3, 8)**

BENTLEY, J. L. and J. H. FRIEDMAN: "Algorithms and Data Structures for Range Searching," *ACM Computing Surveys*, 11 (4), Dec. 1979. **(8)**

BENTLEY, J. L. and C. C. McGEOCH: "Amortized Analyses of Self-Organizing Sequential Search Heuristics," *Comm. ACM*, 28 (4), April 1985. **(8.1)**

BENTLEY, J. L. and D. F. STANAT: "Analysis of Range Searches in Quad Trees," *Inf. Proc. Letters*, 3 (6), Jul. 1975. **(6, 8.2)**

BERGE, C.: *Graphs and Hypergraphs*, North-Holland, Amsterdam, 1973. **(9)**

BERGE, C.: *Theory of Graphs and its Applications*, Methuen Press, 1962. **(9)**

BERZTISS, A. T.: *Data Structures, Theory and Practice, 2d ed.*, Academic Press, New York, 1977. **(D)**

BIRD, R. S.: "Improving Programs by the Introduction of Recursion," *Comm. ACM*, 20 (11), Nov. 1977. **(3.4)**

BIRD, R. S.: "Notes on Recursion Elimination," *Comm. ACM*, 20 (6), Jun. 1977. **(3.4)**

BITNER, J. R.: "Heuristics that Dynamically Organize Data Structures," *SIAM Journal of Computing*, 8 (1), Feb. 1979. **(8.1, 8.2)**

BITNER, J. R. and E. M. REINGOLD: "Backtrack Programming Techniques," *Comm. ACM.*, 18: 651–56, 1975. **(3.3)**

BLUM, M., R. W. FLOYD, V. PRATT, R. L. RIVEST, and R. E. TARJAN: "Time Bounds for Selection," *J. Comput. Sys. Sci.*, 7: 448–61, 1973. **(7.3)**

BOOTHROYD, J.: "Algorithm 201 (Shellsort)," *Comm. ACM*, 6: 445, 1963. **(7.4)**

BOOTHROYD, J.: "Sort of a Section of the Elements of an Array by Determining the Rank of Each Element: Algorithm 25," *Compr. J.*, 10, Nov. 1967. **(7.2)**

BRENT, R. P.: "Reducing the Retrieval Time of Scatter Storage Techniques," *Comm. ACM*, 16 (2), Feb. 1973. **(8.4)**

BROWN, M.: "A Storage Scheme for Height-Balanced Trees," *Inf. Proc. Lett.*, 7 (5): 231–32, Aug. 1978. **(8.2)**

BRUNO, J. and E. G. COFFMAN: "Nearly Optimal Binary Search Trees," *Proc. IFIP Congress 71*: 99–103, North-Holland, Amsterdam, 1972. **(8.2)**

BURGE, W. H.: "A Correspondence Between Two Sorting Methods," *IBM Research Report RC 6395*, Thomas J. Watson Research Center, Yorktown Heights, N. Y., 1977. **(7.3)**

BURSTALL, R. M. and J. DARLINGTON: "A Transformation System for Developing Recursive Programs," *Journal of the ACM*, 24 (1), Jan. 1977. **(3.3, 3.4)**

BURTON, F. W. and G. N. LEWIS: "A Robust Variation of Interpolation Search," *Inform. Proc. Letters*, 10 (4, 5): 198–201, July 1980. **(8.1)**

CARTER, J. L. and M. N. WEGMAN: "Universal Classes of Hash Functions," *J. Comp. Sys. Sci.*, 18: 143–154, 1979. **(8.4)**

CESARINI, F. and G. SODA: "An Algorithm to Construct a Compact B-Tree in Case of Ordered Keys," *Inform. Proc. Letters*, 17: 13–16, 1983. **(8.3)**

CHANG, C. C.: "The Study of an Ordered Minimal Perfect Hashing Scheme," *Comm. ACM*, 27 (4), Apr. 1984. **(8.4)**

CHANG, H. and S. S. IYENGAR: "Efficient Algorithms to Globally Balance a Binary Search Tree," *Comm. ACM*, 27 (7), July 1984. **(8.2)**

CHEN, W. C. and J. S. VITTER: "Analysis of Early-Insertion Standard Coalesced Hashing," *SIAM J. Comp.*, 12 (4), Nov. 1983. **(8.4)**

CHEN, W. C. and J. S. VITTER: "Analysis of New Variants of Coalesced Hashing," *ACM Trans. On Database Sys.*, 9 (4), December 1984 (see also 10 (1), March 1985). **(8.4)**

CHERITON, D. and R. E. TARJAN: "Finding Minimum Spanning Trees," *SIAM J. Comput.*, 5: 724–742, 1976. **(9.4)**

CHERRY, G. W.: *Pascal Programming Structures, An Introduction to Systematic Programming*, Reston Publishing Co., Reston, Va., 1980. **(P)**

CICHELLI, R. J.: "Minimal Perfect Hash Functions Made Simple," *Comm. ACM*, **23** (1), Jan. 1980. **(8.4)**

CLAMPETT, H.: "Randomized Binary Searching With Tree Structures," *Comm. ACM*, **7** (3): 163–65, Mar. 1964. **(8.2)**

COLEMAN, D.: *A Structured Programming Approach to Data*, Macmillan, London, 1978. **(P, D)**

COMER, D.: "Analysis of a Heuristic for Full Trie Minimization," *ACM Trans. on Database Sys.*, **6** (3): 513–537, Sept. 1981. **(8.3)**

COMER, D.: "A Note on Median Split Trees," *ACM TOPLAS*, **2** (1): 129–133, Jan. 1980. **(8.2)**

COMER, D.: "Heuristics for Trie Index Minimization," *ACM Trans. on Database Sys.*, **4** (3): 383–395, Sept. 1979. **(8.3)**

COMER, D.: "The Ubiquitous B-Tree," *ACM Computing Surveys*, **11** (2): 121–137, June 1979. **(8.3)**

CONDICT, M.: "The Pascal Dynamic Array Controversy and a Method for Enforcing Global Assertions," *SIGPLAN Notices*, **12** (11), Nov. 1977. **(1.2)**

CONRADI, R.: "Further Critical Comments on Pascal, Particularly as a Systems Programming Language," *SIGPLAN Notices*, **11** (11), Nov. 1976. **(P)**

COOK, C. R. and D. J. KIM: "Best Sorting Algorithm for Nearly Sorted Lists," *Comm. ACM*, **23** (11), Nov. 1980. **(7.5)**

COOK, C. R. and R. R. OLDEHOEFT: "A Letter Oriented Minimal Perfect Hashing Function," *ACM SIGPLAN Notices*, **17** (9), Sept. 1982. **(8.4)**

COOPER, D.: *Standard Pascal User Reference Manual*, W. W. Norton & Co., New York, N. Y., 1983. **(P)**

DALE, N. and S. C. LILLY: *Pascal Plus Data Structures, Algorithms and Advanced Programming*, D. C. Heath and Co., Lexington, Mass., 1985. **(D)**

DANTZIG, G. B. and D. R. FULKERSON: "On the Max-flow Min-cut Theorem of Networks in Linear Inequalities and Related Systems," *Annals of Math. Study 38*: 215–21, Princeton University Press, Princeton, N. J., 1956. **(9.2)**

DAY, A. C.: "Balancing a Binary Tree," *Comp. J.*, **19** (4): 360–361, Nov. 1976. **(8.2)**

DEO, N.: *Graph Theory with Applications to Engineering and Computer Science*, Prentice-Hall, Englewood Cliffs, N. J., 1974. **(9)**

DIEHR, G. and B. FAALAND: "Optimal Pagination of B-Trees with Variable-Length Items," *Comm. ACM*, **27** (3), Mar. 1984. **(8.3)**

DOBKIN, D. and R. J. LIPTON: "Multidimensional Search Problems," *SIAM J. of Computing*, **5** (2), Jun. 1976. **(8)**

DOBOSIEWICZ, W.: "Sorting by Distributive Partitioning," *Inform. Proc. Letters*, **7** (1): 1–6, 1978. **(7.5)**

DOBOSIEWICZ, W.: "The Practical Significance of D. P. Sort Revisited," *Inform. Proc. Letters*, **8**: 170–172, 1979. **(7.5)**

DOBOSIEWICZ, W.: "An Efficient Variation of Bubble Sort," *Inform. Proc. Letters*, **11** (1): 5–6, 1980. **(7.1)**

DRISCOLL, J. R. and Y. E. LIEN: "A Selective Traversal Algorithm for Binary Search Trees," *Comm. ACM*, **21** (6), Jun. 1978. **(6.1, 6.2, 8.2)**

DU, M. W., T. M. HSIEH, K. F. JEA, and D. W. SHIEH: "The Study of a New Perfect Hash Scheme," *IEEE Trans. Software Eng.*, **SE-9** (3), May 1983. **(8.4)**

EARLSON, I. M.: "Sherlock Holmes and Charles Babbage," *Creative Computing*, **3** (4): 106–13, Jul.–Aug. 1977. **(3.3)**

EDMONDS, J. and R. M. KARP: "Theoretical Improvements in Algorithmic Efficiency for Network Flow Problem," *Journal of the ACM*, **19**: 248–64, 1972.   (9.2)

EPPINGER, J. L.: "An Empirical Study of Insertion and Deletion in Binary Tree Search," *Comm. AMC*, **26** (9), Sept. 1983.   (8.2)

EVEN, S.: *Graph Algorithms*, Computer Science Press, Potomac, Md., 1978.   (9)

EVEN, S. and R. E. TARJAN: "Network Flow and Testing Graph Connectivity," *SIAM J. of Computing*, **4** (4), Dec. 1975.   (9.2)

FAGIN, R., J. NIEVERGELT, N. PIPPENGER, and H. R. STRONG: "Extendible Hashing—A Fast Access Method for Dynamic Files," *ACM Trans. on Database Sys.*, **4** (3): 315–344, Sept. 1979.   (8.4)

FILLMORE, J. P. and S. G. WILLIAMSON: "On Backtracking: A Combinatorial Description of the Algorithm," *SIAM J. of Computing*, **3** (1), Mar. 1974.   (3)

FINDLAY, W. and D. WATT: *Pascal: An Introduction to Methodical Programming*, Computer Science Press, Potomac, Md., 1978.   (P)

FINKEL, R. A. and J. L. BENTLEY: "Quad Trees: A Data Structure for Retrieval on Composite Keys," *Acta Informatica*, **4**: 1–9, 1975.   (6, 8.2)

FISHMAN, G. S.: *Concepts and Methods in Discrete Event Digital Simulation*, Wiley, New York, 1973.   (4.3)

FLORES, I. and G. MADPIS: "Average Binary Search Lengths for Dense Ordered Lists," *Comm. ACM*, **14** (9), Sept. 1971.   (8.1)

FLOYD, R. W.: "Algorithm 245 (Treesort3)," *Comm. ACM.*, **7**: 701, 1964.   (7.3)

FLOYD, R. W. and R. L. RIVEST: "Algorithm 489 (Select)," *Comm. ACM*, **18** (3): 173, Mar. 1975.   (7.3)

FLOYD, R. W. and R. L. RIVEST: "Expected Time Bounds for Selection," *Comm. ACM*, **18** (3), Mar. 1975.   (7.3)

FORD, L. R. and D. R. FULKERSON: *Flows in Networks*, Princeton University Press, Princeton, N. J., 1972.   (9.2)

FOSTER, C. C.: "A Generalization of AVL Trees," *Comm. ACM*, **16** (8), Aug. 1973.   (8.2)

FRANKLIN, W. R.: "Padded Lists: Set Operations in Expected O(log log N) Time," *Inform. Proc. Letters*, **9** (4): 161–166, Nov. 1979.   (8.1)

FRANTA, W. R. and K. MALY: "A Comparison of Heaps and the TL Structure for the Simulation Event Set." *Comm. ACM*, **21** (10), Oct. 1978.   (4.3, 7.3)

FRANTA, W. R. and K. MALY: "An Efficient Data Structure for the Simulation Event Set," *Comm. ACM*, **20** (8), Aug. 1977.   (4.3)

FRAZER, W. D. and A. C. McKELLAR: "Samplesort: A Sampling Approach to Minimal Storage Tree Sorting," *J. ACM*, **17** (3), Jul. 1970.   (7.3)

FREDKIN, E.: "Trie Memory," *Comm. ACM*, **3** (9): 490–499, 1960.   (8.3)

FULKERSON, D. R.: "Flow Networks and Combinatorial Operations Research," *Amer. Math. Monthly*, **73**: 115, 1966.   (9.2)

GALIL, Z. and N. MEGIDDO: "A Fast Selection Algorithm and the Problem of Optimum Distribution of Effort," *Journal of the ACM*, **26** (1), Jan. 1979.   (7.2)

GAREY, M. R.: "Optimal Binary Search Trees With Restricted Maximal Depth," *SIAM J. Comp.*, **2**: 101–10, 1974.   (8.2)

GARSIA, A. M. and M. L. WACHS: "A New Algorithm for Minimum Cost Binary Trees," *SIAM J. Comp.*, **6** (4), Dec. 1977.   (8.2)

GHOSH, S. P. and V. Y. LUM: "Analysis of Collisions when Hashing by Division," *Inf. Syst.*, **1**: 15–22, 1975.   (8.4)

GHOSH, S. P. and M. E. SENKO: "File Organization: On the Selection of Random Access Index Points for Sequential Files," *J. ACM*, **16**: 569–579, 1969.   (8.1)

GOLOMB, S. W. and L. D. BAUMERT: "Backtrack Programming," *J. ACM*, **12**: 516, 1965. **(3)**

GONNET, G. H.: "Heaps Applied to Event Driven Mechanisms," *Comm. ACM*, **19** (7), Jul. 1976. **(4.3, 7.3)**

GONNET, G. H. and P. LARSON: "External Hashing with Limited Internal Storage," *Technical Report CS-82-38*, University of Waterloo, 1982. **(8.4)**

GONNET, G. H. and J. I. MUNRO: "Efficient Ordering of Hash Tables," *SIAM J. Comp.*, **8** (3), Aug. 1979. **(8.4)**

GONNET, G. H. and L. D. ROGERS: "The Interpolation-Sequential Search Algorithm," *Inf. Proc. Lett.*, **6**: 136–39, 1977. **(8.1)**

GONNET, G. H., L. D. ROGERS, and J. A. GEORGE: "An Algorithmic and Complexity Analysis of Interpolation Search," *Acta Informatica*, **13**: 39–52, 1980. **(8.1)**

GOODMAN, S. E. and S. T. HEDETNIEMI: *Introduction to the Design and Analysis of Algorithms*, McGraw-Hill, New York, 1977. **(A, 3)**

GOTLIEB, C. C. and L. R. GOTLIEB: *Data Types and Structures*, Prentice-Hall, Englewood Cliffs, N. J., 1978. **(D)**

GRAHAM, N.: *Introduction to Pascal*, West Publishing Co., St. Paul, Minn., 1980. **(P)**

GRIES, D.: *Compiler Construction for Digital Computers*, Wiley, New York, 1971. **(3.2, 3.4, 8.4)**

GROGONO, P.: *Programming in Pascal*, Addison-Wesley, Reading, Mass., 1978. **(P)**

GUIBAS, L. J.: "The Analysis of Hashing Techniques that Exhibit K-ary Clustering," *Journal of the ACM*, **25**: 544–55, 1978. **(8.4)**

GUIBAS, L., E. McCREIGHT, M. PLASS and J. ROBERTS: "A New Representation for Linear Lists," *Proc. 9th ACM Symp. Theory of Comp.*: 49–60, New York, 1977. **(8.2)**

GUIBAS, L. J. and R. SEDGEWICK: "A Dichromatic Framework for Balanced Trees," *Proc. 19th Ann. IEEE Symp. on Foundations of Comp. Sci.*, 1978. **(8.3)**

GUIBAS, L. J. and E. SZEMEREDI: "The Analysis of Double Hashing," *J. Comp. Sys. Sci.*, **16**: 226–74, 1978. **(8.4)**

HABERMANN, A. N.: "Critical Comments on the Programming Language Pascal," *Acta Informatica*, **3** (1), 1973. **(P)**

HARARY, F.: *Graph Theory*, Addison-Wesley, Boston, 1969. **(9)**

HALATSIS, C. and G. PHILOKYPROU: "Pseudo-chaining in Hash Tables," *Comm. ACM*, **21** (7), July 1978. **(8.4)**

HANSEN, W. J.: "A Cost Model for the Internal Organization of B^+-Tree Nodes," *ACM Trans. on Prog. Lang. and Sys.*, **3** (4), Oct. 1981. **(8.3)**

HELD, G. and M. STONEBRAKER: "B-trees Re-examined," *Comm. ACM*, **21** (2): 139–43, Feb. 1978. **(8.3)**

HIRSCHBERG, D. S.: "An Insertion Technique for One-sided Height-Balanced Trees," *Comm. ACM*, **19** (8), Aug. 1976. **(8.2)**

HOARE, C. A. R.: "Partition, Algorithm 63; Quicksort, Algorithm 64; Find, Algorithm 65," *Comm. ACM*, **4** (7), Jul. 1961. **(7.2)**

HOARE, C. A. R.: "Quicksort," *Comp. J.*, **5**: 10–15, 1962. **(7.2)**

HOARE, C. A. R. and N. WIRTH: "An Axiomatic Definition of the Programming Language Pascal," *Acta Informatica*, **2** (4), 1973. **(P)**

HOLT, R. C. and J. N. P. HUME: *Programming Standard Pascal*, Reston Publishing Co., Reston, Va., 1980. **(P)**

HOPGOOD, F. R. A. and J. DAVENPORT: "The Quadratic Hash Method Where the Table Size is a Power of 2," *Comptr. J.*, **15** (4), 1972. **(8.4)**

HOROWITZ, E. and S. SAHNI: *Algorithms: Design and Analysis*, Computer Science Press, Potomac, Md., 1977. **(A)**

HOROWITZ, E. and S. SAHNI: *Fundamentals of Data Structures*, Computer Science Press, Woodland Hills, Calif., 1975. **(D)**

HU, T. C. and A. C. TUCKER: "Optimum Computer Search Trees," *SIAM J. Appl. Math.*, **21**: 514–32, 1971. **(8.2)**

HUANG, S. S. and C. K. WONG: "Generalized Binary Split Trees," *IBM Research Report RC 10150*, Thomas J. Watson Research Center Yorktown Heights, N. Y., Mar. 1983. **(8.2)**

HUANG, S. S. and C. K. WONG: "Optimal Binary Split Trees," *IBM Research Report RC 9921*, Thomas J. Watson Research Center Yorktown Heights, N. Y., 1982. **(8.2)**

HUANG, S.: "Height-Balanced Trees of Order (β, γ, δ)," *ACM Trans. Database Syst.*, **10** (2), June 1985. **(8.3)**

HUFFMAN, D.: "A Method for the Construction of Minimum Redundance Codes," *Proc. IRE*, **40**, 1952. **(6.3)**

HUITS, M. and V. KUMAR: "The Practical Significance of Distributive Partitioning Sort," *Inform. Proc. Letters*, **8**: 168–169, 1979. **(7.5)**

HWANG, F. K. and S. LIN: "A Simple Algorithm for Merging Two Disjoint Linearly Ordered Sets," *SIAM J. Comp.*, **1**: 31–39, 1972. **(7.5)**

ITAI, A.: "Optimal Alphabetic Trees," *SIAM J. Comp.*, **5** (1), Mar. 1976. **(8.2)**

ITAI, A. and Y. SHILOACH: "Maximum Flow in Planar Networks," *SIAM J. Comp.*, **8** (2), May 1979. **(9.2)**

JACKOWSKI, B. L. and R. KUBIAK and S. SOKOLOWSKI: "Complexity of Sorting by Distributive Partitioning," *Inform. Proc. Letters*, **9** (2): 180, 1979. **(7.5)**

JACOBI, C.: "Dynamic Array Parameters," *Pascal User's Group Newsletter*, (5), Sept. 1976. **(1.2)**

JAESCHKE, G.: "Reciprocal Hashing: A Method for Generating Minimal Perfect Hashing Functions," *Comm. ACM*, **24** (12), Dec. 1981. **(8.4)**

JAESCHKE, G. and G. OSTERBURG: "On Cichelli's Minimal Perfect Hash Function Method," *Comm. ACM*, **23** (12), Dec. 1980. **(8.4)**

JENSEN, K. and N. WIRTH: *Pascal User Manual and Report*, 2d ed., Springer-Verlag, New York, 1974. **(P)**

JONASSEN, A. and O. DAHL: "Analysis of an Algorithm for Priority Queue Administration," *BIT*, **15**: 409–22, 1975. **(4.1, 7.3)**

KARLTON, P. L., S. H. FULLER, R. E. SCROGGS, and E. B. KACHLER: "Performance of Height-Balanced Trees," *Comm. ACM*, **19** (1): 23–28, Jan. 1976. **(8.2)**

KERNIGHAN, B. and P. J. PLAUGER: *Software Tools*, Addison-Wesley, Reading, Mass., 1976. **(7)**

KLEINROCK, L.: *Queuing Systems*, Wiley, 1975. **(4.3)**

KNOTT, G. O.: "Hashing Functions," *Computer Journal*, **18**, Aug. 1975. **(8.4)**

KNUTH, D. E.: *Fundamental Algorithms*, 2d ed., Addison-Wesley, Reading, Mass., 1973. **(D, A)**

KNUTH, D. E.: "Optimum Binary Search Trees," *Acta Informatica*, **1**: 14–25, 1971. **(8.2)**

KNUTH, D. E.: *Sorting and Searching*, Addison-Wesley, Reading, Mass., 1973. **(7.8)**

KNUTH, D. E.: "Structured Programming with Goto Statements," *ACM Computing Surveys*, **6** (4): 261, Dec. 1974. **(3.4, 7.2)**

KORFHAGE, R. R.: *Discrete Computational Structures*, Academic Press, New York, 1974. **(9.1)**

KORSH, J. F.: "Greedy Binary Search Trees are Nearly Optimal," *Inf. Proc. Letters*, **13** (1), Oct. 1981. **(8.2)**

KOSARAJU, S. R.: "Insertions and Deletions in One-Sided Height Balanced Trees," *Comm. ACM*, **21** (3), Mar. 1978. **(8.2)**

KRUSE, R. L.: *Data Structures and Program Design*, Prentice-Hall, Englewood Cliffs, N. J., 1984. **(D)**

LARSON, P. A.: "Dynamic Hashing," *BIT*, **18**: 184–201, 1978. **(8.4)**

LARSON, P. A.: "Linear Hashing with Partial Expansions," *Proc. 6th Conf. Very Large Data bases*, 224–232, Montreal, Canada, ACM, New York, 1980. **(8.4)** ⟨

LARSON, P. A.: "A Single-File Version of Linear Hashing with Partial Expansions," *Proc. 8th Conf. Very Large Data bases*, 300–309, Mexico City, Mexico, Sept. 1982. **(8.4)**

LARSON, P. A.: "Performance Analysis of Linear Hashing with Partial Expansions," *ACM Trans. on Database Syst.*, 7 (4), Dec. 1982. **(8.4)**

LARSON, P. A.: "Further Analysis of External Hashing with Fixed-Length Separators," *Technical Report CS-83-18*, University of Waterloo Computer Science Department, July 1983. **(8.4)**

LARSON, P. A.: "Analysis of Uniform Hashing," *J. ACM*, **30** (4): 805–819, Oct. 1983. **(8.4)**

LARSON, P. A.: "Performance Analysis of a Single-File Version of Linear Hashing," *Technical Report CS-83-28*, University of Waterloo, Nov. 1983. **(8.4)**

LARSON, P. A.: "Linear Hashing with Separators—A Dynamic Hashing Scheme Achieving One-Access Retrieval," *Technical Report CS-84-23*, University of Waterloo, Nov. 1984. **(8.4)**

LARSON, P. A.: "Linear Hashing with Overflow-Handling by Linear Probing," *ACM Trans. on Database Syst.*, **10** (1), March 1985. **(8.4)**

LARSON, P. and A. KAJLA: "File Organization: Implementation of a Method Guaranteeing Retrieval in One Access," *Comm. ACM*, **27** (7), July 1984. **(8.4)**

LECARME, O. and P. DESJARDINS: "More Comments on the Programming Language Pascal," *Acta Informatica*, **4**: 231–43, 1975. **(P)**

LECARME, O. and P. DESJARDINS: "Reply to a Paper by A. N. Habermann on the Programming Language Pascal," *SIGPLAN Notices*, **9** (10), Oct. 1974. **(P)**

LEWIS, G. N., N. J. BOYNTON, and F. W. BURTON: "Expected Complexity of Fast Search with Uniformly Distributed Data," *Inform. Proc. Letters*, **13** (1): 4–7, Oct. 1981. **(8.1)**

LEWIS, T. G. and M. Z. SMITH: *Applying Data Structures*, Houghton Mifflin, Boston, 1976. **(D)**

LITWIN, W. and D. B. LOMET: "Bounded Disorder Access Method," *IBM Research Report RC 10992*, Thomas J. Watson Research Center Yorktown Heights, N. Y., Jan. 1985. **(8.4)**

LOCKYER, K. G.: *Critical Path Analysis: Problem and Solutions*, Pitman, London, 1966. **(9.3)**

LOCKYER, K. G.: *An Introduction to Critical Data Analysis*, Pitman, London, 1964. **(9.3)**

LODI, E. and F. LUCCIO: "Split Sequence Hash Search," *Inform. Proc. Letters*, **20**: 131–136, 1985. **(8.4)**

LOESER, R.: "Some Performance Tests of 'Quicksort' and Descendants," *Comm. ACM*, **17** (3), Mar. 1974. **(7.2)**

LOMET, D. B.: "Digital B-Trees," *Proc. 7th Conf. Very Large Databases*, 333–343, Cannes, France, 1981. **(8.3)**

LOMET, D. B.: "Bounded Index Exponential Hashing," *IBM Research Report RC 9192*,

Thomas J. Watson Research Center Yorktown Heights, N. Y., Jan. 1982, to appear in ACM Trans. Database Syst. **(8.4)**

LOMET, D. B.: "A High Performance, Universal Key Associative Access Method," *IBM Research Report RC 9638*, Thomas J. Watson Research Center Yorktown Heights, N. Y., Oct. 1982. **(8.4)**

LOMET, D. B.: "DL*-Trees: A File Organization Exploiting Digital Search," *IBM Research Report RC 10860*, Thomas J. Watson Research Center Yorktown Heights, N. Y., Nov. 1984. **(8.3)**

LORIN, H.: *Sorting and Sort Systems*, Addison-Wesley, Reading, M. A., 1975. **(7)**

LUCCIO, F. and L. PAGLI: "On the Height of Height-Balanced Trees," *IEEE Trans. Comptrs.*, c-25 (1), Jan. 1976. **(8.2)**

LUCCIO, F. and L. PAGLI: "Power Trees," *Comm. ACM*, 21 (11), Nov. 1978. **(8.2)**

LUM, U. Y.: "General Performance Analysis of Key-to-Address Transformation Methods Using an Abstract File Concept," *Comm. ACM*, 16 (10): 603, Oct. 1973. **(8.4)**

LUM, U. Y. and P. S. T. YUEN: "Additional Results on Key-to-Address Transform Techniques: A Fundamental Performance Study on Large Existing Formatted Files," *Comm. ACM*, 15 (11): 996, Nov. 1972. **(8.4)**

LUM, U. Y., P. S. T. YUEN and M. DODD: "Key-to-Address Transform Techniques: A Fundamental Performance Study on Large Existing Formatted Files," *Comm. ACM*, 14: 228, 1971. **(8.4)**

LYON, G.: "Packed Scatter Tables," *Comm. ACM*, 21 (10), Oct. 1978. **(8.4)**

MAIER, D. and S. C. SALVETER: "Hysterical B-Trees," *Inf. Proc. Lett.*, 12 (4), Aug. 1981. **(8.3)**

MALY, K.: "Compressed Tries," *Comm. ACM*, 19 (7), Jul. 1976. **(8.3)**

MANNA, Z. and A. SHAMIR: "The Optimal Approach to Recursive Programs," *Comm. ACM*, 20 (11), Nov. 1977. **(3.4)**

MANNILA, H. and E. UKKONEN: "A Simple Linear-Time Algorithm for In Situ Merging," *Inf. Proc. Lett.*, 18 (4), May 1984. **(7.5)**

MARTIN, W.: "Sorting," *Comp. Surveys*, 3 (4): 147, 1971. **(8)**

MARTIN, W. A. and D. N. NESS: "Optimizing Binary Trees Growth with a Sorting Algorithm," *Comm. ACM*, 15 (2): 88–93, Feb. 1972.

MAURER, H. A. and T. OTTMANN: "Tree Structures for Set Manipulation Problems," in *Mathematical Foundations of Computer Science*, J. Gruska (ed.), Springer-Verlag, New York, 1977. **(6)**

MAUER, H. A., T. OTTMANN and H. W. SIX: "Implementing Dictionaries Using Binary Trees of Very Small Height," *Inform. Proc. Letters*, 5: 11–14, 1976. **(8.2)**

MAURER, H. A. and M. R. WILLIAMS: *A Collection of Programming Problems and Techniques*, Prentice-Hall, Englewood Cliffs, N. J., 1972. **(A)**

MAURER, W. D.: "An Improved Hash Code for Scatter Storage," *Comm. ACM*, 11 (1), Jan. 1968. **(8.4)**

MAURER, W. and T. LEWIS: "Hash Table Methods," *Comp. Surveys*, 7 (1): 5–19, Mar. 1975. **(8.4)**

McCABE, J.: "On Serial Files with Relocatable Records," *Operations Research*, 12: 609–18, 1965. **(8.1)**

McCREIGHT, E. M.: "Pagination of B-Trees with Variable-Length Records," *Comm. ACM*, 20 (9): 670–674, Sept. 1977. **(8.3)**

MEHLHORN, K.: "A Best Possible Bound for the Weighted Path of Binary Search Trees," *SIAM J. Comp.*, 6 (2), June 1977. **(8.2)**

MEHLHORN, K.: "Dynamic Binary Search," *SIAM J. Comp.*, 8 (2), May 1979. **(8.1)**

MEHLHORN, K.: "Nearly Optimal Binary Search Trees," *Acta Informatica*, **5**: 287–95, 1975.   **(8.2)**

MELVILLE, R. and D. GRIES: "Controlled Density Sorting," *Inf. Proc. Lett.*, **10** (4, 5), July 1980.   **(7.4)**

MERRITT, S. M.: "An Inverted Taxonomy of Sorting Algorithms," *Comm. ACM*, **28** (1), Jan. 1985.   **(7)**

MILLER, R., N. PIPPENGER, A. ROSENBERG and L. SNYDER: "Optimal 2-3 Trees," *IBM Research Rep. RC 6505*, Thomas J. Watson Research Center Yorktown Heights, N. Y., 1977.   **(8.3)**

MORRIS, R.: "Scatter Storage Techniques," *Comm. ACM*, **11** (1): 38–44, Jan. 1968.   **(8.4)**

MORRIS, R.: "Some Theorems on Sorting," *SIAM J. Appl. Math.*, **17** (1), Jan. 1969.
                                                                                       (7)

MOTZKIN, D.: "Meansort," *Comm. ACM*, **26** (4), April 1983.   **(7.2)**

MOTZKIN, D. and J. KAPENGA: "More About Meansort," *Comm. ACM*, **27** (7), July 1984.   **(7.2)**

MULLIN, J. K.: "Tightly Controlled Linear Hashing without Separate Overflow Storage," *BIT*, **21**: 390–400, 1981.   **(8.4)**

MUNRO, I.: "Efficient Determination of the Transitive Closure of a Directed Graph," *Inf. Proc. Letters*, **1**: 56, 1971–72.   **(9.1)**

MUNRO, J. I. and H. SUWANDA: Implicit Data Structures, *Eleventh Symposium on the Theory of Computing*, Assoc. for Comp. Mach, 1979.   **(8)**

NIEVERGELT, J.: "Binary Search Trees and File Organization," *ACM Computing Surveys*, **6** (3), Sept. 1974.   **(8.2)**

NIEVERGELT, J., J. C. FARRAR and E. M. REINGOLD: *Computer Approaches to Mathematical Problems*, Prentice-Hall, Englewood Cliffs, N. J., 1974.   **(A)**

NIEVERGELT, J. and E. M. REINGOLD: "Binary Search Trees of Bounded Balance," *SIAM J. Comp.*, **2**: 33, 1973.   **(8.2)**

NIEVERGELT, J. and C. K. WONG: "On Binary Search Trees," *Proc. IFIP Congress 71*: 91–98, North-Holland, Amsterdam, 1972.   **(8.2)**

NIJENHUIS, A. and H. S. WILF: *Combinatorial Algorithms*, Academic Press, New York, 1975.   **(A)**

NILSSON, N.: *Problem-solving Methods in Artificial Intelligence*, McGraw-Hill, New York, 1971.   **(6.6)**

NISHIHARA, S. and K. IKEDA: "Reducing the Retrieval Time of Hashing Method by Using Predictors," *Comm. ACM*, **26** (12), Dec. 1983.   **(8.4)**

O'NEIL, P. E. and E. J. O'NEIL: "A Fast Expected Time Algorithm for Boolean Matrix Multiplication and Transitive Closure," *Information and Control*, **22**: 132–38, 1973.
                                                                                       (9.1)

ORE, O.: *Graphs and their Uses*, Random House and the L. W. Singer Co., New York, 1963.   **(9)**

ORE, O.: *Theory of Graphs*, **38**, American Mathematical Society, Providence, R. I., 1962.   **(9)**

OTTMANN, T. and D. WOOD: "Deletion in One-Sided Height-Balanced Search Trees," *Int. J. Comp. Math.*, **6** (4): 265–71, 1978.   **(8.3)**

OTTMANN, T., H. SIX and D. WOOD: "Right Brother Trees," *Comm. ACM*, **21** (9), Sept. 1978.   **(6)**

PAPADIMITRIOU, C. H. and P. A. BERNSTEIN: "On the Performance of Balanced Hashing Functions when the Keys are not Equiprobable," *ACM Trans. Prog. Lang. and Sys.*, **2** (1), Jan. 1980.   **(8.4)**

PERL, Y., A. ITAI, and H. AVNI: "Interpolation Search—A Log Log *N* Search," *Comm. ACM*, 2 1: 550–57, 1978.   (8.1)

PERL, Y. and E. M. REINGOLD: "Understanding the Complexity of Interpolation Search," *Inf. Proc. Lett.*, 6: 219–21, 1977.   (8.1)

PETERSON, J. L.: "On the Formatting of Pascal Programs," *SIGPLAN Notices*, 12 (12), Dec. 1977.   (P)

PETERSON, W. W.: "Addressing for Random-Access Storage," *IBM J. Res. and Dev.*, 1: 130–46, 1957.   (8.4)

PFALTZ, J. L.: *Computer Data Structures*, McGraw-Hill, New York, 1977.   (D)

POHL, I.: "A Sorting Problem and its Complexity," *Comm. ACM*, 15 (6), Jun. 1972.   (7.1)

POKROVSKY, S.: "Formal Types and their Application to Dynamic Arrays in Pascal," *SIGPLAN Notices*, 11 (10), Oct. 1976.   (1.2)

POLYA, G.: *How to Solve it*, Doubleday, Garden City, N. Y., 1957.   (A)

POOCH, U. W. and A. NIEDER: "A Survey of Indexing Techniques for Sparse Matrices," *Computer Surveys*, 15: 109, 1973.   (5.3)

PRATT, T. W.: *Programming Languages: Design and Implementation*, Prentice-Hall, Englewood Cliffs, N. J., 1975.   (1.2, 1.3, 2.3, 3.2, 3.4)

PRICE, C.: "Table Lookup Techniques," *ACM Comp. Surveys*, 3 (2): 49–65, 1971.   (8)

PRITCHARD, P.: "The Study of an Ordered Minimal Perfect Hashing Scheme," (Letter to the Editor), *Comm. ACM*, 27 (11), Nov. 1984.   (8.4)

RADKE, C. E.: "The Use of Quadratic Residue Research," *Comm. ACM*, 13 (2), Feb. 1970.   (8.4)

RAIHA, K. and S. H. ZWEBEN: "An Optimal Insertion Algorithm for One-Sided Height-Balanced Binary Search Trees," *Comm. ACM*, 22 (9), Sept. 1979.   (8.2)

RAMAMOHANARAO, K. and R. SACKS-DAVIS: "Recursive Linear Hashing," *ACM Trans. on Database Syst.*, 9 (3), Sept. 1984.   (8.4)

REINGOLD, E. M. and W. J. HANSEN: *Data Structures*, Little, Brown and Co., Boston, 1983.   (D)

REINGOLD, E. M., J. NIEVERGELT, and N. DEO: *Combinatorial Algorithms: Theory and Practice*, Prentice-Hall, Englewood Cliffs, N. J., 1977.   (7)

REYNOLDS, J. C.: "Reasoning About Arrays," *Comm. ACM*, 22 (5), May 1979.   (1.2)

RICH, R. P.: *Internal Sorting Methods Illustrated with PL/I Programs*, Prentice-Hall, Englewood Cliffs, N. J., 1972.   (7)

RIVEST, R. L.: Optimal Arrangement of Keys in a Hash Table," *Journal of the ACM*, 25: 200–209, 1978.   (8.4)

RIVEST, R.: "On Self-organizing Sequential Search Heuristics," *Comm. ACM*, 19 (2), Feb. 1976.   (8.1)

RIVEST, R. L. and D. E. KNUTH: "Bibliography 26: Computer Sorting," *Computing Reviews*, 13: 283, 1972.   (7)

ROHL, J. S.: *Recursion via Pascal*, Cambridge University Press, London, 1984.   (3)

ROSENBERG, A. L. and L. SNYDER: "Time-and-Space-Optimality in B-Trees," *ACM Trans. Database Syst.*, 6 (1), Mar. 1981.   (8.3)

ROSENBERG, A. and L. SNYDER: "Minimal Comparison 2-3 Trees," *SIAM J. Comput.*, 7 (4): 465–80, Nov. 1978.   (8.3)

SAGER, T. J.: "A Polynomial Time Generator for Minimal Perfect Hash Functions," *Comm. ACM*, 28 (5), May 1985.   (8.4)

SAHNI, S.: *Software Development in Pascal*, Camelot Publishing Co., Fridley, Minnesota, 1985.   (A)

SANDS, P. A.: *Advanced Pascal Programming Techniques*, Osborne-McGraw-Hill, Berkeley, Calif., 1984.   **(P)**

SANTORO, N.: "Full Table Search by Polynomial Functions," *Inform. Proc. Letters*, *5*, Aug. 1976.   **(8.4)**

SARWATE, D. U.: "A Note on Universal Classes of Hash Functions," *Info. Proc. Lett.*, **10** (1): 41–45, Feb. 1980.   **(8.4)**

SAXE, J. B. and J. L. BENTLEY: "Transforming Static Data Structures to Dynamic Structures," *Research Report cmu-cs-79-141*, Carnegie-Mellon University, Pittsburgh, 1979.   **(8)**

SCHNEIDER, G. M., S. W. WEINGART and D. M. PERLMAN: *An Introduction to Programming and Problem-Solving with Pascal*, Wiley, New York, 1978.   **(P)**

SCHOLL, M.: "New File Organizations Based on Dynamic Hashing," *ACM Trans. Database Syst.*, **6** (1): 194–211, Mar. 1981.   **(8.4)**

SCOWEN, R. S.: "Quicksort: Algorithm 271." *Comm. ACM*, **8** (11), Nov. 1965.   **(7.2)**

SEDGEWICK, R.. *Algorithms*, Addison-Wesley, Reading, Mass., 1983.   **(A)**

SEDGEWICK, R.: "The Analysis of Quicksort Programs," *Acta Informatica*, 7: 327–55, 1977.   **(7.2)**

SEDGEWICK, R.: "Data Movement in Odd-Even Merging," *SIAM J. Comp.*, 7 (3), Aug. 1978.   **(7.2)**

SEDGEWICK, R.: "Implementing Quicksort Programs," *Comm. ACM*, **21** (10), Oct. 1978.   **(7.2)**

SEDGEWICK, R.: "Permutation Generation Methods," *ACM Computing Surveys*, **9** (2): 137, Jun. 1977.   **(3.3)**

SEDGEWICK, R.: "Quicksort," *Report no. STAN-CS-75-492*, Dept. of Computer Science, Stanford University, Stanford, Ca., May 1975.   **(7.2)**

SEVERANCE, D. G.: "Identifier Search Mechanisms: A Survey and Generalized Model," *Computing Surveys*, **6** (3): 175–94, Sept. 1974.   **(8)**

SHEIL, B. A.: "Median Split Trees: A Fast Technique for Frequently Occurring Keys," *Comm. ACM*, **21** (11), Nov. 1978.   **(8.2)**

SHELL, D. L.. "A High Speed Sorting Procedure," *Comm. ACM*, 2 (7), Jul. 1959. **(7.4)**

SHNEIDERMAN, B.: "Jump Searching: A Fast Sequential Search Technique," *Comm. ACM*, **21** (10), Oct. 1978.   **(8.1)**

SHNEIDERMAN, B.: "A Model for Optimizing Indexed File Structures," *Int. J. Comptr and Inform. Sci.*, **3** (1), 1974.   **(8.1)**

SHNEIDERMAN, B.: "Polynomial Search," *Software-Practice and Experience*, 3: 5–8, 1973.   **(8.1)**

SINGLETON, R. C.: "An Efficient Algorithm for Sorting with Minimal Storage: Algorithm 347," *Comm. ACM*, **12** (3), Mar. 1969.   **(7.2)**

SPRUGNOLI, R.: "Perfect Hashing Functions: A Single Probe Retrieving Method for Static Sets," *Comm. ACM*, **20** (11), Nov. 1977.   **(8.4)**

STANDISH, T. A.: *Data Structure Techniques*, Addison-Wesley, Reading, MA., 1980. **(D)**

STEPHENSON, C. J.: "A Method for Constructing Binary Search Trees by Making Insertions at the Root," *Intl. J. Comput. Inf. Sci.* **9** (1), Feb. 1980.   **(9.2)**

STRONG, H. R., G. MARKOWSKY and A. K. CHANDRA: "Search Within a Page," *J. ACM*, **26** (3), July 1979.   **(8.3)**

STUBBS, D. F. and N. W. WEBRE: *Data Structures with Abstract Data Types and Pascal*, Brooks/Cole Publishing Co., Monterey, Ca., 1985.   **(D)**

SYSLO, M. M., N. DEO, and J. S. KOWALIK, *Discrete Optimization Algorithms with Pascal Programs*, Prentice-Hall, Englewood Cliffs, N. J., 1983.   **(9)**

TANNER, R. M.: "Minimean Merging and Sorting: An Algorithm," *SIAM J. Comp.*, 7 (1), Feb. 1978. **(7.5)**

TARJAN, R. E.: *Data Structures and Network Algorithms*, Soc. for Indust. and Appl. Math., Philadelphia, PA, 1983. **(D)**

TARJAN, R. E.: "Updating a Balanced Search Tree in O (1) Rotations," *Info. Proc. Lett.*, **16** (5), June 1983. **(8.2)**

TARJAN, R. E. and A. C. YAO: "Storing a Sparse Table," *Comm. ACM*, **22** (11), Nov. 1979. **(8.3)**

TENENBAUM, A.: "Simulations of Dynamic Sequential Search Algorithms," *Comm. ACM*, **21** (9), Sept. 1978. **(8.1)**

TREMBLAY, J. P. and R. P. MANOHAR: *Discrete Mathematical Structures with Applications to Computer Science*, McGraw-Hill, New York, 1975. **(9.1)**

TREMBLAY, J. P. and P. G. SORENSON: *An Introduction to Data Structures with Applications*, McGraw-Hill, New York, 1976. **(D)**

ULRICH, E. G.: "Event Manipulation for Discrete Simulations Requiring Large Numbers of Events," *Comm. ACM*, **21** (9), Sept. 1978. **(4.3)**

VAN DER NAT, M.: "On Interpolation Search," *Comm. ACM*, **22** (12): 681, Dec. 1979. **(7.1)**

VAN DER NAT, M.: "A Fast Sorting Algorithm, A Hybrid of Distributive and Merge Sorting," *Inf. Proc. Lett.*, **10** (3), April 1980. **(7.5)**

VAN EMDEN, M. H.: "Increasing Efficiency of Quicksort," *Comm. ACM*, **13**: 563–67, 1970. **(7.2)**

VAUCHER, J. G. and P. DURAL: "A Comparison of Simulation Event List Algorithms," *Comm. ACM*, **18** (4), Apr. 1975. **(4.3)**

VEKLEROV, E.: "Analysis of Dynamic Hashing with Deferred Splitting," *ACM Trans. Database Syst.*, **10** (1), March 1985. **(8.4)**

VITTER, J. S.: "Analysis of the Search Performance of Coalesced Hashing," *J. ACM*, **30** (2), April 1983. **(8.4)**

VITTER, J. S. and W. C. CHEN: "Optimum Algorithms for a Hashing Model," *Technical Report CS-83-24*, Brown University Dept. of Computer Science, Oct. 1983. **(8.4)**

VITTER, J. S. and W. C. CHEN: "Optimum Algorithms for a Model of Direct Chaining," *SIAM J. Comp.*, **14** (2), May 1985. **(8.4)**

VUILLEMIN, J.: "A Data Structure for Manipulating Priority Queues," *Comm. ACM*, **21** (4), Apr. 1978. **(6.5)**

VUILLEMIN, J.: "A Unifying Look at Data Structures," *Comm. ACM*, **23** (4), Apr. 1980. **(D, A)**

WAINWRIGHT, R. L.: "A Class of Sorting Algorithms Based on Quicksort," *Comm. ACM*, **28** (4), April 1985. **(7.2)**

WALKER, W. A. and C. C. GOTLIEB: "A Top-Down Algorithm for Constructing Nearly Optimal Lexicographic Trees," in *Graph Theory and Computing*, R. Read (ed.), Academic Press, New York, 1972. **(8.2)**

WARREN, H. S.: "A Modification of Warshall's Algorithm for the Transitive Closure of Binary Relations," *Comm. ACM*, **18** (4), April 1975. **(9.1)**

WARSHALL, S.: "A Theorem on Boolean Matrices," *J. ACM*, **9** (1): 11, 1962. **(9.1)**

WEIDE, B.: "A Survey of Analysis Techniques for Discrete Algorithms," *ACM Computing Surveys*, **9** (4), Dec. 1977. **(A)**

WELSH, J. and J. ELDER: *Introduction to Pascal*, Prentice-Hall, Englewood Cliffs, N. J., 1980. **(P)**

WELSH, J., W. J. SNEERINGER and C. A. R. HOARE: "Ambiguities and Insecurities in Pascal," *Software-Practice and Experience*, **7**, 1977. **(P)**

WICHMANN, B. A.: "Ackermann's Function: A Study in the Efficiency of Calling Procedures," *BIT*, **16**: 103–10, 1976.   **(3)**

WICHMANN, B. A.: "How to Call Procedures, or Second Thoughts on Ackermann's Function," *Software-Practice and Experience*, **7**: 317–29, 1977.   **(3)**

WICHMANN, B. A. and A. H. J. SALE: "A Pascal Processor Validation Suite," *Pascal News* (16), Oct. 1979.   **(P)**

WICKELGREN, W. A.: *How to Solve Problems: Elements of a Theory of Problems and Problem Solving*, Freeman, San Francisco, 1974.   **(A)**

WILLIAMS, J. W. J.: "Algorithm 232 (Heapsort)," *Comm. ACM*, **7**: 347–48, 1964.
                                                                                   (7.3)

WILSON, I. P. and A. M. ADDYMAN: *A Practical Introduction to Pascal*, MacMillan Press, London, 1978.   **(P)**

WINKLER, J. F. H.: "Some Improvements of ISO-Pascal," *SIGPLAN Notices*, **19** (7), July 1984.   **(P)**

WIRTH, N.: *Algorithms + Data Structures = Programs*, Prentice-Hall, Englewood Cliffs, N. J., 1976.   **(P, D)**

WIRTH, N.: "Comment on A Note on Dynamic Arrays in Pascal," *SIGPLAN Notices*, **11** (1), Jan. 1976.   **(1.2)**

WIRTH, N.: "The Programming Language Pascal," *Acta Informatica*, **1** (1), 1971.   **(P)**

WIRTH, N.: *Systematic Programming: An Introduction*, Prentice-Hall, Englewood Cliffs, N. J., 1973.   **(P, A)**

WYMAN, F. P.: "Improved Event-Scanning Mechanisms for Discrete Event Simulation," *Comm. ACM*, **18** (6), Jun. 1975.   **(4.3)**

YAO, A.: "On Random 2-3 Trees," *Acta Informatica*, **9** (2): 159–70, 1978.   **(8.3)**

YAO, A. C. and F. F. YAO: "The Complexity of Searching an Ordered Random Table," *Proc. Symp. on Foundations of Comp. Sci.*: 173–76, Houston, 1976.   **(8.1)**

ZADEH, N.: "Theoretical Efficiency of the Edmonds-Karp Algorithm for Computing Maximal Flows," *Journal of the ACM*, **19**: 184–92, 1972.   **(9.2)**

ZEMROWSKI, K. M.: "Difference Between ANS and ISO Standards for Pascal," *SIGPLAN Notices*, **19** (8), August 1984.   **(P)**

ZWEBEN, S. H. and M. A. McDONALD: "An Optimal Method for Deletion in One-Sided Height-Balanced Trees," *Comm. ACM*, **21** (6), Jun. 1978.   **(8.2)**

INDEX

external file, 66, 481, 550, 749
external fragmentation, 702
external hashing, 759, 761
external memory, 548, 551
external path length, 455
external pointer, 186–234, 246, 264, 291, 314, 408, 434, 444, 448, 515, 647, 651, 657, 661–662, 670–677
external read, 478
external search, 429
external storage, 390, 473, 477–479, 497–498, 500, 506, 521, 526, 548–549, 552, 557, 748
extract, 25, 52

fact, 110, 118–122, 151–158
factor, 130–133
factorial, 108–119, 135–142, 153, 157–158, 162, 171–172, 303
Fagin, Nievergelt, Pippenger, and Strong, 552
fast search, 443, 761
father, 278–311, 320, 328–355, 396–398, 406, 453, 467–468, 486–489, 493, 498, 503, 507, 511, 536, 635
father, 283, 292–293, 300–333, 364, 480–484, 493–501, 517–518, 636, 643, 692
fib, 112–113, 117–118, 124–125, 136, 169, 446
Fibonacci buddy system, 715, 718
Fibonacci number, 113, 123, 136, 172, 239, 303, 446–447, 715
Fibonacci tree, 324–325, 471
Fibonaccian search, 446
fifo list, 173
file, 30, 66, 185, 293, 367–369, 374–390, 401–447, 478, 502, 513, 522, 548, 551, 561, 573, 748–765
find, 144–147, 169, 256–260, 482–499, 619–620
findabove, 266–268, 272–274
findcode, 322, 324
findelement, 334, 338–339
findnode, 608–609
findpath, 579–580
first, 17, 627, 633–652
first-fit allocation, 698, 704–705
first-fit method, 696–701, 717
first-in, first-out list, 173
fixed field, 59, 61
fixed part, 59, 62, 207
fleft, 314
floating-point notation, 5
flow, 592–603, 758, 767
folding method, 565, 566, 574
follower, 338–339
for loop, 20, 722, 730, 745
Ford-Fulkerson algorithm, 600, 602
forest, 340–347, 355, 515–519, 628–637
formal parameter, 727–728, 748
FORTH programming language, 88
FORTRAN, 149, 442, 666, 667
forward arc, 596, 628, 631, 637, 639
forward search, 445
forward, 128, 130, 600
fragmentation, 702
free block, 694–717
free list, 195, 697–718
free node, 669
free space, 691, 693, 717
free, 330–331
freearc, 619–621
freelist, 224, 665, 668

freenode, 191–195, 202–205, 213, 222–232, 247–250, 292, 360, 454, 606–608
freq, 320–322, 325
frequency, 317–324
front, 173–177, 185–223, 256–258, 325, 423–425, 643, 649, 702–704, 717
front compression, 511, 521
full expansion, 558–563
full node, 473, 498, 511
fully binary tree, 281

game tree, 355, 358–364
gap, 331
garbage collection, 668, 674–679, 683–684, 691–692, 696
gcd, 133
general coalesced hashing, 543–544
general forest, 623
general list, 646–648, 652, 657, 662–668
general selection sort, 392, 400, 407–408
general tree, 339, 349, 473, 477, 515, 603
generalized Fibonacci sequence, 133
generate, 363
geometry, 1
getarc, 619–620
getblock, 708, 717–718
getempty, 542
getnode, 187, 191–195, 202, 213, 221–223, 229–230, 247–249, 292, 306–307, 353–361, 433, 496, 517, 606–609
getsymb, 129–130
global, 125, 202, 360, 378, 383, 737
global variable, 126, 158, 202, 214, 218, 375, 475, 496, 635, 737
Gonnet, 535
Gonnet and Larson, 550, 564
Gonnet and Munro insertion, 537–538
good, 149
goto, 160, 693, 760
gpi, 751
graph, 429, 575–692, 756–763
greatest common divisor, 16, 133
greedy method, 460

H-tree, 511
halt, 80
hardware, 7–22, 36, 45–46, 228, 719–722
hash, 522–528, 565–568
hash bucket, 547
hash clash, 523–526, 544, 548, 555, 564
hash function, 522–526, 542–574, 755–756, 765
hash indicator table, 571
hash key, 522–523, 531, 552, 556
hash table, 524–573, 613–628, 754, 759, 762
hash, 619–620
hashing, 412, 521–573, 758–759, 762–763
head, 648–692
header, 15–16, 27, 36, 209, 227–237, 625, 659, 672, 745
header field, 689
header method, 657, 659, 663, 668
header node, 207–210, 227–236, 256, 264, 413, 604–627, 657–659, 668–674, 692
headinfo, 663–664
headptr, 664, 686–690
heap, 396–403, 471, 507, 612–613, 622, 758–759
heapsort, 396, 400, 405–408, 415, 767
heapsort, 403–404

height, 461–471
height-balanced tree, 470–471, 756, 759–763, 767
heterogenous binary tree, 311
Hsieh, 571
Huffman algorithm, 315, 318
Huffman encoding, 324
Huffman tree, 318–325
hyperplane, 41

i-block, 707–718
i-buddy, 708–709, 712
i-list, 707–708, 713–716
I/O, 526, 548–549, 555–556, 559
IBM PC, 302–303
imaginary 63
implementation, 8, 14, 17–21, 42–62, 79–86, 93, 108, 175, 181–183, 187, 191–194, 201–214, 238, 244–248, 252–253, 277, 307, 333, 353, 397, 431, 445, 470, 513, 547, 555, 588, 600, 606–611, 625–627, 634, 646–667, 717, 720–722, 744, 753
in operator, 44
in-threaded binary tree, 304
incident, 577, 615–616, 632, 635, 643
increment, 408–415
indegree, 577
index, 179, 184, 202, 241, 246, 256, 307–308, 314, 417, 428, 438–447, 513–515, 521–535, 542, 548, 552–557, 565–574, 626, 722, 727–729, 755, 758
index, 480–484, 493–498
indexed sequential file, 438, 439, 445, 446, 515, 521
inequality, 396, 443, 592
infinite loop, 84, 448
infix, 87–106, 142, 288, 290, 355
inflow, 592–596
information, 1, 6–7, 350
inorder, 285–293, 301–314, 326, 343, 347, 350, 396, 448, 453, 637, 638
inorder general tree, 349
inorder predecessor, 308, 456–457, 471
inorder successor, 304–308, 451–457, 471
inorder traversal, 394, 447, 451, 463–466
inplace merge, 419
inplace sort, 375, 392, 396
input file, 286, 748–749
input list, 653
input-restricted deque, 185
insafter, 196–207, 223, 229, 248, 256–260
insend, 224, 249
insert, 33, 174, 180–226, 253–260, 406–407, 430, 446, 493–501, 517, 533, 639
insertafter, 266, 274
insertion, 173–232, 255–256, 267, 286, 293, 299, 306–315, 325, 333, 353, 391–574, 612, 628, 703, 706, 758–764
insertion sort, 406–407, 420
insertleft, 232, 236–237
insertright, 232
insfull, 484
insleaf, 484, 486–487
insnode, 495–501
insrec, 484
insrtleft, 185
insrtright, 185
internal fragmentation, 702, 707, 716
internal key, 428
internal memory, 477, 479–481, 498, 499, 501, 506, 509, 521, 550, 551

real time, 675–676, 691
real-time garbage collection, 675
rear, 173–174, 185–186, 194, 204, 216, 222–223, 227, 325, 422–425, 643, 706, 716–717
rear compression, 511, 513, 521
rebalancing, 466
reciprocal hashing, 568, 760
recombination delaying buddy system, 715–718
record type, 735
record variable, 64, 744, 745
recursion stack, 124, 303
recursive algorithm, 117–118, 143, 441, 479, 633, 644
recursive chain, 127–128
recursive list, 207, 657, 665, 668, 674
recursive procedure, 119, 141, 153
reference count, 668–670, 674
register, 106–107, 151, 303, 747
registrar, 434–435
rehash function, 523–527, 573–574
rehash path, 527, 532, 540
rehash slot, 533
rehash, 525, 619, 620
relation, 577, 589
relatively prime, 412, 415, 526, 568, 569
remainder, 228, 239, 577, 589
remainder reduction perfect hash function, 568
remove, 185, 190–191, 210
remove, 174–207, 218, 222, 253–260, 533, 639, 706
remv, 577, 581, 607–608
remvandtest, 180, 184
remvnode, 610
remvwt, 577, 582, 608
replace, 351, 352, 499–501
report, 367
reserved word, 245, 567
reset, 749
resistance, 603
retrieval, 366, 368, 429–437, 445, 454, 457–458, 520, 521, 528–544, 566
return address, 151–166
reverse, 209
reverse order, 374, 395, 396, 415, 454
reverse Polish notation, 88
reverse topological order, 637, 644
rewrite, 749
rh, 525–536, 573
right bias, 489–490
right-inthreaded binary tree, 305–307, 313
rightrotation, 463, 467, 469
road, 579
robust interpolation search, 443, 444
rotation, 463–470, 766
Round-Robin algorithm, 643
row-major order, 41
running time, 412

Sacks-Davis, 563
Sager, 571
Sarwate, 573
scalar data type, 20, 719
schedule, 620, 621, 622
scheduling, 613, 619, 623, 637
Schorr-Waite, 680, 683, 693
scope, 72–76, 737–744
search algorithm, 429
search and insertion, 429, 433, 444, 461, 486, 515, 518, 521, 524, 527, 531, 533, 542, 545

search argument, 431, 432, 435, 436, 457, 458, 471, 476, 482, 528, 532
search probability, 461
search time, 439, 454, 457, 506, 509, 530, 705, 717, 718
search tree, 459, 470, 478, 485, 501, 506, 507, 624, 628, 755, 760, 766
secondary clustering, 527, 529–530, 540–541, 755
secondary device, 691
secondary hash function, 523
secondary index, 440–441
secondary key, 429
secondary storage, 691
seed, 219, 556
seek delay, 526
seek time, 549, 550
segmentation, 568, 570, 572
select, 392, 625, 632–636, 639, 644
selection sort, 391–393, 397, 420
semantics, 59
semileaf, 475, 482–485, 502, 506
semipath, 595–602
sentinel, 433–434, 448, 451
separate chaining, 544–550, 566, 572
separator, 503, 515, 550–551, 564
sequence, 17–18, 367, 374, 409, 412, 430, 479, 524, 577, 595, 614, 625, 646, 748
sequence set, 513
sequential access, 513, 550
sequential allocation, 419
sequential file, 749, 758
sequential insertion, 500
sequential key order, 546
sequential search, 114, 431–454, 476, 481, 515, 529, 531, 756, 764, 766
sequential storage, 185
sequential table, 441
sequential traversal, 314, 500, 524, 555, 685
set, 20, 22, 36, 41–50, 95, 318, 366 369, 375–376, 430, 457–461, 511, 515, 520–527, 531, 566, 572, 577, 587–588, 602, 611–617, 638, 661, 719–722, 762
set-containment operation, 45
sethead, 649–659, 665–668, 692
setinfo, 649, 652
setleft, 284, 292–299, 306–307, 313, 320
setnext, 649–652
setright, 284, 293–299, 306–307, 313, 320
setsons, 353
settail, 650–654, 665–668, 673, 692
Shell sort, 408, 411, 412, 415, 756
shell, 410
Shieh, 571
shifting, 200, 397, 400, 408, 414, 441, 707
shortest path, 586–588, 610, 640, 645
siftdown operation, 400, 406
siftup operation, 398, 400
signature, 550, 551
simfact, 156, 159, 161, 165
similar, 290, 471
simple insertion, 412, 420–422, 426–427
simple insertion sort, 393, 406–409, 411, 414–415
simtowers, 163–168
simulation, 97–98, 153–171, 211–220, 390, 471, 493, 541, 574, 620, 634–635, 716, 758, 766
simulation language, 218
singly linked circular list, 239
singly linked list, 326
sink, 590, 593, 598, 600, 603
software, 7, 9, 14, 21, 46, 720

son, 294, 340–363, 397, 451–468, 471, 480, 487, 497–498, 506, 515, 518, 520, 603, 635, 639–640, 644
sort by counting, 390
sort decision tree, 376
sorted file, 367–368, 380, 389, 393–394, 407, 415, 420, 437–438
sorted linear list, 205, 413
sorting by address, 367
sorting time, 370
source, 590, 593, 598–603
space, 56, 62–64, 77, 149, 158, 169, 193–203, 228, 233, 244, 253, 300, 321, 336, 342, 369, 375, 379, 390–392, 405–408, 413, 419–425, 438, 477, 486, 501, 506–507, 511, 520–522, 530, 538–552, 602–603, 654, 663–693, 702, 707, 721–729, 747–748
space bit, 502
space utilization, 511, 555
space/time trade-off, 234, 524, 552
spanning forest, 623, 628–639
spanning tree, 628, 631–644
sparse, 520, 603, 628, 766
sparse graph, 612
sparse matrix, 260, 262, 264, 275, 610, 621, 764
speed, 379, 407
split, 487–495, 498, 503, 506–509, 515, 557–558, 697, 702, 707–717
split key, 461
split node, 501
split sequence linear rehashing, 530
split tree, 461
split bucket, 552, 555
split, 493–501
Sprugnoli, 567, 568, 570
srchinsrt, 210
stable, 367, 375
stack, 67–222, 248–253, 304–314, 385–396, 419, 479–481, 634–651, 672–693
stack operation, 205
standard coalesced hashing, 541–544
standard deviation, 219–220
standard Pascal, 30, 33, 80, 251, 663–664, 690, 727, 729, 759
static evaluation function, 357–358
storage allocation, 717
storage block, 477–480, 499, 548, 702
storage management, 646, 675–676, 707, 717–718
storage utilization, 509, 550, 556
store, 25–26, 52, 275
straight merge, 417, 419, 420
straight selection sort, 392–393, 405, 408
straight-line tree, 471
strictly binary tree, 278–283, 287, 320–321, 325, 336, 355
strictly lower triangular array, 50
string, 2–4, 10–32, 54–55, 73–76, 90, 97–105, 143–144, 147, 209, 211, 225, 356
sub, 18
subfile, 382, 386–391, 408–418
subrange, 23, 36, 41–43, 122, 143, 258, 720–721, 729, 750
subset, 277, 340, 720
substr, 19, 30–34, 54, 144, 210
substring, 19, 33, 54, 145, 209, 355
subtask, 613–616, 622
subtract, 22
subtree, 278, 284, 288, 290, 305–307, 326, 336, 347, 352, 361, 406, 447, 451, 457, 461–487, 495–502, 632, 637–638

774